D1440768

History

of the

World Christian Movement

MKLM Library

History
of the
World Christian Movement

Volume II: Modern Christianity from 1454 to 1800

DALE T. IRVIN
SCOTT W. SUNQUIST

ORBIS BOOKS

Maryknoll, New York 10545

Founded in 1970, Orbis Books endeavors to publish works that enlighten the mind, nourish the spirit, and challenge the conscience. The publishing arm of the Maryknoll Fathers and Brothers, Orbis seeks to explore the global dimensions of the Christian faith and mission, to invite dialogue with diverse cultures and religious traditions, and to serve the cause of reconciliation and peace. The books published reflect the views of their authors and do not represent the official position of the Maryknoll Society. To learn more about Maryknoll and Orbis Books, please visit our website at www.maryknollsociety.org.

Copyright © 2012 by Dale T. Irvin and Scott W. Sunquist

Published by Orbis Books, Box 302, Maryknoll, NY 10545-0302.

All rights reserved.

No part of this publication may be reproduced or transmitted in any form or by any means, electronic or mechanical, including photocopying, recording, or any information storage or retrieval system, without prior permission in writing from the publisher.

Queries regarding rights and permissions should be addressed to: Orbis Books, P.O. Box 302, Maryknoll, NY 10545-0302.

Manufactured in the United States of America

Library of Congress Cataloging-in-Publication Data

Irvin, Dale T. 1955–
    History of the world Christian movement / Dale T. Irvin, Scott W. Sunquist.
        p. cm.
    Includes bibliographical references and indexes.
    Contents: v. 2. Modern Christianity from 1454 to 1800.
    ISBN 9781570759895 (pbk.)
    1. Church history. I. Sunquist, Scott, 1953– II. Title.

BR145.3 .I78 2001
270—dc21

                                 2001041424

Contents

Introduction

The history of the world Christian movement has always been greater than what any of its participants ever imagined it to be. It is also greater than what anyone who tries to write about it ever manages to convey. Like all written histories, this one is incomplete, as we can never exhaust either the data or our interpretations of the data. When it comes to history, there is always more to research, more to study, and more to write, just as there is always more to do. Recognizing that such surplus exists both in the history that is lived and in the history that is researched and written serves as both a warning and an incentive to keep the historical project open and the rich conversations going.

At some point in time, however, the writing must come to an end, even if for a time, in order for the project to be seen. After more than a decade of work that included input from a sizable number of scholars and practitioners from around the world, you now hold the product of their efforts as volume two of *History of the World Christian Movement*. The two authors of this volume offer it as a contribution to the conversation that we do not expect to end any time soon. This is not the last word in the history of the world Christian movement of the fifteenth through eighteenth centuries by any means. We offer it instead as one more contribution intended to increase the collective understanding of the history of Christianity throughout the world.

Running through the first two volumes of *History of the World Christian Movement* is the undergirding insight that Christianity was not a European religion that spread to other parts of the world for the first time after the year 1500, as it has often been portrayed. Christianity was born at the juncture of three continents and within its first century had become deeply established on each of them. By the year 1500 it was already something of a world religion. It had also become the dominant and established religion in western Europe, as it continued to be in the East Roman (or Byzantine) empire that had Constantinople as its capital. Volume one ended with the fall of Constantinople in 1453 to the Ottoman forces and the corresponding end of the East Roman (or Byzantine) empire. Only a few decades before Portuguese ships had begun to venture out into the Atlantic Ocean south along the coast of Africa, opening up a new era in world history. This new era was soon characterized by a global imbalance in power that allowed Europeans to dominate many other regions of the globe.

The subsequent movement of peoples, goods, and ideas that those ships facilitated quickly spread Christianity further across the globe than it had previously been as well. Christian communities began to develop in regions on earth where they had not previously been located, most notably in the hemisphere that came to be called South and North America. While in most cases these communities of faith in new locations continued to be related in both character and expression to churches in western Europe, they were never only duplicates of them. In a number of places across Asia and Africa, Christians from western Europe also encountered indigenous Christian communities of various Orthodox traditions that had lived in these places for over a millennium. The results of these encounters were significant for both parties. Churches in western Europe itself meanwhile began around 1500 to experience new efforts for reform that in some cases lead to significant changes, even as they sought to maintain continuity with the historic Christian past, or at least that portion of the Christian past that they considered to be authoritative for their identity. Thus the Christian movement throughout the world found itself after 1453 dealing with compelling forces of change and continuity in new and contextually specific ways.

Trying to tell a fuller story of the Christian movement from the fifteenth through eighteenth centuries has been more difficult than either author of this volume could have predicted a decade ago when the effort to write volume two began. To accomplish the goal we have followed a methodology that shaped volume one that has called for considerable collaboration with colleagues from around the world and from several academic disciplines. Several consultations were held over the past decade in which women and men from Asia, Africa, South America, North America, and Europe representing diverse ecclesiastical traditions and academic disciplines gathered to work together first on the broader historiographical issues entailed in researching and writing the history of world Christianity from the fifteenth through eighteenth centuries, and to work together on initial versions of various chapters in the volume. The consultations were held in Pittsburgh, Pennsylvania, USA (October 2002); Techny, Illinois, USA (January 2003); Pasadena, California, USA (October 2003); New York, New York, USA (March 2004); Port Dickson, Malaysia (August 2004); Graymoor, New York, USA (October 2005); and Princeton, New Jersey, USA (August 2007).[1] The last two in particular involved careful and critical reading of the manuscript in draft form with numerous suggested changes and revisions.

The number of individuals who participated in one or more of these gatherings is far too great to list here. In addition, a number of individuals were consulted one-on-one regarding specific sections as the text was revised. Some of our colleagues provided substantive research notes or even suggestions for rewriting entire paragraphs. Others read entire sections or the entire draft of the manuscript and gave helpful critical responses. Still others have used portions of the manuscript in classrooms and have provided feedback from students as to the usefulness of the text. In all cases we note that responsibility for the final draft falls upon the authors, and all errors are strictly our own.

In volume one of this project the authors made a decision to limit the use of footnotes. We have followed that procedure in volume two to an even greater

---

1. These consultations were made possible by major grants from the Henry Luce Foundation and a grant from the United Board for Christian Higher Education in Asia. We are thankful to both organizations for their support.

extent. We decided early in the project that citing sources would quickly over-
whelm the text and the reader with references. There are numerous places
throughout the volume where a specific detail is offered without the usual cita-
tion in historical works like this to point to the source in an archive where the
information can be found. Instead we have depended upon the collective reading
of our colleagues as well as one another to provide the assurance that typical
citations in footnotes provide that the facts are accurate, giving us the confidence
to dispense with specific references. This is not to say that we can guarantee the
work is without error. There are numerous occasions in a work of this magnitude
and breadth where factual errors will no doubt soon be found. Ongoing historical research continues almost monthly to uncover new information that renders
what we have written obsolete. These realities do not dim our confidence that the
work that is now before the reader is a faithful history of the fifteenth through
eighteenth centuries of the Christian movement.

Throughout the volume we have struggled with the perplexing question of the
spelling of names when they are given in different languages. In numerous cases
in the past people spelled their names differently, or their names were rendered
differently in other languages. The problem is made much more complex when
names are transliterated from one script to another, with either multiple pos-
sibilities for transliteration or where conventions have changed. We have tried
throughout this volume to render names as often as possible in the language and
form that the persons who originally possessed them used, but at times even
this has been difficult to discern. In some cases we have opted to use a form of
a name that is most recognizable to English readers, especially where these are
well established by convention. In numerous cases throughout the text we have
listed alternative renditions of a name in parentheses to try to help the reader
make connections with other histories and language traditions.

A similar problem has confronted us throughout the text in naming geographical locations. As much as possible we have tried to identify political entities from
the past using the names that are being used in the first decade of the twenty-first
century. Where there are alternatives, we have tried to identify these as well in
parentheses throughout the text. Myanmar and Burma generally refer to the same
political and geographical entity for instance. Where we have used Myanmar, we
have tried as well to identify it as Burma, the name that was commonly used in
most English-language texts in the past.

All dating in this text is given in terms of the year of the Common Era. We
have tried as much as possible to locate accurate dates for the birth and death
of every individual named in the pages that follow. That of course has not been
possible to do in all cases. Where we have not yet been able to locate a specific
date of birth and death for an individual, we have endeavored to provide at least
a date of death (indicated by "d" next to the year). In some cases we either have
only been able to locate, or it makes more sense to refer to the dates an individual
political or ecclesiastical authority held office. These dates we have indicated by
prefacing them with the symbol "r" (for "ruled"). In cases where an exact date
is not clear (at least to us), we have used the conventional Latin "c" for *circa* or
"around." In several cases we were unable to locate a precise date of death, which

we have indicated by a simple question mark ("?"). In a few cases we have simply not been able to locate any documented date of birth and death. Those individuals, whose names we often have, are simply identified by "dates unknown" in parentheses after their name. We have endeavored for the most part to provide the dates for individuals the first time their names appear in each chapter, unless that person comes from an earlier century and is being referenced only for theological purposes.

Why only go to the year 1800? The question is a complex one that the authors have struggled with from the inception of the project. Initially we planned to cover the entire period of the fifteenth through the twentieth centuries in one volume. By the time we were finishing an initial outline of the work, however, questions both as to method and to amount of information had emerged. Both the co-authors and the majority of those involved in consultations around the project agreed that the level of detail that we were seeking to provide was necessary for a history that was close to the sources and provided concrete details about peoples' lives. We have consciously sought in numerous places to minimize the level of historical interpretation that we provide as authors and have tried to maximize the effort to tell the stories of living women and men who populate this history. That has resulted in a text with an enormous number of names of people from all regions of the world. The level of detail that we have sought to provide has made for a much longer book than we had initially intended. The amount of detail necessary to understand the history of the nineteenth and twentieth centuries is even greater, as the Christian movement explodes with new initiatives, new forms of leadership, and new community expressions throughout the world.

We also chose initially to organize the text of volume two by employing the combined chronological and continental geographical method we followed in volume one. The method allows us to tell the story of Christianity in various continents of the world as it unfolds across centuries in more or less parallel narrative form. It works fairly well until we reach the nineteenth century when advances in transportation and communication technologies begin to bring the continents of the world closer together, facilitating greater interaction among them and requiring more references to events beyond the immediate context. National borders and continental identities remain, but the manner in which these interactions accelerate and the world as a whole begins to shrink in time and space make it more and more difficult to tell the story of the nineteenth and twentieth centuries through regional narratives. It is not a shift in demographic composition of world Christianity brought about by growth in Christian numbers in Africa and Asia in the last centuries that makes regional narratives less compelling. As important as that shift is, it does not require that we abandon the continental organization of the text. One can still find numerous examples of churches and histories that are "regional" in identity and practice. Nationalism in many places grew stronger as a political force. But even the most local histories in the nineteenth and twentieth centuries become engaged in global conversations in a way that was without precedent in earlier centuries, requiring a more transnational and transregional method for narrating the history of the world Christian movement.

For these reasons the authors and our editors at Orbis Books have decided to end volume two around the year 1800, and to publish a third and separate volume on the history of the world Christian movement in the nineteenth and twentieth centuries. That third volume is expected to appear in print in reasonably short order. In the meantime we provide a brief epilogue at the end of this current volume two that will serve to provide a preliminary overview of the direction as well as significant themes that volume three will entail.

Finally, the authors wish to thank our editor, William R. Burrows, who until recently was at Orbis Books, for the work he has provided over the years in guiding this project, and in seeing volume two through to conclusion. At points Bill almost became a co-author, working with us to think through problems, addressing concerns raised by readers of the text from various national and confessional locations, and always encouraging us to finish. Bill gave us a final substantive reading of the entire draft of volume two, helped break longer passages into separate sections, and suggested numerous sub-headings for chapters. Without him this project might still not be finished. We are truly grateful for his support.

Part I

1454-1600

Two Major Transformations

Residents of the port city of Kozhikode (or Calicut as it was once known) in the region of Kerala on the southwest coast of India were greeted by an unusual sight early in the fifteenth century c.e. A fleet of large and ornate ships, filled with goods from imperial China, had come to trade. The ships were enormous, measuring from 50 to over 125 meters in length. Constructed under order of Ming Emperor Yongle (birth name Zhu Di, 1360-1424) they represented a significant departure from the traditional Chinese trading practices. While Chinese had been involved in trade across east Asia for centuries, and Chinese immigrants were living in present-day Vietnam, Indonesia, and Malaysia, the Chinese had never established colonies or "factories" for trade in foreign lands, nor had the imperial government previously launched such expeditions overseas. Now the Chinese were seeking to expand their trade and diplomatic reach to geographically distant regions. By the middle of the century as many as seven voyages had been undertaken, not just to Kozhikode but to other major ports in Japan, Korea, India, Persia, Arabia, and the eastern coast of Africa as far as present day Madagascar. A giraffe was returned as a gift to the emperor, who considered it an auspicious sign.

Almost as quickly as the ships had appeared, the Chinese naval effort ended. Following the death of Yongle in 1424 the Confucianist literati, who had largely been shut out of decision-making during his reign, reasserted their traditional control within the imperial government. The emperor had sought to build China's strength through sea voyages rather than through agriculture. The Confucianists saw this as an abandonment of traditional Chinese culture, as well as a challenge to their own power. Within a decade of the emperor's death, the navy, which may have numbered as many as 3,500 vessels, was reduced by half. By 1500 it was gone, and building ships of more than two masts was made a capital offense in China. By 1550 it was a crime for the Chinese even to go to sea to trade in a multimasted ship. Seeking to close China off to the rest of the world, the Confucianists had successfully eliminated one of the primary sources of Ming power.

Unlike the Chinese, the Muslims had been plying the waters of the Indian Ocean and in the South China Sea for centuries. Muslim trading colonies along these coasts had for hundreds of years served as sources of wealth for the Islamic world. Muslim merchants had settled as far down the coast of East Africa as Mozambique, and Muslim pilots knew well the trade winds that crossed the Indian Ocean. One of these Muslim merchants was pressed into service in 1498 by the crew of the Portuguese explorer Vasco da Gama (1460-1524) and forced to pilot their small Portuguese fleet across the Indian Ocean, thereby opening up a new era in Asian history.

Vasco da Gama sailed into the harbor of Kozhikode in May of 1498. Two Muslims from Tunis who could speak Castilian and Genoese were soon located to serve as translators. The Portuguese came hoping in part to find a Christian kingdom in Asia that would become an ally in their centuries-old war against Islam. Letters from the king of Portugal, written in Portuguese and Arabic, were presented to the local rulers, whom da Gama mistakenly believed to be Christian. A tour of the city was arranged, including of a temple most likely dedicated to Kali, the Indian mother goddess of destruction. Da Gama mistakenly believed the building to be a Christian church, and the deities represented within it to be the Virgin Mary and other Christian saints.

Upon his return to Portugal six months later, da Gama's report opened up a new era in the history of Asia. Portuguese warships soon dominated the Indian Ocean and effectively controlled all trade passing through it. Subsequent trips corrected for the Portuguese da Gama's misconception that Kozhikode was under Christian rulers, but they soon established contact in South India with other Christians who claimed the memory of St. Thomas. These Thomas Christians held to the ancient traditions of the church of the East with its Syriac liturgy. Over the next several decades the two communions, Syriac and Latin, grounded respectively in the apostolic traditions of St. Thomas and St. Peter, began to interact in ways that eventually reconfigured Christian identity in the South Indian context.

Portuguese ships had made their way down the coast of western Africa and around the Cape of Good Hope into the Indian Ocean over the course of almost one hundred years. The effort had begun in 1415 when Prince Henry the Navigator (1394-1460) seized the port city of Ceutra on the coast of Morocco. The Portuguese did not attempt to move any farther inland from the coastal city, but its bustling markets convinced them of the wealth that lay farther to the south. Soon the Portuguese were moving in that direction by sea, sailing along the coast of West Africa and establishing settlements on several islands in the Atlantic. From these island bases they began exploring the West African coast. In the 1440s they brought their first African captives back to Iberia to sell as slaves. By 1482 the Portuguese had built a permanent fort at Elmina in modern Ghana.

That same year Portuguese ships reached the mouth of the Kongo River. An official Portuguese envoy was sent to the *manikongo* (king of Kongo) Nzinga Nkuwu (d. 1506) who in turn soon sent his son, Mvemba Nzinga (1456-1542) to Portugal to be educated. King Nzinga Nkuwu, known in Portuguese as João I, was baptized a Christian in 1491, but later returned to the faith of his ancestors. His wife was also baptized and took the Portuguese name Eleonora (dates unknown). Mvemba Nzinga took the name Afonso upon his baptism. After Afonso became king in 1506 he made Christianity the religion of Kongo, tearing down the traditional temple in the capital city, building a new church that would serve as a cathedral, and renaming the capital São Salvador (Our Savior). He also sent his son, Henrique (c. 1495-c. 1526), to Lisbon to study for the priesthood. Henrique was ordained a bishop before returning to São Salvador in 1521. Meanwhile the Portuguese continued to send priests, builders, artisans, and educators to help build a Christian kingdom in Central Africa. They also continued to engage in slaving, destroying the social fabric of that same kingdom.

Gold and other goods were high on the list of desired items that the Portuguese sought, but by far the most profitable commodity they discovered along the coast of West Africa came to be the human flesh that they enslaved. Some of the enslaved Africans converted to Christianity in Portugal, and some in the Portuguese church hierarchy began to look for ways to train Africans in theology with the expectation that they would eventually become a Christianizing presence in Africa. The number of enslaved Africans taken to Portugal and sold in the fifteenth century was relatively small compared to what was soon to follow. The market for enslaved labor in Europe was not very strong, and would never have supported the massive development of the slave trade that took millions of Africans overseas in forced labor and brought about the death of many millions more. Those markets opened up across the Atlantic in the lands that Europeans named "America" beginning in the early 1500s.

The year 1492 stands as a watershed in world history. Several years earlier King Ferdinand of Aragón (1452-1516) and Queen Isabella (1451-1504) of Castile had been united in marriage, thereby joining the two powerful monarchies in Iberia into one nation that became known as Spain. In 1492 their army defeated the last Islamic kingdom on the southern tip of the Iberian Peninsula in Grenada. That same year they issued an order expelling all Jews and Muslims from Spain. A Genoese-born explorer known in Spanish as Cristóbal Colón (d. 1506), better known in the English-speaking world as Christopher Columbus, appeared before the throne that year as well to make the case for financing a voyage of exploration to the east. His plan was to test the thesis that the world was round and that by sailing to the west he would in fact arrive at the east, in India. The purpose of the trip was to gain a direct route to the profitable trade to the east, bypassing both the Muslim nations and Portugal. His journey was also meant to extend the Spanish realm. Any land that he came upon that was not already under the rule of a legitimate Roman Catholic monarch was to be claimed for the crown of Spain. In the back of his mind lay the ultimate purpose of financing the final crusade to the Holy Land to reclaim Palestine for Christendom.

Columbus succeeded in reaching land several months later. He called the islands the Indies, and the indigenous inhabitants "Indians," but in fact he had arrived in the Caribbean. He returned to Spain a year later, taking with him several captives from among the native Taíno people to display in the court of Spain. Subsequent voyages were undertaken, and within a decade the conquest and colonial settlement of the region that came to be known as America was begun. The effect upon the indigenous peoples was devastating. The Spanish conquistadors ("conquerors" or soldiers who carried out the military conquest of America, many of whom were veterans of the war against Grenada) and colonists who followed them brought new diseases such as smallpox, which quickly spread among the Taínos, Caribs, and other native inhabitants. Within a few decades the indigenous population was reduced to a fraction of what it had been. Those indigenous peoples who were not killed by violent conquest or disease were often brutally forced to work under slave conditions in agriculture and later mining.

In 1519 the conquistador Hernando Cortéz (or Hernán Cortéz, 1484-1547) entered southern Mexico with around five hundred soldiers. With the assistance of a Franciscan priest who had been shipwrecked a decade earlier and had learned the local Mayan language, he marched inland on a journey of conquest. In one of the villages he defeated Cortéz was given as tribute some twenty young enslaved women to accompany his soldiers. One of these captives, a young Nahua woman named Malinalli (c. 1500-c. 1530), underwent Christian baptism (taking the name Marina), and soon became Cortéz's common-law wife. Through these first conquests in Mexico the Spanish also learned of an enormously wealthy city to the north known as Tenochtitlan (today Mexico City), which was the capital of the Aztec empire under the rule of Moctezuma II (1466-1520). As the Spanish made their way north toward Tenochtitlan they found a considerable resistance movement against the Aztec empire already under way. Assisted greatly by Marina (or "La Malinche" as she became popularly known) who spoke both Mayan and Nahua, Cortéz joined his own small army to the larger resistance forces that were gathering.

When they reached Tenochtitlan, the Spanish alone were allowed to enter the city, leaving their indigenous allies on the outskirts. Moctezuma may have reasoned that allowing the Spanish to see first-hand the practices of human sacrifice that went on in the city would help secure their eventual submission to his rule, as it had for other peoples that the Aztecs had conquered. Whatever his purpose might have been, he did not count on the superior weaponry of the Spanish that allowed them to establish a stronghold inside his gates. The Spanish guests in turn soon proved to be the critical factor in destabilizing Moctezuma's hold over both the city and the empire. The following year the emperor was dead, executed according to some accounts by the Spanish and according to others by dissenting members of the ruling Aztec nobility in the city. Cortéz and his soldiers moved quickly in the aftermath of Moctezuma's death to secure their hold on the city. Smallpox and other diseases were by now ravaging the wider population and significantly weakening the ability of other indigenous forces to respond. Within two years the Aztec empire virtually disappeared, leaving the Spanish militarily in control of the entire region under Governor Cortéz.

A decade later a similar story ensued to the south as Spanish forces under Francisco Pizarro (1476-1541) conquered a second great empire in America, that of the Incas in Peru. Spanish forces had first begun to explore the region along the western coast south of Panama in 1522. Reports of great wealth from the Inca empire farther south drew them back. After several unsuccessful expeditions, Pizarro was finally able to reach Peru in 1532. Outside the town of Cajamarca he met the Inca emperor Atahualpa (1497-1533), who was returning from having recently suppressed a rebellion led by his brother. Lulled into complacency by the overwhelming advantage that his tens of thousands of troops seemed to provide against the less than two hundred Spanish soldiers, Atahualpa agreed to meet the Spanish conquistador face to face, accompanied by a contingent of some one thousand troops. The Spanish pulled a surprise attack, however, and with their superior weaponry quickly wiped out the Incan forces and took the emperor prisoner. The emperor then agreed to pay an enormous ransom of silver and gold, expecting to receive his freedom. Pizarro accepted the payment but six months later he executed the captive emperor, even though Atahualpa had by that time undergone baptism.

A younger brother of Atahualpa, Manco Yupanqui (1516–1544), assumed the throne as ruler of the Inca empire in the capital city of Cuzco (or Cozco), and for a time cooperated with Pizarro. Eventually Manco rebelled, however, going into hiding in the mountains from where he continued to lead sporadic resistance. The internal instability of the Inca empire at this point worked in favor of the Spanish. The Inca rulers had only recently come to power, and they exercised considerable violence against the other peoples they had subjugated in the region. Torn by internal civil wars, facing continuous rebellion, and now ravaged by smallpox and other diseases that had spread ahead of the Spanish from Central America, the Inca empire was simply too weak to stand. By the 1570s the last resistance to the Spanish in Peru was eliminated, and the entire western region of South America was fully under Spanish control.

Evangelization followed in the wake of conquest and colonial settlement in the Americas. Friars, priests, and bishops came from Spain not only to serve the religious needs of the conquistadors and colonizers, but to catechize the indigenous peoples and establish churches for them. The conquered indigenous peoples began as well to appropriate Christian faith as their own. Emblematic of this latter process was the development of the cult of the Virgin. In Mexico, for instance, the Spanish conquistadors brought with them from Spain the light-skinned figure of the Virgin Mary, whom they called Our Lady of Guadalupe. Within a hundred years the descendants of the conquered peoples of Mexico had identified her with aspects of the Aztec goddess Tonantzin and converted the mother of Christ to La Morenita, the brown-skinned Lady who was the mother of the violated people.

There were individuals on the colonial side who took up the cause of the conquered peoples. Most notable among them is that of Bartolomé de Las Casas (1484-1566). Arriving in Hispaniola in 1502, he participated in a number of expeditions, which resulted in his being rewarded with his own *encomiendero,* a "trust" or land grant set up to exploit the labor of indigenous peoples under the guise of "civilizing" or "evangelizing" them. The experience gave the young de Las Casas, soon to be the first priest ordained in the Americas, a special sensitivity and concern for indigenous peoples. By 1515 he was back in Spain, protesting the cruel treatment of the indigenous peoples and arguing for reform.

De Las Casas made his case for the rights of the indigenous peoples before the authorities in Spain. His case won a hearing with the archbishop of Toledo, on whose behalf de Las Casas returned to America the following year to gather further information about the situation of the indigenous peoples. Two years later he was back in Spain, and this time was able to have an audience with the young Carlos I (1500-1558), son of the German emperor and grandson of Ferdinand and Isabella. Carlos I was the ruler not only of Spain but of Burgundy (where he was raised), the Netherlands, Naples, and Milan. To this was being added the lands being conquered and settled in America. In December of 1518 de Las Casas finally met with Carlos and pleaded with him regarding the terrible plight of the indigenous Americans. The greed and insatiable desire for gold of the Spanish were killing the people of the islands. De Las Casas defended the humanity of the indigenous people, arguing for their capacity to receive the faith, practice self-government, and exercise reason. Carlos seemed to have been influenced. In response to the situation, the young king, who had just been elected Holy Roman Emperor as Charles V, condemned (although he did not outlaw) the cruel *encomienda* system whereby indigenous peoples were forced into labor, and called for the creation of free towns.

Eighteen months after Carlos I of Spain met with de Las Casas, he had to preside as Charles V, newly elected Holy Roman Emperor, over the case of another priest who was also a reformer. This time the location was along the Rhine River in the city of Worms, where the Diet, or Assembly of the ruling imperial estates, was in session. An Augustinian monk in Wittenberg named Martin Luther (1483-1546) had created a different, if equally challenging, problem for the emperor. Luther had come to oppose what he believed to be the church's exploitation of the faith of the local population in the selling of indulgences, and the theology that reinforced such practices. Indulgences were a form of penance that the church distributed in exchange for set offerings. But penance is not something that can be granted by the church because money was paid for prayers or indulgences, Luther argued. Penance is something that is a daily attitude of all Christians, and forgiveness is granted by the grace of God in Christ, not by the church. On April 17, 1521, Luther stood before the emperor at the Diet of Worms and declared his refusal to change his position. He would, he said, be guided only by the testimony of scripture or clear reason, not by the teachings of pope or council, and would not go against his own conscience. His effort helped to launch what has come to be known as the sixteenth-century Protestant Reformation.

Western Europe in the fifteenth and sixteenth centuries was a patchwork of kingdoms and peoples stitched together by a common Latin Christian culture and faith. By 1500 this common culture was in the process of being transformed by the pressure of new emerging vernacular traditions and new political states. To the east the Ottoman empire had solidified its control over the former Byzantine empire. The ecumenical patriarch now oversaw a church that had to contend with its newfound status as *dhimmi* ("protected minority"), joining other eastern Orthodox communions that were under Islamic rule. Ethiopia not only found itself contending with increasingly Islamic pressure, but after the fifteenth century had to deal with the disruptive presence of representatives of the Roman Catholic Church in its midst.

The kingdom of Muscovy, on the other hand, in the fifteenth century was emerging from under several hundred years of foreign Mongol rule. A new Russian dynasty was now in power, and a new national identity was emerging among Russian Orthodox Christians. In time Russia began expanding its political influence to the east across Siberia in northern Asia, with Russian Christianity following en route.

Farther south in Asia the Portuguese followed the trade routes that took them farther east to the port city of Malacca (or Melaka) in Malaysia in 1509, which they seized. By 1557 they established their presence in Macao off the coast of China. Portuguese ships were trading with China, Indonesia, and Japan regularly by the middle of the sixteenth century. Meanwhile Spanish ships under the command of a Portuguese captain named Ferdinand Magellan (1480-1521) succeeded in reaching the Philippines from the west in 1521. Magellan was killed in battle in the Philippines, but a remnant of his fleet completed the journey, thereby proving in an empirical manner that the world was indeed round. Not only was the world proven to be round, but by the sixteenth century it was already well on its way to becoming a single integrated network of commercial, political, and religious forces.

The pages that follow tell the story of world Christianity at the beginning of the modern era by starting with the conquest of the Americas. The story then moves across the Atlantic to Africa where the Portuguese explorers were bringing Christianity along the coastal regions west and south, and engaging Ethiopia in the east. It continues following the Portuguese to India and other areas of east Asia where they began to spread Christianity through their colonial efforts. Through these various colonial expansions a major transformation of Christianity was under way, one that would take the rest of the modern era to complete. By the end of the period, however, what was in 1500 a predominantly European religion would once again be global.

Christianity did not stop being a Western religion during this period. The pages that follow will trace that story as well, paying particular attention in the western European context to another major transformation that was taking place. At the onset of the sixteenth century, Christianity could still be characterized as flowing through two major streams, one being the Latin or Roman Catholic tradition in the West, and the other the various members of the Orthodox family of churches in the East (stretching from the Ottoman empire and Russia through Persia to India). During the course of the sixteenth century a host of reforming movements burst forth in Europe. The results were several new confessional formations that separated from the Roman Church thereby fracturing the institutional unity of Western Christendom, and a number of enduring reforms within the Roman Church itself. The rise of new confessional identities had political effects, some of which were felt among the Orthodox churches of the East. Developments within these various Orthodox churches in the sixteenth century within the Ottoman empire, in Russia, and farther east will be examined at the end of this section. Part I then concludes with an overview of world Christianity at the end of the sixteenth century, providing something of a snapshot of the growing interaction that was taking place among various geographical regions, confessions, and identities.

1

Christian Beginnings in America

The preconquest era

Human beings had inhabited the region of the world now called America (North, Central, and South) long before the fifteenth century c.e. Over many millennia migration had populated every section of the hemisphere. The inhabitants of the Americas spoke several hundred different languages and were culturally quite diverse. Hunting and agriculture were the main forms of production, supplemented by a minor trading economy. Social life in the Americas before 1500 was organized mostly by clan and tribe. Most people lived in small settled villages, or were nomadic within a particular geographical region. The major exceptions to this were the urban formations in the southern hemisphere, among the Mayans in what is now Central America, the Incas in Peru, and the Aztecs in Mexico.

We know little about the Mayans today. Archaeological evidence dates their presence in Central America as far back as 1000 b.c.e., but their empire flourished from around 250 to 900 c.e. After that it rapidly declined for reasons that are not clear. The Mayans were the only people to have a fully developed written language in the Americas prior to the sixteenth century. Their cities included plazas, pyramids, temples, palaces, observatories, and stadiums for ball games. While the Mayan political empire rapidly declined after 1000 c.e., their language and culture continue to live on to the present day.

The Inca empire, which arose from one of many tribes living along the mountain plateaus of the Andes, began to expand after 1400 and eventually stretched for 4,000 km in distance, making it the largest empire in the Americas prior to the Spanish conquest. With the rise of the Inca came an elevation of their worship. Pachacutec (1438-1472), the first ruler of the empire, built the magnificent temple to the Sun, which the Spanish called *Coricancha* ("Court of Gold"), called such because the temple was filled with gold statues and its exterior was covered in sheets of gold. The Inca empire, as with empires in other parts of the world, was built around a capital city, Cuzco, the center that represented the place of divine presence.

The Aztec empire emerged in the 1300s when leaders of the Mexica peoples formed an alliance with the two other peoples, the Acolhua and the Tepaneca, and began subjugating neighboring peoples and extracting tribute from them. The Aztec, or Mexica, built their empire around a religious center, the twin cities of Tenochtitlan-Tlatelolco. At its height when the first Europeans arrived in the region, the twin-city capital had a population of 300,000 or more, rivaling any other urban complex on earth for its time. The largest building in the city was the Great Pyramid, which was fifty meters high. Tenochtitlan was the home of the emperor and the center for the cosmic sacrifices of divine rebirthing. Aztec religion revolved in no small part around the shedding of blood through rituals of divine self-sacrifice that resulted in cosmic regeneration. Human beings, often warriors captured in battle, would be ritually transformed into divine beings who would then be sacrificed in order to be reborn.

North America had no such urban empires in the fifteenth century. In the southeastern areas there were more organized cultures, with religious and agricultural development that were made possible by a common language system. Along the east coast, across the Great Lakes and out to the Great Plains, tribal groups seldom developed communities larger than three thousand people. Most were hunters and gatherers, although some practiced slash-and-burn farming. The exception was the Iroquois League, or Nation, a confederacy that emerged around the eastern Great Lakes a century before the arrival of Europeans and had a largely settled form of life.

Religion was thoroughly integrated into the everyday life of North American indigenous peoples. Ritual practices such as the snake dance, the sun dance, or the sweat lodge were communal events that gave order and meaning to life. Many nations, like the Osage (central Mississippi region) practiced an ecological and seasonal faith, based on the close relationship with and dependence on the earth, sun, and water. The Osage honored sky and earth as the two great vitalizing cosmic forces. Although they are opposites, these two forces must come together for there to be life, the Osage believed. Society was organized accordingly, into sky (peace) people and earth (war) people. Similar social-religious ordering of life could be found among the Acoma of the southwest, or the Tlingit of the northwest. For many, rituals accompanying or requiring spilling of blood were significant to religious life.

Population figures for the Americas prior to 1500 are difficult to establish with certainty. Estimates for lands north of the Rio Grande range from five to ten million people. South of the Rio Grande the population was much higher, with a total of sixty to sixty-five million people. Mexico alone, with the more advanced systems of Aztec government, trade, and agriculture, had about seven million people. This means that about 15 percent of the world's population lived in South America in 1492, the year the first Europeans arrived. Within several decades of that date, however, due to the violence and disease brought about by the European conquest, the indigenous population had declined to a fraction of that number. Overall decline in Native American numbers continued for the next four hundred years.

The conquest begins

The history of Christianity in the Americas, as in Asia and Africa in the early modern period, became inseparably tied to the voyages and migrations of European peoples that began in the fifteenth century. Where in Asia and Africa Europeans encountered other Christian communities, sometimes in small numbers but at other times in significant numbers, in the Americas they found themselves in lands where no memory or experience of Christianity existed. The first experience of Christianity in the Americas was linked to brutal conquest and colonization. Christianity arrived as the religion of the conquerors.

The European adventurers who began the conquest of the Americas in the fifteenth and sixteenth centuries were driven by a strange mixture of desire for exploration and trade, national rivalries for territorial expansion, and a desire to spread Christian influence. This last desire was predominantly shaped in the Iberian experience by a long Christian memory of engagement with, or struggle against, Islam. The voyages undertaken by Portugal and Spain in the fifteenth century were understood religiously by many who supported and many who undertook them to be first and foremost a continuation of four hundred years of crusading against Islam. In Iberia the Crusades had taken the form of the *Reconquista* ("Reconquest"). Pope John XXII (1244-1344) had recognized the *Ordinis Christi Militia* ("Order of the Knights of Christ") in 1319. Its purpose was to establish outposts south of Spain and Portugal to encircle Muslims who were still in the Iberian Peninsula. Pope Eugene IV (1383-1447) had sought to encourage the Portuguese by promising that spiritual jurisdiction over all lands conquered by them would be placed under this order. The idea of encirclement was an essential element of the religious strategy that fueled the drive to find a sea route to India. The Renaissance pope Nicholas V (1397-1455), who established the Vatican Library and began the construction of St. Peter's in Rome in the middle of the fifteenth century, called upon the Christian nations of Europe to send out voyagers to discover a sea route to India in order to make contact with the Christians whom he believed might live there, in hopes that an alliance could be made with Christian powers in Asia to encircle and finally defeat Islam. These hopes for a final successful Crusade against Islam informed in part the efforts not only of the Portuguese as they launched their global colonial venture in the fifteenth century but of the Spanish as they first arrived in the Caribbean and Central America.

The Portuguese under Prince Henry the Navigator (1394-1460) led the way. Forces under Henry successfully crossed the Straits of Gibraltar to capture Ceuta off the coast of North Africa in 1415. Advances in navigation and in ship building allowed them to venture out farther into the Atlantic, making use of offshore trade winds to move swiftly across open seas without having to hug the land. The Spanish soon followed the Portuguese into the Atlantic, taking the Canary Islands off the northwest coast of Africa, which became in effect the first overseas "evangelistic" outpost of the Roman Catholic Church. The indigenous inhabitants, known as the Guanches, were subjugated by the end of the fifteenth century, and the islands were completely "evangelized," making the Canary Islands an extension of southern Europe.

As important as the religious motive was, it was not by itself enough to inspire or to explain the expansion that was under way. What drove the efforts of such explorers as Bartolomeu Dias (1451-1500), who arrived at the Cape of Good Hope in 1487, Cristóbal Colón (better known as Christopher Columbus, 1451-1506), who arrived in what he took to be the Indies (but turned out to be the Caribbean) in 1492, and Vasco da Gama (c. 1460-1524), who navigated around Africa and arrived in India in 1498, was not just religion but wealth. The possibility of discovering new sources of gold and precious gems, and the hope of cutting out Muslim intermediaries from the spice trade were critical issues in Portugal's and Spain's expansion. Gold was not just a commodity but the primary currency for exchange, while spice was used in the preservation of meats, which allowed European peoples to sustain the long winters. Together they symbolized the quest for wealth that helped define what has come to be known as the modern era. The fact that Muslims in the fifteenth century controlled both the major sources of gold coming into Europe from West Africa and the spice trade from India indicates how matters of religious and material economy were intertwined.

Christopher Columbus was born in Genoa and spent his first years at sea sailing for Portugal in the Mediterranean. By the middle of the 1480s he was convinced that the world was round, and had developed an apocalyptic sense of the necessity to discover a western route to India. Although he had never served as a ship captain, he succeeded in convincing Queen Isabella of Spain in 1492 to underwrite an expedition to the east. His estimation of the distance was far too optimistic. Columbus calculated the island of Japan to be about 6,200 km west of the Canaries, whereas the actual distance to Florida (not Japan) was approximately 19,000 km.

As with most other European explorers of his era, religion played a critical role in motivating Columbus. His apocalyptic vision was made clear years later, after his third trip across the Atlantic, when he was returned to Spain a broken man in chains. Through visions and the study of texts, Columbus had become convinced that he had been specially called by God to bring about the final age of human history when Christianity would be fulfilled by surrounding Islam; the terrestrial paradise would be discovered, and Jerusalem would be established as the City of God where all the nations would stream to worship. While his own grand apocalyptic vision never came about, what Columbus brought to what he thought was Asia was apocalyptic in a different sense for the indigenous peoples of America.

Columbus set off on his voyage with only three small ships and a company of ninety sailors. Among the crew on board were a Jewish interpreter who spoke Hebrew and Aramaic, a notary, and a representative of the Spanish court. None were priests or monks. The ships arrived in Hispaniola, in what is now the Dominican Republic, in October of 1492. After exploring several islands that he claimed for the Spanish crown, losing one vessel, leaving forty sailors to build a fort, and taking several of the indigenous Taínos captive to show back in court, he returned to Spain. The following year he returned to the Caribbean with a veritable flotilla of seventeen ships and more than one thousand settlers, who brought seeds, pigs, and sheep. Included in their number were two friars and several lay brothers who came to evangelize the indigenous Taínos and Caribs. Finding the forty sailors left from the first voyage dead and their settlement burned in response to their violence and rape of indigenous women, Columbus retaliated. The Taínos were forced to surrender before the superior military power of the Spanish and be enslaved, with five hundred taken captive to be sold back in Spain.

Within a decade the Spanish had established control over the Caribbean islands of Cuba, Jamaica, Hispaniola, and Puerto Rico. The indigenous people living in the Caribbean were of three major groups, all of whom had recently migrated from regions in the Brazil basin: the Ciboney, Caribs, and Taínos. Prior to the appearance of the Spanish they lived mostly off of yucca, yams, fish, and crustaceans. Most of their communities were small and near the sea. Holding superior military weaponry, the Spanish were able to subdue and enslave these indigenous people quickly. Within a few decades, however, disease overtook direct violence, and the indigenous populations of the Caribbean were almost entirely wiped out.

Church and crown both had as a lofty goal the stated purpose of evangelization of these new territories. Their deeds, however, were often at odds with their rhetoric. In a letter dated February 15, 1493, Columbus was the first to suggest enslaving the natives, including them in the other forms of wealth that he expected to bring back to the court in Spain. Enslaving subjugated peoples was not without legal problems for Europeans at the time. Ancient Roman law, which European nations still claimed to follow for precedent, had allowed for "barbarians," which had been understood by the church to mean non-Christians, to be enslaved. But these Caribbean peoples had not rejected the Christian faith, at least not yet. In 1500 Queen Isabella sought the advice of her confessor, Jimenez de Cisneros (1436-1517), who ruled against enslaving the indigenous peoples, whom he considered to be subjects of the queen. Only those captured in a just war could be enslaved. But this loophole proved large, as any rebellion staged by indigenous people could be used to justify enslavement. It would not be until 1542 when the New Laws were established that the indigenous peoples of the Americas were protected from such acts. Furthermore, as will be seen below, these laws were never applied to enslaved Africans brought to the Americas.

Columbus proved to be a poor administrator of the original settlement in the Caribbean. After his third voyage he was arrested by a new governor of the colony appointed by the crown and returned to Spain in chains. He apparently died without ever realizing he had not reached Asia. Others soon realized the significance of his voyage, however. Another Italian captain, Amerigo Vespucci (Americus Vespucius in Latin, 1454-1512), charted the South American coast in the first years of the sixteenth century. A German publisher in 1507 produced the first western European map to show that the continent was a separate body. The mapmaker gave the continent Americus's name, thereby in effect inventing the Americas. Meanwhile, the flow of Spanish colonists into Hispaniola, and then Cuba, was steady. Within two decades over ten thousand Europeans had immigrated to the Caribbean. The number of priests and friars who came with them remained relatively small.

Spanish monarchs had been granted by papal decrees dating to the earlier *Reconquista* the powers of royal patronage (*real patronato*) in territories that came under their control. This meant that the monarchs had the power to nominate bishops for the churches in lands that they conquered. In effect it gave the Spanish kings power of episcopal appointments. Papal bulls of 1501, 1508, and 1511 strengthened these powers under Ferdinand, giving the Spanish crown nearly absolute authority over the creation of churches and monasteries, the appointment of priests and bishops, and even the collection of church taxes in their colonies. Such authority did not extend entirely over the members of the religious orders, the Dominicans and Franciscans, who began to arrive in the early sixteenth century, but it did shape overall the life of the church in its first decades in the Americas.

In 1512 the first bishop arrived in America, setting up his see at Caparra in Puerto Rico. The second arrived in Concepción, in Hispanolia, in 1513. Both returned to Spain by 1516, leaving Franciscan and then Dominican friars to carry on their work without episcopal oversight. The king sent Dominicans specifically to ensure heresies did not gain a foothold in his new lands. The presence of this Order of Preachers meant that Christianity in the new Spanish lands would be characterized by a strong emphasis on teaching. Franciscans also came in these early years, many of them influenced by new reforms that were beginning to spread through Spain. On the whole these early Franciscans were better educated and more disciplined than the Dominicans.

While the Franciscans might thus have been expected to take prophetic leadership regarding the indigenous peoples, given the history of Francis that informed the community, it was the Dominicans who first raised critical prophetic voices against what was happening to the indigenous people. By doing so they inadvertently became the catalyst for one of the most important documents in the early history of Christianity in America, *Las Capitulaciones de Burgos* ("The Capitulations of Burgos") of 1512, the document signed by King Ferdinand and several bishops that set the governing parameters for the early development of churches in the Caribbean. The *Capitulaciones* were in part designed to institutionally contain the Dominicans, whose protests were already being heard.

The rapid decline in the native populations, the mistreatment of local people working in the mines and fields, and the lack of financial support for the missionary work were all evidence of a lack of ecclesiastical oversight to at least some of the Dominicans. Pedro de Córdoba (1482-1521) and Antonio de Montesinos (c. 1486-1530) were among the first in the order who had arrived in 1510. By Advent of 1511 they were both overwhelmed by what they had seen and began to speak out. The Spanish thirst for wealth required a large labor force to search for and extract gold. The local people were gathered onto *encomiendas* ruled by a conquistador and forced to work in the fields or mines. Although the *encomienda* was established in part to ensure that the local people were instructed in the Spanish religion, in fact this was a very low priority of the *encomienderos* who ruled them. The women often became concubines of the *encomiendero,* and the harsh conditions led to local populations gradually fading away either by death or escape at night. It was slavery in all but name.

On December 21, 1511, in Santo Domingo in what is now the Dominican Republic, de Montesinos delivered a sermon that was to be heard far beyond his local congregation. Present were many of the Spanish officials and *encomienderos* who controlled the economic, military, and missionary enterprise of the colony. The text for the day was Matthew 3:3, "A voice of one crying in the wilderness. . . ." The Dominican's sermon was direct and prophetic. By what right, he asked rhetorically, are the indigenous people being subjugated and oppressed. Are they not human with rational souls, and thus are the settlers not bound to treat them with Christian love? De Montesinos suggested that the settlers' state of salvation was comparable to that of Turks and Moors, which was to say, to that of unbelieving Muslims. He concluded by charging them with living in mortal sin.

The sermon was like an arrow shot from the pulpit, and it soon hit its target, the king of Spain. The king's response was two-fold. First he condemned the sermon as theologically erroneous and made sure that the Dominican provincial in Spain did the same. He then moved to strengthen the claims of royal patronage, convening a group of scholars in Spain to examine the complaint and produce a document that would guide Spanish rule in the conquered regions.

The *Capitulaciones* was the result. Signed in the Castilian city of Burgos, the document set the direction for the development of Christianity in Spanish America. It affirmed the earlier papal bulls of donation, *Inter caetera* and *Eximiae devotionis*, which had given the kings of Portugal and Spain spiritual authority in what Europeans considered newly "discovered" lands. It also made explicit that the state was in charge of all evangelization, appointment of clergy and friars, and any arbitration in theological disputes. No appeal was to be made to Rome.

Important for the development of the church was the clear statement that clergy were to be from Spain, or were to be descendants of the Spaniards. In America, indigenous people and Africans were excluded from the ordained ranks of church leadership. Finally, the *Capitulaciones* made it clear that clergy, including Dominican friars, were not to resist the use of local people to mine gold. Extracting gold and bringing the people to God were not conflicting goals. Priests were to support the work of extracting gold by telling the people that more gold would translate into increased ability to go to war against infidels, who were generally understood to be Muslims, but could also be the indigenous peoples who refused to be baptized. The subjugation of the people, racial separation and hierarchy, the priority of gold, and the marginalization of the papacy in these new lands were all put in print as it were in this original "constitution" for the Americas.

Subduing the Aztecs

Mesoamerica had a long history prior to the sixteenth century. The Aztecs were one of the newer immigrant cultures in the region of present-day Mexico and Guatemala. By the time the Aztecs arrived in the fourteenth century, there had already been a succession of previous kingdoms in Mexico, including the Olmec, Toltecs, Mixtecs, and Mayas. Some had declined as a result of outside conquest, others possibly by disease. The Aztec's religious beliefs and practices were nearly identical to those of their predecessors in the region, but they had formed a political state that was ruled by a king rather than by priests. They succeeded in forming an alliance with two other peoples and then together set about to conquer the entire region of Mexico, exacting tribute and maintaining what amounted to a permanent state of war on their frontiers. Their military aristocracy redistributed the land to the benefit of the nobility within the Aztec nation itself, creating greater class divisions than were found among their neighboring states.

The Aztecs claimed to be descendants of Huitzilopochtli, the god of war, who was thereby raised to the level of the god of creation. The mission of the Aztecs was to subdue all other nations and provide sacrificial blood to nourish the one whom they considered to be the supreme giver of life. These two pursuits came together in the sacrifice of prisoners taken in war, an aspect of Aztec culture that the Spanish Christians later exploited as a justification for their conquest. For their part the Aztecs believed that they were the specially chosen people of the sun. Being the chosen people, they had the responsibility to provide the vital energy that would keep the sun and the earth alive. The sun's energy came from blood sacrifice, without which cataclysmic events such as earthquakes, hurricanes, and fires were bound to occur. War, sacrifice, and imperial expansion were thus woven together in the purpose of their existence, and to a degree all of the other gods partook of this blood economy. Among these other Aztec gods was the prophet and god-man, Topiltzin Quetzalcoatl, who was depicted as a young prince and feathered serpent. He was said to have had a miraculous birth, possess miraculous powers, and have ecstatic experiences. He built a great capital city before being deposed and killed, but was later transformed into the Morning Star. Another important Aztec figure was the goddess Tonantzin. Later tradition identified the appearance of the Virgin of Guadalupe on an ancient site dedicated to her worship.

With Hispaniola, Cuba, Puerto Rico, and other islands of the Caribbean under their control, the Spanish turned their interest to conquest of the mainland. In 1519 Hernando Cortéz (1484-1547), who had already established himself as a conquistador, sailed from Cuba with eleven ships, six hundred Spaniards, sixteen horses, and fourteen pieces of artillery. His first encounter on the mainland was in Tabasco, where his forces met with minor resistance. The Tabascan leaders gave him gifts as tribute, including the enslaved woman named Malinalli (known after her baptism as Marina or "La Malinche," c. 1500-c. 1530). As noted above, she not only became Cortéz's common-law wife, but played a critical role as his translator as he moved north against the Aztec capital of Tenochtitlan.

Reports of the wealth of Moctezuma II (1466-1520) drew Cortéz and his soldiers to the north. Along the way they formed an alliance with others who were motivated by resistance to Aztec aggression and domination. Entering the city of Tenochtitlan late in 1519 as visitors, the Spanish were able to turn the tables on Moctezuma. Within a year the emperor was dead. The Spanish forces escaped from the city in the aftermath of the emperor's execution and then engaged in an attack on the city that was supported both by reinforcements of Spanish from the Caribbean and by warriors from other tribes that the Aztecs had oppressed. In 1521 Cortéz finally captured the capital city and executed Moctezuma's successor as emperor. By the end of 1521 most of Mexico was under Spanish control.

Conquering the Incas

In 1533, a little more than a decade after Cortéz defeated the Aztecs in Mexico, another Spanish conquistador, Francisco Pizarro (1476-1541), with several hundred Spanish troops seized control of the capital city of Cuzco in Peru, thereby bringing about the effective administrative end of the Incan empire in South America. Driving the expedition was the quest for Incan gold, about which Pizzaro had heard stories in Panama more than a decade earlier. This was his third incursion into Incan territories and came at the time of Incan civil war. Pizzaro reached the city of Cajamarca in the Andean mountains in 1532 and with the vastly superior military weaponry of his small number of troops he captured the recently victorious emperor, Atahualpa (1497-1533). Pizarro demanded from Atahualpa a room filled with gold, but even after obtaining it Pizarro executed him. The Spanish then installed his younger brother on the throne, but he too was soon in rebellion.

The Incan empire was a mountain kingdom that stretched across more than 4,000 km in the Andes. Given its size, Pizarro's success was not as quick and decisive as that of Cortéz. His conquest never had the finality, both militarily and religiously, that characterized the conquest of Mexico. Rather than destroying the capital city of Cuzco, which played such an important role in Incan religious and cultural life, Pizarro left it and established a new capital at Lima. The effect was to allow the Incas to continue in much of their ancestral religious and cultural life while claiming to be loyal subjects of the Catholic monarch. Revolt and resistance to Spanish rule continued throughout the sixteenth century. The younger brother of Atahualpa whom Pizzaro had allowed to take the throne, Manco (1516–1544), escaped to establish a shadow Inca empire in the mountains, complete with the revival of Inca worship. One of his sons continued the resistance after his death. Finally, in 1572 the last Inca ruler, Túpac Amaru ("Royal Serpent" in Quechua), was captured and beheaded in the center of Cuzco, bringing organized resistance to an end. Túpac Amaru became a powerful symbol for the resistance of indigenous peoples against colonial rule and domination in later independence movements in the eighteenth and nineteenth centuries.

Colonization of Brazil

The conquest of the Caribbean, Mexico, and Peru had all been carried out by Spanish armies, bringing these regions into the Spanish colonial empire. The conquest of Brazil, in contrast, was by Portuguese forces and as such was a continuation of the conquest and evangelization of the Atlantic world begun with the Portuguese settlements on the eastern Atlantic, in Madeira, and in the Azores. The Portuguese initially tried to cultivate grains on these islands, but soon discovered that sugar cane, which they considered a spice, yielded a far greater profit. The colonization of Brazil followed a similar economic pattern.

Portuguese sailors landed in Brazil as early as 1500, when thirteen ships under the command of Pedro Álvares Cabral (1468-1520) attempting to sail around Africa were blown off course and arrived in what is today Porto Seguro. Under the terms of the Treaty of Tordesillas that had been negotiated between Portugal and Spain in 1494 and specified the line of demarcation between Spanish and Portuguese colonies at 370 leagues west of the Cape Verdes islands, the Portuguese claimed the region. Naming the region after a tree that they found there that had the color of an ember (*pau-brasil*), the Portuguese showed little interest in developing a permanent presence over the next several decades. It was not until French explorers began to make their presence known in the region that Portugal in 1530 decided to plant a permanent colony. Shortly after that they began the cultivation of sugar cane. Sugar cane soon changed the face of Brazil.

The indigenous people whom the Portuguese encountered in Brazil lived in isolated communities and were technologically far less developed than the Portuguese. Brazil did not offer valuable gems or precious metals, and the Portuguese found that the indigenous peoples knew the land too well to make their enslavement profitable. Trade from Brazil was controlled by the Portuguese crown, but the king leased the work initially to Fernáo de Loronha (1470-1540), a former Jew who had converted to Christianity. Under his leadership the colony's production expanded.

The first Portuguese ships to arrive in Brazil carried Franciscan missionaries who celebrated a Mass that was observed by some indigenous peoples. Two years later the first indigenous peoples in Brazil were baptized by a chaplain who was part of an expedition under Gonçalo Coelho (1451-1512). The names of those who were the first to be baptized have not been handed down, and one can only imagine what they thought about the act they were undergoing. A handful of missionaries, mostly Franciscans, continued mission work sporadically through this period. It was not until the pope formally granted to the Portuguese crown patronage over Brazil in 1551 that a more fully organized mission effort was undertaken.

The Franciscans established villages where local inhabitants were invited or enticed to come and live. Within these villages the Franciscans conducted catechism classes and sought to provide pastoral oversight for their converts. They reported large numbers, both children and adults, were undergoing baptism. Converts were being instructed that they could no longer eat human flesh, and husbands could now have only one wife. Soon they were establishing schools for the indigenous peoples, for girls and boys alike. The Franciscans also provided religious services to the Portuguese colonial settlements that began to grow after 1530, which were mostly inhabited by traders and *degredados* (castaways, deserters, or convicts). For several decades all of the European settlers in Brazil were men. Many cohabitated with indigenous women, making for a mixed race, multilingual, multicultural, and even multireligious colony.

Administrative challenges after 1550 led the king to divide the colony into fourteen districts drawn as latitudinal regions or strips that were handed over to proprietary captains to be governed almost as private fiefdoms. These captains and their progeny were given authority to rule their territories in perpetuity, making laws, punishing criminals, and establishing taxes. The administrative reorganization of Brazil and the never-ending search for slave labor encouraged settlements to move farther inland. But the single most important factor in the changing colonial situation was the rapid development of sugar plantations. The Portuguese settlements quickly expanded from small factories to large plantations. Large tracts of land were needed for growing and processing sugar cane, resulting in large-scale displacement of indigenous peoples. The sugar that Brazil produced made its way almost entirely into the European economy. European hunger for sweetness literally transformed the face of Brazil, as it later would the Caribbean.

The results of the growth of sugar production in Brazil were devastating for the local peoples. A strongly adversarial relationship emerged between colonial immigrants and natives. The Portuguese used cannons to subdue the people, burning villages and enslaving survivors. Many among the indigenous peoples retaliated. During the 1540s there were revolts against the Portuguese at Bahia, São Tomé, Espírito Santo, and Porto Seguro, although none was effective. Contact between European immigrants and Native Americans meanwhile introduced diseases such as the deadly smallpox into the region, which soon led to the decimation of whole tribes.

With the loss of local people because of disease and conquest, new sources of labor were sought for the production of sugar. Indigenous people often knew the local terrain and so could easily escape. By the middle of the sixteenth century there were fewer and fewer Native Americans to enslave, sending slavers farther and farther inland for captives. Meanwhile, the Portuguese had been selling and using enslaved Africans for more than half a century by 1500. Africans began being shipped to Brazil to work on sugar plantations in the 1530s, and with the huge increase in sugar production the importation of Africans increased as well. Sugar literally darkened the complexion of Brazil. By the end of the sixteenth century between ten thousand and fifteen thousand enslaved persons were arriving from West Africa per year. They came from what is now Sierra Leone in the north to Angola in the south. Nearly 40 percent of all Africans brought across the Atlantic ended up in Brazil.

Preoccupation with wealth often marginalized religious concerns and rendered evangelistic efforts adversarial in the eyes of the plantation owners, military leaders, and ruling officials in Brazil. The work of priests and bishops was marginal to the first generations of colonists and their descendants, many of them of mixed ancestry as European men fathered children with Native American and African women. Nevertheless the work of the church went forward. By 1550 there were over ten parishes established. The efforts of the first generation of Franciscans among the indigenous peoples did not survive the rapid transformation that took place in Brazil during the latter half of the century, due mostly to the growth of the sugar plantations. Nevertheless, those early efforts were significant. Records from a later period indicate that prior to 1550 as many as forty thousand indigenous peoples may have been baptized.

Requerimiento, encomienda, and conquistadors

Throughout the fifteenth and sixteenth centuries one of the expressed goals of the Spanish (less so of the Portuguese) in America was always the conversion of the "Indians," as the disoriented explorer Columbus had called the indigenous peoples. Understanding the religious dimensions of the conquest requires some understanding of Spanish Christianity of the period, for Spanish Christianity was brought to the Americas with little adjustment to the new local context. A larger discussion of Iberian Christianity will follow in a later chapter, but for understanding religion in the conquest, a few comments are necessary.

First, the relatively harmonious state of relations among Islam, Judaism, and Christianity that had coexisted for centuries in Spain had began to decline sharply with the *Reconquista* and came to an end the year Columbus sailed to the west. In 1492 all remaining Jews were expelled from Spain and the last Muslim kingdom in Spain, Granada, was defeated. The expulsion included many Jews and Muslims who claimed to have converted, whom the Spanish called *conversos*. The Spanish court and many church officials often doubted the authenticity of such conversions. There is sufficient evidence to suggest that their suspicions were not without warrant as many *conversos* continued to practice the Jewish and the Islamic faiths in secret. Spanish Christian anxieties about the true state of faith among converted peoples and their descendants led Queen Isabella to reestablish the Inquisition in Spain, a two-hundred-year-old institution that sought out Jews, Muslims, and (later) anyone with leanings toward the new Protestant teachings who were coming from other parts of Europe. In some ways Spain remained the most committed of the European lands to the old feudal structures. The tradition of royal control of the church that had been a heritage of the *Reconquista* made direct papal interference unlikely.

It was in this context in Spain that debates over the conquest of "Indians" took place in the sixteenth century. One of the documents shaped by them was *el Requerimiento* from 1510. Dominicans in Hispaniola had complained that a war of crusade against indigenous peoples, which the conquistadors claimed to be carrying out, was unjust. The document was intended to address the moral problem of going to war against indigenous peoples without provocation. It identified the papal donation to the king and queen of Spain as the basis for the Spanish claims to sovereignty over the lands that were being occupied, and called upon its hearers to submit immediately both to Christian belief and to Spanish rule. Against any who refused or even delayed it declared immediate war, allowing the Spanish to enslave them and seize all possessions.

It was the intention of *el Requerimiento* to satisfy the moral demands of a just war, but in fact it served only as a thin moral veneer to cover Spanish aggression.

The document appears to have made its way into usage by 1513 in the Americas. A member of the attacking force would stand outside a village or even be on board ship while still at sea, and would read it, often inaudibly and always in Spanish to an indigenous people, who in most cases did not understand the language. Immediate devastation most often followed, as the Spanish with their superior military power marched against the inhabitants, justified in part by the demand of *el Requerimiento* that its hearers refrain from a malicious delay in conversion.

A second method of royal evangelization that emerged in America is one that has already been noted, the *encomienda*. These "relocation camps" were used both to provide slave-type labor and to preach to a captive audience. Local populations were made to relocate to provide labor for sugar plantations or mines. Secular priests or friars lived on the *encomienda* to provide religious instruction under the guise of saving the souls of the indigenous people. The *encomienda* emerged early in the conquest in 1503 when the rulers of Hispaniola, under instruction from the Spanish crown, first gathered local laborers to educate them in how to behave and what to believe. The free and uncontrollable lifestyle of the local people, who bathed naked, wore few clothes, and often wandered off, must be brought under Christian control, the Spanish reasoned. *Encomiendas* were never but a small step away from full slavery.

Defending the rights of indigenous peoples

The overall impact of the conquest upon indigenous peoples was nothing short of genocidal. Disease, enslavement, and warfare all contributed to the decimation of the local populations during the first decades. In 1542 the king of Spain issued a new set of legislative rules governing the treatment of Native Americans that were known as *Leyes Nuevas* ("New Laws"). The *Leyes Nuevas* called for greater protection of the indigenous peoples, forbid their enslavement, and called for the dissolution of the *encomiendas*. The response by the colonists in America was either to ignore them or violently resist them, and within several years the more drastic reforms were all but abandoned.

The name that is most often identified with the defense of the rights of indigenous peoples in sixteenth-century America is that of Bartolomé de Las Casas (1484-1566). A Dominican who became known as the "Apostle to the Indies," de Las Casas had first crossed the Atlantic in 1502 at age eighteen, seeking his fortune as an *encomenderos*. A decade later he was ordained a priest, apparently the first person to be ordained to the priesthood in America. De Las Casas continued for several years to run his own *encomienda*, using local people to work in mines while providing them with some religious instruction. By 1514, however, he had firmly turned against the cruel system. Releasing his conscripted Native American workers, he returned to Spain to press the case for the rights of the indigenous peoples. His cause won the support of the archbishop of Toledo and confessor to the queen, Francisco Jimenez de Cisneros, who labeled de Las Casas "Protector of the Indians" and appointed him to a special commission to further investigate the plight of the indigenous. In December of 1518 the young priest finally met the new king of Spain, Carlos I (1500-1558), to present the case for the Native Americans.

Over the course of the next several decades, de Las Casas would labor intensely on both sides of the Atlantic on behalf of the indigenous peoples. In 1522 he joined the Dominican order, and several years later began what would become his monumental book, *Historia de las Indias* ("History of the Indies"), which was not published until after his death. Back in Spain he was influential in getting Charles I to publish the *Leyes Nuevas* in 1542, the same year he completed his short account, *Brevísima relación de la destrucción de las Indias* ("The Devastation of the Indies: A Brief Account"). The following year he was appointed bishop of Chiapas, in Guatemala, where he sought to enforce the *Leyes Nuevas* rigorously. Opposition to such acts such as denying the sacraments to anyone who held an *encomienda* forced de Las Casas finally to return to Spain in 1547 where he spent the rest of his life arguing the cause. In 1550 Carlos I convened an assembly of theologians and lawyers in the city of Valladolid and invited de Las Casas to debate the cause of the indigenous peoples with another Spanish theologian, Juan Ginés de Sepúlveda (1489-1573). The debate took place over several months in 1550 and 1551, and by contemporary accounts was without a clear winner. Nevertheless, it provided de Las Casas with an opportunity to present his case again before the Spanish court.

Throughout the course of his life, de Las Casas made his case for the rights of the indigenous peoples in three ways. First, he argued against the violence by giving ample and graphic details of the evidence of the tragedies that had occurred. The genre of his writing in this regard was important. There were others arguing in defense of the indigenous peoples, but the vivid descriptions of violence in the work of de Las Casas won him a hearing. His books are important historical works still today for documenting the extent of the destruction.

Second, de Las Casas argued on biblical, theological, and philosophical grounds that Native Americans were rational beings and equal in humanity to the Spanish. The people of America were generally peace-loving and avoided war. They were capable of learning to worship God. In his debate with de Sepúlveda, de Las Casas did not reject Aristotle's doctrine that some people are slaves by nature, but he argued that Aristotle's analysis did not fit Native Americans. They had demonstrated the arts of civilization in their cities, languages, customs, and more. The Spanish, on the other hand, were in danger of incurring the judgment of God if they continued to oppress the people of the Indies. The Spanish in fact risked becoming as low and vile as the "Moors" (Muslims) if they continued on in the conquest. Warfare, argued de Las Casas, could only be carried out legitimately in self-defense or against those who persecute Christians and work for the destruction of the Christian faith. The indigenous peoples had done none of these and thus were wrongly being conquered.

Finally, de Las Casas gave specific counsel on how to carry out missionary work among the indigenous peoples. Accepting the Native American peoples as equal and equally "teachable" of things divine, he argued that they must be given time to reason over the great truths from God, and not be forced through violence so as not to be occupied by sorrow or anger. He advocated free towns in which they would be allowed to live in peace and work profitably to the benefit of their own ends. He forcefully argued that conversion could only be genuine if it were not coerced but was a free act.

In his defense of the indigenous Americans de Las Casas was a strong and consistent voice. His defense of Africans who were being enslaved and oppressed, on the other hand, was never as forceful. In his early writings de Las Casas had actually advocated the use of enslaved Africans for labor in place of Native Americans in the Indies, a stance he later came to reject. Various explanations have been offered for his initial support of African labor, such as that he had been misled by the Portuguese to believe Africans had been legally enslaved, or that he never expected the number of Africans being imported to be so large. De Las Casas never offered a defense of Africans on the grounds that he defended the rights of the Native Americans. He came to oppose the African slave trade, but not the holding of peoples of African descent in bondage. By all accounts he appears to have accepted the legitimacy of the perpetual enslavement of Africans in America.

There were others who defended the rights of the indigenous, some who held positions of ecclesiastical authority. Juan de Zumárraga (1468-1548) was the first bishop and then in 1527 the first archbishop of Mexico, or New Spain as the region was called with the appointment of a viceroy in 1535. De Zumárraga exercised his authority to defend the remaining Aztec and other indigenous peoples in his district. Facing opposition from other settlers, he placed all of Mexico under ecclesiastical censure and journeyed to Spain to defend his actions. Upon his return to Mexico he recruited artisans and teachers to help develop the indigenous society, established schools for girls as well as boys, founded hospitals, and even laid the foundations for a college that opened after his death. Zumárraga brought the first printing press to America, with which he published catechisms and other materials. He left a legacy of strong leadership with moral integrity.

Not all church leaders were successful in their advocacy for the indigenous peoples. Antonio de Valdivieso (1495-1550) found out the hard way the risk of opposing the colonialists. Valdivieso was the third bishop of Nicaragua and Costa Rica, assuming the office after it had been vacant for eight years. In 1544 he attempted to implement the reforms called for in the *Leyes Nuevas*. Understandably his efforts were not well received by the *encomenderos* in the diocese. Large portions of his bishopric were controlled by members of a single wealthy family that stood to lose a great deal if the *Leyes Nuevas* were enforced. One of his opponents traveled to Spain to argue for the retention of the *encomiendas*, to no avail. The local *encomenderos* then rose up in opposition and killed Valdivieso in 1550, making him arguably one of the first true Christian martyrs in the Americas.

Notable among the efforts to protect the rights of indigenous peoples in the mid-sixteenth century were those of a newly organized religious order from Europe, the Society of Jesus, otherwise known as the Jesuits. The first six Jesuits arrived in Salvador de Bahia, Brazil, in 1549, less than ten years after the founding of the order in 1540 by Ignatius of Loyola (1491-1556). Because their members answered directly to Rome, they were not under the *patronato* and could operate with a greater degree of autonomy than could the other clergy in the region. It quickly became clear to the Jesuit priests that if they wanted to convert Native Americans, they would have to move inland, away from the influence of the colonizers. Here they began developing independent villages for Native American converts that were called *reducciones* ("reductions"), with members of the Jesuit order serving as governors. Their intention was to create self-sustaining Native American communities that would keep the indigenous people free from the cultural domination and enslavement of other European colonists. One of the signs of success was the large number of indigenous peoples who joined the order in Brazil. By 1600 nearly 17 percent of the Jesuits in Brazil were of indigenous descent. Their ring of schools along the coast for preparing Jesuit missionaries trained indigenous and Portuguese settlers alike.

There were a number of important church leaders who spoke in defense of indigenous peoples and their descendants in sixteenth-century America. The same cannot be said for church leaders defending the rights of persons of African descent, on the other hand. Even the Jesuits held African slaves without expressing much reservation in the first century of the conquest in America. Numerous legal and religious documents published in Europe during the fifteenth and sixteenth centuries distinguished between the situation of Native Americans and Africans. Native Americans were depicted by their defenders as free and peaceful, and therefore were wrongly enslaved, while the enslavement of Africans was overwhelmingly defended as being legitimate in both the eyes of the church and of the law. The Portuguese, who long dominated the African slave trade, routinely defended their cargo as being legitimate captives taken as prisoners of war and purchased by Portuguese merchants to be sold. Papal bulls from the fifteenth century put Africans alongside Muslims, thereby making them legitimate targets of warfare and violence.

There was nothing on the order of the work of Bartolomé de Las Casas in defense of the Africans who were enslaved and held captive in the sixteenth century in America. The closest one comes to finding such is the 1556 publication by Domingo de Soto (1494-1560), *De justitia et jure*, which spoke of the treatment of Africans in terms of missionary concerns. Christianity must not be forced upon people, but instead must be accepted freely. Since the primary concern for all people is that they become Christian, Africans should not be enslaved, he argued. Alonzo de Montúfar (1489-1572), the archbishop of Mexico who succeeded Zumárraga, wrote an appeal to the king around 1560 asking that the enslavement of Africans immediately cease. A number of other appeals and theological statements were made in the 1560s and 1570s, but the arguments were not sustained and there was no royal will to challenge an institution that had become so necessary to global economics. Religious protest against slavery grew in the seventeenth century, but even then the voices were few and hardly heard.

Characteristics of Christian life in sixteenth-century America

Christianity came to America in the sixteenth century completely intertwined with the conquest. The conquistadors and settlers in the Americas for the most part sought to reproduce all aspects of life, including religion, as they knew of it from Portugal and Spain. Churches and cathedrals were built to resemble those in Iberia. Bishops and priests came from Spain and Portugal and sought to maintain a high degree of continuity with the form of Christian faith that they knew from Iberia. By the middle of the sixteenth century bishoprics and diocesan structures were fairly well established throughout the entire continent. After 1600 there would only be fourteen more dioceses formed in the next three hundred years in South America, an indication of how stable the early structure was.

The conquistadors and settlers were Christians, lay persons mostly, but nevertheless faithful members of the church who received its sacraments and according to their own understanding lived under its teachings. The churches that began to be built in America after 1500 were firmly under the authority of friars, priests, and bishops, who in turn, for all practical purposes, were under the authority of the Spanish or Portuguese crown. The vision and goal of the Iberian settlers were to construct upon the land they were conquering replicas of the Christian societies of Spain or Portugal that they had left behind. For the Spanish especially, to be Christian one had to farm, learn to make certain crafts, and attend Mass in a church or cathedral located in the center of the village, town, or city. America was to be built to replicate Spain or Portugal.

From the very first decade of the conquest, another form of Christianity began to take root in America, slowly at first, and without much in the way of historical record or documentation. Indigenous peoples were the targets and victims of extraordinary violence. Their numbers were drastically reduced by the diseases that the Spanish and Portuguese brought with them. In many places the indigenous population was reduced to one-tenth of its pre-conquest number. From the very first decades of the conquest, the Spanish and Portuguese directed missionary efforts toward indigenous peoples as well. Perhaps the most surprising historical fact to note is that these efforts were to some degree successful. Indigenous people in America began to become Christian, undergoing baptism and seeking to follow what they considered to be Christian ways of life.

Conflicting opinions regarding the degree to which certain cultural practices of indigenous peoples could be accommodated within a Christian society arose from time to time among church leaders. There was never a question, however, in the mind of friars, priests, conquistadors, governors, administrators, and others who were part of the Iberian colonial enterprise that indigenous peoples, if they were to be allowed to survive, must become Christian in an Iberian way. A paternalistic "civilizing" model of evangelism, accompanied and reinforced by extraordinary degrees of violence, dominated. Among the conquered, many accepted Christianity as the new religion that had to be followed. Aztecs had dutifully followed their religious priests, so they transferred that obedience to the newer Christian priests and were baptized by the thousands. Others, often in mountainous regions, resisted Christianization more explicitly, and still others found ways to maintain subjugated traditions surreptitiously.

Concerns about the condition of church life in Central and South America led the first archbishop of Lima, Gerónimo de Loayza (c. 1498-1575), to call the first two general church councils for the Americas, both of them held in Lima. The constitutions of the First Lima Council in 1551 were divided into two parts. The first dealt with the context of Native Americans and the second with organizing the Spanish colonial churches. According to the council's constitutions all local people were to be catechized before being admitted to baptism and they were to be taught in the local language. Parish structure was to follow the tribal configurations already present in the Americas. This did not mean Native Americans were to be equally received into what was being called the new "Christendom of the Indies." The second part of the constitutions gave eighty guidelines for organizing the Spanish and *criollo* (a person of European descent born in America) church. Local converts were not to receive the sacrament of the Eucharist, and Native Americans were to attend separate churches. Loayza provided leadership again for the much larger Second Lima Council in 1567. Here the use of local languages for instruction was once again affirmed. Loayza was aware of the decrees of a reforming council that had recently concluded in Europe, the Council of Trent, and tried to put some of them into practice as well. No steps, however, were taken to overcome the two-tiered system of Spanish and *criollo* churches on the one side and indigenous on the other.

In Brazil the importance of the local language was also a priority in evangelistic work. José de Anchieta (1534-1597), known as the "Apostle of Brazil," became proficient in the Tupí and Guarani languages spoken in that region. Seeking to help others who might follow in his footsteps, Anchieta published the first grammar book and dictionary in Tupí. This concern for languages was still evident at the end of the sixteenth century in the constitutions of the Third Lima Council of 1582-1583. At this gathering, arguably the most important of the Lima councils, the question of how to better evangelize the indigenous Americans was high on the agenda. Gentle persuasion in the language of the people was the rule of the day, and the need for catechetical materials in the local languages was recognized.

Alfonso de Mogrovejo (1538-1606), known as "Toribio," and the archbishop of Lima who called the third council helped to produce a catechism in three languages, Spanish, Quechua, and Aymara. As with other advocates of language acquisition, Toribio was critical of the treatment of the indigenous peoples both by the government officials and by the *encomiendas* who virtually enslaved the local population. The concern for learning the local languages to better communicate Iberian Catholicism stopped short of translation of the Bible into local languages. Except for occasional portions of scripture and the Lord's Prayer, the Bible itself was never translated into local languages by church leaders in America in the sixteenth century. Bernardino de Sahagún (1499-1590) came the closest with a translation of all four Gospels, plus a catechism and prayer books with sermons that he rendered in the Nahuatl language of Mexico.

Multilingual approaches to church life were not to become the norm in the sixteenth century in America. From the beginning of the century a policy of "hispanization" was taking place. Spain and Portugal were understood to be the model for their respective colonial territories. A Spanish royal order in 1550 required friars to teach the local people not just the Spanish language but Spanish practices and customs as well.

Hispanization required schools, especially for the *criollos*, or children of first-generation colonists. Schools were soon established for all children of European descent for basic literacy, but there was resistance to educate Native Americans or Africans at any level. Several early universities were founded by *peninsulares,* or immigrants from Iberia. Zumárraga's College of Tlatelooco was established to train local priests in 1536, but Zumárraga doubted if it was possible for indigenous people since, he believed, it was so difficult for them to remain celibate. In 1555 the First Council of Mexico forbade anyone who was not fully European from taking holy orders. This local or provincial ruling was affirmed for the entire Spanish empire in America in 1578. The First Council of Lima, while encouraging the use of local languages, paradoxically prevented a person of indigenous descent from receiving Holy Communion. A special dispensation from the bishop was required for an indigenous American to receive the Lord's Supper.

The first colonists brought with them crops, farm animals, and crafts from Iberia. The purpose was to have familiar foods and products for their own consumption. For the missionaries the new crafts and foods were introduced to help develop a local Christian economy for people who were often not used to being sedentary. Missionaries presented the Christian faith not only in catechetical instruction, but also through paintings and other artwork. Religious instruction was also provided in the transplanted rhythm of the Catholic life. Holy days, Mass, sermons, and confession were all re-enforced, giving a religious dimension to all of the life in the villages that friars sought to build among the indigenous peoples.

The traditional Christian saints of Catholic Europe soon came to serve double duty as local Native American deities became identified with particular Catholic figures in religious remembrances. Local indigenous religions were considered evil, and so idols, old temples, and other religious artwork were generally destroyed. The destruction of the pyramids of the Aztec nation and rebuilding of a cathedral from the same stones is a fitting example of how local religious cultures were perceived. However, indigenous American as well as imported African cultures not only survived, but have had a vibrant existence up to the present. Enslaved workers often continued African religious practices in the Caribbean islands and in Brazil, providing spiritual continuity in the midst of apocalyptic change. In Peru Pizzaro had defeated the Inca kingdom, but instead of building upon the old Incan capital of Cuzco, he established a new capital in Lima and thus allowed for the survival of Inca spiritual life in the ancient capital alongside Catholic faith.

Most Native Americans did not take Communion during the celebration of the Eucharist on a regular basis, if at all. As late as the end of the sixteenth century, indigenous Americans were generally only admitted to the Eucharist on Easter and only if they convinced the priest that they had a clear understanding of the sacrament. For most of the sixteenth century Native Americans and Africans were also excluded from joining religious orders. One of the first persons of mixed African descent to break through the barrier and to eventually be recognized as a saint in America was Martin de Porres (1579-1639). Born in Lima, Peru, his father was Spanish and his mother a freed African from Panama. Because his parents were not legally married, he was considered in the eyes of the church to be illegitimate. At age eleven Martin became a servant in a Dominican monastery and at fifteen he became a lay brother. He spent the rest of his life as a laborer, and developed a reputation for his spirituality, which extended far beyond the confines of his community and city, earning him official canonization by the church after his death.

Women in Catholic America

In the early stages of the conquest very few European women were to be found in America. Only 10 percent of the colonists before 1570 were women. The result was a high degree of sexual relations, in either marriage or concubinage, between Iberian conquistadors, sailors, traders, and colonists and Native American or African women. The resulting generations of offspring made America a racially diverse people. Many of the women who lived with Spanish and Portuguese men became Christian in name, if not in identity. Spiritual practices among these women, even those living with Christian men, tended to be more open to indigenous influences.

Spanish spirituality of the sixteenth century was militant, deeply opposed to heresies (including the new one called Protestantism, which was spreading in Europe) and devoted to the Virgin Mary, the mother of Jesus. This type of devotion directed the spiritual formation of women on the "frontier." It was devotion to Mary that was most important in guiding the spiritual life of women. The conquisidors brought with them from Spain their devotion to Our Lady of Guadalupe, who was depicted as a light-skinned supporter of the Spanish conquest. By the beginning of the seventeenth century, however, she had been converted through popular piety and in a well-known story of a vision given to a Native American *campesino* ("peasant") by the name of Juan Diego (1474-1548) into La Morenita, the brown-skinned Lady, who was the mother of the violated Indian people who had been orphaned and deprived of their religious identity. Several versions of the legend survive from the middle of the seventeenth century, but in most of them she speaks Nahuatl, the indigenous language of Mexico, and appears near the sacred mountain of the Aztec deity Tonantzin.

Little instruction in religion was provided for women of the lower classes and the *criollos*, although those who came from Spain might have had opportunities for greater instruction in Iberia. Women's religious orders were unknown in the Americas during these first decades, and in general women's religious orders when they did arise in the Americas were not transplanted from Europe but were founded in the Americas. They were also usually contemplative.

It was not self-sacrifice but the performance of pious duty that was the religious standard of these women. Two basic structures of spiritual formation developed in South America: convents and *beaterios* (spiritual communities for lay women). The former were of two types: large convents or *conventos grandes*, and smaller *conventos recoletos*. The former became important institutional domains of women devoted to the deeper religious life and living behind walls and closed doors within the larger male-dominated society. By the early seventeenth century many of these large convents had become bustling towns of wealthy women who entered the convent with maids and slaves to serve them. The smaller *conventos recoletos* were often formed in reaction to their larger, more secular counterparts. In the smaller convents the daily pattern of Mass before dawn, silence during meals, singing of the psalms, and long periods of meditation was more strictly followed. These traditional monastic structures were largely transplanted from Spain.

Beaterios were a more specifically American development as a type of lay home for women committed to living a devotional life but were not cloistered. By the seventeenth century there was one or two in almost every town. Women who joined, known as *beatas*, were often devoted to living a life on the model of Mary. They remained virgins, wore a religious habit, and were fully active in religious services of devotion in chapels and churches. These women often became role models for other women. Many *beatas* became women of considerable influence. Wealthy women and men of influence would come and visit the *beatas* as a way of drawing near to God or to receive a blessing.

One of the most influential *beatas* of the late sixteenth and early seventeenth centuries was Isabel Flores de Olivia (1586-1617), better known as the "Holy Rose of Lima." Rose, as she was legally renamed in 1597, was born to a very common family. One day while she was sleeping, a Native American woman servant came into her room and saw two roses outlined, one on each cheek. Several family members and other close friends were called in to witness the miracle. Clearly it was a sign from God, for the rose was understood to be a symbol of divine love, and the Virgin Mary a "rose without thorns."

Rose was confirmed in 1597 at eleven years of age. Almost immediately she began serving as a spiritual guide for others. Her identification with Mary was of great importance in this regard. Donning the brown robe of a Franciscan and later the habit of the Dominicans, Rose provided spiritual direction for people of all levels of society. As a *beata* she lived in a small cubical next to a family garden, spending much her spare time in embroidering and gardening. In addition she wrote songs of divine love, transforming secular songs and poems into songs of love to God. She was especially devoted to Mary, visiting the three most revered Madonnas in Lima almost daily. These Madonnas were small statues that were dressed in robes and jewels and cared for only by a select few *camareras* (maids in waiting). Rose was one of them. Her close identification with Mary and religious devotion, together with the miraculous appearance of the roses on her cheeks as a child, combined to give her significant power. To many she seemed to be a living extension of Mary herself.

Although there were many miracles reported in connection with people who experienced Rose's spiritual guidance, the most important occurred just months before her death. While praying in a small chapel, other worshippers noted that a recently painted oil of Jesus on the cross had begun to sweat from the head. They attributed the miracle to Rose's intense devotion to the suffering Christ. Four months later she died and her funeral caused a near riot as people scraped to take some relic of her grave clothes. One devoted faithful even lunged forward to bite off one of her fingers as a personal relic. While such forms of popular devotion were not sanctioned by the church, their occurrence testifies to the depth of feeling among those who followed her.

Not all *beatas* were considered so worthy of devotion. Spiritual power as exercised by someone like Rose could indeed lead others to greater devotion to God, or to pursuing purer motives or being more faithful in their religious practices. Other *beatas* exercised such spiritual power for baser motives. One such woman was Doña María Pizarro (d. 1572), sister of a Jesuit and distant relative of the conquistador Pizarro. From an early age Doña María claimed to have direct revelations from God through saints and angels. Others would seek her out for fresh revelations or a new word from God. A large group, mostly women but also some influential men, gathered around her. They saw themselves as a specially chosen company who were not bound by the normal doctrines and moral teachings of the church. By 1570 this group was practicing a variety of forms of erotic mysticism or sacred sexuality. Some claimed that intercourse with a priest was the best way to reach God. A number of priests apparently were involved, and at least one *beata* gave birth to a child conceived in this way. In 1572 the Inquisition condemned the group and imprisoned a number of the devotees, including Doña María herself who died in prison from neglect. Although this particular movement was not the norm, it illustrated the extent of influence these holy women exercised.

In the first century of colonial life in South America Christian women's education was very limited. Whereas there were some schools opened for men, hoping in the early years that some would be trained for the priesthood, there were no schools opened for women until much later. At first, only the wealthy could afford to provide education for their daughters by hiring a private tutor. Quite often these tutors were priests or monks. The girls would learn to read and write, do math, sing, and read Latin. The first grammar schools did not open until late in the sixteenth century, and teachers had to be licensed to make sure they had real knowledge of the subject matter, and to be sure they were Christian. Education was a matter for the church.

Toward the end of the sixteenth century, two forms of education for women developed: convent schools and private schools set up by a benefactor. Convent schools developed as brothers and sisters of nuns began to send their young girls to study with their aunt. The young girls were, in fact, given to the convent for six or seven years during which time they lived almost as nun apprentices. They accepted the regulations of the convents and were not to leave or receive visitors without permission of the headmistress. The young girls were taught basic skills of reading and writing, but they also learned the religious practices of the holy life. Many of the convents became centers of music because of the training of music for young girls. As one might expect, many of the young ladies petitioned to join the order upon graduation. The convent had become their world. Although convent education began as a school for relatives of nuns, it also was used by nobility and royalty and by the early decades of the seventeenth century became a place for unwanted baby girls. Many of these babies were mestizo children, and so a small class of well-educated, mixed-race women began to develop.

Private or lay schools did not have the strong religious education that a convent had, but without other models for women's education, they imitated the convent schools. The girls lived in an enclosed community and often wore the habit of Carmelite nuns. Basic skills of reading and writing were taught, but the girls also learned domestic skills necessary for marriage. Often these schools evolved into trade schools with an important economic component: making or producing items to sell that provided supplemental support for the institution. In both schools religious education was included, but the Bible was not part of the curriculum. It would be centuries later before women would have the same educational opportunities as men, and before they would study the Bible.

Beginnings of the transformation of Christianity in America

The first century of Christian presence in the Americas dramatically transformed the cultures, peoples, and ecology from Terra del Fuego past the Rio Grande river. In many regions whole populations had been decimated by enslavement and foreign diseases. Diet had changed by the introduction of new crops and animals. Churches and monasteries now dotted the landscape. Not only Iberians but Africans were part of the local population, especially in the Caribbean and Brazil. A social hierarchy had become entrenched by 1600 where the *peninsulares* (those born in Iberia) and *criollos* (those of full Iberian descent but born in America) were on top; mixed-race mestizos (of Iberian and Native American descent) or *mulatos* (sometimes used for persons of mixed Iberian and African descent) were next, and Native Americans and Africans were at the bottom. Christianity reflected this social structure to a fault. Africans and Native Americans were seldom treated equally, and were generally excluded from ministry and even from the Eucharist. Education for the priesthood was well established, but with few exceptions it was entirely for the *peninsulares* and *criollos*.

Events in Europe had a direct bearing on the development of Catholicism in America. In Europe the Council of Trent, which met from 1545 to 1563, was designed both to purify the Roman Catholic Church and to restrict the spread of Protestantism, but it also had the unintended effect of restricting the development of indigenous forms of Christianity in America. Trent required that the Mass continue to be offered only in Latin and required scriptures to be read only in Latin as well, thus restricting the development of more contextual forms of theology at that time. Although other religions were targets of violence and where it could the church sought diligently to extinguish them in America, indigenous American and imported African beliefs and practices survived either surreptitiously or by being incorporated into Catholic forms. Roman Catholic devotion to the saints and to Mary was more readily embraced by indigenous peoples, and later by Africans brought to America. Even when the skin color and accent changed in a region, familiar local practices persisted. And yet, it must be noted that it took less than a century for most of Spanish and Portuguese America to become at least nominally Catholic, making it the most rapidly Christianized continent in the history of the Christian movement.

The transformation of the Catholic faith from its Spanish to its South American form is nowhere better illustrated than in the story of the Virgin of Guadalupe, which was referred to above. The Spanish brought with them from Guadalupe, Spain, the image of a light-skinned Virgin Mary, the Mother of Christ. She was portrayed by them as a *conquistadora*. In Mexico she was transformed into La Morenita, the dark-skinned Virgin who was concerned for the indigenous people.

The account of her appearance was first recorded in the indigenous language of Nahuatl in 1649, but the story itself is much older. According to these early sources, in December of 1531, only a decade after the conquest of the Aztec empire, Juan Diego (1474-1584), who was a *campesino* (or peasant) of Aztec descent, had gone to pray at Tepeyac, the sacred mountain of the Aztec goddess Tonantzin, near Mexico City. As he approached the hill, Diego heard singing and then his name being called. Following the voice to the top of the hill, he met a lady whose clothing shone like the sun. Speaking in Nahuatl and not in the Spanish of the conquistadors, she told him that she was the Virgin Mother of Téotl Dios, or the True God, and that he was to go to the home of the bishop with a message. The Queen of Heaven wanted a temple built in her honor on Tepeyac, for she had heard the lamentations of the suffering people who were native to the land and wanted to communicate her love and compassion to them there.

Twice Diego did as the Virgin had told him, and twice the bishop refused to see him. La Morenita then appeared to Diego a third time. She directed him to a craggy peak where, despite the fact that it was December, various flowers were in bloom. He gathered some into his cloak and then went off to see the bishop once again. This time the bishop received him and when Diego opened his cloak the petals fell out, leaving impressed upon its inside the perfect image of the Virgin. The bishop immediately recognized the sign as a miracle and ordered the shrine to be built on the site. The earliest recorded version of the story, published in Nahuatl by Luis Laso de la Vega (dates unknown) in 1649 and titled *Huei tlamahuiçoltica* ("The Great Happening"), went on to tell of the further numerous miracles performed by the Virgin for her dark-skinned children.

The historiography of the legend remains a matter of scholarly debate. While no written texts attesting to the story that date before 1649 have been found, the chapel to the Virgin on the site at Tepeyac has been dated as early as the 1550s. Furthermore, Laso de la Vega's version was written in the indigenous language of Nahuatl and not Spanish. The fact that the story survived in Nahuatl long after that language ceased to be the dominant tongue of Mexico points toward the antiquity of the legend.

Whatever its authenticity, the significance of the story and of the centuries of devotion and pilgrimage to the shrine that followed can hardly be overstated. One can see both the struggles and the identity of what has been called "the Other Spanish Christ." Diego is repeatedly identified as poor, in contrast to the distant and unbelieving bishop who lives in a palace and has servants. Both the local peasants and the Spanish prelate were devoted to a woman, Tonantzin for the indigenous people and Mary for the bishop. Devotion to both of them involved pilgrimage, gifts, and healing miracles. In Diego's experience the two devotional streams met and merged (*encuentro* in Spanish) into one, creating a new mestizo ("mixed") spirituality. The description in Laso de la Vega's text of the local flora, the references to the first generation figures, and even the location of the appearance of the Virgin (a former Aztec shrine) all reveal how Christianity had taken on local characteristics and was speaking to the local sensitivities. The prophetic aspect of La Morenita's care for those who were suffering and the missiological aspect of her desire to communicate this to them were one and the same. Its enduring effect is reflected in the decision of Pope John Paul II in 2002 to canonize the Mexican peasant, Juan Diego, as the first totally indigenous saint of the Americas.

Suggestions for further reading

Bethell, Leslie, ed., *The Cambridge History of Latin America, I: Colonial Latin America.* New York: Cambridge University Press, 1984.

Dussel, Enrique, ed., *The Church in Latin America, 1492-1992.* Maryknoll, NY: Orbis Books, 1992.

Goodpasture, H. McKennie, *Cross and Sword: An Eyewitness History of Christianity in Latin America.* Maryknoll, NY: Orbis Books, 1989.

Kamen, Henry, *Empire: How Spain Became a World Power, 1492-1763.* New York: HarperCollins Publishers, 2003.

Penyak, Lee M., and Walter J. Petry, *Religion in Latin America: A Documentary History.* Maryknoll, NY: Orbis Books, 2006

Rivera Pagán, Luis, *A Violent Evangelism: The Political and Religious Conquest of the Americas.* Louisville: Westminster John Knox, 1992.

Williams, Eric, *From Columbus to Castro: The History of the Caribbean, 1492-1969.* New York: Vintage Books, 1970/1984.

2

African Christianity in the Sixteenth Century

Ancient roots of Christianity in Africa

The history of Christianity in Africa reaches back to the pages of the New Testament. The Gospel of Matthew tells the story of the young boy Jesus being taken to Egypt as a refugee, and a North African named Simon being forced by Jesus' Roman executioners to carry his cross to Calvary. According to the book of Acts, a court official from the ancient kingdom of Meroë underwent baptism at the hands of one of the first apostles. Christianity arrived in Alexandria early in the apostolic era. During its first three centuries the movement spread through Egypt, across North Africa, and up the Nile to Ethiopia. The names of Origen, Clement of Alexandria, Athanasius, Shenoute, Perpetua, Cyprian, Donatus, and Augustine all bear witness to Africa's rich contributions to the collective heritage of the world Christian movement.

A number of factors played a role in weakening the African churches from within after the sixth century. Political struggles, changing cultural patterns, economic realignments, and theological differences all were at work. But the rise of Islam in the seventh century more than any other factor led to the eventual decline of Christianity in Africa. Christian churches all but disappeared in North Africa and in the ancient kingdom of Nubia. In Egypt the Coptic Church continued to survive as a minority community under Islamic rule. Only in Ethiopia did an independent Christian church and Christian state survive, making it an emblem of African independent Christianity.

By the fifteenth century the Ottoman Turks and the Mamelukes in Egypt controlled much of the trade passing within the Mediterranean region. Enslaved persons and gold were the two most important commodities Muslim merchants sought. Cross-continental trade routes linked the northern Africa kingdoms of Songhay, with its capital of Timbuktu; Mali, which crushed Songhay in the fourteenth century; and the Mossi and Hausa states, east of the Niger River. Several kingdoms along the western coast had established new regional trading centers by the fifteenth century and were experiencing a growing Muslim presence, while the eastern coast of Africa was integrated into the economic fabric of the Indian Ocean. All of these trade routes and the patterns of intercultural engagement that they fostered were radically transformed by the appearance of the Portuguese along the shores of Africa after 1500.

Africa south of the Sahara was made up of hundreds of tribal cultural communities, nations, and linguistic groups, of varying sizes. Centuries of migration had helped make the diversity of languages, cultures, and religious practices even more complex throughout the continent. By the thirteenth century Muslim traders were traveling by land as far as the Senegal River in West Africa and all the way to Mozambique in East Africa, taking Islam beyond the borders of the caliphate in the north into a new form of diasporic existence. The Portuguese came by sea in the fifteenth century, bringing European Christianity for the first time directly into contact with peoples along the coastal regions.

West African culture and Portuguese incursions

Unlike North Africa, Egypt, or Ethiopia, western Africa had no long history of Christianity when the Portuguese first arrived in the fifteenth century. Most of West Africa was made up of small kingdoms, with a few larger nations dominating. The only transnational religion in the region was Islam. West Africa had long provided natural resources such as gold to Islamic traders in exchange primarily for salt, which was a valued commodity in the region. Islamic traders had also exported enslaved captives from the region. Kingdoms in the region such as Fouta, Dahomey, Kongo, Matamba, Mali, Songhai (Songhay), Ghana, and Sokoto had accumulated significant amounts of wealth through the centuries. These were not as old as the kingdoms of Nubia, Ethiopia, and Egypt in the east, but their rise in the period prior to the arrival of Europeans meant that the Portuguese traded with kingdoms, not with local peoples.

The early fourteenth century Muslim King Mansa Musa (1307-1337) of Mali was wealthy enough that on his pilgrimage to Mecca he is reported to have sent five hundred enslaved persons ahead of him to prepare the way. His overflowing gifts of gold as he passed through Egypt had the effect of reducing the value of gold overall in North Africa. Iberian explorers heard stories of such wealth and found it a powerful incentive to reach the region that the Portuguese called the Guinea coast. The wealth that eventually flowed from West Africa to Europe was enormous, and was reflected in the names that Europeans gave to these regions of West Africa: the Ivory Coast, the Gold Coast, and the Slave Coast.

Musa's kingdom declined in the fourteenth century, and the Songhai empire of Gao (on the Niger River) rose on its remains. One of the most influential West African leaders of Gao, Sonni Ali (c. 1464-1492), is remembered for his plundering and expanding of the empire, along with his local religious devotion. The Muslim leaders and scholars in Timbuktu reportedly fled when Ali's troops arrived. The king's cruelty served to control West Africa's trade, but his disrespect for Islam created an environment for a strong orthodox Muslim reaction.

The next ruler of the Songhai empire, Askia Muhammad I (1442-1538), used the plundered wealth to rebuild Timbuktu as a Muslim center for learning and to fund a major two-year pilgrimage to Mecca. Muhammad I extended his empire to include the Hausa to the east and reached to within two hundred miles of the Atlantic Ocean in the west. For their part, the Portuguese avoided these Islamic rulers but made use of the numerous and culturally diverse smaller kingdoms along the coast that had been relatively untouched by Islam to help wrest the gold trade out of Muslim hands in the fifteenth century.

Although there was a great deal of diversity in the religious practices and beliefs of West Africans in the fifteenth century, some general comments about these are possible. For most Africans, in the fifteenth century as well as today, all of life is religious. The African view of the world is consistently communal and world-affirming. The world is full of divine life and activity, animated by spiritual beings who move among the living.

Most traditional African religions share the belief that the world was created by a great or high God who fashioned humans out of the earth (from clay or from a hole in the ground). At some point in mythic time, however, a separation between God and humanity set in. Numerous stories tell of how this came about, either through an act of evil or an unfortunate occurrence. In part because of this separation humans do not or cannot relate directly to the supreme God. A range of lesser gods and spirits who animate trees, rivers, mountains, and other elements of the environment, and who are near and personal, mediate the divine-human relationship. African religionists in the fifteenth century as much as today have understood such spirits and lesser deities to be channels of communication to the divine. The Igbo of southeastern Nigeria have a proverb that says, "God is like a rich man. You approach him through his servants."

Priests, diviners, healers, and prophets help mediate between the world of spirits and human society. Employing incantations, rituals, and natural substances, they seek to influence (for good or evil) spiritual forces. Mediators are called on at important moments of transition in life, such as birth, adulthood, marriage, and death, to assist in the passage. They can be called on to bring healing upon one's self or others, appease evil spirits, remove spells or curses, or in the case of witches, to put a spell or curse on someone else, thereby bringing spiritual harm on one's enemies. In many African societies women as well as men serve in these religious roles as priests, diviners, healers, or prophets. The Yoruba of Nigeria and Benin speak of the "Great Mothers," who are holy women with considerable, if at times ambivalent, powers.

Ancestors, the "living dead," have long played a significant role in the African religious world. The living dead are those who have died in the past few generations (four or five) and who are said to have a foot in both worlds. These spirits of the recently departed are unpredictable as they come and go among the living. Having not yet made the final translation to the spirit world, they must be fed and cared for, but they are also able to link the living with the dead, thereby enabling the living to "return to the future." In most cases, ancestors come to help the living by speaking through dreams or in visions, giving advice or warnings. Some African societies believe that only those who lived well become "living dead." They are honored in death in order to be encouraged to continue to help the living. In other African societies (mostly central and southern Africa) ancestors may return to haunt or bring illness because they were not properly buried, or were not cared for when they were alive.

Ritual sacrifices and offerings are central elements in traditional African religion. Sacrifice helps to negotiate communal harmony by restoring social relationships and appeasing harmful spirits. For some African cultures, sacrifices and offerings are made to the Supreme God, but in most cases they are made to spirits or to the living dead. Blood sacrifices in particular are considered sacred gifts to God or to the spirits that cover human misdeeds and restore the sacred flow of life.

The earliest Europeans to arrive in West Africa in the fifteenth century had no understanding of the African religious world that they were encountering, and for the most part lacked any interest in gaining such. They were Portuguese explorers, financed and organized by Prince Henry (1394-1460), who were looking for wealth and to extend Portuguese political influence. They were also driven by Henry's desire to spread the Christian faith. In 1415, at the age of twenty-one, young Henry led a crusade against the port city of Ceuta, which was across the Straits of Gibraltar and part of the Muslim caliphate of North Africa. The Portuguese took the city, discovering in its markets a wealth of goods that had come from the trade routes to the south. Two years later, the pope named Henry the grand master of the *Ordinis Christi Militia* ("Order of the Knights of Christ"), whose roots went back to the fourteenth century and the *Reconquista.*

Turning his attention to the sea, Henry began financing expeditions in the Atlantic in the 1420s. His ships soon reached the previously uninhabited island of Madeira where they established a permanent colony. The development in the 1440s of a new, smaller, swifter ship called the caravel was a critical factor in the Portuguese expansion, for these ships could better tack or sail against the wind, and thus return more easily from longer voyages south along the African coast. Portuguese expeditions financed by Prince Henry reached the uninhabited islands of Cape Verde in 1445, on which they established a colony. By the 1450s Portuguese ships had reached Guinea on the west coast of Africa.

Portuguese explorers brought the first African captives back to Portugal to be sold as slaves in 1441. In 1444 another expedition brought back 235 captured Africans who were sold in the port city of Lagos, the base of Henry's operation. Some of these captives were given to the bishop to serve the church. Africans were closely associated with Islam in the sixteenth-century Iberian worldview, and as such were considered unbelievers who could justly be enslaved for their opposition to the Christian faith. For some among the Portuguese, the desire to evangelize these Africans served as a further justification to capture and sell them as slaves in Portugal and Spain. There were more than a few among the ranks of church leaders who hoped that by educating West African captives in Iberia, the Christian faith would eventually be spread back through the African region. The papacy was especially zealous for this crusading missionary work, providing important spiritual coverage for the baser economic motives that lay behind these exploits. On their part, many of these Africans, who became known as *ladinos*, embraced Christianity and underwent baptism. By 1500 they were forming confraternities for support. Some were even able to obtain their freedom. Juan Garrido (1480?-1550), a conquistador who participated in the conquest of Tenochtitlan in the 1520s, was a free man of African descent.

Fifteenth-century popes repeatedly called for the evangelization of the peoples that the Portuguese explorers were encountering, but left it as a matter of royal responsibility. Rome provided no organized means for missionary outreach, and popes had little power to undertake any initiative on their own. The rulers of both Spain and Portugal were constantly reminded that it was their Christian duty to bring Christianity to the peoples that their expeditions encountered. In some cases we have evidence of at least an effort on the part of a Portuguese explorer to evangelize in West Africa. In 1457 Diogo Gomez (1420?-1500) visited the kingdom of Mali where he reportedly engaged in a debate with a Muslim scholar. Gomez reported that he had convinced the Mandinka (or Mandingo) chieftain of the region, Nomimansa (dates unknown), to convert to Christianity, but no further evidence to support the claim has been found.

The Portuguese continued to move south along the Atlantic coast of Africa, establishing settlements for trade. Chapels or churches were built in these settlements to provide religious services for the Portuguese. In 1482 they established their first tropical fort at Elmina, on the Gold Coast in present-day Ghana. Upon landing, a priest with the expedition said Mass, the first known celebration of the Eucharist on Ghanaian soil. Following the Mass, the Portuguese implored the local chief to be baptized while the local chief implored the Europeans to go away. Both were disappointed.

The local ruler, Nana Kwamina Ansa (dates unknown), was eventually convinced to allow the foreigners to stay and build a fort, which became known as Elmina Castle, as a way to help the king rebuff his enemy, the Shama people. The Portuguese, lacking knowledge of local custom, quickly offended the religious sensibilities of the people by crushing rocks that were in a local sacred area. The rebellion that followed nearly ended the Portuguese presence. The fort, which included a chapel, was eventually built and named São Jorge de Mina. During its first years a Mass was said every day for the soul of Prince Henry the Navigator, who had died two decades earlier. It may have been on Ghanaian soil, but clearly the Christian worship and devotion that were practiced had the soul of Portugal in them.

Further south along the coast of Africa, the Portuguese reached the mouth of the Kongo River in 1483. The Portuguese exchanged emissaries with the Kongolese *manikongo*, or king, Nzinga Nkuwu (d. 1506), taking two Kongolese back to Portugal where they studied for several years. In 1491 the Portuguese returned with several Franciscans. In May of that year Nzinga Nkuwu, was baptized, taking the name of the king of Portugal, João I. His wife, Nlaza (dates unknown), was baptized and took the name of Eleonora, while their son, Mvemba Nzinga (1456-1542), was baptized and took the name Afonso. A large bonfire was built following the royal baptisms and a number of traditional religious artifacts were burned.

After several years Nzinga Nkuwu returned to his traditional African beliefs. Afonso, however, continued to follow in the Christian faith. With the assistance of the Portuguese he defeated his brother upon the death of his father, and ascended to the throne in 1506. Among his first acts as king was to order the traditional temple in Mbanza Kongo, the capital city, destroyed and a new church built. The capital was renamed São Salvador (Our Savior). Afonso sought to spread his new Christian faith, often doing so at the end of a spear, but he also sought to introduce educational, social, and even medical practices that he learned from the Portuguese. The king of Portugal responded to the news from Kongo by sending more priests, builders, artisans, and educators.

Over the next several decades Afonso ruled over a Christian kingdom in Central Africa. The degree to which Christianity took root among the people has often been debated, but by the same token the degree to which the Portuguese sailors were Christian can also be debated. Over the course of the following century, a majority of the people under the rule of the Kongolese kings came to identify themselves as Christians. At the same time the form that Christianity took among them was not the same as it had been among Europeans. Traditional African practices were freely mixed with devotion to Christ and the saints in a manner that prefigured a host of independent African Christian formations over the next several centuries.

From the beginning there were mixed signals about the Portuguese intentions in the region. European priests got off the same boats that by 1502 were loading African captives being sold into slavery. By the middle of the sixteenth century, some three to four thousand Africans annually were being sold into slavery to the Portuguese in West Central Africa. A number of priests were directly engaged in the slave trade, prompting the king of Kongo at one point to complain to the king of Portugal that Christ was being crucified anew by those sent to be ministers of his body and blood.

Afonso sought as quickly as possible to see an African clergy trained to minister to his people. His request would not be fully met for at least another 350 years, but before his death he received at least a glimpse of a hopeful sign of indigenous clergy. Henrique (c. 1495-c. 1526) went to Portugal to study for the priesthood. In 1514 he had an audience with Pope Leo X (1475-1521), who would soon be embroiled in controversy with a German monk named Martin Luther (1483-1546). With Pope Leo's support, Henrique was ordained first as a priest, and then in 1520 as a bishop. The next year he returned to São Salvador, but he did not live long enough to make a lasting impact in leadership of the church. As the son of the king, he was always more of a political figure there than an effective ecclesiastical leader. Nonetheless, he was the first African bishop to serve in São Salvador, in West Central Africa, doing so before Calvin wrote his *Institutes* and before Loyola formed the Society of Jesus.

Following Afonso's death Portuguese political domination of the Kongo increased. War with a neighboring Jaga (or Yaka) people broke out in 1568, further weakening the central Kongolese government. After a brief distraction with new lands in Brazil and in Asia, the Portuguese returned to help restore order and to expand the slave trade. Although there were exchanges with Rome from time to time, serious attention to Christian growth had to wait until the arrival of the Capuchins in 1645. Afonso's vision of an indigenous clergy would be delayed considerably longer.

Faced with growing Portuguese pressure, in 1575 the Kongolese king Álvaro I (d. 1587) permitted the Portuguese to establish a new colony at Luanda (also known as Loanda), to the south of his kingdom on the Atlantic coast. Eventually the Portuguese took control of the broader coastal region and established the colony of Angola. During these years a new order, known as the Society of Jesus, or simply as the Jesuits, became involved in the efforts to evangelize along the West Central African coast, replacing the Military Order of Christ in the region. The Jesuits, as will be seen in the next chapters, reflected the humanist's love of learning more than the crusader's concern for conquest. Their approach was accordingly different. Rather than establishing a military presence and staying within the colonial city, the Jesuits, under the leadership of Pero (or Pedro) Tavares (1591-1670), purchased tracts of land and developed a string of Christian villages among peoples whom they then converted and baptized in Angola. The experiment lasted into the middle of the seventeenth century.

Portuguese ships under the command of Vasco da Gama (1460-1524) made their way around the southern cape of Africa and reached Mozambique in 1498. Seven years later the Portuguese established a permanent settlement in Mozambique, which eventually grew to be their second largest colony, after Angola. The Portuguese settlement began trading with nearby Zimbabwe, and in 1560, a Jesuit mission from South India under Gonçalo da Silveira (1526-1561) traveled up the Zambezi River to the kingdom known as Mwene Mutapa. The young king, Chisamhura Nogomo (dates unknown), welcomed the Jesuits, who, while being Portuguese, did not come to capture slaves or to demand women and gold. The Jesuits' spiritual disciplines and ascetic piety appear to have been particularly attractive to him. Silveira was granted an opportunity to explain the Christian faith. Aided by a series of visions that were understood to be of the Virgin Mary, the king along with his mother and some three hundred other members of his people underwent Christian baptism in 1561, less than a year after the Jesuits' initial arrival.

Silveira no doubt thought that the conversion was sincere, but he did not count on the resistance of Muslim traders in the region who convinced Nogomo that the Jesuit was a Portuguese spy who had special powers to bewitch Africans. Less than two months later Nogomo had the Jesuit strangled in his sleep and his body thrown into the river.

Africa, Christianity, and the slave trade

The Portuguese launched their excursion out into the Atlantic and down the coast of Africa with a crusading mind. Their end was the extension of their Christian kingdom and, not incidentally, gaining wealth. Wealth came in the form of gold first and foremost, for it was the most valued medium of European exchange as well as a commodity. Spices were also sought by the Portuguese, but they knew that these came from beyond Africa, from the East Indies, making the quest to find the southern end of Africa a means to reach a greater end. Midway through the fifteenth century the Portuguese with little reflection or stated intention took captives from the West Africa coast back to Portugal where they sold them in the markets as slaves. The slave trade was not the main reason that the Portuguese set out to explore the coast of Africa. Within a few decades, however, driven in no small part by the explosive demand for agricultural labor to work the plantations of America and by the enormous profits that could be accumulated when the labor was forced, that is, provided by enslaved people, the slave trade soon overtook everything else in the Portuguese economy in West Africa.

Slavery is one of the most enduring human institutions in world history. Although its form and severity varied from culture to culture and in different eras, the underlying premise, that some human beings could exercise absolute ownership and control over the body and labor power of others, remained constant. The modern institution of chattel slavery was a juggernaut of ethnic arrogance, material greed, and religious hubris, undergirded by violence and terror. People of the continent of Africa bore by far the brunt of this modern holocaust, while people of European descent became after 1500 the main perpetrators of the practice and the benefactors of its profits. The development of the Atlantic African slave trade in the fifteenth and sixteenth centuries is without question one of history's greatest tragedies. The role that religion played in authorizing and sustaining it poses a challenge to the very heart of the Christian movement.

Christians were not the first to enter into the lucrative market of the African slave trade. Europeans before 1400 had little use for slaves on their own territories. The main markets for European slave traders were Muslims in the Mediterranean world. Their captives were mostly non-Christian peoples bordering on the Christian kingdoms of Europe. Inside Europe itself the slave population was quite small and quite diverse prior to the fifteenth century. Greeks, Sards, Tartars, Russians, Caucasians, Turks, Armenians as well as North Africans were all bought and sold in the markets of Genoa and elsewhere. Muslims were the first to actively engage in transporting and selling slaves from the African continent to Europe. For Muslim society, however, slaves as a general rule were regarded as a sign of wealth but were not used as a means for producing wealth. They were employed for the most part in forms of servitude or labor that were considered nonessential and not resulting in production of wealth. The two major exceptions in the Islamic world were women enslaved as concubines who were kept as captives for the pleasure of their male owners as well as for reproduction of children, and the use of slaves in the military as soldiers.

Europeans began in the fifteenth century to use slaves as field workers in plantations, thereby transforming the institution of slavery to make it the primary means of creating wealth. Again the Portuguese led the way in this transformation, forcing enslaved persons to work in the agricultural fields of Madeira beginning in 1520, in the Azores after 1527, in Cape Verde in 1560, and in São Tome, which was settled in 1570. At first the main goods grown on these islands were grapes and grains, but sugar cane quickly became the most important. The economic incentive for this transformation was enormous. Enslaved persons provided the labor power that drove the first phase of a global agricultural revolution in the fifteenth and sixteenth centuries, a revolution that undergirded the emergence of the modern global economy.

Slavery, within certain parameters, had long been an accepted practice within both Muslim and Christian societies. In both cultures the primary sources of captives were combatants taken captive in warfare. Enslavement was an alternative to execution, and thus could be seen as a humanitarian act. The earliest justifications for the modern African slave trade were based on this argument. Since Christians were at permanent war (Crusade) against Muslims and other infidels, the reasoning went, those peoples taken captive by Christian military forces could legitimately be enslaved. The argument can be found in the papal bull of 1455, *Romanus pontifex*, for instance. The bull praised Prince Henry the Navigator and the nation of Portugal for the military advances being made along the coast of Africa. It noted in passing that the Holy See had granted the king of Portugal permission to invade and subdue those whom it called enemies of Christ, be they Muslim or indigenous religionists. Since this was considered war, permission was granted to capture and enslave these enemies of Christ and to seize their property as booty. Whether they had been purchased from local rulers or taken captive directly by the Portuguese, such Africans, since they were not Christian, could lawfully be enslaved, the papal bull stated.

Isidore of Seville (San Isidoro de Sevilla), a Christian writer of early-seventh-century Spain, had argued that all people were born free according to both the law of nature and the divine law, but slavery existed by the law of nations. There were, on the other hand, a host of ancient theories that argued the opposite, holding that some human beings were by nature inferior to others and destined for servitude. By the fifteenth century the latter argument tended to dominate, and it was applied especially to people of African descent to justify their perpetual bondage.

Both Christian and Muslim law generally forbade enslavement of fellow religionists. Enforced servitude of a fellow Christian or Muslim was allowed for a number of reasons, but such persons were considered indentured servants and were expected to be set free after a specified number of years of labor. Prior to the fifteenth century, enslaved persons in Europe who converted were considered indentured servants after conversion and a specified point of manumission was generally expected following baptism. For this reason the subtle yet significant change in European laws from non-Christian to non-European (or African) in defining who could properly be forced to serve in perpetual bondage represented a monumental shift in consciousness and culture.

In Spain and Portugal prior to the fifteenth century enslaved persons were permitted to purchase back their freedom. Such self-purchase (*coartacion*) required that the enslaved person and the owner agree upon a price, which the enslaved person then would meet by performing additional work or raising funds in other ways (such as theft, or grants from other family members) to gain the needed currency. Many of those forced into service in Spain were Christians who were indentured servants who could not pay their debts, and thus their time in servitude was counted against the amount that they owed. This was not generally the case in the Americas, where most of the Africans who were taken captive eventually ended up being sold. Although there were individual cases of manumission, freedom for those enslaved in the Americas in the fifteenth and sixteenth centuries generally came in the form of rebellion and escape.

Although there were numerous debates among both Christian and Muslim scholars over the treatment of the enslaved, in general a master's treatment of his or her enslaved property was considered mostly a matter of piety. Among Muslims, an enslaved person was to be treated well, and if he or she was not a believer, the owner was to encourage conversion. Similar encouragement was found among Christian writers, although after the fifteenth century as Christians became major holders of enslaved persons, ambiguities regarding conversion grew. Various justifications for Christians holding slaves came to be offered in the vein of piety, such as the African slave trade serving the larger providential purposes of bringing African peoples into contact with Christian teaching, or individual Africans having their lives improved by working for so-called Christian masters.

For the Roman Catholic Church in the fifteenth century, evangelization was always a primary concern. Papal bulls such as *Inter caetera* in 1493 stated the evangelistic principle forcefully. The kings of Portugal and Spain (the only two Christian nations at the end of the fifteenth century venturing out in exploration beyond Europe) were instructed by the Holy See to send virtuous agents to instruct the indigenous peoples of the various lands they were conquering in the Christian faith. Both kings complied.

The advance of the Portuguese along the west coast of Africa and then the Spanish across the Atlantic Ocean provided the routes along which the Atlantic slave trade would grow over the next several centuries. Portugal at first controlled it. The papal bulls of 1493, *Inter caetera* and *Eximiae devotionis*, stated that the lands to the west of the Atlantic Ocean belonged to Spain to be colonized and evangelized. The lands to the east, including Africa, were the responsibility of Portugal. While it might seem unimaginable today for the pope to be able to grant ownership and political control over lands that were inhabited and fully under indigenous forms of government, in the fifteenth-century worldview of European Christendom, the pope was the supreme religious authority on earth and thus could properly exercise such power. The Treaty of Tordesillas in 1494 between Spain and Portugal confirmed that the African slave trade was under Portuguese control. All of Spain's enslaved Africans for use in the Americas had to be procured by licenses given to Portuguese merchants.

After their initial excursions the Portuguese came to rely less on capturing slaves along the African coast. Instead they came to rely on local African rulers, who traded bodies for European goods such as iron products or cloth, goods that ironically the African nations themselves often already produced. These local rulers in turn engaged in raiding parties directed against neighboring nations or tribes to supply the captives for the European traders, hence giving the Europeans the thin justification that their captives had been legitimately enslaved according to Christian law as prisoners of war. Such rationalizations persisted long into the modern period.

Initially enslaved Africans were forced to labor in Spain, Portugal, and the islands off the Atlantic coast of Africa that were colonized. After 1515 they became increasingly forced to work in America. Enslaved Africans were used on the plantations and in the mines, replacing the Native Americans who were quickly dying off due to violence and disease, or who could escape because of their knowledge of the local terrain. African death rates were also quite high, but Africans already had developed important resistance to diseases that were ravaging the Native American population; and the Africans who were imported did not know the land as well as Native Americans, making escape more difficult.

Between 1500 and 1850 from ten to fifteen million Africans are estimated to have been transported across the Atlantic to the Americas, making it the largest forced migration of humanity in human history. Millions more died in captivity before they reached the Americas, most of them in the middle passage at sea, making it one of the greatest holocausts in human history as well. The Atlantic Ocean became in effect an African lake, as Africans came to inhabit the Americas. In some areas, such as some of the islands of the Caribbean, the local inhabitants died off entirely from disease and violence, and Africans became the new dominant population.

Transatlantic trade from Portugal was conducted in a triangle. Ships from Portugal traveled to West Africa with manufactured goods that were exchanged for human cargo. The captives were held in colonies or stations such as Elmina, in Ghana, before being transported in the middle passage across the Atlantic to the Americas. Stripped naked, crammed into cargo vessels so tightly that their legs could not be stretched, and without room even to stand, the captives were sent on the sixty- to ninety-day crossing. Disease, starvation, and abuse took the lives of many. Their bodies would simply be thrown into the sea. Others, when presented with the opportunity, jumped overboard, taking their own lives rather than endure the torture of their captivity any further. Those who made it to the markets in the Americas were sold at tremendous profit, earning as much as 300 percent on the initial investment of a merchant. The third leg of the voyage in the trade triangle involved taking raw materials back to Europe from America. It is estimated that fifty-four thousand voyages were made in this triangle of trade in the four hundred years of the African slave trade.

Enslaved Africans in America were treated differently than slaves held by Muslims or Christians in Europe, Asia, or North Africa during the same period. Furthermore, Africans held by the Portuguese and Spanish in America were treated differently than European or North African captives in Iberia. Both the long distances the captives were transported across the Atlantic to the Americas and the prejudice against dark-skinned peoples reinforced the more dehumanizing treatment. Linguistically the difference can be expressed as a shift from serfdom or indentureship, the form slavery generally took as practiced in Europe, to chattel slaves or humans as commodity as practiced in America.

Under such oppressive conditions, enslaved Africans often found their only solace in religion. African religion crossed the Atlantic in the hearts of the captives to be reconstructed in their new location in America. When all else seemed to be lost and the African was brought close to death, it was often the religion of the ancestors that spoke to the heart. Many of the basic elements of West African religion, including devotion to ancestors, spirit possession, ritual practices, and divination, survived the passage. Often they were merged with forms of the Catholic religion that enslaved Africans encountered in America when they first arrived. Magical charms, spells, and divination often became a liberating force in opposition to the slave master. African religion both pacified and empowered the captives.

As African families and clans were broken up, new configurations emerged in America, beginning in the slave markets and continuing on the plantations where they were shipped to work. The larger plantations often had a religious cult house, coexisting as a parallel religious expression with the prescribed Iberian Catholicism. Enslaved women often fulfilled the role of healers and community mothers. Enslaved men took on the role of *brujos,* or sorcerers, who would use incantations and spells to try to control slave owners. These *brujos* (*bruxos* in Portuguese) also were the leaders of some of the first revolts by the enslaved that occurred in Colombia, Cuba, Haiti, and Brazil.

From almost the beginning of the period, Africans in America found ways to integrate their ancestral religions with the Catholicism that they encountered among their captors. Rosary beads were used as amulets or fetishes. Holy water, prayers, and statues were used as access to spiritual power. The saints of Catholic practice became identified with divinities and ancestors from Africa in creative ways, allowing for a high degree of continuation with traditional African practices. A highly complex cultural and religious mix was forged in the Americas, and a new transcontinental form of Christianity developed. Christianity was forced out of the local tribal or ethnic enclaves it had as a European religion to become something new. Over the next several centuries the creativity of this African genius, in Africa and America, would continue to unfold.

Ethiopian Christianity

Ethiopia has a powerful claim to being the flagship of African Christianity. For centuries it was the only land on the continent where Christianity received political support and was freely practiced. Christianity was the national religion of Ethiopia, but the churches there had a long history of being continuously enriched by outside contacts. The liturgy, buildings, and church order all bore the marks of both a distinctive Ethiopian cultural identity and of influences from wider Christian currents. The tradition of the patriarch of the Ethiopian church, or *abuna*, being appointed by the Coptic pope in Alexandria (later Cairo) gave visible form to this transnational identity, as did the continuous engagement of its monastic communities with other ancient Christian monastic traditions.

By the fifteenth century these outside connections were being strained by the growing presence of Islam on all sides of the Ethiopian nation. Nubia (northern Sudan) had been taken over by the Mamelukes of Egypt, who then restricted contacts with Christians passing through Egypt to Ethiopia. Pilgrimages to Jerusalem and other holy cities, including Rome, continued to provide an open window to the wider world Christian movement. A number of Ethiopian envoys were in western Europe around the time of the fall of Constantinople to the Ottomans in 1453. But contact with other parts of the Christian world was becoming more difficult.

The fifteenth century witnessed one of the most powerful emperors in Ethiopia's long history, Zara Ya'iqob (or Zar'a Ya'eqob, r. 1434-1468). Raised under the tutelage of his father and a reforming monk named Abba Giyorgis of Gascha (or Sagla, d. 1425), Zara Ya'iqob proved early on to be a bright and capable student of political and religious affairs. His childhood teacher, Abba Giyorgis, in 1424 penned *Mashafa mistir* ("The Book of the Mystery"), which offered a systematic presentation of Ethiopian theology. As a young man Zara Ya'iqob was imprisoned by a jealous brother who had succeeded their father. Upon the death of his brother, however, he was released to assume the throne. He quickly set about to ensure regional peace, employing a combination of military force and Christian teaching. During his thirty-five years of rule he reorganized the government, enforced a greater uniformity in religious belief and practices, and strengthened Ethiopia as an island Christian nation in the sea of Islam.

In 1449, Zara Ya'iqob (who had by this time taken the royal name of Constantine) called a special church council at his newly built monastery at Dabra Mitmaz in Shoa. An auspicious day was chosen for opening the gathering, the feast of Mary, August 15 according to the Ethiopian calendar. Ethiopia was a large nation, and the previous centuries of monastic and theological revival had left the country fragmented in various monastic loyalties. The emperor had determined that recognition of both Sabbath (Saturday) and Sunday observances for liturgy, and universal support for devotion to Mary and the cult of the cross were necessary steps in the direction of unifying the land.

Sabbath observance had been a matter of controversy in Ethiopia for over a century. The practice of maintaining Saturday rather than Sunday as the holy day had grown over the previous several centuries. But there were those who also kept the more traditional Christian liturgical holy day of Sunday. Now finally a definitive answer was given: not one or the other, but both days would hereafter be observed in Ethiopia.

Mary and the cross had long been the focus of strong devotional practices in Ethiopia, but the degree of the emperor's support was now something new. Imperial leadership of the council and the church at large was troubling to some monks and priests who saw reform as needing to be closer to traditional theological and biblical formulas. One such imperial irritant (later flogged and sent into exile to die) was a monk named Estifanos (1380-1450). Estifanos was troubled by the increasing control of the royal court over the church. Monks and priests should not be providing secular counsel for the king, he argued. He refused to raise Mary to such a level of devotion if for no other reason than to refuse to bend to political control of religion. In the end his followers, known as the Stefanites, survived as a small Christian sect, their monastery almost inaccessible to the outside world. The royal reform of Zara Ya'iqob regarding increased devotion to Mary became the Ethiopian Orthodox norm.

Zara Ya'iqob's writings and courtly intrigue provide a window into the ongoing relationship of Christianity and local African cultures. Much of the region the emperor ruled was newly acquired territory. Many of his subjects were only nominally Christianized by conquest. The emperor took on responsibility of building churches and monasteries and providing literature to evangelize these regions. Some of his new subjects were former Muslims, while others were Jews (called Falasha), and still others followed traditional African religions. The emperor was ruthless in his pursuit of Christian purity. One of his assumed names was "Exterminator of the Jews."

As great as his hatred of Jews and Muslims was, however, it was his hatred or fear of traditional practices, and of the temptation of new converts to return to local religions, that were of greatest concern in his theological writings. Long sections of his work were devoted to decrying the practice of magic and divination. The Bible, it seems, was being used as an amulet or charm by many of the people. The emperor was especially concerned that these "magicians" were often priests and monks who were, in his view, idolaters and Jews—idolaters because they worshipped other gods and Jews because they denied the deity of Jesus.

His writings alone do not appear to have been effective, for Zara Ya'iqob also employed force, declaring that killing adherents of other religions was not sin. Numerous so-called pagans (who were often in fact Christian reformers) were flogged to death. Even his own family (one wife and several sons and daughters) was not spared when accused of such practices. Despite these excesses, however, this powerful and pivotal leader of the Christian empire of Ethiopia was later canonized.

The story of Zara Ya'iqob provides a window to understanding the imperial nature of Ethiopian Christianity in the fifteenth century. Christian identity and royal identity mutually reinforced each other. The emperors were crowned in a celebration reminiscent of Jesus' arrival in Jerusalem. Emperors, like regional bishops, traveled around to "tabernacle" with their people and even oversaw the annual rebaptism of the nation. The *abuna* of the church also traveled around the nation with two large white umbrellas as a spiritual shadow of royal power. From the fourth century the *abuna* had been an Egyptian appointed by the Coptic patriarch of Alexandria. As a result the head of the Ethiopian church was often not fluent in the local language, and the position was often vacant for years as the appointment was held up by the Muslim rulers in Egypt. During those periods when the Ethiopian church was without a leader, the most powerful monastic leader or the emperor's personal clergy assumed greater powers. The pattern of absentee *abunas* tended to magnify the political nature of Christianity in Ethiopia and the role of rulers in the affairs of faith. Political rulers exercising theological judgment also worked to preserve Ethiopian Christian identity, on the other hand. This was particularly important as Europeans began to arrive in Ethiopia by sea.

Prior to 1500, Ethiopia's ecumenical relationships, especially with the Latin church, were restricted by the Islamic countries through which envoys had to pass. An Ethiopian abbot from Jerusalem sent a delegation to attend the Council of Florence in 1441, and one of the monks, named Peter (dates unknown), spoke at the council, declaring that the Ethiopian king desired greater unity with the church of Rome. Little came of his efforts, but the Europeans were moved enough by the presence of the Ethiopians to represent them on the doors of St.

Peter's in Rome. By 1460 there was a small Ethiopian chapel near the Vatican, St. Stephen's, where Africans were worshipping in the Ethiopic language, Ge'ez. In 1513, an Ethiopian Psalter was printed in Rome.

The Europeans were drawn as much by myth as by mission to explore relationships with Ethiopia. The myth was a legendary Christian priest-king, Prester John. European travelers spent more than a century searching for this legendary figure not only in Ethiopia but also in central and eastern Asia. In the minds of many Europeans, contact with a Christian kingdom on the other side of Islamic territories would make it possible to surround and crush Islam forever, finally realizing the goal of the Crusades. The king of England sent a letter to the king of Ethiopia in 1400 seeking such a Christian alliance.

One of the goals that occupied the Portuguese as their ships made their way down the west coast of Africa was to find a river passage to Ethiopia. Some had hoped the Niger River would provide such a throughway. Shortly after Vasco da Gama returned from India, the Portuguese were able to send their first envoy to Ethiopia by sea, arriving in 1493. Little further contact ensued for more than a decade, however, until 1509 when the Ethiopians, feeling the pressure of Islam on its eastern and northern borders, sent an embassy to Portugal requesting a coordinated effort against Islam. Their proposal was that Ethiopia would fight Muslim forces on the land and be joined by the Portuguese on the sea.

The Portuguese king did not respond until 1520. The Ethiopian emperor, Lebna Dengel (r. 1508-1540) received a Portuguese embassy that year, and for the next six years the delegation remained in his kingdom, acting more like tourists than a political ally. With little military work to pursue one of the members of the Portuguese delegation, Francisco Álvares (c. 1465-c. 1540) was able to write extensively about his observations and experiences, providing some of the best detailed records of Ethiopian life during this period. Both sides, Portuguese and Ethiopian, were able to observe each other's Mass, and both expressed approval. The Portuguese raised questions regarding the Ethiopian practice of circumcision and its non-Chalcedonian theology, but there was little sustained discussion.

The Muslim kingdom of Adal (located in what is now part of Somalia) to the southeast of Ethiopia had for half a century been growing in political and economic strength, with continuous raids back and forth between the two nations. In 1529 under the leadership of Imam Ahmad ibn Ibrihim al-Ghazi (c. 1507-1543), Adal launched a major attack against Ethiopia, targeting churches and monasteries in particular for destruction. The Ethiopian army was defeated at Shimbra-Kure (or Chembra Kouré) and an Islamic governor installed in the capital. Christian sites throughout the country were looted and burned, and St. Mary of Zion, the great sixth-century cathedral in the ancient capital of Aksum, was completely destroyed. Over the next three years, tens of thousands of Christians converted to Islam. Many written records and documents of Ethiopia's long history were lost during this period, greatly diminishing written Ethiopian sources dating from before 1530.

As bleak as the conquest was, Ethiopia did not die. Emperor Lebna Dengel was never captured; and upon his death in 1540 his eighteen-year-old son, Galawdéwos (r. 1540-1559), assumed the throne. Several years before, in 1535,

Lebna Dengel had helped a Portuguese physician named João Bermudez (d. 1570) escape to seek European Christian aid against the Muslim insurgents. In 1541 the Portuguese arrived with four hundred soldiers and cannons, led by Vasco da Gama's son, Cristóvão da Gama (1516-1542). The Muslims turned to the Ottoman Turks, who sent some eight hundred troops. This proved to be decisive in turning the tide against the Portuguese and Ethiopian forces. De Gama and 160 other Portuguese were captured and beheaded, the Turks were released to return home, and the war seemed to be over.

The Ethiopians turned the tide one more time, however. Led by Queen Mother Sabla Wangel (d. 1568), and her son, Galawdéwos, thousands of Ethiopians and a handful of remaining Portuguese soldiers marched against an overly confident Islamic army. At the Battle of Woguera in 1543 Imam Ahmad was killed by a Portuguese musket. Without their leader, the Muslim forces scattered and the Ethiopians claimed victory, reestablishing their rule over the nation.

Despite the success of the Ethiopian-Portuguese alliance at war, relations between the two Christian nations did not go well over the next several decades. By the middle of the sixteenth century the Portuguese had firmly established themselves militarily in the Indian Ocean from the island of Goa, off the coast of South India. The Portuguese viewed East Africa from the Indian Ocean. Thus, East Africa, Arabia, and West India were to them a single coastline. East Africa, beginning in 1534, was part of the Latin diocese of Goa. Rome had appointed a Portuguese archbishop over the region, and expected the ancient churches of South India and Ethiopia alike to conform to the Latin tradition.

In 1555 without any conversation with the Ethiopian king or church hierarchy, Rome appointed three bishops, João Nunez Barreto (d. 1562) and Melchior Carneiro (d. 1583), who were both originally from Portugal, and Andre de Oviedo (c. 1517-1577), who was from Spain, to assume leadership of the Ethiopian church. Barreto was appointed by Rome to be the new patriarch for the Ethiopian church, ignoring the long tradition of the patriarch being an Egyptian appointed by the patriarch of Alexandria. The three Iberian bishops traveled to Goa, but before they made the final trip to Ethiopia ambassadors were sent ahead to communicate to the emperor the actions of the pope.

Galawdéwos responding by going off for a month with his mother, Sabla Wangel, who seemed to have been his chief advisor, to write a brief but significant confession. The statement affirmed the Councils of Nicaea, Constantinople, and Ephesus, and the full humanity and divinity of Jesus. The Ethiopian practices of Sabbath observance, circumcision, and not eating pork were defended. Galawdéwos stated that the Ethiopians kept the Sabbath on Saturday not as Jews do, but as instructed in the ancient *Didascalia*. The practice of circumcision was carried out as Ethiopians had always carried it out. It was a local custom, not a religious custom from the Jews. Finally, regarding pork, the emperor said that the Ethiopian tradition does not condemn those who do eat this meat, and pointed to the Apostle Paul who in Romans said that the one who eats should not despise the one who does not eat. What the Latin church saw as Judaizing, the king identified as local custom or a practice with clear scriptural command. On the other hand, the emperor rejected what he considered to be theological innovations from Europe, among them the appointment of a patriarch by Rome. It was unthinkable that the Ethiopian emperor would ever allow a Latin patriarch to rule over his people.

Following this exchange it was decided in Goa that attempting to send a Latin patriarch would not be a good idea at that time. The dialogue was continued by the Spaniard Oviedo, however, who proved to be more contentious than gentle. After the polite dialogue turned into accusations, Oviedo penned an unambiguously confrontational piece defending Roman primacy against Ethiopia's supposed errors, and proceeded to pronounce the Ethiopian emperor excommunicated. Following the death of Galawdéwos in 1559, Oviedo supported the Ottoman Turks, who were Muslims, against the Ethiopian Christian forces during a period of civil war. Soon after that, Oviedo was appointed by Rome as the Latin patriarch of Ethiopia. He spent his final days until his death in 1577 in Ethiopia, serving as a local priest to the growing foreign and mixed-race community.

The first three bishops sent by Rome to take over leadership of the Ethiopian church were all members of the newly founded Catholic missionary order known as the Society of Jesus, or the Jesuits. Founded in 1541 by a Spaniard named Ignatius Loyola (1491-1556), the Jesuits quickly grew to become a force throughout the world. Loyola himself had come in contact with the Ethiopian church while in Rome and offered his services for this work. Because of his age and the need for him to direct the work from Europe, he remained in Rome but drew up detailed instructions for the members of his order, who were the first to go by the name "missionaries." Although the approach he described was to be gentle or sweet (*con dolcezza*), the aim of the effort in East Africa was nothing less than to bring the Ethiopian church under the full authority of, and into uniformity with, Rome.

The first chapter of Jesuit missionary work in Ethiopia came to a close by the end of the century. As in many other places where Portuguese and Spanish traders had gone around the world, a mixed-race community of mixed-religious affiliation soon developed. Most of the Jesuits who came to Ethiopia worked among these mixed communities. By 1597 this mixed-race group had mostly become Ethiopian Orthodox in their religious faith, observing the Sabbath, circumcising children, and no longer speaking Portuguese. These characteristics point back to the distinctive shape of Christianity that continued to live in Ethiopia despite foreign interventions. The close identification of Ethiopia with the ancient King Solomon, its relative isolation from the broader currents of the world Christian ecumenical church for several centuries, and the adaptation of many local African customs into the life of the church all contributed to this unique Christian formation.

Ethiopian church life continued to be organized by a patriarch, or *abuna*, at the head. Under him were the priests in the emperor's palace, the heads of the various orders of monks, and then the monks, nuns, hermits, and the lay clerics. A more complex episcopal hierarchy never developed as it did in other communions. Consequently, the power of a foreign patriarch was greater, and the church was much more localized through the leadership of local monasteries and charismatic monks and priests.

The number of monasteries and churches in Ethiopia in the sixteenth century appeared overwhelming to foreign travelers. Monasteries were often located in inaccessible terrain, as much in response to the threat of conflict as in search of spiritual solitude while churches occupied more prominent locations. Priests, with shaven heads and carrying crosses in their right hands, could marry in Ethiopia, but never remarry. In the sixteenth century the number of priests was increasing rapidly, and, more often than not, priests were the sons of priests. Most of the clergy were not wealthy, but those who were attached to principal churches and monasteries had large estates and incomes. Clergy had no special dress, and many of the poorer clergy had to work in the fields to supplement their income.

Priests could only be ordained by the *abuna* since there was no second tier of bishops under him. If there was no *abuna* for a number of years, as was often the case, the new patriarch would lead large ordination services even before he was fluent in the language of Ge'ez. Álvares describes an ordination service where 2,357 priests were ordained, and he was told it was a smaller number than the usual five or six thousand. At the ordination service three lines of ordinands would come forward, and each would read a brief section from one of three open Bibles. After having proven his literacy, each candidate would then enter the *abuna's* tent to have hands laid on him by the *abuna* alone. The Eucharist would then be celebrated for the thousands of new priests.

Monks and nuns played an important role in the life of Ethiopia. The power behind the throne was often a key monk whose interpretation and advice were sought. The number of monks generally outnumbered the number of priests in any given region. Nuns were likewise numerous in Ethiopia, living in their own convents but excluded from holy sites. Nuns had their own separate churches where the Eucharist was celebrated by ordained monks. Unlike the priests, monks and nuns had special dress that identified them as set apart. Most wore yellow cloth or goat skin, and the monks often had a full, flowing cape and hat. Large gatherings of monks at special festivals and holy days were common. Álvares describes the arrival of Emperor Lebna Dengel as he migrated through the land, with twenty to thirty thousand monks and priests to greet him.

Worship in the Ethiopian churches evidenced a number of distinct character-istics. Most of the churches were round with an outer region for the laity (*qene mahalet*), a second region toward the center marked off with curtains for the officiating priests (*maqdas*), and then the center and most holy section (*qeddasta qedasan*) where the holy altar slab (*tabot*) and the Eucharistic elements were kept. Many of the churches in their outer architecture imitated local homes and buildings, but in sacred space imitated the Jewish tabernacle or temple.

Worship consisted in recited prayers (sung or chanted), readings from the Psalms, and music provided by bells, drums, and the human voice. Dance was part of the worship, as was a procession of priests carrying censers in the right hand and crosses in the left. There were no seats. People stood in worship, at times bowing to kiss the ground. Scriptures were read, or shouted, by the priest who would be standing in the doorway to the outer chamber (*qene mahalet*). Communion was served to the monks in the middle chamber and then to the laity in the outer chamber. As with other Orthodox churches, the bread and wine were mixed and then served with a small spoon, followed by some water. The water was to be swished around in the mouth and then swallowed.

The Sabbath, as seen above, was honored on Saturday and Sunday, and fasting was rigorous and frequent. The Portuguese visitors were surprised not only by the celebration of two Sabbaths and the strict fasting regulations, but also by the practice of circumcision and annual baptism. Circumcision seems to have been practiced as a continuation of African ritual adopted into the Christian faith. Even those Ethiopians who were convinced by the Portuguese to become Roman Catholic continued the practice. Infant boys were baptized at the age of forty days and girls at eighty days. They were baptized at the entrance to the church with water poured over the infant and were then given Communion. There also developed in Ethiopia a practice of annual rebaptism, which was practiced in regional centers in large baptismal pools. Once again there may have been a similar local practice that was incorporated into the Ethiopian church, for the defense given by the emperor was simply that it provided an annual reminder to repent of all the sins committed during the previous year.

Other beliefs appear to have been local practices that persisted even after a millennium and a half of Christianity in Ethiopia. Belief in augury, sacred sayings, and auspicious days and times seem to have been deep-seated in the local cultures. It was considered a bad omen if, while going on a trip, one heard a bird singing on the left of the path. Emperors, priests, and monks struggled against such superstitions. Spirit possession continued to be a concern, although for many it was identified with the spirits of Christian saints, Mary, or the Holy Spirit who gave commands to the people. One of the critical issues for the churches of Ethiopia was literacy. Beyond the priests and members of the royal family, few in the nation could read. Both the scriptures and the liturgy continued for centuries in the same ancient Ethiopic (Ge'ez) language. Few of the newer tribes that were brought into greater Ethiopia understood the language of Christian worship or could read any of it. Increasingly the Christian faith was being defined by liturgy that was not fully understood and by opposition to Islam.

During this period Christianity in Ethiopia struggled not only for survival but also with its own identity over against Islam. The problem of reintegrating thousands of former apostates in the middle of the sixteenth century required a new understanding of Christian identity and community. The imperial nature of Ethiopian Christianity was strengthened since it was the emperor and his mother and his father who had been the defenders of the faith. But the uneasy relationship with European Christians that emerged in the middle of the sixteenth century intensified in the seventeenth. Ethiopian Christianity now had to engage not only the customs and beliefs of recent African converts and Islam, but now European religious imperialism.

King Galawdéwos's confession provided an important response to this last challenge. The king's teacher and friend, Enbaqom, provided an equally important response to Islam. Enbaqom, an Arab Christian probably from Iraq who lived in Ethiopia, wrote *Anqasa Amin* ("Door of Faith") in response to Ahmad of Adal, who was pursuing him in 1540 and was possibly going to be his new ruler. *Anqasa Amin* is a Christian apologetic work written in Arabic and was one of the only works ever written in Ethiopia with an extensive discussion of Islam, even quoting from the Qur'an. Christianity is defended on the grounds that it is a superior moral faith (driven by love for the poor, not war against unbelievers) and a truly universal faith (based upon the many languages into which the Bible is translated). While it was not a typical theological work, the book provides a window on how one important Ethiopian thinker in the sixteenth century understood Christianity and Islam.

Suggestions for further reading

Agbeti, J. Kofi, *West African Church History: Christian Missions and Church Foundations, 1482-1919*. Leiden: E.J. Brill, 1986.

Baur, John. *Two Thousand Years of Christianity in Africa: An African Church History*. 2nd ed. Nairobi: St. Pauls.

Gray, Richard, *Black Christians and White Missionaries*. New Haven: Yale University Press, 1990.

Hastings, Adrian, *The Church in Africa, 1450-1950*. Oxford: Clarendon Press, 1994.

Isichei, Elizabeth, *A History of Christianity in Africa: From Antiquity to the Present*. London: SPCK, 1995.

Kalu, Ogbu, *African Christianity: An African Story*. Pretoria: Department of Church History, University of Pretoria, 2005.

Sundkler, Bengt, and Christopher Steed, *A History of the Church in Africa*. Cambridge: Cambridge University Press, 2000.

Werner, Roland, William Anderson, and Andrew Wheeler, *Day of Devastation, Day of Contentment: The History of the Sudanese Church across 2000 Years*. Nairobi: Paulines, Publications Africa, 2000.

3

Christianity Re-encounters Asia

Christians were no strangers to the Asian continent when the Portuguese arrived in the fifteenth century. Christianity had been born in western Asia. During its first centuries the movement had spread along trade routes through the Persian empire into India and up the Silk Road through central Asia, reaching as far as the imperial capital of China by the seventh century. Persecution by the Zoroastrian rulers of the Persian empire and later by Islamic rulers in various parts of Asia had deterred the growth of churches over the centuries, but Christianity never ceased being an Asian religion.

Asia has never been a unified cultural world. For thousands of years the continent and its surrounding islands had been home to a vast number of languages, cultures, and religions. Major centers of urban civilization in Mesopotamia, Persia, India, and China had emerged several thousand years ago. By the beginning of the Common Era they were actively trading with one another across the continent. Arab rulers successfully joined Arabia, Mesopotamia, Persia, and much of central Asia under a common Islamic government in the seventh and eighth centuries for the first time, but eventually regional rulers rose to become more important. The Mongol empire in the fourteenth century had come closest to unifying the entire continent of Asia under a single ruling dynasty, reaching from China to Europe and into northern India. By the fifteenth century it too had split into several political and cultural factions.

Western Christianity comes to Asia

By the fifteenth century the shoreline of the Indian Ocean and South China Sea had become an integrated trading zone that was mostly controlled by Islamic rulers and dominated by Arabs and Persians on its west. Christians in the Persian world had been reduced to a small minority community and had lost most of their former wealth and prestige. An East Syrian patriarch in Baghdad was still being appointed; but he was little more than a figure, and his office had lost much of its ability to function effectively.

The Christian community along the southern Indian coast in Kerala was doing well, on the other hand. These "St. Thomas" Christians, as they were known, had carved out a protected political place in the larger society and enjoyed a fairly profitable life as merchants. India in the fifteenth century was ruled by numerous kings, sultans, and other royal figures who were mostly either Muslim or Hindu. As a small but important minority community of less than 100,000, Christians were protected by local Hindu rulers in the south. Christian bishops had the political status of local military chiefs. As a minority people, the St. Thomas Christians could still be exposed to the will and power of their rulers. Nevertheless, they enjoyed political favors, such as being exempt from paying duty on imports and manufactured goods, a significant benefit in light of the fact that they were predominantly merchants. The St. Thomas Christians were critical actors within the South Indian economy, controlling most of the pepper trade in the region. There is some indication that this protected and favored status was slipping in the late fifteenth century, but at the time of the Portuguese arrival, the St. Thomas Christians were still relatively wealthy and influential.

The Portuguese entered the Indian Ocean several decades after the last Chinese imperial ships had sailed through its waters. The Chinese had carried out a series of official imperial trade and diplomatic missions under the Ming ruler, Emperor Yongle (1360-1424). After the 1420s, however, the Chinese had ended such major seafaring expeditions, falling back upon the tradition of expecting merchants from other lands to come to them in the port cities of China. At the end of the fifteenth century a small number of Chinese merchants lived in settlements in port cities such as Malacca (also known as Melaka) on the Malaysian peninsula, but they did so as expatriates with little or no contact with the Chinese imperial government.

Muslim seafarers of Arab, Persian, and Indian cultural descent controlled most of the trade in the Indian Ocean prior to the arrival of the Portuguese. No single Muslim ruler exercised political control over the sea lanes at the time. For the most part the ships were small vessels that were owned by the merchants, carrying goods as well as passengers back and forth between ports throughout the region. These merchants came on behalf of different national cultures, and they established trading colonies in each port they visited, creating a permanent foreign presence. As Muslims, they also sought to spread their religion where they traveled through south Asia, bringing Islam to the seacoast regions of Indonesia and as far as the Philippines by 1500.

The Portuguese quickly established trading colonies or factories like those of the Muslim merchants. Unlike the Muslim-dominated trade that had preceded them, however, the Portuguese effort was directed and coordinated by a single political entity. The Portuguese also quickly spread beyond the Indian Ocean, passing by way of the Strait of Malacca to the South China Sea. Like the various Muslims who had traded in the region before them, the Portuguese were driven by the pursuit of wealth; but they also brought their religion. Indeed, it can be said that the modern histories of Africa and Asia were determined as much by matters of religious belief as they were by material economy or military might. The fifteenth century was critical for the religious development in this region of the world in part because of the competition that emerged here between the religious ideologies of Christianity and Islam. One result was that the smaller, poorer, and in many ways less technologically advanced countries of Portugal and Spain, not the mighty empire of China, ended up colonizing far from home and spreading their religion to Africa, Asia, and the Americas.

The Portuguese arrived in India at a critical moment in the subcontinent's religious history as the region was undergoing a political transformation that still in part shapes it today. India had never been a united kingdom or empire, but to a greater or lesser degree large portions had been united by various, often foreign, powers. In 1526 Zahir-ud-din Muhammad Babur (1483-1530), a grandson of Tamerlane (1336-1405) and ruler of a small kingdom in central Asia, launched an attack against a fellow Muslim, the sultan of Delhi. Babur's victory at Panipat marked the beginning of the Mughul empire. Babur's grandson, Akbar the Great (1542-1605), assumed power in 1556 at the age of fourteen. Over the next five decades he extended Mughul rule from Afghanistan to central India. By the end of the seventeenth century the Mughul empire controlled all of India except for the extreme south and a few European settlements. The Mughuls were Sunni Muslims, and although the first generation exercised a relative degree of religious tolerance, their later rulers were more strongly orthodox. In the south of India the Vijayanagar empire, whose rulers were Hindu, exercised a significant degree of toleration, which allowed the Christians of Kerala to prosper.

St. Thomas Churches and Indian Christianity

Christianity first came to India in the first centuries of the Common Era. According to ancient tradition it was brought there by St. Thomas the Apostle. The earliest firmly documented evidence of a permanent Christian community in South India comes from the fourth century. For hundreds of years these Indian churches, located along the southwest coast of Kerala, had been nourished by a continuous flow of Christian traders and monks from other parts of Asia. The Persian church provided them with priests; and like their Persian Christian neighbors, the Indian community worshipped in Syriac. By the tenth century Christianity had been eclipsed in most of Asia east of Persia, and by the fifteenth century had almost disappeared entirely from Persia and central Asia. India was the most notable exception. Christians in Kerala had become integrated into the Indian culture as a distinct caste, and, although not widely spread through the region, were quite strong and influential.

Most of the evidence suggests that Christians in India were relatively high in their caste location. Because of the rigid caste structure in India, Christians remained there for the most part, identified by their dress and employment (agriculture, trade, and military), just a step below the Brahmins in South India. The Christian men wore their hair long, tied up on top of their head into a knot into which a metal cross was inserted. Except for the cross, they could be mistaken for any Hindu upper-caste member of the village. Newborn children, like their Brahmin contemporaries, were fed a mixture of powdered gold, honey, and ghee in keeping with upper-class habits. Christians had become well adapted to the culture of India.

Indian Christians continued to worship in the fifteenth century much as they had for a millennium before. The liturgy was carefully followed in Syriac, a language even many of the priests no longer understood. Christians, however, were very devout. Portuguese observers described the Indian Christians as lovers of fasts and long sermons. They were also devoted to the cross (depicted in the East Syrian tradition without a body) and to their prayers. Churches had no images such as those found in Roman Catholic churches, and, before the arrival of the Portuguese, churches were built in the local style, resembling a Hindu *pagoda* (or temple) with a cross on the top. The floors of churches were "painted" with cow dung in the manner of the *pagoda*, and they had lamps and umbrellas in the local style.

Inside the churches in South India one would also typically find a copy of the Syriac Bible, often in gold leafing on an elaborately carved stand, and no statues or other images depicting the divine. Men and women sat on opposite sides of the church, and everyone bowed in three directions upon entering: forward to honor the cross, to the right in the direction of the baptismal font, and to the left where the Eucharistic bread was located. Unison prayers were said in a loud voice, but then personal prayers were said quietly in a prostrate position.

The St. Thomas Christians, along with all eastern Christians at the time, allowed their priests to marry (although not their bishops), but they also had orders of monks and nuns who were celibate. Fasting was important, with a total of 98 fasting days per year. Christians were marked as being a different community, not only by the limited diet, but also through the proscription of touching during their fasts, for a fasting Christian was not to touch a non-Christian.

The Christian marriage ceremony was, like the building in which it was celebrated, a very Indian affair. As in a Hindu wedding ceremony, the St. Thomas Christian ceremony involved "the giving of the dress." At the climax of the ceremony, the groom would give the bride a cloth, a beautiful piece of a wedding gown laced with gold threads, placing it on her head. Threads that had been taken from the cloth were then placed upon the bride and groom as a necklace. The wedding liturgy was full of images from the biblical book the Song of Songs, with the constant reminder of the couple being also in covenant relationship with the bridegroom, Jesus Christ.

In language, theology, and church order, Indian Christians were a part of the "Church of the East," the Assyrian or Chaldean Church. The St. Thomas Christians were still under the headship of the patriarch of Baghdad (Indians called him *catholika*) in Persia. Indian Christians would talk about their prelates, whom they greatly revered, as coming from Babylon. As was the case in Ethiopia where the head of the church was appointed by the patriarch in Egypt, the Indian Church depended upon a foreign nation, in this case Persia, for its episcopal leadership. These foreign bishops were by most accounts both respected and honored by the Christians of India, in part because they were so rare a sight. Often decades would pass without a new bishop from Persia being appointed, one reason the Indian Church favored ordination of young boys as priests, who could then be expected to serve for a greater length of time. Dependency on an outside cultural church and using a language different from the one the people spoke hampered the life of the St. Thomas Church at times. At the same time the foreignness of the liturgy and episcopal leadership help preserve the distinctive identity of Christians within the dominant religious culture, helping to prevent their being entirely absorbed within the dominant surrounding Indian religious context of Hinduism.

The St. Thomas Christians had historically looked toward the west, to the patriarch in Baghdad as the ecclesial head of their own church. This suddenly changed in the spring of 1498 with the arrival of Europeans who looked not to Baghdad but farther west to Rome for the head of their church.

Arrival of the Portuguese

Religion, politics, and food all played a role in bringing Portuguese ships to India in May of 1498. With the collapse of Constantinople in 1453 at the hand of the Ottoman Turks, the overland route of pepper to southern Europe was cut off. Other products were also missed, but it was pepper that was identified as the main concern because Europeans used it to preserve meat in an edible form during the long winter months. One can easily understand the desire to circumvent the Muslim traders and tax collectors who controlled the overland trade between Europe and Asia, but religion and politics were also motivating factors in the Portuguese expansion. Southern Europeans continued to support the notion of a crusade against Muslims, as we have noted in the motivation for Columbus's voyage and for the Portuguese attack on Ceuta. The Iberians continued to hope to find Christian communities on the other geographical side of the world in Ethiopia and even India who could help them encircle and eventually strangle Islam. Europeans thought that in India, or in some country near India, there was a Christian kingdom whose legendary king, Prester John, would join them in this new alliance against Islam. Asked in 1498 why Vasco da Gama (1460-1524) had come to India, one of his scouts replied, in search of Christians and spices. Both were found.

Four Portuguese ships under the command of da Gama made their way around the southern tip of Africa and up the eastern coast in 1497. Then with the help of a Muslim pilot who was pressed into service, in 1498 they crossed the Indian Ocean to arrive in the port city Kozhikode (or Calicut as it was generally known in the West). Aided by several North African Muslim merchants in the city who spoke both the Iberian languages and Malayalam, the language of Kerala, the Portuguese were able to tour the city and meet the local rulers. They visited a local temple that da Gama mistakenly took to be a Christian house of worship, adding fuel to his hopes for finding Prester John. De Gama returned later that year to Portugal, where he organized a second voyage to India in 1502.

In between these two voyages a second Portuguese fleet of ships, this one with nineteen missionary priests, eight of whom were Franciscans, and sailing under the command of Pedro Álvares Cabral (c. 1468-1520) left for Africa in 1500. Cabral decided to sail farther out in the Atlantic than his predecessors, thereby landing by accident on what eventually became Brazil and claiming it for Portugal before continuing on around the southern tip of Africa into the Indian Ocean. He arrived at Kozhikode later that year, but his ignorance of local customs combined with his crusading mentality soon led him into trouble. To quell a local riot that had likely been precipitated by the presence of so many Portuguese, Cabral opened fire on the city with his cannon. For two days the Portuguese ships fired upon the city, killing not only Muslims and Hindus but three of the Franciscan missionaries who had come on board his own vessels.

In the aftermath Cabral and the Portuguese had to flee to Cranganore, in the region of Cochin. There they found a large community of St. Thomas Christians who were friendlier toward the western Christians, whom the St. Thomas Christians considered co-religionists. For a short time the Portuguese and the St. Thomas Christians found grounds for cooperation, and a fragile trust was established. Without understanding each other's language well, they observed each other's Eucharistic celebrations with approval. The Indian Christians were pleased that God seemed to be sending Christian support against the "Ishmaelites," as they referred to Muslims. With time, however, the Indian Christians learned that both the morals of Portuguese sailors and the goals of the *parangi* (foreign) missionaries were a threat to the ancient Christian churches of India. Marginal support is all that the Portuguese needed, on the other hand, as they expanded their control of ports and trade routes in India, and eventually to the Pacific.

During the first few decades of the sixteenth century, the Portuguese solidified their hold along the coastlines in the south (taking Cochin in 1503 and Goa in 1510), in the Persian Gulf (taking Ormuz in 1515), and over to Malaya (taking Malacca in 1511). The Portuguese in Asia did not seek to build a land-based empire as the Spanish did in America, so direct conflict between local Mughul or Vijayanagar rulers and the Portuguese was minimal. Indians, both Hindu and St. Thomas Christians, saw the Portuguese as possible deliverers as well as trading partners. On the other hand, the Portuguese soon controlled the Indian Ocean. Their warships practiced what amounted to piracy, raiding and destroying the lightly armed Muslim trading ships that had previously sailed the Indian Ocean without a great deal of fear. A little more than a decade after their initial arrival in India, Portuguese warships were in control of the entire Indian Ocean and were becoming a presence in the South China Sea.

Five bishops from the East Syrian Church had recently been appointed to serve the churches in the south of India just prior to the Portuguese arrival in the sixteenth century. We know very little about any of them except for Mar Jacob, the Metropolitan of Cranganore (r. 1504-1551), who was a key figure in the emerging relationship between the St. Thomas Christians and the Portuguese. Mar Jacob helped to negotiate treaties for both trade and land, and introduced (or translated) the Latin form of confession into the Syriac language for Indian Christian worship. He was respected by the Franciscan friars and later by the Jesuit priests, as well as by shipping captains, and he believed that relations with the Portuguese would be good for the Indian Christians because of the Portuguese's knowledge about both the world and theology.

Indian Christians as a whole, however, were soon of two minds about the

Portuguese. Some of the leaders like Mar Jacob could see that there was much to gain from good relationships. However, the lifestyle of the Portuguese sailors and their misunderstanding of local practices were irritating to the Indians, especially the Indian Christians. The term for the Portuguese foreigners was *parangi*, which at first was merely descriptive but soon became derogatory. What began as hope and even admiration soon turned sour. The Portuguese were building an empire at the initiative of pope and king, and the Indian Christians were useful only to the degree that they could adopt the Portuguese plan. The work that the Portuguese friars undertook in India quickly came to focus on shifting the alliance of the St. Thomas Christians from Baghdad (or Chaldea as they called the patriarchal see) to Rome, an effort that was similar to the Portuguese initiative toward Ethiopia, which has already been noted.

The Portuguese initially concentrated their military attention along the extreme southwest coast of Kerala. In 1510, however, they succeeded in removing the Mughul Muslim rulers from the island port of Goa, farther north along the west coast. Goa, along with Malacca in Malaya and Macao off the coast of China, soon became one of the major centers of Portuguese power in Asia. Christianity in Kerala remained strongly attached to the identity of St. Thomas while Goa became strongly Roman Catholic. After the death of Mar Jacob, there was no one of equal stature and diplomacy to keep the very different groups together. Several church leaders were sent by the St. Thomas community to Rome, to seek recognition of the eastern tradition, without success. In India some of the leaders of the Christian community accepted the Latin tradition in worship, but others refused to submit, claiming that the authority of St. Thomas in the East was comparable to that of St. Peter in the West. The strong ethnic association and historical identity with India meant the latter group generally had the heart of the people. The issues that divided the two sides were always as much cultural and linguistic as they were theological.

The initial policy of the first Portuguese governor of Goa, Afonso de Albuquerque (1453-1515), toward other religions on the island was one of tolerance that allowed religious freedom for all. After a short period he reversed himself and sought to annihilate all Muslims, but then in 1513 reversed himself again and welcomed Muslims (especially Persian and Arab traders) back to the island. Hindus on the island initially praised the protection and profit Portuguese rule appeared to have brought. Hindu festivals appear actually to have increased under the initial Catholic rulers. One of the few restrictions of the Portuguese was that of outlawing the practice of *sati,* or the burning of widows on the funeral pyre of their deceased husbands. The tolerance toward the Hindu religion at least did not last for long, however. In 1540 a new policy, the "Rigor of Mercy," was introduced, ordering all Hindu temples in Goa to be demolished. By the end of the year there were none to be seen.

The following year in Portugal the Confraternity of the Holy Faith was established, the first order dedicated to evangelizing India. The statutes of the confraternity outline a variety of inducements to conversion, negative as well as positive. In territories under Portuguese control, for instance, Hindus were not to rebuild their temples; Muslims were not to convert their slaves to Islam; non-

Christians had heavier tax burdens; and enslaved persons who were baptized were to be freed. In a more positive vein, the confraternity was to provide Christian instruction and preaching, and ministries of mercy and benevolence. The confraternity even planned to establish a college to train future Indian priests.

Another order that was influential in Goa in the sixteenth century was the Misericordia. Although the roots of this order went back to Florence, Italy, in the thirteenth century, it had been introduced to Lisbon at the end of the fifteenth century and by the sixteenth century had become predominantly Portuguese. Its members traveled with Portuguese sailors around the world, establishing hospitals and places of rest and refuge in the various settlements that the Portuguese founded. Where they did not start hospitals, they were often asked to take over hospitals that others had established, so highly regarded was their work. Medical care at this time was mostly a matter of providing food, drink, and comfort while easing the dying person's journey to the next life. The Misericordia excelled in such ministries of compassion. Members of the order lived completely off of alms collected from parishioners. The brothers ensured that the sick and the imprisoned received sacraments and food. The desperately poor received donations of food three times per week. In addition the brothers took care of the burial of the poor and cared for those who were condemned to death.

During these first years in India the Portuguese effort succeeded in converting a small number of Hindus and Muslims to the Christian faith, mostly in Goa. Converts were brought into the western Latin rather than the Indian form of Christianity. After the "Rigor of Mercy" policy was introduced, Hindus on Goa turned to Christianity more rapidly. A number of factors still worked against conversion, however. For one thing, the Portuguese sailors and rulers alike generally set a bad example and actually discouraged conversion. Prominent Hindus on Goa spoke against conversion and encouraged Hindus and Muslims to retain their own religion. Priests and monks discussed separating the converts from the local population to insulate and preserve the church. Others suggested removing the influential and upper-caste Hindus who discouraged Christian conversion. Those who did convert to Christianity were mostly lower caste and peasants. The wealthy and respected Brahmans in particular saw no reason to leave their religion to adopt a western religion of a lowly Jesus.

Francis Xavier and the Jesuits

One of the most significant Christian figures in Asia in the sixteenth century was Francis Xavier (1506-1552). Xavier was the first Jesuit to arrive in Asia, landing in Goa in May of 1542, just two years after the new order under Ignatius of Loyola (1491-1556) had been approved in Rome. Ignatius was a Spaniard who had studied in Paris. While serving in the military he had been wounded in battle. During his recuperation he had undergone a spiritual experience that resulted in a process of spiritual reflection. Ignatius later set out the process in a book titled *Spiritual Exercises*, through which he sought to prepare both himself and others around him to become more faithful witnesses to the true faith. The result was a new order, known as the Society of Jesus, or Jesuits. Xavier was one of the original members of the group.

Xavier arrived in Goa with no other experience than a few years of teaching in Paris, followed by a time of caring for the sick in Venice. Xavier, like Loyola, was a native of Navarre, Spain, but he had been sent by the king of Portugal as Apostolic Nuncio to Asia to assist in the work of converting Indians to the Christian faith. Upon his arrival in Goa, Xavier immediately began to work with young children, ringing a bell to attract them to attend lessons on the Lord's Prayer and the catechism. But Xavier was as restless as he was creative in his missionary spirit. He was only in Goa for six months before sailing south around Cape Comorin to the Fishery Coast in southeast India. Thousands of low-caste pearl divers (*paravas*) and fishermen had already become Christian under Portuguese rule in the region, but demonstrated little apparent understanding of the faith. Aided by three Indians who had been accepted as students for the priesthood in a new seminary, Xavier worked for one year, translating a basic doctrinal statement into the local language, Tamil, and writing a sermon in Tamil on what it meant to be a Christian. His efforts quickly began to show results. At the capital of Tuticorin he preached so much and baptized so many that he complained that he was losing his voice and his arms were aching.

In September of 1543 Xavier left Tamil Nadu to return to Goa, but he did not remain there for long. For the next two years he continued to catechize neglected children, visit the imprisoned and the sick, and preach against the immorality of the Portuguese. At one point he wrote to the king of Portugal that the voices of India were raising a complaint to heaven because the king was being stingy in spending his material wealth on the spiritual needs of their land. It was the voice of a prophet against unjust profits, and it raised what became a common, if not dominant, theme for many in the Jesuit order during the early modern colonial period in Asia.

Even after several years of work, Xavier had no confidence that the church would survive or grow in Asia after the European leadership left. Although his approach was more responsive to the Indian context than that of the Franciscans before him, he still bore marks of the western mindset, which considered Latin ways of thinking to be essential to the faith. This would eventually change as he encountered other cultures and languages. In 1545 Xavier heard about some of the first Christian converts from Islam in the Maluku Islands (or the Moluccas, as the islands were formerly known) in what is now Indonesia. He had previously heard of the islands from a former sultan from the region named Tabarija (1521–1542) who had been deposed and was in exile in Goa, where he had become a Christian. Xavier determined that there were others farther east who had become Christian through contact with the Portuguese but who were without sufficient pastoral care, and that he should be visiting them. Following the expanding Portuguese shoestring empire, he journeyed east, stopping off first in Malacca on the Malay Peninsula before heading off for the port of Ambon, located on an island by the same name that is now part of Indonesia.

In two separate trips he managed to visit the islands of Ambon, Morotai, Halmahera, and Ternate, teaching, writing songs with which to teach Christian doctrine, and baptizing many local people. He promised to send more Jesuits, which he did, thus helping to begin the Jesuit Moluccan Mission in 1545, whose work established large Christian communities throughout the Maluku (or Molucca) Islands. Xavier was popular not only among the young Christian converts but also among local Muslims. One of his major contributions during this period was the further development of the Goan Seminary of the Holy Cross for training young converts. The school had been founded in 1541 by two priests who had established the Confraternity of the Holy Faith. In 1548 it was turned over to Xavier, and soon it was divided into two schools. The Seminary of the Holy Faith was for ordinary students while the College of St. Paul was for the formation of Jesuits. The college opened its door to non-Jesuit students in 1558, and soon it became a training center for Asian and African priests. Some of the first priests to serve in what would become Indonesia were trained alongside Africans and Indians at this seminary.

Christian beginnings in Japan

Returning to India in 1547, Xavier stopped off in Malacca where he met a Japanese fugitive named Yajiro (or Yajir, also identified in early Jesuit writings as Anjiro, 1511-1550). Xavier's horizons were immediately expanded, and his attention turned toward bringing the Christian message to that nation in the east. He arrived two years later in 1549 at a time when a new age in Japanese history was dawning. Oda Nobunaga (1534-1582) was the son of a minor Japanese lord who had recently inherited his father's estate. For over two centuries Japan had been divided by such local warrior rulers, called *daimyo,* who were often aided by militant Buddhist monks. A long history of militant Buddhist activism by these warrior-monks had plagued the islands of Japan, preventing political unity and cooperation among the numerous provinces. The Buddhist communities overlooking Kyoto were especially pugnacious and troublesome, often threatening and even raiding and burning the noble city.

Buddhism had come to Japan from Korea in the seventh century and had slowly been integrated into the indigenous religion of Shintoism, or "the way of the Superior Beings." Acceptance of Buddhism into Shinto religion was made possible in part by the identification of many of the Shinto beings as various incarnations of the Buddha, a practice that had long characterized Buddhism in east Asia. At the time of the arrival of the Portuguese, Nobunaga had come to the conclusion that the more militant form of Buddhism sponsored by temples such as the one at Mt. Hiei was the major threat to his consolidation of power. Portuguese ships had already stopped in Japanese ports and were seeking to open up trade. Nobunaga saw the new foreigners, with their ships, guns, and foreign monks, as potential allies.

This was the context for the arrival of the Jesuits in Japanese history. The decisive leader in this effort was not Xavier, however, but the young criminal-turned-evangelist, Yajiro. Yajiro wrote to the Jesuits in Europe in 1548 what is most likely the first Japanese Christian testimony to be recorded. After murdering a man in Japan, he fled to a Buddhist monastery, was ushered out of the country on a Portuguese ship, and ended up in Malacca, he said. He learned about the Christian faith from the Portuguese on the ship going to Malacca, and later in China where ships would stop off before making the dangerous trip to Japan. By the time he met Xavier, on his second trip to Malacca, he was eager to become a Christian. Xavier was soon just as eager to go to Japan.

The two companions traveled to Goa, off the coast of India, where Yajiro was baptized by a Portuguese priest and was given the name "Paul of the Holy Faith." Between March of 1548, when he traveled to India, and November of that same year, when he penned his testimony, Yajiro had translated the Gospel of Matthew into Japanese, having divided it into four memorable sections and committed the Gospel to memory. His instincts as an evangelist and missionary thinker had a considerable impact on the Spanish Jesuit. Unsure of the welcome that he would receive in Japan, for instance, Xavier asked the young convert that if he went to Japan would the people become Christian. Yajiro responded with a thoughtful reply that his people would not immediately become Christian. They would first want to ask questions and carefully weigh the answers. They would also want to observe the Christian's behavior. But if the answers they received and observed were suitable, he assured Xavier, within six months the educated would quickly become Christian.

Yajiro may have been overly optimistic about his own people, but the basic direction of his argument, to approach the rulers and to demonstrate good deeds to prove the faith, became the pattern for the Jesuits in east Asia. Yajiro raised questions about the relationship of the church to merchants, on the other hand. Merchant ships had often provided the transportation and support for the work of monks in east Asia, but the merchants seldom showed respect for the local cultures and for morality in the way that the monks did. When it became clear to Yajiro, Xavier, and the others in their party waiting in Malacca for Portuguese transport to Japan that no Portuguese ship would soon be available and that they would have to travel to Japan on a Chinese junk, Paul was elated. He was eager to keep Xavier and the message of Christianity separate from the European Christian merchants, whose greed contradicted Christian teachings so clearly.

Yajiro understood that Christianity was not synonymous with Iberian culture, but that it was also different than both Iberian and Japanese culture. After his encounter with Yajiro, Xavier's letters demonstrated greater concern with these issues and expressed confidence that Asians could do the work of the church themselves, something that was not even being considered by other Western church leaders at the time. He wrote appreciatively of Japanese culture, which had commanded his sincere respect. The task he set for himself as a Spaniard was to study Japanese ways and adapt the Christian message to that culture. Xavier came to believe, for instance, that his dress in apostolic poverty was not appropriate in Japan, for the message would only be heard by local rulers if he showed them proper respect by wearing silk and bringing gifts. Yajiro deserves much of the credit for being the early pioneer in this method of missionary adaptation. Back in Japan, however, he continued to suffer from persecution under Buddhist warrior-monks, forcing him eventually to flee the country. By the end of his life he had apparently abandoned Christianity as well, dying as a pirate (*bafan*) in China.

Xavier only spent twenty-seven months in Japan, but during that time, much was accomplished. He began translating creeds and prayers, and preached to Buddhist monks and *daimyos*, some of whom had become Christians. One of the key lessons he learned and passed on to the other Jesuits was that the emperor should not be the focus of missionary activity. He believed that local *daimyos* were the key to reaching local peasants. In his discussions with Japanese, he came to the conclusion that the Japanese imitated the Chinese. This led him in 1551 to head off for China, believing that if the Chinese would be converted then the Japanese would follow. Xavier died before reaching China, but he left behind three small yet strong and growing communities of Japanese Christians.

Christianity reaches the Philippines

The Portuguese military advance by sea created a shoestring empire made up of port cities and settlements that by the middle of the sixteenth century stretched around Africa and across Asia. For the most part the Portuguese did not seek to develop an extensive land-based colonial empire as the Spanish had done in America. The colonies of Brazil, Angola, and Mozambique were the Portuguese exceptions to what was otherwise a string of small port cities and settlements from Portugal to China. The tactic proved to be highly profitable. From their strategic ports the Portuguese controlled the major sea lanes of Asia through which trading ships now regularly passed.

As the Portuguese were expanding their trading empire in Asia by sea from the west, sea captains sailing for the Spanish crown sought to extend that nation's colonial reach into Asia, doing so by coming from the other side of the world, from the east. In 1519 a Spanish expedition of five ships under the command of a Portuguese explorer named Ferdinand Magellan (1480-1521) left Spain, traveling west. In March of 1521 his ships arrived in Leyte, on the island of Cebu, in what is now the Philippines. His crew fired off weapons in a show of force and celebrated the Eucharist on board ship in view of indigenous peoples gathered on shore. Within several days Magellan had succeeded in convincing the local ruler, or *datu*, of Cebu, Rajah Humabon (d.c. 1522), whom Magellan called a "king," to undergo baptism. A month later Magellan decided to support Humabon in a local conflict against a neighboring island of Mactan. With a force of forty men he launched an attack against a rival chief who had close to three thousand warriors. Magellan was killed in the battle. Three years later, the one remaining ship of his expedition with eighteen men aboard returned to Spain, having circumnavigated the globe. The ship was loaded with nutmeg that it had stopped to pick up from the Spice Islands, worth enough to pay for the entire cost of the expedition.

The archipelago where Magellan had been killed and that the Spanish eventually named the Philippines, after King Phillip II (1527-1598), is composed of over seven thousand islands, of which some two thousand are inhabited. The inhabitants of the islands are ethnically quite diverse, a result of the waves of migrations that populated the region over the centuries. Many of the earliest inhabitants came from the neighboring islands to the south, while others came from Vietnam, Taiwan, and China to the north and west. Most settled along the coasts and rivers, although a number of tribes made the rugged mountains their homes for millennia. Separated by rivers, mountains, and ocean expanses, the peoples of the Philippines represent a wide range of local tribal identities, customs, dialects, languages, and religious beliefs developed over time. Prior to the arrival of the Spanish in the sixteenth century the Philippines never developed a larger urban-based empire such as was known in Japan, China, or Vietnam.

Local religious practice prior to the sixteenth century followed a pattern common among many East Asian peoples. Daily life was carried on in a world inhabited by spirits of creation (trees, hills, streams) and spirits of ancestors. Proper relationships to the spirit world were often negotiated through mediums (most often women) through whom the spirits spoke to the living. When spirits had been offended, purposefully or accidentally, amends had to be made through sacrifice. There were (and still are) many variations related to creation stories and various myths of the spirit world in the Philippines. Some of these traditions and practices continue to be observed by Christians.

To this diversity came the unifying religious culture of Islam in the south after the tenth century. Although Islam spread through imperial and militant expansion in the first centuries across North Africa and Persia, in Southeast Asia Islam spread peacefully through trade. Arab Muslim traders were in Sumatra by the late seventh century and were actively trading with Tang-dynasty China. Muslim and Christian (East Syrian and Armenian) trade with China largely came to an end with the collapse of the Tang dynasty in the tenth century, as China closed its doors for a time to the outside world. Trading ships from the west subsequently looked elsewhere to buy and sell goods. Sumatra, Java, and the Malay Peninsula all became major centers for Muslim merchants from Arabia, Persia, and India from the eleventh through the fifteenth centuries. Muslims settled in trading ports, married local women, established *masjids* (mosques), and often rose to become local rulers, or *datus*. In this way Islamic culture took root and developed all along the coasts of Southeast Asia.

Islam came to the Philippines from the Brunei Sultanate and Malacca. The earliest Muslim missionaries, or *makhdumin*, as opposed to traders who settled in with local women, arrived late in the fourteenth century in the Sulu archipelago, a string of islands that had at one time been a land bridge bringing earlier Malay peoples from northeast Borneo to the Philippines. Through the fourteenth century the Sulu islands as far as Mindanao in the southern Philippines were ruled by Muslim *tuans* (chiefs) and other *orang kayas* (persons of means). The turning point in Muslim history in the region came when a scholar from Mecca named Sayyid Abubakar Abirin (often known simply as Abu Bakr, r. 1450-1480) arrived in Sulu and married the local Princess Paramisuli (dates unknown). Being well received, he established the Sultanate of Sulu with most of the local inhabitants (including parts of Mindanao) accepting the new religion and leader. Islamic influence continued to spread farther north through trade, reaching the islands of Cebu and even Luzon. All this was happening in the middle of the fifteenth century, the very time the Spanish were removing the last Muslims from Iberia by force. Islam was becoming a new unifying cultural force in the Philippine Islands just one or two generations before the Spanish sailed into its waters from the east.

Two decades after Magellan first landed a second Spanish fleet arrived in the Philippines. But the Spanish conquest of the islands did not begin until 1564 when Miguel Lopez de Legazpi (1510-1572) arrived from Mexico, having been sent by the king of Spain to find pepper. The price of spices was rising rapidly in Europe and Philip wanted a part of the profits. Economics and taste drove Spain to what became a very rapid evangelization of the Philippines.

Legazpi's ship was piloted by an Augustinian friar named Andres de Urdaneta (1498-1568), who brought four other Augustinians along on the voyage to evangelize the Philippines. Urdaneta had been in east Asia, or what the Spanish called the Western Islands, before as a soldier, and had charted the first sea lanes from Mexico to the Philippines. He now returned in the role of a missionary.

At Cebu the Augustinians found a welcome response from the niece of Rajah Tupas (1497-c. 1570), son of Rajah Humabon, who had earlier befriended Magellan. Legazpi and his troops met with resistance from Tupas on the other hand and defeated the Cebuans in battle, burning Tupas's town to the ground. Such violence was not a standard procedure as the conquest of the Philippines unfolded, as little force was normally required by the Spanish. Five years later Legazpi decided to move his headquarters from Cebu to the island of Luzon, which boasted a much better harbor at Manila. The Spanish quickly defeated the local inhabitants in the region, including a Muslim settlement at Tondo. The following year Legazpi built a new walled city at the mouth of the harbor and with the help of both the Augustinians and the Franciscans established himself as administrative governor of the Philippines. The new colony was officially Catholic in religion. Manila eventually became the center of Roman Catholicism in all of east Asia.

The rest of the conquest of Luzon island was led by Legazpi's grandson, Juan de Salcedo (1549-1576), who was later honored with the title "Conqueror of Luzon." By the time of Salcedo's early death at the age of twenty-seven, the Philippines were under the general control of Spain. The conquest took only eleven years, and, except for the southern islands of Mindanao and Sulu (as well as many of the mountainous inland regions), the Philippines were made a part of the Spanish empire, which stretched from Spain to the Caribbean, across Mexico all the way to these islands.

Europeans in the East Indies and Indochina

Nineteen Portuguese ships under the leadership of Afonso de Albuquerque (1453-1515) arrived in the Muslim port city of Malacca, on the Malay Peninsula, in 1511. On board were eight hundred Portuguese and six hundred Indians, with eight chaplains. De Albuquerque was the second Portuguese governor or viceroy of Portugal's Asian empire. His goal was to control each step along the spice trade from the East Indies to Europe. He had seized the island of Goa in 1510, and now Malacca in 1511. Four years later in 1515 he would take Hormuz. These victories were seen by the Portuguese as victories of Christianity over Islam and were celebrated as such in Lisbon. The crusade was moving from military confrontation to economic conquest.

Malacca was an international city made up ethnically of Gujaritis, Javanese, Chinese, and local Malays. It quickly became the second major Portuguese city in Asia, after Goa. As such it was the launching point for missions (military, economic, and religious) that reached to the East Indies, Japan, and eventually Macao and China. In typical pattern the Portuguese sought only to control the coastal cities, which served as the base for their military forts and trading factories. Malacca was one such city, and soon was saddled with one of the worst moral reputations of any city in the world. The vicar of the city, Alfonso Martinez (d. 1549), was a friar who had been appointed by the king of Portugal in 1515 to serve Our Lady of the Annunciation, the first church in Malaya. In addition to parish duties he built a pauper hospital and a Misericordia to meet the needs of widows, orphans, and the poor. By the end of his life he had developed a reputation for having become a lapsed ecclesiastic, as Xavier discovered when he administered the vicar's last rites and confession. Many of the local Hindus and some of the Javanese underwent baptism during these first years, but very few Muslims became Christian.

Francis Xavier made five visits to Malacca. During his first stay in 1545-1546, he chose to lodge in the hospital rather than with the viceroy or the parish priest in order to make a statement regarding his ministry. He is credited with establishing the first Christian school in Malaya, St. Paul's College, during this visit. Reportedly the school attracted over 180 pupils within two days of opening. Even though Xavier's ministry in Malacca had an impact on the city, it did not help much with the wider reputation Malacca had throughout Asia. Nevertheless the city was recognized as an important center for the overall governance of the church throughout Asia. In 1557 Malacca became a suffragan see under the see of Goa with responsibilities over Burma, Siam, China, Japan, Malaya, and the East Indies. By the end of the sixteenth century the city had about 7,400 Christians, many of whom were of European Christian descent. Most of the converts were Chinese and Indians.

While Malacca was itself a city of poor Christian repute, it was for the next century a gateway to east Asia, sending missionaries to all regions where Portuguese ships could safely travel. Under the bishop Jorge de Souza de Santa Luzia (r. 1561-1576), who was a Dominican, missionaries were sent to reinforce the work in Flores and Timor. In these islands east of Java, over five thousand conversions had already been recorded under the work of other Dominicans, and there was a need to provide assistance in teaching and other pastoral work. Both Dominicans and Franciscans, and later Jesuits, established churches in the Celebes (Makassar), the Moluka Islands (centered on Ternate), and Flores and Timor. One of the strongest churches and a mission center for other parts of the East Indies was Solor, a mission run by the Dominicans from Goa. Solor was a regional center for mission to the East Indies the way Malacca was for east Asia. Following a Portuguese pattern of bringing Asians and Africans to the West, four Celebes students were brought back to the college in Goa in 1545 to study and prepare to be missionaries to their own people. The venture was fairly successful, and since two of the young men who converted were of royal blood, the impact was much greater when they returned. A number of other rulers in the Celebes converted after their return from Goa, but on many occasions conversion of local royalty was nearly impossible because of the violent behavior of the Portuguese sailors and soldiers.

The sixteenth century was a transforming time for Christianity and for Asia. Within one short century the number of Christians speaking to God in Malay, Japanese, Chinese, and many other languages increased dramatically. The first recorded history of Christian communities had begun in Japan, Siam, Malaya, the Philippines, and hundreds of other islands. A handful of kings, rajahs, and *datus* had been converted, their subjects following closely behind. The Catholic Church was in the first stages of a transition from a conquering and crusading mode, as was still seen in the Philippines, to a missionary mode, where representatives of the Western church in regions beyond its traditional homelands were more than royal agents. Christianity spread to new places along the trade routes of the east, but its Western missionaries in some places pushed ahead and beyond Western merchants.

One subtheme that was constantly in the background of these experiences was the relationship with Islam. In India the Mughul empire under the rule of Akbar the Great from 1556 to 1605 extended a form of Islam that adapted itself to the Indian context at the very time the Portuguese arrived. Akbar became a patron of some of the Jesuits, even building the first church in Lahore, and the missionaries, for their part, prayed and worked for his conversion. It never happened. Islam was spreading to the north from the East Indies as the Spanish arrived from America. Their approach was to try to turn the Muslims back with canons. The confrontation with Islam continued also in western Asia and eastern Europe, reaching the geographic heart of early Christianity, Constantinople, which was now under Ottoman control. The Ottoman Muslims were at the door of western Europe at the very time Roman Christianity was struggling with its own unity and its own renewal.

Suggestions for further reading

Brockey, Liam Matthew, *Journey to the East: The Jesuit Missions in China, 1559-1724*. Cambridge: Harvard University Press, 2007.

Cary, Otis, *A History of Christianity in Japan: Roman Catholic, Greek Orthodox and Protestant Missions*. 2 volumes. Tokyo: Charles E. Tuttle Company, 1909/1976.

Chew, Maureen K. C., *The Journey of the Catholic Church in Malaysia*. Kuala Lumpur, Malaysia: Catholic Research Centre, 2000.

Moffett, Samuel Hugh, *A History of Christianity in Asia, II: 1500-1900*. Maryknoll, NY: Orbis Books, 2005.

Mundadan, Matthias, *History of Christianity in India, I*. Bangalore: Church History Association of India, 1989.

Ross, Andrew C., *A Vision Betrayed: The Jesuits in Japan and China, 1542-1742.* Maryknoll, NY: Orbis Books, 1994.
Standaert, Nicolas, ed., *Handbook of Christianity in China, I: 635-1800.* Leiden: Brill, 2001.
Sunquist, Scott W., ed., *A Dictionary of Asian Christianity.* Grand Rapids, MI: Eerdmans, 2001.
Thekkedath, Joseph, *History of Christianity in India, II.* Bangalore: Church History Association of India, 2001.

4

Europe in an Age of Reform

A changing Europe steps onto a global stage

The colonial expansion that Portugal and Spain launched in the fifteenth century ushered in a new era in world history. Other European powers followed their lead, and soon the entire world was feeling the effects. The social, political, economic, cultural, and religious impacts of this expansion affected every part of the globe, including Europe itself. Europe's global colonial expansion was taking place at the same time as a relatively unified western European Christian civilization was beginning to break apart internally. The overseas empires that Spain and Portugal had embarked upon in the fifteenth century were the opening chapters of what soon became a global era of European colonialism. At about the same time, beginning early in the sixteenth century, new currents of religious thought led a number of churches throughout Europe to separate from the authority of Rome, in effect fracturing of the unity of Western Christendom. Europe was in the throes of a cultural transformation that brought about the end of the unified church and culture of Christendom, and the beginning of modern European nation-states, whose overseas colonial expansion was to prove critical to national economic development. These two major historical processes, western Europe's modern colonial expansion and the internal fragmentation of the unified European church that had for so long provided its peoples with a common culture, were related. The implications for world Christian history are still being felt today.

A number of factors were involved in the emergence of what we can now call early modern Europe. Technological advances in shipbuilding, navigation, and weaponry played a major role in extending European political power on a global scale. New technologies also played a role in fracturing the intellectual unity of Christendom in the West, most notably the printing press, which quickly disseminated new ideas on an wide scale. Urbanization in the West by the sixteenth century had resulted in much greater social differentiation among classes, a factor reflected in the emerging differentiation of religious beliefs. Historically there had been always been a symbiotic relationship between land-based monarchs and urban-based merchants and guilds in Europe. By the beginning of the sixteenth century a new urban class (what the Germans called *Burghers* and the

French called the *bourgeoisie*) had in a number of places successfully gained control of cities through their councils, laying the foundations for a new political order that would eventually challenge the old landed aristocracy. In many parts of Europe the new urban leaders latched onto the efforts for religious reform that were being undertaken as a means of wrestling control of the churches away from the older feudal order in which the church hierarchy was so interwoven.

This is not to say that the monarchs were quickly passing from the historical scene. On the contrary, the sixteenth century was a period of regional political consolidation and the development of newly strengthened national identities under powerful kings, queens, and princes. National political formation found expression in the fixed vernacular traditions that are still recognized today as the languages of modern Europe: English, Spanish, French, German, Italian, Dutch, and others.

A new generation of powerful royal families that emerged during this period made their lasting mark far beyond the borders of their own kingdoms. This was the age of the Hapsburgs of Austria, the Valois of France, the Medicis of Italy, and the Tudors of England. The marriage of two of these monarchs in Iberia created one of the most powerful political alliances that Europe had yet seen when Isabella (1451-1504), queen of Castile, married Ferdinand II (1452-1516), king of Aragon in 1469, thereby uniting most of the Iberian Peninsula under one royal household. Only the kingdom of Portugal along the western coast and the Muslim kingdom of Grenada at the southern end of Iberia remained outside their control. Twenty-three years later, in 1492, the army of Isabella and Ferdinand defeated the last Muslim caliph in Grenada. That same year Christopher Columbus (1451-1506) departed Seville on his expedition to the Indies, a project that the Spanish crown financed and that soon led to Spanish conquest and colonial control of a large section of the Americas.

Another powerful monarch in the first decades of the sixteenth century was the king of France, François I (r. 1515-1547), who was of the House of Valois. Although he was staunchly Catholic, he maintained considerable political distance from the papacy. In the fifteenth century French kings had gained administrative control over the churches in their land, including regulation of church taxes and the ability to conduct councils. François I assumed the power to make ecclesiastical appointments throughout all of France, which included ten archbishops, eighty episcopal sees, more than five hundred monasteries, and the faculties of the universities of Paris and Sorbonne.

Kings, princes, and city councils all assumed greater administrative control over the churches that existed within their territories over the course of the sixteenth century, creating new challenges for the papacy while heightening the national identities of churches. The epitome of national control of the churches was the Iberian system of patronage by which monarchs reserved to themselves the power to nominate bishops in their colonial territories. In 1504 Pope Julian II (1443-1513) tried to create several dioceses in the Caribbean, but the Spanish crown blocked him. Responding to the reports of abuses, Pope Paul III (1468-1549) in 1537 issued the bull *Sublimis Deus*, which affirmed the humanity and asserted the rights of the indigenous peoples of America. Carlos I (1500-1558), the grandson of Ferdinand and Isabella who was king of Spain and who had become Holy Roman Emperor Charles V in 1519, sought to limit its effects, asserting his right to control the churches of his colonial domain.

Ironically the same political authority over matters of church affairs was soon claimed by a number of the German princes who were electors of the emperor, but in support of reforms that Charles did not approve. Likewise in England Henry VIII (1491-1547) took control of the churches in his realm, ending papal authority and appointing the archbishop of Canterbury himself. The system of Spanish and Portuguese royal patronage of the church in their colonies, the protection provided by German princes for the efforts of a reformer named Martin Luther (1483-1546) and his followers within their territories, and the assumption of control of the church of England by the English monarch were all expressions of national political power being reasserted over religion in sixteenth-century Europe.

Social differentiation led by changes in political economy and regionalization was matched by rapid intellectual changes taking place in sixteenth-century Europe. A number of new universities were founded at the beginning of the century, making for unprecedented development in intellectual life. More and more men and women were able to read and write, creating a new intellectual market for the ideas being disseminated by publishers. Printing presses meant increasing numbers of people could also publish books that they had written, giving even common people a chance to become prolific authors with an influential following. Among the churches in the north of Europe the rapid dissemination of printed Bibles in vernacular translations did much to affect the fundamental spirituality of the people. Traditional artifacts that had given religious life material expression were stripped away in favor of a more verbal form of religiosity. A new spiritual aesthetic that was centered on reading the word began displacing an older spirituality that was expressed through rosaries, relics, and the sacramental mysteries of the church. The pattern of worship among the "evangelical" churches (as a number of the reformers chose to call themselves) underwent a transformation, the rapidity of which was unparalleled in Christian history. All of this happened while monarchs and merchants continued expanding their military and economic reach beyond the borders of western European territorial Christendom, thus providing a ready vehicle for the global dissemination of the new diversity of Christian ideas and practices.

One of the results of accelerating changes in society and culture was an increase in overall social anxieties. Some of these found expression in popular apocalyptic expectations that sometimes led to violence. Such expectations were fanned by a number of popular teachers throughout the century, such as Girolamo Savonarola (1452-1489), Thomas Müntzer (1489-1525), and Melchior Hoffman (1495-1543), who will be discussed in the pages below. Far more insidious was the popular anxiety regarding witchcraft and magic that exploded across Europe during this period. Witches were believed to be behind any number of social and natural calamities, and any woman who showed signs of independence was in danger of being labeled such. Especially targeted were women who served as midwives or who practiced traditional healing using natural remedies, for their healing arts were often regarded as magic and their lives placed in peril.

The publication in 1486 of the infamous *Malleus malificarum* ("Hammer of Witches") was both a symptom and a contributing cause to the hysteria that swept the continent over the next two centuries. The book was a manual authored by Heinrich Kramer (1430-1505) and James Sprenger (1436-1495), two Dominicans from northern Germany who were members of the Inquisition and had been authorized by a papal bull two years earlier to undertake the project. The work was blatantly misogynistic, providing the rationale for and spelling out methods of torture and violence to be used against women suspected of witchcraft. Torture was authorized as a means of gaining confessions, and the stated purpose of the authors was to burn as many witches as possible to free the land of their evil. Those convicted had no rights of appeal, executions were to be as painful as possible, and any property owned by the accused was to be confiscated. Not everyone believed in the existence of witches in Europe, but enough church leaders did to make for several centuries of terror. While the number of women (and men) who were eventually executed is uncertain, it is likely that over a four-hundred-year period more than forty thousand were killed.

The humanists and European cultural transformation

The story of the cultural transformation that produced modern Europe is often told as if it began with the Protestant Reformation in the sixteenth century. The Protestant Reformation itself, however, was part of a wider intellectual movement that had begun several centuries before in Italy before spreading to other countries in Europe. In the nineteenth century, historians of European life came to call it the Renaissance, but proponents at the time called themselves humanists. The term referred to the disciplines of arts and letters, or the humanities, which were their primary interests.

Francesco Petrarch (1304-1374) of Italy was the most notable name among the early ranks of the humanists. As a scholar, he had pioneered the search for forgotten texts of antiquity that were scattered throughout monasteries and libraries of Europe. Petrarch was also an accomplished poet, and his works joined those of others such as his older Italian contemporary, Dante Alighieri (1265-1321), in shaping a new wave of literary activity.

Humanists in the fifteenth century championed the study of grammar and rhetoric over the more focused study of logic that had occupied the earlier scholastics. Where scholasticism had been concerned almost exclusively with the pursuits of theology and philosophy, the humanists expanded their interests into other areas of culture and learning. The scholastics had devoted themselves primarily to Aristotle in their classical studies, while the humanists of the fifteenth century preferred Plato. Especially important to the humanists was the study of ancient texts in their original languages, leading to a significant growth in Greek and Hebrew studies among their Christian ranks in western Europe. *Ad fontes* ("to the sources!") was their motto in this regard.

The fall of Constantinople in 1453 aided these efforts as a wave of intellectual refugees from the Byzantine East fled westward. A number of monks and scholars resettled in Italy where they were able to aid in the revival of Greek learning. A new academy dedicated to the study of Plato opened in Florence under the direction of Marsilio Ficino (1433-1499), and was soon spreading its influence to other parts of western Europe. The study of Hebrew among Christian scholars was significantly advanced by Johann Reuchlin (1455-1522) with the publication of his Hebrew grammar textbook in Germany in 1506.

A humanist scholar in Rome, Lorenzo Valla (1405-1457), demonstrated the power of this knowledge, and not so incidentally the manner in which it could challenge authority in the church when applied to the sources of tradition. Valla undertook a comparative evaluation of Jerome's Latin translation of the Bible, the *Vulgate*, and the Greek text of the New Testament, a project that led him to question the adequacy of that time-honored Latin text. The same fifteenth-century scholar turned his attention to the *Donation of Constantine*, a document that had for centuries been cited as the basis for papal political authority. Based on linguistic and historical evidence within the document itself Valla proved it to be a forgery, demonstrating the critical effect such studies could have on traditional textual sources of authority.

The authority of papacy and church was at times the object of the humanists' criticisms, but then there was often much to criticize in Rome. Although some fifteenth-century popes were identified with the humanist agenda, others were more concerned with intrigue and power. The institution of the papacy came through the fourteenth century stronger than ever. The fifteenth century was a time when several national monarchies were rapidly consolidating power, but several of these monarchs learned that a powerful international papacy and its curia could work in their interests. Such an arrangement benefited the monarchs of Spain and Portugal, especially in their overseas expansion by providing powerful ideological justification for their actions. The fact that Pope Alexander VI (1431-1503), who was elected to the papal throne in 1492, was able to mediate between Spanish and Portuguese claims regarding colonial possessions demonstrated the degree of power the centralized papacy commanded.

The corruptive effects of wealth and power in Rome were obvious to many. Popes handed out appointments to the College of Cardinals to family members in shameless fashion, and engaged in unseemly political practices that were at odds with the spiritual nature of their office. This is not the whole story, of course, and there were popes whose successes came to define the age. Pope Nicholas V (1397-1455) promoted humanist efforts in learning and began the reorganization of the Vatican Library, which served succeeding generations of scholars well. A number of popes were patrons of the arts and sponsored significant new building projects in Rome, such as the basilica of St. Peter's, whose cornerstone was laid in 1506 and whose dome was set in 1590. These projects required funds, this at a time when land (of which the church owned much) was no longer the most important source for generating wealth. One of the plans that the papacy promoted as a source of church revenues was the sale of indulgences, a practice that would soon irrupt in controversy in Germany.

New political winds were blowing in the fifteenth century in a number of places. In the city of Florence, a popular preacher rode these winds of unrest to their heights, but then crashed as they proved to be undependable. Girolamo Savonarola (1452-1498) had been educated in humanism and medicine before deciding to enter the ranks of the Dominican order and taking up the vocation of a public preacher. His itinerary took him to several cities before he finally settled in Florence, where he soon gained a following as a popular preacher. Savonarola took upon himself a prophetic mantle and claimed to be receiving divine instructions that foretold of coming judgment. Much of what he had to say was addressed to the inequalities of the city. Florence's civic leaders supported him at first, but as the popular preacher began to speak out for reforms such as the need to aid the city's poor or to redistribute its wealth, things began to change. Savonarola's challenge to the city's upper class soon spilled over to include the church hierarchy and the papal court itself, which he viewed as being corrupted by its wealth and power. Excommunication from Rome came swiftly, and with it the collapse of Savonarola's support in Florence. In 1498 he was executed by the city leaders in the town square. To some he represented a rabble-rouser, but for others he was a prophet and the harbinger of a new age of European political reform.

Humanist learning in the fifteenth century quickly spread from its fertile soil in Italy to Holland, France, Germany, and elsewhere in Europe. Among the ranks of the church's hierarchy, Cardinal Nicholas de Cusa (1401-1464) in Germany was a proponent of the study of Plato as well as a student of mathematics and astronomy. De Cusa remains best known perhaps for his metaphysical speculations regarding the manner in which all differences are reconciled and resolved in the perfect unity of God's infinite life, the doctrine of the "coincidence of opposites." In England humanism was well represented by Sir Thomas More (1478-1535). The author of a visionary work titled *Utopia*, More was eventually beheaded by Henry VIII for his allegiance to Rome.

One of the striking aspects of the humanist movement was the absence of attention paid to the world outside of Europe. The parochial nature of the effort had a significant effect on how Europeans engaged others who were not a part of Western Christendom. Centuries of warfare with Islam, which surrounded Europe on three sides, had diminished the flow of both material goods and intellectual ideas to and from the West. European Christendom turned inward in its efforts to advance culturally and intellectually during these centuries. The humanists and their followers in the religious reforms of the sixteenth century alike tended to look primarily or solely to what they perceived to be Europe's religious and cultural past in Greco-Roman antiquity, concealing the debt they owed to Islam as a principal mediator of that heritage to Europe for several centuries.

Francisco Ximénes de Cisneros and reforms in Spain

One of the greatest champions of the humanist movement during this period was Francisco Ximénes de Cisneros of Spain (1436-1517). Born a member of the noble class, he studied at the University of Salamanca and then went to Rome for several years before returning to Spain and entering the ranks of the Franciscans in 1484. Eight years later he was appointed by Queen Isabella to be her confessor, a position that entailed being her personal chaplain and advisor on matters of both church and state. In 1495 he became archbishop of Toledo, the highest ecclesiastical position in the kingdom, and was soon made a cardinal by Rome. Under Ximénes de Cisneros a number of pastoral reforms in the Spanish church were instituted. Concubinage among the clergy was banned, for instance, and priests were ordered to restore preaching to the Mass.

Among the most important reforms that the cardinal supported was the requirement for increased education of the priests. A significant outcome of this particular effort was the founding of a new university at Alcalá in 1500. Like most humanists, Ximénes de Cisneros recognized the authority of classical texts from antiquity, which in the case of religion meant the Bible. Not only was it necessary that one read scriptural texts, but one needed to be able to study them in their original languages. Under his sponsorship a polyglot edition of the entire Bible in its original languages was completed in 1517 and published in 1522. The work was dedicated to Pope Leo X (1475-1521). In the prologue Ximénes de Cisneros wrote that words had their own unique character and that no translation could express their full meaning. The letter of scripture by itself appears dead, he continued, but this is because the Spirit of Christ is concealed within the words, enclosed within them like in a womb. Learning the original languages and studying the Bible in them was a vital spiritual exercise.

For a variety of reasons the influence of humanism only partially reached the churches in Spain's colonies. The first dioceses in the Americas were established while Ximénes de Cisneros was archbishop of Toledo, but this did not mean his influence was felt across the Atlantic. The system of patronage was partly responsible, as Ferdinand and Isabella were looking not for humanists to lead the church as much as they were looking for administrators to manage affairs in the Americas. Humanist impulses did make their way into the churches in Spanish America by way of several Dominicans who had been educated at Salamanca and who were among the first preachers appointed in 1512 to the church in Hispaniola, in the Caribbean. The legacy of the humanists in colonial America is ambiguous at best. While they were often the advocates of clerical reforms and educational advance in Europe, humanists were also strong supporters of a classical anthropology (especially indebted to Aristotle) that argued the suitability of some peoples for servanthood and slavery. The arguments of the humanists were often mustered to support the enforced servitude of Native Americans and later Africans. In this regard one can count Bartolomé de Las Casas (1484-1566) as an opponent of humanist reformers. His *Plan for the Reform of the Indies* challenged significant humanist assumptions in the colonial context.

The violence that accompanied Spain's colonial enterprise in the Americas did not necessarily contradict the humanist goal of restoring the classical religious foundations of knowledge. Violence appeared to have clear biblical support, as did the right of kings to exercise power to maintain order. As archbishop of Toledo and head of the church of Spain, Ximénes de Cisneros played a significant role in overseeing the apparatus of the Spanish Inquisition, which was one of the most notorious institutions of systematic violence that Christendom had ever seen.

To understand the Spanish Inquisition, one must look back into history of Spanish Christianity. The Iberian Peninsula prior to the fifteenth century had been among the most religiously and culturally pluralistic regions of Europe. For several centuries Muslims, Christians, and Jews lived side by side under Islamic rulers. Christians and Jews bore the burden of minority status; but while there were occasional periods of persecution, for the most part they found Spain to be a relatively hospitable place to live. Things had begun to change for Jews and Muslims as Christian kings pushed south in their crusade in Iberia. Desiring to unify their kingdoms religiously, Christian rulers pressured Jews and Muslims to convert, a process that intensified in the fourteenth and fifteenth centuries. A new class of former Jews and Muslims who had undergone baptism and were now known as *conversos* emerged. Questions remained about the depth or authenticity of such conversions, and many were suspected of secretly maintaining their previous religions.

Ferdinand and Isabella had succeeded in unifying most of Spain politically. Now they sought to complete the task religiously. In 1478, at their instigation Rome authorized the establishment of the office of the Spanish Inquisition whose purpose was to root out heresy, especially among the *conversos* throughout the kingdom. Of major concern to the crown was the continuing presence of Muslim and Jewish communities in Christian territories, for they provided a place to which the *conversos* could return. The same year that their Christian forces took Grenada, 1492, the Spanish crown ordered all remaining Jews, perhaps as many as 100,000, expelled from Spain. The explicit purpose was to remove the temptation they posed to Jewish *conversos*. The result was an exodus of Jews to other cities in Europe and across the Mediterranean.

Meanwhile, the Inquisition continued its work of rooting out actual and perceived deviations in belief among Christians in Spain. By the middle of the 1520s it was systematically seeking out not only the hidden remnants of Jewish or Muslim belief among *conversos*, but similar ideas among mystics and other spiritual teachers. Among the individuals who fell afoul of the Inquisition was Isabella de la Cruz (c. 1490-c. 1530), a woman from a family of Jewish *conversos*. By 1515 Isabella was a member of the Third Order of Franciscans and had gained a small following on her own as a teacher. Much of what she taught was shared by other mystics, who by the 1500s were being called *alumbrados* ("illuminated ones") in Spain. Among the controversial positions Isabella shared with these spiritual mystics was the belief that the soul can reach complete union with God thereby by-passing the ministry of the church and its sacraments, that an eternal hell was incompatible with the idea of a loving God, and that the divine Spirit lives within each person in a way comparable to that in Christ. Her tendency to disparage religious images and the external sacraments of the church are what drew the attention of the Inquisition in particular, which investigated her over a period of four years before submitting her to torture and forcing her to recant, and sentencing her to life imprisonment in 1529.

In 1536 the crown in Portugal established a similar office of Inquisition to root out suspected heresies, especially among the *conversos* in that kingdom. In both countries ecclesiastical agents by the 1540s had investigated tens of thousands of people suspected of being unfaithful to the teachings of the church. Their methods of investigation included formal tribunals as well as the extensive use of torture to gather information. Since ecclesiastical law prevented the church from carrying out death sentences, those so condemned were turned over to the secular political rulers for execution. Several thousand individuals were eventually put to death for heresy. The most common forms of punishment that were meted out, however, ranged from confiscation of property, an act that resulted in financial ruin for its victims, to periods of imprisonment. At first the Inquisition was directed mainly against former Muslims and Jews who were suspected of secretly holding, or reverting to, their original religious convictions. The scope of its inquiry was extended in 1525 to include Illuminists and other spiritual or mystical teachings that seemed to contradict the external authority of the church. After 1540 it began to turn its attention increasingly toward the new evangelical heresy whose ideas were seeping in from Germany and Switzerland, executing in 1543 the first suspected proponent of the new Protestant teaching.

Erasmus of Rotterdam and the broad current of humanist learning

The name that eventually became almost synonymous with sixteenth-century European humanism was that of Desiderius Erasmus of Rotterdam (1466-1536). The son of parents who were not legally married (his father was a priest), Erasmus later in life applied for and received from the pope a dispensation so he could be ordained despite his "illegitimacy." As a child he was educated by members of the Brothers of the Common Life, an order that had been founded toward the end of the fourteenth century in the Netherlands. Members of the Brothers and Sisters of the Common Life were both lay and ordained. Some lived in their own homes while others lived together in common houses. They practiced celibacy and obedience, but did not take life-long vows or beg as those in mendicant orders did. Support came from individual members of the community working in secular jobs, such as providing their services professionally as scribes. Although the Brothers and Sisters provided some outreach to the poor, their efforts were mostly directed toward the cultivation of the inner spiritual life. Alongside the more traditional practices of preaching and education, they pursued various devotional exercises and literary endeavors that were collectively known as *devotio moderna* ("modern devotion"). Among those whose names were associated with the Brothers of the Common Life was that of Thomas á Kempis (1380-1471), whose book, *De Imitatione Christi* ("Imitation of Christ"), is still considered by many to be a classic of Christian spirituality. Erasmus himself was eventually ordained to the priesthood in 1492 in one of the communities of the Brothers.

Following his sixteenth birthday and the death of his parents, the young Erasmus lived for several years in an Augustinian monastery. There he continued to study and write, but was unwilling to abide by the discipline of the community. In 1495 he entered the University of Paris to study theology, but was soon involved in supporting new educational reforms. Corporal punishment of students who did not perform well ought to be banned, he argued, for instance, while younger children ought to be allowed periods of play during the day while they are studying. In 1499 he moved on to Oxford without finishing his degree at Paris, and began a life of itinerant scholarship that took him from city to city across Europe until he finally ended his days in Basel, Switzerland. Erasmus never served as a priest in a church nor held a formal teaching position in a university. He supported himself by his writings as an independent scholar. Through these numerous books, and a copious body of letters (he corresponded with hundreds) his influence spread throughout Europe.

Erasmus's major concern was to bring about reform in Christian life and in the institutions of the church. He criticized many of the traditional religious practices of his day that seemed to him to hold little in the way of moral value. Traditional moral virtues such as sincerity and honor, on the other hand, he steadfastly defended. To this end he called for a relaxation in the institutional authority that the hierarchy exercised over thinking within the church and encouraged scholarly freedom. One of the most influential treatises from his pen in this regard was *Enchiridion militis Christiani*. The title of the work means both "Handbook" and "Weapon" of the Christian Soldier. In its pages Erasmus argued for an inner spiritual discipline that went beyond the external aids of religious life, such as relics, fasts, and even the church's sacraments. These external aspects of religion were meaningless apart from internal spiritual experience. It was in the inner life of virtue that the fruits of the Spirit were to be found. External aids were but a means to cultivate the inner life of faith. Another reform Erasmus undertook was to encourage a more systematic study of the New Testament in its original language, and the publication of new Latin and Greek translations of the New Testament. His insistence on ascertaining the meaning of scripture directly from the text of the New Testament itself, and not necessarily guided by church tradition, laid the foundation for later generations of biblical scholarship.

One of Erasmus's best-known works was a satirical book titled *Moriae Encomium* ("In Praise of Folly"), first published in 1509. Its pages subjected to ridicule many popular religious beliefs and practices of the period, including invoking the protection of saints or purchasing indulgences to release others from punishment in the afterlife. Especially targeted for ridicule in its pages were the perceived vanities of religious leaders, although he did not spare peasants, artisans, monastics, or even intellectuals from the satire of his pen. These criticisms won him his share of enemies within the church, but Erasmus never wavered in his commitments to the Catholic faith and the hierarchy, and especially to the authority of the pope. His great desire was to see reforms being instituted that would lead to greater piety and learning. It was a vision that continued to inspire long after his passing.

Martin Luther and the Protestant Reformation in Germany

Among Erasmus's conversation partners was a young German theologian named Martin Luther (1483-1546). Born of a peasant family, Luther had studied law before entering an Augustinian monastery at the age of twenty-two. Six years later he was appointed to a teaching post at Wittenberg University, in Saxony, which had only been recently established by the German prince and elector of the Roman empire, Frederick the Wise (1463-1525). During these years Luther professed to have been troubled by a conscience that could not find consolation. The church offered an elaborate sacramental system for dealing with sin that began with baptism and reached all the way into afterlife, in purgatory, where the church could still remit punishments for sin. Grace was understood to be something infused or poured into the individual through the sacraments that the church administered. Its authority to do so was regarded as having been handed down by Christ himself, and this belief provided the ultimate legitimacy for the Catholic papal-episcopal-sacerdotal system.

Salvation, in the Catholic view of the matter, was a process in which sinners received sanctifying grace (sometimes called "habitual grace") in baptism and had that state restored after sin in the sacrament of penance (confession). Sanctifying grace moved one toward becoming righteous (*iustitia*, justification) and holy, thereby enabling them to receive "actual graces," which empowered them to live a virtuous life. Through the sacraments of the church, God provided what was needed to lead the Christian and, when one failed, offered the sacrament of penance to gain forgiveness of sins and assure the guilty conscience of pardon. By practicing proscribed acts of penance, furthermore, one "merited" the remission of post-mortem punishment for sins and lessened the time one had to spend in purgatory before being cleansed of the effects of sin and entering heaven.

The problem for Luther was that he could not find assurance that his sins were ever truly forgiven, and thus could not be assured that he had truly been made righteous or justified. During the first six years at Wittenberg he began to retrieve what he felt was the authentic New Testament doctrine and to propose a different framework of understanding that did not rely on the action of the church or the authenticity of the individual's act of repentance. The answer for the troubled conscience was not in further acts of penance, Luther would say, but in a trusting reception of God's promise of salvation by faith. Justification, Luther interpreted the Apostle Paul to say, did not depend on any work of one's own, including the sacramental work of penance. Nor did it depend on a human being's experience of it. Justification was a free gift, given by God. The good news of the gospel was God's promise of forgiveness because of the obedience of Jesus unto death, and righteousness was not infused or poured into sinful persons, but imputed to them in an act like a judge's declaration of innocence. Human beings, Luther taught, remain sinful this side of eternity. The only righteousness they can claim is the righteousness of Jesus Christ, who is sinless; this righteousness is imputed or applied to them. But this in turn meant for Luther that salvation did not depend on the mediation of the church or on the merit that persons could accrue. It depended only on Jesus Christ and his merits alone. The means of appropriating Christ's salvation were through absolute trust in the promise of God. Here in brief form was Luther's doctrine of justification by faith, a doctrine he believed had been obscured through the centuries.

From this position it was a natural step to challenge the church's claim to exercise authority over the dispensation of grace. The inevitable conflict with the hierarchy erupted in public in 1517 when Luther nailed to the door of the Wittenberg Castle church a list of ninety-five theses challenging, among other practices, the sale of indulgences (church-granted pardons from time served after death in purgatory for the effects of one's sins). In an effort to raise funds to build a new Basilica of St. Peter, the pope had authorized the sale of these ecclesiastical indulgences. A papal representative, the Dominican friar Johann Tetzel (1465-1519), was peddling them throughout the countryside, assuring those who purchased that their coins would release the souls of loved ones from purgatory. Luther proposed a debate over the matter, a practice that was common among the faculty. He posted his theses on the door of the Castle church, which served as a community bulletin board.

Word of his challenge quickly spread beyond the university's walls, and a much larger debate over the question of the authority of the church erupted, reaching all the way to Rome. Answering Luther's challenge was Johann Eck (1486-1543) of the University of Ingolstadt, whose refutation was soon in print. Pope Leo X responded by issuing a bull in 1520 giving Luther sixty days to recant or be condemned as a heretic. In Wittenberg, Luther publicly burned a copy of the bull.

A series of published treatises from Luther's pen followed quickly, arguing for the authority of the laity and appealing to the German nobility to exercise national leadership over the church. The notion that the Eucharist was a sacrifice and the Communion practice of withholding the cup from the laity were both rejected. Even the doctrine of transubstantiation was questioned. Luther could find only two sacraments being instituted by Christ in the scriptures, baptism and the Eucharist (or Lord's Supper), although he allowed that penance could be defended as an extension of baptism. The sacraments were not means by which the church offered the sinner grace, but means by which the church proclaimed Christ's grace in response to what Christ had accomplished with his perfect sacrifice.

The reformer was summoned to appear before the newly elected emperor Charles V at the Diet (or Assembly) of Worms, in 1521. Luther made his case for the doctrine of justification by faith alone, apart from any mediation that the church administered. His support, he claimed, was found in scripture, which he argued was the only legitimate authority for doctrine. Again, it was Johann Eck who made the case for Rome against Luther. The assembled members of the Diet condemned the Wittenberg theologian, sending Luther into hiding for almost a year. He returned to Wittenberg in 1522 when word of new turmoil among his followers reached him in hiding, and after receiving assurance of protection from his prince, Frederick the Wise.

By this time Wittenberg had become a seedbed for reforming ideas. A younger scholar named Philip Melanchthon (1497-1560) had joined the faculty in 1518, and by 1521 had published a major textbook in systematic theology, *Loci communes rerum theologicarum seu hypotyposes theologicae* ("Common Places in Theology or Fundamental Doctrinal Themes"), often known simply as the *Loci communes*. The work, which was intended to provide theological support for the efforts of the reformers, is often considered one of the first works in Protestant or evangelical systematic theology. In 1522 Luther and his colleagues at Wittenberg published a German translation of the New Testament. The following year Luther published a new guide to worship that simplified the Mass. Worship was now to be conducted in the vernacular language rather than Latin, and lay people were to have a greater role in services. Lay people were also to receive both bread and wine in the Eucharist. Preaching was to have a much greater role in the life and worship of churches that adopted the reforms that Luther proposed. In turn preachers, along with printed books and pamphlets, spread the message of Luther's reforms throughout the German countryside and beyond.

Luther's efforts looked to many to be following a pathway that other humanists were traveling. To a degree Luther himself accepted this depiction of his efforts. Humanism in Luther's hands took on a more nationalistic flavor, however, merging to a significant degree elements of anticlericalism and empowerment of the laity with German nationalism. These converging themes are seen especially in one of Luther's early tracts, *An den christlichen Adel deutscher Nation* ("To the Christian Nobility of the German Nation"). On the other hand the authority of the scriptures for determining doctrine and worship and the need to study them in their original languages were commitments that echoed the wider currents of humanist thought. An exchange of pamphlets between Luther and Erasmus in 1524-1525 drew the line between the two thinkers most clearly, and by extension between the humanists and the new reformers. The exchange centered on the question of human free will, an issue that had been debated in Western theology since Augustine. Late in 1524 Erasmus published a book titled *De libero arbitrio diatribe sive collatio* ("Freedom of the Will") that defended the capacity of human beings to make free moral choices for the good. Erasmus did not suggest that this capacity could supplant the church's role in mediating eternal salvation. His purpose was to articulate a clearer moral basis for the legitimate exercise of human reason and knowledge. Luther read the work and responded the following year with a book of his own titled *De servo arbitrio* ("The Bondage of the Will"). Following Augustine, he claimed that the individual's will is irreparably bound by sin because of the fall. A human being is therefore incapable of making a free decision for the good or for God. Faith, not reason, was the only viable vehicle.

To Luther, Erasmus's position seemed to be a new expression of the Pelagianism that St. Augustine had so thoroughly criticized. Human beings could not through the exercise of their will participate in their own salvation, he believed. Erasmus, on the other hand, thought Luther's position to be too extreme in that it denied the possibility of reason and knowledge attaining a measure of moral or intellectual good. More important, Luther's attack on Erasmus had been personal and inflammatory. The exchange turned acerbic, ending any hope of the two reformers joining forces.

That same year the German countryside became embroiled in social turmoil, which drew Luther into another controversy, this time with more radical supporters of reforms from among the peasant class. The situation for rural workers and artisans was becoming increasingly difficult as nobility and church alike sought to extract wealth from them. For centuries the nobility had exercised their rule and acted as courts of law without much resistance, but the new urban political model of city councils formed from among the guilds was filtering out into village and countryside. Conflict was also exacerbated by the infusion of chiliastic religious impulses stemming from the covert commentary on the apocalypse from the thirteenth-century Calabrian monk Joachim de Fiore. Fighting between peasants and administrators in the service of the nobility broke out in southern Germany in 1524 and soon spread to other regions. Leading in the peasants' cause in a number of places were clergy who had been inspired by Luther's teachings. In village after village, parish priests and monks along with the ruling nobility became the target of peasant revolt.

A list of articles published by the leaders of the rapidly spreading peasant revolt in 1525 registered their demands: the right of the people to choose their own pastors in churches; the right for workers to be paid for services beyond their traditional obligations to the lords; the right to hunt, fish, and gather firewood from the land; access to courts of law beyond the immediate dictates of feudal lords; relief for the poor; and an end to serfdom in which peasants were bound by law to the feudal lands on which they were born. Luther responded with cautious support for a number of these peasant demands. Although he was uneasy with the claims of some following his reforms among the peasant leadership, and was particularly concerned to enjoin obedience to all political authority that he believed the gospel required, Luther called upon the princes to limit their harsh treatment of the peasants when it amounted to tyranny and to treat them with greater kindness so that God would not ignite further the fires of rebellion throughout the land. He concluded by inviting both sides to see that they were partially in the wrong and would have to give up something to achieve a just peace.

Peace was not to be, however. In the spring of 1525 rebellion broke out as bands of peasants began taking control of village churches and attacking the retainers of the ruling nobility they found among them. The princes responded by sending an army against the peasants and crushed the rebellion and its leadership. The peasants were no match for professional soldiers. Estimates of the number of peasants who died run between 50,000 and 100,000, while casualties on the princes' side numbered at most in the low thousands. Meanwhile, Luther had responded to the first wave of revolt by rushing a new pamphlet into print, written in German and titled *Wider die räuberischen und mörderischen Rotten der Bauern* ("Against the Thievish, Murdering Hordes of Peasants"). The pamphlet called the peasants "mad dogs" who deserved death for having taken up arms against legitimate civil authority and for doing so in the name of the gospel. He called upon the princes to suppress the revolt with violence, and to slay all that they could. Such rebellion was, in Luther's view, intolerable.

Controversy with Erasmus and the humanists on one side and the peasants and their leaders on the other was not all that occupied Luther's attention during 1525. That same year he married a former nun named Katherine von Bora (1499-1552). Katherine was a member of an order located in Saxony when she encountered Luther's new teachings. Along with several other members of her community, she decided to escape the convent, which at the time was illegal, and make her way to Wittenberg. Single women in sixteenth-century Germany were without legal, social, or economic protection. One of the tasks Luther undertook was to arrange marriages for the former nuns who were arriving in his city. Two years after Katherine had appeared in Wittenberg a husband had still not been found for her, leading Luther himself to propose marriage. Katherine accepted.

Some among Luther's opponents criticized the former monk and nun for having broken their vows of celibacy and succumbing to the temptations of the flesh. By most accounts the beginning of their marriage was not a romantic affair so much as it was a mutual duty the two undertook. Yet by all accounts the two soon fell in love. The prince gave them the former monastery in which Luther had lived at Wittenberg, a forty-room building that Katherine worked hard to manage. The house was constantly occupied by guests, refugees, students, and various relatives. Katherine ran the couple's farm, which produced the food needed to feed all these people as well as to provide income. She not only managed the affairs of the house and played the major role in raising their children, but also took an active part in the theological conversations that went on around the household table. Luther eventually willed the property to Katherine, an act that was significant in light of the fact that women did not typically own property in their own name in sixteenth-century Germany. Toward the end of her life Katherine was even able to purchase several additional plots of land, which she held as an investment. One of the most important contributions she and her husband made was to model for others a new form of married pastoral life.

In the years following 1525 Luther's reforms spread from the territory of Saxony to other parts of Germany, gaining support from a number of other princes and electors of the Roman emperor. During these years the attention of Charles V was largely occupied by conflict on one side with the king of France, who had entered into an alliance with the cities of Italy, and on the other with the Ottoman Turks, whose armies by 1529 were marching into Austria and threatening to take Vienna. The German imperial assembly had refused to take action against Luther when Rome had earlier demanded it. A number of electors now supported Luther. In their regions bishops were being removed from authority, monastic properties were being confiscated, and churches were being reorganized following Luther's proposed reforms. Charles V, however, remained steadfast in his support of Rome; and a majority of the German princes still sided with him against Luther.

In 1529 the imperial assembly met to consider the religious situation in the empire and voted a series of measures intended to slow or even stop the progress of the Lutheran party's efforts at reform. Bishops loyal to Rome were to be restored, traditional worship in Latin allowed, and properties of monasteries restored. The princes who supported the Lutheran effort entered a protest against the decision, leading their party to be known as the "Protestants." By this time their party was also being dubbed "Lutheran," a designation Luther and his colleagues resisted. They preferred to speak of their position as being "evangelical" since they looked to the Good News ("evangel") as the final source of authority in all that they did. Luther himself never believed he had left the Catholic faith, only that he had opposed what he considered the excessive authority exercised by the pope in Rome and the traditions that supported this.

The following year the emperor again turned his attention to the reformers, calling for all parties to present their case before him at Augsburg. Luther could not attend as he was still under imperial ban. The case for the evangelical position was left to be made by Melanchthon, who drew up a statement to be read before the emperor and the rest of the assembly meeting in Augsburg. The document, which was written in both German and Latin and was known in Latin as *Confessio Augustana* ("Augsburg Confession"), remains today the foundational statement of Lutheran confessional identity. Its several articles articulated the evangelical party's understanding of justification by faith, the nature of the church, and the number and meaning of the sacraments. Theologians representing the Roman Catholic side were given a chance to prepare a refutation of the confession, in response to which Melanchthon then drew up and published a defense of the Augsburg Confession the following year. The emperor still refused to recognize the evangelical stance as legitimate, and the princes supporting the Lutheran cause in turn formed a new alliance known as the Smalkaldic League.

One of the critical debates that emerged during this period concerned the nature of the Eucharist. In 1529 Luther participated in a theological colloquium in Marburg, Germany, with another emerging leader of evangelical reform named Ulrich Zwingli (1484-1531) from Zurich, Switzerland. Luther and Zwingli had earlier exchanged pamphlets debating the nature of the Eucharist. At the heart of the matter was the question of whether Christ could be said to be bodily present in the sacrament of bread and wine. According to the Gospels, at the Last Supper Jesus had said, "This is my body." Zwingli understood this to be a figurative manner of speaking, but Luther insisted that Christ had intended it to mean his real corporeal presence in the elements of bread and wine. According to reports of the Marburg conversation, Luther had written *hoc est corpus meum* ("this is my body," from the Latin Mass) on the table that evening and returned insistently time and again to his singular point, that Christ is really present in bodily form in the sacrament.

The doctrine of real presence for Luther was closely related to the *communicatio idiomatum* or "sharing of attributes" that was a part of the heritage of the Council of Chalcedon from 451. In Jesus Christ both natures (the human and the divine) were said to share their attributes with the other. Luther extended this understanding to bread and wine in the Eucharist, arguing that Jesus Christ was corporeally present in, under, and around the physical elements on the altar, a position that came to be known as consubstantiation (as distinct from transubstantiation, which was adopted as official doctrine in Roman Catholic understanding). The affirmation of Christ's ubiquitous presence came to be associated closely with Lutheran sacramental theology. Unlike transubstantiation, the Lutheran doctrine did not rely on priestly intercession to effect the transformation of the elements of the Eucharist into Christ's body and blood. It sought, instead, to affirm that the promise of the preached word of God, conjoined to the sign of the elements and acknowledged by faith, effected a new manifestation of Christ's incarnation, all this fitting in closely with one of Luther's central insights that the good news of Jesus Christ comes to humanity in the form of a promise. In this way the Eucharist became the visible means of receiving the gift of Christ's righteousness and accepting God's promise. The joining of word and sign, not the alteration of the substance of the elements, was the basis for asserting the real presence of Christ for the gathered congregation, Lutherans argued.

Over the course of his life Luther gave shape to a distinct theological legacy. Luther himself, however, insisted that the ultimate authority was to be found in the word of God in scripture. Creeds and other theological statements were authoritative only to the degree to which they conformed to that standard. The doctrine of justification by faith was at the heart of the theological system. Luther's own understanding of this position was one that was set amid the paradoxes of life and faith that he encountered and embraced. Human beings are justified by God, who pronounces them free in Jesus Christ. But human beings also remain always sinners in their old nature, and thus live as both sinners and justified at the same time (Latin: *simul iustus et peccatur*). As sinners, humanity stands condemned under the Law, which Luther readily admitted he found in the Bible. But humanity also finds in the Bible the good news that they have already been justified by God. These two, law and gospel, Luther said, are found in the scriptures. They must both be proclaimed without being confused.

The same sense of paradox and contrast informed much that Luther had to say concerning the state. God's rule over the world is carried out in two forms, Luther argued. He termed these the kingdom of the right hand (in which God rules through the gospel) and the kingdom of the left hand (in which God rules through the governing authority of kings). The kingdom of the right hand, which is under grace, is characterized by the rule of powerlessness and love. The rule of grace is hidden from our eyes in the world for the most part, Luther said, noting that grace often comes under the sign of its opposite. The greatest testament to this is the sign of the cross. For Luther the theology of the cross and its hidden power of grace concealed in humiliation were the proper knowledge of God.

Luther was careful not to reduce the saving work of Jesus Christ to his death on the cross. Just as important for salvation was the resurrection of Jesus Christ whereby he became the first fruit of God's new age. The transforming effects of the resurrection, Luther believed, were communicated through preaching. Recalling the ancient teachings of Athanasius, Luther argued that as the word became flesh in the incarnation, so the flesh becomes word in proclamation. The glorification of the believer, what the ancient theologians of the Greek church called *theosis*, Luther understood to be union with Christ and only fully realized in an eschatological sense. Deification, or glorification, was experienced now only in the form of the promise of what is one day to be, and hence was attainable now only through faith.

It was the central task of the church to give flesh to the word by proclaiming the message of Jesus Christ in the world. To this end Luther labored to produce a translation into German of the entire Bible, a project that was completed in

1534 and remains one of the greatest works of German literature in history. The gospel, argued Luther, comes to us primarily through the means of the preached word. Language is the sheath in which the sword of the Holy Spirit is contained, he contended. Christ is truly present wherever his word is preached, a point that allowed Luther to affirm both the doctrine of the real presence and the evangelical meaning of the Eucharist. Evangelical and catholic, faithful to ancient tradition yet attentive to the pastoral needs of the present moment, willing to embrace all the contradictions that life had to offer because the gospel had already promised he was free from these—this was the Luther whose spirit lit a pathway to wider reforms.

Spread of the Lutheran reform beyond Saxony

Nowhere was the power of the newly invented printing press made more evident than in the rapid dissemination of Luther's books and pamphlets throughout the Latin-speaking world of sixteenth-century Europe. The printed book soon proved to be a most effective information delivery system. It could be easily produced and sold in mass quantities, smuggled into restricted lands, hidden from investigating eyes, and passed from person to person. The universities in Europe proved to be ready territory for the reception of many of Luther's ideas in the sixteenth century. Within months of their publication Luther's writings were often being read by faculty members in various other schools. Wittenberg itself was also an effective means of spreading these ideas into the churches throughout Europe. Matthias Devay (d. 1547) was a student in the university; he returned to his homeland of Hungary in 1531 where he started the first evangelical congregation and began to spread Luther's teachings. Through books and personal contacts Protestant teachings spread to the cities of Danzig, Thorn, and Elbing in Poland in the 1540s where they took root.

Luther's influence spread rapidly through other parts of Germany, taking hold in a number of states with the support of sympathetic princes. North of Germany, in Scandinavia, Luther found an early champion in Christian II (1481-1559) of Denmark, for reasons that had to do mostly with consolidating political control within his kingdom. Hans Tausen (1494-1561) had been a student at Wittenberg before returning to his native Denmark, where he became the chaplain to the king and played a major role in advancing the Lutheran cause. By 1530 a Danish translation of the New Testament was prepared and a Lutheran confession was presented before the Danish king. Seven years later the Danish church was reorganized along Protestant lines, without, however, incurring any break in the succession of its episcopal leadership. Norway and Iceland were both under the Danish crown during this period, and their churches were brought into the Lutheran fold. Although worship and devotional practices continued to be conducted as they had previously been done, on a formal or institutional level the lands of Denmark, Norway, and Iceland had by 1540 become Protestant lands.

During these years Sweden, which had won its independence from the Danish crown in 1523, also embraced Lutheranism. Two Swedish brothers, Olaf Petersson (1497-1552) and Lars Petersson (1499-1573), were also students at Wittenberg before returning to their native land. Lars became a professor in the University of Uppsala, while Olaf was appointed to be preacher in Stockholm. Together they produced a Swedish translation of the Bible that was published in 1541. King Gustaf Vasa (1496-1560) supported the Lutheran effort, and by 1530 had instituted the evangelical reforms. While some Swedish bishops departed from the country, most remained. The office of the archbishop was retained, although appointment to the post was taken over by the king of Sweden. In 1531 Lars Petersson became archbishop of Sweden, without a break in the line of episcopal succession with his predecessors.

In Silesia a former knight of the Teutonic Order, Kaspar Schwenkfeld (1490-1561), convinced his local ruler, Friedrich II of Liegnitz (1480-1547), to support the Lutheran movement. While Friedrich became a Lutheran, Schwenkfeld himself moved further in a spiritualist direction, understanding the sacraments in a far more dualistic manner. The inner or spiritual nature was all that mattered to Schwenkfeld, and by 1526 he no longer even participated in the actual Eucharist, or Communion. His movement attracted few followers, but his spiritualist impulse became quite influential in following centuries.

Ulrich Zwingli and the city of Zurich

Erasmus ended his life in relative peace in Basel, Switzerland. Five years earlier, in 1531, outside another Swiss city, Zurich, another advocate of religious reform died a much more violent death while serving as chaplain to his city's troops in a battle against other Swiss cantons. Ulrich Zwingli (1484-1531) was born in a village in the Swiss countryside to a peasant family who made their living raising sheep. As a young boy he was sent away to school, and after attending the University of Vienna for a time, returned to Switzerland to graduate from the University of Basel. In 1506 he was ordained to the priesthood and assumed a position as a parish pastor. He continued his studies of Greek, early Christian writings, and classical literature, however, journeying to Basel to call on Erasmus whose Greek edition of the New Testament was published in 1516. Zwingli entered the fray of ecclesiastical reform in 1518 by opposing the local sale of indulgences by agents from Rome. That same year he was invited to assume the pulpit as the "people's priest," or the public preacher, in the city of Zurich.

Toward the end of the thirteenth century several small districts, or cantons, at the headwaters of the Rhine had formed a confederation that had been able to remain free from the feudal encroachments of stronger neighboring states. By the first decades of the sixteenth century the confederation had grown to thirteen cantons and a number of independent cities. Zurich, which was one of the cities in the confederation, was ruled by a council that was elected by the guilds, or unions, of the city. The members of the city council exercised a great deal of control over matters of church as well as civic life in Zurich. The appointment of Zwingli came after an interview with this council, and a vote taken in his favor.

Shortly after assuming the main pulpit of the city, Zwingli announced that he would no longer follow the pattern of preaching from biblical readings assigned by the lectionary for each week, but would institute instead a program of expository preaching that followed the text of an entire book of scripture. He soon earned a reputation as both a brilliant orator and a biblical scholar. In line with his humanist leanings, Zwingli understood the scriptures to be the primary source of authority for doctrine and worship. He could find no basis in the Bible for a number of church doctrines, including the universal authority of pope, the celibate priesthood, transubstantiation, mandatory fasting during Lent, or the role of the saints in Christian spiritual life. He emphasized, on the other hand, the need for both moral and spiritual regeneration of the city, which he said could be brought about only by a renewed trust in God through Jesus Christ.

Controversy broke out in 1522 when several lay persons in the city began eating sausage during Lent. Zwingli defended their action, leaving the matter of abstaining from meat up to the individual conscience to determine. That same year he secretly married a widow named Anna Reinhard (c. 1487-1538), an act they acknowledged two years later when Zwingli began publicly to challenge clerical celibacy. Opposition to the position on fasting during Lent came from the bishop of Constance, whose representative traveled to Zurich to engage in an open disputation. Word of Zwingli's activities also reached Rome, where the pope decided against open confrontation. Zurich's council was beyond papal intervention. Rome could do little to prevent Zwingli's teaching. At one point the Swiss reformer submitted a statement of belief before the emperor, but it was simply ignored.

A number of Zurich's citizens thought Zwingli was not going far enough in the application of his principle of appealing to scripture alone as the authority for doctrine and worship. Two specific issues around which controversy ensued were infant baptism and the use of images in the church. Zwingli defended the practice of infant baptism on the basis of a covenantal understanding of the rite, but there were others who rejected it and began baptizing only adults. The council ordered the practice to cease on pain of death, a punishment that was eventually carried out by public drowning. Regarding the presence of images in the church, Zwingli had argued for their validity and allowed for those such as a cross, while rejecting others such as images of saints.

The one issue that separated Zwingli and his supporters in Zurich most radically from the vast majority of other Christians of the world at that time was their understanding of the meaning of the sacrament of the Eucharist. According to Zwingli, the Eucharist commemorated Christ's death, and was not a reenactment of his sacrifice. The reformer rejected the doctrine of transubstantiation, which was official Roman Catholic teaching. In his debate with Luther, Zwingli allowed no room for any understanding of the real corporeal presence of Christ in the sacrament. He argued instead that following his resurrection and ascension Christ was physically located only in heaven. The bread and wine constituted a memorial to Christ. Zwingli began teaching as much, and administering both elements to the laity in worship. Differences regarding the exact meaning of the sacrament soon became grounds for separation. It continues to divide churches of the world today.

The Zurich city council supported Zwingli and his efforts, instituting his reforms while silencing those who opposed them. At Zwingli's urging, Zurich sponsored preachers who traveled to other cities and throughout the surrounding cantons to spread the new message. Several other cities in Switzerland, including Basel and Bern in the late 1520s, proved to be receptive to the types of reforms Zurich was adopting. The collaboration among preachers and councils representing these cities was a key element in securing the foundations for an enduring Reformation tradition in Switzerland. Zurich's preachers in the countryside met with considerably less success. Their efforts stirred resistance, which soon led to armed conflict. In 1531 Zurich was attacked by an army from several other cantons seeking to end its efforts to push its reforms beyond its own gates. Zwingli, serving as chaplain to his city's troops, died from wounds he received on the battlefield. The efforts he began continued in the city, however, under his successor, Heinrich Bullinger (1504-1575).

The first Anabaptists, the Swiss Brethren

In January of 1527 the city council of Zurich, with the support of Zwingli, had one of its citizens, Felix Manz (1498-1527), executed by drowning. The son of a priest, Manz was an early supporter of Zwingli and shared his views on most matters. The issue they disagreed most about was the practice of infant baptism. In January of 1525 a group of some fifteen persons meeting in the home of Manz's mother in Zurich underwent baptism as adults. One of the leaders of the group, Conrad Grebel (1498-1526), baptized another member who in turn baptized the rest. Word of the group's actions soon reached the city council, which decided the following year that "rebaptism" was illegal and punishable by death. Manz was arrested and in 1527 was executed for the act.

Manz, Grebel, and the others in their group argued that baptism was only properly administered to those who had undergone repentance of their sins. The administration of the rite to infants was thus in their view an empty gesture, void of any spiritual value or meaning. The true church, they believed, was composed of those who had undergone proper baptism and committed themselves to following Christ in a life of discipleship. Within a short period of time these "Anabaptists" (or "Rebaptists," a name given to them by their opponents) were organizing new congregations of believing men and women in the villages near Zurich.

The Swiss Brethren (as they preferred to call themselves) soon began to articulate a fuller understanding of Christian faith and community. Since the true church was formed only by believing Christians who had undergone baptism after repenting of their sins and expressing their commitment to follow Christ, it was not subject to secular political authority. The city council thus had no right to collect the church tithe, and Christians were not to serve in the civil military. Zwingli and Luther both supported the secular magistrates playing a major role in guiding the reform of the church. The Swiss Anabaptists rejected such a role and argued that the true church was composed of believers apart from both the secular magistrates and the ecclesiastical hierarchy. The Brethren shared Zwingli's position on the authority of scripture, but accused him of having failed to go far enough in following its teachings. Like Zwingli they rejected the use of images in the church and sought to reform worship, but they also fostered a strong anticlericalism and believed the common people had a right to read scriptures, call their own pastors, and exercise leadership within the church. The Anabaptists' vision of the church was much more egalitarian than either Zwingli or Luther had allowed. Common Christian believers and not priests, monks, or nuns were the true models of Christian piety.

Their ideas spread quickly throughout the region around Zurich. The message won a following, especially among craftspeople and farmers in the countryside. Notable among the first adherents were a number of women such as Margret Hottinger (c. 1514-1530), of Zollikon, a village on Lake Zurich. Margret's father, Jakob (d. 1530), was a farmer who had a reputation for anticlerical sentiments even before 1525. He and his daughter were among the first to join the new congregation in Zollikon that was organized by Manz and Grebel that year. In November Margret and several men were arrested by Zurich officials and imprisoned for their actions. Six months later Margret was released after publicly recanting, but she was soon spreading the Anabaptist teachings again in the villages. Like other early Anabaptist women, Margret believed she was being guided by the Holy Spirit to interpret Scriptures and speak words of inspired prophecy in the houses where believers gathered. After several years of these activities, Margret and her father decided to immigrate to Moravia, where Anabaptists were reportedly being given refuge. Arrested en route, they both were executed in 1530.

One of the early Anabaptist leaders in Zurich was a former Benedictine monk named Michael Sattler (c. 1485-1527). Sattler had been for a short time the prior of St. Peter's monastery in the Black Forest near Freiburg. By 1525 he had left the monastic community and the following year was in Zurich where he was identified with Manz and Grebel. The following year he left Zurich to travel through the region north and west of the city, staying for a short time in Strassburg, the Alsace city on the Rhine. In February of 1527 Sattler and a handful of other Anabaptists arrived in the town of Schleitheim, Switzerland, which was under Austrian rule at the time. A conference among these Swiss Brethren produced a short confession of their common faith written in German and titled *Brüderlich vereinigung etlicher Kinder Gottes: Sieben artikel betreffend* ("Brotherly Association of Several of God's Children: Concerning Seven Articles," better known in English as either the Schleitheim Articles or Schleitheim Confession). The document set forth in seven brief articles a statement of the Anabaptist position, which was then circulated in the countryside in hand-copied form. Before the year 1527 was out, however, Michael Sattler and his wife, Margaretha (d. 1527), a former Beguine, were arrested by local Austrian authorities. Both were quickly tried and sentenced to death, Michael by having his tongue cut out and then being burned to death, and Margaretha by drowning.

Although Michael Sattler is credited with being their principal author, the Schleitheim Articles summarize a much wider consensus that had emerged among the Swiss Anabaptists by 1527. The various sections set forth their basic beliefs regarding baptism, which was to be administered only to believers; church discipline, including the practice of the ban in place of excommunication; the Lord's Supper, which was understood to be a commemorative meal; and the nature of the church, which was a community separated from the world. Pastors were to be chosen by the people and ordained by them, not by bishops or secular authorities. Christians were forbidden to participate in the exercise of the power of the sword or to use violence on behalf of the state, an article that rejected the fundamental premise that the state could be Christian or a legitimate means of furthering the work of the gospel. Christians were to exercise passive resistance by means of their witness, accepting persecution, suffering, and even death as authentic marks of true Christian faith. They were to refuse to hold civil office in secular government, or to participate in secular courts. The unity of the Christian community was not one found through legal or coercive means, but one that could be expressed only through peaceful bonds of love that tied believers together in their faith.

The Schleitheim Articles appealed to biblical sources as their sole source of authority. Preaching the gospel as it is found in the scriptures was perceived to be the only legitimate means by which the Christian community could be formed. The scriptures provided the only adequate rule for Christian life as well, a position that echoed Sattler's own earlier experience of living under and administering community life guided by the *Rule of Benedict*. Indeed, the Anabaptists were forging a form of disciplined life in the Spirit that reflected the form of community known to monasticism in earlier Christian centuries. Anabaptists placed a great deal more emphasis than did monasticism on the need to bring the gospel to the common people, however, putting them in many ways in the tradition of the Third Order Franciscans, the Beguines, and other spiritual renewal movements among the laity from earlier centuries.

Wide diffusion of the Anabaptists

As Manz, Grebel, the Hottingers, and Sattler were spreading their teachings in the region around Zurich, a similar but unconnected group was emerging in southern Germany in the region of Thuringia between the Rhine and Elbe rivers. Expressing ideas that were similar to those of the Swiss Anabaptists, the German group was strongly influenced by Luther's early teachings, which were circulated in written form throughout the region. Especially important in this regard were Luther's defense of justification by faith, his challenge to the church's institutional control over the administration of the means of grace, and his early defense of the priesthood of all believers. This last position was one Luther came to modify after seeing the manner in which it was being interpreted by the Anabaptists.

Among Luther's early associates at Wittenberg was Andreas Karlstadt (1480-1541). During the period of Luther's absence of 1521-1522, Karlstadt introduced further changes in worship, rejecting vestments, images, and musical instruments in the church. A group of radical preachers who had been forced out of the town of Zwickau soon arrived in Wittenberg and joined forces with Karlstadt, which in turn alarmed Frederick, Wittenberg's secular ruler. Upon Luther's return to Wittenberg, Karlstadt was forced to depart the city, but he continued to exercise considerable influence among the Anabaptist believers.

One of the preachers from Zwickau who come to Wittenberg was Thomas Müntzer (1488-1525). After a dispute with Luther, Müntzer moved on and resettled in the city of Allstedt, in Thuringia, where he organized a new church. Like Luther and Zwingli, he affirmed the authority of scripture and conducted worship in German. With the Anabaptists he expressed opposition to infant baptism, although he did not move to end its administration. Most important for Müntzer was the belief that the poor were granted special insights into revelation by virtue of their suffering. This last conviction led him to side openly with the peasants in the rebellion that broke out in 1524. Believing the times to be entering the last days, Müntzer embraced an apocalyptic view of their struggle as being the forces of Christ against those of anti-Christ. The suppression of the revolt by the German princes reached apocalyptic proportions as tens of thousands of the peasants were killed. Müntzer himself was captured in the city of Frankenhausen and executed in 1525.

The suppression of the peasant uprising in southern Germany failed to address the fundamental causes of the rebellion. Luther's support of the princes only served to alienate many from among the lower classes. The religious spirit that had been a part of the rebellion, exemplified in leaders such as Müntzer, did not die. Müntzer supported armed rebellion, but others among the religious leadership of the peasants had not. In the years following 1525 a number of these leaders survived to begin quietly organizing new communities of believers in southern Germany, following the pattern of the Swiss Brethren. From the leadership of these communities the Anabaptist movement in southern Germany was reborn.

One of the centers for Anabaptists in Germany after 1525 was the imperial city of Augsburg. The religious situation of Augsburg was dominated by the struggle between Lutheran and Roman Catholic parishes. Anabaptists tended to attract less attention and were able to organize for a time with less persecution than in other places in Germany. One of the Anabaptist leaders who settled in the city for a time was Hans Denck (1495-1527), whose advocacy of internal spiritual experience reflected an older German mystical religious tradition. Another was Hans Hut (1490-1527), a bookseller who was in Frankenhausen when Müntzer was captured, and who was one of the more active missionaries of the Anabaptist cause in Germany. Augsburg's rulers were never willing to tolerate what they considered to be the seditious teachings of the Anabaptists, and a large number were arrested, many of them women who were active as missionaries and teachers. Women who owned their own homes provided lodging for other Anabaptists traveling through the region, and held clandestine meetings under their roofs. They played a key role in maintaining communication among members and in providing support for those in need, helping extend what was emerging as an underground church connected by a host of itinerant missionaries and teachers of the Anabaptist way.

Another city where Anabaptists were found in significant numbers before

1530 was Strassburg. Like other urban centers in Europe at the time, Strassburg was ruled by a council made up mainly of representatives from the city's various guilds. A portion of the seats on the council was reserved for members of the nobility. Members of the merchant and landlord classes dominated the political affairs of the city in the sixteenth century, while unskilled laborers working in areas such as gardening and hauling were at the bottom of the social order. The lower classes, while lacking meaningful representation in the city council, could exercise political power from time to time by rioting. One of the parishes, made up mostly of gardeners in the city, in 1524 called to its pulpit, without the approval of the city council, a preacher named Martin Bucer (1491-1551). Bucer was a former Dominican who had been educated at Heidelberg where he was converted to the evangelical cause by Luther's writings. With a group of other leaders in the city who had evangelical sympathies, Bucer was able to secure a degree of religious toleration from the council to allow their evangelical preaching to be heard.

Hopes for religious toleration attracted a number of Anabaptists to Strassburg. Bucer himself seemed in some of his writings to favor their position by acknowledging that adult baptism was the usual practice in early Christian experience. On the other hand Bucer was strongly committed to the concept of an integrated Christian society and a unified church, positions that the Anabaptists opposed. Many Anabaptists refused to take oaths or serve in the military defense of the city, and considered the true church to consist of believers who had separated themselves from the false church that baptized infants. Although Bucer was willing to engage in an exchange of views with Anabaptists like Michael Sattler who passed through Strassburg in 1526, he supported the imprisonment and exile of Anabaptist leaders when they were arrested. In Strassburg, like in Augsburg, Anabaptist congregations had to remain clandestine faith communities.

A number of the first generation of Anabaptist leaders in Switzerland and Germany had university educations, but others were without significant theological training. A number of these early leaders had formerly been members of monastic communities, but the majority of those who joined were lay people without previous involvement in the spiritual life of a religious community. Anabaptists drew heavily from among the social ranks of craftspeople, laborers, and clerical administrators throughout the region. But they could also boast from time to time a significant name from among the ranks of the upper classes.

One such person was Helena von Freyberg (c. 1485-1545) from Münichau in Austria. In 1528 she underwent baptism and opened her castle to Anabaptist preachers. It took two years for officials to prove her Anabaptist connection, but when they did the archduke sent her into exile. For the next two years she lived in Constance, where she was expelled again for her religious activities and forced to return to her home in the Innsbruck area. There she was forced to recant before a public official, a deed she performed in order to buy time. By 1535 she had resettled in Augsburg and was once again holding Anabaptist meetings in her home. She spent the last decade of her life in Augsburg, supported in part by her husband, who was a Lutheran.

Helena von Freyberg carried on a lively correspondence with a number of other Anabaptists, with leaders of the evangelical cause, and with some whose spiritual teachings did not fit any of the major party definitions of the day. Her social status proved useful to the Anabaptist effort by providing its leaders with social contacts and at times material resources. At the same time, she willingly gave up both wealth and status to follow Christ in a deeper life in the Spirit. Toward the end of her life she wrote a brief confession, in which she laid bare her own inner spiritual struggle with the memory of sin and asking her congregation to forgive her (a common Anabaptist practice that replaced the practice of saying confession to a priest). Its pages provide an insight into the spirituality that made the Anabaptist movement attractive to many. Among the sins she confesses, for instance, are personal bitterness and behaviors that are not Christ-like. Christ teaches us to leave ourselves behind and to follow him, she implores her readers. Believers are to be childlike, without falseness and without deceit.

In city and countryside Anabaptists were hunted down, imprisoned, tortured, exiled, and executed in Swiss, German, and Austrian territories during the 1520s. The only territory in central Europe where they found their teachings tolerated by local authorities was Moravia, a region located east of Bohemia. A century before the region had witnessed the formation of *Unitas Fratrum* ("United Brethren") following the execution of the popular preacher from Prague, John Hus. Those earlier Brethren had gained the support of the local Bohemian nobility, forging an alliance that was successful in defeating the invading forces of German Catholic emperors who were determined to extinguish them. Thus there was a precedent for Moravia's territorial rulers to extend permission to the early Brethren from Switzerland and Austria to resettle in their lands. Word spread quickly among the Anabaptists, and by 1528 many were heading east to resettle.

One of these was an Austrian hat maker named Jakob Hutter (1500-1536) from what is now western Austria. Upon his conversion to Anabaptist teachings in 1529, he began to organize members to form a local congregation. Two years later he moved to Moravia to escape persecution, where he continued to organize Anabaptist congregations. Hutter turned out to be a gifted community organizer, developing a model of community life that other Anabaptists quickly began to adopt. The most distinctive characteristic of the communities of Hutter's followers, who soon became known as Hutterites, was the practice of sharing all property and goods in common. Like other Anabaptists, the Hutterites refused to participate in the use of violence and believed in separating themselves as much as possible from the political life of established Christendom, which they deemed sinful and worldly. Nowhere had Anabaptists been able to develop an alternative model for social life that demonstrated in a positive way their understanding of community life, however. This was Hutter's contribution. The concept of communal sharing of property and goods allowed his followers to adhere in a literal fashion to Christ's command to sell all and give to the poor, thereby implementing the radical form of community life that had been established by the apostles in the book of Acts.

In 1535 Jakob Hutter and Katharina Purst (d. 1538), a woman who had worked as a maid and whom Jakob had baptized several years earlier in Austria, were married. A year later political pressures from the Austrian archduke caused the local Moravian ruler to withdraw his support for Hutter's community. Jakob,

Katharina, and other members of their congregation set off to return to Austria, hoping to find refuge among the clandestine Anabaptists still living there. Unfortunately, Jakob was soon discovered because of his preaching and baptizing. The couple was arrested outside the city of Innsbruck. Jakob was tortured and burned at the stake in 1536. The authorities tried to persuade Katharina to recant, and she appears to have been allowed to escape from the prison. Two years later she was taken into custody again on the charges of being part of an Anabaptist community and was executed.

The deaths of Jakob and Katharina Hutter did not bring about an end to the Hutterite community. Others carried on the leadership in Moravia, expanding the numbers of those who followed Hutter's model to the tens of thousands eventually. A short confession of faith was eventually drawn up that set forth the principles of adult baptism, communal ownership of lands and goods, nonviolence, and separation from the world. In the Hutterites the Anabaptist movement found an abiding form of Christian social life and community development that would continue for many centuries to come.

The Hutterites sought to build a Christian society on the principles of nonviolence and communal sharing of goods. In 1535 a group of radical Anabaptist preachers who believed Christ was about to establish his millennial kingdom seized control of the city of Münster in western Germany and set about to implement a different model of a Christian society. The road to Münster began several years earlier in Strassburg with a furrier named Melchior Hoffman (1495-1543), who had been converted to the Anabaptist cause. Hoffman was convinced that he was living in the last days, that the Holy Spirit was being poured out in new ways, and that among the spiritual gifts he and his followers had received were prophecy and the ability to interpret the mysteries of scripture. Through several books and an effective program of new congregational organizing, Hoffman's influence spread quickly to other cities in the region. By the time authorities in Strassburg arrested him in 1533, the foundations had been laid for an underground network of churches across northern Germany and the Netherlands. Hoffman himself spent the rest of his days in prison in Strassburg, dying in 1543.

Following Hoffman's arrest, a baker from Amsterdam named Jan Matthijs (d. 1534) stepped forward to claim the mantle of leadership among these congregations. By means of prophetic inspiration Matthijs came to the conclusion that the city of Münster was the New Jerusalem from which Christ's rule would be exercised over all the earth. Deserting his wife, he took off with a young woman named Divara van Haarlem (1511-1535), who was the daughter of a brewer. Together with a group of followers they resettled in Münster. By early 1534 Matthijs had won over the council and a number of religious leaders in the city. Worship was reorganized along Anabaptist lines, common ownership of goods was proclaimed, and a large number of citizens underwent baptism. Those who resisted were banished or executed. Outside the city the Roman Catholic bishop of Münster was able, with the aid of the prince, to raise an army and lay siege to the city, cutting off Matthijs and his followers from the outside world. This did not discourage them, however, for Matthijs set the day of Christ's return for Easter of that year.

When Easter came and went without Christ appearing, Matthijs decided to take matters into his own hands and confront the besieging army. Upon leaving the city he was immediately killed. At that point a tailor named Jan van Leiden (1509-1536), who had been among the followers who came from the Netherlands, took over the leadership role. Almost immediately he married Divara, and then a month later declared that polygamy was the law of God and all males were required to take more than one wife. He himself took fifteen more women as wives. Before the year was out van Leiden was declared to be the new King David who was appointed by God to rule all the earth, and Divara was the queen.

The experiment lasted only six months. In June of 1535 the besieging army entered the city and executed the entire population. The leaders were tortured and paraded throughout the countryside for more than a year. Word of the excesses of the leaders in Münster and of the manner in which they were crushed unnerved the Anabaptists in the region. The cause of their movement throughout central Europe looked even more hopeless than it did immediately after the peasant's rebellion a decade before. With Lutherans and Roman Catholics alike persecuting them, their future looked bleak.

The person who stepped into this situation to lead the Anabaptists in northern Germany and the Netherlands in a new direction was Menno Simons (1496-1561). A priest from Utrecht, he was converted to the Anabaptist faith in 1536 and ordained an elder the following year. From that point on he began to travel incessantly throughout the region, organizing new churches and spreading Anabaptist doctrines. Soon he had a price on his head, but it did little to deter him. Preaching at night and in homes to avoid detection by civil authorities, and remaining constantly on the move, he succeeded not only in rebuilding the network of underground churches but also in laying the foundations for an enduring institutional structure. Elders were ordained, overseers (or bishops) appointed, and prophetic inspirations curtailed. A new body of hymnody emerged, and a new confessional identity was articulated as the Mennonites (as they were soon known) grew in number.

The Anabaptist commitments were forged by the fire of numerous testimonies of suffering and martyrdom. In sixteenth-century Christendom, baptizing an adult who had previously undergone the rite as a child was a capital offense, punishable by death, for evangelicals and Roman Catholics. Evangelicals and Roman Catholics alike considered the integration of religion and political life to be divinely mandated, and thus Anabaptists were by definitions enemies of the state. For their part, Anabaptists considered themselves members of the true church who could expect persecution for their faith. Suffering was understood to be a part of the work of redemption. Christ himself had suffered in the flesh, so why should a Christian who followed him expect any less? The ancient tradition of martyrdom was given new expression within Christendom by these radical believers, accounting in part for the spread of their ideas.

For Anabaptists, the church was a body of regenerate Christians, and believers were to have as little as possible to do with the unregenerate world around them. Of course most Anabaptists still had to make a living, which usually meant having some dealings with the wider social world. As far as possible they sought to form new communities that lived apart from the world and engage the wider society only when necessary. The major forms of engagement were preaching to win new converts and witnessing before public officials when one was arrested. It was a powerful vision of an alternative kingdom of God on earth that inspired the movement then and now.

In addition, Anabaptists exhibited a greater degree of social egalitarianism than was typical in that age. Openness to the Spirit and its inspiration provided an opportunity for women to exercise more of a leadership role in Anabaptist communities than they could in the Catholic or Protestant churches. Women never experienced full equality in leadership with men even in Anabaptist communities in the sixteenth century, but by all accounts they shared fully in the lay aspects of community life. Women played an equal role with men in deciding to impose a ban on someone for sinful behavior, for instance. The process of initiation in baptism was the same for women and for men, requiring them to repent and confess their faith before the whole community. The decision to enter an Anabaptist congregation was one that a woman had to make apart from her husband or father, thereby challenging in some cases his legal control over her life and even leading to divided families.

John Calvin and the Geneva Reformation

The first quarter of the sixteenth century found much of Europe in the midst of upheaval. Preachers calling for change were appearing in cities throughout Germany and Switzerland, many of them inspired by reading Luther. Reform was the order of the day, with matters such as a simplified liturgy, the use of the vernacular language in worship, and the removal of images or artifacts (relics) from churches being everywhere debated. The influence of the humanists could be seen in many of the reformers, especially in the authority they gave to scripture. Preaching and biblical reading were becoming common public practices in many cities. In some cases the emerging political structures of councils formed out of guilds seemed to weigh heavily in favor of changing the established church order under episcopal hierarchy, an order that had been long intertwined with the system of ruling feudal nobility in the West. Reformers were challenging not only their bishops, but the authority of Rome in the definition of catholic.

One of the voices of the new reform was Guillaume Farel (1489-1565), a native of France and one-time student at the University of Paris. After visiting Strassburg, Basel, and Bern, Farel landed in Geneva in 1532. Geneva in the sixteenth century was a free city that was ruled by an elected council, although the duke of Savoy exercised a great deal of influence over its affairs. The churches in Geneva were under the rule of the bishop of Savoy, a situation the city council did not necessarily approve. By the time Farel arrived, Luther's writings were already being debated in the city. A congregation of people committed to evangelical teaching had been formed and was sharing the Lord's Supper on a regular basis. Although he was not ordained a priest, Farel gained control of one of the churches and began instituting reforms similar to those advocated in Zurich and Wittenberg. In 1536 he convinced a younger colleague who was also from France, John (or Jean) Calvin, to join him in his effort.

John Calvin (1509-1564) was born in Noyon, north of Paris. His father was an attorney for the cathedral in Noyon and had substantial political connections. Throughout his school years Calvin was supported financially by two benefices, or income generated by offerings to local chapels. At the age of fourteen he was sent to the University of Paris, where he studied for the priesthood and graduated at age eighteen with a master's degree. The following year in obedience to his father he began the study of law at Orléans, completing his doctorate in the field in 1532. Calvin eventually obtained his license in law but was never ordained to the priesthood. From his days in Paris it was also clear that his interests were heading in the direction of humanistic studies. His first book in 1532 was a critical edition and commentary on Seneca's *Two Books on Clemency.*

The humanism that was flowing through the universities in France at this time has often been termed evangelical because of the degree of attention it paid to biblical texts. Luther had been translated and published anonymously, although his ideas did not gain a significant following. A humanist scholar in Paris named Jacques Lefebvre was much more influential. There was tension in the air, and some were still being arrested and executed for spreading ideas the church considered heretical, but most of the scholars around Calvin considered themselves loyal Roman Catholics intent only on their learning and ideas.

Sometime before 1534 Calvin experienced what he described thirty years later as an unexpected conversion. He wrote of this experience only once, describing it as a turn toward being teachable and away from his strong devotion to the papacy. In his later writings Calvin emphasized the gradual nature of conversion that takes place in life through stages. One would have reason to suspect his own journey to the evangelical cause might have been the same. But if we were to look for a point at which we can date Calvin's turn to the evangelical faith in a definite way, we might find it in the 1533 sermon delivered by his colleague, Nicolas Cop, who was the rector of the University of Paris. Cop made a public case for what was essentially Luther's position regarding grace, and attacked efforts to suppress the new evangelical position. The response was almost immediate. No one less than the king of France called for action against the Lutherans at the university. Calvin was suspected of being a sympathizer, if not actually having contributed to the sermon, forcing him not only out of the university but soon into Basel in exile.

Within three years he published in Latin the first edition of what would become his most important written work, *Institutio Christianae religionis* ("Institutes of the Christian Religion"). From its opening pages the work left no doubt that Calvin was a partisan of the evangelical cause. He wrote the work explicitly to make a case before the king of France for the evangelical reforms. That same year, 1536, he made a brief trip to Italy, and was passing back through Geneva when he made the acquaintance of Farel, who convinced him to stay and help in the city. Geneva's council was gaining considerable power, including power over the churches. Farel and Calvin proposed a series of what they perceived to be reforms, including monthly administration of the Eucharist in worship, appointments of special ministers who would enforce moral laws, and publication of a new catechism. Resistance against them was strong, however, and in 1538 both were banished. Farel found a pastorate in Neuchatel, while Calvin went to Strassburg, where he met Melanchthon.

Three years later the citizens of Geneva through the council invited Calvin to return as a minister in the city, which he did, settling there for the rest of his life. One of the first tasks he undertook upon his return to the city was to draft a report in French titled *Les ordonnances ecclésiastiques de l'église de Genève* ("Ecclesiastical Ordinances of the Church of Geneva"), which was presented to the city council. The ordinances recognized four offices of leadership in the church: pastors, teachers, elders, and deacons. While ministers were to obey God in all things, they were expected to swear allegiance to the civil magistrates as well. Regular weekly meetings of the ministers for study and mutual edification were to be established. Most of the affairs of running the churches were to be put in the hands of lay elders, who together with the ministers were to form a consistory that would oversee teaching and discipline throughout the city.

Calvin's plan was adopted with little change, and over the course of the following decades Geneva embarked on implementing its vision for a Christian city. Calvin himself never held any position other than one of the ministers in the city. He was often at odds with members of the city council, and was not even awarded citizenship until near the end of his life. Nevertheless, his influence proved to be enormous as he set about not only leading his urban congregation but publicly addressing matters of religious reform throughout the city. The power he exercised was usually that of persuasion. His biblical expositions, delivered in sermons several times a week and published in numerous volumes of commentary, as well as his theological writings, most notably the *Institutes*, which he continued to revise and publish, provided the foundation for Geneva's religious reorganization. Over the course of his decades in Geneva Calvin guided the city toward a comprehensive and coherent understanding of Christian life that engaged social, political, spiritual, and theological dimensions fully. The name that came to be associated with the endeavor was simply the "Reformed" faith.

No better expression of what the Reformed faith looked like in its sixteenth-century inception can be found other than Calvin's *Institutes*, as they are most often called in English. He published the first edition in Latin in 1536 and in French in 1541, but he continued to revise the work until the final edition was published in Latin in 1559 and in French the following year in 1560. Organized into four books, the *Institutes* covered the totality of Christian belief in systematic fashion. The work opened by examining the question of knowledge of God as creator and the corresponding doctrine of creation. Book II went on to address the knowledge of God as redeemer, covering both the giving of the law as well as the person and work of Jesus Christ. Book III considered grace and redemption, while Book IV examined the church and its sacraments.

At the heart of the *Institutes* was Luther's doctrine of justification by grace through faith, a doctrine for which Calvin acknowledged his debt to Luther. Faith united the believer directly to Christ, by-passing the need for the sacramental mediation of the church, Calvin argued. Union with Christ had a double effect, however, for it deemed a person justified by God and it began to make the person become like Christ in moral and spiritual nature. Faith was principally the work of the Holy Spirit, and it manifested itself primarily in the form of assent to the gospel. It rested entirely on knowledge of Jesus Christ, which in turn could only be gained through the scriptures. The scriptures by themselves were not enough, Calvin argued. They were the external witness, but required an internal work that Calvin called the witness of the Holy Spirit that made the knowledge they contained effective. There was thus an inseparable relationship between faith, the word, and the Spirit for Calvin. The knowledge that resulted produced both comprehension and assurance.

The *Institutes* opened by arguing that knowledge of God has been implanted in every human being and could be found in creation. Such knowledge of God has been smothered or corrupted by human sin, however, making it impossible to know God sufficiently apart from revelation. Enough knowledge of God remains only to condemn us and to leave us without an excuse, Calvin asserted. In the *Institutes*, Book II, Chapter 1, Section 8, the doctrine of sin that accompanied this position is often referred to as one of "total depravity" (a doctrine that he somewhat qualifies by insisting that the *imago Dei* is tarnished but not destroyed after the fall into sin). According to Calvin, every aspect of human existence, both soul and body, was defiled by the pervasive effects of concupiscence, or inordinate desire. Calvin saw the doctrine of original sin and total depravity as being a hedge against the self-sufficiency of his age and the notion that people are capable of resolving their predicament through their own efforts.

Calvin was equally capable of affirming the beauty and goodness that were in the world and had been brought about through human endeavors. He affirmed the truth that could be found in other religions and philosophies as well. All of these were in reality gifts of grace given by the Spirit of God for the benefit of all people. In and of themselves, however, the grace that one found through creation was not capable of sanctifying humanity, and thus apart from Jesus Christ did not have enduring or eternal value.

In order to reach us, Calvin noted, God had condescended to meet us on our own level, the heart of the doctrine of the incarnation. Christ paid the penalty of sins on the cross (Calvin asserted a doctrine of penal substitution), thereby enabling one to live a righteous life. Since no one is capable of initiating salvation, it follows that God must be the sole cause of it. God's election is not universal, argued Calvin, for there is both salvation and reprobation. Calvin defended the justice of God by noting that all deserved damnation on account of sin, but that the mercy of God was manifested by God electing some to salvation. Like God's governance of history, called providence, the election of those who are saved is mysterious and cannot be inquired into. Calvin understood this doctrine to be a comfort to the Christian who could trust God and leave salvation in God's hands.

Regarding the sacraments of the church, Calvin followed Luther and accepted only two. For Calvin, the sacraments were covenantal in meaning, sealing to the heart what was heard in the Word of preaching. Although he agreed with Luther that Christ was really present, he understood this to be a presence at the table rather than a presence "in, under, and around" the elements of bread and wine, as Luther had argued. On the other hand Calvin rejected Zwingli's doctrine that the bread and wine are only a memorial to Christ's body and blood. Christ's physical presence was indeed in heaven with the Father, but through the Holy Spirit Christ was communicated to the faithful through both preaching and sacraments.

Concerning civil government, Calvin sought a more integrated order of the civic and religious realms. Church and state were not separate realms, for Christ was Lord over all. Spiritual and temporal realms, on the other hand, were not identical and ought to be properly ordered. The law that had been delivered to Moses in the Ten Commandments, Calvin argued, was divided into two tables. The first concerned spiritual matters, while the second concerned temporal matters. This provided an organizing principle for church leadership as well. Elders were the spiritual leaders in charge of preaching and teaching, while deacons carried out a wider ministry in the world.

Ordained ministry for Calvin, as for Luther, was an office that belonged to the whole church and not to an individual priest. The church conferred on some the ministry of word and sacrament as a matter of good order, doing so through the laying on of hands by other elders. One is called to ministry through a double process that was similar to the experience of coming to faith. The individual was expected to have received an inner call of the Spirit that was then to be confirmed by an external call by a congregation. One of the interesting questions that was raised in this connection for Calvin was whether women could be ordained. His response was that in the spiritual realm, in Christ there was neither male nor female. However in the temporal realm, the need for good order seemed to him to require that women not be ordained. The prohibition of women in leadership in the church was a matter of practical polity and not of spiritual or theological necessity.

Like Luther before him, Calvin opposed monasticism and the organization of separate religious orders for the spiritual estate. Both envisioned a church in which all members of the laity would have access to the spiritual benefits that were found in monastic discipline. Both also understood every Christian to be called to ministry in the secular world, a move that tended toward a radical democratization of the notion of Christian vocation. Every human being is called by God to a particular work in life, be it administering justice, fixing wagons, or raising a family. Whatever work is performed in the world is lifted to the level of a spiritual vocation when performed for the greater glory of God, Calvin argued. This notion of what some have called a "worldly asceticism" in Calvin in particular informed later developments in social life regarding the inherent value of labor.

On many of these points Calvin shared a great deal with Luther, whose career preceded his. The differences that emerged between them were often subtle, yet they were significant enough usually to prevent the followers of the two reformers from being in communion with each other. Furthermore, Luther and his followers were not the only ones among the reformers with whom Calvin did not agree. As noted above, Calvin opposed Zwingli on some matters. Geneva during Calvin's time attracted numerous dissidents from across Europe, many whose teachings Calvin opposed. For one of them, Michael Servetus (1511-1553), Calvin's opposition proved deadly.

Servetus was a Spaniard who had published a treatise denying the doctrine of the Trinity. Forced to leave Spain because of the work, he was attempting to travel through Geneva undercover when he was identified, arrested, convicted by the city council of heresy, and burned at the stake in 1553. Calvin served as a witness for the prosecution against him and later published a book that defended the punishment of death in cases of heresy. His approval of such punishments rested on the same grounds as other crimes that Calvin saw as endangering the social order, including repeated adultery and prostitution. The discipline that Calvin sought to impose by the church upon life in the city of Geneva became a later model for other European states as they entered the modern age.

Spread of the Reformed faith

Calvin's *Institutes*, it was noted above, was addressed to the king of France. It was the Genevan pastor's hope that the French king would be swayed to undertake evangelical reforms along the lines that his book had outlined. The hope was never realized, but there were significant pockets of early French support from among members of the French nobility. One supporter was a woman named Renée of Ferrara (1510-1575), a sister-in-law of François I married to the Duke of Ferrara in Italy. She carried on a lively correspondence with Calvin in Geneva and opened her home in Italy to some of the first of Calvin's followers to seek refuge from France. After the death of her husband, Renée returned to France where she held a small principality that continued to offer refuge to Protestant or Reformed believers. She is usually regarded as holding moderate Reformed leanings herself, but continued to attend Roman Catholic worship, and refused to condemn others who were committed to the Roman Catholic faith. Unfortunately her voice of moderation was a minority on all sides of the widening religious divides that were opening up across Europe.

François I opposed evangelical teachings strenuously because they threatened the unity of the church of France. He ordered a number of arrests and even executions, and many of the first evangelical supporters went into refuge. Some found safe haven inside France while others went to Geneva or other cities beyond the king's reach. François was not against negotiating with German Protestants if it meant weakening the German emperor's position, but within his own realm Protestants were not welcomed.

After the death of François, his son, Henri II (1519-1559), assumed the throne. Henry was married to Catherine de Medici (1519-1589), an Italian who was the niece of Pope Clement VII (1478-1534). Protestantism was now seeping into France, with several congregations formed by the 1550s, one even in Paris in 1555. The members of these congregations refused the ministry of Roman Catholic priests and called their own pastors, mostly from Geneva. The evangelicals in France were called "Huguenots" by their opponents, a term whose origins are unclear.

Marguerite of Navarre (1492-1549) was the older sister of François I. A woman of letters, she was conversant with scholarship of her day and was reportedly moderate in her evangelical leanings. Her daughter, Jeanne d'Albret (1528-1572), was more public in her support of the Huguenot cause. At fourteen years of age Jeanne was forced by her uncle, François I, into marriage with Wilhelm I, duke of Jülich-Cleves-Berg in northern Germany. The marriage was annulled by the pope, however, as it had been performed without d'Albret's consent. She then married Antoine de Bourbon (1516-1562), and in 1560 at thirty-two years of age she announced her embrace of the Reformed faith. Navarre, which was located in southern France along the border with Spain and was the home of the couple, thereafter became a base for Huguenot political efforts.

The year before their marriage, in 1559, some fifty representatives of Huguenot churches throughout France gathered secretly in Paris to draw up articles and discipline for a national church. Elders and deacons were to be elected from among the people in the new church order and were to jointly govern the local congregations. Elders and pastors formed regional colloquies, or conferences, that were to meet at least four times a year to oversee churches within their region. Representatives from all the churches were to meet once a year in a national synod. In effect, the Reformed Churches had moved beyond the conciliar theology of the past to embrace a new form of collective episcopacy. The structure was intended to provide oversight of churches, ensure lay participation, and create a vehicle for ongoing work of reform. From the early Huguenots in fact (although exactly who or when is not known) came the motto *ecclesia reformata semper reformanda* ("the church reformed and always reforming").

Matthias Devay, who as was noted earlier had introduced Lutheran teachings to his native Hungary in 1531 when he returned from Wittenberg, traveled to Switzerland a decade later. Upon his return to Hungary he began supporting a view of the sacraments that was closer to that espoused by Zwingli, dividing the evangelical community there but marking the beginnings of the Reformed tradition in that country.

The Seventeen Provinces that are now the Netherlands, Belgium, and Luxembourg were the site of some of the first executions of followers of the evangelical cause in the 1520s. Three members of an Augustinian monastery in Antwerp, Henry Vos and John van den Esschen in 1523 and Lambert Thorn in 1524, were burned at the stake for preaching evangelical doctrines. The Netherlands were joined into one administrative unit by Charles V, who had been raised in one of them, in Flanders. His son, Philip II of Spain (1527-1598), a staunch supporter of Rome, continued to rule the region after 1556. Yet Amsterdam and Antwerp provided more of an open door to Lutheran, Anabaptist, and Reformed teaching than any city in Spain, due mostly to the number of merchants who flocked to these northern ports from other parts of Europe. The Reformed position was set forth most clearly in the region in 1561 in a statement that came to be known as the Belgic Confession. Addressed to Philip II, it was written by Guido de Bres (1522-1567), who had returned from Geneva in 1559. The Belgic Confession condemned Anabaptist teachings, argued for the word of God as the sole governing standard for the church, and posited church discipline alongside preaching and right administration of the sacraments as a third identifying mark of a true church.

The evangelical cause found increasing political support in the Netherlands during the 1560s among the regional nobility, many of whom resented Spanish rule. Led by William of Orange (1533-1584), who was also known as William the Silent, they organized a Confederacy of Nobility in 1565 and presented their case before the governor, Margaret of Parma (1522-1586), who was the half-sister of Philip II. William had been baptized a Lutheran and raised a Catholic, but by the 1560s he was supporting the Reformed cause and expressing considerable tolerance for the other evangelical churches. Resistance to Spanish rule by these "beggars," as their opponents called them, broke into open rebellion in 1568 and lasted for eight decades. The military base for the rebels was in a fleet of small ships that acted as an independent naval power; the rebels were thus regarded by their opponents as pirates.

In 1572 William took the city of Brill and the northern territories. An alliance with France was formed, aided by the marriage of Henry of Navarre (1553-1610) to Margaret of Valois (1553-1615). In 1577 William extended official recognition to the Anabaptists, making the Netherlands a refuge for a variety of groups embracing that branch of Christian faith from across Europe. At William's death, Spain still held claim on the provinces, but Spanish control had declined significantly and continued to do so until the Netherlands finally claimed independence in 1609. Eventually the Netherlands divided into a Reformed north region (modern Netherlands) and a Roman Catholic south (modern Belgium).

Separation of the Church of England
from Rome under Henry VIII

The English had long been acquainted with traditions of popular dissent and reform. Since the days of Wycliff and the Lollards in the fourteenth century the Catholic Church had faced significant dissent and even opposition on the island. England's universities had provided fertile ground for humanism and other ideas that challenged traditional theological thinking as well. None of these forces played a major role, however, in bringing about the separation of the Church of England from Rome in the sixteenth century. The single most decisive factor was the Tudor king, Henry VIII (1491-1547).

Henry was no Protestant when it came to theological sympathies. In 1521 he took it upon himself to publish a pamphlet titled *Assertion of the Seven Sacraments,* which attacked Luther's position on the matter. The issues that led him to sever the relationship between the churches of his kingdom and Rome were much more mundane. The year he had assumed the throne, Henry had married Catherine of Aragon (1485-1536), the daughter of Isabella and Ferdinand of Spain and an aunt to Charles V. Catherine first came to England in 1501 to marry Henry's older brother, Arthur the Prince of Wales (1486-1502). She was sixteen, and the young prince fourteen at the time of their wedding. Several months later Arthur died of respiratory illness. According to Catherine the marriage had never been consummated. Still it had been a legal union, and since church teaching held that a man could not marry his brother's wife, a dispensation had been secured from the pope annulling Catherine's marriage to Arthur if Henry were to marry her. The dispensation was granted and Henry and Catherine married in 1509.

Fifteen years of marriage produced only one living offspring, however, a daughter named Mary (1516-1558). Henry wanted a male heir. By 1525 the probability of Catherine having a son seemed remote, given her age. Henry petitioned Rome for a legal annulment of his marriage to Catherine on the technical grounds that she had previously been married to his brother, and that the book of Leviticus forbade their own union. Catherine would not agree to the annulment, however, complicating matters for the pope, who could not afford to anger her nephew, Charles V. The pope's solution was to stall. Henry responded by turning to the faculties of theological schools for support. Soon professors of theology in universities across Europe were being asked to weigh in on the question of whether the Bible permitted a man to marry his brother's wife (citing Leviticus 18:16 and 20:21 over against Deuteronomy 25:25), and if not, whether a pope could grant a dispensation to divine law. In England one of the most visible supporters of the annulment was Thomas Cranmer (1489-1556), one of twelve university preachers appointed to Cambridge. Cranmer himself had once been married, but after his wife and child both died in childbirth he had taken holy orders as a priest and had been appointed to the university position.

A compromise of some sort might have been found had Henry by 1530 not fallen in love with another woman, Anne Boleyn (1501-1536). Anne was a member of a powerful family among the nobility, and she refused to be a mistress of the king as had other women with whom Henry had been stricken. Failing to receive an annulment of his marriage to Catherine, Henry moved to sever Rome's authority over the churches of England. Catherine was forced into seclusion, separated even from her daughter, Mary. In 1533 Henry appointed Thomas Cranmer archbishop of Canterbury and secured Rome's approval. For two years prior to that Cranmer had been Henry's ambassador to Charles V in Germany, and had himself been secretly married for a second time, to a Lutheran woman from Germany named Margarete Hetzel (c. 1511-1576). By 1533 Henry had also secretly married Anne Boleyn, who was pregnant. Soon after his consecration as archbishop, Cranmer ruled that Henry's marriage to Catherine was annulled, thereby denying Mary's legitimacy under law. The act would come back to haunt him twenty-three years later when Mary ascended the throne upon the death of her half-brother. Meanwhile, Anne was soon to bear Henry a second child, again a daughter, this one named Elizabeth (1533-1603).

By the end of 1533, a convocation of English theologians was ready to declare that the pope had no authority over the churches in England. The final step was taken by parliament when it issued the Supremacy Act in 1534. The Act declared that the monarch who ruled England was the supreme head of the Church of England, with power to determine heresies, appoint the archbishop, and oversee the church's administration throughout the land. Many of those who opposed the Act, including the great humanist scholar Thomas More, were arrested and executed for high treason. Henry moved to close the monasteries throughout England and confiscate their properties, which were then given to his supporters.

In Rome, Pope Clement VII had given his final refusal to grant an annulment earlier in 1534. A bull of excommunication was drawn up against Henry, Cranmer, and Anne the following year, but Clement did not publish it. Unable to convince François I in France and Charles V in Germany to take military action against England, the pope realized that the excommunication would only expose Rome's weakness in England. Clement hoped that a future council at which all the heads of Christendom would meet would determine to take such action against England. Henry in the meantime worked the diplomatic channels to keep Charles and François from launching any attack against him.

Throughout the whole affair it was clear that Henry harbored little, if any, sympathy for the evangelical cause. Several minor changes in the doctrine of the church were introduced by him in 1536. The authority of scripture, the creeds, and the first four ecumenical councils was acknowledged, for instance, but not the authority of the tradition of Rome. Mass was to be said in Latin, however, and images were to remain in the churches of England. There were several executions of Protestants who were judged to be spreading heresy. Cranmer himself succeeded in keeping any strong evangelical sympathies he might have secretly held, and remained unmolested. One of his acts was to oversee the publication in 1537 of an English translation of the Bible, but this did not amount to much in the way of introducing theological change.

Henry's interest in Anne meanwhile had waned, and in 1536 he had her beheaded on fabricated charges of adultery and high treason. A third marriage, to Jane Seymour (1508-1537), ended with her death after the birth of her son, Edward (1537-1553). A fourth wife, Anne of Cleves (1515-1557), brought ties with Saxony and for a brief moment hopes on the part of some of a united front with Protestants in Germany. That marriage was soon annulled as well, however, as Henry moved on to his fifth wife, Katherine Howard (1520-1542). She was a devout Catholic but like one of her predecessors, Anne Boleyn, was beheaded on charges of adultery that were of a highly dubious nature. A sixth wife, Katherine Parr (1512-1548), managed to outlive the Tudor king.

During these years, despite Henry's antipathies, evangelical ideas were slipping into England. Henry's response in the last decade of his rule was to try to move the Church of England in a more Catholic direction, this despite his continuing dispute with Rome. Parliament passed the Six Articles Act in 1539, affirming the doctrine of transubstantiation, forbidding the marriage of priests, and supporting private confessions. Public dissent was to be punished by death. Cranmer himself was still married at the time, and in order to avoid problems sent his wife, Margarete, home to Germany. The execution of prominent proponents of Protestant doctrines in 1540 and 1541 drove home the extent to which Henry was willing to go to preserve Catholic teachings. Only Cranmer managed to survive among the advocates for Protestant reforms, and this due mostly to his long service on Henry's behalf.

Upon Henry's death, his ten-year-old son, Edward, ascended to the throne in 1547. The advisors who ran the government in Edward's name moved quickly in a more evangelical direction. The Six Articles were repealed, and a new *Book of Common Prayer* that had been drawn up by Cranmer was introduced. This edition retained the language in the Eucharist that referred to the real presence of Christ. A second, revised version that was approved in 1552, however, introduced more decidedly Protestant elements. The 1552 version referred to the Eucharist as a memorial, and seemed to some to avoid a direct statement of the doctrine of the real presence. That same year Cranmer introduced a list of Forty-Two Articles of religion that were intended to take the church more in a Protestant direction. Among the theologians who worked on these with Cranmer was a Scottish church leader named John Knox, who was soon to lead the Reformed effort in his native country.

Edward did not live long. His death in 1553 brought his half-sister, Mary, to the throne. Daughter of Catherine of Aragon, Mary was staunchly Roman Catholic in her commitment. The following year she married Philip II, son of Charles V (her cousin) and king of Spain. Soon she was busy undoing the changes that had been introduced during the reign of Edward. Parliament officially recognized the pope again as the head of the Church of England. Archbishop Cranmer was excommunicated by Rome, and in 1556 was burned at the stake as a heretic. Others joined him in a wave of executions, with many evangelicals going into exile in the cities of Germany and Switzerland. By the time Mary died in 1558, several hundred executions had been carried out against Protestants. The effect was to create a new host of evangelical martyrs whose memory continued to inspire their cause in England for generations to come.

Mary's sister Elizabeth, child of Henry VIII by Anne Boleyn, ascended the throne in 1558. The following year she began cautiously to reinstate changes that had been made under her father and brother. She first reclaimed title to being head of the Church of England, and removed from power those who supported Rome. A new edition of the *Book of Common Prayer* was brought out, one that both affirmed the real presence in the Eucharist and referred to it as a memorial. A new archbishop of Canterbury was consecrated in unbroken succession with previous episcopal leaders, but with the approval of the monarch and not the pope. Under Elizabeth the monarchy consolidated administrative power over the churches throughout England. Over the course of the next four decades a distinct Anglican theological tradition blossomed, one that drew upon both Catholic and evangelical strands of faith but was expressed in the vernacular of English life and culture.

Reform in Scotland

The churches of Scotland remember Patrick Hamilton (1504-1528) as being among the first to bring Luther's teachings there. He was burned at the stake for his efforts. For the next three decades a handful of Protestant preachers entered Scotland to little avail, as its rulers were allied with France and the Catholic faith of Rome. In 1547 a French force attacked the castle of St. Andrews where a priest named John Knox (1514-1572), along with a handful of others holding Protestant leanings, had taken refuge. Knox was taken captive and spent the better part of the next two years as a galley slave on a French ship. Freed in 1549, he made his way to England, which was then under the rule of Edward. While there he was given the opportunity to review the *Articles of Faith* and the revised *Book of Common Prayer* that Archbishop Cranmer had labored to prepare.

After Mary Tudor ascended to the throne of England, Knox made his way to Germany and then Geneva, were he served an English-speaking congregation as its minister. Knox became a close collaborator with John Calvin, working with him on projects such as the printing of a popular English translation of the Bible known as the Geneva Bible. He made a brief trip back to England to get married, then on to Scotland in 1555 where Mary of Guise (1515-1560) was serving as regent. Back in Geneva, Knox wrote *The First Blast of the Trumpet against the Monstrous Regiment of Women*, a book that attacked on grounds of both natural law and religion the rights and ability of women to govern. Intended as a piece of propaganda against Mary Tudor and Mary of Guise, the book was published just as Elizabeth ascended the throne. Needless to say, Knox was not welcomed back in England.

Instead he returned to Scotland, where in 1559 he began preaching throughout the country. With England's help, Scottish resistance forced the French out of the country in 1560. The Scottish parliament then turned to Knox, who had settled as minister of St. Giles Church in Edinburgh, to draw up a new confession of faith. The document that the parliament approved later that year showed the influence of Calvin and Geneva in virtually every article. The Scot's Confession affirmed eternal election and salvation by grace, the authority of scripture, and the marks of the church being word, sacrament, and discipline. The mystical presence of Christ at the Lord's Supper was likewise affirmed in language that Calvin would have approved.

A *Book of Discipline* was soon drafted and adopted by parliament as well, establishing a combination of lay and ordained leadership over the churches. Ministers were to be elected by the congregations they were to serve. Superintendents were assigned to oversee the churches, although their function was soon replaced by local councils. Ministers were to be educated and had to be publicly examined before being ordained. To this end schools were to be established. Funds were to be set aside for the poor (a part of the *Discipline* the nobility strongly resisted). Preaching, teaching, and catechetical instruction were all enjoined on the ministers, as was the task of overseeing the moral condition of church members. The power of excommunication was in the hands of a board composed of lay and ordained leaders in the church. The whole church was to be governed by neither monarch nor the pope but by a general assembly resembling the Scottish parliament.

A few years later, in 1564, the parliament adopted the *Book of Common Order*, whose text again was written mostly by Knox. The liturgy it established drew from the traditional Western Mass a number of elements that were given a distinctive Reformed expression. As in Zurich and Geneva, only the Psalms were allowed to be sung in worship. Preaching was central to worship. The Lord's Supper was to be celebrated only four times a year, and by members of the church sitting around a table, partaking of both bread and wine. One of the important steps for rooting the reform effort beyond the cities came in the form of a translation of the *Book of Common Order* into Gaelic, the language used in the Scottish highlands among Celtic people.

Such changes were being introduced with little resistance from the monarch, Mary, even though she had strong Catholic sympathies. Mary's personal life after 1565 fell into disarray, as she first married one man, then fell in love with another, whom she married after he arranged for the death of her former husband. Forced to abdicate the throne, Mary took refuge in England, where she was executed two decades later by Elizabeth on charges of conspiracy. Back in Scotland, Mary's infant son, James VI (1556-1625, later to be James I of England as well), became king in 1567. John Knox preached the coronation sermon.

Early Unitarians

The execution of Michael Servetus in Geneva for Unitarian views has already been noted. The teachings of Servetus were not unique. A number of people came to radical conclusions in this great century of rethinking Christian doctrine from the ground up. In an attempt to rediscover the real gospel, many theologians reopened the early theological controversies of Christianity, putting even the central tenets of the doctrines of the Trinity and Christology on the table for re-inspection. Some, like Servetus, did not find Nicene Christianity taught in the Bible.

Another theologian who challenged trinitarian thinking was an Italian named Lelio Sozzini (1525-1562). With both a wandering mind and a wandering body (buoyed by his father's wealth he traveled throughout western Europe) Sozzini corresponded with a number of Reformers, including Bullinger, Melanchthon, and Calvin, on the sacraments, the resurrection of Jesus, predestination, and the Trinity. By the mid-1550s Sozzini was being investigated by the Inquisition on the Roman Catholic side, and he was being questioned by his Reformed friends in Switzerland on the Protestant side. Sozzini died in 1562 before a case was finally prosecuted against him. His nephew, Fausto Sozzini (1539-1604), picked up his uncle's scattered notes and systematized his teachings into a doctrine that became known as Socinianism. Like his uncle, Fausto Sozzini was also a traveler and a creative, speculative theological thinker. His christological ideas gave rise to what can be described as a fully developed Unitarian position, namely, that God is not three persons but one, and Jesus Christ was not divine but only human. Holding to such teachings made him vulnerable to persecution on all sides in sixteenth-century Europe, but he found refuge in the borderland region known as Transylvania. With the Hapsburg empire on one side and the Ottoman empire on the other, Transylvania was something of a safe haven for a variety of dissenters in the sixteenth century. The emerging Unitarian cause was especially welcomed there by a sympathetic prince, John Sigismund, and the bishop of the Reformed Churches in the region, Ferenc Dávid (or Francis David, 1510-1579), who by the 1560s had also become a Unitarian. Transylvania's eclectic community of worshippers paved the way for a social doctrine of tolerance, which was confirmed in the 1568 Edict of Turda. Sozzini remained in Transylvania until the prince's death, after which the region came under a Roman Catholic ruler. Forced to leave Transylvania, he moved on to Poland, where he spent the remainder of his days defending his Unitarian understanding of God and his rational approach to theology.

Ferenc Dávid came to Unitarianism from a very different direction. Born into a Hungarian family, Dávid studied in Wittenberg and returned home to become a superintendent of the new Lutheran churches in Hungary. Soon he came under the influence of the Reformed preacher Péter Melius Juhász (1532-1572), converted to Calvinism, and began serving as a Reformed bishop in Hungary (one of the few places Calvinists retained bishops). By the 1560s he was coming under the influence of other speculative thinkers, however, who led him to begin questioning the doctrine of the Trinity. Councils were called, debates were held, and in the end the Reformed Churches in and around Transylvania split into Unitarian and Calvinist factions.

Catholic reforms led by religious orders

The search for a more meaningful faith that would correspond to the growing appreciation of the classics among the educated led to a renewal of biblical studies and humanistic learning throughout Europe. Closely related to this was the search for greater spiritual discipline and vitality. In cities and towns the desire for institutional reform was being propelled among the new urban classes who were not satisfied with church structures that seemed to foster corruption and moral laxity. In some places efforts for reform were closely related to rejection of the authority of the papacy over the churches of Europe, and a corresponding diminishment of church tradition as authoritative teaching. Generally these churches and their theologians called themselves evangelical because of the manner in which they looked to the Bible as the unparalleled source of authority for doctrine, worship, and practice. In Germany they were soon to be known as Protestants, while in Switzerland the various cities and leaders formed themselves into a more or less coherent communion that called itself Reformed. Some from the Reformed movement went so far as to reject the doctrine of the Trinity, becoming Unitarian. Some congregations and leaders refused to recognize the validity of infant baptism and argued that a pure church consisted of those who had been baptized after coming to belief on their own, and was organized apart from worldly powers. The Brethren, or Anabaptists as they were more generally called, advocated a form of Christian discipline in community that resembled the reforms of earlier generations of monasticism. Like the Lutheran, Reformed, and Unitarian churches, Anabaptist congregations came to be separated from the Roman Catholic Church in communion.

There were also a number of theologians and church leaders throughout Europe in the sixteenth century who did not reject the authority of the papacy and of the accumulated body of the Latin theological tradition in the West, but who still sought to foster reform from within. The humanists were largely in this camp. Because their reforms were largely confined to the realm of scholarship, however, their impact did not reach far beyond the walls of the universities and academic life. Far more important for Roman Catholic Church life in Europe were movements for spiritual renewal that emerged in the form of new orders or associations. A number of spiritual writers and mystics found willing and eager ears among western Europe's disenchanted but loyal Roman Catholics. Several new monastic orders emerged as well to carry forward the spiritual renewal of the age within the Roman Church.

Monasticism as an institution was attacked by evangelical reformers from every direction in the sixteenth century. Monastic houses in territories under Lutheran and Reformed rulers were closed and their lands confiscated by secular authorities. Even in England, where the evangelical cause was not strongly supported, the monasteries were closed by Henry VIII and the lands confiscated as part of his reform of (or assumption of power over) the Church of England. At about the same time and seldom because of Protestant criticisms, on the other hand, the institution of monasticism experienced a new outburst of energy and reform throughout Europe.

The Capuchins were organized in Italy in 1525 in an effort to renew Franciscan spirituality. Matteo de Bascio (1495-1552) appealed to Pope Clement VII that year, asking him for permission to follow a strict Franciscan observance, including restoration of being discalced (going shoeless), begging for food, and working on behalf of the poor. In 1528 his request was granted, with permission given for the new order to wear a pointed hood, or capuche. In the early years this reform order of Franciscans attracted a number of unreliable leaders (one became a Calvinist), but soon the order grew dramatically, reaching out to regions of Europe that had become Protestant. By 1619, when they became an independent order, there were over 1,500 houses. The Capuchins were centered mostly in Italy, but members of the order were influential in the development of churches in East Africa and in Kongo. In Europe they joined the Jesuits in active outreach among Protestant, Orthodox, and Turkish lands.

In Brescia, Italy, a woman named Angela Merici (1474-1540) in the early decades of the sixteenth century began visiting hospitals and taking orphans into her own home. Merici was not married but had not taken monastic vows. She appears to have been educated since she established reading classes for girls. At some point she received a vision for starting a new order of women who would serve in the world but not remain cloistered. That vision came to fruition in 1535 when she organized the first community of Ursulines. The Ursulines were the first women's order established solely for education. At the time of Merici's death five years later the community numbered around 150. Growth continued to be at a slow pace at first, even after Pope Paul III approved the order in 1544. It would take several more centuries until the Ursulines would become a major Catholic mission order, but they eventually did, realizing more fully the originating vision of their founder.

Other reforms in Roman Catholic spirituality took place within existing orders. Among the most important was the renewal that took place among the Order of the Brothers and Sisters of Our Lady of Mount Carmel. The Carmelites, as they were better known, had been founded in the twelfth century on Mount Carmel in

Israel by pilgrims. The order spread across Europe but for several centuries had been in decline. From the highlands of central Spain near the provincial capital of Avila in the sixteenth century, however, two spiritual giants emerged to lead a renewal of the entire order. Juan de Yepes Álvarez, better known as Juan de la Cruz (St. John of the Cross, 1542-1592) and Teresa de Jesús, better known as St. Teresa of Ávila (1515-1582), were both of Jewish descent. They each combined in their teaching a stricter monastic observance with a more mystical understanding of Christian living as union with God.

Teresa entered the Carmelite order at the age of twenty. Almost immediately she began to suffer from severe illnesses that inflicted her with debilitating pain. She also began to receive spiritual visions that aided her through the suffering. The visions endured even after she partially recovered from her illness, and around 1550 she began to write them down. She also began to undertake efforts to reform the Carmelite order from within, to strengthen its spiritual discipline. In 1562 she received permission from the Carmelite superior to found her own convent of Discalced Carmelite Nuns of the Primitive Rule of St. Joseph at Avila. Within a few years she was organizing other convents throughout Spain that were characterized by their adherence to stricter standards of spiritual discipline, including a more rigorous adherence to vows of absolute poverty and the discalced practice of going without shoes. As important as these reforming efforts were, it was the body of written work that eventually emerged from St. Teresa that spread her influence far beyond her native Ávila, making her one of the most important figures in the history of modern Christianity. That significance was confirmed in 1970 when Teresa became the first woman ever to be named a Doctor of the Church by Rome.

Teresa's writings offered a pathway for devotion that moved the soul through four stages from contemplation to ecstatic rapture. Her image of the spiritual journey was that of the soul moving through a house or castle with its many rooms through which the soul must pass before reaching the innermost chamber, the place of full communion with God. The vision of communion she offered was at once mystical, sensuous to the point of being erotic, and fully embodied. The spiritual journey she imagined was more of a movement through concentric circles than the traditional hierarchical ladder journey of ascent that other mystical writers before her employed. To her final days she was inspired by vivid visions of Jesus, one of which reportedly lasted for two years.

Juan de la Cruz also came from the region of Ávila. He had studied at the University of Salamanca, and was already ordained as a priest and about to enter another order when he met Teresa in 1567. She convinced him to join the Carmelite order instead and help her in reforming it throughout Spain. Resistance among others in the Carmelite order who considered the efforts of the two reformers to be too severe mounted, and in 1577 Juan was arrested in Toledo on the instigation of opponents within the order on the pretext of having disobeyed his superiors by organizing new houses. In prison he was beaten regularly and kept in an isolated cell. During this period he composed one of his most famous works, a poem titled *Cántico espiritual* ("The Spiritual Canticle"). After nine months of imprisonment and torture he was finally able to escape by breaking through a small window. Even this experience could not stop him from his reforming efforts, as Juan spent the last years of his life organizing new houses.

Juan's spiritual writings, like those of Teresa, are among the classics of Christian literature throughout the ages. *Cántico espiritual* tells of a bride, which is the soul, searching for the bridegroom, who is Jesus Christ, with whom the bride finally unites. The work is often seen as a Spanish vernacular version of the biblical Song of Songs, a story of passionate lovers that is interpreted as a vehicle for mystical experience. The other poem for which Juan is known is *La noche oscura del alma* ("Dark Night of the Soul"). It too narrates the journey of the soul to God, a journey that takes place in the dark of night and reaches its climax at the light of dawn. During the dark night the soul encounters various difficulties, which are overcome as it journeys on toward God. Both poems portray the mystical union of the human soul with God as the pinnacle of salvation, and both set forth the pathway as one of inner meditation and journeying. One can see the application of these mystical themes in the inner lives of both Juan and Teresa, but one can also see their effects in their outer lives as public figures and reformers. Like many of their Protestant contemporaries, Teresa and Juan were writing in a European vernacular language (Spanish in their case), and not just Latin, indicating the growing importance of use of the vernacular languages for spiritual and intellectual life in Europe, and charting reforms in new vernacular directions.

Ignatius of Loyola and the Jesuits

Teresa and Juan were both breathing the air of spiritual renewal in Spain. They were joined in this effort by another reformer, Ignatius of Loyola (1491-1556), who was the founder of one of the most important Catholic orders in the history of world Christianity, the Society of Jesus, or the Jesuits. Ignatius was born in the Basque region in northern Iberia. His name was originally Iñigo until a university official registered him as Ignatius. His first career was that of a soldier in the Spanish army, but it ended in 1521 when he suffered severe wounds from a cannonball while defending a Spanish fort against French forces. During the lengthy convalescence that followed, he came across two books that changed his life, one on the life of Christ and another on the lives of the saints. After recovering from his wounds, he retired to the village of Manresa in the Spanish countryside where he spent almost a year engaged in inner spiritual reflection. He began to chart there the pathway of an inner encounter with God that led one into the glory of perfect union with Christ. From this experience emerged *Exercitia spiritualia* ("Spiritual Exercises") whose text Loyola continued to work on for the next twenty-five years.

The *Spiritual Exercises* is a guidebook designed to take one through a four-week spiritual retreat. Its readings for each week begin with a prayer and opening reflection that are followed by a series of considerations. Each section concludes with instructions regarding specific affections one is to experience, or affirmations ("colloquies") that one is to consider. Each day of the retreat a person is to read a section and then spend time meditating on it, taking up to several hours with each passage if necessary. Although the volume is organized around this four-week setting, it is not confined to this. Loyola and his early companions themselves employed it as a guide for their own regular devotions and meditation.

The goal of the *Spiritual Exercises* is not merely to increase one's theoretical knowledge of God and doctrine, for if that were the case, one could read it once and be done. The exercises are intended to bring one into a fresh encounter or experience with God, and to provide a plan for deepening one's response to God throughout a lifetime. Indeed, the *Exercises* are not meant to be read. Instead, the one introduced to them (the "exercitant") is counseled to return to being directed in the *Exercises* by a skilled director year after year. Illumination of the mind and activation of the spiritual imagination are two aspects of the single objective of the *Exercises*, which seek to engage the senses and emotions of the exercitant to partake of God's grace in a manner that reflects human beings' manifold faculties. The purpose of the exercise is to draw down on the exercitant the fullness of the grace of God in all its dimensions, for of the plenitude of grace there is always something more to gain.

The content of the four weeks of exercises move from repentance through contemplation to direct engagement with Christ. Week number one focuses on creation and sin, week two on the life of Jesus Christ, week three on the suffering and death of Jesus Christ, and week four on the resurrection life and glory of Jesus Christ. In this way the exercises guide one through the entire experience of salvation and bring one to the glory of God that is the end of all creation. As Ignatius wrote in the section dedicated to preparing for the retreat, human beings were created for a certain end, which is to praise, to give reverence, and to serve God, and by these means to arrive at eternal salvation.

Although the first week's exercises open with consideration of God's acts of creation, the nature and effects of sin within an individual's life quickly dominate. The attention paid to sin in the opening pages of the handbook reminds one of the emphasis given to the doctrine of total depravity by Calvin in his *Institutes*. In both cases the purpose is to challenge notions of self-sufficiency. Loyola invites the retreat participant to pay particular attention to the personal and individual dimensions of sin, bringing the effects of sin into view in order to bring about a purification of the soul through repentance. Interestingly, the first week's exercises do not call for confession to another, either in private or public. The conversations that one is directed to undertake through its pages are ones that are to take place within oneself. The meditation on sin is specifically designed to bring to mind one's actual individual sins, and the horrors that await the unrepentant person in hell.

The second week shifts the focus to the life and attitudes of Jesus Christ, while the third week guides one in meditation on the suffering of Jesus. In both cases the intention of the various exercises is to bring one into full (sensual as well as intellectual) engagement with Jesus in his incarnation and passion. Through prayer and meditation, and at this point without the sacramental elements of bread and wine, one is led to encounter the presence of Christ in both its incarnational and sacrificial dimensions in a way that is spiritually transformative. This encounter continues in the fourth week, during which the focus of the meditation is on the resurrection and glory into which Jesus has passed. But the real point of the four weeks is to bring the exercitant face-to-face with the opportunity to choose to become a follower of Christ and to gain clarity about precisely what Christ is calling one to do. The exercises conclude with a short list of recommendations regarding one's return to ordinary life and directions for further spiritual development. Among the latter are daily prayer and devotions, weekly participation in the sacraments of penance and Communion, intentional conversations with a spiritual director (or confessor), regular reading of devotional literature, cultivation of a virtuous life, special attention to devotion to Mary, and annual renewal through retreat.

The heart of the Jesuit order was found in the *Exercises*. Members were required to repeat them annually in an eight-day retreat and to discuss with their superiors the movement of their souls brought about through the exercise. Superiors in turn were expected to guide exercitants so as to bring into harmony the inner work of the Spirit working upon the soul and the work in the world to which superiors assigned each member. Furthermore this spiritual work was not confined to the priests and brothers who were members of the order, for Jesuit work among the laity introduced both men and women who were outside the order to the *Exercises,* using them to help instill that same sense of devotion and vocation to them in their work in the world.

Ignatius of Loyola's *Spiritual Exercises* drew on deeper traditions of mystical reflection and spiritual direction that had long been nurtured in monasticism within Catholicism. The individualized application and the manner in which the *Exercises* were designed to help Catholics integrate faith and life in a rapidly changing world fit better the pattern of civil society that was emerging in the sixteenth century in Europe. The *Exercises* also led one into a deeper and more reflective engagement with the biblical narratives of the life and work of Jesus found in the Gospels. While there were no direct connections between Ignatius and the Protestant reformers of his era, his *Exercises* drew from the same wellsprings of renewed evangelical fervor as did they. Luther and Calvin regarded the Christian's work in the world as being a spiritual vocation through which one could give greater glory to God. Loyola preserved the more traditional dimensions of monastic retreat from the world while envisioning the integration of the ancient spirituality in the wider social world with an evangelical spirit.

After his year at Manresa and the conception of *Spiritual Exercises*, Loyola set off on a pilgrimage to the Holy Land. By some accounts his goal was to evangelize among the Muslim population, apparently without much success. By 1523 he was back in Spain, where he entered the University of Salamanca. His educational career continued at the University of Paris, where he graduated with a master's degree in 1534 several years behind Calvin. During this period Ignatius (as he was now known) gathered around him the nucleus of a group that would soon become the Society of Jesus. After graduation, Loyola set off again for the Holy Land but wound up instead in Italy. There the vision for a deeper spiritual life coupled with active ministry in the world crystallized. The result was the new order, the Society of Jesus (or Jesuits), which was granted official recognition by the pope in 1540. The *Spiritual Exercises* took the place of a founder's *Rule* within the order.

Taking the path trod by the mendicants one step further into a life lived totally in the world, Jesuits did not exercise their pattern of life within the confines of a monastery. And unlike the mendicants, they dispensed with the recitation of the divine office in common, thus freeing members to an even greater degree. The first companions of Loyola liked to say that the whole world was their house, and indeed within a few years of their founding, members of the new order, such as François Xavier (1506-1552), were traveling throughout Asia and other parts of the world. Where earlier Catholic orders were primarily contemplative, the Jesuits were what came to be called an "activist" congregation formed in the mysticism of the *Spiritual Exercises* for life in the world. Education was one of the most important of activities in which they engaged; they founded and staffed schools wherever they went. Public preaching was another.

The Jesuits from their inception understood themselves to be an order that served the pope directly. A cadre of specially chosen and prepared members took vows to go "on missions" wherever the pope sent them in the world, making theirs one of the most effective missionary orders the Catholic Church has ever known. It is to Ignatius of Loyola and the Jesuits in fact that we trace the first use of the term "missionary" as referring to the work of agents of evangelization and expansion of the church. By the end of the sixteenth century they had become a truly global missionary force.

The Council of Trent and Catholic institutional reform

Ignatius Loyola, Angela Merici, Teresa of Ávila, Juan de la Cruz, and others embodied an important stream of Roman Catholic spiritual renewal in the sixteenth century. Institutional reform within the Roman Catholic Church was the task of the Council of Trent, which met off and on from 1545 through 1563. Hopes for a general council surfaced early in the century as numerous efforts for reform began to sprout. During the period immediately after his excommunication, Luther had appealed for such a general council to be called. Princes who supported the evangelical effort in Germany had supported his call, and even Charles V had in 1530 spoken hopefully of such a gathering.

Through the first decade of the Lutheran struggle Rome was reluctant to call such a council. The lingering effects of what was called "conciliarism" (the idea that councils were superior to the pope) still echoed from the previous century. While conciliarism had little support from the pope, monarchs and others favored the position as it gave greater power to local bishops over whom kings and princes could in turn exert greater power. One of the ways popes had responded to conciliarism was by increasing the number and power of the cardinals they appointed, creating a counterweight to regional episcopal leadership.

Rome was in no hurry to call a general council in 1520, but by 1530 the crisis of German and Swiss territories departing from Roman Christendom turned the tide. Shortly after he was elected in 1534, Paul III, who supported humanist studies and educational reform, made it known that he intended to call such a council. It was Paul III who commissioned Michelangelo to paint "The Last Judgment" for the Sistine Chapel in Rome, and he who authorized the Jesuits in 1540. This same pope in 1542 instituted the Roman Inquisition to stop the spread of the Protestant heresy, and published the first index of prohibited books the following year in 1543. The council he called for reflected all these concerns. Its purpose would be to extirpate heresies, reform morality, restore peace in Christendom, and prepare for war against the unbelieving (that is, Muslim) Turks.

Warfare and political intrigue on European soil prevented the council from taking place immediately. Protestants demanded it be held in German territory and that the pope not preside, while Paul III was determined to keep it close to Rome. Finally in 1542 the pope issued a bull calling for a general council to convene at Trent (*Tridentum* in Latin), a city in the Italian Alps that was technically within the German emperor's domain. Representatives were dispatched to courts and cities throughout Europe to inform them of the decision. The call that they carried betrayed the sense of crisis that now beset not only a church but a continent. The affairs of Christendom were daily becoming worse, it stated. Hungary was being oppressed by the Turks, and Germany was endangered. The nations of Europe could no longer wait for a single king to save them, but acting together had to look to God for the good of the Christian commonwealth (*Christianae reipublicae*).

The council opened in December of 1545 and continued its work through 1547. It convened again from 1551 through 1552, and then a decade later from 1562 through 1563. These were eighteen troubled years in Europe. War at home in Germany and with the Ottoman Turks in Hungary occupied the emperor, Charles V. The plague forced delegates out of Trent at one point, while the threat of war between France and Germany did so at another. Paul III died in 1549, and his successor to the papal throne had a stroke during the final session in 1563. The Lutherans had already separated from Rome by 1545, and their princes and theologians refused to participate in the council. No one even expected the Swiss Reformed districts to send representatives. Nevertheless the council went forward. Fewer than one hundred bishops and heads of orders participated in the first session, and not more than three hundred bishops in all participated in the span of eighteen years. About two-thirds of those who attended came from Italy, with French, German, and Spanish bishops making up the remaining number. Two Portuguese Dominicans represented their king, but no one from the overseas colonial dioceses of Portugal or Spain participated. Charles V, who was also King of Spain, explicitly refused to allow anyone from his colonial empire to attend on the basis that the issues being addressed did not affect them. A trio of papal representatives chaired the council.

The work of the council was conducted in twenty-five sessions. Little was accomplished during the first three of these, but with the fourth issues of substance began to emerge. One of the first of these was the question regarding the authority and interpretation of scriptures. The final statement of session four recognized both the written books of the Bible and the unwritten traditions of the church as being the vehicle of the saving truth of Jesus Christ. The Latin Vulgate was reaffirmed as being a trustworthy translation, while the council warned against allowing individuals relying on their own judgment to interpret the scriptures. Over against the plethora of new interpretations that were showing up across Europe, Trent asserted that authority to determine the meaning of scripture belongs to the church. Along these lines it called for the legal imposition of restraints on publishers whose works were inducing many to follow grievous errors in doctrine.

More positively, the council called for establishing programs throughout the church for instruction in scriptures and training in biblical interpretation, conducted under qualified teachers. All bishops were instructed to improve preaching in their churches, and if necessary to establish and fill specific offices of preachers. Preaching was to be in a vernacular tongue, although the rest of the liturgy was to be conducted in Latin. The sacraments were to be explained to those who participated in them, as were the scriptures that were read in worship. A later session instructed all bishops to set up special colleges that would serve as seminaries for ministers of God (*Dei ministorum perpetuum seminarium*), according to Session 23, Chapter 18, the origin of seminaries.

The sixth session in 1547 addressed the question of justification, which together with the issue of papal authority was at the core of the controversy with Protestants. Trent had earlier affirmed the doctrine of original sin, which the decree on justification now assumed. Though Christ died for all, not all receive the benefits of his justification, but only those to whom his merit is communicated, the decree stated. Justification is the translation from the state of sin to the state of grace, brought about through the washing of regeneration of baptism or by the desire for baptism. Sinners are justified by grace through Jesus Christ. The beginning of justification is found in the predisposing grace of God that illuminates and empowers sinners to participate in their own justification through their assent and cooperation. Furthermore, justification entails both the remission of sins and the sanctification or renewal of life. Neither faith nor the good works that might precede justification merit grace. Rather, grace is the foundation of both faith and good works. The ability that human beings have to cooperate with God in their salvation is itself a gift of grace that can be refused. The resulting assurance of faith is not the basis for salvation, but is nevertheless a desired response. By the same logic, faith does not exempt one from obedience and the law but is integral to them.

Human beings cannot presume to know whom God has predestined or chosen to justify, the decree continued. Nor can they presume to be preserved in their salvation if they depart from proper norms of living and belief. In other words, human beings can sin and forfeit the grace of justification they received in baptism. By the same token they can also receive the grace of repentance through penance, which Session 6, Chapter 14 called a "second plank after the shipwreck of grace lost." On both counts, our trust is not in what human beings can do, but in what God does for us. God arouses the human will through predisposing grace. The fear of hell or the grief experienced in repentance is a work that results from such prevenient grace, but nevertheless is a work that we perform. Works of charity are not just the fruits or signs of justification, but they are also the means by which grace is increased. Among the Decree's concluding anathemas was one that condemned anyone who would say that we do not cooperate in our salvation, or that the preparation and disposition do not involve an act of the will of the person who is to be justified.

There was much here with which Lutheran and Reformed theologians agreed. Indeed, from a perspective located five centuries later, one can see that regarding the doctrine of justification the two sides shared far more in common than either side was willing to admit. The differences were subtle, and certainly the theologians of the day who were in the thick of things were skilled at picking them out and apart. Disagreement repeatedly came back to the question of whether any activity on humanity's part (including the act of receiving grace) is a necessary part of the total event of justification, and if so, how one ought to understand theologically the value of that activity that participates in divine grace. The differences became much clearer when the focus was placed on the necessity and role of the church as the agent of salvation. Roman Catholics insisted on the church being empowered by Christ to be the channel of grace, while Protestants on all sides (Lutheran, Reformed, and Anabaptist) argued for a more immediate relationship with Christ for grace. The differences between Catholics and Protestants on the sacraments and ministry were very clear.

Trent reaffirmed the traditional seven sacraments of Roman Catholic life, as well as the sacrificial understanding of the Mass. Above all, the council insisted that the sacraments conferred grace when they were properly celebrated and that they were not "mere" symbols of a promise. More particularly, the doctrine of transubstantiation holds that in the consecration the whole substance of bread and wine becomes the substance of the body and blood of Christ, while the accidents (that is, the appearance) of bread and wine remained. Since the substance of both bread and wine become fully the substance of Christ's body and blood, lay persons did not have to receive both elements in Communion. They were not necessarily forbidden to do so, however. The decision to continue to withhold the cup from the laity appears to have been one made more to distinguish Catholic from Protestant practice than one that had any pressing doctrinal reason behind it. Over against the Anabaptists, Trent affirmed the validity of infant baptism, but advised that children who were not of the age of reason were not required to take Communion.

Regarding the priesthood, Trent reaffirmed its sacramental status and the centrality of priests in the life of the church. Other pressing issues that confronted the bishops regarding the priesthood, however, were found in the overwhelming evidence of abuses that were running rampant. Here the council focused its greatest attention for reform. The council began by strengthening the power of the bishops over priests, while at the same time condemning the extravagances that were known to be too common among bishops. Training of priests in proper seminaries was insisted on. Targeted for reform were such practices as bishops furnishing their quarters in a luxurious manner, or using their office to assist the enrichment of family members. Bishops and priests were required hereafter to live within their dioceses and parishes. Bishops could reside away from their diocese only under special circumstances, as when appointed to serve in Rome.

Priests were no longer to serve in more than one parochial church or cathedral, or bishops in more than one diocese. Trent ordered an end to the practice of church benefices, or the income received from offerings or endowments assigned to particular churches or chapels being used for the support of persons other than clerics or members of religious communities. It also prohibited any individual from receiving funds from more than one benefice. The disciplinary requirement of a celibate priesthood was affirmed, and priests were explicitly forbidden to have concubines. Those who were living in such relationships were ordered to end them, and no exemptions were to be given. If they did not end such relationships, they were to be suspended from their duties and cut off financially. If they persisted, they were to be excommunicated.

On the question of indulgences, the council affirmed the church's power to grant them, while recognizing that there had been abuses. It recommended that indulgences be handled with moderation, and ordered that their indiscriminate sale be abolished. A warning was registered regarding superstitions and popular practices that were not a part of the faith. At the same time, popular devotional practices involving images and relics of saints were reaffirmed, for these carried the sanction of the faithful through the ages. As noted above, the sacraments were not to be practiced without explanation, nor was scripture to be read without giving its interpretation. To this end Trent called for a renewal of catechism in the church. This was realized with the publication of a new catechism in 1566, followed by a new missal (a book containing the worship services for the year) in 1570.

Reading through the decrees of Trent, one sees abundant indications of the challenge that the Protestants posed to Roman Catholic faith and practice. The storm that had broken over Germany dominated the institutional horizon of Rome in the first half of the sixteenth century, far more so than the Reform efforts in Zurich and Geneva, or events taking place in England. Trent's theologians had read the Lutheran documents, even if they failed to understand fully or to agree with their concerns. The challenge of this movement that was claimed to be a Reformation was real, and Trent rose to the occasion of responding to it.

At the same time, it would be a mistake to see the council as simply a reaction to the Protestant challenge. Trent responded on Roman Catholic grounds and proceeded with its reforms following Catholic principles, and the reforms that it instituted lasted long after the threat of further Protestant territorial gains in Europe had subsided. The educational initiatives it instituted at the level of dioceses and parishes, the directions it gave for priestly vocation, and even the enthusiasm it instilled for renewed biblical study were all lasting gains that served the church well. The council provided a new charter for Roman Catholic life, one that was translated into numerous new situations across the world. So effective was it in this regard that the structures it bequeathed to what eventually became known as the Tridentine church were to endure for another three centuries, carrying Roman Catholics through some of the most turbulent waters in its history.

The legacy of a turbulent century

Christianity in the first half of the sixteenth century in Europe became far more diverse than it had ever been before. In 1500, Christianity worldwide could still be divided into two major streams of Roman Catholic and Orthodox life. Among the Orthodox there were several communions, but they shared a general sense of belonging to a common ancient tradition. In western Europe at the beginning of the sixteenth century there were several communities that had formed themselves outside the Roman Catholic Church. Waldensians had survived mostly because of the inaccessibility of their homes in the mountains of northern Italy. The Hussites and Lollards lived in eastern Europe and England, but were often forced to do so underground. By 1600 these small marginal movements in the West were joined by major new Lutheran, Reformed, Anglican, and Anabaptist streams of tradition. The first three of these churches and communities had the support of magistrates or of city councils. Two of them, the Lutheran and Reformed streams, shared a much stronger evangelical commitment to the authority of scripture, setting them somewhat apart from the Anglicans in their Protestant identity.

The fourth stream, the Anabaptists, which later historians would also call the Radical Reformation, had roots in earlier Christian experience, but only became a separate stream of tradition in the sixteenth century. Those within this fourth stream tended to look to the scriptures to guide them in recovering what they considered to be the authentic church. Some, such as Mennonites, became enduring fellowships, or organized bodies of churches. The Mennonites in particular provided an important connection with a movement in England in the seventeenth century that would later claim simply to be Baptist. A second group of Radical Reformers looked for immediate inspiration of the Holy Spirit and the imminent reign of God on earth. Few of these groups, like the followers of Thomas Müntzer and Kaspar Schwenkfeld, developed strong and enduring followings, and yet they provide a link in the long tradition of Holy Spirit churches that today identify themselves as Pentecostal or Charismatic, as well as many indigenous Spirit churches around the world. A third group that emerged from the Radical Reformation can perhaps be termed "evangelical rationalists," and provide the foundations for what eventually became Unitarianism. These three streams of the Radical Reformation together formed the foundation of a powerful new stream of Christianity that was independent of magistrates and spiritual in orientation. They joined those who remained faithful to the dominant tradition in the West of Roman Catholic faith in making up European Christianity in the sixteenth century.

Suggestions for further reading

Duffy, Eamon, *The Stripping of the Altars: Traditional Religion in England 1400–1580*. New Haven, CT: Yale University Press, 1992.
Hillerbrand, Hans, *The Division of Christendom: Christianity in the Sixteenth Century*. Louisville, KY: Westminster John Knox, 2007.

Lindberg, Carter, *The European Reformations.* Oxford: Blackwell Publishers, 1996.

MacCulloch, Diamaid, *The Reformation.* New York: Viking Books, 2003.

O'Malley, John W., *The First Jesuits.* Cambridge: Harvard University Press, 1993.

O'Malley, John W., *Trent and All That: Renaming Catholicism in the Early Modern Era.* Cambridge: Harvard University Press, 2000.

Ozment, Steven, *The Age of Reform (1250-1550): An Intellectual and Religious History of Late Medieval and Reformation Europe.* New Haven, CT: Yale University Press, 1980.

5

Orthodoxy amid the Empires

The sixteenth century was a time of global Christian transformations. In South America, Africa, and east Asia, Christianity was being introduced or re-introduced in connection with a new global colonial enterprise, while in western Europe the integrated complex of Latin Christendom was fracturing. During this same period Christianity along the border of eastern Europe and western Asia was undergoing a new era of persecution. Those Orthodox churches that looked to the office of the ecumenical patriarch for leadership were struggling with the political and cultural ramifications of that ancient office now being firmly under Ottoman Muslim rulers. Other Orthodox churches farther east struggled with changing tides in the Persian empire. At both ends of the continent of Asia the spread of Islam in the fifteenth and sixteenth centuries (by trade in the east and by military force in the west) was affecting the affairs of Orthodox Christian churches.

Islamic empires

Two great Islamic empires defined much of the political life of western Asia in the sixteenth century. The Ottomans, who were Sunni Muslims, ruled much of western Asia and parts of eastern Europe while the Safavid dynasty, a Shi'a dynasty that came to power in 1501, controlled Persia. A third Muslim empire, the Mughals, ruled farther east, in India. A fourth formidable Islamic power was located in Africa, the Mameluke dynasty in Egypt. Although these Islamic states struggled with one another politically, they formed a continuous Islamic cultural and religious zone of influence that extended from southeastern Europe, across northern Africa, and into southern Asia. The internal divisions within the Islamic world became more important politically for Christianity in western Asia and eastern Europe through the course of the sixteenth and seventeenth centuries as the Ottomans turned toward the West and away from their Islamic co-religionists. Throughout all of these regions, however, Christians lived as minorities under conditions that often amounted to outright persecution. In the sixteenth century most Orthodox churches were located within Islamic political empires. Only the Russian and Ethiopian churches were under Christian political rulers.

Orthodox churches in the fifteenth and sixteenth centuries were organized into several major communions. The divisions that separated them reached back deep into the historical past to the fifth century and the controversies around the nature of Jesus Christ that had been debated at the Council of Chalcedon in 451. The African churches of the Copts and the Ethiopians were non-Chalcedonian in theology. Often called Monophysites in the West, they shared a common theology (although a separate hierarchy) with the West Syrian and Armenian Orthodox communions that lived mostly under Ottoman rule. The churches that were under Persian Islamic rule were members of the East Syrian tradition and included in their communion, prior to the arrival of the Portuguese in the sixteenth century, the St. Thomas Christians of South India. The East Syrian tradition also rejected the decisions of the Council of Chalcedon, but for reasons on the other side of the Ethiopian, Coptic, Armenian, and West Syrian churches. They were usually called Nestorian in the West.

The churches under Ottoman rule in western Asia and eastern Europe that were Chalcedonian in theology were in large measure inheritors of the Greek Orthodox tradition and under the authority of the ecumenical patriarch. After 1453 the ecumenical patriarch was the head of a *dhimmi* community under an Islamic ruler. The ecumenical patriarch in effect became a political head of a minority community within an Islamic state. The Ottoman sultan appointed the ecumenical patriarch from a list of candidates nominated by the Holy Synod, but removed the patriarch at will, which often happened. The Orthodox Church in Russia, which in the sixteenth century was located almost entirely within the kingdom of Muscovy, shared a common faith and tradition with the Greek church. The head of the Russian Orthodox Church had for centuries been a metropolitan who was technically considered to be under the ecumenical patriarch in rank. In 1589 the Russian Church elevated that office to the rank of a patriarch, in effect separating the Russian Orthodox Church from the Greek Orthodox administratively. The communion between the two churches was not broken. Russian and Greek Orthodox could still worship together. But the ecumenical patriarch in Istanbul (which the Greek Orthodox Church continued to refer to as "Constantinople") no longer played a role in the selection of the head of the Russian Orthodox Church.

The history and identity of the ecumenical patriarch had since at least the fifth century been inextricably intertwined with the Byzantine empire. The Ottoman forces that entered Constantinople in 1453 brought the last remnants of the ancient Byzantine empire to an end, setting the patriarchate within an entirely new context. The Ottomans quickly consolidated their power through most of the Balkans, reaching deep into the nation of Hungary the following century. In language that was reminiscent of the Christian crusades, the Ottoman rulers understood their effort to be a religious struggle (*jihad* in Arabic) against the Christian West. Symbolic of their mission to spread Islamic culture was their removal of all Christian symbols from the nine-hundred-year-old cathedral of Hagia Sophia in the city of Constantinople (which the Ottomans renamed Istanbul) and the transformation of the great basilica into a mosque. The westward expansion of the Ottomans reached its end in the sixteenth century. Their rule in eastern Europe came to be especially tenuous and fragile. But the division, distrust, and destabilization it brought to the church, especially in the Balkans, were significant.

With the loss of Christian control of Constantinople in 1453, both Rome and the "Third Rome" (Moscow) became more important in providing Christian leadership worldwide. In eastern Europe Christian identity became even more closely identified with ethnic identity. Ottoman rule in the first years after the conquest of Constantinople was by most accounts oppressive. Christians living under Safavid rule in Persia were treated with more respect and had greater freedom. Conditions began to improve somewhat for Christians in the Ottoman empire toward the end of the sixteenth century as the Ottoman rulers became more involved both politically and economically with western Europe. In both the Ottoman and Safavid empires, Christians continued to live as minority people. Church leaders learned to make the compromises necessary to ensure the survival of their communities.

Christians under Ottoman rule

The Ottoman expansion to the West can be seen as something of a historical counter-crusade. In waging it, Ottoman rulers were among the first to use the language of *jihad*, which is often translated as "holy war" but in Arabic simply means "struggle," to unite the various ethnic factions in their armies in a common mission. By the time of the fall of Constantinople under Sultan Mehmed II (1451-1481), the Ottomans had already taken control of most of the Byzantine empire. Constantinople was ransacked for three days before its reorganization as an Islamic city began. The new Muslim rulers renamed the city "Istanbul," the popular term used by Muslim merchants prior to the fifteenth century that derived from the generic Greek word for a city (*polis*). Chief among the concerns of the new Muslim rulers of Istanbul was the appointment of an ecumenical patriarch who would be the head of the newly subjugated Orthodox Christian community that was now *dhimmi,* or a "protected minority." Meanwhile Mehmed was not about to rest content with his conquest of Constantinople but pressed on with the goal of eliminating Christian political rule from the face of the earth. His last great effort before his death was to dispatch an army against Rome in 1480. The army was on Italian soil the following year but turned back when news came that the sultan had died.

After the death of Mehmed II the Ottomans suspended further military efforts in the west against Europe, at least for a time. Selim "the Grim" (1466-1520), grandson of Mehmed II, turned his attention first toward the new Safavid rulers in Persia who were Shi'a Muslims. Selim captured the Persian capital of Tabriz in 1514, but then withdrew when it was clear he could not hold the city. He then turned his attention toward the Mamelukes who ruled Egypt and Syria, defeating the Mameluke army in Syria in 1516 and in Egypt the following year, in 1517.

Selim had a taste for the artistic. He brought some of the finest works of art and artisans from Syria and Egypt to Istanbul, resulting in a collection of magnificent works that remain in Istanbul today.

The golden age of the Ottoman empire was arguably that of the Suleiman I (1494-1566), who came to power in 1520. Known as "the Magnificent" to Europeans, but as "the Lawgiver" to his subjects, Suleiman not only consolidated Ottoman rule with great splendor, but he also conquered a large part of Hungary in 1526, laid siege to Vienna in 1529, dominated the north coast of Africa, and drove the Portuguese navy out of the Red Sea. This cosmopolitan ruler on three continents even entered the religious wars in Christian Europe, responding to a call at one point from Protestant princes to go to war against the Catholic emperor Charles V. Following Suleiman I, however, the Ottomans began to decline in their territorial reach. In Persia the Safavid rulers recovered from their defeat and consolidated their hold over their territories. The Ottomans continued to exercise nominal rule over Egypt and Syria, but they found that they could not effectively govern without the collaboration of members of the Mameluke nobility. In 1571 the Ottoman navy was handed a decisive defeat by Roman Catholic forces in the last major battle of galley ships in the Battle of Lepanto (in the Gulf of Corinth, off the coast of Greece). Over the next 350 years they continued to rule an empire that reached from Bosnia to Persia and included Palestine and Arabia, but they could no longer claim to be an expanding power.

Christians within the Ottoman empire were organized into two different *millet* communities in the fifteenth and sixteenth centuries. The Greek-speaking Orthodox were under the political and social rule of the ecumenical patriarch, who became as much the political representative of Greek-speaking Orthodox Christians before the sultanate as he was head of the Greek-speaking Orthodox community in the Ottoman empire. The Orthodox Christian millet, which the Ottomans called the *Rum Millet*, or Roman Nation, was the largest of the religious minorities in their realm. The Ottomans also recognized the Armenian patriarch in Cilicia, in the city of Sis (modern Kozan, Turkey) as head of the Armenian Orthodox churches under their rule, and thus as the one who represented Armenians politically in the court of the sultanate. This was a different patriarch than the catholicos in Etchmiadzin, the historic administrative see of the Armenian Orthodox Church in the Armenian homeland. Because the Ottomans did not exercise direct rule over Egypt and Syria even after 1516 but allowed the Mameluke nobility to exercise a degree of autonomy, they did not become directly involved in either West Syrian or Coptic Orthodox affairs. The Ottomans placed all Slavic-rite churches under the ecumenical patriarch, increasing the power of his office and creating greater tensions between what had been smaller autocephalous communions and the Greek church. Roman Catholic and East Syrian Christians who lived under Ottoman rule were represented by the Armenian patriarch. A separate Jewish millet community was headed by a rabbi elected by the rabbinical council in Istanbul and approved by the Ottoman rulers.

Election of the ecumenical patriarch remained nominally under the control of the Holy Synod in the new city of Istanbul, but in fact the Sultan played the most significant role in his selection. To assume office a patriarch was required to have an official document from the sultan known as a *berat*. The *berat* was not easy to procure and generally involved a significant bribe, the expense of which was passed on to the bishops and local churches. Furthermore, once elected, the patriarch served entirely at the whim of the sultan. Of the 150 patriarchs selected from the fifteenth to the twentieth centuries, 105 were driven from office by ruling sultans. Many others were removed from office by the bishops, went into exile voluntarily, or were murdered. Only twenty-one died in office.

Limitations were placed on the size of church buildings and the repairs that were allowed under Ottoman law. Christian women were often forced into marriage with Ottoman men, many of whom under Islamic law took several wives. Christians of both genders were restricted in the means of travel they were allowed (no horses), the colors of their textiles and clothes, and even what types of clothes that could be worn. On top of all of these regulations were the annual taxes. Christians were to pay an annual head tax (*cizye*) for every male over twelve years old. Every seven years the sultan would also require a special levy called a *devsirme*, a special human tax where fit youth were selected by the sultan's household to be enslaved, converted to Islam, and educated for the military or for use in the administration. It was to the benefit of the empire to keep the *dhimmi* numbers high, for it meant more revenue and more future soldiers.

The tense and complex relationships that developed between the Ottoman Turkish overlords and the persecuted millet community in Serbia came to be associated with the memory of the first archbishop of the Serbian Church, Sava I, who had died several centuries earlier in 1235. Two years after having been initially buried in the Cathedral of the Holy Forty Martyrs in Trnovo, Sava's body was disinterred and moved to his homeland where he was set to rest at the Mileshevo monastery. While workers were preparing the body for reburial, as the story went, the casket was opened and the body was found in life-like preservation, a delightful smell filling the sanctuary all the while. Word spread rapidly and St. Sava began receiving thousands of guests, including (according to the tradition) Roman Catholics, Greek Orthodox, and even Jews.

The Mileshevo monastery became an even more important place of pilgrimage after the arrival of the Turks in 1389. St. Sava became a figure of national hope and solidarity. His image was often put on Serbian flags, and even Turks reportedly began to tell of his healings. The unity built around the national veneration of St. Sava (called *Svetosavlje*) became an even greater irritant to the Ottoman authorities in 1595 when his memory helped to inspire a revolt against their rule. The insurrection of St. Sava was led by Jovan (John) Kantul (r. 1592-1613), a bishop whom the Serbian Orthodox considered to be their patriarch. The revolt was put down, but in its aftermath the Ottoman rulers determined it was best to take away its inspiration. On Holy Friday in 1595 Turkish troops descended on the Mileshevo monastery, removed the body of St. Sava, and had it burned. As is often the case, the desire to quench the nationalistic religious spirit of a people only serves to inflame it. Serbs continued to hold the memory of the burning of the relics of St. Sava with great passion.

The Armenian community felt the impact of the divisions between the Ottoman and Safavid empires most acutely. The historic Armenian homeland was on the border between these two Islamic powers that were often at odds with each other, if not engaged in outright war. Over the previous millennium, the Armenian Orthodox Church had been fractured into several competing hierarchies, each being under a different political power. The Ottomans added to their number in 1461 when Mehmed removed the Armenian archbishop from Bursa in the Caucasus, established his seat in the new Ottoman capital of Istanbul, and gave him the title of "patriarch." After Selim I's further conquests in the Caucasus, the seat of the Armenian catholicos was removed from Sis to Istanbul.

One of the most important Armenian leaders of this period was the catholicos Michael of Sebastia (1545-1576). It was Michael who brought the printing press to the Armenian community. An emissary was dispatched to Venice in 1562 to learn about the new technology. Three years later the first book was published in the Armenian script in Italy. Very quickly Armenian printing houses sprang up across Europe in cities such as Rome and Amsterdam, as well as in western Asia in Istanbul, Isfahan, and Echmiadzin. Scattered and divided, the Armenian Church had long been held together by its literature, its religion, and national heritage. To this was now added the power of the printing press.

The first generation of Ottoman rule in eastern Europe had the effect of sending Orthodox Christians to the West. The new divisions among Christians in the West in the sixteenth century had the effect of sending both Protestants and Catholics to the East. Both Protestant and Catholic rulers sought to court the ecumenical patriarch as a potential ally. Luther's interest in the Greek New Testament and the Greek theologians of the first several centuries underscored his belief that the Orthodox Church was closer to following the tradition of Jesus than was Rome. Several of his disciples, including Melanchthon, sought to make contact directly with their contemporaries in the Greek Orthodox Church, although no genuine theological exchange occurred until the 1570s. The exchange was initiated by Lutheran theologians from Tübingen, who were accompanying a German embassy to the Ottoman court and called upon the patriarch, Jeremiah II (1530-1595), in 1575. The Lutherans brought a translation of the *Augsburg Confession,* which the patriarch read and penned a critical response to. More correspondence followed without the two parties achieving anything that could be remotely considered an agreement. Nevertheless, the exchange in the 1570s can be considered the first bilateral dialogue between Protestants or evangelicals and the Orthodox.

The Coptic Church in Egypt

The Coptic Church had struggled under Mameluke rule for centuries, but it had survived. Its survival in part was due to the fact that Copts played an important role in Egyptian society. Coptic Christians in Egypt were forced by the very logic of their existence as a marginal and taxed community to turn to mercantile activities in order to survive. They were also better educated than many of their Egyptian neighbors. The Mamelukes relied on educated Copts for civil administration, tax collection and accounting, and legal counsel to a considerable extent. Mameluke rulers often provided financial incentives to Copts to convert to Islam, but few did, leaving the Egyptian rulers no choice but to hire Christians to administer their government. Its relationship with Ethiopia was also helpful for the Coptic Church. Ethiopia, as a Christian nation, had Muslims under its territorial rule, and threatened to persecute the Muslims if the Mamelukes persecuted the Copts. Although such diplomatic threats provided only a very limited security blanket for the Coptic community at any given time, they were important. During the Mameluke reign, persecution of the Coptic Church never fully abated. The Mamelukes put an end to the important Coptic celebration of the Feast of the Martyrs, for instance, and engaged in periodic destruction of Coptic Church buildings. By some accounts, no Coptic Church building escaped at least partial destruction at the hands of the Mamelukes during the centuries of their rule. Nevertheless, the community and its churches survived.

Mameluke rule came effectively to an end in 1517 when the Ottomans under Selim I invaded and conquered Egypt. The Coptic community greeted the change with hopeful anticipation at first, but they were soon disappointed. Selim forced a number of builders, craftpersons, artists, and scholars to be relocated to Istanbul, many of them Coptic Christians. The effect was to weaken Egypt as a whole in the long run. Under the Ottomans the Coptic community suffered increasing hardship. A large number of ancient Coptic manuscripts were destroyed, resulting in a significant loss for later generations of historians of the church. The Ottoman rulers introduced a number of new measures that restricted the Coptic pope's exercise of authority within the church and community. Popes found their time to be increasingly occupied with collecting taxes and trying to protect the Christian community from further persecution. Some turned to questionable financial transactions in an effort to raise the necessary funds that their rulers demanded. Finally, the Ottomans never succeeded in placing their own rulers in positions of government in Egypt, but they tended to rely on the older Mameluke aristocracy. Change in the end did not bring much in the way of change for Coptic Christians in Egypt.

One of the more famous Coptic popes during the sixteenth century was the long-reigning Gabriel VII (r. 1525-1568). Gabriel is often remembered for his efforts to rebuild monastic life, including physically rebuilding the famous monasteries of St. Paul and St. Anthony. These two institutions had been destroyed in 1484 by Muslim opponents. The buildings had been greatly damaged, and many of their manuscripts had been burned. Gabriel arranged to have the monasteries rebuilt and monks from the Monastery of the Virgin Mary (*Deir El Surian*) to help develop monastic life within their walls again. Tragically, both monasteries were again raided and destroyed. All of the monks who had been sent to live there were killed. Still Gabriel would not be deterred. Once again he organized the rebuilding of the monasteries, this time renovating the Maimoun and El-Mouharak (St. Mary's) monasteries in Upper Egypt and the famous monastery of St. Anthony along the Red Sea as well. As a result of this rebuilding, the church in Egypt was strengthened by the well-educated leaders that these institutions eventually produced. St. Anthony's in particular became an important center for training future popes for the Coptic Church, doing so well into the middle of the nineteenth century.

During Gabriel's reign, the Ottoman rulers increased the *jizia* (*cizye*) taxes required of all those in the millet communities by one thousand dinars per year. The annual taxes were to be collected by priests, and the Coptic pope was responsible for ensuring that they were paid. Gabriel simply could not secure the funds. In an effort to avoid torture and probable death, he took flight to the fortress-like monastery of St. Anthony, dying on the way.

The Coptic community living on the island of Cyprus seems to have been reduced almost to oblivion during the sixteenth century. There are records of Coptic bishops leading the Coptic community in Cyprus in the early decades of the century. When the Turks invaded Cyprus in the middle of the century, the Coptic community was targeted for persecution. Soon after the Turkish invasion, Armenian Christians took over former Coptic churches and monasteries such as St. Anthony in Nicosia and St. Makarios (*Sourp Magar*) in the north of the island, with no apparent Coptic presence in them remaining.

The pressures put on the Coptic Church by the Ottoman Turks were bad enough, but from Rome came a different kind of pressure, similar to that being placed on both the Ethiopian and South Indian churches. Rome sought to subsume all of these Orthodox churches under the authority of the Roman pope. Envoys from Rome wooed all four of the sixteenth century's Coptic popes. At one point the Coptic Church nearly took the Roman offer, hoping for protection from the Ottomans and their Egyptian rulers in exchange for submission to the Roman pope. Gregory XIII of Rome (1502-1585) sent a delegation to Egypt to try to convince John XIV of Cairo (r. 1573-1589) to accept the offer. A special council was called, and bishops and monks met at the city of Menph in February of 1583. The council was divided. Those who refused to submit reminded the council that their ancestors had resisted other churches and other religions, and that there was now a long line of martyrs praying that the church would remain faithful. On the other side were more practical and political arguments. The church was suffering under Muslim rulers and needed protection. An alliance with Rome could bring support. No decision was made at this time as John XIV died suddenly, cutting the conversation off. His successor, Gabriel VIII (r. 1587-1603), did not pursue it.

Christians under Safavid Persian rule

Orthodox Christians living under Ottoman rule faced significant challenges, but they hardly compared to those faced by East Syrian Orthodox Christians living within the adjacent Safavid empire of Persia in the sixteenth century. The only significant contact that the East Syrian Church had with other Christians for several centuries had been with the St. Thomas Christians of South India, and even this amounted to little more than the occasional consecration of metropolitans or bishops from Persia. By the founding of the Safavid dynasty in 1501, the East Syrian Church had been reduced to scattered groups of believers, many in the mountainous regions of present-day eastern Turkey and northern Iraq and Iran. The massive destruction a century earlier under Timur the Great (or Tamerlane) had left them severely weakened. The Safavid, like other Muslim rulers, continued to mark the Christians as a separate community with diminished rights. The fact that these scattered and struggling Christian communities of the East Syrian communion survived at all is astonishing.

The Safavid dynasty began when a thirteen-year-old named Isma'il (1487-1524) from a Sufi Muslim family in northern Iran converted to the Shi'a branch of Islam and rose to power. Many among his Shi'a followers believed that he was the mystical Hidden Imam of Shi'a Islamic tradition, a messianic figure who was a direct descendant of the Prophet Muhammad, and who would come in the final days of history to restore the true faith over all the earth. These followers quickly proved to be a formidable force. After taking Azerbaijan they moved south into Iran. A decade later his army was conquering deep into central Asia. He was also intent on spreading his Shi'a faith, the main reason why the Ottoman rulers invaded his realm and took his capital city of Tabriz. The Ottoman army did not hold the city long, but their efforts effectively stopped for a time the westward spread of Shi'a beliefs into Ottoman territories. Meanwhile under Isma'il, Sunni leaders were expelled or killed, leaving the Shi'a party dominant in Persia.

The scattered Christian communities that survived the destruction of the fourteenth century had little opportunity to regroup under the Safavid rulers. Although the Safavids did not engage in direct persecution, the continued pressures of Islamic rule prevented any reorganization, much less growth, on the part of the East Syrian Church. The normal method of passing on leadership through elections by the bishops by the first decades of the fifteenth century had come to an end. It was simply impossible for bishops of the church to gather in a synod to elect or consecrate new episcopal leadership, even a patriarch. Out of necessity East Syrian bishops (who were celibate) would simply pass the office down to a nephew or younger brother. This hereditary pattern made for a severe narrowing of church leadership and opened ecclesiastical appointments to abuses, but it became the only effective means for ensuring episcopal succession.

The East Syrian Church was further weakened by a major division in 1552. Patriarch Shimon (Simon) VII (r. 1539-1558) was accused by other bishops of serious moral failings. Apparently he had also named his twelve-year-old nephew to be his eventual successor. A number of prominent leaders (including three bishops) used this as an occasion to launch a protest and proceeded to elect an alternative candidate named Yohannan Sūlaqa (c. 1510-1555) as patriarch. In the meantime Shimon VII's nephew died, so the patriarch designated another nephew, this one fifteen years old, to succeed him. Although Shimon VII was still living, a number of bishops recognized instead as their patriarch Yohannan Sūlaqa, who took the name Shimon VIII. In 1558 Shimon VII died and his designated successor, Eliya VII (c. 1537–1591), claimed the patriarchal title as well, meaning there were now two patriarchs, Shimon VIII's "new line" and Eliya VII's "old line."

Things became even more complicated when the Franciscan missionaries in the region, who were intent on bringing East Syrian Christians under the authority of the Roman Church, backed the "new line" Shimon, Sūlaqa. With Franciscan support Sūlaqa traveled to Jerusalem and then on to Rome, where he made a confession of faith before the pope and was appointed "Patriarch of the Chaldeans." Upon his return home he located his patriarchal see in the city of Amid (now Diyarbakır, in Turkey) but within two years was arrested by the local governor (perhaps at the instigation of Shimon VII), tortured, and executed. Upon his death, Abdisho IV Maron (r. 1555-1570), whom Sūlaqa had previously consecrated as a metropolitan, became patriarch of the Chaldeans in the new line that was now in communion with Rome. In 1562 he traveled to Rome and received the papal blessing. The new line came to be called Chaldean Catholic. Its churches continued to use the ancient Syriac liturgy in worship and maintain Orthodox practices. Rome expected to appoint the patriarch, however, who located the patriarchal see in monasteries for protection.

The Russian Orthodox Church

As the Orthodox churches in Egypt, Anatolia (modern Turkey), and the Balkans were entering this long period of domination under Muslim Ottoman rulers, the church of Russia was coming out from under several centuries of Muslim Mongol rule. The "Golden Horde," as the Mongol conquerors had been known in Russia, had never been as aggressive in promoting the Islamic faith as were the Ottomans. The Mongols (or Tartars as they were sometimes known) in Russia had not turned churches into mosques, for instance, and had not taxed churches and clergy as other Muslim rulers in other parts of the world had done. Under Mongol rule, which ended in 1480, churches and monasteries remained repositories of art treasures. Christian educational institutions continued, and the hierarchy of the church was allowed to continue its work more or less unmolested. Although the Mongol rulers in Russia had formally converted to Islam several centuries before, they remained strongly shamanistic in their religious beliefs and practices, and continued to follow the older Mongol practice of religious toleration in their realm.

Five years before the fall of Constantinople, in 1448, the Russian bishops took the step of appointing their own metropolitan apart from the ecumenical patriarch in Constantinople. It was this step that finally established the Russian Church as autocephalous. The separation did not happen suddenly. Signs of it were apparent already at the Council of Florence a decade before, when delegates from Constantinople agreed to enter into communion with Rome, but the Russian hierarchy refused to do so. The union that the council achieved ended with the fall of Constantinople in 1453 and the Ottomans forced the selection of a new ecumenical patriarch. After 1453 the Russian Church conducted its affairs apart from the patriarch in Istanbul.

In 1480 the Grand Duke of Moscow, Ivan III (1440-1505), succeeded in overthrowing the last of the Mongol rulers and established a new independent kingdom. In a telling indication of the significance he believed his rule to hold, Ivan took the title of *tsar* (or *czar*, Russian for Caesar) and used the symbol of the double-headed eagle of Byzantium to represent his glory. Eight years earlier he prepared for this enthronement by marrying Zoe Palaiologina (1455-1503), the niece of the last Byzantine emperor. Under Ivan III Russia took on the mantle of the ancient Christian Byzantine empire. Moscow was now to be "the Third Rome."

The church in Russia played an important social and political role under Mongol rule. It often served as mediator in disputes among the Russian princes, or between princes and Mongol *khans*, and intervened on behalf of the Russian people with the Mongol tax collectors. With the emergence of a new Russian national dynasty the role of the church became even more important. More than any other institution, the church was seen as the heart of Russian national unity and the foundation for rebuilding Russian society.

Princes and other rulers in Russia for several centuries played little role in church affairs. Under the Mongol rulers, Constantinople made the appointment of the head of the Russian Church. Things changed in 1448 when Metropolitan Ionas (or Jonas, d. 1461) was elected by the other Russian bishops at a council that was called by the Grand Duke of Moscow. The political association with Moscow was telling, for the historical center for Russian Christianity had not been in Moscow, but in Kiev, farther south. By the end of the fifteenth century the center of the Russian Church had decisively moved north to Moscow and was identified closely with the new national independent political state under Ivan. From that point on Russia's political rulers began to play a more active role in governing church affairs.

The symbol of Moscow as the Third Rome became widely associated during this period with the popular story of "the white cowl." This legendary tale told of a white cowl, or hooded cloak, that Constantine had supposedly given to Pope Sylvester I in Rome in the fourth century as a sign of Rome's authority. The cowl then passed on to Constantinople after the city of Rome had fallen to invaders the following century. With the fall of Constantinople, the story went on, the cowl appeared in Novgorod where it was worn by the archbishop of that city. The political significance of this theological passage was made even more explicit by a monk named Philotheus of Pskov (1465-1542), who first recorded the story in 1510. The Russian ruler was one of only two Christian emperors left on earth. The true church was no longer led by Rome or Constantinople, but now by Moscow. A number of Christians throughout the world in the sixteenth century believed that Jesus would one day return to earth to reign over the Christian empire that had already been formed on earth. For many Russians, theirs was now that church and empire over which Christ would reign upon his return.

One of the more unusual theological developments in the last decades of the fifteenth century in Russia was a Judaizing movement (*zhidovstvuiushchie*) within the church. Mikhail Alexander Olel'kovich (r. 1479-1500) was an Orthodox Christian from Kiev of Lithuanian royal descent who had settled in Novgorod. He brought with him his Jewish doctor, Skharia (Zachariah, dates unknown), and two Jewish merchant friends. In the 1470s these three well-educated Jews, supported by Olel'kovich, began to engage in theological debates with church leaders in Novgorod, arguing for the superiority of the Old Testament (Jesus himself said he came to fulfill the Law, meaning the Old Testament), and the impossibility of God becoming human. Christ was only a prophet, they asserted, and the doctrine of the Trinity was really a belief in three gods. Not only did they oppose icons in the churches, but even the image of the cross. Their teachings took on both an air of secrecy and of superiority. Some of the men in the city were secretly circumcised, and privately enrolled in the new society.

The movement soon spread thanks to the surprising support of Grand Prince of Moscow Ivan III (1440-1505). On a visit to Novgorod in 1479 two Judaizing priests managed to arrange a meeting with the Moscow ruler. Ivan was impressed with them, and as protector of the church of Russia appointed the two to be rectors of the main cathedral in Moscow. Anti-trinitarian belief was thus brought into the very heart of the Third Rome. It appears that Ivan, his daughter-in-law Helen of Moldavia (1485-1505), and others in the royal family all converted to this teaching. Ivan's ambassador to Hungary during this period, Feodor Vasiliyevich Kuritsyn (d. c. 1500), upon his return to Moscow likewise became a supporter of the anti-trinitarian belief. Kuritsyn apparently already had contact with similar teachings among Unitarians in Poland. In Russia he became a leader of the Judaizers.

The Judaizing movement reached its peak in Russia in the 1490s. In 1490 a Judaizing metropolitan named Zosima (r. 1490-1494) was elected. Zosima joined the Judaizing movement with its apocalyptic expectations, the belief that Moscow was now the Third Rome, and various doctrines of astrology and alchemy. In Novgorod Archbishop Gennady (r. 1484–1504), who was a man of more zeal than erudition, and an abbot of considerable theological gifts named Joseph of Volotsk (or Joseph Volotsky, 1440-1515) led the attack against the movement. Joseph made his case in the pages of *Prosvetitel* ("The Enlightener"), which was written to refute the Judaizers. Councils to address the movement were held in Novgorod, out of the reach of the Muscovites, in 1488 and 1490, the latter being the same year as the elevation of Zosima. The teachings of the Judaizers were condemned. Gennady and Joseph sought the death penalty for nine of the movement's leaders in Novgorod, but in the end the council determined that their punishment would be banishment to a monastery. Moscow remained under the control of the Judaizers until the death of Ivan III in 1505 removed their political support. Several trials were held, resulting in six leaders of the movement being condemned to be burned at the stake, while others were banished to monasteries. By 1510 the movement had all but died, even in Moscow.

While the Judaizers had a brief reign in Russian Orthodox history, their presence left a lasting theological legacy in the form of Abbot Joseph's work, *The Enlightener*, and other treatises defending the Orthodox Christian faith. Also notable from this period was the effort to translate the Bible into Slavonic. Archbishop Gennady was one of the strongest proponents of this endeavor. The project was completed by 1500, predating Luther's translation of the German Bible by several decades, but because of the late arrival of the printing press in Russia, it was not made available to the wider church until 1582.

Spirituality, property, and wealth were intertwined in one of the most protracted struggles in Russian Church life during this period. At stake was the extent of influence monasteries exercised in the church. Under Mongol rule, churches and monasteries had actually grown in the wealth that they controlled in Russia, but such wealth, along with the political involvement that the church exercised, was seen by a number of monks as having a corrupting spiritual influence. Reforming monks would move away from the cities and towns out into forests and wilderness regions to escape these corruptions. Once such monks settled in remote areas, however, peasants would often follow them, building small communities that would later become towns with governments and military outposts. The semi-eremitic monks, sensing a new worldliness, would then move farther out into wilderness areas. In this way the Russian empire expanded. Contact with Turkik, Mongolian, and Finnic peoples on its frontiers came about as well over time by this monastic migration.

By the end of the Mongol period in 1480, monasteries controlled (often as good-sized fiefdoms) about one-third of the land in Russia. Much of it had been acquired through the growth that followed these migrations. Monastic life in the past had been patterned after the most famous Russian saint, St. Sergius of Radonezh (c. 1314-1392), who as an advisor to the grand duke modeled ascetic detachment and humility in his service. After centuries of accumulating lands and wealth, monasteries became wealthy, and monks became more concerned with crops, servants, and the price of agricultural goods than living the self-denying life of Jesus.

This was the context for one of the most important monastic reformers in Russian history, Nilus of Sorka (or Nil Sorskii, 1433-1508). Nilus was of peasant background, and he had dedicated himself to the life of the forest hermit, living beyond the Volga River. Much of the monastic life in Russia at the time was beholden to the *hesychastic* tradition associated with the community at Mt. Athos in the Mediterranean region. He had spent time at Mt. Athos and was a strong advocate of a rigorous *hesychastic* lifestyle. His concern to live a life of true humility extended even to his death. Nilus left no records of his own life so that no one could write of him. He requested that his body be cast into the wilderness to be eaten by animals so there would be no pilgrimages to his grave site.

Russian monks did not have religious orders or congregations as monks in the Latin tradition did. Most heads of monastic communities developed their own rule to guide the faithful. Nilus's rule sought to be more spiritual than legalistic, more inward than outward. He counseled repetition of the Jesus Prayer, self-denial and repentance, and the mental exercise of living in the shadow of one's own death. He even developed a new monastic architectural style to support this spirituality. Called a *skete*, the house was in fact a small cottage where only two to four monks lived in community. Located between the anchorite form of monastic isolation and the cenobitic form of monastic community, the *skete* ensured accountability and support, but of only a few companions and located away from the temptations of the world.

Nilus reportedly used the occasion of a church council in 1503 to launch an attack on monastic land ownership, a practice that had become a national issue in light of the vast monastic holdings. He spoke as a devotee of the tradition of Mt. Athos. On the other side of the debate was Abbott Joseph Volotsky, who earlier had a prominent role in opposing the Judaizers and who was the head of a large cenobitic establishment. Joseph responded in defense of monasteries possessing lands. The conflict thus soon became known as the "Possessors" (those who followed Joseph) and the "Non-Possessors" (those who followed Nilus) controversy.

Joseph's rule was rigorous and harsh. He made strenuous demands of his monks in terms of labor, service to the poor, and ascetic lifestyle. Women as well as young men without beards were strictly prohibited from being on the grounds of his monastery, which was located 70 km from Moscow, but he welcomed the presence of the wealthy and landed because they were the source of support for his ministries of charity. He was quick to criticize the wealthy for harsh treatment of servants or slaves, however, and he argued that it was the church's spiritual responsibility to establish schools and hospitals to care for the social needs of the poor. Wealth had to be directed toward its proper spiritual ends. At one point he is reported to have stated that even the wealth of the church actually belonged to the poor. But still he defended its accumulation. Large, wealthy monasteries and strict discipline were the best means of serving the pressing needs of the masses, he believed.

Aberrations in doctrine were considered by Joseph to pose an even greater danger than wealth to the church. He argued that heretics should be executed for they were murderers of the soul. Nilus, on the other hand, was an advocate of reeducation and penance for heretics, a stance that during the Judaizing controversy had for a time won the day. Joseph's view of Orthodoxy was in the tradition of institutional church and royal government working hand-in-hand to better represent the kingdom of heaven on earth. Nilus opted for an alternative relationship between monastery and state, one where the monks, in their detachment from the world and attachment to Christ, become models of holiness for all people. The contrast came to characterize the struggle between the Possessors and Non-Possessors in their controversy.

In 1503 most of the "Trans-Volga" hermits, along with other individual monks, supported Nilus and the Non-Possessors. But the overall majority of monks supported Joseph and the Possessors. The Non-Possessors had a difficult time making their argument since the work of the larger land-holding monasteries was visible to all. Joseph's monastery in particular was feeding some seven hundred people a day and helping to provide homes for the aged and orphans, seemingly overwhelming evidence of the truth of his claims for the value of property ownership. Joseph reasoned that large monasteries and aristocratic bishops were needed for the church to have a place and a voice in the larger society. Princes and other boyars (nobles) would respect those of their own class and social standing, and this respect must be assured if the church was to lead in society. Nilus, defeated by this reasoning, was still resolute that such attachment to the world led to worldly preoccupations and a denial of the suffering Christ. In fact, such attachment to the world turns the Christian into one who causes suffering and torture. No warrant could be found in the gospels, among the apostles, or in the church fathers for enslaving the peasants, the Non-Possessors argued.

The end of the conflict came in 1525-1526 when the Non-Possessors launched an attack on Grand Prince Vasili III (or Basil III, 1479-1533) for divorcing his wife without just cause. The tsar's reason was that the queen was barren, but this was not recognized by the Orthodox Church as legitimate grounds for divorce. Basil responded by sending many to prison and closing many of the Trans-Volga hermitages. The Non-Possessors, from that time on, were driven underground by the tsar with the support of most of the church leaders.

The Non-Possessor controversy in Russia had the effect of dichotomizing the central commitments of the monastic tradition. Monastic self-denial, humility, and detachment were set in conflict with service to the poor and needy in ways that were foreign to the ancient traditions. In its spiritual formation, the Russian Church drew closer to and more comfortable with the socially affluent and urbane elite. The loss of the prophetic witness of the followers of St. Nilus was the price to be paid.

One of the monastic figures who mediated between the two parties through this period was St. Maximus the Greek (c. 1470-1556). Maximus, a Greek by birth, was received in Russia after a time of theological development in the Italian cities of Florence and Venice. While in Italy he drank deeply of the various political, cultural, and theological movements of the period. From 1504 until 1517 he was an Orthodox monk at Mt. Athos and learned, like Nilus, from the hesychastic tradition. His writings and translations became widely known, not only in the Ottoman empire but as far as Moscow, leading Vasili III to invite him to come to Russia to translate Greek theological works into Latin. Maximus was more than happy to do so since his brief foray into the Roman monasticism of the Dominicans had turned him against the Roman Catholic Church. At Mt. Athos he had already begun writing works against Latin Christianity. In Moscow Maximus made his contribution as one of the greatest scholars in Russian Church history, writing a number of theological treatises, correcting Russian service books, and translating other liturgical and theological works.

Strong opinions not only about the First Rome (he was anti-Latin), but also about the Third Rome and her independence from the Second Rome, along with some careless translations into Slavonic (a language he was just learning) landed Maximus in hot water with Metropolitan Daniel (c. 1492-1547), a student of Abbott Joseph and a strong supporter of the Possessors. Caught in the middle of Russian theological disputes, Maximus found himself identified with the Non-Possessors; and in 1525 he landed in prison, where he remained for the next twenty-six years. Although imprisonment allowed him the freedom to write and freely worship, he was still restricted from movement and was never allowed to return to his beloved mother church in Constantinople.

Two new rulers rose to power during Maximus's imprisonment. Both were important historically, although Ivan IV (1530-1584), known as the "Terrible" (*Groznyi* in Russian), is remembered more today for his deeds than the Metropolitan Makarii (r. 1543-1563). Ivan was only three years of age when he assumed the title of Grand Prince of Moscow. His mother ruled in his stead for the first four years, whereupon she was poisoned by her opponents. From age seven to sixteen the boyars ruled for the young prince, but Ivan learned not to trust the courtly aristocracy. In 1547 Ivan assumed control of the government on his own, taking the title of tsar, the first Russian ruler to do so formally. After his coronation Ivan married Anastasia Romanovna Zakhariina (1530-1560), whose grand-nephew later became the first of the important line of tsars to take the name "Romanov."

Makarii became metropolitan of Moscow just as Ivan was coming into power, and is credited with having encouraged the young Ivan to assume the new title. As metropolitan, Makarii stood firmly within the Josephite tradition, which meant he was a strong supporter of the church wielding worldly power. To this end he was unwilling to release Maximus from his arrest. Makarii worked closely with the tsar to centralize both government and church administration. In 1551, one year after a new law code was passed, a special *sobor,* or council, was called to aid in a similar process for the church. A year later, in 1553, the *Stoblav Sobor,* or Hundred Chapters Council, adopted a new church constitution. Of note were the reforms in the area of education, whereby a national network of schools at each local parish was to be established which would provide basic literacy for all people. Colleges for training priests were to be set up under each bishop. Most of these required the government's backing and did not take place until a century later owing to Ivan's preoccupation with military expansion and defense.

One of Ivan's accomplishments was his conquest of the Tartars on his borders (by now mostly turned Muslim). In 1552 the Kazan Khan was destroyed, and in 1556 the Astrakhan Khan was turned back. This conquest was for Ivan a type of crusade against invading Muslims. Ivan understood himself to be a defender of the faith as well as the leader in propagating the Orthodox Church. Upon the completion of Ivan's conquest of Kazan, he commissioned a church to be built in memory of the victory on the feast day of the Intercession of the Virgin. Ivan wanted the church named the Cathedral of the Intercession of the Virgin on the Moat, but the Muscovite masses were more enamored by the colorful Basil the Blessed (c. 1468-1552), better known as Basil the Holy Fool (*yurodivy*), an eccentric who wandered the streets of Moscow naked as he begged on behalf of the poor, and who had ridiculed Ivan for not paying enough attention to building the church. The Holy Fool won out. The church eventually came to be known as St. Basil's, and the *yurodivy* himself is buried in it.

The architecture of St. Basil's showed complex theological levels of meaning. Heaven was represented by its eight towers, and then a ninth, much larger, tower in the center was built to unite the structure as a single sanctuary. The cathedral was positioned in such a way as to symbolize the geographical and cultural placement of Moscow, looking both to Europe and to Asia. The towers represented Persian, Turkish, Kazak, and Indian motifs, which were woven in to represent the expansion of the Orthodox Church throughout all of Asia.

Upon his wife's death in 1560 (a death that Ivan suspected was caused by poisoning and that has recently been confirmed by tests on her remains) the tsar became despondent. He retreated from the city for a period of time, and then filled with zeal and paranoia, returned to lead his country in a reign of terror that earned him the moniker "Terrible" throughout history. Ivan established a special private police force called the *oprichnina,* who dressed in monks' robes, wore hats like Mongols, and spread terror among the boyars, who were his main opponents. During this reign of terror it was difficult to find a metropolitan who would serve such a tsar. The first two choices requested that the *oprichnina* be reigned in or disbanded. Both died rather suddenly in monastic exile.

A third respected older monk named Feodor Stepanovich Kolychev (1507-1569), but better known by his monastic name, Philip, had already achieved renown for his engineering feats in building a monastery far to the north on the White Sea, as well as for his agricultural feats on behalf of the Arctic peoples ("those of the north"). In 1567 he agreed to accept the position as Metropolitan of Moscow on the condition that he would be free to speak up on behalf of the poor and oppressed, and that Ivan would abolish the *oprichnina*. Ivan accepted the arrangement, but then failed to change. Less than a year after becoming metropolitan, at a Sunday service during the celebration of the divine liturgy with Ivan present, Philip spoke out. He condemned the tsar in no uncertain terms for shedding innocent blood in the streets, warning him of the judgment of God that awaited such deeds. The tsar responded with a verbal blast of his own against the cleric. Philip, with the dispassion of a Non-Possessor, quietly responded that he was willing to suffer for the truth. A short time later Philip was arrested at the Cathedral of the Dormition (also known as the Cathedral of the Assumption). The tsar had the metropolitan deposed by a synod. The following year Philip was strangled in the monastery in Otroch by Ivan's chief *oprichnik*, Maliuta Skuratov (d. 1573).

The church could not resist the tyrannical rule of this type of a royal Russia. The irony was of course that Ivan saw himself as a religious leader even though he summarily rejected both the church's guidance and her leadership. In his last days, feeling remorse for the thousands of innocents he had slaughtered, he entered a period of repentance which included paying for prayers to be said for the dead, and then he had himself rechristened as "Monk Jonah." Ivan the Terrible was buried in a monk's habit, carrying the name Jonah.

Russia ended the sixteenth century in something of a state of political disarray. Ivan's son Feodor (or Theodore, 1557-1598) assumed the throne in 1584. He was religiously devoted, but was of generally poor health and left no heirs. Consumed with religious observance, in large part praying for the sins of his father, he left the task of ruling the country to his brilliant and creative brother-in-law, Boris Godunov (1551-1605). Following the death of Feodor, Godunov was crowned tsar.

In 1587 Godunov oversaw the election of a former abbot named Job (d. 1607), who was bishop of Kolomna, to be the new metropolitan of Moscow. The following year Patriarch Jeremias II of Constantinople (1530-1595) visited Moscow. The Ottomans had allowed the patriarch to travel to Poland and Russia, where he was seeking to raise funds for the Greek churches under Ottoman rule. Upon his arrival Jeremias was treated with great honor, but he soon discovered that he and his party were being held captive until he extended his recognition of autocephaly to the Russian Church. Godunov convinced the Greek patriarch to elevate the office of the metropolitan in Moscow to the rank of patriarch as well. Jeremias agreed, apparently offering his own name for the position. Godunov convinced him otherwise, and in 1589 Jeremias participated in the service of consecration that elevated Job to be the first patriarch of Moscow. The synod in Constantinople confirmed the action in 1593. Moscow was now ranked alongside the other ancient patriarchates of Jerusalem, Constantinople, Antioch, and Alexandria in dignity. Unfortunately, Job soon proved to be little more than a pawn in the hands of Godunov. His weakness would lead to trouble for the church down the road.

The fifteenth and sixteenth centuries saw a number of new developments in both Russian religious art and architecture. The eclectic and multicultural design of St. Basil's in Moscow was one example of this. It is one of four main cathedrals to be built in the Kremlin and one of two that were built solely by Russian architects within a sixty-year period. The other two churches built in this period were designed by Italians who incorporated newly developed Renaissance designs into Russian themes. The Cathedral of the Dormition, where Ivan IV was crowned in 1547, was started a number of times in the fourteenth and fifteenth centuries, but it was finally completed in 1479 by an Italian named Aristotele Fioravanti (c. 1415-c. 1485). Annunciation Cathedral, completed in 1489, was built as a chapel for the grand princes of Moscow and might well be described as the embodiment of royal Orthodox Russia. Designed by the best architects of Russia, four domed side chapels were added by Ivan IV, and the nine total domes were entirely coated in gold. The last great cathedral, dedicated to St. Michael the Archangel, was built between 1505 and 1509 by another Italian architect.

Designed and built by Italians, these cathedrals nevertheless reveal something of Russian Orthodox Christianity. Generals, grand dukes, and tsars are honored in the frescos and sculptures the way the apostles were often honored in other cathedrals. Like Hagia Sophia in Constantinople, the Russian cathedrals are grandiose representations of the New Jerusalem, intended to turn one's mind to the heavens and to reflect on the hope of the return of Christ the King. Looking at these magnificent structures even today, one can see something of the European Renaissance mixed with Russian and Asian hues.

Art for the Russian Church at this time generally meant frescos, and more importantly, icons. During the fourteenth and most of the fifteenth centuries, there was a renewal of iconography in Russia. The collapse of Constantinople, where Kiev and Moscow had previously looked for icons and icon painters, resulted in Moscow developing its iconography more on its own. By the sixteenth century, painters like Dionisii (Dionysius, c. 1440-c. 1503) had created a uniquely Russian style of iconography that was softer and more saturated in color, more realistic, and which used elongated figures and different proportions for the bodies. His painting titled "The Crucifixion," which is found in the cathedral of the Pavlo-Obnorsky Monastery, is perhaps the best known of his works. Influences from the West would continue to increase in the seventeenth century, but even then Russia's own unique form of iconography would remain a cultural heritage it bequeathed to all of world Christianity.

The Ukrainian Church on the borderlands

The name "Ukraine" means "borderland." The term is an appropriate appellation for a place where Christianity developed in a borderland of crossing populations. The Ukraine had long been an important crossroad linking greater Russia and Asia with the Byzantine world and also with Europe. Home to the city of Kiev, it was where the heart of Russian Christianity was lodged until the Mongol invasions in the middle of the thirteenth century. The early saints of Russia were not monks or ascetics but Kiev's rulers, such as St. Vladimir and St. Olga, the first Christian ruler of Kiev. As Moscow began to rise as the second metropolitan see in the Mongol period, Kiev entered a period of decline. Kiev eventually was cut off from trade to the east and south by the Mongols, while from the west Lithuania and Poland began to move into the territories of the Ukraine.

Christianization had been a fairly smooth process, although a number of historians talk about a long period of *dvoeveriea* or "double faith" whereby the local deity, Perun (god of thunder and lightning), continued to be honored while churches were being built. By the fourteenth century, Ukrainian Christianity had taken much of the form of Byzantine Christianity and "Russified" it. The Russians adapted by making wooden churches rather than stone. Worship was in Church Slavonic or Old Russian, not in Greek. Most of the early artwork was copied from Byzantium, but when it came to theology, Russians did not have a long tradition of philosophy, so early writings reflect more of the South Russian hero tales that were turned into the lives of saints. Two of the most important saints of the Ukraine are the founders of Russian monasticism, St. Anthony (c. 982-1073) and his disciple St. Theodosius (d. 1074). Anthony was the founder of the more ascetic and anchorite tradition, while Theodosius developed communities that were available to serve the poor, feed the hungry, and advise (or condemn) those in power regarding their behavior. Throughout Russian history, the famous Monastery of the Caves, near Kiev, has been seen as foundational for Russian spirituality and monastic life.

The Ukraine's position as a borderland was becoming more obvious in the sixteenth century. In the fifteenth century the Grand Duchy of Lithuania succeeded in taking political control over much of the Ukraine, displacing Mongol rule in effect. With the end of Mongol rule in Moscow in 1480, the Ukraine and Moscow were now at odds. The presence of the Ottomans to the south put additional pressure on the region. In response to the growing presence of foreign powers in the region, a group of "freedom fighters," called *Cossacks* (from the Turkic word for "free people"), formed in the region of the Dnieper River late in the fourteenth or early in the fifteenth centuries. The actual origin of the movement is unclear, but wherever they came from, by the sixteenth century the Cossacks had become a significant force to deal with.

The Ukraine, like the rest of Russia, had long looked to the south and east, toward Byzantium and the Orthodox Church of Constantinople, for theological guidance. The growing influence of the Duchy of Lithuania and the separation politically of Kiev from Moscow did not significantly affect the Orthodox character of the churches in the Ukraine. Lithuanian rulers were generally tolerant of the Orthodox faith of their Russian subjects, although they tended to favor an independent Orthodox Church in the Ukraine. By the middle of the sixteenth century, however, increased influences from the West were being felt. Roman Catholic missionaries were entering the Ukraine from Lithuania and Poland, and even the most secure borders could not entirely stem the flow of the new Protestant ideas that were beginning to infiltrate from Germany and Switzerland. These Western influences increased dramatically after 1569 with the formation of the Polish-Lithuanian Commonwealth. The Polish-Lithuanian Commonwealth was one of the most religiously tolerant and progressive republican governments of the period (with an elected parliament and a powerless king). It nevertheless was a foreign power, and by the end of the century was intent on a policy that amounted to colonization of the Ukraine. Poland in particular supported the flow of Roman Catholic missionaries to the Ukraine. By the end of the sixteenth century, the Ukraine was becoming fertile ground for Roman Catholic missionary efforts. Like many others in the Orthodox world, Ukrainian Orthodox found themselves ironically facing increased pressures not just from other religions but from fellow Christians intent on converting them from their ancient Orthodox tradition.

Suggestions for further reading

Atiya, Aziz S., *A History of Eastern Christianity*. London: Methuen, 1968.

Brock, Sebastian P., *The Hidden Pearl: The Syrian Orthodox Church and Its Ancient Aramaic Heritage*. Rome: Trans World Film Italia, 2001.

Hupchick, Dennis P., *The Balkans, from Constantinople to Communism*. New York: Palgrave MacMillan, 2002.

McGuckin, John Anthony, *The Orthodox Church: An Introduction to Its History, Doctrine, and Spiritual Culture*. Oxford: Wiley-Blackwell, 2010.

Runciman, Steven, *The Great Church in Captivity*. Cambridge: Cambridge University Press, 1985.

Ware, Timothy, *The Orthodox Church*. New York: Penguin Books, 1963.

Zernov, Nicolas, *Eastern Christendom: A Study of the Origin and Development of the Eastern Orthodox Church*. London: Weidenfeld & Nicolson, 1961.

6

World Christianity at the End of the Sixteenth Century

By the last decades of the sixteenth century, the expansion of Western forms of Christianity beyond their territorial homelands was well under way. Meanwhile, at home in Europe, the unity of Western Christendom had been decisively shattered. The conflicts in Europe had often been violent. Warfare between Catholic and Protestant armies and numerous executions of Anabaptists marked the period throughout the continent. The Western church, first in its Roman Catholic form but eventually in its Protestant form as well, spread into other regions of the world on the back of Europe's new colonial venture. In parts of both Africa and Asia these colonial forces brought Western missionaries into regions where Orthodox Christian communions had previously been established. Catholic missionaries sought not only to bring peoples who had never been baptized (Muslims, Hindus, indigenous religionists in Africa and South America) under the discipline of their respective Western communions. They sought to convert those who were Orthodox as well. In the sixteenth century, Rome began to appoint its own bishops as patriarchs in regions that had historically been home to Orthodox churches in Africa and Asia. Eventually in both western Asia and eastern Europe entire churches would come into communion with Rome, maintaining their own Orthodox liturgy and theology. These "unitate" churches (as they came to be called) represented another level of Catholic missionary efforts in Asia. The presence of Western Christian missionaries combined with the continued pressure of the global Islamic expansion in the sixteenth century made for considerable stress in Orthodox churches throughout the world.

Protestant confessional formations in Europe

By the end of the sixteenth century the Protestant churches had proven to be unable to agree on a common theology and practice and were forming themselves into several confessional communions. The process was not peaceful. In Germany, princes who supported Lutheran reforms along with leaders of several free cities had formed a political alliance in 1531 called the Smalkaldic League. Open

145

war between Protestants and Catholics was avoided for another fifteen years, but finally broke out in 1546. Catholic forces had the upper hand until 1553, when a Protestant army nearly captured Charles V (1500-1558). The emperor, weary of the struggle and sick with gout, abdicated his throne, which was turned over to his brother, and retired to a monastery in Spain. The two sides then signed the Peace of Augsburg in 1555. It extended imperial recognition to Lutheran territories (but not to other evangelicals). No further territories were to become Lutheran, while no Lutheran territory was to be forced to become Catholic. The document established the principle of *cuius regio, eius religio* ("whose region, his religion"), meaning that the religion of the ruler was made the religion of the churches of that region. Dissenters were invited to immigrate to a place where their faith was established.

Philip Melanchthon (1497-1560) was the dominant theological voice among the Lutherans during these years, and he guided these Protestant churches through to the rise of the next generation. One of the most ecumenical figures of the age, Melanchthon labored hard to find common ground not only with Calvin and other Reformed theologians but also with Roman Catholics. In the north in the city of Magdeburg Matthias Flacius Illyricus (1520-1575), a Croatian who had studied at Wittenberg, emerged in the 1550s within the Lutheran communion as a leader of the opposition against Melanchthon. Flacius is best known for the *Magdeburg Centuries,* which he set to print in that city during this period.

At the same time in the Palatinate region in southwestern Germany, the theological influences of Jean Calvin (1509-1564) and others in what was becoming known as the Reformed Church were making inroads. They did so with the support of Frederick III (1515-1576), who was also an elector of the emperor. Two theologians from Heidelberg, Kaspar Olevianus (1536-1587) and Zacharias Ursinus (1534-1583), prepared a new catechism, which was adopted by Frederick for the churches under him in 1563. The *Heidelberg Catechism*, as it was known, sought to bridge the Lutheran-Calvinist divide and bring about an irenic integration of questions of faith and works.

Seeking to unite the various Lutheran parties and address the continuing controversy with Calvinist teaching, a group of theologians led by James Andreae (1528-1590) and Martin Chemnitz (1522-1586) drafted a new confessional statement to serve as a basis for agreement among the various Lutheran factions in the 1570s. Called the *Formula of Concord,* that statement was signed by fifty-one princes, dukes, counts, and barons, who were joined by mayors or representatives of councils from thirty-five German cities. The Scandinavian kings soon adopted it as well. Two years later, in 1577, the Lutheran *Concordia* (*Book of Concord*) was published, bringing together (among other documents) the *Augsburg Confession*, Melanchthon's *Apology*, several of Luther's catechetical efforts, and the *Formula of Concord.* The *Concordia* quickly became the fixed collection of confessional writings that defined Lutheran orthodoxy.

In Switzerland Calvin's reforms became institutionalized in Geneva. The city became a center for spreading these ideas elsewhere as visitors and refugees poured in. Calvin's successors in Switzerland solidified his teachings through several new confessional statements for the churches, including the First and

Second Helvetic Confessions. The First Helvetic Confession was drawn up in Basel by Heinrich Bullinger (1504-1575) and others in 1536. The much more authoritative Second Helvetic Confession was originally a longer, private statement by Bullinger, written in 1562, but it quickly became a Reformed standard.

When Henry II of France (1519-1599) died, his son, Francis II (1544-1560), husband of Mary of Scotland (1542-1587), became king. Francis lived only another year. He was succeeded by his ten-year-old brother, Charles IX (1550-1574), but their mother, Catherine de Medici (1519-1589), was in reality the effective ruler of France. Catherine arranged the marriage of her daughter, Margaret of Valois (1553-1615), to Henry of Navarre (1553-1610), known to be a Huguenot, in 1572. In August of that year Huguenots from across France arrived in Paris to celebrate the marriage of one of their own to the daughter of the queen. Five days later, on August 24, Catherine and the Catholic nobility unleashed an attack against the Huguenots in Paris on the evening of St. Bartholomew's Day. It was quickly followed by others throughout the city, and spread to other urban centers. The resulting slaughter of Huguenots numbered in the tens of thousands, although Henry of Navarre was spared

In 1589 Henry of Navarre inherited the throne, assuming the title Henry IV. A Huguenot as king of France would be faced with enormous challenges, leading Henry to decide to enter Roman Catholic communion in 1594, which was followed by his formal coronation. As king he sought to steer a third way between Reformed and Roman Catholic parties that soon became identified with a new party of *politiques*, a new generation of nobility who had tired of the wars of religion and argued that in matters of confession, government ought to remain neutral. The first wave of a new civil and political philosophy that would soon be called "secular" emerged from their efforts.

Henry of Navarre, now King Henry IV of France, issued the Edict of Nantes in 1598, which legalized the Reformed faith in France for the first time. Huguenots were permitted to work in the government, worship in public except in a handful of cities (including Paris), and be free from forced catechesis in the Roman Catholic faith. Several independent Huguenot towns were recognized, giving them a military base. Relative peace ensued in France until 1685 when a new edict outlawed the Huguenots, and a massive exodus of Protestants from France ensued.

Anabaptists made their way into the Netherlands during the first half of the sixteenth century and found an underground reception. The emperor had been more effective in preventing the spread of Lutheran ideas in the Netherlands after they first appeared in the 1520s. Reformed teachings eventually found a hearing, especially in the cities, and in 1562 a Reformed confession was published and circulated by a group of theologians. In 1566 a synod in the city of Antwerp adopted an edited version of that confession that Guido de Bres (1522-1567) had written five years earlier, called the Belgic Confession, followed by a second in 1572. In 1575 the University of Leyden was founded by Prince William of Orange (1533-1584) with strong Reformed influence.

Worship in Reformed Churches in the Netherlands from its inception was marked by its simplicity and by its expressive use of the Bible. The Reformed faith in the Netherlands was also marked by a strong iconoclastic tendency as well. Beginning in the 1550s and continuing on and off for more than half a century, marauding bands broke into churches and destroyed images within them, defacing works of religious art by gouging out representations of the Eucharist or faces of sainted figures.

Upon the abdication of Charles V in 1555, governance of the Netherlands passed on to his son, Philip II of Spain (1527-1598). Sea trade with England and other parts of Europe brought a great deal of prosperity; and by the middle of the sixteenth century a common but very international culture was emerging as the basis of national identity in the region. Philip was Spanish in culture and identity, and had little relationship with his subjects in the Netherlands. The increased control he sought to impose over churches and cities was greatly resisted. Philip was often distracted by other concerns during these years, maintaining an American conquest, fighting Muslims in the Philippines, and deftly taking over the entire Portuguese empire. Still he did not entirely abandon his interests in northern European politics. In 1588 he sent a massive armada against his sister-in-law, the strong-willed Protestant Queen Elizabeth of England (1533-1603). English resistance combined with unfavorable winds ended up routing the Spanish Armada, which became a significant benchmark in what would be the long, slow decline of Spanish sea power and the vast overseas empire.

In Hungary, the writings of Martin Luther (1483-1546) reached the university by 1523, and had almost immediately been banned. Three years later, in 1526, the Ottoman ruler Suleiman (or Suleyman) the Magnificent (1494-1566) with an army of 100,000 appeared in Hungary, defeating a much smaller army under King Louis II (1506-1526) and bringing a large portion of the nation under Ottoman rule. The Ottomans did not impose direct administrative control over the country, nor did they suppress Christian worship or seek to transform church buildings into mosques. But the Ottoman Muslim influence was protracted, pervasive, and persistent. Under the Ottomans the local Hungarian nobility found their attention toward evangelical churches significantly diverted. Reformed congregations began to spread, especially in cities.

The Ottomans made Transylvania a Turkish vassal in the 1550s. Like Hungary, Transylvania remained a Christian territory, and its nobility was able to exercise great control over internal affairs. In 1572 a national Diet extended official recognition to four different communions: Roman Catholic, Lutheran, Calvinist, and Unitarian. The Orthodox were not officially recognized, but Orthodox churches were able to continue their life and ministry relatively unimpeded in the country. Transylvania's religious tolerance was an important harbinger of the political and religious theory of toleration that would follow in other places in the West in subsequent years.

The Polish-Lithuanian empire that formed in the middle of the sixteenth century was another place where religious tolerance was practiced in Christendom. Poland's Diet voted in 1555 to allow Lutheranism, and the estates of some of the nobility were soon supporting Lutheran churches. The Jesuits entered Poland under Sigismund II (1520-1572) in the 1560s and began efforts to bring the

Lutherans and others into the Roman Catholic Church without forced coercion. Jesuit mission to both Lutheran and Orthodox territories continued to grow in the seventeenth century.

England too began to experience a degree of religious tolerance toward the end of the sixteenth century. Elizabeth, who became queen in 1558, showed moderate sympathies for Protestants, although many of the nobility and priests continued to support Rome. The established Church of England came firmly under her control, including the right to appoint the archbishop of Canterbury, and she gained ascendancy over parliament, which passed the laws governing the church's affairs. In 1570 the pope declared Elizabeth excommunicated, and the following year the first of what would be several unsuccessful attempts on her life was made. Leading Roman Catholics were implicated in the effort, which induced parliament to strengthen Elizabeth's control over the church and to impose new restrictions on Roman Catholics in England. English Roman Catholic exiles had established a center for their work at Douai, France, producing there a Roman Catholic translation of the scriptures in English, which became known as the Douai Bible. Congregations of Roman Catholics continued to gather in England, but bishops were forced to reside in exile, and priests had to come across the channel surreptitiously to provide the sacraments.

On the Protestant side, a party called Puritans first appeared in the 1560s to press for more extensive reforms in a Calvinist or Reformed Church direction for the Church of England. By the 1580s the number of dissenting groups and congregations outside the official Church of England was considerable. Many of these were led by charismatic teachers or church organizers, and their work was from time to time interrupted by the authorities, but they often had the support of powerful individuals, especially from among the rising merchant class, giving them a degree of freedom to operate in England.

The English Reformed translation, called the Geneva Bible, which had been produced there by John Knox (1514-1572) and other exiles in 1560, was well received in England. Among other features, it included numerous marginal notes throughout the text to help a reader interpret various passages. Many of the notes on Israel's kings were critical of human monarchs, giving the text an antimonarchical tone. In 1568 a new translation, known as the Bishop's Bible, was published in England without such notes, and was supported by Elizabeth. A revised *Book of Common Prayer* was also published, seeking to show an Anglican "middle way" between Reformed and Roman Catholic positions.

Queen Elizabeth had Mary of Scotland (1542-1587) executed in 1587 for her alleged involvement in another attempt on Elizabeth's life. Elizabeth left no heirs and was succeeded in 1601 by James VI of Scotland (1566-1625), a member of the House of Stuart and son of Mary whom Elizabeth had executed. In England the new king was known as James I. King James continued to guide the Church of England along Elizabeth's "middle way," rejecting a number of Puritan proposals that would have taken the church in a stronger Calvinist and congregational direction and began to close independent congregations with Reformed sympathies. One of the leaders of such independent congregations in London was

John Smyth (1570-1612), who went into exile in Amsterdam. There he came into contact with Mennonites who convinced him that baptism was properly administered only to believers, and not to infants. Smyth (or Smythe as the name was also spelled) baptized himself and then others in his congregation in Amsterdam before returning to England where he became the leading theological voice for the new movement. Within a few decades, despite royal displeasure, a number of congregational churches embraced the doctrine of adult baptism and began gathering in associations that called themselves Baptists.

King James I saw early in his reign the need for a new translation of scriptures. The result, the King James Bible, was published in 1611 and became one of the most important literary events in the English language. It filled the need that the king of England felt for a translation authorized by himself, and it became the dominant translation not only in Britain but also in English-speaking churches worldwide, as well as becoming a landmark event in the formation of English-speaking cultures.

The evangelical movement in its various Lutheran, Reformed, Anabaptist, Anglican, and Baptist forms and expressions made hearing and reading the word, rather than observing the celebration of sacraments, central to Christian religious life. Daily devotions, reading scriptures in the home and in church, and listening to sermons in a worship service became the mainstay of evangelical or Protestant Christian life. Finding no authorization for revering the saints in these scriptures, most segments of the evangelical camp rejected material representations of the saints and their veneration, including that of the Virgin Mary, the mother of Christ. Uneasy with any theological description of the Eucharist that seemed to indicate it was a material representation of Christ's sacrifice on Calvary, worship was stripped of elements suggesting what many called "papist superstition." The real presence of Christ for many was no longer in the bread and wine, but was found in the sense that he was seated at table in a memorial fellowship meal. Church buildings became plainer, resembling meeting halls, and new hymnody carried added vitality to the stripped-down liturgy, while Protestant church life became more democratic.

The evangelical movement also tended to be critical of monasticism and doubted that this form of religious life under vows represented a more perfect way. This in turn paved the way not only for the closing of monasteries, but for the search for ways of bringing the spirituality of an ordered Christian life to bear in the day-to-day world of the laity. For kings and princes, an added reason for dissolving monasteries lay in the rewards to be gained in taking over their lands. More idealistically, however, the shift from monasteries to the laity was intended to highlight the fact that for evangelicals in general the gathered congregation took the place of the monastery as the place for spiritual development. Attention to holiness marked Calvin's teachings in particular, and subsequent developments in Reformed Churches bore this out. Believers came to scrutinize their own and one another's day-to-day lives, looking for marks of holiness that could be interpreted as signs of divine election. They learned to interpret the work they did in the world as a spiritual vocation. Pastors were expected to be educated, and were regarded as both members and leaders of this ascetic worldly community. In established churches pastors' salaries were paid by the state, while in the new free churches that were emerging support came from free contributions. Pastors were expected to be married men, usually with families. Women were still not given any significant leadership role, even in Anabaptist churches, and since the monasteries were being closed traditional avenues of service and leadership through convents were lost. A number of powerful women emerged in national political leadership in western Europe in the sixteenth century, but this did not generally carry over into the churches.

Roman Catholic reform and development

Roman Catholic Church life in the sixteenth century did not undergo the revolutionary reorientation toward the spoken and written word that marked Protestantism. Instead, sixteenth- and seventeenth-century European Catholics continued to emphasize the sacraments while attempting to purify them of superstitious accretions. The growing popularity of the feast of Corpus Christi among European Catholics is one example of this, as is the increase in the laity's participating in the Eucharist overall. Devotional practices directed toward Mary and the saints continued to be important to Catholic life, along with pilgrimages, especially to Rome. The development and desire of such practices were important elements to Roman Catholic renewal.

Large sections of the decrees of the Council of Trent revolved around the sacraments. A number of regulations concerning the celebration of the Mass were made. Marriage was reaffirmed as an indissoluble sacrament, excluding any possibility of divorce or remarriage while a partner was still alive. A matrimonial ceremony was to be conducted in public and with two or three witnesses in addition to the priest. Both parties had to enter into marriage of free assent, and the union was to be registered in parish records. Forced marriages were determined to be invalid, and a marriage could be annulled if it had not been consummated. Adultery and concubinage were also severely condemned, punishable by excommunication. Roman Catholic teaching overall through this period sought to pay greater attention to nurturing family life.

Trent also restricted nuns to the cloistered life, although the very attempt to do so seemed to signal the bishops' wariness concerning the rising demand of women that they be involved in service in the world. The regulations of Trent included the provision that nuns were not to be permitted to leave their convents for even brief periods for visit without the approval of the bishop, a decree that appears to have been unevenly enforced.

In one of its last sessions, Trent condemned dueling, on the threat of excommunication. Deaths through duels were to be treated as homicides, it ruled, and those who died in dueling were to be refused a Christian burial. One can see through this brief ruling more than a response to the rising problem of social violence brought about by the increased availability of firearms in Europe.

Traditional practices of swordplay among the nobility had long been a part both of military training and the social ordering of chivalry. At the heart of the social order of feudalism, which was supported by the ethics of chivalry, had been the twin virtues of loyalty and honor. Honor was also at stake in the social practice of dueling. By condemning dueling the church was in effect calling into question the value of a social order built upon "honor." By the sixteenth century a new social order was emerging in Europe, and the church was beginning to address its cultural ramifications.

A new political ordering was also apparent in Europe as the modern nation-state was emerging. The church was slower to embrace elements of this new national consciousness if they harbored a move from its established political position. A new Roman Inquisition was begun in 1542 that was intended to root out heresy in all of Christendom. In effect, it only ever operated in Italy, and even there in the papal estates, for Europe's other Catholic monarchs did not recognize its jurisdiction in their lands. In Italy the Inquisition carried out a handful of executions, and by the end of the century had turned its attention from rooting out Protestants entirely to rooting out witches, an indication of its ineffectiveness. On the other hand Rome found in the Jesuits a far more effective force for combating Protestantism and other heresies. Some Jesuits supported strong or even violent methods, but generally sought to win unbelievers through methods of argument, persuasion, and education.

Chief among the challenges the Roman Catholic hierarchy faced was the rising tide of new publications, many of them espousing views contrary to official church teaching. Bishops and university faculties needed to sift through them to guard against errors in both moral and intellectual content. To help guide and protect its members against grievous errors, in 1557 Rome established an official Index of Forbidden Books, which was overseen by the Holy Office of the Inquisition.

Orthodoxy and the Ottoman empire

The Ottomans, as we have seen, were increasing their European political presence in the sixteenth century. Kings and emperors from various European nations began exchanging diplomatic missions with the Ottoman rulers as the various powers sought to affect the direction of one another's foreign policies. Among the imperial ambassadors from the Hapsburg court in Germany to Istanbul in 1573 were two Lutherans, Baron David Ungnad von Sonnegk (1530-1600), who came as an ambassador, and his chaplain, Stephen Gerlach (1546-1612) of Tübingen University. Through an Orthodox scholar named Theodosius Zygomalas (1544-1614) they gained an audience with Patriarch Jeremias II (1530-1595). Upon their return to Germany the two Lutherans began to advocate opening relations with the Orthodox. In 1574, Gerlach wrote to his friend, the Greek scholar Martin Crusius (or Kraus, 1526-1607) of Tübingen, requesting a Greek translation of the *Augsburg Confession*. A positive introductory letter was attached to the copy that was sent to the ecumenical patriarch, emphasizing the orthodox nature ("no innovations") of the German confession. A Greek translation of the *Augsburg Confession* had actually been completed earlier in 1559, indicating the clear interest of at least some among the Lutherans in theological dialogue with the Orthodox.

The response came from Istanbul two years later, in 1576, just one year before the signing of the *Formula of Concord*, in a letter from the ecumenical patriarch. After careful and thorough consideration by the Holy Synod, the Orthodox found a number of deficiencies in the Lutheran position. The Orthodox believed the Holy Spirit proceeded from the Father alone, and that baptism was to be by triple immersion immediately followed by an anointing with oil, signifying the seal of the Holy Spirit. On matters of grace and faith the ecumenical patriarch quoted the ancient church fathers, affirming the need for holy Scriptures and seven sacraments, but arguing that good works must necessarily follow. Predestination was rejected (the *Formula of Concord* would soon agree), but so was the Lutheran opposition to seeking the mediation of the saints in prayer. The mother of God, by virtue of her holiness and her special relationship to her Son, should be asked to intercede on our behalf. She and the many saints are not to be ignored or belittled. Concerning monastic life, even though it is not possible for all, it is a better way to live in complete devotion and service to God, the patriarch explained. In the end, a humble, if slightly condescending, olive branch was held out, inviting the learned Germans to join themselves to the most holy church of Christ and subject themselves as children to the Orthodox teaching and tradition. Letters continued to pass between the Germans and the Greeks until 1581 when Patriarch Jeremias requested that the correspondence cease, although he invited friendship to continue.

The exchange did not initially accomplish much, but it was an important opening to future ecumenical dialogue. On a number of points the Lutherans found the differences they had with Catholics were ones they had with the Orthodox as well, such as devotion to Mary and the saints, or the place of monasticism in Christian life. On other matters, such as the procession of the Holy Spirit from the Father and the Son, or the practice of confirmation several years after baptism rather than chrismation immediately after the rite, the Lutherans found they were firmly part of the Western Latin tradition and against the Orthodox East.

Farther north in the region surrounding Kiev, the Orthodox faced growing pressures from the West in the sixteenth century. The newly formed Polish-Lithuanian empire annexed a large section of western Ukraine in the middle of the century, and by 1560 Jesuits had entered the region seeking to win both Lutheran and Orthodox congregations over to the Roman Catholic fold. Supported by members of the nobility, the Jesuits opened new schools and disseminated literature that was published in the vernacular. The Orthodox churches in the region, though Russian in their culture, were under the jurisdiction of the ecumenical patriarch, whose administrative effectiveness after 1453 had been greatly diminished. Seeing trouble on the horizon, Patriarch Jeremias II, after visiting Moscow in 1589, visited the Ukraine to shore up Orthodox faith.

Despite these efforts the patriarch's influence among the churches was slipping. Within a year a number of Orthodox bishops in the area gathered in a synod to consider which direction they would take. At the conclusion they voted to submit to the authority of the pope in Rome, asking to be allowed to maintain their own rites and ecclesiastical status. The decision was supported by the Polish king, who was Roman Catholic, but required several years of negotiation. The Russian bishops went to Rome with the model of the Council of Florence in mind, which had sought to bring about a reunion of separated churches. In effect, however, Rome, now in the midst of the struggle with the Protestant Reformation, had undergone a shift in its thinking regarding such unions. Rome received the Russian Church leaders as individual converts, granting the Russians privileges that they understood to be their legitimate Roman apostolic patrimony. Nevertheless, in 1596 agreement was finally reached and the Union of Brest declared, bringing a number of Russian-speaking churches in the Ukraine and Lithuania into communion with Rome. The Union of Brest established a Roman Catholic Ukrainian Church (called uniate or Ukrainian Catholic today) whose priests were allowed to be married. Churches were allowed to maintain their ancient liturgical rites. Worship continued to be conducted in Slavonic with the Eucharist offered in both kinds. Nevertheless, Latin was soon being taught and Thomas Aquinas was being studied in the theological schools in the region. Many Orthodox Church leaders and lay people resisted the Union of Brest and the resulting uniate church that emerged. A special envoy named Kyrillos Loukaris (often known in the West as Cyril Lucaris, 1572-1638) was appointed as the patriarch's official representative to the area to try to counter the uniate efforts. A new chapter in the troubled history of Catholic-Orthodox relations had been opened.

Conflicts in world Christianity beyond Europe

The Catholic-Protestant conflict that was dividing western Europe spilled over into the Americas in the sixteenth century. In November of 1555 about six hundred Frenchmen (but no women) arrived at the Bay of Guanabara (modern Rio de Janeiro) led by a Catholic named Nicolas Durand de Villegaignon (1510-1571). Funded by the admiral of France, the expedition included both Roman Catholics and Huguenot ministers and craftsmen, reflecting the admiral's hopes to start a colony in which Catholics and Protestants could live together. The colonists soon encountered problems, and Villegaignon sent a letter to John Calvin in Geneva requesting help. Calvin responded by selecting two ministers to go with a larger group of colonists, who were French refugees living in Geneva. As soon as this second group of Calvinists arrived, conflict erupted. Theological arguments over the proper celebration of the sacraments led to a number of Genevans being expelled and three of them being killed. For two months, the Huguenots lived on the mainland, struggling to survive and getting to know their new neighbors, the Tupinamba Indians. Villegaignon then sent them all back to France, with orders to have them imprisoned. The captain told the Calvinists of the plot and allowed them to escape. One of their number, Jean de Lery (1536-1613), wrote a detailed history of the efforts in Brazil titled *Histoire d'un voyage fait en la terre du Brésil* ("History of a Voyage Made in the Land of Brazil") in 1578. The book provided an important early written description of the Tupinamba.

The French effort, which was in part driven by the desire to stem the growth of Portuguese and Spanish influence in South America, ended in failure. By the end of the century, the Portuguese had established control over most of the coastal territory of Brazil. Sugar income was on the rise, more enslaved Africans were being imported, and the periodic attacks of the French were on the decline. Spain was off and on at war with France during much of the sixteenth century, and this conflict too spread to the Americas as the French crown encouraged corsairs to capture Spanish gold and other treasures being brought back to Europe. Many of the corsairs were Huguenots, and their efforts took on a religious dimension. French ships in 1554 attacked and captured Santiago, Cuba. A year later they sacked Havana, destroying a number of churches and killing several priests.

During the 1570s the Netherlands and England became Spain's primary belligerents in America. The English and Dutch were largely Protestant by this point. The defeat of the Spanish Armada in 1588 cleared the way for them to begin to establish their own empires by sea, to the Caribbean, North America, Africa, and Asia. By the end of the century Sir Walter Raleigh (1554-1618) was sponsoring English excursions into the Caribbean, and the Anglican theologian Richard Hakluyt (1552-1616), in works such as *Discourse on Western Planting*, was paving the way for Protestant expansion in the Americas. The motives, as with the Spanish a century earlier, seemed to express a religious zeal for purity. Hakluyt in particular looked forward to colonial settlers and ministers becoming defenders of the faith, not just spreading the Christian religion to the Native Americans but purifying the church back in England. Hakluyt defended the need for Protestant settlements based on the poor treatment of the local people by the Spanish in the Caribbean. He let the Spanish speak for themselves as he quoted from an English edition of Bartolomé de Las Casas's (1484-1566) *Account of the Destruction of the Indies*.

During this entire period the Society of Jesus was increasing its work in South America. One of the Jesuit leaders, Inacio de Azevedo (1527-1570), came to believe that for priests to be fit to work in Brazil, they had to actually grow up in the land, learning the local languages and customs. In 1570 he set sail from Portugal for Brazil with sixty-nine young recruits aged fourteen to sixteen. The group was attacked by French Huguenot corsairs and all were killed. But the memory of Azevedo became part of the larger Jesuit legacy in America that was searching for new missionary approaches to local cultures and developing a more indigenous form of Christianity among Native Americans.

Within the borders of Europe the Jesuits focused their energies on educating the laity, while members living in proximity to Protestants were active in developing strategies to combat Protestantism by accentuating Catholic traditions. Outside Europe they were more willing to listen and adapt to local cultures than the diocesan priests and members of the mendicant orders, many of whom were content to be chaplains to their fellow Europeans and to give evangelization of local peoples a lower priority. In Spanish and Portuguese territories in America as well as in Africa and Asia, Jesuits pioneered a model of mission that was not dependent on political power. The implications were particularly important in America, where the Jesuits first entered Brazil in 1549, and then during the following decade began working in Mexico and Peru. Members of the society were not under the *real patronato* system, but answered through their own hierarchy directly to Rome. They were also free from the Inquisition. In Mexico, Brazil, and eventually Paraguay the *reducciones* that they organized became self-sustaining agricultural villages. By 1610 the Jesuits were quietly arming the Native Americans in these villages for self-defense against colonial raiding parties.

The Jesuits, like other priests and bishops in the Americas, held African slaves during these first years of conquest. By the eighteenth century, indeed, they were among the most extensive owners of slaves in the Americas. Nevertheless, there were a number of individual Jesuits who opposed slavery in America beginning in the seventeenth century. Alonso de Sandoval (1577-1652) and Pedro Claver (1581-1654) both began working around 1610 in the city of Cartagena (in modern Colombia), one of the major ports where slave ships from Africa to Spanish America brought their cargo. In his final vows as a Jesuit back in Europe Claver had added the phrase *Aethiopum semper servus* ("slave of the Black Africans forever"). In 1627 Sandoval published *De instauranda Aethiopum salute: Naturaleza, policia sagrada i profana, costumbres i ritos, disciplina i catechismo evangelico de todos Etiopes*, known in English as *A Treatise on Slavery*. Over the course of four decades these two Jesuits worked among the slaves passing through the markets of Cartagena. They boarded arriving ships to reach those who were dying, and they cared for sick Africans awaiting sale in the city. They attempted to set up catechism classes for slaves, and traveled to the surrounding plantations to continue these efforts. Such individuals do not make up for the overall failure of the Jesuits to oppose the growing African slave trade that was part of the European heritage in the Americas, but they did point the way to an alternative mission.

By the first decades of the seventeenth century Christianity in South America was firmly established institutionally with its own councils of bishops, operating under the oversight of the Spanish or Portuguese rulers. Outside the diocesan structures Dominicans, Franciscans, and Jesuits all provided ministry to the diverse Native American, European, and African peoples that now populated the region. The establishment of *Congregatio de propaganda fidei* in 1622 in Rome began the long effort to bring all missionary work outside Europe under the single administrative office of the Vatican. In South America the intent of *Propaganda fidei* was to counteract in some degree the system of the *patronato*.

Among the names of the faithful in South America during the first century stands out that of a Creole woman, St. Rosa of Lima (1586-1617), who was the first canonized saint in the Roman Catholic Church from the Americas. A member of the Dominican tertiary movement, she was noted for the degree of piety that she practiced. One of her contemporaries, also from Lima, was Martín de Porres (1579-1639). His father was Spanish and his mother a free African. Martin grew up in poverty and sought at a young age to enter religious life. The Dominicans at that time did not allow Africans to become members of the order, so he was permitted to enter only as a servant in the monastery. Eventually he was allowed to practice the discipline of the order and became well known for his care of orphans and stray animals. Before the end of his life Martin had several miraculous healings credited to him. Devotion to him and recitation of the so-called "little stories" that became his legacy would later be mined to show the way in which mestizos and Indian converts became Catholics with an understanding of the faith and the equality it revealed that were actually quite subversive of the colonial ideology of the civil and religious Spanish authorities.

In the 1570s a new Portuguese missionary congregation of Augustinians called the Hermits of St. Augustine arrived at Hormuz in the Persian Gulf. Members of the order had begun studying the Persian languages and by 1602 had established a residence in Isfahan. Among their early efforts were a translation of the missal and the four Gospels into Arabic. The mission did not amount to much, however, as the center of Portuguese efforts in the Indian Ocean in the first decades of the seventeenth century remained at Goa, and not in Persia or on the Arabian Peninsula.

The Portuguese tended to bring with them an understanding of Christianity that left no room for the ancient churches of the East. In a move that was highly symbolic of that lack of understanding, in 1575 the Portuguese archbishop of Goa, speaking for the Portuguese *padroado,* proclaimed that the head of the St. Thomas Christians, the metropolitan of Angamale, would no longer be appointed by the East Syrian (or Chaldean) patriarch. The St. Thomas Christians, who still referred to the Portuguese as *parangi* ("foreign"), sent word to the East Syrian patriarch anyway, asking that five new bishops be ordained for their churches. No new bishops from Persia were forthcoming, however, leaving the St. Thomas Christians increasingly dependent on the Portuguese hierarchy for their sacramental needs.

Relations between the Latin and the St. Thomas Christian communities took a decidedly bad turn with the arrival of the Portuguese archbishop Aleixo de Menezes (1559-1617) in 1595. Menezes, who was given the title "Archbishop of Goa and Primate of all India" by the pope, was adamantly committed to bringing the Indian Church in line with the Roman Church. At one point he even wrote that Syriac was a channel through which heresy flowed and thus needed to be extinguished. Shortly after his arrival in Goa and with the support of the Hindu rajah of Cochin, who ruled the region of Kerala, Menezes ordained eighty-eight Indians as priests and had them swear allegiance to Rome.

A critical point came in 1597 when the last metropolitan from Persia, Mar Abraham, died. Following the ancient St. Thomas tradition, an archdeacon, Parambil George (or George of the Cross, d. 1640), who had been ordained by Mar Abraham several years earlier, became the new administrator of the Indian churches. At an assembly of the St. Thomas Christians at Angamale, delegates from these churches took an oath of allegiance to him. Archdeacon George was then convinced to come to the Roman Catholic Church of the Blessed Virgin at Vaipin to give a public profession of faith. It is not clear how much of the proceedings he understood since they were held in Latin and Portuguese, but the outcome was a public declaration of shared faith.

Archbishop Menezes moved quickly to secure Roman control of the churches. Acting as the senior ecclesiastical officer in the region, he called for a synod, to be held at the church of Diamper (*Udayamperoor*) shortly after Pentecost in 1599. Ancient Indian Christian custom called for laity and clerics alike to participate in such synods, a custom Menezes was forced to follow. Some 650 lay people joined the 150 or so clerics at the gathering. Menezes presided as the highest-ranking ecclesiastical officer in the region. He conducted the proceedings in Latin and Portuguese, languages most of the Indians could not understand, and thus effectively shut the Indian Christians out of the discussion.

Although the official record of the synod would lead one to believe that all decisions were reached in an open, honest, and mutually acceptable manner, this was not at all the case. What actually happened is that demands were read in Portuguese, and agreements to them were coerced with little understanding on the part of the Indians. Some of the documents were completed or edited after the synod and treated as if they had been ratified there. Some two hundred decrees were approved over the seven days of proceedings, most predictably focused on issues that paved the way to the ascendancy of Roman Catholicism and degraded Indian Christianity. Theological points accentuating the human suffering of Christ and canonical-theological issues such as the pope in Rome being the single head of the universal church, the Mass being said only in Latin, and mandatory celibacy for all priests were underscored. To enforce its decrees, the Inquisition was extended to the St. Thomas Christians. Christians who were culturally Indian had to prove their allegiance to European language and religious customs or be disciplined as heretics. The effect was all the more tragic if it is recalled that the Portuguese were originally welcomed as allies against the spread of the Islamic Mughul empire in India.

Menezes's intention was to enforce subjugation of the Indian Christians to Roman Catholic rule in all essential and a host of nonessential matters. His actions created instead deep and long-lasting divisions among Christians in India and had the devastating effect of denigrating a centuries-old historical memory and damaging the future of Christianity in India. Following the synod many Syriac liturgical, theological, and historical books and records belonging to the Indian Christians were destroyed. A number of churches refused to accept the Roman Church's authority and continued to follow their ancient traditions, but they found themselves in a severely weakened situation. Latin Christianity came to be seen as a foreign religion in India, and the long memory of indigenous Indian Christianity was eclipsed.

Japan was in a period of change when the Jesuits had first arrived in the middle of the sixteenth century. One of the major struggles of mid-seventeenth-century Japan was between the shogun, who was the power behind the emperor, and the local Buddhist warrior-monks. The powerful warlord Oda Nobunaga (1534-1582) accepted gifts from the Jesuits and encouraged Christian work in his home region near Kyoto, not because he favored Christianity but because he found relations with the Christians helpful in his conflict with the Buddhist monks. It has to be said that the initial positive reception of the Jesuits was for reasons completely extrinsic to their own reasons for coming.

Nobunaga was assassinated in 1582. His successor, Toyotomi Hideyoshi (1536-1598), further unified Japan under his regime and initially continued to show favor toward the Christians. His views changed, however, in 1587 after a night of drinking with a companion. The companion reportedly told the Japanese ruler that Christians were destroying Buddhist temples and Shinto shrines, enslaving Japanese, and resisting the shogun's use of Christian women for pleasure. In short, Christianity was portrayed as unraveling the fabric of Japanese society.

The situation was made worse by a conversation between the emperor and a Spanish sea captain who had come from the Philippines. The sea captain described the Spanish conquests that were encircling the globe, recounting how Spain, which also ruled Peru, Mexico, and the Philippines, was far more powerful than the Portuguese. Concerning the spread of Christian faith, he explained that the kings of Spain first sent out teachers of religion and, when they had won the hearts of the people, the king would dispatch his troops to complete the conquest.

The message confirmed Hideyoshi's fears. The powerful ruler responded to what he perceived to be both the internal and external threats posed by Christianity by issuing an Edict of Expulsion against the Christian missionaries. The edict, which actually came in two versions, one addressed to the Japanese and one to the foreign Christians, demanded that the foreign missionaries leave in twenty days. Buddhist *daimyos* ("warlords") were forbidden to convert without permission, and symbols of the foreign God were ordered removed. The emperor's concern was to stem the threat of social unrest and to bring unity to the nation, but the effect of the edict was to damage the Christian institutions that had been started and to end efforts to convert the Japanese. In 1587 there were already five Christian *daimyos* supporting conversion among their subjects. They were all now exposed and their Christian subjects made vulnerable.

After 1598, the situation for the nascent Christian community became more difficult. Following Hideyoshi's death, the newly united nation came under the rule of Ieyasu Tokugawa (1542-1616). Ieyasu consolidated his power, moved the capital to Edo (Tokyo), and took the title of *seii-taishogun* ("supreme commander in war"). Working closely with three advisors, the Buddhist shogun Ieyasu sought to institute a tight Confucian social order and a new national form of religious devotion. This marked the beginning of the end of toleration for Christianity in seventeenth-century Japan. Only Ieyasu's desire for trade with Portugal and, in his last years, with Spain and the Netherlands prevented persecution from coming earlier in his reign.

In January of 1614 Ieyasu finally issued an edict banning the practice of Christianity in the realm. Written by his anti-Christian Zen monk advisor, Konchiin Süden (also known as Ishin Süden, 1569-1633), the edict starts with a memorable passage. It maintains that Christians have come to Japan not only for trade but to spread evil and overthrow the government so they can possess the land. They are described as enemies of the gods and the Buddha alike, and must leave Japan immediately or suffer the penalty of death. All *daimyos* were ordered to send foreign Christians to the port of Nagasaki (which had become such a heavily

Christian city that some visiting foreigners called it the "Rome of the Far East"). From there they were to be deported. How many Christians were there? It seems that, in a country of about 20 million people, Christianity had grown to about 2 percent of the population (400,000), mostly in the region of Kyushu. Although there were only fourteen Japanese priests ordained at this time, many more were being trained, and the indigenous leadership was on the rise.

The growth of Christianity in Japan was clearly hampered by its foreignness. Japan was a land filled with the spirits of ancestors and gods that continued to defy the European Christian imagination. Europeans had encountered such religiosity elsewhere in Asia, in India for instance. The attraction of European missionaries to Japan had an additional component that is important to note. The Jesuit visitor for the Far East, Alessandro Valignano (1539-1606), came to Japan in the 1580s after a brief stay in India, convinced that the Indians and other "darker" peoples were disorganized and didn't learn well, leading him to the more promising "lighter" peoples of Japan and China. Skin color was clearly a factor in determining European Christian attitudes toward other peoples.

Valignano sought to follow the lead of Francis Xavier (1506-1552) in establishing a policy of limited adaptation for the Jesuits in Asia. Local leaders and shogun rulers were all to be honored with gifts appropriate to their position. Christian priests were to dress in ways (normally in silk) that showed that they were also deserving of respect. Concerning eating pigs or cows, the Jesuits were quick to adapt by no longer eating these animals, which the Japanese found offensive. As in Europe, religious paintings were used, but very soon, within the first generation of missionaries, Japanese artists were beginning to paint Japanese-styled Christian religious paintings of the madonna and child, the crucifixion, and other scenes. Regarding worship, on the other hand, there was very little adaptation. The liturgy was generally (though not solely) taught in Latin, the office was chanted as it was in Europe, and Western instruments such as harpsichords, viols, and even organs were used in churches.

Where adaptation was most clearly seen was in the early catechisms that were written for Japan. Xavier and Yajiro (1511-1550) receive credit for producing the first such Japanese catechism, a translation of an earlier Indian catechism. Valignano, during his first visit to Japan, began work on a catechism that spoke specifically to the Japanese context. Considering that Japan was not the only land under the visitor's supervision and that he had only been in the nation a year when it was finished, the catechism, which was completed in 1581, shows a relatively significant degree of sensitivity to the indigenous culture and society. Written first in Portuguese and then translated into both Latin and Japanese, the document employs a narrative style rather than the traditional question-and-answer format of most other catechisms. Although its discussion of Japanese religions, including Buddhism, is rather polemical, the section on cosmology reflects sensitivity to Japanese concepts. Valignano and other Jesuits in Buddhist contexts in east Asia were concerned to communicate the necessity for a creator, a created order, and ethical responsibility to this creator. On matters of traditional doctrine, the catechism, as well as later and more popular works, closely followed the catechism that had been produced by the Council of Trent and varied only its contextual concerns regarding cosmology and local religions. Both were used mostly in leadership training.

In contrast to the attitudes of the Portuguese and Spaniards in Latin America, the Italian Valignano believed that Japanese could and should be educated to lead the Japanese Catholic Church. The policy was articulated in a series of resolutions that emerged from his discussions with missionaries held at a conference in Nagasaki in February 1582. The resolutions express a vision of Japanese Christianity being self-governing and self-propagating (without actually using these nineteenth-century expressions). A local bishop was to be appointed as soon as possible, Jesuits should be the exclusive order at work in Japan, and a native clergy should be nurtured. Because of financial problems, it was even envisioned that the mission would become self-supporting through agricultural work. With these goals in mind, Valignano had two colleges and two seminaries established.

The first seminary for boys at Arima was established in 1580, during the first visit of Valignano when he also wrote the catechism. The school was an old Buddhist monastery, given to Valignano by a local lord in return for the visitor's aid in procuring European weapons. A total of twenty-two students were enrolled that first year. A strict routine was followed, starting at 4:30 each morning and lasting until 8:00 at night. Students studied Latin, Japanese, and music, and were given time for recreation, the Eucharist, vespers, and catechism. By the end of the 1580s a more advanced *colegio* (college) was established in Funai. Both theology and preaching were taught in Japanese at this institution. Religious workers lived a monastic life using the Buddhist term for living together, *dojuku*. The *dojukus* were lay helpers or novices. Some were taught how to catechize lay people and to preach, extending the work of a local priest by helping with pastoral duties. In many ways they functioned as lay ministers until enough Japanese priests could be trained.

Valignano's strategy for educating leaders and developing multiple training centers proved prescient. Another of his strategies proved more spectacular, but less helpful. The Jesuit visitor reasoned that if some of these Japanese Christian youth could visit Europe, they would be impressed with the grandeur of Christian Europe. He also believed that Europeans would be impressed with the civility of the Japanese and would want to support the work of Jesuit missions. Thus in 1582 four Japanese youth left for Europe via Goa. Two were sent as official legates of local Japanese lords. During their thirteen-month stay in Europe the boys met two popes, a king, and numerous cardinals, dukes, archbishops, prelates, and ambassadors. All this was in keeping with Valignano's explicit directions to the Jesuits that the boys should see the best of Christian Europe and its leaders. With their exotic Japanese dress and swords lashed to their sides, the boys excited both the Iberians and the Italians whom they met. According to Valignano's design the young men were to be received in private, not in public displays, but when they finally returned to Japan with Valignano in 1590, there was a huge celebration in Nagasaki where they were paraded in their European attire to meet the great emperor Hideyoshi.

Internal divisions rooted in the West played an essential role in diminishing the growth of the Christian movement in Japan during the last decades of
the sixteenth century. It was Valignano's clear design that there be unity among
Catholics in Japan. For him this meant that only the Jesuits would work in the
country. However, Valignano was not the pope, the Jesuits were not the totality
of Catholicism, and his mission was not insulated from European expansion and
trade. Spanish ships with Franciscans aboard began to dock in Japanese ports.
The first Franciscan to come to Japan was a Spaniard named Juan Pobre (d. 1615),
on his way from Macao (off the coast of China) to Manila in 1580. His lifestyle
of poverty and apparent dedication of spirit was so highly regarded that he was
invited by some local Japanese to return. Two years later he and three other
mendicants, one a Franciscan and two Augustinians, did so. The local ruler, Lord
Matsuura of Hirado (1529-1599), saw the Spaniards as possible links to the Spanish trade. The Jesuits had not met expectations for improving his local economy,
and he hoped the Spaniards might correct that. Accordingly, Hirado wrote to the
Spanish governor of the Philippines asking him to send both merchants and (if
he must) more friars.

The Jesuits protested that they had papal law on their side, since the Vatican
clearly reiterated in 1576 what earlier papal bulls had decreed regarding the par-
titioning of the world between Spanish and Portuguese powers. China and Japan
were under Portuguese patronage and were to be evangelized under the direction
of the Portuguese, who were backing the Jesuits. The conflict escalated when the
emperor Hideyoshi demanded tribute from the Philippines, which meant from
the king of Spain. The Franciscans were in effect called on to be ambassadors
representing the kingdom of Spain to Hideyoshi. When their embassy failed,
the Franciscan presence in Japan was officially proscribed. They kept coming,
nevertheless, expanding their work from Kyoto to Nagasaki with the encouragement of both Japanese rulers and Japanese Christians. The Portuguese and Italian Jesuits were furious. The zealous Spanish Franciscans were largely ignorant
of the local politics, the Jesuits charged. The shogun was soon to ban Christianity
altogether.

There were women converts among the Japanese during these first years, but
no women's orders in these first generations. Only in the last two decades of the
sixteenth century did groups of consecrated women begin to arise, alongside
the *confraria da misericórdia* (confraternity for charity work). These cells of
lay people were established at the encouragement of the monks beginning in
the early 1580s. In 1596 a women's *confraria* was organized in Kyoto. As in
Latin America, it was for women from upper-class families. The women took
vows of poverty, chastity, and obedience and engaged in work on behalf of the
hungry, naked, sick, refugees, and the dead. The cell structure of the order and
the emphasis on servanthood were important for its survival during the severe
persecutions of the 1600s.

The pattern of colonization in the Philippines followed that of Spain's empire in
the Americas, from where it was launched. Various orders divided up the islands
and set about to catechize indigenous peoples using Spanish, although worship
was always in Latin. Cathedrals were built, a few hospitals were started, but all

was under the authority of the Spanish religious and secular priests. Unlike the long and struggling growth of Christianity in regions that had organized empires with a literate upper class, evangelization in the Philippine Islands occurred with great speed at a surface level. Of an estimated 700,000 people in the islands, about 250,000 had been baptized by 1591. Infants were often baptized, however, with no provisions made for later instruction. Jesuits set up a small school for Filipino converts, but for the most part training of priests was not a priority.

The first bishop appointed for the Philippines was Domingo de Salazar (1512-1594). Two decades before coming to the Philippines he had eloquently argued against the abuses of the *encomiendas* in South America. In the Philippines Salazar quickly won the hearts of the indigenous people on whose behalf he intervened repeatedly. In 1582 a synod in Manila under his direction even questioned the legitimacy of the king of Spain's claims to rule the Philippines. The Spanish had the obligation only to evangelize the region, the synod ruled, and thus to protect the friars and churches, but not to claim direct rule over the lands. Salazar compared the mistreatment of the local people by the Christian Spaniards with the treatment by the Muslim rulers in Luzon, concluding that the Filipinos would be in a better condition and happier people if they had the more gentle Muslim rulers. Pope Gregory XIV (1535-1591), influenced by Salazar, decreed in 1591 an end to slavery in all Spanish possessions. Despite the bishop's efforts, the confusion of conquest and missions, or soldiers and friars, plagued the development of Christianity in the Philippines.

At the end of the sixteenth century Christianity was both fragmented as never before and spreading as never before. New Christian beginnings were evident on five continents. A religion that had been mostly confined to western Europe in 1453 with only struggling remnants in Africa, western Asia, and India was now spreading across the globe. The divisions and intra-European conflict in the West were significant, and they were carried over into the Christian diffusion to Asia, Africa, and the Americas. At the same time new attempts to study, understand, and indigenize the Christian message in various new contexts were emerging. Christianity was becoming global in new ways. The pace would accelerate over the course of the next century.

Part II

THE SEVENTEENTH CENTURY

Global Religious and Secular Encounters

The sixteenth century witnessed the emergence for the first time of an understanding of the world as global. Theories that the earth was round had existed earlier in various cultures of the world, but the concept remained mostly an abstraction. In the sixteenth century, for the first time, human beings circled the earth and recorded the experience in a way that effectively brought into consciousness the reality of the world as a global whole. The fact that it was Europeans who first achieved this feat led them to place themselves at the representational center of the new global picture that was emerging. The rest of the world was literally marginalized or rendered peripheral in the new maps that portrayed the emerging European perspective. There was a lag in the communication of this new global perspective across the world. In some places it took hold quickly, while in others, both in Europe and in other locations, the implications of the new picture were slower to set in. Eventually those implications did come to be grasped, however, reflecting to various degrees the dominance of a European or Western world perspective that would last several centuries.

Most of the European explorers and merchants who were building this new global nexus in the sixteenth century thought of themselves as Roman Catholic Christians. Supported by the various national courts of Europe, these explorers took their version of Christianity with them institutionally in the form of priests and friars who accompanied them on their voyages to Asia, Africa, and the newly named continent of America. The modern missionary movement that emerged in the sixteenth century was closely connected to Europe's colonial and mercantile global expansion. The long-range impact of this association would be both to link Christianity to Western colonialism and later to imperialism in significant ways, but also to transform Christianity from a mostly Western religion to a truly global or world religion.

The form of Christianity that these Europeans brought to other parts of the world in the sixteenth and seventeenth centuries was overwhelmingly Roman

Catholic in character, since there was very little Protestant activity going on outside Europe in this period. These Catholic Christians, both lay people and priests, were loyal not only to the papacy but to the national courts that sponsored them. Tension often resulted from that dual allegiance. And over the course of the seventeenth century, they began to find themselves having to honor commitments made to their fellow expatriates in the lands to which they had gone, as well as to their catechumens and converts in places as diverse as China, Japan, Angola, Peru, and Canada. Catholics began to have to negotiate their way through local, national, or imperial governing structures and within the cultures and religions of these hundreds of different peoples.

The encounter of Christianity with other religions and cultures inevitably became much more complex and multifaceted. Orthodox churches had a long history of living as minorities, especially under Muslim rulers. Christians from western Europe had little such experience. For the most part, Western Christians came from situations where Christianity was the dominant and ruling "religion," and where heretics, Jews, and Muslims were regarded as apostates, infidels, and nonbelievers. Their communities were thought better suppressed in order to strengthen Christendom. With the spread of Christianity to places like Vietnam, Japan, Ghana, and Mexico, interreligious encounters and even tentative forms of dialogue began to expand rapidly as the sixteenth slipped into the seventeenth century. Proposals on how the accidentals of Christian worship and practices could be altered to make Catholicism more at home began to emerge as missionaries worked in new cultural situations and indigenous Christian believers began questioning whether their traditional practices were not incompatible with their new-found faith.

At another level, the transition from the sixteenth into the seventeenth century was marked by the emergence in the West of what can somewhat anachronistically be termed "secularization." Rulers began systematically to reduce the public role of the church in many parts of Europe. Trends that began to take shape several centuries earlier among those who called themselves "humanists" joined forces with the beginnings of experimental sciences and improved technologies through this period. In the background and enabling the entire enterprise was the rapid expansion of wealth—wealth earned in "trade," if one's perspective was that of the colonial powers; wealth earned by exploiting the weakness of those whose resources were coveted if one's perspective was that of Asians, Africans, and Native Americans whose lands fell under the power of Portugal, Spain, Britain, France, and the Netherlands.

Behind the changes in Europe were minds numbed by the destruction and bloodshed of the great wars of religion that began in the mid-sixteenth century and reached their crescendo in 1618-1648 in the Thirty Years War. A new group of concerned thinkers, shocked at the bloodshed, sought to free their states from entanglements with particular confessional forms of Christian faith. The intellectual movement that emerged from these events eventually became known as the Enlightenment, and in many places, it successfully challenged the hitherto universal European assumption that Christianity was good and its beliefs were the foundations of Christendom's organization of the ecclesiastical and political economy.

7

Eastern Asia in the Seventeenth Century

The doors of China swing open . . . and shut

Fifteenth-century China had the ability to colonize far beyond its imperial borders. The Ming dynasty (1368-1644), however, like the majority of dynasties before them, had little need or desire to do so. China was the center of the world as far as its rulers were concerned. These rulers sought to extend military influence over regions that bordered China, but they did not press to build an overseas colonial empire in the way that European nations had begun to do. Foreign merchants brought to the Middle Kingdom what the Chinese wanted and their rulers permitted, trading these goods for silk and other goods that they transported to markets across Asia and into Europe. The Ming rulers, like their predecessors, carefully controlled the access foreigners had to China. Both the Ming and their successors in the Qing (or Ch'ing) dynasty (1644-1911) were especially concerned to maintain control of their eastern borders against western Europeans who began to appear in armed ships in the sixteenth century, pressing to pry China open with guns, science, opium, and the Christian religion.

Confucianism had long been the ruling social and political philosophy in China. By the fifteenth century it had become a full-fledged system of religious devotion and philosophy as well, or what is often referred to as Neo-Confucianism. Its learned scholars, or literati, exercised enormous influence over the royal household in China through this period. Toward the end of the Ming period both Buddhism and Taoism came to be seen as enemies of the state by the Confucian scholars. Islam had spread from central Asia into the western regions of China by the sixteenth century, and it too came to be considered something of a threat by the Confucian leaders. Most of the population adhered to popular religious beliefs and practices that dealt with local spirits and the ancestors. These popular traditions often gave hope and meaning to the farmers, the peasants, or others who suffered under imperial policies and the demanding meritocracy of the Confucian social order. From time to time they played a role in the rise of leaders who launched rebellions against China's rulers, but for the most part the Confucian literati ignored them. In the sixteenth century Christianity was represented in China by only a small number of foreign adherents, such as the Armenian merchants who resided within the Middle Kingdom, and was hardly viewed by the Confucian scholars as being any cause for concern.

For centuries the imperial state sought to control religion in China with various degrees of success. The policy reached its peak under the Manchus rulers in the Qing (Ch'ing) dynasty in the seventeenth and eighteenth centuries, under the code known as *Da Qing Luli* (or *Ta Ching Lu-li*), whereby all religions were brought under the Board of Rites. But China's rulers were already moving in this direction during the late Ming period, when as a way of controlling what the rulers feared to be various "heretical" religious influences, all who worked in the civil service, which meant those with the most influence within the social order, were required to pass rigorous civil service exams. The exams were administered in regional centers as well as in the shadow of the emperor in the Forbidden City in Beijing. Students were required to reproduce with ink and brush the exact Chinese characters from large sections of the Confucian classics, such as those known in English as the *Great Learning, Doctrine of the Mean, Analects of Confucius,* and *Mencius.* Long and dedicated study of the classics was believed to be the best way to ensure that religious superstition would be purged, and that tradition would be reinforced. There was little room in this system for creativity or innovation. The supreme cultural value of China was social order, and the examination system was one of the chief methods for ensuring its continuity.

China found itself internationally at a significant political crossroads at the end of the sixteenth century. To the north, Russia was pushing across the continent east to the Manchurian border. The Manchus in turn were moving into China, the Great Wall proving to provide little in the way of a deterrent any longer. Europeans were sailing up from the south and had recently settled in their own colony in Portuguese Macao, while others were sailing from the east, from the Spanish Philippines. The Japanese were making a move to invade Korea, from which it appeared they planned to move militarily against China. Finally, all of these external forces were being exacerbated by the internal political corruption and moral decay that had come to characterize late Ming rule.

In 1583, a twenty-five-year-old tribal leader named Nurhaci (1559-1626) came to power in Manchuria. A devotee of Chinese culture, he united the various tribes in the Manchurian region into a single powerful army. They slowly moved into China, helping Korea and China turn back the Japanese invasion of 1592-1593 before moving to assume control of large portions of China themselves. By 1616 Nurhaci had taken the name of *Tien-Ming* ("Heaven-designated Emperor") and was calling his new dynasty-in-the-making "Qing." In his last year of life he defeated the Ming general using a new cannon that had been cast by Jesuit missionaries. A year later, in 1644, his successors finally took Beijing, thus officially inaugurating the new Qing dynasty.

The lure of China had long been a common theme in Western literature and history. The romantic draw was in part a result of Marco Polo's *Livres des merveilles du monde* ("Description of the World," also known in English as his "Travels"), which had first appeared in French in 1298. European interest in the sixteenth century was further spurred by the writings of a Portuguese soldier named Galeote Pereira (dates unknown), who had been arrested by the Ming rulers for smuggling and sent into exile in the interior of China. He escaped in 1553 and was able to publish a report of his experiences that was soon being read in Goa by Jesuit missionaries preparing to go farther east. Translated into Italian and English, the work noted the large numbers of Chinese people and the strict legal system, which was part of his bane but had earned his respect. In 1570 another account of China was published in Lisbon by Gaspar da Cruz (1520-1570), a Dominican who had spent only a few weeks in Canton while traveling throughout Asia in 1556, but whose *Treatise* proved to be both accurate and enticing. Da Cruz described life, politics, handicrafts, food, and daily sanitary practices.

Jesuits enter the Middle Kingdom

For Francis Xavier (1506-1552), China, with its teeming masses and high degree of civilization, represented the supreme missionary call. The Jesuit visitor who oversaw all Jesuit mission work in Asia during the last decades of the sixteenth century, Alessandro Valignano (1539-1606), shared this positive view of East Asian civilization, advocating the adaption of Christianity to local Asian cultures and languages in order to facilitate the growth of Christian communities in the region. In 1579 he sent an Italian Jesuit by the name of Michele Ruggieri (1543-1607) to Macao, the Portuguese trading city on the southeast coast of China, in order to learn the Chinese language and culture. Three years later in 1582 Ruggieri wrote to ask that another Italian, named Matteo Ricci (1552-1610), join him. Ricci soon overshadowed his older colleague in the Jesuit order in his contributions to Chinese Christianity.

Matteo Ricci was born in Macerata, Italy, where he was educated by the Jesuits before going to Rome in 1568 to study law, mathematics, astronomy, and philosophy. After joining the Jesuits in 1571 and completing further studies in Rome, he set sail for Goa, off the southern coast of India, where he studied for the priesthood and was ordained in 1580. In 1582 Ricci then sailed for Macao.

The Ming dynasty in the last decades of the sixteenth century was undergoing severe stresses on a number of fronts, and foreigners of any kind were not generally welcomed. Nevertheless, Ruggieri and Ricci were permitted to move to the city of Zhaoqing on the mainland after only a year in Macao. They continued there to study Chinese language and culture, and especially Confucian doctrines. During this period they wore the garb of Buddhist monks and shaved their heads, hoping to be identified as having a religious purpose and not to be confused with Spanish soldiers or traders. The invitation from the Chinese authorities was revoked, but six months later it was extended again, this time with permission to build a temple. A sign on the building that was eventually constructed, which was a gift of the local magistrate, Wang Pan, identified it as "Temple of the Flower Saint," a name that was intended to sound Buddhist.

The temple was intended primarily to be a way to reach out to local Chinese officials and the literati. Members of the Chinese literati were not allowed to visit a foreigner in a private home, but could visit at a temple or chapel. Hence, the identification of the Jesuits' building, which was a means of opening doors for contact. The Jesuits eventually learned, however, that Buddhist monks were not held in high regard by the Ming authorities, that often in Chinese history Buddhist monks had even been expelled for disrupting the social order, and that by identifying with Buddhists they were not going to be truly considered scholars by the literati. In 1588 Ruggieri returned to Europe, but Ricci remained in China and by 1595 was dressing as a Confucian scholar, presenting himself to the literati as being a Western man of letters rather than as a priest or monk.

Ricci proved to be a remarkable student of Chinese. He committed to memory the four ancient classics of Chinese philosophy and adopted the Chinese name Li Madou (Matou). He knew that unless official permission was given ultimately by the emperor himself in Beijing for Christianity and its representatives to stay in the country, they would be expelled. Ricci's goal was thus to meet the emperor and receive official approval for the work of the Jesuits. He could not do this, however, without earning the respect of local officials. The only way was to show proper respect to the authorities by speaking their language, observing their cultural practices (including engaging in the proper kowtow when meeting authorities), and honoring officials with gifts appropriate to their status. The foreign Christians would gain a hearing only if they proved themselves worthy in terms of the dominant Chinese culture, Ricci reasoned.

Winning the hearts and minds of the Chinese literati and presenting Christianity within the Chinese intellectual framework became the warp and woof of the fabric of the Jesuit mission in China. To these ends Ricci worked both to understand Chinese relationships and to impress the Chinese with Western knowledge, especially mathematics and science. Helped by Chinese scholars, he and Ruggieri translated into Chinese in 1584 a catechism that Ruggieri had begun. *Tianzhu shilu* (or *T'ien-chu shih-lu,* "A True Account of the Lord of Heaven"), which is sometimes simply called "Ruggieri's Catechism," was the first Chinese catechism in the modern era. A more sophisticated philosophical introduction of Christianity in Chinese, titled *Tianzhu shiyi* ("The True Meaning of the Lord of Heaven") and set in print in wood-block carving, was published by Ricci in 1603. Written as a dialogue between a Western and a Chinese scholar, the work reads like a synthesis of Thomistic and Confucian teachings.

The focus for Ricci was on the Chinese concept of "heaven." The true Lord of Heaven was known in original Confucianism, he argued, opening up the possibility that Chinese ancestors had been saved through their knowledge of natural law, though not without an accompanying special gift of grace from God. Christian theology must place itself on the side of the conservative Confucian scholars and in opposition to Neo-Confucianism, he argued. Neo-Confucianism as a religious philosophy had no place for a personal God, but Ricci, after studying and translating large portions of the Confucian classics, had come to the conclusion that Confucius himself did believe in a personal God. This was the philosophic bridge that he worked to build with Chinese Confucianism. By 1595 Ricci had also published a more popular book, *Jiaoyou lun* ("On Friendship"), which consisted of quotations from various Western and Chinese philosophers (including

Jesus and St. Paul). That book sought to build further bridges of understanding by finding common ground between Western and Chinese cultures.

In 1601, after a period of five years in Nanchang and Nanjing, Ricci and several associates were granted permission by Emperor Wanli to enter Beijing, the imperial city. The Jesuits brought with them maps from Europe, paintings, and clocks to give to the emperor as gifts of tribute. The clocks were immediately considered most valuable, and Ricci was given a stipend to look after them. He began working on a new world map that located the Middle Kingdom in the actual middle of the world. The final edition of this *Mappamondo* was published in 1602, and thousands of copies were soon available in both China and Europe.

Ricci always kept in view his main purpose, which was to convert the emperor of China to Christianity. To those who expressed an interest in learning more about the Christian faith Ricci and his associates provided further instruction, and in some cases this led to baptism. For the most part, however, he kept his missionary profile low and represented himself at court as a philosopher rather than as a missionary of the Christian religion. The tactic has sometimes been criticized as disingenuous and even deceitful, but Ricci never denied his Christian allegiance. He simply sought as much as possible to present the message of Christianity as being compatible and even in agreement with the classical teachings of Confucianism.

The main problem Ricci faced in this regard was that the Confucian teachings of his day did not consider the Lord of Heaven to be a supreme deity. Heaven was much more an impersonal reality, a primordial energy, and an order of existence that was connected to earth in the person of the emperor for the Chinese philosophical tradition. The Confucian concept of heaven did not include a creating or intervening God. Heaven acted indirectly on the destiny of humanity. Human beings on earth were to seek to live in harmony through their behaviors involving rites and morality. There never was as close a fit between Catholic Christianity and Confucianism on these grounds as Ricci wanted to believe. Catholic Christian teaching in the sixteenth century placed significant emphasis on getting to heaven in the afterlife. Confucian teaching held that everyone got to heaven in the afterlife. The purpose of religion for the Confucian thinker was to bring life on earth into harmony with heaven, doing so mainly through the rituals prescribed by the ancient tradition.

The Chinese knew about the religious beliefs of India and the Arabs, and had learned what those people believed regarding heaven. The Christian notion, on the other hand, that the Lord of Heaven was nailed to a wooden *ten* (a cross in Chinese) and died seemed to most to be utterly stupid. The vast majority of those of the Chinese imperial court could never accept the Jesuits and their philosophical doctrines as being anything more than the vulgar beliefs of strange, Western barbarians.

Of far more interest to the Chinese scholars in the imperial city was the scientific knowledge that the Jesuits brought. Foremost in this area was their astronomical knowledge, since one of the principal duties of the emperor and his administration in China was to set the calendar. By doing so accurately, the emperor ensured that human activity followed the cycles of the cosmos. The accuracy of the calendar was a token of dynastic legitimacy and power. Private individuals were even forbidden to study the heavens on their own or to try to set the dates for particular events. The emperor's work of establishing the calendar each year, thereby calculating the equinox and other ritual days, played a critical part in the Confucian imperial rites, which were vital to maintaining the social order. Ricci had noticed in his first visit to Nanjing that there were astronomical instruments left from the days of Arab scientists under the Mongol rulers that were no longer being used. In 1610, shortly after Ricci's death, the Jesuits proved to be more accurate than the Chinese astronomers in predicting an eclipse. Again in 1629 their ability to predict an eclipse more accurately proved the superiority of their knowledge, earning them an appointment to the *Qintianjian* or "Astronomical Bureau," located within the Bureau of Rites. In 1644 at the beginning of the new Manchu dynasty the Jesuit scholar Johann Adam Schall von Bell (1591-1666) proved once again to be more accurate in predicting an eclipse than the Chinese Confucian and Muslim astronomers. Schall was appointed director of the important Astronomical Bureau.

The knowledge that the Jesuits brought proved to be quite helpful for establishing a more accurate calendar, thereby ensuring greater harmony throughout the empire and in turn winning for the Jesuits a degree of imperial support. At the same time this knowledge was a source of opposition, for the Jesuits were foreigners and barbarians, and having them play a role in the imperial service was seen by some as a cause for alarm. The Jesuits brought with them the theory that heaven was composed of seven concentric spheres, directly contradicting the Confucian doctrine that heaven was a harmonious and integrated whole. Ricci introduced Euclid's geometry to China, translating works on the Greek philosopher into Chinese for the first time. What won them an initial place in the imperial city of Beijing was their scientific and technical knowledge, which helped the emperor's administration in concrete, practical ways.

Through the Jesuits' efforts a small number of Chinese eventually became Christian, undergoing baptism and identifying with the new teaching. Those Chinese who did so for the most part were attracted to the moral element in Christianity that Ricci and the other Jesuits lifted up, and secondarily to the scientific knowledge that appeared to accompany the Christian religion. Christianity seemed to some Chinese not only to be in agreement with the Confucian classics, especially regarding control of passion and reverence for authority, but to go beyond them in its effectiveness. Essentially, Christianity was introduced as a new sect of Confucianism at a time when there were some among the Chinese intellectual class looking for reform.

Sixteen Jesuit priests came to work with Ricci in the first decades of the mission, a surprisingly small number. By 1650 they had baptized perhaps as many as 2,500 Chinese, also a low number when compared to other areas of Asia at the time such as Japan where the number of converts was considerably higher. Among the baptized, however, were several important members of the literati, including three that the European Jesuits called the "Three Pillars" of the Chinese church, a name given to them during a period of official persecution in 1616-1617.

One of the Three Pillars was Xu Guangqi (1562-1633). A native of Shanghai, he met Ricci in 1601 as they were both journeying to Beijing. Two years later Xu was baptized, taking the Christian name of Paul. During his earlier years he had studied Buddhism, Taoism, and Neo-Confucianism. In 1604 he passed the highest national examination, the *jinshi*, and went on to become a high-ranking official and advisor to the emperor, toward the end of his life serving as grand secretary (the prime minister). Xu worked with Ricci to translate a number of Western scientific texts, including the works on Euclid, into Chinese. He later wrote several texts on his own that drew on Western scientific knowledge. It was through him that the Jesuits' knowledge of astronomy was brought to the imperial office that took care of the calendar. During an extended visit to Shanghai in 1608, Xu was instrumental in establishing the first Catholic congregation in that city, with many of its first members coming from among his own family.

Li Zhizao (1565-1630), the second of the Three Pillars, was born in Hangzhou and passed the *jinshi* in 1598. He too had come to Beijing to work in the imperial bureaucracy. There he met Ricci and other Jesuits and converted to Christianity, undergoing baptism in 1610. In 1626 he authored *Tianxue chuhan* ("Collection of Heavenly Studies") and collaborated with Xu to write another book, but is best known for his 1630 "Preface" to Ricci's *The True Meaning of the Lord of Heaven.*

The third of the Three Pillars, Yang Tingyun (1562-1627), was also a native of Hangzhou and passed the *jinshi* in 1592. For seven years he served as a district magistrate before taking a position as government inspector of public works, a censor. One of the prime concerns in his governmental positions was to reduce taxes, thereby alleviating some of the burden that the common people bore. After a period of intense interest in Buddhism, Yang Tingyun converted to Christianity in 1611. In his writings he explicitly interpreted Christianity as a Neo-Confucian sect, reformulating central Confucian metaphysical and ethical concepts. His reconception of the Christian understanding of God as Father/Mother (*dafumu*) introduced a more personalized notion of heaven into Confucian thought. His interpretation of Jesus in light of the history of Chinese civilization provided a more universal framework for understanding salvation than the Western Jesuits had provided. He defended the Jesuits' practice of celibacy and their obedience to their kings while traveling to other lands as being compatible with Confucian social ethics.

Xu Candida (1607-1680) was the granddaughter of Xu Guangqi and was converted under the influence of her grandfather. A woman of remarkable gifts, she is credited with having founded thirty churches in China, along with two communities of women catechists and several orphanages. A member of the upper class, she was involved in extensive work for the poor as well as in supporting the Western Jesuit missionaries. The story of her life, including extracts from her letters and the story of her conversion, was the subject of *Histoire d'une dame chrétienne de la Chine* ("History of a Christian Woman in China"), written by Philippus Couplet and published in Paris in 1688.

There were a handful of others from among the Chinese scholarly class who became Christians and began building a library of Chinese Christian works in the sixteenth century. The church was slow to allow Chinese to enter the ranks of its clergy on the other hand. The first Chinese Roman Catholic bishop was not consecrated until 1685. Luo Wenzao (known in the West as Gregorio López, 1611-1691) was born in Fujian province. Baptized in 1633 by Franciscan missionaries, he traveled to Manila where he was educated by the Dominicans and ordained in 1656, becoming the first Chinese Roman Catholic priest. He returned to China, where he was an active supporter of the Jesuits' efforts at home and in Rome. In 1685 at the age of seventy-four he became the first Chinese Roman Catholic to be consecrated as a bishop. Luo in turn became the first bishop to elevate Chinese clerics to the priesthood within China proper when in 1688, more than one hundred years after the first Jesuits had arrived in China, he ordained three Chinese priests. Another 240 years would pass before Rome consecrated another Chinese bishop, an indication of the difficulty Catholic Christianity had becoming fully identified as a Chinese religion.

The issue of Chinese Christians being members of a religious association under foreign authority was cause for considerable concern in the Chinese imperial court. Especially troubling for the Chinese rulers was the fact that those who became Christian were supposed to pay honor to *jiaohuang* (the "emperor of the religion," or the pope), a shadowy figure who lived far away and whom the Jesuits professed to obey absolutely. In 1616 a persecution broke out, and the Jesuits were ordered to leave Beijing and return to Macao. The intervention of the Chinese Christians in the imperial bureaucracy was critical in their gaining permission to return the following year. By 1620 they had gained permission to begin working in the provinces, and had begun to move among the lower classes especially. The attraction of Christianity to the lower classes was connected with schools as much as anything else, for the imperial educational system bypassed most common people entirely.

Always there was opposition to the new Christian teaching in China, published in works such as *Poxie ji* ("Collection for the Destruction of Vicious Doctrines"), which appeared in 1640. *Poxie ji* targeted the notion that one man, Jesus, who lived in the West among the barbarians during the period of the great Han emperor, was Lord of Heaven. To any educated Chinese person this seemed utterly absurd. For some critics, the Christians' teachings were an immediate threat to Confucian social order, which clearly defined separate classes. To some, the Jesuits were simply seducers with their scientific knowledge and toys such as clocks. Mostly these Westerners were simply viewed as barbarians by the more civilized Chinese.

Controversy over adaptation of Christianity to Chinese culture

The Jesuits seemed to be particularly intent on attacking Buddhism, which they considered to be nothing more than vulgar idolatry, and Taoism, which they considered superstition. The metaphysical concepts of Buddhism in particular escaped the Jesuits entirely as they cast their lot with the imperial ideology of Confucianism. Some of the most significant attacks on the new Christian teaching in the seventeenth century came from Chinese Buddhists who resided not only in Beijing but throughout China. The barbarians' claim that the Lord of Heaven had attributes and had a personality contradicted the statement that he had no beginning and no end, they said. The absurd doctrine of the incarnation attached a self to the absolute, a condition that Buddhism fundamentally rejected. The Christian doctrine of creation was, in their mind, easily refuted by Buddhist metaphysical teachings regarding "conditioned arising."

Opposition to Christian teaching could also be found among the Confucianists. The work of one Confucian scholar, Yang Guangxian (1597-1669), warned about how the Jesuits were destroying the fabric of society. The Jesuits claimed the realm had two sovereigns, he argued. One was political and ruled the Chinese kingdom, while the other was religious and ruled over all the kingdoms of the earth. This is like having two suns, he said. Such a doctrine could only disturb the unity of China. On the contrary, he argued, China, or the Middle Kingdom, was organized around the emperor and all religions were under the control of the imperial government. For this reason if there really were a Lord of Heaven, the long-standing Chinese social order would be seriously disrupted.

In their approach to presenting Christianity in China, Ricci and his Jesuit colleagues were conscious of engaging in a major new encounter between Christian faith and a well-developed literary and philosophical tradition, perhaps unlike anything in the history of Christianity since the early days of its encounter with Hellenism in the Mediterranean world. One of the difficulties that the Jesuit mission in China faced in this regard concerned the choice of the Chinese word that they used to name God. In traditional Chinese culture, although there were many gods, spirits, and bodhisattvas, there was no common concept or word for a personal high God. The closest concept the Jesuits found was *Tian* ("Heaven"), which was totally transcendent, all-powerful, and unapproachable. Traditional Chinese cosmology understood the land of China to be the Middle Kingdom that stood between heaven and earth. The transcendent principle and power of heaven were mediated specifically through the emperor of China, who was the Son of Heaven.

Ricci argued that at one time the Chinese did believe in a personal God and this needed to be rediscovered. But he was then faced with the question of what was the name of this Heaven-God. The Chinese classics used two titles for heaven, *Tian* ("heaven") and *Shangdi* ("Emperor" or "Lord on High"). At first Ricci chose to use *Tianzhu* ("Lord of Heaven"), but some Chinese scholars told him that *Shangdi* was more appropriate and so he ended up defending the use of both. Others among the Western missionaries thought that God should simply be called *Tian* or *Deus*, the Latin term. Roman Catholics officially accepted the term *Tianzhu* in 1628, and to this day the Roman Catholic Church in China is known as *Tianzhujiao* or the "Religion of the Lord of Heaven."

Another internal controversy that marked the Jesuit mission, which has come to be known as the "Rites Controversy," and entailed the veneration of Chinese ancestors was not resolved so quickly. Ancestral rites were deeply rooted in Chinese culture, having a central place in the Confucian order of relationships. After passing the literary civil service exam all candidates were required to honor Confucius at a ceremony that often involved animal sacrifice. Children were to honor their parents, even after death. This "honoring," usually called filial piety for the devotion of a son for his parents, entailed in part bringing gifts for the dead ancestors. For most Chinese this was understood to actually mean feeding their souls to satisfy them in the other world. Paper money, called "hell money," was often burned to help pay the ancestors' way out of suffering and hell. The living had an ongoing relationship with deceased parents and grand-parents, and it was especially the duty of the first-born son to care for the tablets that represented the various ancestors. The practice of honoring the ancestors was done either in the home or at a family or regional temple. To neglect these rites was to unravel the social fabric.

Ricci argued that these various Confucian and ancestor rites were consistent with the Christian religion. Honoring the genius of Confucius could be seen as a patriotic duty, and remembering parents could be seen as showing respect, in line with the biblical commandment to honor one's father and mother. The Jesu-its proscribed certain practices. A Christian was not to pray to the ancestors as if they could hear or could act on one's behalf. Chinese Christians were not to bring food to feed the ancestors and were not to participate in animal sacrifice to Confucius. But they were allowed to honor their ancestors in accordance with traditional Chinese practices, argued Ricci.

Not everyone was as sure as Ricci that the family altars were simply a matter of remembrance or veneration. Ricci's exposure was to the educated elite, but among the villages and throughout the countryside such "remembrance" could more accurately be called ancestor worship. Dominicans and Franciscans began arriving on the coast of China around 1630. Before long they heard about the Jesuits' decision and were appalled. Word spread among the Spanish from the Philippines that the Jesuits allowed Chinese converts to worship all sorts of gods as long as they hid a crucifix under their robe. Soon letters were sailing off to Rome.

In 1643, Juan Bautista de Morales (1597-1664), a Dominican, carried to Rome seventeen charges against the Jesuits and their work in China. Pope Innocent X (1574-1655) responded in 1645 with a decree against the Jesuit practice. The Jesu-its countered with an appeal, and a new pope, Alexander VII (1599-1667), in 1656 issued a decree supporting the Jesuit practices in China. Soon the issue was a point of discussion among scholars throughout Europe and in the imperial court in China. Some 260 works were published in Europe on the controversy, while several emperors in China weighed in with official statements in support of the Jesuits' practice.

By the late seventeenth century Augustinians and missionaries of the Société des missions étrangères de Paris (the "Paris Foreign Mission Society," MEP) had arrived in China and were taking the side of the Dominicans and Francis-cans in opposing the Jesuit position. Back in Rome, the Sacred Congregation for the Propagation of the Faith, better known simply as *Propaganda fidei*, which had been established in 1622 to bring all Catholic missionary activity directly under the authority of the Vatican, began weighing in. Instructions from *Propaganda fidei* generally called on missionaries to refrain from imposing their own national identities on the churches that were being formed in other parts of the world, and to allow for indigenous customs and cultural practices as long as they did not directly contradict church teachings on doctrine or moral practice. Regarding the Chinese rites, however, *Propaganda fidei* changed its ruling several times. When the Jesuits presented their case, it ruled in their favor, but it then reversed the ruling when others gave their understanding of the rites. A strong supporter of the Jesuits, the Qing emperor Kangxi (1654-1722) in 1692 issued an edict protecting Christianity in China. In 1704, the controversy took a turn for the worst for the Jesuits when Bishop Charles Maigrot (1652-1730), who had already prohibited the Chinese rites in his vicariate of Fujian, convinced the Holy Office of the Inquisition to issue a universal condemnation. The ruling was promulgated in Nanjing in 1707 by the papal legate Charles Maillard de Tournon (1668-1710). Kangxi and his successors on the throne of China were angered by Rome's measures against the rites. Emperor Yongzheng (1638-1735) in 1724 ordered all missionaries except those employed at the court to be deported to Canton and Macao. In 1736, his son, Emperor Qianlong (1711-1799), imposed the death penalty for anyone practicing and embracing Christianity.

The conclusion of the Rites Controversy did not come until almost the middle of the eighteenth century. After decades of debate, Rome finally issued a papal bull in 1742 that condemned the practice of Chinese Christians commemorating their dead with traditional ancestral rites. The Jesuits were instructed to forbid the practice. Ever obedient to the Holy Father, they did so, but at great cost because this then made Christians subversive in the eyes of the Confucian state in a manner that had not previously been the case. Only a handful of Jesuits remained at the imperial court as foreign advisors. All other missionaries were ordered to leave China, although a few remained in hiding, working in the countryside. Despite the restrictions on Christianity, a number of Catholic Christian communities were able to sustain themselves in China.

One of the most surprising aids that the Jesuits had in China during the first half of the seventeenth century turned out to be a gift from the East Syrian Church that was 734 years in the waiting. In 1625 a large stone with a lengthy inscription in Chinese and Syriac was unearthed near the Tang dynasty capital city of Xi'an (previously Chang'an). The stone, situated on the back of a large turtle, held a lengthy inscription that told the story of the coming of Christianity to China in 635 and its acceptance by the Tang dynasty emperors. A statement of faith and the names of members of the community (in Chinese and Syriac) were included on the monument. Here was the evidence that proved that Christianity was not a new religion to China, and that it had been previously approved by emperors. The Jesuits made much of the discovery while skeptics in Europe, including Protestants, denounced it as a Jesuit plant to support their work. In winning support for the Christian work in China, this surprising discovery helped encourage the Jesuits, empower Chinese Christians, and open the ears of Chinese intellectuals.

In the seventeenth century there were no women's orders established in

China. Worship followed the European pattern in buildings that were built in Italian style but with Chinese readings and devotions. Worship was conducted partly in Chinese during much of the seventeenth century. In 1615 Pope Paul V (1552-1621) approved the use of Chinese for the administration of the sacraments, but the translation of liturgical books lagged behind. In the midst of the Rites Controversy, the mood shifted and more Europeans began to argue for the Mass being said only in Latin. At the same time, a growing number of Chinese wanted to learn Latin, reinforcing the decision to use this language. In the end Rome recalled the privilege of using Chinese in worship, thereby ending in China, as in Latin America, the experience of Catholic worship in the indigenous languages for several more centuries.

For all of the effort to reach the rulers and the literati, the church in China remained clearly Western in worship and devotion. Even though much of the mission work had been conducted among the male literati, most of the local churches were made up of members of their families. At the time of Ricci's death there were, it is estimated, 2,500 Chinese Christians. By the end of the century there may have been as many as 100,000 Chinese Christians. Even with periods of internal conflict and persecution the Christian population maintained itself into the eighteenth century. However much it remained a minority religion, Christianity this time had come to China to stay.

Korean beginnings

Korea's encounter with Christianity did not begin with missionaries or merchants but with invading Mongol armies, as archaeological evidence indicates that there were Mongol rulers who gained control of portions of Korea in the thirteenth and fourteenth centuries. Christians were also among the Japanese army that attacked the "Hermit Kingdom" (as Korea was often called due to its isolationism) in the sixteenth century. During the Japanese invasion in 1592 under Hideyoshi (1536-1598), the soldiers of General Konishi Yukinaga (1555-1600), who led the march against the Korean city of Pyongyang, were mostly Japanese Christians. A European Jesuit, Gregorio de Cespedes (1551-1611), accompanied by a Japanese brother, Foucan Eion (dates unknown), came after the main battles were over to encourage the troops. De Cespedes is possibly the first European to step on Korean soil, arriving in December of 1593, and he was quite possibly the first person to celebrate the Eucharist in Korea.

Upon their retreat, the Japanese took a number of Koreans as prisoners to be sold as slaves. Some became Christian, as evidenced by a small Korean church that was built in Nagasaki in 1610, the first-known Korean church ever built. One of the first Korean martyrs, Vincent Kwon (d. 1626), was the son of a high-ranking military officer from Seoul who was taken from Korea by General Konishi and raised as a Christian in a Jesuit community in Japan. He was given the opportunity to return to Korea, but instead remained in Japan where he was martyred at Shimabara during a period of persecution in 1626-1627.

There were two other brief Korean encounters with Catholicism in the seventeenth century, neither of which led to a permanent community. A Korean embassy visited Beijing each year as part of Korea's vassal status to its more powerful neighbor. During one of these visits several Korean Confucian scholars came across Ricci's *The True Meaning of the Lord of Heaven*. One of the Confucianists, Yi Syu-Kwang (d. 1627) wrote a summary of it for Korean use, but nothing of his influence or if he wrote anything else about the Christian faith is known. A second contact in this period came about when Manchu invaders took Crown Prince So-hyun (1612-1645) as a hostage in response to Korea's support for the dying Ming dynasty. When the Manchu finally ended the Ming dynasty and established their rule as the new Qing dynasty in Beijing in 1644, So-hyun was with them. During his brief stay in Beijing, the prince became acquainted with Schall von Bell, from whom he learned about both science and religion. So-hyun returned to Korea without any explicit indication that he was considering conversion to the Christian faith, but accompanying him were several Chinese Catholic eunuchs and Chinese Catholic women. Two months after his return to Korea in 1645 the crown prince died suddenly, ending any known official Christian presence in Korea for another 150 years. Christian teachings, however, in the form of the Jesuit books and under the guise of a Neo-Confucian school, began to circulate among members of the scholarly class.

Christian twilight in Japan

Japan, as noted earlier, was relatively open to Christians during much of the sixteenth century, for reasons as much to do with internal political struggles and the promise of Portuguese external aid as with interest in Christianity. In any case, the result was the sudden emergence of a significant Japanese Christian community. During the last years of Hideyoshi's rule the situation began to change. The arrival of Spanish friars in 1593 brought a new approach to mission and conflict among the Europeans seeking influence. The Franciscans were primarily concerned with ministering to the poor, whereas the Jesuits had focused their efforts on members of the upper ruling class. The Jesuits were fearful that if the Franciscans didn't follow Japanese customs and respect those in authority, they would all be expelled from the country. The Franciscans, on the other hand, were suspicious of the Jesuits. Both were beholden to traders from their respective supporting kings of Portugal and Spain and upon the Japanese desire to purchase the goods that had opened the Japanese to consider Western ideas.

The Jesuit fears began to unfold when the Spanish galleon, San Felipe, ran aground in 1597, loaded with weaponry and missionaries. The captain, questioned by the Japanese, in the words carried back to Hideyoshi himself, said that the Spanish were now enlarging their field of conquest from Mexico and the Philippines to Japan. Six Franciscans who had been on the ship and three Japanese Jesuits who may not have been on it were seized, along with another fifteen Japanese Franciscans from a hospital. Two others voluntarily turned themselves in to the authorities. Each of the twenty-six Christians had an ear sliced off, and all were paraded through the streets before being executed by crucifixion. The emperor ordered that their bodies be left on the crosses for nine months as a warning to those who might think of befriending Christians.

With the rise of Tokugawa Ieyasu (r. 1598-1614), Christians in Japan experienced a brief period of relative calm. During his first years, Ieyasu was preoccupied with uniting Japan under his rule. The Christian population experienced a reprieve and grew. In the territory of the Christian *daimyo* and leader of the war against Korea, Konishi Yukinaga, some twenty-five thousand baptisms a year were being reported by the Catholic priests. There may have been as many as 300,000 Christians altogether in Japan by 1614. But the shogun, Tokugawa Ieyasu, and local warlords then turned suddenly against Christians, both Japanese and foreign. Suspicions mounted that the Spanish were planning to take over Japan, and that missionaries were the first wave of colonists. An English navigator, Will Adams (1564-1620), arrived and quickly became the chief trade negotiator for the shogun, further undermining both the valuable Portuguese trade and the Roman Catholic missionaries who were dependent on Portugal for support and protection. The shogun himself had begun to turn away from both Christianity and Buddhism to adopting a form of Neo-Confucianism as a way to bring order to his realm. Finally, the Japanese civil war that began in 1600 pitted the new shogun, Ieyasu, against the supporters of the heirs of Hideyoshi. Unfortunately, the Christian *daimyo* Konishi and his forces fought against Ieyasu with the consequence that Christians were perceived as enemies of the state.

In 1614 a vigorously anti-Christian edict was issued proclaiming that all churches were to be closed, all missionaries were to leave the country, and all practice of Christianity, public or private, was banned. The religions recognized in Japan were to be Shintoism, Buddhism, and Confucianism, the edict declared. Christianity was the religion of foreigners who wished to take over the country. All Japanese were to be enrolled in one of the Buddhist sects, initiating a Buddhist revival and leading to more Christian martyrdoms and defections from the faith. One of the defectors, Fukansai Habian (or Fabian Fukan, 1565-1621), had been an apologist against Buddhism and Confucianism. After a long period of silence he left the Jesuit order and began with equal vigor and zeal to write against Christians and the Europeans.

The authorities used torture and slow death as a way to dissuade people from continuing as Japanese Christians. Descriptions of the tortures were gruesome, and include mention of Koreans. The actual number of those who suffered is difficult to assess. Jesuit records indicate that the number of Christians had grown from 3,000 in 1551 to 30,000 in 1561, and then to 300,000 in 1614, out of an estimated total population of about 20 million Japanese. There were never more than seventy European Jesuits working in Japan at one time. Approximately sixty of the missionaries who refused to leave were caught and decapitated or crucified upside down. Estimates of Japanese martyrs range from two thousand to five thousand, making it a significantly small percentage of the total number of Christians reported by the Jesuits at the time. Many of those who escaped martyrdom and who refused to recant their confession went into hiding. Some were ministered to by foreign priests who remained in the country and moved about at night to administer the sacraments and encourage the faithful. The vast majority of those who had been baptized simply renounced their Christian faith and followed the shogun's orders.

If there were to be an epilogue to what is often called the "Christian century" in Japan it would be the Shimabara Rebellion in 1637. Led for the most part by Japanese farmers, the rebellion symbolized the matrix of issues that affected Japanese Christianity. Arima province had been a Christian province but had come under the rule of an anti-Christian *daimyo*, Matsukura Shigeharu (1598-1638). Taxation ran as high as 80 percent on crops, which combined with bad harvests and extreme violence directed against their families led the farmers to revolt in December of 1637. Most of these farmers were Christians. Led by a fifteen-year-old prophetic leader named Amakusa Shiro (1622-1638), who also went by the Western Christian name of Jerome, they marched into battle under Christian banners with crosses and angels unfurled against the samurai army.

At first the samurai suffered heavy casualties. With reinforcements from the shogun the samurai then returned and defeated the rebels, killing more than a thousand. Several remaining thousands of rebels retreated to Shimabara, taking over Hara Castle. Besieged and starving, a reported thirty-seven thousand Christians held out at Hara Castle until April of 1638. Those who surrendered were beheaded (over ten thousand) while the rest remained and were burned to death in the castle. Iron crosses, glass, and thousands of heavily burned skeletons have been unearthed in recent years from the site, attesting to the size of the debacle. The following year, the final anti-Christian edict was announced, and Japan closed her doors to all outsiders, ending a ninety-five-year period of trade and Christian development.

Japan's Christian century was marked by several important characteristics. Even though the converts came from among the lower classes, including many farmers and peasants, the conversion of the *daimyos,* or local rulers, was crucial for allowing Christianity to spread. Ironically, this is what also led to the eventual downfall of Christianity in Japan. When the Christian *daimyos* lost in battle, Christianity lost its place in society. For a very brief period of time Christian leaders were educated and were influential in evangelizing whole regions of the country. It is no exaggeration to say that Christianity was becoming the dominant religion in the south, and had the overall political climate continued as it had been, there is no reason to believe that Christianity would not have become a major religious presence throughout Japan.

As in many other places in the world, women played a significant role in Japan in the early development of Christianity. A number of Japanese women were catechists and evangelists. They baptized new believers, heard confessions, and formed women's communities. One of these Japanese Christian women was Kiyohara Ito Maria (1565-?). Her father was a Confucian scholar, and she was a personal attendant to another prominent upper-class woman, Hosokawa Tama (1563-1600), who also became a Christian in 1587 and added the Christian name Gracia to her own. A third Japanese woman from this period was Naito (c. 1565-1627), a Buddhist nun who became a Christian in 1595 and took the name Julia. Naito Julia organized one of the first women's communities in Japan, Beatas of Miyako, in Kyoto in 1606. She was also recognized for her missionary work among the consorts and wives of the *daimyo*. Naito was expelled in 1614 and spent the remainder of her life in Manila, where she and several other Japanese nuns organized a new convent. There were many more women who were important to the story of Christianity in Japan during this period whose names are not yet known.

During this period few churches were built. Those that were constructed were built with local materials and resembled other religious buildings in Japan. Religious paintings of Jesus, Mary, and the saints were particularly important in the religious devotions of the Japanese. The Jesuits wrote repeatedly to Europe' to ask for more religious art. Buddhist converts especially requested Christian religious art to replace the images they had in their homes. Recognizing the need for these images, the Jesuit visitor Valignano established a Seminary of Painters in Japan in 1583 at Arima. Under the leadership of Giovanno Nicolo (1563-1626), who was originally from Naples, the school trained many Japanese Christian artists and even some early Chinese Christian artists. Although they were teaching the European style of art, with shading, rounder figures, and European facial features, one finds some Japanese features in later works in some of the few surviving images.

Japan's Christian century came to a close in 1639. Little evidence exists to tell what happened to any Christians who remained after the persecution. Some may have survived in rural areas or in the mountains, but the history of Christianity in Japan from 1639 until the nineteenth century when mission work again began is mostly blank. One small window can be found in a practice that arose during the persecutions in 1633. The government of Nagasaki initiated a way to ensure that there were no longer any Christians in the region. Each January all local citizens were required to participate in a "foot-treading ceremony" (*fumi-e*) whereby they would, one-by-one, have to walk on top of paintings of images of Jesus, Mary, and the saints. Japanese religious devotion was so closely tied to these images that such an act was a clear sign of rejection of Jesus Christ. Many citizens were tortured and killed because they refused to do so, indicating the continuing presence, if underground, of Japanese Christians.

Vietnam

Like Japan in the sixteenth and seventeenth centuries, Vietnam (whose northern region at the time was called Tonkin, and the southern region Cochinchina) was strongly influenced by China. Chinese emperors at times exercised direct rule over portions of northern Vietnam, but more often they simply demanded, and received, tribute. The Vietnamese had their own indigenous religion that was similar to that of the Chinese regarding both the ancestors and heaven. *Ong Troi,* or "Mr. Heaven," was a transcendent, benevolent, and just being who was the source of all that existed. Unlike the Chinese, the Vietnamese believed Ong Troi to be a personal being, eventually making it easier to identify Ong Troi with the creator in Christian teaching. The Vietnamese also recognized the ongoing spirit realm of the ancestors who "resided" in wooden tablets that had the names of the deceased on one side and dates of birth and death etched on the other. Ancestors were venerated (*tho*) through offerings and lighting of joss sticks, or incense.

The Vietnamese also practiced the religions called the *tam giao* of Buddhism, Confucianism, and Taoism. Of these religions, Buddhism was in decline in the seventeenth century, in part because the founder of the later Le dynasty, Le Thai To (1385-1433), opposed it. Taoism, which often took on aspects of a romantic and mystical reaction to the sterile and strict social order of Confucianism, had become an indigenous Vietnamese religion with Vietnamese heroes and great spirits. Confucianism dominated the civil service with the same type of examination system (begun in the Tran dynasty, 1225-1400) that existed in China.

Among the first Christians known to have sought to bring Christianity to Vietnam was the Portuguese Dominican Gaspar de Cruz, who was mentioned earlier and who arrived in the country around 1550. Other Franciscans and Augustinians followed in the 1580s and 1590s, but little was accomplished by them. Refused permission by the local rulers to work among the Vietnamese, they provided ministry only to Portuguese and Japanese in the seacoast areas.

Vietnamese Christianity does not really begin until the arrival of the Jesuits in 1615. The first of them, Fathers Francesco Buzomi (1576-1639) and Diego Carvalho (1578-1624), along with several brothers, landed in the country in the middle of January that year. By Easter they were ready to baptize the first ten Vietnamese converts. Within three years there were over three hundred Christians, with one new Jesuit arriving each year to help with the work. Joining them as well were a number of Christian refugees escaping persecution in Japan. Many of these Japanese refugees settled in an international port city of Hai Pho (Faifo), where the work of the Jesuits was strong.

Portuguese ships carrying both merchants and missionaries were well received in both north (Tonkin) and in the south (Cochinchina) during the second decade of the seventeenth century. By this time it was evident to rulers throughout east Asia that the European boats brought valuable goods for trade. In addition to their treasures, they also had armaments and military know-how that most Asian governments were pleased to gain access to. Although the Le dynasty was in name ruling over all of Tonkin and Cochinchina, the regions were in fact ruled by two different clans, each of whom was seeking to gain ascendancy over the other. Christian missionaries and European merchants both found themselves caught in the middle of this civil war, at one moment being used as advocates, and the next moment imprisoned as traitors. In addition, Cochinchina was expanding its empire into the southern regions of Champa and Cambodia. Portuguese cannons and muskets were being sought to assist these efforts. As in other regions, merchants, missionaries, and the military competed to gain the advantage in what each specifically sought: spices, souls, and cannons. When the missionaries did not seem to be helping the Vietnamese rulers get what they wanted, they were simply expelled. It was a delicate dance, especially for the missionaries.

Although Jesuits began their work in Vietnam in 1615 it was in 1624 that the story of Vietnamese Christianity began in earnest. The occasion was the arrival of Alexandre de Rhodes (1593-1660). Born in Avignon to a family of Jewish origin, de Rhodes joined the Jesuits and studied at the Quirinal in Rome in preparation to be a missionary to Japan. Upon ordination to the priesthood, he continued his studies in mathematics and astronomy in the grand tradition of Jesuit academic work in east Asia. After a few years in Goa, de Rhodes traveled to Macau in 1623 to head for Japan, but persecution in that country prevented him from heading farther east. Instead his superior sent him south, to Cochinchina, to help with the work that began almost a decade earlier.

De Rhodes immediately began studying the Vietnamese language, with great success. Less than two years later, he, along with the other foreign missionaries, was expelled, setting up a pattern of hard work, positive response, and then expulsion. During his first brief stay, however, several important accomplishments were recorded. While assisting Francisco de Pina, S.J., de Rhodes witnessed the conversion of Lady Minh Duc (1568-1648), the last concubine of Lord Nguyen Hoang (1525-1613), the founder of the Nguyen dynasty. She took the Christian name of Marie Madeleine and became an important supporter of the Jesuit's work. A bright young boy, who was eventually given the name Raphaël de Rhodes (dates unknown), also became a Christian and taught Alexandre de Rhodes proper pronunciation of the Vietnamese tones. The younger de Rhodes later accompanied the European missionaries on their first journey to Laos, which meant that one of the first Christian missionaries to Laos was Vietnamese.

The older de Rhodes learned mostly by error how important it was to show respect for the cult of the ancestors. Opponents of Christianity were already attacking Christians for threatening to divide the country because Christians did not appear to pay sufficient respect to the souls of departed ancestors. De Rhodes became convinced that there was very little in Vietnamese cultural practice that was sinful. Thus, he was disposed from his first years to accommodate the cult of ancestors and believed there was no way for the work to continue otherwise. The approach the French Jesuit pursued, described in his book published in 1651, *Histoire du royaume de Tunquin et des grands progrez que la predication . . .* ("History of the Kingdom of Tonkin and of the Progress of the Preaching . . ."), can be described as one of enculturation. He understood his mission to be identifying for the Vietnamese the God they worshipped but did not know.

Another decision of de Rhodes had long-term implications not only for the survival of Christianity but for the spirituality that developed in Vietnam. Early Vietnamese converts wanted to wear crucifixes, crosses, rosaries, and images as a witness to their new faith. The Vietnamese ruler sought to outlaw the practice. A number of Christians indicated that they were willing to die for their "witness." De Rhodes, however, reasoned that such offending items were not essential to the faith and that it would not be brave, but foolhardy, to retain them. The counsel meant that lives were saved and the Christians given more time to continue their work.

In 1627 de Rhodes moved north to Tonkin, where he stayed until 1630. Unlike Ricci who spent seventeen years gaining the confidence of the Chinese rulers, de Rhodes was immediately received by the royal household in the village of An Vuc, where he had discussions with members of the royal family and with local Buddhist monks. In the course of three years he oversaw the building of the first church in the village of An Vuc, established a residence for other Jesuits, began a program for training catechists, and then was expelled for life from the kingdom. By then he had succeeded in baptizing 5,602 people, however. De Rhodes was accompanied during his three years by only one brother, Pero Marques (1577-1657), who previously worked in Cambodia.

Women played an even more prominent role in the development of the Christian community in Vietnam than they did in other East Asian countries in the seventeenth century. The name of Minh Duc Vuong Thai Phi, the last concubine of Lord Nguyen Hoang, has already been noted in this regard. Another early convert, given the Christian name Lina (dates unknown), lived in the town of Van No (present-day Thanh Hoa), where she opened a residence for the poor, perhaps the first such ministry in Vietnam. The sister of Lord Trinh Trang (1577-1654), who took the name Catherine (d. c. 1650) upon baptism, had been a devout Buddhist and a teacher of that faith. After her conversion she continued as an instructor, but now of Christianity, for other women in the royal court. Upon her conversion she applied herself to the study of Christian scripture, using her gift of poetry to write a book of poems that was set to music as a type of catechism. The poems described the biblical story of salvation and ended with the coming of Christianity to Vietnam. The songs became popular and were sung by Christians and non-Christians alike.

The experiences of these women reveal de Rhodes's strategy of immediate instruction and the empowering of converts so that the Vietnamese church would be built by Vietnamese. De Rhodes was cognizant of the fact that Vietnamese who were leaders in the court and in the temples would make the best evangelists and teachers. His conversations with Buddhist monks proved to be particularly fruitful in this regard. At least one Buddhist monk converted and became a Jesuit catechist in Vietnam during the period de Rhodes was working there.

De Rhodes's sojourn in Tonkin was cut short by suspicions, rumors, and finally a royal decree. The Portuguese were aiding Cochinchina in its war against Tonkin, and eunuchs in the court spread the rumor that the Jesuits were agents of the Portuguese. The local lord listened. By then opposition to the Jesuits was mounting on several fronts. Catholic teaching did not allow concubinage, arousing opposition among the upper classes. The Buddhist monks were fearful of their temples becoming vacant, and the Christians were confronting, if not confounding, local magicians. The Jesuit missionary was put under house arrest and banned from engaging in any further evangelistic activities. He and his colleagues continued to communicate by letters, however, which were read at house prayer meetings and passed along.

Eventually de Rhodes was permitted to leave Tonkin and return to Cochinchina. His second period of ministry in the south consisted of four different visits between 1640 and 1645. The Lord Nguyen Phuc Lan (1601-1648) allowed him into the country not because he favored Christian missionary activity but because of the gifts that de Rhodes brought. When he first arrived, the Jesuit found that the community he left behind had been faithful and growing, in part due to the work of Minh Duc, who had proven to be a highly competent leader. Ninety-four new converts were ready for baptism under her instruction, for instance. During this period the Christians conducted most of their religious work carefully out of the sight of officials, often in secret and at night. The Vietnamese Christians themselves carried out most of the work of evangelism, teaching, and apologetics.

A sudden turn came in 1644 when an order came from the capital to put to death one of the Vietnamese catechists, a former mandarin and scholar of the Chinese classics named Ignatius. Ignatius was not found, but another catechist, named Andrew, was, and he was executed in July 1644. De Rhodes was arrested, but soon released. After two more catechists were beheaded, however, de Rhodes left Vietnam for the last time. Although he continued to follow events of the church there, he never returned to east Asia. Nearly sixty years of age, he began a new mission to the royal court of the Moghul emperor in what is today Pakistan.

Over the course of two decades de Rhodes had spent a total of less than ten years actually in Vietnam. During those years, according to his own records, he had personally baptized 9,002 people. More important, however, he had empowered Vietnamese catechists to baptize on their own. When de Rhodes departed Tonkin in 1630 he left behind a community he counted at 5,602 Christians. Ten years later there were nearly 100,000 Christians in 235 churches. In Cochinchina in 1639 there was a community of about 15,000 Christians and 20 churches, but after de Rhodes's second visit persecution slowed the growth dramatically. When de Rhodes reported on Vietnam to *Propaganda fidei* in Rome in 1650 he said the church had about 300,000 Christians and was growing at a rate of about 15,000 per year.

Two of the most important contributions of de Rhodes to Vietnamese Christianity were a dictionary and a catechism. The *Dictionarium* (in Latin, Portuguese, and Vietnamese) and *Catechismus* were both works in progress when he left Vietnam, but he eventually published them in Rome. *Catechismus* benefited from the work of Ricci but was adapted for Vietnam. It included Vietnamese proverbs and even quotes from Vietnamese authors, and used the name *Chua Troi Dat* or "Lord of Heaven and Earth" for the creator and ruler of all things. Various teachings of the Buddhists, Taoists, and Confucianists were refuted, indicating a clear awareness of the interreligious nature of the context. This first theological work in Vietnamese was written in a Latin script and used a vocabulary intended for the common people. Christianity was thus presented not in the language of high Vietnamese or Chinese as was used in the royal court, but in a language for the peasants and soldiers.

The *Catechismus* was regularly used in the semimonastic institution of catechists de Rhodes organized that he called a "seminary." The catechists in the community were organized into groups with a head catechist chosen by de Rhodes for each. Members took vows of chastity, poverty (interpreted as self-support), and obedience. Supported locally and not from foreign mission funds, these catechists carried out most of the ministry of baptizing, teaching, and evangelizing and eventually became a model for other indigenous orders in Asia. Invented out of both necessity and theological design, the pattern gave the fledgling church in Vietnam a structure and order that the churches in Japan and China lacked.

On one of his trips back to Rome de Rhodes made an appeal for a church hierarchy to be established in Vietnam so that the sacrament of confirmation could be carried out for the thousands of new believers he said were coming into the church. As a Frenchman, he believed that the apostolic oversight of the kings of Portugal and Spain was less than ideal. There needed to be direct oversight appointed from Rome. After several appeals and a rejection of the request that a bishop be sent, a new structure for Roman Catholic missions in Asia was established with François Pallu (1626-1684), given by Pope Alexander VII (1599-1667) in 1658 the title of bishop of Heliopolis and vicar apostolic of Tonkin, Laos, and southwest China. At about the same time a new vicar apostolic of Cochinchina was chosen, Pierre Lambert de la Motte (1624-1679). The two Frenchmen, who were friends, were the primary founders of MEP (Société des missions étrangères de Paris). De Rhodes met Pallu in Paris when de Rhodes was recruiting missionaries for Vietnam. Pallu was convinced that secular priests would be more effective than religious (such as Jesuit or Augustinian) priests in planting churches in non-Christian lands. MEP was established with this goal in view.

Pallu set out for Vietnam in 1662 with nine other missionaries and arrived in Ayutthaya, capital of Siam, in 1664 with four who survived the long trip. In Thailand Pallu met with de la Motte in what has been called the Ayutthava Synod of 1644. The two new overseers of the work in Vietnam were joined by a number of Vietnamese Christians, most likely some of de Rhodes's catechists, and decided on a cooperative strategy for mission in the region. This arrangement was later approved by the pope, which meant that all oversight was directly under the French bishops, leaving the king of Portugal out of the picture.

In 1669 de la Motte, who was the vicar apostolic, finally visited Tonkin, since Pallu had been unable to visit this region, to oversee the work. Seven Tonkinese priests were ordained and a number were received into religious orders. Two years later de la Motte established a new women's religious order, known in Vietnamese as *Dong Men Thanh Gia* and in French as *Amantes de la croix* ("Lovers of the Cross"). The order took as its task evangelizing women, teaching the catechism to young girls, baptizing infants who were dying, and caring for the sick. It quickly became an important structure for providing continuity to the life of a persecuted church. Eventually the order was spread by the MEP missionaries to Siam, Burma, and China, but its largest numbers were always in Vietnam.

Siam and Cambodia

The borders of the other kingdoms of Indochina, as with Vietnam, were in constant flux during the sixteenth and seventeenth centuries. European military support and trade partners were both a promise and a problem to the rulers in the region. Among the first Europeans to visit Siam (Thailand) were Portuguese Dominicans who arrived in 1567, but when the Burmese conquered the capital of Ayutthaya in 1569, the Dominicans were executed. There is also a record of a Franciscan work beginning in 1585, but it was the Jesuits arriving in 1607 who started the first, if brief, chapter of Christianity in Siam. Although Jesuits arrived under the *padroado* system that the Portuguese had put into effect in Siam, their toehold was tenuous, and no resident missionaries were established until 1655. The next year the situation changed dramatically under the new leadership of King Narai (r. 1656-1688).

King Narai was concerned about the rising influence not only of the Portuguese but of the newly arriving Dutch in the region. One of the advisors he retained in his court was a colorful character named Constantine Phaulkon (1648-1688), a Greek who had been baptized as a Roman Catholic and at the age of ten set off on a life of travel and adventure, eventually working on British ships and becoming a Protestant. Phaulkon later married a Japanese Catholic and returned to the Catholic fold. By intrigue and hard work, by 1674 he had made his way into employment in the court of King Narai. Meanwhile, France was moving in on the lucrative trade in Asia, and in 1685 King Louis XIV (1638-1715) sent an embassy that was received by Narai, with Phaulkon at his side. The embassy included the French envoy, Alexandre Chevalier de Chaumont (1640-1710), along with Jesuit Guy Tachard (1651-1712) and a priest, Benigne Vachet (1641-1692), of the MEP. The envoy was rigid and difficult, the missionaries were hopeful and pleased, but the Siamese were cautious.

Tachard later wrote up a lengthy report of this and two subsequent voyages that he made to Siam. The report was eventually translated into English and read throughout Europe. Like de Rhodes, Tachard appealed for missionaries. During his three trips to Siam over a fifteen-year period he introduced in Jesuit fashion the study of astronomy and modern mathematics to Siam, sought the approval of the king, and evangelized as he could. Narai allowed the Jesuits to establish a seminary in the capital that would train priests for countries in the region. The Jesuits were hopeful that the king might himself become a Christian, a hope that was never realized. In the end the change in royalty sealed the fate of the religion. Christianity was not tolerated under subsequent rulers and was not allowed to return to Siam until the nineteenth century.

Cambodia had since the fifteenth century been struggling against the oppressive suzerainty of their western neighbor, Siam, and had turned to the Portuguese for help. Faced with an increasing international population of traders and refugees, Cambodia's rulers requested the Portuguese in Malacca to send missionaries as well to work with the foreign communities. Beginning in 1555, missionaries, mostly Portuguese Dominicans, began to arrive in Cambodia, where they were permitted to work under limited conditions. There was very little interest in the foreign presence among the royal family, except if they could bring weapons and goods. Among the general population there was growing unease. The international presence of Japanese Catholics, Chinese traders, Portuguese, Spanish, and even Vietnamese Catholics became so great and was perceived as such a threat that upon the arrival of Spanish priests to negotiate a Spanish protectorate over Cambodia in 1599, popular riots broke out in Columpe (today's Phnom Penh).

Christian ministry in Cambodia in the early decades of the seventeenth century can be described as tenuous, regional, and multi-ethnic. It was tenuous in that the European powers were struggling for control of the region, and that in turn made local authorities suspicious of foreign missionaries. In addition, the missionaries were caught between the older pattern of *padroado*, whereby the Portuguese and Spanish kings appointed bishops, and the newer pattern of leadership provided by the *Propaganda fidei*, which brought episcopal appointments directly under Rome's control. The work was regional rather than just national because a strong base was not possible in Cambodia. Leadership came from the Thai city of Ayutthaya; priests and monks were sent from Malacca, and soldiers, priests, and monks were dispatched from Manila. Finally, the work was multi-ethnic because of the many foreign communities and religious refugees. Second- and third-generation Catholic Christians from the Celebes were being severely persecuted by the new colonial power in Asia, the Dutch, and many fled to Cambodia. Some of these had Portuguese blood, and many of their relatives first heard about Christianity through Francis Xavier. Compared to the Spanish, Portuguese, Chinese, and Japanese Christian communities, the pure Khmer church was very small.

These complex cultural issues are illustrated in the tragic ministry of Louis Chevreul (1627-1693). Chevreul was sent to Cochinchina by Lambert de la Motte in 1664 to minister to the Japanese Christians now living there. Because of the persecution in Vietnam, Chevreul ended up first in Ayutthaya and then, after falling ill, in Columpe in Cambodia where he was cared for by a Vietnamese Catholic refugee family. He was then joyfully welcomed by a struggling refugee church of mixed-race Portuguese from the Celebes. Still, Chevreul wanted to reach out to the Cambodians, but he did not know the language and could not find an interpreter. Unlike many of the other Jesuits, Father Chevreul had great admiration for the Cambodian Buddhist monks, and even found them a positive role model for Christian monks. Tragically, Chevreul was caught in European church-state struggles. He was accused of preaching without the orders from the king of Portugal and was then tried by the Inquisition in Goa. The charges were dropped but the priest fell into deep depression and died in Siam in 1693. Christianity in Cambodia in the seventeenth century was caught in the midst of competing kingdoms, competing colonial empires, and competing European churches that were already exporting their divisions to Cambodia.

Catholics and Reformed in the East Indies

Indonesia in the seventeenth century was a string of independent island kingdoms. Their religious ecology was a mixture of Hindu, Muslim, Buddhist, and (after 1500) Christian influences, all of them overlaying a strong system of *adat*, or local customs and beliefs. In 1511 the Portuguese conquered Malacca on the Malay Peninsula and opened up a century of cultural influence in the region. The Portuguese established themselves in the Straits of Malacca and along the eastern islands, where they had control over the valuable spice trade. The Dutch arrived in 1601 and conquered the Portuguese at Sumatra. They moved east in 1605 to Ambon and in 1619 conquered Jakarta on the island of Java, renaming it

Batavia. By 1641 the Dutch had also established ports in Sri Lanka (then Ceylon), Taiwan (or Formosa), and Malacca, giving them, to the dismay of the Portuguese, British, and Spanish, control of the valuable trade of cloves, nutmeg, and other spices that could easily command a 3,000 percent mark-up from the Banda Islands to Amsterdam or London.

Under Portuguese influence the Catholic Church had strengthened in the region under the Solor Mission, so-named because it was centered on the island of Solor where the Portuguese had built a fortress. Operating from Solor, Dominicans built strong Christian communities on Adonara, Flores, and Timor. When the Dutch arrived, the Portuguese had only recently thrown off Spanish rule. The Dutch began following the Portuguese trade route around the coasts of Africa and Asia, setting up their own competitive posts and destroying the Portuguese centers as they came upon them.

Where the Portuguese had originally come with pope and crown to trade, the Dutch at first came only as traders. Dutch traders and sailors did not travel directly under the crown of the Netherlands, but for a private company, the Verenigde Oost-Indische Compagnie ("Dutch United East India Company," or VOC), which was founded in 1602. This was a private trading company that was given extraordinary powers by the Dutch government to operate as a colonial power. The Dutch at first also lacked the interest in missions that Rome had helped fan among both Portuguese and Spanish excursions. For the Dutch the priority of profit over everything else was evident in each port city where the VOC was soon operating.

The VOC charter was altered in 1623 when it was mandated that the company provide religious care for those aboard ships and those who lived in the Dutch trading cities. A strong Reformed Christian presence soon developed in the Dutch communities in places such as Colombo, Batavia, Malacca, and Ambon, with large European church buildings being erected. The revised charter also included instructions to spread or extend the Christian faith as the company spread its influence. Such mission work was costly, however, since the missionaries were to be paid by the private company, and so the instruction was largely ignored until the end of the seventeenth century.

A number of Dutch church leaders in the seventeenth century accepted the argument that the command to evangelize all nations had been concluded with the apostolic age. The peoples of Asia, they reasoned, had already rejected the gospel. The all-consuming passion of the Dutch was for material profits, and they tolerated the faiths of others in order to minimize any disruption in their trade. The first Asian Reformed Classis, or Presbytery, was formed in 1625 as a result not of Dutch evangelistic activity but of Portuguese and Roman Catholic attrition. In Amboina the Portuguese Catholics had been removed, and many of those Catholics who remained joined the Dutch Reformed Church, enough to form several congregations and a governing Classis. Under Dutch rule, Islam was generally protected. In negotiating a treaty on Ternate, one of the former strongholds of the Portuguese, the VOC accepted the provision that outlawed Muslim conversions to Christianity. In some places Islam under the Dutch, as it was at times under the British, was protected and even strengthened. The few chaplains who came in the seventeenth century had very little concern or interest in work among local people, and even the few who did had very little impact until the eighteenth century.

Spain and Catholic religion in the Philippines

The seventeenth century in the Philippines witnessed the end of what some call the "Golden Age" for Christian missions in that country. The period of 1576 to 1609 was one of dramatic expansion of the Roman Catholic faith throughout the islands. It ended with the onset of Dutch attacks against the Spanish colony in 1609, which continued until the middle of the century. Muslims from the south, called "Moros" by the Spanish, also began attacking the colonialists to the north. Under the first Spanish governor, Miguel López de Legazpi (1502-1572), the Catholic faith had expanded at a fairly steady pace with a degree of ethical rectitude. In the period after 1609 a number of problems appeared.

First, there were not enough priests and catechists to instruct the thousands of Filipinos who converted to the Catholic faith. Lacking both instruction and pastoral oversight, their conversions and baptisms meant very little. The Spanish empire in Asia was proving to be far less profitable than the nation had hoped. Spain's original design had been to move into Asia through the back door of the Pacific to seize some of the valuable spice trade from Portugal. The Philippines had proven not to be the Spice Islands, however, and while they were the largest European colonial holding in Asia, they were also one of the poorest. The limited earnings from trade and agriculture that the Philippines produced for Spain did not support expansive religious work in the eyes of the crown and the church. On top of this the moral life of those friars who did reside in the colony was in decline. Both the accumulation of land, and therefore wealth, and the lack of supervision made for a low moral situation. In 1619 frustrated Augustinian monks actually murdered the provincial superior of the order, Vicente de Sepulveda, for exposing their shortcomings and for his demands for reforms in the order.

Divisions among the friars and priests grew. Much of the conflict was over authority and territory. A dispute called the "Visitation Controversy" developed over whether or not the bishop had the right or authority to visit and thus oversee the regular clergy who were doing most of the pastoral work in the *encomiendas* that had been established. The Council of Trent in 1563 had determined that clergy who were members of orders but were involved in pastoral duties were to be under the jurisdiction of a local bishop. Many in the orders in the Philippines resisted this directive, which meant that friars were supervised only by their own superiors. Each of the five orders working in the Philippines (Dominicans, Franciscans, Jesuits, Augustinians, and a new order called Recollects, which had arrived in 1606) was building its own ecclesiastical kingdom, thus fragmenting the church overall as a result. The problem was heightened by the large amounts of land that were being developed by the various orders, who had become some of the largest landowners in the islands, and had very little interest in training leaders to take over the large missions connected to the *encomiendas*. Within the orders further problems arose. A division within the Augustinians emerged, for instance, between those who were pure Spanish (born, raised, ordained in Spain) and those who were considered *creole* (raised in Mexico).

The Filipino church throughout the seventeenth century remained Spanish controlled and Spanish led. At one point it looked like a seminary would be established, but even the impetus for this did not come from the Spanish. It was the ever-present Frenchman and founder of the MEP, François Pallu, who initiated the idea. Pallu was on a ship heading for China in 1672 when it was blown off course and found refuge in Manila. The Spanish were none too friendly toward the Frenchman, who represented Portuguese mission territory, and so they locked him up and decided to put him on the next boat for Europe. While in prison, the industrious priest learned of the situation of the church in the Philippines and came to the conclusion that local, indigenous leadership needed to be trained and ordained as quickly as possible. To this end the local church needed a seminary where candidates could study to prepare for the priesthood.

The Spanish kept their promise, and Pallu ended up back in Spain, where he put his case for a seminary in the Philippines before the king. The king agreed and signed a decree to this end, which in turn only angered the archbishop in Manila, who never put it into effect. In 1700, 130 years after Legazpi first arrived, there was still no seminary for training local priests in the Philippines. As a result indigenous leadership was severely lacking. In 1698 the archbishop ordained the first Filipino priest, Francisco Baluyot (d. c. 1625). The next year he ordained several more candidates, but without a seminary, these would remain only isolated instances of Asian church leadership development in the Philippines.

In this situation the persistence of older pagan beliefs and Filipino identity continued in spite of the efforts of teaching the converts the new prayers and catechisms. The relationship of the newer Catholic faith to indigenous religious practices in the Philippines is a complex issue. Many historians have noted that there were natural bridges to belief since Filipino culture honored ancestors (saints), was aware of *anitos* (spirits), and honored those who could heal. Much of the early evangelical work was expressed in healings and other types of miracles. A basic view of the cosmos was shared by the monks and indigenous Filipinos. However, some of the beliefs and practices that Roman Catholicism opposed also persisted. There were problems with the continuance of polygamy, for instance, and with the keeping of certain amulets and religious charms to fend off evil spirits.

Closely related to this persistence of indigenous beliefs and practices was the larger question of Filipino identity. As long as the Spaniards came with an oppressive and violent demeanor, there would always be those who longed for the days of freedom from domination to be real Filipinos again. A number of revolts beginning in the seventeenth century were rooted in just such longings. In 1621 Jesuits were opposed by a number of the Bohol people who, led by a local priest named Tamblot (dates unknown), rose up in rebellion against Christianity and the Europeans. The rallying cry was for the people of Bohol to return to their native gods. Another rebellion, a type of religious revolt, was led by a sorcerer named Tapar (dates unknown). Tapar brought together local myths and practices with some of what he knew about Christian teachings. His new religion attracted large numbers of people. An Augustinian friar tried to dissuade him, but the people killed him. These and other rebellions were put down by Spanish arms, revealing further the heavy-handed, colonial approach in this complex religious milieu.

Many of these early missionaries, trained in some of the best schools in Europe, preserved valuable information about the cultures, climates, flora, and fauna in the Philippines. Francisco Ignaci Alcina (1610-1674) arrived in 1632 and served as a parish priest in the Visayan Islands of Leyte and Samar until the last two years of his life. He composed a number of books on the Visayan language to aid future missionaries and devotional books for lay Christians in the islands. His major work, though, was a great undertaking, providing what some have called one of the best descriptions of a small area of the Philippines ever written, *Historia natural del sitio, fertilidad y calidad de las Islas, e Indios de Bisayas* ("Natural History of the Site, Fertility, and Quality of the Visayas Islands and the Indigenous Inhabitants"). The volume also contains one of the best early descriptions of indigenous beliefs and practices in the Visayas.

The Jesuit Pedro Chirino (1557-1635) was another missionary who made careful observations and preserved much of the knowledge of the culture and language of precolonial Filipinos. Chirino arrived in the Philippines in 1590 and established one of the first sedentary missionary works when most of the missionaries were still itinerant. His major work, titled *Relación de las Islas Filipinas* ("An Account of the Philippine Islands"), was completed in 1604, two years after he left the Philippines. In it he described how Chinese traders grew dwarf trees by planting them in coral, why the Tagalog language is more dignified than the Visayan language, what the particular skin tones of various island peoples were like, and even how the Filipinos took to flagellation (a new sixteenth-century practice in Spain) with such zeal and vigor they at times had to be restrained. According to Chirino, the Filipinos, who were already literate in Tagalog, would write down Bible stories or sermons after Mass, using the traditional Philippine script.

Chirino's observations provide an early account of the literacy of Filipinos and make it clear that language preservation and study were important to missionary work. One also learns from Chirino's pages why he thought so many people in the region of Taytay converted so quickly. According to his account, miraculous occurrences, both healings as well as confrontations with spirits that were calmed or exorcized, were decisive. Reading his *Relacion* one is reminded of the some of the highest ideals and aspirations of the missionaries in the only region of Asia colonized by a Catholic nation.

Christianity, a West Asian religion from its very beginnings, was becoming much more of an East Asian religion in the seventeenth century. In countries such as Japan, faithful disciples laid down their lives for their faith commitment. In the Philippines, Jesus was beginning to speak in Tagalog, and worship was becoming more Filipino. Large communities of Vietnamese continued their faithful worship, evangelizing and teaching using the newly minted Vietnamese Romanized script, with virtually no foreign leadership. Chinese Christians were rediscovering Christianity and reading apologetic writings that appealed to the highest ideals of Confucianism that were revealed by a personal Lord of Heaven. Many of the lessons that were learned in China by Matteo Ricci, or in Vietnam by Alexandre de Rhodes, were applied in India under the Mughul empire just decades later.

Suggestions for further reading

Brockey, Liam Matthew, *Journey to the East, the Jesuit Mission to China: 1579-1724*. Cambridge, MA: Harvard University Press, 2007.

Moffett, Samuel Hugh, *A History of Christianity in Asia, II: 1500-1900*. Maryknoll, NY: Orbis Books, 2005.

Mungello, D. E., ed., *The Chinese Rites Controversy: Its History and Meaning*. Nettetal, Germany: Steyler Verlag, 1994.

Phan, Peter, *Mission and Catechesis: Alexandre de Rhodes and Inculturation in Seventeenth-Century Vietnam*. Maryknoll, NY: Orbis Books, 1998.

Phan, Phát Huôn, CSsR, *History of the Catholic Church in Viet Nam, I (1533-1960)*. Long Beach, CA: Privately published by author, 2001.

Ronan, Charles E., S.J., and Bonnie B. C. Oh, eds., *The Jesuits in China, 1582-1773*. Chicago: Loyola University Press, 1988.

Ross, Andrew, *A Vision Betrayed: The Jesuits in Japan and China, 1542-1742*. Maryknoll, NY: Orbis Books, 1994.

Standaert, Nicolas, ed., *Handbook of Christianity in China, I: 635-1800*. Leiden: Brill, 2001.

Sunquist, Scott W., David Wu Chu Sing, and John Chew Hiang Chea, eds., *A Dictionary of Asian Christianity*. Grand Rapids, MI: Eerdmans, 2001.

8

South Asia in the Seventeenth Century

Disputes over Roman Catholic and St. Thomas rites

Christianity in India was at a crossroads at the beginning of the seventeenth century. The Synod of Diamper in 1599, over which the Portuguese archbishop Aleixo de Menezes (1559-1617) presided, sought to bring the St. Thomas Christians of India under the authority of Rome. The decisions of the synod called for Indian Christians to adopt a European form of Christianity, shunning their own language, culture, and tradition. Indian priests, or *kattanars,* who accepted the decisions of the synod began to say the liturgy in Latin and looked toward Rome as their apostolic office. Sermons began to be heard criticizing the patriarch of the Chaldean or East Syrian Church under whose spiritual authority the Christians in South India had been for more than a thousand years. Anyone in the churches now aligned with the Portuguese who spoke against the pope in Rome was threatened with the Inquisition. Most of the Christians of South India appear not to have accepted the decisions of the synod, but enough did so as to divide the churches in the region.

The most effective leader of the Indian Christians in resisting the imposition of Roman and Portuguese control over the churches was the Archdeacon George of the Cross (d. 1640). George was excommunicated in 1609 by Menezes's successor. The Portuguese clerical leaders were nevertheless forced repeatedly to cooperate with George who, as leader of the Indian churches, resisted their efforts to bring them under Roman authority.

A new Portuguese archbishop, Stephen de Britto (r. 1624-1641), was appointed by Rome in 1624. An irenic man of creative disposition, de Britto nevertheless continued the Portuguese effort to westernize Indian churches. One of the initiatives de Britto undertook in this regard was the establishment of an Indian religious order, the Congregation of St. Thomas the Apostle, as a way to reduce the number of ordained Indian priests, known as *kattanars.* It was supported by Archdeacon George because it furthered one of his long-standing goals, raising the level of spiritual devotion among Indian Christians. George also saw it as a means of training Indian Christian leaders in the absence of other options.

Despite the support of both European and Indian Church leaders, the new order failed to take hold. Its numbers were always small, and within a few years it faded away completely. One reason for the demise of the order was the extreme standard of discipline that it sought to maintain. Members were required to observe 150 days of fasting per year and abstain from meat, fish, eggs, and wine. In addition to the austerity that it fostered, the congregation was criticized by *paranghi* ("foreigners," i.e., the Portuguese) as being a place where Indian Christians could meet in community and vent their frustrations about foreign rule of their churches. Whether or not the Portuguese archbishop was accurate in his assessment that the order provided space for venting antiforeign sentiments, his withdrawal of support put an end to this experiment in Indian religious life.

Confusion and conflict marked the changing configuration of the South Indian churches in the early seventeenth century. Archdeacon George of the Cross and later his nephew, Archdeacon Thomas Parambil (or Thomas de Campo, 1637-1673), carried the hearts and minds of most of the Indian Christians. Given the disappearance of their own episcopal hierarchy, they were dependent on the Latin bishops for ordination of priests and sacramental services. The archdeacons responded by seeking to undermine the authority of the European archbishops in every way that they could, often showing great skill in turning friars and priests against one another, and to keep alive opposition in the churches toward Rome and the Portuguese.

Added to these ecclesiastical dynamics in the region was the growing presence of other European colonial powers in India. The Dutch had established their presence in Sri Lanka by 1640, and although they did not take control of Cochin in southwest India until 1663, their presence in the south of India was being felt. The English East India Company had entered India in the north by way of the Gujarati coastal city of Serat, at least as early as 1612. By 1640 the English had also established a foothold in Chennai (long known as Madras), in the southeastern region that is now Tamil Nadu. These new colonial powers were Protestant and often at odds with the Catholic Portuguese. Eventually the Portuguese would lose control over the churches in their colonial empire to the *Propaganda fidei* (the congregation in Rome that was becoming the Department of Missions for Catholics internationally). In the 1650s signs that the situation for the Portuguese-dominated churches was changing were clear.

Religious orders continued to play an important role in the life of the churches during this period in South India. In most places in Asia in the seventeenth century, the Jesuits were advocates of early forms of adaptation and contextual approaches to theology. In the South Indian Christian arena, however, they were defenders of European authority against Indian culture and theology. The main reason for this was that while in other areas of Asia the Jesuits understood their work to be primarily evangelical by spreading Christianity among adherents of other religions, in the south of India they understood their work primarily as that of unifying the church, which meant bringing the South Indian Christians more fully into the Roman fold. In opposition to the Jesuits, Archdeacon Thomas appealed to Rome for Carmelites and Dominicans to come and labor among them. The Jesuits, Thomas complained, prevented the Indian archdeacon from exercising his authority. Not finding help from other Catholic orders, Thomas turned to the heads of other churches in the East. Secret letters were sent in 1648-

1649 to the Coptic patriarch in Alexandria, the East Syrian patriarch in Baghdad, and the West Syrian patriarch in Antioch, stating that India was without a bishop and asking that one be sent.

Three years later, in 1652, Thomas received a letter from a prelate named Mar Atallah (1590-c. 1653), who claimed to have been appointed by the pope to be Ignatius, Patriarch of All India and China. The letter was carried by three Indian seminarians who had gone on a pilgrimage to the grave of St. Thomas in Mylapore, on the southeast coast, and had stayed at the Jesuit college there. Mar Atallah was originally from Aleppo, in Syria, and was an archbishop of Damascus, Ems, and Nicomedia in the West Syrian Church. In 1632, however, under the influence of Franciscans, he entered the fold of the Roman Catholic Church and journeyed to Rome for a period before returning to Damascus and claiming the rank of patriarch. Mar Atallah then made his way across Persia and, supposedly in response to the letters from Thomas to the Coptic patriarch in Cairo, came to India to help the churches there. He was detained by Jesuits, who sent him to Goa to be tried by the Inquisition.

The Indian Christians protested that the Jesuits were imprisoning an ecclesiastical authority who had been sent by the pope. Not willing to concede authority, Archbishop Garcia declared that he should still be detained because he had not been appointed under the *padroado* by the king of Portugal. When word came that Mar Atallah was being transported to Goa, the Indians staged a protest and demanded a meeting with him at the port city of Cochin (contemporary Kochi), where his ship was scheduled to land. The Portuguese intervened and prevented the captain of the ship from allowing Mar Atallah to come ashore. The ship instead set sail for Goa. It was later rumored that the Portuguese drowned Mar Atallah at sea rather than bring him to Goa for trial before the Inquisition.

The struggle for control of the ancient church in South India came to a second crisis point in what is called the General Revolt of 1653. It was a defining moment for the church of Kerala, on the southwest coast, for it gave rise to the Syrian Orthodox and Syrian Catholic divisions that can still can be found there today. Early in January of 1653, at Our Lady at Mattancherry Church near Cochin, many *kattanars* and thousands of other faithful Indian Christians gathered to consider the situation. Many of the Indians gathered immediately took an oath of allegiance to the archdeacon as governor of their church, and denounced Garcia and the Jesuits. According to contemporary records, several of the most prominent *kattanars* took the oath in the church in front of a crucifix over the Bible. Later accounts, not necessarily contradictory, cite hundreds or even thousands taking the oath while holding onto ropes tied to the famous Coonan Cross, hence giving the name "Coonan Cross Oath" to the establishment of the church. The event marks the clear division in the Indian Church with the emergence of a distinct communion claiming the heritage of St. Thomas.

A month later, a number of these Indian Christians gathered again to reaffirm their support for Archdeacon Thomas. Four prominent *kattanars*, or priests, Kaduthuruthy Kadavil Chandy (dates unknown), Angamali Vendoor Geevarghese (d. 1670), Kuravilingad Palliveettil Chandy (also known as Parambil Chandy, d. 1687), and Anjilimoottil Itty Thommen (d. 1659), were named to form an advisory council to support him. Several months later another gathering of church leaders was convened. This time a letter was produced, supposedly from Mar Atallah but most likely a forgery, elevating Thomas from being an archdeacon to the rank of archbishop with a dispensation regarding marriage, and conferring on him all of the powers of the office. Twelve priests then laid hands on him to ordain the archbishop, who took the title of Mar Thoma I.

Rome responded by sending more acceptable bishops with no taint of Jesuit involvement. An Italian Discalced Carmelite named Joseph Sebastiani (also known as Joseph of St. Mary, r. 1657-1665) was sent to India to try to reconcile the Indian Christians to Roman authority. Sebastiani failed to win over a substantial portion of those who supported Archbishop Thomas. Upon hearing a report of the situation, the pope decided to designate the region as the Vicariate of Malabar under Carmelite care and appointed Sebastiani its administrator with the title Bishop of Hierapolis and Vicar Apostolic. Churches under his pastoral oversight were permitted to worship in both Latin and Syriac.

The struggle over the Indian Church was further complicated when Sebastiani, still working to bring about the submission of churches in the region to Rome, suddenly discovered he was standing in Dutch territory when the Dutch forces seized Cochin in January 1663. Being Protestants, they ordered all Carmelites to leave Kerala. Sebastiani quickly ordained Parambil Chandy, one of the four *kattanars* who had served as councilors to Mar Thoma I and who was also a cousin of the Indian archbishop, as bishop in the Roman tradition. Roman Catholic ministry at this point began to be carried out with effectiveness under local, indigenous leadership that had been properly ordained. The move was critical in helping to ensure the endurance of what became known as the Syrian Catholic Church. Even after the Carmelites later returned, a strong indigenous leadership continued to characterize the churches.

Chandy's industrious cousin, Mar Thoma I, did not easily give up. Once again his ecclesiastical authority was given a boost by another answer to his 1648-1649 letters. A West Syrian bishop named Gregorios (dates unknown) arrived at Calicut in 1665 claiming to have been sent by the Antiochian patriarch as an answer to Thomas's earlier plea. Although the West Syrian tradition had historically been out of communion with both the Roman Catholic Church and with the East Syrian Church that had previously provided episcopal leadership for the Indian Christians, Gregorios was embraced in part because he represented an Asian church tradition. Efforts were made to begin to restore aspects of the ancient Syrian tradition that had been lost after the Synod of Diamper, thereby joining the Indian Church again to its Asian roots. After the 1670s the liturgy among the churches following Mar Thoma I was again celebrated in Syriac, using leavened bread for the Eucharistic host. Priests were allowed to marry. Both the Orthodox fast in Advent and the old Syrian Church calendar were restored.

A subtle change occurred with this new-found connection to the West Syrian tradition. Although the South Indian Church had been under the East Syrian (or Chaldean) patriarchate (called "Nestorian" in the West) for centuries, the bishops showing up now in the seventeenth century were from the West Syrian patriarchate (called "Jacobite" in the West). Both communions had rejected the decision of the Council of Chalcedon in 451, but for opposite reasons (one nature or two persons). The fact that the liturgy of both church traditions was in the ancient Syriac tongue helped conceal the differences in part. Slowly, with almost no resistance, the ancient East Syrian Indian Church tradition shifted theologically to the West Syrian tradition. The major concern among the Indian Christians was not so much theological as it was cultural and national, that is, to have a hierarchy and tradition that was Syriac and Asian.

A deep divide now appeared in Christianity in South India. Under the leadership of Chandy, who assumed the title of *malpan* (a Syriac term for a bishop), and with the support of Rome and the Carmelites, the Syrian Catholic Church took much stronger root. Because of the ongoing delegations from west Asia, the Syrian St. Thomas Christians continued to grow in numbers and in unity as well. The Asian prelates, separated from the Roman West for over a millennium, were clear that the Syrian Church must resist Roman domination. Mar Gregorios appealed to Indian priests in letters and in sermons, calling Rome idolatrous and denouncing those who were part of the Syrian Catholic Church as heretics and under the influence of the king of Portugal. A deep divide now separated Thomists and Romans.

The struggle between Syrian Catholic and Syrian Orthodox churches in India was more about Asian autonomy and Asian identity than theological orthodoxy. Ironically, in the end Asian identity won on both counts, in both communions. The Syrian Catholic Church, which grew to be the stronger of the two communions, allowed for a Syriac Eucharistic rite; and although foreign-born monks populated the ranks of its orders, they were fluent in local languages and provided consistent pastoral care. By the end of the seventeenth century the Syrian Catholics were estimated to have some 400,000 communicants, outnumbering the Orthodox by two to one. The Syrian Orthodox (often called the Mar Thoma) Church on the other hand could claim in years to come greater continuity with the St. Thomas Christian past, and an identity that was non-Western and even anticolonial.

Christian witness in the Mughul empire

By the end of the seventeenth century, several European nations were vying for control of the southern and western Indian coastal regions where they were building competing colonial empires in Asia. At stake in these struggles were prestige, trade, religion, and social order. In the northern part of India, however, the struggle did not involve so much the rising European sea powers and the forms of Christianity that they sponsored against local Indian political and religious (including Indian Christian) realities. Northern India, instead, was an arena in which the newly founded Mughul empire and the Islamic faith that it sponsored in a traditionally Hindu society were expanding.

In the seventeenth century, Islam was also expanding, not only in its Turkish dress in the West in the form of the Ottoman empire, but also in its newer Mughul form in India. The founder of the Mughul empire, as we noted above,

was a descendant of Tamer the Lame (Tamerlane) named Babur. Babur had originally come from Afghanistan but had moved into the regions of the plains of the
Multan region in northern India. In 1523 he led the Mughul forces toward the
Punjab, near present-day Lahore in Pakistan, and then on to Delhi. Following
his death, Babur's son, Akbar (1556-1605), secured his rule and established what
came to be known as the Mughul empire. In a relatively short period of time,
most of northern India, the land of thousands of gods and historically the home to
Hinduism and Buddhism, came under the rule of a foreign monotheistic Islamic
empire.

Akbar the Great followed the path of Sunni Islam, but was also greatly influenced by both Shi'a and Sufist traditions. He initiated the Mughul pattern of com-
bining Islamic and Hindu art and architecture, making use of some of the finest
local materials, including marble and gems. Establishing his capital at Agra, near
Delhi, Akbar had nearly five hundred buildings constructed in a short period of
eight years. He was a tolerant Muslim leader, who, like his Mongol predecessors
of old, appreciated many different religions and entertained different religious
leaders at court. He did not impose the religious tax on Hindus and other religionists, and streamlined the massive administration of an empire that by the end
of his life stretched from Dacca in the east to central India and all the way across
Lahore past Kabul in the west.

The Jesuits were welcomed in Akbar's court along with priests of various
other religious traditions in northern India. In 1594 he actually requested that
the Portuguese in Goa send several Christian priests to his court. Several went.
Arriving in 1595, the group set up a chapel, celebrated the Eucharist, and began
what became a long, if for them sometimes frustrating, engagement with the
emperor. Akbar refused to talk about religion until the Jesuits could speak Persian, the language of his court. When they finally learned it, he gave them little
opportunity for dialogue. Nevertheless, they earned the emperor's respect, and
in 1602, Akbar decreed that his subjects were free to convert to Christianity if
they so chose. This was one of the first times a Muslim ruler had done so in a
territory as large as the Mughul empire. Through a small school set up in Lahore,
an indigenous Roman Catholic community under the pastoral leadership of the
Jesuit missionaries began to grow.

The next emperor, Jahan-gir (r. 1605-1627), continued to exercise religious tolerance. Like Akbar, he maintained the patronage of Jesuits at the Mughul court.
Jahan-gir admired the Western Christian paintings that the Jesuits brought, and
was reported to have had many framed pictures of Mary and her child, Jesus, as
well as depictions of Old Testament stories, in his possession. In 1610 he even
had three of his nephews baptized as Christians, although the motive for this was
most likely to get Portuguese wives or to prevent any of the young men from later
becoming emperor. Three years later he forced all three to apostatize.

This was the last of the easy years for the Jesuits and other Christians in
the Mughul empire. In 1615 an embassy from King James I of England (1566-
1625) arrived in the court in India. Accompanying the English ambassador, Sir
Thomas Roe (1581-1644), was a chaplain from the Church of England, Edward
Terry (1590-1660). Terry had little tolerance for the Mughuls and no desire to

convert them. He is reported to have said to the Jesuits that he was mostly troubled by what he called the Muslim "libertie for women." The Jesuits reportedly convinced the Anglican that the Europeans should quietly tolerate each other so as not to hurt the witness of Christians in the royal court. Apparently the ambassador and the chaplain agreed, making for one of the first episodes in which Roman Catholics and Anglicans exercised a degree of cooperation on behalf of a united Christian front.

Christianity grew in northern India during the reign of these two Muslim emperors. Churches were built in Agra, Lahore, Cambay, and Thatta. A number of royal officials and their families developed a positive view of Christian presence, and some members of royal families were baptized. Most important, the Jesuits extended their influence by serious cultural studies, including learning local languages and grasping the mindset of the Mughuls. Jerónimo Xavier (1549-1617), grandnephew of Francis Xavier, did the most to build a literary foundation for Christianity in India during this period. By 1611, Xavier had published in Persian a life of Christ titled *Mirat-ul-quds* ("Mirror of Holiness"), a detailed apologetic work titled *A'ina-yi haqq-numa* ("The Truth-Showing Mirror"), *Dastan-I ahwal-I hawari-yan-I hazrat-I Isa* ("History of the Vicissitudes of the Apostles of the Lord Jesus"), a catechism, a translation of the Psalter, and a detailed commentary on the creed titled *Bayan-I iman-I' isawiyan*. In all of these works, the concern was to present a clear witness in the Persian language to the Muslim rulers of northern India. In addition, Xavier produced a Hindustani catechism in 1611, while a German Jesuit produced a Sanskrit grammar to begin ministry among Hindus.

With the reign of Shah Jahan (1627-1658) both the height of Mughul architectural grandeur and the end of Christian tolerance were reached. Jahan was a devout orthodox Muslim ruler, not given to accepting other religions in his court and committed to spreading Islam. In 1632 he issued an anti-Christian edict that appeared to close the door to the approach the Jesuits had developed over the previous forty years in the Mughul court. In terms of religion it initiated what turned out to be a reign of persecution under the guise of purification. In terms of architecture, it was the beginning of a period known as the "Reign of Marble." Churches were destroyed, but mosques and other buildings, including the most famous grave site in the world, the Taj Mahal, which was completed in 1648 for Shah Jahan's second and favorite wife, Mumtaz Mahal (1593-1631), were constructed.

The final Mughul emperor of the seventeenth century, Aurangzeb (1658-1707), extended restrictions on Christians, Hindus, and other non-Muslims, and reinstated the poll tax. Nevertheless, it was during his reign that Alexandre de Rhodes, known as "the apostle to Vietnam," finished studying Persian in Isfahan and began a new mission to the court of Aurangzeb. The presence of de Rhodes in northern India is but one more illustration of the manner in which the Jesuits were building a pan-Asian and pan-global network and consciousness.

Partly in response to the spread of the Mughul empire, and partly by their own inspiration, two relatively new streams of religious devotion that had emerged in northern India came to prominence during this period. The first was the religion of Sikhism, and the second was a devotional tradition within Hinduism that was known as *bhakti*. Both were to have a significant impact on Christianity in India and later in what is now Pakistan.

Sikhism is a monotheistic religious faith tradition that was founded by a devout mystical seer in Punjab named Sri Guru Nanak Dev Ji (1469-1538). Around the year 1500, Nanak received in a vision what he understood to be a divine call to preach devotion to the one God in purity of heart, and to show care for the poor. Nanak recognized both Islam and the religious traditions of Hinduism as having valid elements within them, and advocated a relatively high degree of religious tolerance. Nanak's message was radically egalitarian. He taught that all human beings were equal before God, and that through righteous actions and compassion all human beings may achieve peace and salvation.

Over the course of the next two centuries, nine other gurus followed Nanak, the last being Guru Gobind (d. 1708). These gurus passed down the teachings of Nanak. Their followers, the Sikhs, believe the divine light that had been revealed through Nanak continued to shine continuously through the lives of these gurus, or prophets. The tenth and final guru, Gobind, is believed to have transferred this light to the eleventh guru, the sacred Sikh scriptures that are known as *Guru Granth Saheb.*

Sikhs rejected the use of any images in worship and the social divisions of caste, both of which are important to Hinduism. They worshipped a single God (known as Hari, Sat Guru, or Sat Nam) and accepted the doctrines of *karma* and reincarnation. Over the course of the first ten gurus, the Sikh community grew largely among the lower classes. Although the original message was given in the vernacular, the second guru, Angad Dev, is credited with creating a new alphabet with which the scriptures were eventually written, thereby strengthening the separate identity of the community. Various Mughul rulers tried from time to time to stop the spread of the teachings of the gurus, culminating in the martyrdom of Guru Gobind, the tenth guru. Such persecution, however, appears only to have strengthened the new religious community.

Closely related to the emergence of the Sikh tradition, and even seen by some Sikhs as a part of their movement, was *bhakti*. *Bhakti* is a Sanskrit word meaning "sharing" or "participation." Its scriptural roots lay in ancient texts such as the *Bhagavad Gita* and the *Bhagavata Purana*. Historically, bhakti had been associated with devotion directed toward the specific deities Shiva and Vishnu in southern India; and in its simplest expressions, it offered devotion of heart as an alternative to knowledge as the pathway to salvation.

Under the Mughul rulers, bhakti rose in prominence in northern India as a distinctive practice. One of the most important bhakti poets of this period was Surdas (c. 1478-1581). Blind from birth, Surdas was a devotional singer who began composing poems dedicated to Vishnu, and to his incarnation in Krishna. Eventually his poems numbered into the thousands. They were collected in volumes such as *Sur Sagar* ("Ocean of Melody") and even found their way into Sikh scriptures.

Another well-known bhakti saint, and one of the best-known women mystics in India, was Mirabai (c. 1498-1550). Born in Rajasthan in the northwest to a noble family, she famously refused to submit to *sati* (the practice of widows being burned upon a pyre with their late spouses) when her husband died in 1516. According to tradition, her father was killed in 1527 resisting Mughul advances into the region and soon after that she left the court to become a wandering poet and dancer, devoted to Giridha Gobal (a form of the Lord Krishna). Modern scholars accept over 200 poems as authentically hers, but more than 1,300 have been attributed to her. She may have written in Gujarati, but her poems were almost immediately translated into Hindi and other languages, sung at first throughout the north but later through all of India.

Bhakti had much in common with Sufi Islam, which the Mughul rulers had brought to India. The goal of both practices was achieving a loving union with God, which was most clearly portrayed in the analogy of the love of a wife for her husband. Bhakti entailed meditation, singing, poetry, and devotion, practices in which Muslims as well as Hindus could engage. As a means of direct encounter with God, bhakti turned away from the images that characterized much of Hinduism. It also opened the door for the poor and uneducated to experience direct and immediate union with God, opening the door for social criticism based on the ideal equality among human beings. Setting aside the paths of asceticism and knowledge (understood as a form of *gnosis*), the bhakti path of devotion made salvation accessible to the masses. It found a home also in a popular form of Hinduism associated with the god Vishnu and his incarnation as Krishna and would later develop affinities with mystical forms of Christian devotion as well.

Both Sikhism and bhakti devotion were built on written scriptures, or texts of praise and worship. The presence of Islam, for whom the written text of scripture commanded so much authority, was undoubtedly a factor in this. Within Hinduism the bhakti movement promoted translation of religious writings from the dying Sanskrit language into the vernacular language that was being used during this period. This renewed devotional movement in India became even more important when Hinduism later encountered Protestant Christianity in the eighteenth and nineteenth centuries.

In the context of late-seventeenth-century Mughul India, local religions were in the process of change. Sikhism became an identified, militant community, while the Maratha Hindu movement arose chiefly to oppose the Mughul efforts to spread Islam in the western region of the Deccan plateau south of the Indo-Gangetic plain. Shivaji Bhonsale (1627-1680), an indefatigable fighter, defended the region and became known as the father of the Maratha nation. Bhonsale and his followers were what might be called today "freedom fighters," committed to defending their land and their religious traditions. Their war cries were *swaraj!* ("freedom"), *swadharma!* ("religious freedom"), and *goraksha!* ("cow protection"). The Maratha, inspired by a vision of a return to a Hindu Maharashtra Kingdom, never developed a kingdom, for they were loosely connected bands of fighters defending the Hindu way of life against Islam. Throughout the seventeenth century they were a militant Hindu force to be reckoned with, by the Mughuls and Europeans alike, but by the middle of the eighteenth century their revolt had been put down.

Roberto de Nobili and Christian adaptation in Hindu Madurai

At approximately the same time that Matteo Ricci was seeking to gain entry to the Chinese imperial court in Beijing as a Confucian *literatus* and Jerónimo Xavier was writing apologetic works in Persian for the Mughul emperor, another Jesuit, Roberto de Nobili (1577-1656), who had entered the Jesuits in 1596, began to undertake the intellectual and cultural adaptation of Christianity in the Hindu heartland of Madurai, in far southern India, a region that had not been conquered by the Muslims, the heart of Tamil literary and religious culture. Born into an aristocratic Italian family, de Nobili was the nephew of the well-known Jesuit Cardinal St. Robert Bellarmine (1542-1621) and was related to two popes.

He arrived in India in 1605 and was first assigned to continue work that had been started nearly half a century earlier by Francis Xavier among the fisherfolk of Parava Coast. This was Portuguese territory, and the Christians were all of lower castes. Within a year, however, de Nobili was sent by the Jesuits out of Portuguese territory to the small, inland Vijayanagar empire to begin work in Madurai. At this point, after a century of Western Christian missions in India, the Jesuits and other Westerners had worked among Indian Christians (who were from higher castes), among poor lower-caste fisherfolk, and in the immediate vicinity of the Mughul court. There had been virtually no effort, however, to engage the educated and higher-caste Hindus in dialogue or to seek their conversion.

Another Jesuit, Gonçalo Fernandes (1541-1619), had been at work in Madurai, but his efforts had been directed toward the pastoral care of a small group of Portuguese and Parava Coast Christians who lived there. The message implicitly transmitted to Hindu aristocrats, accordingly, was that Christianity was a foreign religion and that to become a Christian one had to become a *paranghi,* or foreigner. De Nobili decided that this perception had to change. With the permission of his bishop, he committed himself to six concentrated months of studying classical, literary Tamil. Within this period, he was able to master the language sufficiently to preach, write, and converse proficiently, earning the respect of local Brahmin scholars. As he wrote in 1613 to his uncle, Cardinal Bellarmine, his goal was not only to learn Sanskrit, which he recognized held a position in India comparable to that of Latin in western Europe, but to become intimately familiar with the teachings of the Brahmins in order to discuss with them matters of religion.

In order to carry out the task of speaking to the Brahmins, de Nobili argued that one had to become a scholar of Sanskrit. He went further to maintain that one also had to become a full participant in the Brahmin culture. As long as Christians were viewed as *paranghis*, it would not be possible for the Brahmin to become Christian, de Nobili reasoned, for to convert would mean that they had to put off what made them Indian. He instead sought to become *sannyasi* ("renouncer"), the highest level of Brahmin ascetic.

When asked about his identity, de Nobili said he was not a *paranghi,* because that term was generally used of Portuguese. De Nobili said he was of *raj* ("royal") Italian blood, and therefore was of the *kshatriya* class. He had come to teach a new spiritual law as a *sannyasi*. Such identification made it possible for other teachers and upper-caste members to listen to him and to eat with him. De Nobili lived the life of a *sannyasi*, one who had renounced the world, eating no meat, fish, or eggs and drinking no wine. He limited himself to one meal of rice, milk, and some vegetables per day and did not wear the black cassock of the Jesuits. Instead, he dressed as an Indian *sannyasi* and avoided contact with leather and with people of lower castes. Although cut off from the lower-caste folk by his still-controversial cultural adaptation, de Nobili could now be visited by teachers and high-caste members in his little mud hut built in the Brahmin quarter of town.

Over time, de Nobili became known as a well-versed Indian *sannyasi*, so much so that people traveled from throughout the region to engage him in discussions about religion. De Nobili would impress them with his knowledge of their own scriptures, and he both composed poetry in classical Tamil and sang songs that taught his Christian understanding of God. The results were not dramatic, but one of the early converts was his own language teacher, a man who had been a teacher at Gonçalo's school, who took the name Alberto after his baptism. Like many of the other conversions that eventually occurred, this one took place after weeks of long discussions. De Nobili reported a total of ten conversions from the upper castes in 1607 after his first year of work, fourteen in 1608, and sixty in 1609. The numbers were not large, but they were the first upper-caste Hindus to become Christian. Commenting on the validity and value of the ministry, another Jesuit who spent some time with de Nobili and his converts noted that the converts were well instructed, pious in their lifestyle, and had become Christians only for the salvation of their souls, not to receive gifts or material rewards. He also noted that they continued to have good relations with their Hindu friends even after conversion.

Still de Nobili's move was the beginning of controversies surrounding how Christians should adapt to the Indian caste system and the separation of the poor and outcasts that this system promoted. The issue quickly became the equivalent of the Chinese Rites Controversy for India. Was it acceptable for some Christians for the sake of being able to make contact with Brahmins and members of other high castes to separate themselves from the poor or lower castes? Was this a denial of something essential about the Christian faith? De Nobili struggled with this and came to the conclusion that in allowing all Christians to worship together in the same building, even though the lower-caste members were separated from the upper castes by a balustrade and stood in a lower place, he was adapting without denying the Christian gospel. The Jesuit reasoned that all people were equal and had equal access to God, but that did not have to mean that they had the same social conditions on earth. In this way he felt he had adapted the teachings of Jesus without denying their essence.

Not all agreed. By 1610, de Nobili was encountering significant opposition from other European Christians, from many Brahmins, and from some of his converts. Leading the attack from the European side was Gonçalo Fernandes, who wrote numerous letters and memoranda to Goa and Rome, stating that de Nobili's work constituted a denial of essential elements of the church's constitution.

Franciscans working with the fisherfolk charged de Nobili with becoming Hindu. These letters got the attention of Roman authorities, who demanded a thorough examination of the issue. Thus, the first meeting took place in Goa in 1619. Attending were the archbishop of Goa and both Franciscans and Dominicans opposed to de Nobili's approach. Only the archbishop of Cranganore and the Jesuits defended de Nobili's identification as a Christian *sannyasi*. After years of conflict, de Nobili and his approach were finally approved by order of the pope in 1634, allowing not only the new form of Indian Catholicism to continue in Madurai but also in other regions of India as well.

The Christian movement also advanced by popular movements and not only through the efforts of missionaries, as is shown by what happened when the *nayak* (ruler) of Madurai showed such respect for de Nobili and his work that in 1616 he moved his court, along with a number of recent converts, to Tiruchirappalli, in Tamil Nadu. A civil war was going on, and Muthuvirappa Nayak moved his army to punish Raghunatha Nayak of Thanjavur. For a total of three years, up until 1627, de Nobili provided pastoral care and received members of the *nayak's* court into the church. On a few occasions, converts of de Nobili brought about the conversions of other gurus, and when this happened, many of their disciples followed them into the church.

These new and, in some cases, rapidly growing communities were a cause of alarm for other local Hindu authorities. One such popular movement in Tiruchirappalli, led in part by a convert named Muthudayan (dates unknown), became so large that baptisms and meetings were held in secret to avoid drawing unfavorable attention from the Hindus. Nonetheless, this group of over three hundred was discovered. Many were arrested and beaten, their small church was burned down, and Muthudayan himself was beaten before he escaped. Still full of zeal for his new faith, he ended up in Karur, where he established a small congregation of converts.

De Nobili sought to make it possible for upper-caste Hindus to become Christian while remaining Indian. The reality was, however, that many lower-caste people were also becoming Christian through efforts like his in Madurai. In effect, the method of adaptation persuaded a few Brahmins to convert, but it also opened the door for people of other castes to see an Indian form of Christianity. Members of lower castes also, it must be said, often found Christianity to be a means of social advance. In any event, one should not imagine that the issue of caste or the foreignness of missions, enjoying their colonial government support, was resolved in India in the seventeenth century. The problem of Christian mission complicity—real and imagined—in colonial and imperial projects was only to grow more acute in the eighteenth and nineteenth centuries as Western nations seized more and more control over India's territories and peoples. De Nobili's commitment to studying Sanskrit texts and to transforming Christianity into a cultural form that was acceptable to the high Brahmin caste provides an important missionary model, but it was not the only model, as the following stories show.

The history of Robert de Nobili's work highlights the encounter between European and Indian cultures. The story of Christianity in the seventeenth century, however, was already becoming more complex through multiple cultural engagements. Miguel de Apresentacão (d. 1670) was a Dominican friar, and by the time of his death, a master of theology and the vicar of Santa Barbara in Goa. He was also a member of the Shona peoples from East Africa. The son of a local king against whom the Portuguese fought in battle, he was taken prisoner to Goa where he had been educated by the Dominicans. In 1630 he was received into the Dominican order in Lisbon, and returned to India where he was ordained a priest to serve in the Portuguese fort city of Bacaim. Two decades later, he was serving the Santa Barbara church in Goa. Offered the chance to return to his native Africa, he declined, stating that India had become his home. A report from one of his contemporaries, an Italian named Ardizone Spinola (1609-1697), who claims to have known de Apresentacão well, indicates that while respected as a teacher and priest, the African experienced opposition from other members of the order solely because of the color of his skin.

The story of Joseph Vaz (1651–1711) illustrates the growing complexity that Europe's colonial enterprise was giving rise to as European conflicts between Roman Catholics and Protestants spilled into Asia. Vaz was from a Brahmin family in Goa that had converted to the Roman Catholic faith. After attending Dominican and Jesuit schools in Goa he was ordained to the priesthood in 1676, but according to prevailing Portuguese policies, was not admitted into a religious order. A group of Indian priests who had begun to meet on their own as a community invited Vaz, who had already shown a deep devotion to Mary, to become their superior and to write their rule and develop their spiritual exercises. His passion on behalf of Roman Catholics who were being discriminated against by the Protestant Dutch in Ceylon (modern Sri Lanka) was strong. The problems he was facing came as a result of the Dutch East India Company taking control of the Portuguese colony in the north of Sri Lanka in 1658. They closed the Catholic churches and forced Catholic priests into exile. After several efforts to reach the island, Vaz finally did so in 1687 under the cover of being a migrant worker. For the next three years he worked clandestinely among the Roman Catholics in Jaffna, hiding by day, traveling by night, celebrating Mass in secret, and battling illness.

In 1690 he moved to Buddhist Kandy, a safer kingdom in central Sri Lanka than Protestant Jaffna. At the instigation of the Dutch, however, the ruler of Kandy had Vaz imprisoned, a move that soon proved positive for his missionary work. He learned the Sinhalese language and was able to start a new Catholic church among his fellow prisoners. Eventually he earned the trust of the king, Vimaldharna Surya II (d. 1707), and his son, King Narendrasimha (r. 1707-1739), who recognized Vaz as a genuinely religious leader. For the rest of his life Vaz worked in Sri Lanka, returning several times to Jaffna, welcoming other priests who joined him in Kandy, translating works from Portuguese, writing new catechetical materials in Sinhalese and Tamil, and planting Catholic churches, thereby earning for himself eventually the title of "Apostle to Ceylon."

The life and work of Vaz took place in the context of growing northern European colonialism, which was moving in as Portugal's colonial efforts declined. Unlike the Portuguese and Spanish, the Dutch and British East India Companies often resisted missionaries working in their territories. These trading companies were in Asia only for financial gain. They often saw missionary efforts, be they Protestant or Catholic, as an obstacle to their commercial purpose. Vaz's missionary career, on the other hand, illustrates the manner in which the Roman Catholic Church was becoming indigenous in the south of Asia despite the indifference and opposition of European trading interests. He was from an indigenous Asian Catholic family. He composed literature in Sinhalese and Tamil. He traveled though Sri Lanka disguised as a migrant worker and later was recognized by a Buddhist king—a Sinhalese Buddhist ruler—as a legitimate religious person. And this Buddhist was more congenial to his missionary efforts than Dutch Protestants were to Indian Catholics. Christianity, which had long been at home in Asia in its Orthodox expressions, was now in its Roman Catholic form finding itself at home there as well. And the spread of the world Christian movement was the result of a much more interesting and complex process than a colonial imposition.

Suggestions for further reading

Firth, C. B., *An Introduction to the Indian Church History*. Madras: Christian Literature Society, 1961.

Moffett, Samuel Hugh, *A History of Christianity in Asia, II, 1500-1900*. Maryknoll, NY: Orbis Books, 2005.

Mundandan, A. Mathias, *History of Christianity in India, I*. Bangalore: Church History Association of India, 1989.

Neill, Stephen, *A History of Christianity in India, I: The Beginnings to A.D. 1707*. Cambridge: Cambridge University Press, 1984.

Panikkar, K. M., *Asia and Western Dominance: A Survey of the Vasco Da Gama Epoch of Asian History 1498-1945*. London: George Allen & Unwin, 1953/1959.

Thekkedath, Joseph, *History of Christianity in India, II*. Bangalore: Church History Association of India, 2001.

9

African Christian Kingdoms

Africa in the emerging global slave trade

Africa was an integral part of the new global political economy that was emerging in the seventeenth century. Among the currents of global commerce that were part of this emerging new economy, none affected the African peoples more than the expanding slave trade. Christianity in Africa was deeply intertwined with the sale of humans for the exploitation of labor. Christians were both perpetrators and victims of the growing commerce in African bodies.

The Portuguese dominated the African slave trade through much of the 1500s, but by the end of the century, other European nations were beginning to encroach upon Portugal's virtual monopoly. In 1592, the first English began carrying enslaved Africans across the Atlantic, followed by the Dutch in 1597, the French in 1640, the Swedes in 1649, the Danes in 1651, and finally the Germans (Brandenberghers) in 1685. By 1707, Ireland, Scotland, and Wales had joined in as part of the United Kingdom. The trade became virtually pan-European and involved a wide array of banking houses, investors, shipping companies, and governments.

Christians from Europe were not alone in conducting the industry. Some of the funding for European ships came from wealthy Jewish merchants. For their part, Muslim slave traders often clashed with Europeans in both West and East Africa. By the last decade of the sixteenth century, the trans-Atlantic slave trade had surpassed the trans-Sahara slave trade, both in terms of numbers of individuals taken and in the loss of human life. For the next three centuries, it was Europeans who dominated the global slave trade, and the vast majority of those involved directly or indirectly in the capture, transport, sale, or holding of African slaves were pious and professing Christians who were regarded by most of their churches as being in good standing.

While most of Christian Europe eventually found a way to join the profitable global trade in goods of all kinds, the Dutch were most successful at breaking the Portuguese monopoly in Asia and Africa in the early seventeenth century. The Dutch challenged the Portuguese militarily at key points throughout the Portuguese empire, taking over their factories and routing goods and profits back to northern European seaports. Dutch warships seized control of Jakarta (and renamed it Batavia) in Indonesia in 1619, Formosa (now Taiwan) in 1624, Cochin in India in 1633, Elmina in Ghana in 1637, Ceylon (now Sri Lanka) in 1638,

Luanda in Angola in 1640, Malacca in Malaysia in 1641, and the Cape in South Africa in 1652. In each location, Dutch companies ousted Portuguese colonial rule and took over governing functions.

Where the Portuguese expansion in the fifteenth and sixteenth centuries had been sponsored by the crown and had been both national and religious in character, the Dutch empire of the early seventeenth century was a multinational corporate affair, driven solely by profit. The Verenigde Oost-Indische Compagnie (VOC, "United East India Company") that was established in 1602 was chartered by the Dutch government to operate in East Africa and the Indian Ocean. It was joined in 1621 by the Geoctroyeerde Westindische Compagnie (WIC, "Chartered West India Company"), whose charter allowed it to operate from West Africa to the Caribbean. Both companies were allowed to form private armies, negotiate treaties with heads of states, and exercise colonial power over any lands that they seized and could hold. Both also enlisted members of other nationalities to sail for them. The Dutch government granted these companies the power to wage war, coin money, and establish colonies in order to extend Dutch trade in Africa, the Caribbean, and Asia.

One of the crucial differences in the new Dutch colonial enterprise concerned missions. Where the Portuguese had included the spread of Christian faith and the church as an intrinsic part of their colonial efforts, the Dutch were strictly businessmen and traders whose sole concern was for profits. But while the Dutch merchants showed little interest in mission work, this did not mean they had no concern for matters of religion. The Netherlands had embraced the Reformed faith as its national religion by 1620, and its companies were committed to carrying on the religious war against Portuguese Roman Catholics. Wherever the Dutch companies established their control, they sought to restrict Catholic religious activities, in effect spreading western Europe's wars of religion globally.

The Dutch established a trading port at the Cape of Good Hope on the southern tip of Africa in 1652 in order to have a supply station for their ships traveling between Rotterdam and Batavia. Within a few years they were importing enslaved Africans from other parts of the continent, in several cases seizing Portuguese slave ships to redirect their human cargo for labor at the southern African port. Within a few decades they had expanded the slave holdings to captives taken from Madagascar, Mozambique, India, Ceylon, and Indonesia. Many of these early slaves brought to the Dutch-held region of South Africa were Muslims. The Cape quickly became one of the most ethnically and religiously diverse regions of the world, with the African and Asian population surpassing the number of European colonists. The Dutch did not seek to capture the indigenous inhabitants of the Cape, the Khoikhoi (whom the Dutch called Hottentots), as slaves, but the Khoikhoi were severely oppressed by Dutch encroachments on their lands, and by smallpox, which the Europeans unwittingly introduced.

Central Africa

During the middle years of the seventeenth century, the WIC succeeded in setting up a series of trading posts along the coast of West and Central Africa from the region just south of the Sahara to Angola, challenging the Portuguese dominance in the region. Like the Portuguese, the Dutch did not engage directly in the capture of Africans for sale into slavery. Local African chieftains provided this service for them, collaborating in the trade by taking captives from less-powerful neighboring states and in turn selling them to the Europeans at the port cities. By the 1660s the Dutch were purchasing and selling about three thousand Africans annually for export around the world, but mainly to the Americas. Ships from other European nations joined in the trade, but the Dutch and Portuguese controlled most of the business from their port cities along the western coast of Africa.

Central Africa was organized politically into a number of national kingdoms in the seventeenth century. The largest and most powerful was the kingdom of Kongo, which had been ruled by African Christians since the end of the sixteenth century. To the north along the coast was the kingdom known as Loango. To the south along the coast was the Portuguese colony of Angola, under the administrative control of the city of Luanda. Inland from Angola was the kingdom of Ndongo. A cluster of smaller kingdoms known as the Dembos were on the border between the kingdoms of Kongo and Ndongo.

São Salvador was the largest city in the region. As many as 100,000 people are estimated to have lived in its neighborhoods and surrounding districts in the early decades of the seventeenth century. The pope elevated the status of the main church in São Salvador to the ranks of a cathedral in 1596. A report of its resident bishop in 1619 is instructive regarding the condition of Christianity in the region. The *manikongo*, the report complains, came to Mass with all of his wives, and many of his subjects carried on religious practices that the bishop considered un-Christian. There were only twenty-four priests in all of Kongo and Angola at the time. The *manikongo* and bishop both thought that there was a need for many more. A small school for training priests had been opened in 1596 in São Tomé, the Portuguese-ruled island off the coast in the Atlantic, but only twenty candidates had gone through the program, most of them Europeans. Only a handful of mulatto and African priests had been trained for the entire region.

Into this situation stepped the Jesuits. The Jesuits sought to establish their work in the region as early as 1548 in Kongo, but conflicts with the *manikongo* led to their departure a decade later. They returned to the region to work in the Portuguese colony of Angola in the 1570s, and opened a college in 1607 in its capital, Luanda. In 1624 the Jesuits opened their second college in Central Africa, in São Salvador. The first rector of the college in São Salvador, Mateus Cardoso (d. c. 1635), was fluent in Kikongo, and translated the Roman catechism into the language that same year. An earlier catechism in Kikongo had been printed in 1556, but it was used mostly to instruct slaves in other Portuguese colonies. The new one, which was published in Portugal, was intended for use primarily in the churches of Kongo.

Unlike the catechisms that were written in Vietnam and China, which reflected the worldview of local converts, the Kongolese catechism of 1624 was a translation of a European document and did not address local religious beliefs as directly. As in Asia, however, the Catholic missionaries took the risk of using a local word for God and for various elements of the Christian religion. This allowed for a significant degree of continuity in understanding and belief between traditional African and Christian religiosity. Sections of the Kongolese catechism were set to music, inviting its readers to sing the doctrines.

The Kongolese catechism supported the use of local languages for prayers and in worship. As they did in other places, the Jesuits in Africa placed the symbol of the cross both physically and theologically at the center of their work. Along with the cross, images of Mary and the saints were also important. In cities and villages where churches were established, the cross, the Virgin Mary, and the saints became the Christian counterpart to traditional African images of deities. The main agents for teaching Christian faith and providing pastoral leadership in Kongo during these first years were the *maestri*, or local teachers. These lay catechists were usually bilingual and did much of the work that a friar or secular priest did in other places. Unlike the catechists in Vietnam during this same period, the *maestri* were not permitted to baptize. They did, however, do most of the catechetical training.

By the middle decades of the seventeenth century, Rome was working to remove from the kings of Portugal and Spain the authority to appoint episcopal leadership throughout their empires. The major work of overseeing the church in these colonial regions fell to the Congregation for the Propagation of the Faith, or *Propaganda fidei*, which was established in 1622. In West Africa, *Propaganda fidei* relied on the Capuchins, a reforming branch of Franciscans, to provide pastoral services for many of the churches that had been started. The first Capuchins arrived in Kongo in 1645. Over the course of the next two centuries these friars were closer to West Africans and developed a more intimate knowledge of African Christianity than any other European order.

The Capuchins who were sent to Kongo and its smaller client kingdom of Soyo were mostly Italians. Twelve arrived at Mpinda (the port city of Soyo) in 1645. Their coming was a cause for celebration for the *manikongo* Garcia II (1641-1661) and his subjects, even if it was short-lived. It quickly became evident that Portugal was not going to give up spiritual control of the region to *Propaganda fidei* easily. Although both Garcia II and the Capuchins sought more missionary help, the Portuguese, who controlled transportation, balked. Bishops found it difficult to enter Kongo or Soyo. Without a resident bishop, the Capuchins, who had assumed responsibility for many of the churches and who were much more conservative than the Jesuits regarding ecclesiology, would not allow training of local clergy. The Dutch took control of Luanda briefly in the 1640s and disrupted much of the work that the Jesuits sought to carry on in the region. After regaining control of the city, the Portuguese demanded that Soyo remain under the bishop of Luanda. As a consequence of these factors, Soyo and Kongo constantly suffered from a lack of indigenous trained leadership.

The contrast between the earlier Portuguese work and the later work of the Capuchins under the direction of *Propaganda fidei* was as much a matter of motives as it was anything else. The earlier Portuguese efforts were concerned mainly with service to the king, to extend Portuguese political rule, and to increase profits from trade. *Propaganda fidei* was single-minded in seeking to establish Christian communities and catechize local people. The friars worked closely with the royal family and often became involved in political struggles in the region, but to a lesser degree than the Portuguese before them. The Capuchins also brought more of an international presence. Most of the Capuchins were Italian, and some even came from other European nations as well.

The Capuchin approach to indigenous African religions was more confrontational than adaptive. The Capuchins simply regarded local religions as evil. They sought to exorcize the spirits they encountered in traditional African religionists and destroy what they regarded as the Africans' idols. The Capuchins introduced the Western Christian calendar, with days for commemorating the Western Christian saints. One member of the order, Luca da Caltanissetta (d. after 1700), wrote at the end of the century that he baptized as many as two or three hundred people a day. According to his report, he baptized 2,373 Africans in 1698 alone. He remarked that the Soyo believers were quite enthusiastic in the penitential self-flagellation called "The Discipline." During the singing of the Gloria in the Mass, the Soyo would beat drums, play instruments, and even shoot guns in the air. Caltanissetta also reported that of their own accord people would bring *calabash* filled with water for the priests to bless. After the blessings they would drink the water for healing.

During the first several decades of Capuchin work in Central Africa, more people were baptized than had been in the previous century of Portuguese activity in the region. It is estimated that by the end of the seventeenth century, over 300,000 persons had undergone the rite of Christian initiation in the region. Although it was by no means the exclusive religion, Christianity was the official religion of the royal families of Kongo and of a majority of the people in the region.

Through these decades the Portuguese interest in the region did not diminish. They held the island of São Tomé and their colony of Angola. As was noted earlier, the Dutch captured Luanda and held it for six years from 1641 to 1647. After the Portuguese recaptured Luanda in 1648 they sought to expand their influence in the region, putting increased pressure on the kingdom of Ndongo to the west. Several new fortified Portuguese cities were established, including Ambuila, near the border of Kongo, which soon gained the notorious distinction of being a dumping ground for Portuguese criminals.

The Portuguese presence in the region after 1650 amounted to little more than military forts, slave traders, and criminals, but it was effectively putting new political pressures on Kongo. Both Garcia II (1641-1661) and King António I (1661-1665) of Kongo were supportive of the work of the Capuchins, but both were also increasingly concerned about Portuguese expansion and the growing Portuguese slave trade. In 1665 the Portuguese helped to foment a rebellion in one of the southern provinces of Kongo. António, along with his Christian chaplain and a number of allies, went to war. Outside the city of Mbwila they engaged the Portuguese in battle. António was killed, and in the aftermath the uneasy federation controlled by the Kongo kings collapsed. For the next forty years Kongo was divided by continuous civil war. The Christian capital of São Salvador was abandoned in disarray, left to be overgrown with weeds.

Among the important political and religious figures in Central Africa in the seventeenth and early eighteenth centuries, several powerful women stand out. One of these was Queen Ana Nzinga (or Njinga, c. 1582-1665), who in 1624 became the ruler of Ndongo. It was a time of unrest for Ndongo. From the west, the Portuguese were putting increasing pressure on her border. Farther east, several other African nations were causing trouble along the frontier. Two years earlier, Nzinga had gone to the port city of Luanda on behalf of her brother, who was king, to negotiate peace with the Portuguese. Luanda at the time was a city with an estimated fifty thousand inhabitants. Africans dominated the population, with a scattering of mulattos and Europeans, many of them exiled convicts from Portugal. Impressed by the power of the Portuguese, the buildings in the city, and the rituals of Christianity, Nzinga, after successfully negotiating the treaty, underwent baptism, taking the name Dona Ana de Souza. The Portuguese governor served as her godfather.

Upon her departure, the Portuguese quickly broke the treaty, and the queen abandoned any further relationship with the Portuguese or their religion. After she assumed the throne she allied her people with the Yaka (Jaga) tribe on the border of Matamba to the east and launched what became a thirty-year war against the Portuguese. Under her rule Ndongo became a haven for freed or returned slaves, as well as a number of Portuguese-trained soldiers who had deserted. An elite group of youth who renounced all family ties and were raised in a warrior community served as her inner guard.

In 1656 two Capuchin priests were captured and brought in by her warriors. Their capture coincided with an oracle she received from the spirit of her dead brother who said that if she accepted the Christian faith again, the Europeans would no longer fight and there would be peace. Following the advice of her ancestor-brother, Queen Nzinga reconverted and placed herself under the spiritual guidance of the Capuchins. By all accounts the conversion seems to have been genuine. Traditional Jaga laws that were opposed to Christian teachings were changed, and many of her soldiers were baptized in the weeks that followed. A central Christian building, the Church of Our Lady of Matamba, was erected. The queen reportedly worked side by side with workers on the project, with musicians playing sacred songs in the background. Started in 1660, the church was finally completed in the year of Queen Ana Nzinga's death in 1665. Upon her death, her husband assumed political rule and out of fear of the Portuguese, who had just recently killed the king of Kongo, returned his people to their traditional religions. The city of Santa Maria de Matamba, including the beautiful Church of Our Lady, was destroyed and the experiment in Christian rule brought to an end.

Two prophetic Christian women would play an important role in Kongo early in the eighteenth century. After the defeat of the Kongolese by the Portuguese in 1665, the Christian capital, São Salvador, had been abandoned. For the next four decades Kongo was in chaos as various rulers contended for control. The Capuchins began working with the Portuguese more closely. By 1700 the strongest of the Kongo rulers, Pedro IV (r. 1694-1718), located his court at Mount Kibangu while the forest retook the streets of São Salvador.

In the midst of this situation, in 1704, a Kongolese woman named Muffata (exact dates unknown), who was also known as Apollonia, began to relate to her people a vision she had of the Virgin Mary. According to reports from the period, the Holy Mother told her that her son, Jesus, was deeply saddened to know that the holy city of São Salvador was no longer inhabited. Muffata gave voice to the spirit and concerns of many of the common folk for whom Christianity had become their indigenous faith. She proved her visions through various works of power, including healings, then produced a rock from the river that had on it the appearance of the face of Jesus, verifying her vision in the eyes of many. Her message called for the royal court to come down from Mount Kibangu and rebuild the city of the savior, São Salvador.

Later that same year, another young woman in Kongo named Kimpa Vita (1684-1706), who was also a *nganga,* or a woman with spiritual gifts, fell into a trance. While in this spiritual state Kimpa Vita, or Dona Beatriz as she was later known by the Portuguese, was possessed by the Portuguese patron saint Ántonio. Ántonio told her that he needed her body to preach. When she arose from the trance she explained to her family what had happened, and set off on a mission to Pedro IV at Kibangu, where the king had established his court. She succeeded in gaining an audience with the ruler and relayed to him the message from the saint. Pedro was to restore the capital city of São Salvador.

By this time the moral status of many of the Capuchin priests had sunk fairly low. Drunkenness was rampant among them, and the priests were constantly meddling in political affairs or now pursuing their own personal economic interests. Some were even involved in the slave trade, helping to foster internal warfare among various African rulers as a means of generating prisoners of war to be sold off in the slave ports, and in some cases were themselves reported to be conducting slaving raids farther inland. By the year 1700 the number of Kongolese being sold into slavery reached seven thousand annually.

By 1700, Kongo had also been a Christian kingdom for nearly two hundred years. Most of the priests were poorly trained nationals of mixed Portuguese-Kikongo descent or Capuchins from Italy. Throughout the Kongolese countryside priests were still rare, often visiting villages only once every several years to administer baptisms. The Kongolese often put salt in the baptism water, appropriating a traditional African spirituality that understood salt to be a means of warding off evil spirits. Local catechists conducted classes to teach the basics of the Catholic faith in villages throughout the kingdom, but for the most part the religion of the people was a blend of traditional European Catholic teaching and traditional Kongolese spirituality. It was a situation of spiritual decline that Kimpa Vita also believed she was called to reverse.

Much of our information on her comes from a Capuchin priest named Bernardo de Gallo, who worked in Kongo from 1699 to 1717. De Gallo was a missionary who also served as an advisor to Pedro IV and who later recorded Kimpa Vita's story after interviewing her. According to this woman who believed she was the spiritual messenger of St. Anthony, the priests were in error when they claimed that the church had its origins outside Kongo and that the Christian saints were all Europeans. Jesus had been born in São Salvador, Ántonio had told her, and she was to tell this to the people. Jesus and Mary were both black

Africans, not white Europeans. The priests had distorted the faith for their own purposes.

Kimpa Vita began teaching a new catechism in Kikongo, called the "Salve Ántoniana." It called God *Nzambi a Mpungu*, the Kikongo name for the high God that the Jesuits had earlier appropriated, but it denied the inherent power of the sacraments performed by the priests and stressed instead the intentions of the heart as being what mattered in religion. At the core of her message was a call to conversion, coupled with the promise of political unification of the country that would be achieved by the physical restoration of the capital of São Salvador. This type of conversion, it was foreseen, would bring an end to the perpetual civil war among the various *manikongo* vying for the throne, which in turn would mean an end to taking prisoners of war which was feeding the Portuguese appetite for slaves.

When Kimpa Vita was possessed by Ántonio she was reported to have appeared to levitate and was heard to speak in unknown tongues. She also began performing physical healings, with curing infertility among women being the most prominent. Her movement spread as she wandered from village to village preaching and teaching the new catechism São Ántonio had delivered to her. The message that Jesus and the saints were black, and that the priests had lied about them being European, found a ready hearing.

Late in 1704 Kimpa Vita announced that she and her followers would begin to repopulate the ancient capital of São Salvador on their own, and then invite the various *manikongo,* or leading rulers, of whom Pedro IV was the most prominent, to come and join her there. The city's houses had become overgrown with foliage, its churches were in disrepair, and its fields were lost to the forest. No *manikongo* had been able to occupy the city for a quarter century due because of the constant warfare among the rival groups. When Kimpa Vita announced the restoration had begun, a popular following of several hundred marched in to reoccupy the city. She had enough support from several local rulers and enough of a popular following to prevent any of the various warring factions from marching against her unarmed followers. Finally, rumor had spread that she had obtained the *Santíssimo Sacramento*, a small bag containing several papal bulls with indulgences granted to the *manikongo* Diogo I (r. 1545-1561) in the 1550s, and that it had been housed in the cathedral of São Salvador for more than a century. Were the rumor true she would have had the legitimate insignia of national leadership.

Over the next two years Kimpa Vita preached to her followers in the ruins of the cathedral of São Salvador about the true religion of Jesus. She began to commission them to be little Ántonios, sending them out through the countryside. Through them the movement spread among the Kongolese catechists and lay teachers, and even some of the members of the royal households.

Late in 1705 Kimpa Vita discovered that she was pregnant. Although she had been married twice before her spiritual calling, both relationships had failed, and she was no longer legally married. Seeking to hide the pregnancy, Kimpa Vita left São Salvador with a trusted lieutenant named Barro (d. 1706), who was also presumably the father of the child, to find a hiding place in a neighboring village where she could deliver her baby. Shortly after giving birth to a son she was discovered by enemies and taken captive to Pedro IV. A trial was held according to Kongolese law, but with the involvement of the Capuchin priests. Kimpa Vita was condemned by the king to death. In July of 1706, along with her companion, Barro, she was burned at the stake. Their baby was spared. Before her execution she told much of her story to the Italian priests, who recorded it in full, providing a historical record of sorts for the Antonian movement.

Within days of her execution, Pedro IV marched on the city of São Salvador and routed the Antonians. Several thousand were sold into slavery, while others were forced into exile across the Kongo River. Still the movement was not stamped out. Long after Kimpa Vita had been burned and her remains burned a second time to prevent any collection of relics, Kongolese continued to tell her story and to spread the message of St. Anthony coming to them with an authentic African form of Christian faith. The story of Kimpa Vita and the Antonian movement can still be heard in Central Africa today as a call for a unified spiritual community from one of the first founders of an African Initiated Church movement.

Ethiopia

The ancient Christian kingdom of Ethiopia was much reduced in its territories by the seventeenth century. Repeated incursions of neighboring Muslim rulers over several centuries were taking their toll. All three traditional centers of Ethiopian authority, its monasteries, *abuna* (the Ethiopian patriarch), and *negusä nägäst* ("king of kings," the Ethiopian emperor) had weakened. Externally the presence of Portuguese guns and soldiers along the coast were creating a new dynamic in the region. The Portuguese and the Jesuits shared the same religious mission in Ethiopia in the seventeenth century, to bring the nation and its churches under Roman papal rule. In 1603 Rome again appointed its own patriarch to head the Ethiopian church, a Spaniard named Pedro Paez (1564-1622), and sent him to East Africa. He had studied at the Jesuit college in Goa and was influenced by the experience of the Jesuits in eastern Asia. Paez learned both written Ge'ez and spoken Amharic, and worked to establish good relations with the emperor.

Two emperors eventually took Paez into their confidence as an advisor. The first was Za Dengel (r. 1603-1604), who had just come to power in 1603 when Paez arrived. Za Dengel was immediately impressed by the Spaniard, and announced to him his plans to recognize Rome's authority. Most likely hopes of protection and increased economic trade were major factors in the decision. By all measures it was a very political conversion, and one his people did not share. Za Dengel sent letters to both the pope and the king of Spain seeking support, but when word leaked out about them *Abuna* Peter (d. 1607) excommunicated him. Soon afterward, others among the nobility took up arms, and civil war ensued. Although he had the support of two hundred Portuguese armed with guns, Za Dengel was killed.

Over the next three years Za Dengel's cousin, Yaqob (d. 1607), received sufficient support from leading members of the Ethiopian nobility to plausibly be called emperor. His leading contender for the throne was a member of another aristocratic family, Susenyos (1572-1632). The two sides finally met in battle in 1607. Susenyos proved victorious. Yaqob and *Abuna* Peter, who supported him, were both killed.

Susenyos was enthroned in Axum the next year, and before long was pursuing Za Dengel's policy of cooperating with Paez. Ethiopia needed military, educational, and spiritual resources, to say nothing of the desire of the emperor for increased trade. The Ottomans were exerting military pressure along the East African coast. Egypt was under Ottoman control, and although the spiritual attachment of Ethiopia to Alexandria was still strong, the Coptic Church could provide little in the way of spiritual support. Susenyos wanted to convert immediately and bring Ethiopia more fully under Rome. The Latin patriarch counseled caution and patience on the other hand. He had seen the disruption that the conversion of Za Dengel had created. Ethiopia would have to turn slowly toward Rome, Paez reasoned, not suddenly and by imperial fiat. Meanwhile, Paez was proving influential in helping to bring masons and other craftspersons to Ethiopia from India. Trade in general with India increased, in large part because of the Portuguese and Jesuit influences.

Working closely in ruling the Ethiopian nation and in developing relations with Rome through this period was the king's brother and confidant, Cela Krestos (or Se'lä Krestos, d. after 1635), advisor to the king and governor of Tigre. In 1612 Cela Krestos, along with several other members of his family, publicly joined the Roman Catholic Church. Paez convinced the king not to follow his brother's example yet, however, and so Susenyos refrained from officially converting. During this time there were never more than six Jesuits in the country, but they had an impact that far outweighed their numbers. Four of them served as royal advisors.

Finally in 1622, after a number of major military victories and with his popularity at its height, Susenyos converted to the Roman Catholic faith. At first the timing seemed providential to Jesuits and king alike, but six weeks after his conversion the irenic Paez died. His successor, Alfonso Mendez (r. 1624-1632), was far more rigid and irritating. Rome gave Mendez the title of Patriarch of Ethiopia, increasing the tension in the land. Susenyos's conversion coupled with Mendez's title brought all of the theological divisions between Ethiopia and Rome to the fore. A thousand years of Ethiopian tradition were at stake. The African Christians celebrated the Sabbath on Saturday as well as on Sunday. They honored Mary far more than the Romans did, and they circumcised young boys, a habit the Roman Catholics thought was full of ancient superstitions. Above all, Ethiopian Christian identity was marked by its rejection of Chalcedon's doctrine of the two natures in Jesus Christ, a doctrine that the Ethiopians viewed as "Nestorian." Mendez, coming not from India but directly from Spain, supported the rigid application of Tridentine theology and practice. He also demonstrated complete ignorance regarding cultural adaptation. His only redeeming quality was his inflated self-confidence. It soon proved to be a lethal formula for seventeenth-century Ethiopia.

Mendez arrived with a retinue of dignitaries, great pageantry, and blasts of canons in 1626. King Susenyos made a public declaration of submission to the pope, and Mendez clarified just what this meant. In his first proclamation as the newly arrived patriarch, Mendez wrote that the faithful Ethiopians must be rebaptized and priests must be reordained. In addition, the Roman liturgy had to be followed, although he allowed that it could be said in Ge'ez. Circumcision was prohibited, and Saturday was no longer to be the Sabbath, but a fast day. All of this was too much for most of the royal family as well as for the monks and the masses of Christians whose faith had been supported by these ancient rituals and practices. Rebellions soon sprang up. At first Susenyos put them down decisively, but a general peasant rebellion broke out in 1632 that shook the confidence of the emperor. Finally it became clear that his people would not abide the foreign influence in religion. Before abdicating his throne to his son, Fasiledes (1603-1667), Susenyos issued a proclamation allowing both types of Christian worship (Ethiopian and Roman) to continue, but celebrating his own return to Ethiopian worship. Clergy were to be allowed to return to their churches and say the liturgy in either language.

The response was far-reaching. In the first years of Fasiledes' reign several Roman Catholic priests, including two Capuchins sent by Rome, were executed. Eventually he ordered all Western priests expelled, and all Latin theological books to be burned. Ethiopia from that point turned decisively away from Rome and the West, and looked even more toward India and the Orthodox traditions of the East. For the next few centuries the East African nation for all practical purposes remained cut off from any important relationship with Europe. Kings now looked to India for artwork, architects, clothes, and other products. Fasiledes changed the Ethiopian tradition of the ruler and his entourage traveling throughout the country, housed in hundreds of tents that formed a pilgrim capital. He eventually built a new capital city at Gondar just north of Lake Tana. On the one hand, this move tended to isolate the royal family and the government from the people. On the other, the splendor of the capital with its palace and many churches enhanced the sense of royal authority. Most of the laborers who built the new capital were Indians and at least a few were Muslims from the Mughal court. Not only the buildings but even the dress of the Ethiopian court now came from India. Ethiopia's rulers adopted Indian silk and Indian slippers. Even the peasants began eating papaya and figs that had been imported from India. Ethiopia turned east. Meanwhile, the handful of Portuguese who had settled and remained in the country were increasingly marginalized.

Even though Ethiopia was turning away from the West, one European managed to make an important contribution to the nation while making a home for himself in East Africa. Peter Heyling (1607-1652) was a German Lutheran medical doctor and theologian. Heyling had been part of a small group of students in Germany who had made a commitment to help the ancient churches of the East that were facing severe challenges. He had first gone to Egypt, where he befriended the future Ethiopian *abuna* Marqos (r. 1635-1672), studied Arabic, and lived in Coptic monasteries in the desert. After a year in Egypt, Heyling arrived in Ethiopia in 1634 where he was received with appreciation because of

his medical skills. Heyling did not believe that the Ethiopian church was heretical, as most European church leaders claimed, but that it was in need of the Bible
in Amharic, the language that the people now spoke. He proceeded to translate
the Gospel of John in booklet form for wide distribution. Heyling finally left
Ethiopia in 1652, going by way of the ancient Christian kingdom of Nubia, or
what is now the Sudan. Along the way he was captured by a Turkish pasha and
beheaded. Heyling was thus the first Protestant missionary to Ethiopia, one of
the first modern biblical translators in Africa, and the first Protestant martyr in
Africa.

Heyling's translations helped to reignite an older Ethiopian theological debate
regarding the manner in which the two natures of Jesus Christ had become one.
The Apostle Peter, according to Acts 10:38, in the house of Cornelius had said that
"God anointed Jesus of Nazareth with the Holy Spirit and with power." On the
one side of the debate in Ethiopia were the monks who were collectively known
as the House of Takla Haymanot, after a thirteenth-century Ethiopian monastic
leader by that name. They claimed that this anointing referred only to the manner
in which Jesus Christ became the Messiah, and not to his united nature. On the
other side were the Ewostathians, who claimed the tradition of the fourteenth-
century Ethiopian monk Ewostatewos, better known for his support of observing
the Sabbath on both Saturday and Sunday. They believed that this anointing of
Jesus Christ was the moment of the divinizing of his humanity, or the point at
which the two natures, divine and human, had come together as one. The position of the Ewostathians thus became known as qibatoch, or "unctionist." The
House of Takla Haymanot, who were "unionists" and claimed that their position
was truer to the ancient Tewahido ("United") position of the non-Chalcedonian
communions of Ethiopia and Egypt, charged that the Ewostathian's position led
to subordinationism or adoptionism.

Behind the renewed debate, which continued for two decades, was the stimu-
lating effect of a newly translated Gospel of John, as well as the increased exposure of Ethiopians to Western Catholic liturgy and theology. For those involved,
the debate was not simply a matter for monks. The emperor was soon a participant in the controversy. Two synods were held in an effort to maintain the unity
of the kingdom, with little effect.

Fasiledes then took matters into his own hands, and in 1654 declared that
the official position of the empire would be that of the Ewostathians, or the unctionists. The next emperor, Yohannes I (r. 1667-1682), continued to support the
unctionists and gave those who disagreed time in prison to reconsider. His son
and successor, Iyasu I, called "the Great" (1682-1706), reversed this decision and
demanded that all of the Ewostathians support the House of Takla Haymanot,
or the unionists. In the end neither side was able to claim a clear-cut victory, but
the Ethiopian church overall experienced renewed christological reflection. In
retrospect, the Roman Catholic influences as well as the new Lutheran emphasis on Scriptures were important catalysts for these new theological stirrings in
Ethiopia.

Although we have little in the way of writings concerning the history of
women in Ethiopian Christianity during this period, we do have a few brief

glimpses recorded for us. Royal women in particular were sometimes active in theological discussions and even intrigue. In the unctionist-versus-unionist controversy, Queen Seble-Wengel (d. c. 1700) was fully involved alongside her husband, King Yohannes I, and in opposition to her son, Iyasu I. She shared the theological views of her husband but was apparently unable to influence her son, who demanded that the country support the unionist position.

A glimpse into the lives of Christian women in Ethiopia at this time is provided by a fascinating book, *Vita di Walatta Pietros* ("Life of Walatta Pietros"). Although written in the style of hagiography, its pages reveal much about seventeenth-century Ethiopian ideals of Christian womanhood, if not the actual facts of a particular woman. Walatta was a woman of means who was described as actively involved in both secular and religious leadership of her time. She spent much of her time reading spiritual literature, and had miraculous powers of both healing and killing. On a number of occasions she was depicted as slaying people from a great distance, either for their own good to protect them from greater harm or for the good of others. All three of her children died in youth, and her husband converted to Roman Catholicism, allowing her, according to the author of the volume, to take up the highly regarded life of a nun. She founded her own monasteries for men as well as for women and established a rule that gave her considerable control over decisions, even involving the priests.

Although her husband turned to Rome, Walatta persisted in providing support for local priests and monks who remained faithful to the Ethiopian tradition. The work portrayed her as a saint who while being persecuted by the Romanists was able to build churches, establish monasteries, and serve the poor. Even though church leadership in Ethiopia was all male, her final vision before she died involved her appointment by Jesus Christ to be "Head of the deacons." *The Life of Walatta Pietros* is one of the earliest full biographies of an African Christian woman, and it provided a model for women in leadership positions in the church.

The seventeenth century was a period of intercontinental and intercommunion struggles that ended with the Ethiopian church turning inward and eastward. The monastic confederations continued to exercise considerable spiritual and theological authority, while the *negusä nägäst* was in many ways an equal to the *abuna*, or patriarch, who was at the head of the church. Christianity in Ethiopia would, until the 1970s, be a religion of the *negusä*, *abuna*, and monks working together.

East and southeast Africa

The eastern coast of Africa south of Ethiopia was opening up for trade in the seventeenth century. Islamic merchants were increasing their presence, especially in the kingdom of Mombasa in present-day Kenya. In 1597, one of Vasco da Gama's grandsons, Francisco da Gama (1565–1632), became viceroy of India. One of his first acts was to order missionaries to be sent from India to plant the Christian faith along this coastal region in Africa. The candidates who came were mostly from India and had been trained at Goa. Among the first were

Augustinians who began missionary work in the ancient capital of Mombassa, an island city on the coast. They established a Portuguese military outpost named Fort Jesus and within its walls a church, a monastery, and a Misericordia fraternity to meet the needs of the sick, poor, and destitute. By the end of the first year, they had recorded over six hundred baptisms.

Other missions were started along the coast from as far north as Faza and Pate to the island of Mozambique. Christianity spread in the region mostly, however, through Portuguese traders, soldiers and sailors, and their slaves. The relationship with Islam was especially important along this coast. A Muslim sailor had originally guided Vasco da Gama to India, and although the Portuguese controlled much of the open sea, Muslims still dominated the coast and many other places. As Christianity was developing along the east and southeast coasts of Africa, it did so in constant contact with Islam. Two illustrations demonstrate how varied their relationships were in the seventeenth century.

Along the coast of present-day Kenya lie a series of islands from Lamu in the north to Zanzibar in the south on the Kenya-Tanzania border. These were areas that had long been undergoing Islamicization. With the arrival of the Portuguese and then the call from the viceroy of India for missionaries, however, many monks, most of them Augustinians, began to arrive to undertake Christian missionary work. One of the islands at the north end of the chain is Faza, and it is where an Augustinian friar named Diogo do Espirito Santo (d. c. 1630) arrived at the beginning of the seventeenth century. Because of the contentious relationship with Islam, Faza was the only island in the region where a missionary could stay, and even then life was not secure. Father Diogo not only managed to establish a mission in Faza, but his ministry in this Islamic region lasted over thirty years.

The Portuguese had earlier sacked the town of a local sultan on the island in response to the Islamic ruler's call for military resistance against the uninvited Europeans. The sultan later developed a strong relationship with the friar, however, going so far as to help Diogo build his new church. Reportedly the sultan even carried stones on his own back, claiming that the church would be like a wall of protection to help him live in peace, and the Catholic fathers like spiritual soldiers to defend it. In a similar way, the Augustinian work in Zanzibar was remarkable for the peaceful and respectful relations they had with a local sultan. There were good relations with the Muslims in part because most of the ministry the friars undertook was with non-Muslims, most of whom were currently or formerly enslaved.

Relationships between Christians and Muslims were seldom clear and simple during these years, however, and they rarely entailed religious dialogue or shared community values. Matters of religion usually overlapped with political and economic issues among local populations. Mombassa in 1600 was one of the many island centers along the coast that were ruled by sultans or kings, mostly of Arab or Persian descent. The rulers, both religious and political, were considered foreigners by the local African population. These cities looked not into Africa but out across the Indian Ocean to south and west Asia for trade and political relations.

In 1614 the sultan of Malindi offended a Portuguese sea captain, who in turn had the sultan slain. The sultan's son, Yusuf bin Hasan (d. 1638), was then taken captive to Goa. There he was raised in the Augustinian convent, and after much instruction, baptized into the Christian faith and given the name Jerónimo Chingulia. This son of a sultan soon proved to be an excellent gunner for the Portuguese navy. In 1625, after being away from Mombassa for eleven years, Jerónimo was made a knight of the Order of Christ and returned with his Portuguese wife to assume the position of sultan of Malindi. To the Portuguese this seemed to bode well politically, economically, and religiously. A Portuguese-trained Christian sultan was to be ruling over one of the key port kingdoms in Africa. The sultan wrote the pope in 1627 to assure him that he was being received well by his Muslim citizens and had already succeeded in converting a number of them to the Christian faith. Such, however, was only the Christian side of the story. The local Muslim record offers a different perspective on his rule. It was recorded in the Arab chronicles that he was a cruel ruler, and that his people suffered greatly.

Whether it was hearing again the familiar Arabic prayers, the complaints from his own people, or the visits to his father's tomb, we may never know, but within several years of his return, Christian Jeronimo had returned to his home faith of Islam as well, retaking the name Yusuf bin Hasan. His reacquired Islamic sympathies were soon raised before the Inquisition, but Rome could do nothing against him. In August of 1631, Sultan Yusuf killed the Portuguese captain and many of his soldiers who were stationed at Fort Jesus. Christians, looking for a place of protection, ran for the monastery. After five days, negotiations between the sultan and the friars failed. Yusuf bin Hasan gave an ultimatum for the Christians to accept Islam or die. Only one person escaped through conversion. The rest of the Africans, Portuguese, and mulattos who refused the order were either killed or sold off as slaves, some four hundred of the latter to Mecca alone. An estimated three hundred persons, including men, women, and children, half of whom were Africans, died and were soon known as the Mombassa Martyrs. Most of those who were Africans among their number were enslaved. The fact that they chose death over conversion is an indication of the sincerity and depth of their Christian faith.

Within a year the Portuguese returned and retook Fort Jesus. Their rule was not popular, however, especially since they began populating the fort with *degredados*, or criminals. The people of Mombassa soon turned to the sultan of Oman to release them from the yoke of the Portuguese. The sultan responded by first attacking Zanzibar and then helping to set off a number of rebellions along the coast. As Portuguese influence on the seas began to decline, the rebellions could not be put down, the missionaries could not be protected, and East Africa came entirely under the sway of the sultan of Oman. Fort Jesus itself was besieged and fell in December of 1698, bringing Portuguese influence in East Africa to an end. Most of the members of the small, struggling, and isolated Christian community died in the end by the sword.

Farther south still, along the coast of Africa, were the Portuguese settlements north and south of the Zambezi River, at present-day Mozambique and Zimbabwe. This region of Africa was not particularly profitable for the Portuguese, although for decades they pressed ahead on rumors of silver and gold. Of greater economic interest, as elsewhere in Africa, was the lucrative slave trade. Numerous enslaved Africans from the Zambezi region, stowed on ships and sometimes baptized, ended up each year in Brazil. The regional center for Portuguese activity was in India. Their traders, monks, soldiers, and priests all sailed from Goa to the outposts in South Africa. Missionaries to the region sought to speak to and with the local cultures less here than in almost every other area of Africa in the seventeenth century.

Along the Zambezi settlements of Sena, Tete, Chikova, and Zumbo, Jesuits and Dominicans accumulated land, ran large estates called *prazos*, which were worked by slave labor, and ministered mostly to the Portuguese, their local wives (often Africans), and their children. Writing near the end of the seventeenth century, Friar João Frausto (d. c. 1700) described his work in the Mutapa kingdom hearing confession and administering the sacraments to the Christians scattered throughout the kingdom who were engaged in trade, whether they were Portuguese, mulatto, or African.

Recent archaeological work in the region has confirmed some of these descriptions of the missionary work. Near present-day Harare was a small trading center known as Dambarare. The settlement was little more than a fort and a church, with a few Dominican priests. The church was a brick building with graves beneath the clay floor and around the outside of the building. There were no coffins. The bodies of Europeans were buried, crowded together under the church floor. Some still had gold rings on their fingers when they were set in the ground. Outside the church were buried the bodies of African females and some mulatto men and women who wore only copper or bronze jewelry. There were no African men, so we can conclude that this Christian site was made up of Portuguese men and their African wives and concubines. The community was wiped out in a raid in 1693, the Dominican priest being flayed alive.

The foreign Christian community was for the most part involved in disreputable trade, either employing or enslaving local people to do their work. Monks and priests occupied themselves mostly with the slave trade. Those local rulers who were baptized and took Christian (that is, Portuguese) names did so mostly for political reasons. It was the surest way to identify with the Portuguese for both trade and military protection. In some instances priests took young royal family members away to immerse them in a foreign Christian culture in Goa, hoping to return them as "Christianized" rulers in the land. As with the case of Yusuf bin Hasan, the strategy generally did not succeed.

While the behavior of European priests in southeastern Africa often left much to be desired during this period, there were prophetic figures who stand out. António da Conceição (d. 1700) was one such individual. Da Conceição was appointed ecclesiastical administrator of the Zambezi River region during the late 1680s. Being an Augustinian, he could do a better job than most in navigating between the two major religious orders working in the region, the Jesuits and the Dominicans. His concern was mainly for ministry to the local African peoples. He vigorously contested the general assumptions of his colleagues that Africans were not intelligent and could not learn about Christianity, arguing that they had to be instructed in their own language. To this end he worked to translate the catechism into the local language and argued strongly that all church leaders should become fluent in it, something that was almost unheard of in seventeenth-century southeast Africa.

Da Conceição asserted that missionaries must not be involved in local business and they must be primarily involved in catechizing the local people. For all of his appeal for reform in the mission work, little was done because of the suspicion on the part of the other orders that da Conceição was only making room for more of his own Augustinians to enter the region. Little was accomplished after nearly fifteen years of appeals. The Dominicans, working south of the Zambezi, did appoint a visitor and sent out some newer friars to focus the Dominican work on the local people, but the accomplishments were minimal.

By 1700, African Christianity was at a major point of transition. The Dutch were quickly becoming a force along the coastal regions while the Portuguese-African Christian kingdoms had passed their zenith. While Christianity seemed to be waning, Islam was healthy and spreading its influence throughout Africa. One of the great tragedies of the era was the growing European-sponsored slave trade, which increasingly involved monks and priests sent from the West to work throughout Africa. Religious division and even violence began to be imported from Europe as Protestants and Catholics conspired against each other throughout the continent. And yet there were faithful friars, African prophets, and a handful of Christian leaders who all pointed to something greater and nobler. Africans themselves began to shape Christianity in places where Europeans had planted missions, but it would be another 150 years before their work would come to real fruition outside the northeastern region.

Suggestions for further reading

Baur, John, *2000 Years of African Christianity: An African Church History.* 2nd ed. Nairobi: Paulines, 2009.

Denis, Philippe, *The Dominican Friars in Southern Africa: A Social History (1577-1990).* Leiden: E.J. Brill, 1998.

Hastings, Adrian, *The Church in Africa, 1450-1950.* Oxford: Clarendon Press, 1994.

Isichei, Elizabeth, *A History of Christianity in Africa.* Grand Rapids: Eerdmans, 1995.

Kalu, Ogbu, ed., *African Christianity: An African Story.* Pretoria: Department of Church History, University of Pretoria, 2005.

Sundkler, Bengt, and Christopher Steed, *A History of the Church in Africa.* Cambridge: Cambridge University Press, 2000.

10

The Caribbean and South America

The Caribbean

The seventeenth century was a time of rapid change in America as it was elsewhere in the world, brought about mainly by developments in the wider global material economy. The decline of profits through extracting the precious metals of silver and gold, and the subsequent rise of profits from sugar and tobacco plantations were the most important factors accounting for these changes in America, and especially in the Caribbean. In the early 1640s, a colony of Portuguese Jews emigrated from Brazil to Barbados. They brought with them knowledge regarding sugar cane farming and production. Sugar soon became a major product in the Caribbean. Tobacco was indigenous to America, but in the sixteenth century it had yet not played a major role in the economy of the Caribbean. That changed, and in the seventeenth century "brown gold," especially from Cuba, joined sugar as a major source of profit and power in the region.

Sugar production was labor intensive, labor that was mainly to come from enslaved people of African descent. In the seventeenth century sugar production more than any other factor fueled the growing Atlantic slave trade. In Barbados in 1627 Africans composed only 10 percent of the population. By 1685 the island had four times as many enslaved Africans as it had settlers from European descent. The average plantation had sixty slaves. Many islands of the Caribbean that had been uninhabited before 1492 or depopulated after the appearance of Europeans had a majority of people of African descent by 1700. One of the consequences was that African-Caribbean culture was much stronger in the region and arguably even predominant in the long run.

Political and religious developments in Europe were continuously spilling over into the Caribbean and along the coast of South America during these years. By the last decades of the sixteenth century Spain's control of the seas was in decline, and the Dutch and English were rising as global military powers. A close relationship between the British and the Dutch developed as the Netherlands freed itself from Spanish rule and began looking to extend its economic reach to other parts of the world. The Caribbean became an active battleground for the struggles among these European nations. British, Dutch, and French ships were often privateers sailing nominally under national flags but operating outside of official royal command, making the Caribbean a sea of pirates and buccaneers as well. The first Dutch to arrive in the Caribbean were looking to intercept goods and take over trade that was being conducted by the Portuguese and Spanish. Their first settlement was in Guiana on the Essequibo River in 1616. After 1621 the effort was brought under the control of the Geoctroyeerde Westindische Compagnie ("Chartered West India Company," WIC), a private Dutch company that was granted powers by the government of the Netherlands to establish colonies, raise a private army, negotiate treaties, and otherwise conduct business as a state-authorized entity. Further settlements were established in St. Martin, St. Eustatius, Saba, Curaçao, Bonaire, and Aruba. Spain conceded these territories to the WIC, and by extension to the Netherlands in 1648.

At about the same time, British settlers began to arrive in the Caribbean. The first English colony was established in 1624 on the island of St. Christopher (now St. Kitts) by Thomas Warner (1581-1649). A year later he received from King Charles I (1600-1649) authority to proceed with his efforts, which included the propagation of the Christian religion. His good friend and adamant Calvinist, John Fealtey (c. 1605-1666), came along as the first resident Anglican minister. These English Calvinists in the Caribbean interpreted their efforts in providential terms. They believed that God had specially chosen them, like Israel of old, to enter a new promised land and to subdue the indigenous inhabitants for God. As Fealtey said in a widely published sermon, it was their Christian duty to possess the land. The English leaders were Joshuas, the Atlantic Ocean was the River Jordan, and the islands were Canaan. These Calvinist Anglicans believed they were to live before the peoples of Canaan in such a way as to represent God to them, serving as role models of sincerity and truth to point them to the one true God. The theological reasoning provided powerful ideological cover for England's conquest.

The English were motivated to take up the colonial mission in part because of what they had learned about the violent and oppressive Spanish conquest and rule. The so-called Black Legend of Spain's violent oppression of indigenous Americans was used by Protestants in England to warrant their nations' intervention in America. Ironically, most of what these English Protestants knew of the Spanish conquest came from a translation of the *Brief Account of the Devastation of the Indies* written a century earlier by the Spanish Dominican, Bartolomé de Las Casas (1484-1566).

One of the English writers who promoted the Black Legend and whose writings proved to be among the most effective when it came to inspiring Protestants to resist the Spanish in America was Walter Raleigh (1554-1618). A friend and confidant of Queen Elizabeth (1533-1603), Raleigh was sent on an expedition to the Orinoco River region and followed up with a brief volume in 1595 titled *The Discoverie of Guianea*. The book not only tempted the English reader with descriptions of gold and other valuables, but also promoted a joint English and Native American attack on the Spanish empire in America.

A second influential English author promoting the Black Legend was Richard Hakluyt (1552-1660). His *Discourse on Western Planting*, published in 1584, was widely discussed in the English court. His appeal was in part religious. It was necessary for the salvation of the poor people of America who had for so long lived in darkness and in the shadow of death to have preachers sent to them, he argued. The Spanish were colonizing and sending their priests and prayer books. Reformed Christians should do the same. Of the twenty-one chapters in the book, however, only four explicitly concerned religion. Most of the reasons given for English colonization had to do with trade, wealth, and national security.

When the English did eventually establish colonies in America, concern for the protection and evangelization of Native Americans was far less of a concern than it had been for the Spanish or the Portuguese. In spite of the English condemnation of the Spanish for the Black Legend, the earliest English groups in the Caribbean did not behave any better. Fearing the local Carib people, for instance, Thomas Warner and the other English settlers on St. Christopher launched a preemptive attack three years after establishing their colony, killing a large number of the local inhabitants, including their ruler, King Tegreman.

English settlers landed at a second Caribbean island, Barbados, in 1625. The Spanish had already enslaved and removed the indigenous inhabitants, but had not settled the island themselves. The English colony quickly grew, due mainly to an influx of poor people from England who came as indentured workers. The third governor of Barbados, William Tufton (d. 1632), organized the island into six parishes, and worked to get priests in each church. He was also outspoken concerning the treatment of indentured servants but unfortunately was ousted from office and executed by his successor, in part for his stance on behalf of the poor.

The first Protestant churches in the Caribbean, like their Spanish and Portuguese predecessors, worked closely with the secular colonial rulers. Governors generally were expected to establish parishes, appoint priests, and ensure financial support for the church. Charters from the king, like that of Charles I for the St. Christopher colony, mandated a missionary responsibility. As with the Spanish, this was easily neglected since it cost money to carry out religious work. Religious orders among the Spanish, however, made evangelization more likely, even when governors and viceroys were not supportive.

British settlers in the Caribbean often had Protestant leanings, and churches tended to function on the model of congregational rule that was emerging in England, with vestries exercising more control among the Anglicans in the islands than they did in England. These were for the most part churches without bishops. Although appeals were made to appoint a resident bishop in the Caribbean, the first did not arrive until 1824, two centuries after the first British settlers. Without the direct line of episcopal authority tying them to the rites of the Church of England, congregations in the British Caribbean adopted a greater variety of worship styles and theology than their counterparts in England.

The combination of scant episcopal ecclesiastical supervision, along with scandal caused by the behavior of the seedier elements of British society who were attracted to Caribbean outposts, contributed to diverging ecclesiastical styles and a fairly low moral tone among the immigrants. One gets a sense of the ethical character of the region in various laws and acts that were passed. An act from the 1640s, for instance, mandated that the Church of England would be the established church in Barbados, and all other churches, especially those that met secretly, were outlawed. Another act from the period required family prayers to be said morning and evening in each home. Church attendance was required two times each Sunday, and servants were required to attend church with their masters. The clergy were required to catechize youth and provide other regular services. People who swore or cursed were to be punished, according to these colonial regulations, and local authorities were to walk every Sunday among the taverns and alehouses, looking for lewd behavior or debauchery, which they were to punish by having the guilty parties arrested and placed in stocks or fined. The fact that such laws were being passed suggests that the civil authorities perceived errant behavior to be, if not rampant, then at least a danger in the colony.

Slavery

The African slave trade was arguably the greatest moral issue of the era. The fact that Christian leaders could so easily ignore the violence and torture that chattel slavery entailed, to say nothing of defending the system, poses a fundamental challenge to the claims of such leaders that they were representatives of a just and gracious God. As England and the Netherlands joined Spain and Portugal among the ranks of colonial European nations, Protestants joined Catholics in defending slavery. The number of enslaved Africans brought to America increased dramatically in the seventeenth century. The economic benefits from the system that were accruing to Europeans made it difficult for those Europeans who opposed it to mount any effective resistance.

Resistance to slavery began first instead among Africans themselves who were being taken captive and sold in America and elsewhere into forced labor. Captives had to be held in chains while they were being shipped across the Atlantic in what was called the middle passage, due to the constant threat that they would rise up in rebellion or commit suicide as the ultimate refusal to cooperate in the degradation. Even after arriving in America and being sold to plantation owners in public auctions, Africans continued to resist, from time to time participating in uprisings, but more often by escaping. Communities of fugitive slaves, called *cimarróns* in Spanish or maroons in English, formed in more remote regions where the colonial authorities could not reach them. Sometimes they developed relations with Native American inhabitants.

The initial steps in evangelization among Africans in the Caribbean went ahead without official church approval or control. Africans observed the religious world of their captors, and some began to adapt their own indigenous religious worldview to that of their new social context. Various African deities began to be identified with traditional saints of the Christian order and with Mary. Traditional African beliefs and practices, including those revolving around spirits, spirit possession, healing practices, and ancestor veneration, were merged with Christian symbols and practices in a variety of ways. All of this happened outside official church sanction, laying the foundations in the seventeenth century for a distinctive mode of African Christian religiosity that would emerge more clearly in the eighteenth.

Europeans fought over many things political and religious, but in the seventeenth century they were in general agreement regarding the legitimacy of slavery. Those few who disagreed and spoke out on behalf of the slaves were usually motivated by religious concerns, but while they might be notable for their boldness and theological consistency, they were far too few in number to be effective. The European social order thought of itself as Christian and accepted hierarchy as part of nature. Enslaved persons were regarded as being at the bottom of a natural social order that many thought to be divinely sanctioned. Ongoing debates as to whether some were born to be slaves, and in some cases whether Africans were fully human, were major topics of European discourse. Most Europeans agreed that Africans were in some sense human and that therefore restrictions on how cruelly they could be treated were in order, but few spoke out to challenge the legitimacy of the institution of slavery in the seventeenth century.

The effort to regulate the violence and evangelize enslaved Africans took the form of "Black Codes" or "Slave Codes" (for example, the so-called *Code Noir* in Haiti) that pertained specifically to African captives. One of the first set of these codes to be promulgated in the Caribbean was in Barbados in 1661. Under it those enslaved were required to be clothed, but denied basic rights that were guaranteed under English common law. Codes became stricter and more inhumane as the century progressed. Slave owners were allowed to beat, whip, brand, or hamstring runaways or slaves who threatened to strike their master without any outside intervention and without any oversight by outside authorities.

Although it reads more like a dream than a law, the Jamaican Code and the Haitian *Code Noire* both required that slaves be taught the Christian faith. Article one instructed the French colonists to "chase from our islands all of the Jews." Article two instructed that all slaves were to be baptized and instructed in the Roman Catholic religion. The Haitian Code was written in the shadow of the revocation of the Edict of Nantes in France, and thus at a time when that country was becoming less tolerant regarding religious diversity. These first two articles reflect that situation in part. Other articles detailed structural matters such as a requirement for keeping slave families together, a regulation that was later abandoned.

One of the major questions that arose in England in relation to the evangelization of African slaves concerned the traditional church teaching that required baptized persons who were indentured or enslaved to be eventually manumitted, or set free. A number of clerics argued that it was the Christian duty of the English in foreign colonies to provide evangelical care for the local peoples. In the seventeenth century this meant catechetical instruction that would lead to baptism. If, as it had previously been held by church teaching, a Christian after baptism could not be held in bondage as an indentured servant or a slave indefinitely, then the slave owners as well as traders and parliamentarians would not support evangelizing the Africans. Slaves would quickly convert, be baptized, and then have to be set free, they argued.

In order to protect the institution of African slavery, which by the middle of the seventeenth century had become a key element in Europe's economic system, and still be able to evangelize Africans, clergy accepted the paradox of conferring baptism while permanently denying freedom to the enslaved. Slaves could attend worship, learn the catechism, and become Christian, but that would not mean that they would then eventually be released from their bondage. Thus, the Lords' Committee on Trade and Plantations directed the governor of Barbados in the 1650s to instruct slaves in the religion of the Church of England and to admit to baptism those who attained sufficient knowledge of doctrine, but explicitly stated that such baptism was not a basis for enfranchisement or manumission.

The result was often a tragic compromise at best. The Anglican clergyman Morgan Godwyn (1640-c. 1700), for instance, sought to be an advocate for enslaved Africans. In his 1680 treatise, *The Negroes and Indians Advocate*, Godwyn argued that enslaved African and Native Americans ought to be admitted as full members into the church. They were to be treated fairly, taught English, allowed to attend worship, and be expected to live up to the same religious standards as other Christians. They were not to work on the Sabbath or to engage in polygamy. Underlying the slave system, as he saw it, was the growing wealth and irreligion of the age. Godwyn carried his attack on the treatment of the enslaved into Westminster Abbey in a well-publicized sermon that he claimed was intended to stir up and provoke English people abroad and at home. Although his solutions did not go far enough, his analysis of the problem that profit was taking precedence over humanity was perceptive.

A more important voice against mistreatment of the enslaved, and later against slavery as an institution, was that of an English society that arose in the mid-seventeenth century known as the Quakers. Facing persecution in England because of their nonconformist beliefs, the Quakers began in the second half of the century to migrate and spread their teachings in America. George Fox (1624-1691), the founder of the Society of Friends, as they were formally known, did not himself call for the abolition of slavery, but many of his followers continued his logic and came to the conclusion that slavery must be abolished. Fox visited the Caribbean in 1671 where he encouraged young Friends communities that had recently formed in Barbados and Jamaica. After visiting the region, he wrote to the governor of Barbados that the Friends did not teach Africans to rebel, answering charges that were being raised against his followers in the region. Elsewhere he argued that enslaved persons were to be considered members of the household and treated as such. A number of Fox's followers went further and arrived at the conclusion that slavery itself was evil and needed to be abolished.

One of the most important English clerics who opposed the institution of slavery in the seventeenth century was the Puritan pastor and writer Richard Baxter (1615-1691). Baxter had personally tasted of the desire for freedom, having been imprisoned for a year in the Tower of London for his dissenting religious views. He spoke with more righteous anger against the whole slave system than perhaps any other English cleric before the end of the eighteenth century. In his pastoral treatise "The Christian Directory," which was published in 1673, Baxter made it clear that the only reason one could buy a slave was for the loving purpose of "delivering" him or her, that is, converting the person. Slave owners were trustees for Christ and were thus to lead the enslaved both to faith in Christ and to freedom. The entire system of slavery, on the other hand, was an evil that had to be crushed. Those who engaged in the slave trade were nothing more than pirates and thieves. They were more fit to be called devils than Christians, he concluded. At the time Baxter was a prophet without a following. Where among the English a choir of voices was needed, he sang the song of emancipation solo.

The efforts of some Dominicans and Franciscans in the Roman Catholic Church on behalf of both indigenous peoples and Africans in America were noted earlier. The prophetic Catholic voice broadened during the seventeenth century to include Capuchins and Jesuits. Four who were members of these latter orders, two Spanish Jesuits, one French Capuchin, and one Spanish Capuchin, stand out in particular as noteworthy. Alonso de Sandoval (1576-1652) was a Spaniard who as a young child accompanied his father to Peru when the elder man was appointed to work with the vice-regal government. While in Lima he joined the Jesuits and in 1605 was sent to the Caribbean port city of Cartagena, the main entry point for African slaves coming into Nueva Granada (present-day Colombia).

Seeing the treatment of the slaves and the needs they had upon arrival, Sandoval dedicated his ministry for the rest of his life to the Africans in Cartagena. His days were spent mainly in catechizing and baptizing slaves, and in trying to help meet their basic human needs. One of the earliest, and longest, treatises published in Europe on the customs and beliefs of African slaves and on methods to evangelize them, *De instauranda Aethiopum salute* ("On Procuring the Salvation of the Ethiopians"), came from his pen. Although not opposed to all forms of slavery, he spoke out unequivocally against the African slave trade as an institution. God created human beings to be free, he wrote. Slavery is evil.

One of the greatest contributions Sandoval made to enslaved Africans was his mentoring of a Jesuit four years his junior named Pedro Claver (1580-1654). Born in Spain, Claver entered the Jesuit order at the age of twenty and was assigned to engage in missionary work in America. In his final vows as a Jesuit he is reported to have added the phrase *aethiopum semper servus* ("slave of the Ethiopian forever"). For more than three decades he carried out that vow in Cartagena, working among those who were arriving in ships from West Africa. Claver would visit the captives as they arrived in the city, seeking to provide relief to those who were suffering from hunger or disease, and comfort to the dying. He not only sought to provide food and clothing, but through translators attempted to teach the basics of Christian faith and to lead Africans to baptism. Later he would visit the enslaved on the nearby plantations where they had been transported in order to continue his ministry to them. It is estimated that he eventually baptized as many as 300,000 Africans in his years of work.

Several Capuchins also took a critical stance against the institution of slavery. Two in particular, Epiphane de Moirans from France (1644-1689) and Francisco José de Jaca from Spain (c. 1645-1688), stand out for their efforts. After working with Africans in the Caribbean region both became convinced that slavery was wrong, and argued against its basis in the Aristotelian logic of social order that had long been used to justify the institution. In doing so, they found themselves opposing the teachings of the church they had vowed to serve. In Cuba they preached publicly against slave holding and even refused to administer the sacraments or to hear confession from slave owners. Their efforts landed them in prison for sedition, as the authorities feared that their actions would incite slave rebellions.

A lengthy imprisonment gave the two Capuchins time to reflect and write. Slavery as an institution is opposed to natural law, divine law, and the law of nations, they argued. Slavery is refuted by scripture, Aristotle, and Thomas Aquinas because it robs human beings of their freedom without just cause. Thus, justice requires not only freeing the slaves, but also restitution in the form of paying them back for the time during which they could not work for themselves. Their arguments were directed not only against the mistreatment of those enslaved but for full abolition.

Brazil

While individual members of Catholic religious orders had begun to speak out against slavery, church and crown alike continued to support it as a social and economic institution. In South America the plantation system was growing in the seventeenth century, with large numbers of enslaved persons being imported and forced to work on plantations. The seventeenth century saw a huge influx of those coming from Africa to Brazil in particular, which became a major factor in both social and religious developments there. Throughout South America the majority of those migrating from Iberia were men. In Brazil the ratio was particularly large, and the number of Iberian women quite small, leading Portuguese men to take Native American, and then increasingly, African women as their wives or concubines. Interracial marriage or cohabitation and the mixed-race population that resulted were much larger in Brazil than in many other parts of South America as a result. African cultural influences were also especially strong in Brazil, and African religions survived there more so than in most other regions of South America.

In northeast Brazil, a handful of Dutch settlers at the beginning of the seventeenth century carved out a small section that grew into a separate colony known as Dutch Guiana. From 1630 to 1654 the WIC controlled the region of Pernambuco, in which the cities of Recife and Olinda are located. The latter was an important early center of Franciscan missionary activity that twenty-five years of Dutch Protestant control could not dislodge. In 1680 the Franciscans had over four hundred friars working mostly with indigenous peoples.

During the sixteenth century Portugal had exiled to Brazil a number of Jews who were supposedly converted but were later found by the Inquisition to have "lapsed." In Iberia Jews who had supposedly converted to Christianity but who were suspected of having either kept or reverted to their Jewish religion were called *conversos* ("converted") or *marranos* (from a Spanish term for "pig"). Such persons, if they were not killed, were forced to attend Catholic Mass and were otherwise watched for signs of practicing Judaism. In Brazil in the absence of any apparatus of the Inquisition, however, many were able to practice their Jewish religion more freely. Brazil, like parts of the Caribbean, proved to be a more welcoming home to Jews of Iberian descent. By the first decades of the seventeenth century, the Dutch had begun to allow Jews in the Netherlands to freely practice their religion, and in 1630 when they took control of Pernambuco, they extended that freedom to Brazil. A number of Jews from Amsterdam immigrated to Brazil where they joined with *marranos* to form a worshipping Jewish community and build the first synagogue in America in Recife in 1636. Several years later, in 1642, the first rabbi in America, Isaac Aboab da Fonseca (1605-1693), joined them. Da Fonseca returned to Amsterdam in 1654 after the Portuguese retook control of Pernambuco. Several members of the synagogue in Recife eventually traveled north to another Dutch colony that had been founded on the island of Manhattan to establish a synagogue in New Amsterdam, the first in North America.

The Portuguese retook Pernambuco in 1654, thereby regaining control of the entire colony. Nowhere else in the world did Portugal develop a colony of the magnitude of Brazil. Portugal's empire in Asia was composed of forts, ports, and trading factories. In Africa they eventually developed fuller colonies in Angola and Mozambique, but those were in many ways still extensions of their initial factories. Brazil was different, but its difference was brought about through a slow and cautious expansion. Portugal in the seventeenth century did not have the wealth of Spain, nor did Brazil have the wealth of Spanish America. For its first century and a half, Brazil depended on sugar for the income it produced, whereas the Spanish had gold and silver mines to exploit. The Portuguese were so involved in their more prosperous African and Asian regions that the number of colonialists willing to make an investment in Brazil was very small. The Spanish were rapidly colonizing and expanding into vast regions of land, whereas Portugal was barely able to hold on to the little land it actually controlled.

This changed after 1693 in Brazil when gold was discovered in Minas Gerais in the south. Tens of thousands of Portuguese poured into Brazil, seeking to gain a part of the new-found wealth. The overall profit that Portugal gained from the gold mining was small. The long-term impact of the *paulistas*, or adventurers from São Paulo as they were called, was to populate the south with Iberians and extend Portugal's control into the region.

The extension of Portuguese claims and control into western regions of Brazil was due mainly to the efforts of missionaries and *bandeirantes*, or paramilitary adventurers. The *bandeirantes* wandered inland looking for local people to capture and enslave, to force them to work either on sugar plantations or as domestic servants in the cities of the east. The Jesuits, in an effort to protect the indigenous inhabitants from these raids, tried to gather these seminomadic people into *reducciones* and develop Christian villages. One of the major groups of indigenous inhabitants in this battle was the Túpi-Guarani. The Guarani lived in a land-locked territory located mostly in present day Paraguay, and extending into Brazil and Argentina. They worshipped a variety of spirits, but their creation story told of a Great Father, Ñanderuvusú, who created human language from his own divine essence before he created humanity. The Guarani were thus sensitive to "beautiful words" and were also highly responsive to visions, dreams, and trances.

The Jesuit approach to evangelizing these indigenous people was innovative as they sought to combine some of the unique qualities of the Guarani with their own seventeenth-century Iberian culture. The *reducciones* that they built were actually small villages of 2,000 to 5,000 people living in long houses with a church in the center. Eventually some thirty of these communities were established, with a total of nearly 150,000 residents. Days were interspersed with work, singing, dance, prayer, and worship. Some European cultural patterns were mandatory, such as wearing clothes, sleeping in rooms only with family members, and building straight streets that met at right angles. But the Guarani were not Europeans, and they were not used to ten or twelve hours of work each day. The normal workday was set for only six hours, and great emphasis was placed on Guarani strengths such as carving, sculpture, handicraft works, and later making watches and musical instruments. Since "beautiful words" were very important, the Jesuits developed carefully worded sermons. Dreams and visions were also important to the local culture, so the Jesuits would share dreams with the Guarani, who often claimed to be having the same ones.

Although the Franciscans had pioneered the idea of settled communities with land ownership as a response to the *encomienda*, it was the Jesuits who built the Túpi-Guarani into self-sustaining economic Christian communities. The people produced handicrafts and grew tobacco, cotton, and the highly prized tea called yerba-maté, which they sold in markets farther east. In this way the communities were profitable even though they were far away from the colonial centers, located deep in the interior of South America. Intermittent raids from *bandeirantes* continued to threaten these experiments in Christian communal existence. Nevertheless, under the leadership of the Jesuits, who acted as governors, they provided a pattern for ministry to indigenous peoples that resisted more aggressive colonial designs.

Antonio Ruiz de Montoya (1585-1652), a mestizo from Lima, is one of the most memorable of the Jesuits involved in the efforts of the *reducciones*. Born as the illegitimate child of a Sevillian captain and a Lima native, Ruiz de Montoya is reported to have had a rather wild youth. But while preparing to enlist to go to war against the indigenous Aravacanians in Chile, he had a mystical experience and was converted to Christ, making his confession at a Jesuit college. He subsequently joined the Jesuits in 1606 with a completely different interest in indigenous peoples. While still a novice he worked both in Paraguay and in Argentina, then in 1613 was appointed to work with the Túpi-Guarani in Brazil. In his years as a missionary and later as superior for work with the Guarani (1620-1637) he founded eleven missions.

Troubles with *paulistas* who were killing and enslaving his villages eventually led Ruiz de Montoya to organize a mass migration of Guarani from the Portuguese territories to the Paraná River in Argentina, nearly one thousand miles away. Ever an activist for the Túpi-Guarani, he even traveled to meet with King Philip IV (1605-1665) to plead on behalf of the indigenous people. After hearing his case the king consented to allow the Guaraní in 1641 to arm themselves, a right they had been denied for over a century. Raiding their communities thereafter became less enticing.

Ruiz de Montoya made a particularly important contribution to Christian history through his book *Conquista espiritual hecha por los religiosos de la C. de J. en las provincias del Paraguay, Paraña, Uruguay y Tape* ("Spiritual Conquest by the Society of Jesus in the Provinces of Paraguay, Parana, Uruguay, and Tape"). The work provided a history of Christian missions in these regions up to 1637, but also provided important information on the local cultures. Ruiz de Montoya made an enormous contribution toward building a fuller library of scholarship on the Túpi-Guarani language, composing the first grammar in 1639 and the first dictionary in 1640, the latter reaching eight hundred pages in length. His scholarship was not only technical and historical. One of his most memorable works was a Christian mystical guide titled *Sílex del divino amor y rapto del ánima en la primera causa* ("Firestone of Divine Love and Rapture of the Soul in Knowledge of the First Cause").

If Montoya's advocacy of the Guarani was personal and supportive, António Vieira's (1608-1698) was political and confrontational. Born in Lisbon, Vieira went to Brazil when still young, studied with the Jesuits there, and then joined the order. Although he sought to work directly among the Guarani, Vieira was instead, due in large part to his oratorical gifts, sent back in 1641 with the viceroy's son to Portugal, to work in the service of King João IV (1603-1656). Portugal had just thrown off the yoke of Spanish rule the previous year and fighting continued between the two Iberian nations. Over the next fourteen years Vieira was involved in military strategizing and international negotiations. He served as tutor to the young prince Dom Pedro and as court preacher, and became known especially for his position defending both the freedom of all people and equal taxation. Before returning to Brazil in 1655 he even spoke out against the cruelty and injustices of the Dominican-led Inquisition in Portugal.

Over the next six years in Brazil, while working with the Guarani and opposing the Portuguese landowners, Vieira managed to translate the catechism and teach arts and basic Christian doctrine. His eloquence and royal connections made him a powerful advocate on behalf of the indigenous Americans, leading the settlers to have him arrested and deported in 1661. Back in Portugal he was tried by the Inquisition and imprisoned, but then later released on the order of the pope himself. In 1681, at the age of seventy-two, Vieira returned to Brazil and was appointed as visitor and provincial of the Brazilian missions, a position he held until he died at the age of ninety.

Vieira's preaching and writing had a great influence on a German-speaking Luxembourger named Johann Philipp Bettendorf (1625-1698). Bettendorf represents the international nature of the Jesuit work, in contrast to the strongly nationalistic colonial work of the Spanish and Portuguese. Joining the Jesuits in 1647, Bettendorf volunteered to work among the indigenous peoples in Brazil but ended up instead at about the same time as Vieira in Portugal where he served in the court first of King João IV, and then of Afonso VI (1643-1683, r. 1665-1667). Bettendorf finally arrived in Brazil about the time Vieira was being deported. He served for a time as the chaplain or rector of the Colleges of Maranhão and Paará before being appointed as superior of the mission, the position that Vieira would later hold. Like Vieira, Bettendorf too was a learned linguist and advocate for the Túpi-Guarani. A treatise on the Christian faith was written in both Portuguese and Túpi-Guarani, while his chronicle of early mission efforts in the state of Maranhão described not only the missions but the local flora, fauna, and mineral resources. Along with a number of other Jesuits, he helped to pioneer indigenous forms of religious art, a project the Jesuits were also pioneering in Mughul India and in China at the time.

In February 1681 a Brazilian mulatto named Lourenço da Silva de Mendonça (1620-1698), who claimed to be descended from royalty in Angola, arrived in Lisbon to lodge a protest against slavery. He was soon recognized as representing the mulattos of Brazil and Castile and appointed to the position of procurator of the "Confraternity of Our Lady Star of the Negroes" with authority to establish new houses. The confraternities were a type of lay apostolate organized to care for the poor and imprisoned, and to guarantee a respectable Christian burial. In both Portuguese and Spanish territories they became important structures for developing African and African-American leadership.

Equipped with his new title, da Silva de Mendonça soon went on to Rome where he made his appeal before Pope Innocent XI (1611-1689). One of Innocent's predecessors, Pope Paul III (1468-1549), had issued a papal bull in 1543 that had long been forgotten but ordered that Native Americans were not to be enslaved. Lourenço did not oppose all forms of slavery, but strongly objected to the idea of perpetual and cruel slavery of fellow Christians such as himself. In his appeal to Innocent XI he argued that those involved in the sale and purchase of these other Christians should be excommunicated, only to be released by the pope himself.

The description of mistreatments provided by the African-Brazilian had an impact on the pope and on the recently formed office of *Propaganda fidei*. Communication from Capuchin missionaries in the Kongo to *Propaganda fidei* in 1685 pressed the case further. The following year Innocent XI issued a general condemnation of the entire Atlantic slave trade. Unfortunately its impact was minimal, as kings and merchants alike throughout the Catholic world ignored the call.

Spanish America

Spanish American and Portuguese American Catholicism developed in geographic proximity and along similar patterns, but with a good deal of conflict in the seventeenth century. From 1580 to 1640, Spain ruled over its smaller and poorer neighbor. The effects were felt globally in the Portuguese colonies in South America, Africa, and Asia. When the Spanish expelled both Muslims and Jews from their lands in the late fifteenth century, many made their way to Portugal where they found a somewhat greater degree of tolerance; and, as seen above, a number of *marranos* ended up in Brazil. Jewish communities played an important role as merchants in Portugal's economy, but they were an irritant to the Spanish, who as early as 1519 brought the Inquisition to America to weed out both Jewish and Protestant belief. As was noted earlier, Jews played a large role in initially developing sugar in northeastern Brazil, and had spread the cultivation of the sugar cane plant to the Caribbean when they were forced to leave during the period of Spanish rule.

Spain throughout the seventeenth century ruled its American empire through two vice-royalties: Peru (which included most of South America) and New Spain (Central America and the Caribbean). Each of these was in turn subdivided into smaller provinces, which were ruled by *audencias*. The church was fully integrated into this order, with bishops working closely with the viceroys and *audencias* to bring about a religious culture as close to that of Spain as possible. Schools were founded to train priests, their curriculum following closely the curriculum of schools in Spain.

America under European colonial rule in all of its locations was a culturally mixed and highly stratified society. In Spanish America *peninsulares* (those who came from Spain) and *criollos* (those whose ancestry was purely Spanish, but who were born in America) were at the top of the social order. Those of mixed Spanish and African or Spanish and Native American ancestry were next in the social order. At the bottom were persons of full African or Native American ancestry. This stratification was deeply ingrained in the higher church officials in America, all pure Spaniards, who worked closely with the wealthy viceroys and governors. People of color, including those of mixed ancestry, were systematically excluded from almost all religious and secular positions of power.

A great deal of effort was devoted by religious orders in the seventeenth century to the extension and consolidation of territories on behalf of colonial governments. Generally the missionaries were the colonial vanguard, making the first contacts with indigenous peoples and, as the kings had hoped, bringing some degree of pacification to the regions. In 1609 the king of Spain entrusted the region of New Mexico to the Franciscans, opening a chapter in the history of Christianity in North America that will be explored more fully in a following chapter. In South and Central America religious orders similarly helped to extend Spanish colonial control and not just Christian presence throughout Peru and New Spain, and into Portuguese territory to the east.

The previous century had seen two universities founded by the colonial governments in the capitals of Mexico City and Lima, and three church-founded universities in Santo Domingo, Quito, and Bogotá. In the seventeenth century the Jesuits founded schools at Santiago de Chile, Córdoba, La Plata, Cuzco, Quito, Bogotá, and Mérida (Yucatán). The Dominicans founded schools at Santiago de Chile, Quito, and Guatemala. The Franciscans founded a school in Cuzco. For the most part these colleges and universities were concerned with the training of priests. The schools also promoted the colonial social order and provided locally trained administrators for colonial governments.

While the clerical orders continued to play a major role in spiritual life during the period, new forms of lay associations, or *cofradias* ("confraternities"), were emerging. Some of these new lay orders came about in response to the growing problems of the sick and destitute in the cities of Latin America. The Hospital

Brothers of the Order of St. John of God, founded in 1602, focused solely on serving the sick and infirm. These *cofradias* became important social service institutions, and, at the same time, they gave greater opportunity for lay involvement in the life of faith.

One of the earliest religious orders founded in America was the Bethlehemites, which was started in 1665 in Guatemala by Pedro de San José Betancur (1619-1667). Betancur was so moved by the suffering of the local people that he began a small clinic for the sick. It eventually developed into a hospital that was dedicated to Our Lady of Bethlehem. From this small but devout beginning a major effort to care for the imprisoned, the sick, the poor, and others who were without means developed. Schooled by the Jesuits, Betancur was also influenced by the Franciscans, taking on the friar's dress and lifestyle. Upon his death, he was buried by the Capuchins.

Some of the orders organized their life around particular devotional practices rather than particular ministries. The Benedictines from Montserrat came in 1592 to Lima and in 1602 to Mexico City with a particular mission dedicated solely to devotion to the image of the Black Virgin of Montserrat, which was one of the most famous images of Mary and Jesus in Spain.

Religious orders in Spanish America in the seventeenth century had control over significant amounts of land and wealth. With these came not just mismanagement but corruption. One of the reformers of the period was a secular priest named Juan de Palafox y Mendoza (1600-1659). Born as the illegitimate son of a Spanish nobleman, Palafox studied at Salamanca and was appointed briefly to the Council of War of the Indies. Renouncing worldly titles, he stepped down and chose instead to be ordained a priest in 1629. Ten years later he was consecrated bishop of Puebla de Los Angeles and visitor general of Mexico, with the task of overseeing the missions. Taking his job of oversight seriously, he quickly offended the Inquisition as well as the Franciscans, Dominicans, and Augustinians by criticizing their privileges and exemptions.

A good deal of money at the time that was supposed to be passing through Mexico and on to Spain was not leaving the hands of the viceroy. The king of Spain, pleased with Palafox's willingness to take on the religious orders, appointed the priest to serve briefly as the viceroy of New Spain. The reforming bishop did so for five months in 1642, during which period he corrected many of the financial mishandlings.

After his short stint as viceroy Palafox thrust himself into one final conflict and challenged the Jesuits on their exemptions and privileges. A number of bishops in Latin America believed that the Jesuits, whose oath of obedience was directly to the pope, undermined local episcopal authority. Palafox appealed directly to Innocent X to address this problem, and received a limited response. Shortly after this the reformer returned to Spain, where he spent the last years of his life.

During his brief tenure as viceroy, Palafox ordered a number of Aztec religious images destroyed. A number of Spanish secular rulers had been fascinated by the Aztec images. Some had shown tolerance and even a degree of appreciation for the Aztec religious works. Clerics on the other hand were almost unanimous in holding that these images were idolatry and the work of the devil, and deserved total eradication. This was not a marginal matter for nuanced disagreement among Tridentine Catholics. The issue was not tolerance but rather the method of eradication. How were the local people to be taught, or forced, to put away their idols and accept the Catholic faith?

The approach of Pablo José de Arriaga (1564-1622) was typical among the priests and orders. Arriaga was a Jesuit who came to Peru from Spain and was appalled that so many in Peru continued to be practicing what he considered idol worship. He took on the issue directly, smashing images and establishing homes for what he considered to be the recalcitrant indigenous religious leaders, the shamans. His published work, *Extirpación de la idolatría en el Perú* ("On the Extirpation of Idolatry in Peru"), which was published in 1621, gave detailed descriptions of the images along with instructions on how to destroy them. Most of the images he described were of stone. These sacred stones, or *huaca* as they were called, were understood by indigenous religionists to protect life, increase fertility, and bring good fortune, depending on where they were placed and how they were honored. Indigenous devotion associated with sacred stones, statues, and even sites was not easily displaced, and remained among many indigenous peoples a symbol of resistance to the rule and religion of the Spaniards.

The effort to eradicate these religious images was part of a wider contest over the meaning of religious symbols in general in South America. A related issue concerned the suitability of indigenous languages for religious purposes of instruction and worship. The various religious orders in general made learning the local languages a priority and sought to communicate the Christian faith in the form of a catechism through them. Seldom, on the other hand, did bishops or secular priests show the same concern for local languages. One notable exception was Alonso de Peña Montenegro (1596-1687), who was appointed bishop of Quito in 1653. Traveling through his diocese in Ecuador, he observed first-hand the challenges of local ministry. He recorded the results of his observations and his pastoral instruction in a lengthy manual intended to guide priests who were working in parishes with indigenous people. *Itinerario para párrocos de Indios* ("A Guide for the Pastors of Indians") was published in 1668 and quickly became a standard tool for church leaders throughout the region.

Women had relatively little role to play in the first century of Christianity in South America. As has been noted already, the first generations of conquistadors and colonialists from Iberia were mostly men, as were the members of the religious orders. Whereas in the sixteenth century there were very few places for women to express and deepen their faith, in the seventeenth century a number of schools were established and new institutions founded to foster spiritual life for women.

There were two basic patterns for women's religious development in seventeenth-century South America, the *beaterio* and the convent. In the *beaterio* women did not actually take vows but lived in semicloistered settings intended to protect them and to facilitate religious devotion and mentoring. The *beatas*, or women in the orders, in turn became spiritual role models for other women and girls who lived in the busy and compromising world. Some among the *beatas* even become mentors for men of means. As one might expect, not all *beatas* were exemplary spiritual models. The *beaterio* was used by some women as a place of refuge from other responsibilities, or, because personal possessions were allowed, even a place of peaceful affluence.

Perhaps as a sign of religious renewal, more women sought out the ordered religious life of the convent and the *beaterio* in the seventeenth century in South America than the society could or would provide. The number of new convents rose rapidly, and the number of women waiting to take vows grew long, leading kings and viceroys alike to try to discourage, and at times, disallow the building of new convents. Convents that followed the rule of St. Teresa of Avila had twice the number of women living in them as they were intended to house. Many religious communities numbered several hundred members, making them small towns of women within the larger society. The movement in turn had implications for marriage and family life, education, and since many Spanish women became unavailable for marriage, even race relations. Most of the convents had schools for young girls, but the demand for education was so great that without connections one could often not get in. Those girls who were accepted were far more likely to take vows later on, further increasing the number of those entering religious life.

One of the best-known women religious of the period was Juana Inés de la Cruz (1651-1695). Raised by her grandparents in the town of Panoayan near Mexico City she was selected to live for five years in the residence of the viceroy of New Spain. While in the royal court she composed plays, sonnets, and songs to entertain the viceroy and courtiers. The poetry reveals a woman who had fallen in love and who knew the life of wealth and diversion. Yet, she was clear that she wanted not the life of the court and family but the solitary life. She was admitted first to a Carmelite convent, but the strict regime threatened her health so she was admitted to St. Paul's Convent in the order of St. Jerome, where she took the name by which she is now known.

The religious life in the order of St. Jerome was relatively flexible, providing Sor Juana the freedom to pursue her studies as she desired. Attended by a slave and servants, and served her meals in private, she could devote her days to reading. She was a voracious student not only of theology, but of music, science, and literature. In the course of these pursuits she collected a sizable library numbering over four thousand volumes, reportedly the largest in South America at the time. From an early age she was fluent in Castilian Spanish, Latin, and Nahuatl (the language of the Aztecs). As an adult she composed literary works in all of them. Secular rulers and religious leaders sought her counsel or visited her to engage in intellectual discussions.

Her fame and influence as a woman brought criticisms as well. A critique she wrote of a sermon by Antonio Vieira that had been delivered some forty years earlier in 1650 was published without her knowledge by a bishop, out of jealously one might assume. Already Sor Juana was in dangerous waters as a well-educated woman, but her audacity at criticizing one of the most famous Jesuits of the period was too much for many church leaders. Others, however, praised the Mexican thinker for decimating the arguments of Vieira, point by point.

For her brilliance and precision in theology she was applauded, but she was also chastised for supposedly wasting so much of her talent on secular poetry, music, and drama. Against these charges she defended herself well, arguing that secular education in the sciences of rhetoric, astronomy (or as she said, astrology), history, law, arithmetic, and music served to help one understand the queen of the sciences, or the study of theology and the Bible. In addition to this integrated view of knowledge in service to God, she argued in her *Respuesta a Sor Filotea de la Cruz* ("Reply to Sister Filotea") that there was one further requirement, "a continuing in prayer and purity of life, so as to be visited by God with that cleansing of the spirit and illumination of the mind which the understanding of such lofty matters demands, in the absence of which none of the rest is any use."

In her last years of life Sor Juana dedicated herself to constant penance and deprivation. She sold off all of her library and gave the money to the poor. She refused to write any more prose or poetry. Her example was a challenge to the archbishop, who sold off his own books, his furniture, and even his bed. In her last days, ministering to sisters who had caught the plague, Sor Juana herself became infected. She wrote her last words in her own blood, using her fingernail as a pen. Sor Juana was one of the greatest and most creative minds in America in the seventeenth century, and even though her work was severely criticized by those in authority, her influence was significant. In her life we see the conflicting views of women in the church, the ambiguities of wealth and poverty, the struggle over slavery and indentured servants, and the mutual development of secular and religious knowledge.

Religious practices in America

Roman Catholic religious life in America generally replicated much that was familiar in Christian experience in Spain and Portugal. Churches were built in the middle of the city, surrounded by a *plaza*, or public square. Houses of worship and residences for priests and bishops, usually constructed with slave labor, were designed as if they were in Barcelona or Seville. Church calendars in America replicated those in Iberia with the liturgical year moving through feast days and holy days of remembrance. The provincial council of Santo Domingo in 1622-1623 established twenty-six feast days per year. Such feasts were celebrated in ways that had been carried over from Iberia, and often included dancing, games, bullfighting, horse racing, parades, and even fireworks. This is not to say that indigenous religious practices of Africans and Native Americans did not survive. They did, often in the form of local festivals and feasts that celebrated indigenous heroes or gods who were reconstituted or reinterpreted through the lives of Christian saints.

The feast of Corpus Christi featured public processing for adoring the body of Christ in the Eucharistic sacrament and was among the most important days in the South American calendar. In Cuzco, Peru, the former capital of the Inca empire, this particular festival took on special significance, especially in the last decades of the seventeenth century under the bishop, Manuel de Mollinedo y Angulo (r. 1673-1699). De Mollinedo y Angulo tried to imitate as closely as possible the magnificent celebrations of Madrid, but the place and date of the celebrations in Peru meshed closely with local Inca religious belief. Cuzco was the center of Inca worship of the Sun God, Inti, and June, the time of the feast of Corpus Christi, coincided with the celebration of the solstice. The Spanish Catholic celebration in the city thus took place at a time and on holy ground dedicated to the Incan deity Inti. Spain had concluded its victory over the Inca empire by dismantling the Inca temples and using the carefully crafted stones to build Spanish government buildings and the cathedral. For the Spanish, this was a display of religious and political domination. For the indigenous people, the stones represented a degree of continuity with their traditional beliefs and religious culture.

All that ambiguity notwithstanding, feasts such as Corpus Christi were embraced by the Peruvians as their own and marked by processions, paintings, and special dress. Five indigenous parishes participated in the Corpus Christi procession. Standard bearers would proudly wear Inca dress, while others were adorned with special headdresses with scarlet fringe, such as were worn by the Inca ruler himself. Thus, Incan traditional culture and religion were part of the transformation of Corpus Christi in the capital of the former Incan empire.

The Sunday Eucharist celebration, or Mass, also took on new social and religious significance in South America. Just as the cathedrals were placed in the center of the cities, so attending Mass became central to the weekly calendar. The celebration of Sunday Mass became both a religious and a social event, a reminder that, for the Indian, religious life was social and social life was religious; later Western concepts of "religion" as something distinct from the "secular" were unknown in either traditional life or the people's understanding of Christianity. The Mass itself would often conclude with general news and announcements. Men would gather afterward at shops or in taverns to socialize. Women and children enjoyed their own company or played.

Sunday Mass became the place to be seen and to maintain social relationships, but also to maintain social order. The Mass in fact reinforced the social caste. Virtually all priests and monks were *peninsulares* or *criollos*. Darker-skinned people were not a part of the religious as well as the political leadership, and the Sunday gatherings reinforced this separation. Worship was costly, involving imported liturgical books, olive oil for lamps, wine for the Eucharist, and many candles. Church vessels were made of precious metals. When possible, an organ was imported from Europe for worship, adding to the beauty but also the foreignness of the Mass to those whose cultural background was not European. Weddings and funerals also reinforced the social stratification by requiring money that only wealthy *peninsulares* and *criollos* could afford. Thus, the way worship was conducted both symbolized and reinforced the marginalization of Native Americans, mestizos, and Africans.

An important element of devotion was provided by the lay confraternities called *cofradías*. These confraternities were often formed around people who shared the same occupation or geographic location. They were voluntary in nature and gave a sense of belonging or identity through religious service and worship. Most urban Spaniards were members of *cofradías*, but in rural areas indigenous *cofradías* were also formed for the pastoral care and devotional life of their members. Most had a patron saint who was honored with an annual festival, and the associations celebrated other festivals and religious holy days as well. Some dedicated themselves to providing for the poor, preparing their members for the Eucharist, or ministering to the dying and the dead.

In 1647, the Cathedral in San Juan, Puerto Rico, had twelve *cofradías*. The wealthiest at the time, *Cofradía Nuestra Señora de la Concepcion* ("Confraternity of Our Lady of the Immaculate Conception"), was attached to the hospital. A number of the confraternities became relatively wealthy, mostly as a result of their members remembering the *cofradía* in their wills. Clerics sometimes registered frustration because money that might have gone directly to the church was instead being given to the *cofradías,* with the result that the position of the priest could be compromised.

Protestant practices in the Caribbean, like their Catholic counterparts, were mostly an adaptation or replication of European practices, but with the nature of the many varieties of Christian bodies, greater tolerance of nonconforming practices was necessary. Thus, although local Anglicans opposed the Quakers and other "spiritualists," they were afforded more freedom in the Caribbean than they had been in Europe or in Iberian-dominated America. The Caribbean was arguably the most religiously and culturally diverse region of the world in the seventeenth century, which may have forced it to be the most tolerant.

Another characteristic of Protestant life in the seventeenth-century Caribbean world was the lack of authoritative pastoral guidance. Protestant countries were commonly short of well-trained leaders. In the colonial regions of the Caribbean, the effect was more pronounced. As a result, religious life was generally lax. Most of the islands had two to four times more Africans than Europeans by the end of the seventeenth century, which meant that European Christians lived in close proximity to followers of African traditions. Although the colonies were ruled by European powers that were officially Christian, European norms for religious practice could not be enforced, and in many places traditional African practices flourished.

How to adapt to the demands of so many different cultures was not immediately apparent. Catholic religious orders, for instance, had to decide whether non-Europeans could be admitted to membership. One of the most notable illustrations of this is found in the story of one of the first persons of African descent to be admitted to a religious order; he also became one of the first persons born in South America to be canonized as a saint in the Catholic Church, Martin de Porres (1579-1639). Martin de Porres was born in Lima, Peru, of a Spanish father and a freed African mother from Panama. Because his parents were not legally married he was considered in the eyes of the church to be illegitimate, a social stigma that was added to his poverty.

At age eleven Martin became a servant in a Dominican monastery but was not allowed to join the order because he was mulatto. Eventually his spiritual devotion and piety won the order over, however, and he was allowed to take his vows and become a full member. The rest of his life was dedicated to caring for the sick and needy. The stories of his personal piety, of nights spent in prayer, of his refusal to eat meat, of his daily flagellation, and of his care even for sick animals became a spiritual model for others who suffered oppression far beyond his native Lima. Three centuries after his death, Martin de Porres was finally canonized by the Catholic Church, a testimony to the continuing effect of his life and witness.

Martin's life and the stories that are associated with his person illustrate the complexities of racial mixing, devotion, and local ministry that characterized Spanish American religious experience. The life and story of another Dominican from the age, Domingo Fernandez de Navarrete (1610-1686), illustrates on the other hand the global and even cosmopolitan nature of Christianity that was beginning to emerge. Navarrete was a Thomistic scholar from Spain who bypassed the opportunity to teach theology at home in order to dedicate his life to missionary work in other parts of the world. In 1646 he passed through New Spain on his way to the Philippines, where he arrived in 1648. In Manila he taught at the Dominican University of Santo Tomás for a period, and then with several other Dominicans relocated to China where the Rites Controversy was under way.

Navarrete studied Chinese in Fujian Province and hoped to turn to scholarship as a means of spreading Christian faith. Local persecution restricted his activities, however, and he ended up spending four years in detention in Guangdong. After this he returned to Rome, where he argued the Dominican position against the Jesuits on the role of Chinese rites in Christian life, winning the admiration of Pope Innocent XI in doing so. Although he was forceful in his opposition to the Jesuits' position, he was always careful to be respectful of Jesuits and of their work. Asked to accept the appointment as bishop of the Chinese mission, he declined. A short time later, however, he was appointed archbishop of Santo Domingo, on the island of Hispaniola in the Caribbean, where he supported the Jesuits in their effort to establish a college.

Navarrete had a global ministry linking Europe, America, and Asia. He wrote a two-volume catechism in Chinese, taught theology in Manila, and supported the Jesuits in the Caribbean after arguing against them in China and Rome. He is also responsible for introducing tofu to the West. Christianity in South America reflected the experiences of both de Porres and Navarrete. It was parochial and hierarchical, but also global and cosmopolitan and on its way to becoming a global religious faith.

Suggestions for further reading

Beebe, Rose Marie, and Robert M. Senkewicz, eds., *Lands of Promise and Despair: Chronicles of Early California, 1535-1846*. Berkeley, CA: Heyday Books, 2001.

Bethell, Leslie, ed., *The Cambridge History of Latin America, I: Colonial Latin America*. Cambridge: Cambridge University Press, 1984.

Dayfoot, Arthur Charles, *The Shaping of the West Indian Church, 1492-1962*. Gainesville: University Press of Florida, 1999.

Desmangles, Leslie G., *The Faces of the Gods: Vodou and Roman Catholicism in Haiti*. Chapel Hill: University of North Carolina Press, 1992.

Dussel, Enrique, ed., *The Church in Latin America, 1492-1992*. Maryknoll, NY: Orbis Books, 1992.

García-Rivera, Alex, *St. Martin de Porres: The "Little Stories" and the Semiotics of Culture*. Maryknoll, NY: Orbis Books, 1995.

Goodpasture, H. McKennie, *The Cross and the Sword: An Eyewitness History of Christianity in Latin America*. Maryknoll, NY: Orbis Books, 1989.

Jaenike, William F., *Black Robes in Paraguay: The Success of the Guaraní Missions Hastened the Abolition of the Jesuits*. Minneapolis: Kirk House, 2008.

Penyak, Lee M., and Walter J. Petry, eds., *Religion in Latin America: A Documentary History*. Maryknoll, NY: Orbis Books, 2006.

Rogonzinski, Jan, *A Brief History of the Caribbean: From the Arawak and the Carib to the Present*. Revised ed. New York: Plume, 1999.

Shepherd, Verene A., ed., *Women in Caribbean History: The British Colonised Territories*. Princeton, NJ: Markus Wiener Publishing, 1999.

Weber, David J., *Bárbaros: Spaniards and Their Savages in the Age of Enlightenment*. New Haven: Yale University Press, 2006.

11

North America

Spanish and French Catholic beginnings in North America

The fall of the Muslim kingdom of Granada in the south of Spain in 1492 brought about an end to the *Reconquista* in Iberia. It also left a number of Spanish soldiers unemployed. For several hundred years soldiers in the Spanish armies had been compensated with lands that had been taken from Muslim rulers which they then occupied and used as a means of wealth. Without additional land in Iberia, these unemployed soldiers in 1492 were left looking for a new place for conquest. A number of them joined Columbus on his second journey to America in 1493. Among them was a soldier named Juan Ponce de León (1474-1521).

After visiting several islands, including one the Spanish called San Juan Bautista, which is now Puerto Rico, Columbus and his company arrived in Hispaniola, the island that the nations of Haiti and the Dominican Republic share today. Ponce de León remained there for several years, establishing an *encomienda* on which a number of indigenous Taínos were forced to labor. In 1508 Ponce de León received permission from Spain to establish a new settlement on the island of Puerto Rico. At first he selected a location for the settlement that was several kilometers inland from San Juan Bay, in what is now the city of Guaynabo, but the following year he moved across the bay to reestablish the settlement in what is now the city of San Juan.

Ponce de León was appointed by the Spanish crown to be the first governor of the new colony. But soon conflicts with Diego Colón (c. 1480-1526), the son of the famed explorer and now viceroy over the entire region, led Ponce de León to look north toward territories he had heard about from Native Americans living under his rule. In April of 1513 he landed on the northeast coast of a peninsula that he named *la Florida* in honor of the celebration of *Pascua Florida*, or "Paschal Flowers," a Spanish term for the Easter festival. While probably not the first Spaniard to have seen the region, he was the first to name it. Eight years later he returned to the southwestern coast of the peninsula, this time with some two hundred settlers and several priests intending to establish a colony. A fierce attack by the indigenous Calusa people brought the experiment to a quick end, but not before the priests had reportedly celebrated the Eucharist, perhaps for the first time, on the soil of what eventually became the United States of America. Ponce de León visited Florida again in 1521, and again was met by fierce resistance from the Calusa inhabitants, resulting in wounds from which he died.

Five years later, in 1526, another group of Spanish sought again to establish a colony along what is now the eastern coast of the United States. San Miguel de Gualdape, whose exact location is unknown but was most likely in what is now South Carolina, had some six hundred residents, included enslaved Africans, and several Dominican priests. Most of the Spanish colonists died in the first few months and the rest returned to Hispaniola. Some of the enslaved Africans who were part of the colony participated in a rebellion and escaped into the South Carolina countryside to settle among the Native American community. One of the Dominicans in the short-lived colony was Antonio de Montesinos (c. 1475-1540), one of the earliest critics of Spanish treatment of Native Americans.

Further explorations in the southeastern region of what eventually became the United States were undertaken by Pánfilo de Narváez (1478-1528) in 1527-1528 and Hernando de Soto (1496-1542) in 1539-1542. The latter took the Spanish conquistadors through Florida to Georgia and Alabama, all the way to Arkansas. Fifteen priests lost their lives during these expeditions. A similar fate awaited Luis Cáncer de Barbastro (d. 1549), a Dominican who had served with Las Casas in Guatemala before sailing for Florida in 1549 to establish a mission to Native Americans. De Barbastro landed near present-day Tampa Bay, where he and the others in his party were quickly killed by the Calusa.

About the time de Soto was exploring Florida and the lower Mississippi River region, the first organized Spanish expeditions north of the Rio Grande river into what is now New Mexico and Arizona were taking place. Among the most extensive was that of Francisco Vásquez de Coronado (1510-1554), who traveled as far as present-day Kansas looking for what the Spanish had heard were seven fabled cities of gold. Coronado returned to Mexico in 1542, leaving behind a group of Franciscans who decided to stay to start a mission among the indigenous peoples in the region that the Spanish called Quivira. Juan de Padilla (1500-1542) was killed later that year while trying to make contact with Native Americans to the north. The exact location of his death is unknown, but it was somewhere in the region of what is now Kansas, Nebraska, and Colorado. Two other Franciscans, Juan de la Cruz (d. 1544) and Luis de Escalona (d. 1544) were killed two years later at their mission near the Rio Grande river.

Human beings had inhabited what is now the southwestern United States for thousands of years before the sixteenth century. During the first millennium of the Common Era the area was home to several cultural groups, one of them a cliff-dwelling people whom archaeologists and historians call the Anasazi. They in turn are believed to be the ancestors of several distinctive cultures, including the Acoma, the Zuñi, and the Hopi, that emerged after 1000 c.e. Collectively called *Pueblos* by the Spanish, the indigenous peoples lived in settled towns or villages atop mesas in the region where they pursued peaceful lives as farmers and hunters. Both the Acoma inhabitants of Acoma, New Mexico, and the Hopi inhabitants of Old Orabi, Arizona, claim their towns to be continuously inhabited from around 1150 c.e., the oldest continuing settlements on the North American continent. Corn, or maize, was the most important crop that was grown among the Pueblos, and the most important religious figures were the divine Corn Mothers.

Several other Native American peoples had migrated into the southwest one or two centuries before the Spanish came. The Navajo (or Dine, as they call themselves) and the Apache were two of the most prominent nomadic groups in the region. The Apache were among the first Native Americans to recapture horses that had escaped from the Spanish conquistadors and ride them in warfare against the Spanish and others in the region. The Spanish contacts were mostly confined to the mesa-dwelling peoples, and only distantly engaged with both Navajo and Apache during the sixteenth century.

Back along the eastern coast, Spanish ships rarely ventured far into the North Atlantic in the sixteenth century. The French took advantage of their absence to launch their own trans-Atlantic trade to the north. In 1534 a French explorer names Jacques Cartier (1491-1557) reached Newfoundland. He returned the following year and explored the St. Lawrence River, deep into the territories of the Huron (or Wendat) nation. The French were initially looking for a passageway to China. What they discovered was a lucrative trade in fur. Cartier took over existing indigenous villages at Quebec and Montreal and turned them into permanent foreign trading settlements. Native American (or First Nation) peoples in the area allowed him to do so, because trade benefited both partners as far as material goods were concerned, although contact with the Europeans began to introduce diseases into the Native American population, and over the next century they had a devastating effect similar to that experienced by the indigenous peoples to the south. The French also became quickly involved in regional warfare among Huron, Algonquin, Mohawk, and Iroquois nations. Seventy years passed before French Jesuits would attempt to bring Christianity to the Huron confederacy, but by that time the death and disruption caused by disease and European arms were already taking a heavy toll on the Huron people's existence.

When the Jesuits, or the "Blackrobes" as they were known among the indigenous people, did arrive in Canada, their missionary labors were quite different from their work in South America. Among the seminomadic Micmacs, Montagnais, Huron, and Algonquins, the Jesuits sought to create a form of Roman Catholicism that could communicate Christianity and at the same time win acceptance by these various First Nations peoples. In 1635 they founded a small school for boys, which in 1663 under the first bishop of New France, François-Xavier de Montmorency-Laval (1623-1708), became the first French-speaking college in North America.

One of these early Jesuits in Canada was Jean de Brébeuf (1563-1649). De Brébeuf lived among the Huron, sleeping in a wigwam even in winter. He was the first to compose a dictionary of Wyandot, the Huron language, and wrote a Christmas hymn in the tongue that is still sung today. The words of the "Huron Carol" reflect Native American experiences. "Twas the moon of wintertime when all the birds had fled / That mighty Gitchi Manitou [Great Spirit] sent angel choirs instead . . . Within a lodge of broken bark, the tender babe was found / A ragged robe of rabbit skin enwrapped his beauty round." Due in no small part to the increasing European presence in these Canadian woodlands, war broke out between the Iroquois and the Huron. De Brébeuf and another Jesuit were captured by the Iroquois in 1649 and were burned at the stake.

Kateri Tekakwitha (1656-1680), known as the "Flower of the Algonquins," was the daughter of an Algonquin Christian mother. Her father was a Mohawk chief who followed the traditional indigenous religion. Both of her parents died of smallpox when she was four. Tekakwitha was left by the disease with scars on her face and impaired eyesight. Following in the way of her mother, she was instructed in the Christian faith by Jesuit missionaries and baptized at the age of twenty, taking the Christian name Kateri. She became known for her practices of extreme self-mortification, which were also common among Native American warriors at the time, as well as for her works among the poor and the healing power of her prayers. Her grave eventually became a pilgrimage site for Catholics, especially from among the First Nations people throughout Canada.

During the middle decades of the sixteenth century the French also sought to establish a presence at the northern end of Florida in a settlement they called Fort Caroline. Spain responded by sending an expedition under Pedro Menéndez de Avilés (1519-1574) in 1565, which wiped out the French settlement. In an effort to protect the northern end of the Spanish sea lanes, de Avilés established a settlement named St. Augustine in Florida. A year later, several Jesuits led by Pedro Martínez (1533-1566) were sent to establish a mission among the indigenous people there. A storm redirected their ship farther north, near Cumberland Island in Georgia. A small band went ashore, where they were met by a group of Native Americans. The first Jesuit to step foot on soil that would later become the United States, Martínez quickly became the first Jesuit to be martyred as well on soil that would later be the United States. The other two priests survived and later returned to work among the Calusa peoples in southern Florida. The story of the martyrdom of Martínez became part of Jesuit lore in America.

In 1570, Juan Baptista Segura (d. 1571), along with six other Jesuits, including several novices who had not yet taken full vows, established a settlement in present-day Virginia in order to begin mission work among the Powhatan. In what seemed like a good decision at the time, the Spanish Jesuits brought along a Powhatan named Paquiquino (1544-unknown), who had been kidnapped nine years earlier and taken to Mexico, then to Spain, where he had taken the name Don Luis de Velasco and undergone baptism. In Virginia the group quickly got settled and built a log chapel in September, but by the end of the winter, the bicultural Don Luis took revenge on his captors by leading a Powhatan rebellion against them. All of the members of the settlement were killed except for a young Spanish altar boy who escaped to tell the story.

Following this experience the Jesuits left the region and concentrated their efforts on Mexico. Franciscans took up further mission work along the eastern coast of the United States, but results were meager during the sixteenth century. By 1602 Franciscans could number in their four stations a combined total of just over a thousand Native Americans. Nevertheless, a string of Spanish forts and Catholic missions among native people extended across north Florida and as far along the Atlantic coast as what is now South Carolina.

The Franciscan century in New Mexico

Following Coronado's expedition in the early 1540s, the Spanish abandoned any effort to extend their conquest north of the Rio Grande from Mexico. In 1573 the Spanish crown issued a set of Ordinances of Discovery that forbade further conquests on the order of Mexico and Peru beyond the borders of their existing empire. Further settlement in New Spain was to be peaceful, and directed by missionaries. The Franciscans responded by sending two expeditions north under Agustín Rodríguez (d. 1582) and Francisco Sánchez Chamuscado (1512-1582) in 1581. Their reports to the king of Spain resulted in the Franciscan order being given charge of extending Spain's colonial control through the region while spreading the Catholic faith. Supported by 125 troops of various European and Native American descent under the command of Don Juan de Oñate (1550-1626), the friars crossed the Rio Grande again in 1598. Seven years later the Spanish viceroy in Mexico forced Oñate to resign his position of governor because of atrocities he had committed against Native Americans, including the destruction of the community of Acoma. A new governor was appointed in 1609 and a new capital established for the colony at Sante Fe. Under the direction of a prelate, the Franciscans were given sole access to outlying areas in order to establish their missions.

From that point on the Franciscans entered an eight-decade contest with indigenous religious beliefs over the soul of the Pueblo peoples. The friars brought with them not only a strict discipline and a readiness to face martyrdom. They were motivated by their powerful millennial belief that Christ was soon to return to earth and that they were on the frontier of the last days of history. They sought to create among their Pueblo converts a pure Christian society that would provide a welcoming home for the returning Christ. To realize this goal they began building missions near the Pueblo villages, seeking to lure the people as much as coerce them to accept the Christian faith. Employing a Pueblo distinction in leadership between "inside" and "outside" chiefs, the Franciscans portrayed themselves as "inside chiefs," with Spanish soldiers under "outside chiefs" far enough away not to interfere with the day-to-day affairs of the people, but near enough to be reached in Sante Fe if called on to bring punishment and destruction.

The Spanish were a formidable presence. Their soldiers had come on horses and used terrifying weapons that shot fire. The friars similarly sought to awe and entice the Pueblos with gifts and other material rewards, signifying what they regarded as their more advanced Christian material culture. Cows, sheep, and pigs soon supplemented a Native American diet that had long depended on hunting for meat. European medical knowledge and Christian prayers for healing were soon being used to lure converts away from the more traditional means of Pueblo medicinal practices and prayers.

Unlike many other regions of Spain's American empire, limited contact with the Europeans and the Franciscans' paternalistic protection prevented the Pueblos from succumbing to mass diseases or being decimated by enslavement. The Franciscans were determined to create a new Pueblo society, however, that was ruled by them and populated by converts. For their part, the Pueblos were forced to allow Franciscans into their villages, but they did not abandon their traditional beliefs. Some did indeed convert and begin to visit or live at the Franciscan missions. Others held fast to their traditional Pueblo religious and cultural traditions, in villages where the Franciscan presence was minimal.

What emerged was a mixed religious and cultural world, a borderland in which Christian relics and statues existed alongside *kachina* figures representing traditional spirit beings. Crosses competed with traditional Pueblo prayer-sticks as symbols of power and prayer. *Kivas*, the traditional Pueblo lodges where men gathered apart from the women for spiritual and cultural matters, continued to be built nearby newly established altars in chapels where the Eucharist was celebrated. Pueblo spirituality looked toward the earth, out of which humanity had emerged, while European Catholic religious culture looked toward heaven, from whence Christ would someday return. Pueblo religious festivals concentrated on planting and harvest, from spring until fall, while the Catholic liturgical calendar moved from Advent to Pentecost, or fall to spring. Nevertheless, there were enough commonalities between the two spiritualities if not their religious practices, such as those between the Corn Mother and the Virgin Mary, for a mixed religious world to eventually come to expression.

By the middle of the century many Pueblos came to accept the Franciscans' religion and Spanish colonial rule at a distance, but continued scattered resistance, sometimes violent in character, could still be found. Native resistance to the Franciscans often had the tacit, if not outright, support of the Spanish governors in Sante Fe who resented the Franciscans' efforts to exploit Pueblo labor for the colonists' financial gain. Several governors were accused of undermining the Franciscans by supporting Pueblo religious practices in the name of freedom of conscience, and ended up facing the Inquisition in Mexico.

The Apaches had gained access to horses by the middle of the seventeenth century and were posing an increased threat to Spanish colonial presence in the region. The Spanish conducted a number of raids against the Apaches out on the plains, mainly intended to gain captives that they could enslave. They succeeded mostly in drawing fierce reprisals against the Franciscans and their missions. Apache reprisals also spilled out against the Pueblos, increasing the overall tensions in the region.

By the 1670s Pueblo native resistance and native religious rites were both becoming more explicit. For their part the Franciscans had weakened over the seven decades in the spiritual condition of their work, especially regarding their vows of poverty and chastity. The growing number of children of illicit relations between Spanish friars and Pueblo women attested to the latter. Several years of drought and crop failure helped secure the growing belief in many that their belief in the Christian God had failed, supporting a return to traditional Pueblo ways. Scattered rebellions increased. In 1680, a medicine man named Popé (c. 1630-1692), who was a member of the Tewsa people, emerged in Taos, New Mexico, to organize a general rebellion. Calling upon all who respected the *kachinas* to join him, he marched against the Spanish in Sante Fe. Within a month his forces had driven out the governor, the colonists, and almost all of the

Franciscans in Arizona and New Mexico. Popé's Pueblo alliance soon fell apart. The medicine man was unable to produce rain in the absence of the Spanish and the Franciscans, as had been promised. Local rivalries and the ongoing hostilities between Apache and Pueblo further divided the peoples. For their part the Franciscans and Spanish decided not to attempt to return to New Mexico for almost a decade. When the Spanish did finally launch a reconquest in 1692 they met stiff resistance outside Santa Fe, but little else throughout the region. Many Pueblos greeted the Franciscans' return by professing their Christian faith and swearing their allegiance to the Spanish crown. Spanish colonization in the area thereafter continued on more traditional patterns of settlers moving into the area. The Franciscan vision of creating a pure Christian society had to be put on hold for the time being.

The English in North America

During the last decades of the sixteenth century the English became eager to exploit the wealth of the Americas as well. They were increasingly in conflict with Spain's expanding empire. In 1586 the English captain Sir Francis Drake (1540-1596) crossed the Atlantic and looted and burned St. Augustine. Spanish control of the settlement was soon reestablished, however, and over the next two decades Spain's dominance along the coast of what is now the southeastern United States was unquestioned. When the English did finally establish a permanent presence in the Americas, it was at Jamestown, Virginia, in 1607, followed by a settlement in 1620 at Plymouth, much farther north in the present state of Massachusetts.

The first attempt to establish an English colony in Virginia had been undertaken in 1585. The effort was ill-fated, as the entire colony disappeared without a trace. A group of London merchants took up the effort again in 1606, forming the Virginia Company for the purpose of searching for gold and looking for a direct passage to China. The following year the company established a small settlement that they named Jamestown near the mouth of the Chesapeake Bay in Virginia. Conflict with the Powhatan peoples, on whose land the settlement was located, internal struggles, harsh winters, lack of supplies, and a population ill-fitted for the task nearly ended the settlement during its first several years. The colonists soon discovered, however, that tobacco brought huge profits back in London, and within several decades its annual production was making Virginia a financial success. While religion was not a motivating factor in establishing the colony, a cleric was among the first settlers and celebrated Communion upon arrival. The Church of England was the established religion.

In England dissenting church groups were increasingly being pressured by the king and bishops to conform on matters of religious practice. In 1620 a band of separatist Congregationalists, already living in exile in Holland for several years, decided to immigrate to America to join those who had started a colony in Virginia. Their ship, the *Mayflower,* landed instead far to the north on Cape Cod, where the group founded Plymouth Colony. They were followed in 1628 by a group of Puritan colonists who landed in Salem and in 1630 by a much larger group organized by the newly chartered Massachusetts Bay Company. Among the leaders of the last venture were prominent Puritan Congregationalist clergy and lay persons, a number of whom had been educated at the universities of Oxford and Cambridge.

The colony they founded was on lands long occupied by the Wampanoag people, which the settlers took without attempting to provide any compensation. A steady stream of immigrants on trading ships from England soon followed, enabling the colony to expand rapidly. More than twenty thousand people crossed the Atlantic over the next decade from England to New England. Their settlements soon spread inland as far as the Connecticut River Valley, putting significant pressure on the indigenous inhabitants. A second colony was established in 1636 as Connecticut. The port city of Boston, which was founded in 1630, emerged as the center of a booming economic enterprise with a strict religious culture.

While not all who came to Massachusetts and Connecticut were Puritans, Reformed theology, Congregational ecclesiology, and Puritan spirituality shaped these colonies into a bold experiment in building a Christian society that leaders imagined would serve as a model for England and the rest of Europe. Puritans on both sides of the Atlantic during these years were generally pessimistic about the historical course that England and the rest of Europe were on. Many feared that the Roman Catholic religion would even be reestablished in England. Employing apocalyptic terms, they spoke of the imminent rise of the forces of anti-Christ. A colony in New England, on the other hand, could serve as a bulwark against such forces. As John Winthrop (1587-1649), the first governor of Massachusetts Bay Colony and a lay person, said in his sermon on board the ship *Arabella* on the way to America, they were to be as a city upon a hill with the eyes of the world upon them.

To this end the Puritans understood themselves to be charged with creating a new society. Local congregations were "gathered" as believers "covenanted" together to be the Church of Jesus Christ. Pastors and other church officers were elected by covenanted members. The pattern was mirrored in civil government at the village and colony-wide level, as the franchise was opened to male church members. Ministers could not hold office in the civil government, but the civil and ecclesial realms were both considered to be under God's sovereign rule over all of life. Because it entailed the participation of all the "saints," what came to be called "the New England Way" offered to male members of the society broader political participation than was otherwise typical for European society at that time.

The Puritan colonies in New England had a higher percentage of university graduates and a higher literacy rate among the population than any other European society. Among their noted leaders in Boston were John Cotton (1585-1652), who had studied at Cambridge; Richard Mather (1596-1669), who had studied briefly at Oxford; and Thomas Hooker (1586-1647), who had also studied at Cambridge and who was the leader of the group that founded Connecticut. Education was such a high priority for them that they not only provided for the education of children but established Harvard College in 1636.

The Puritans were nonconformists or dissenters who opposed the episcopal form of government in the Church of England. In New England they had the opportunity to put their reforms into practice in their churches. Clergy translated and published *The Whole Booke of Psalmes . . . into English Metre* (*Bay Psalm Book*) for singing in worship in Boston in 1640. The spiritual life of New Englanders can be studied in conversion narratives that were offered upon joining a congregation, meditative poetry, devotional manuals, private letters, and journals.

Puritan theology was disseminated at the popular level in lengthy sermons delivered during three-hour worship services in the meeting house twice every Sunday, as well as at other services during the week. Family catechism and neighborhood devotional meetings were also the setting for theological instruction. Delegates from the congregations adopted the Cambridge Platform in 1648, which endorsed the Westminster Confession on all points of its Calvinist doctrine but substituted its own congregational polity, in which governing authority of the church is vested in the local congregation, for Westminster's presbyterian system of polity, in which governing authority of the church is vested in an association made up of representatives of all the churches in a particular region.

The New England way linked a personal experience of the covenant of grace with membership in the body of Christ through the church covenant, and bound all individuals in society, church members or not, together in a social covenant. As in any society with such a dominant, controlling ideology, dissent was a problem in Puritan New England. One of their number, Roger Williams (1603-1683), was forced to leave the colony because he called for a strict separation of church and state. He settled in 1636 along the headwaters of Narragansett Bay on land that he purchased from the Native American tribes in the area. The settlement, which he named Providence Plantations, and the colony, which was eventually chartered in England as Rhode Island and Providence Plantations, became known for its tolerance in matters of religion. Within a short period of time it included Jews as well as Christians. Williams himself joined for a brief time the new Baptist movement and helped found what is considered to be the first Baptist church in America, but he eventually departed from their fellowship, doubting whether the true church even existed on earth any longer.

Dissent was even more distressing to colonial leaders when it came from strong women with diverging religious views. Anne Hutchinson (1591-1643) was an educated woman who took advantage of the Puritan practice of neighborhood home meetings to hold Bible studies in her home in Boston at which she taught her own interpretation of scripture. The gatherings quickly grew, and soon included several prominent men, including the colony's governor. Hutchinson went so far as to dispute the interpretation of other Puritan preachers, condemning what she called their argument for a "covenant of works" that was ignorant of grace. By 1637 political opposition to her in the colony reached a breaking point. Hutchinson was brought to trial, excommunicated, and exiled the following year. She and her family went to Rhode Island for a time, then on to what is now New York, where she was killed by Native Americans in 1642.

Anne Hutchinson's claim to a direct connection with the Holy Spirit and special revelations apart from scripture resonated with the teachings of the Society of Friends, or Quakers, who were making their way from England to America.

Mary Barrett Dyer (1611-1660), exiled like Hutchinson to Rhode Island, returned to England in the 1650s where she met founder George Fox (1624-1691) and became a Quaker. Dyer, along with several other Quakers, soon returned to Boston to preach their message of the guiding inner light of Christ. In 1658 the Massachusetts legislature passed a law banishing Quakers from the colony on pain of death. Despite repeated arrests and expulsions, Dyer and the others refused to obey and continued to preach. In 1659 the Puritan fathers finally handed down a sentence of death. Two Quaker preachers, Marmaduke Stephenson (d. 1659) and William Robinson (d. 1659), were hanged in Boston. Mary Dyer received a reprieve and was banished, but when she returned the following year to preach in the city, she was arrested and hanged. A fourth member of the Society, William Leddra (d. 1661), who had come to Massachusetts from Barbados, was hanged the following year. When news of the executions reached England, Charles II then wrote to the Massachusetts governor to forbid any further executions on religious grounds. Massachusetts was forced to begin to exercise a degree of religious tolerance.

Back in England, civil war broke out in 1640 and lasted almost two decades. The Puritans in England were closely associated with opponents of the crown, but by 1660 their popular support had evaporated. The Puritan sense of destiny, especially in New England, likewise began to decline. By the 1660s a new generation in New England was coming of age, and many of these had been baptized as infants and embraced as adults the basic commitments of the original settlers but lacked a vital personal spiritual experience that would warrant church membership. The notion of a "half-way covenant" was introduced in many congregations to allow these nominal believers to remain in the church fellowship and have their own children baptized. The problem of maintaining Puritan identity deepened as commerce-minded New Englanders became increasingly enamored with English fashions, secular ideas, and more genteel worship practices.

Over the course of the first century of the New England colonial experiment, a number of Puritan leaders interpreted their effort in millennial terms. They were living at the cusp of an age, and their experiment in New England was to play a role in ushering in the reign of Christ on earth. They appropriated the biblical imagery of Israel crossing over the Jordan into Canaan and applied it to their own history of having crossed the Atlantic, allowing them to figure Native Americans as Canaanites and at times allowing the settlers to justify appropriating the Native American lands.

Other Puritan leaders, most notably John Eliot (1604-1690), were no less millennial in their interpretation of history, but they perceived their relationship to Native Americans in different terms. Chief among the stated purposes for the original incorporation of the Massachusetts Bay Colony in England had been the conversion of indigenous peoples to the Christian religion. The original seal of the colony in fact depicted a Native American asking in English, "Come over and help us!" Eliot, who settled in Roxbury, Massachusetts, and accepted a call to serve as pastor of the town's church, took up the task. After years of study with local indigenous speakers he learned the Algonquian language well enough to begin to preach in it in 1646.

Later that year the governing body of Massachusetts appropriated a tract of land for Eliot to build a separate town for Native Americans who converted to Christianity. Eventually fourteen such "praying Indian towns," as they came to be called, were founded. Their purpose was to provide an environment in which Native Americans who had become Christian could effectively learn to become culturally European as well. Residents were required to dress in European clothing, learn European trades, and live in European-style houses.

Meanwhile tensions between the indigenous people and European settlers in the wider colony were growing. In 1662 the Puritan leaders of the colony arrested the Wampanoag leader, Wamsutta (1634-1662), in an effort to force the native inhabitants off more of their land. Wamsutta died while imprisoned, and his brother, named Metacom (1639-1676) but called Philip by the English, became the Wampanoag leader.

By 1675 the situation reached a crisis point. War broke out and spread to the neighboring colony of Connecticut. Fighting lasted a year before Metacom was killed by members of his own people who sided with the English colonists. The outcomes were devastating for the Native Americans, including those who had sided with the colonists. Many who fought on the side of the Wampanoag were sold off in Europe into slavery. Vast amounts of Native American land were taken over by the English for further settlements, and indigenous people seeking to maintain their own way of life were forced to move farther west. Most of the praying Indian towns were abandoned. Those that remained languished.

In England, in the so-called Glorious Revolution in 1688, the English parliament succeeded in bringing William III (1650-1702) and Mary II (1652-1694) jointly to the throne of England, Scotland, and Ireland. The religious effect was to ensure that the Church of England would not return to the Roman Catholic fold. The act of parliament that brought William and Mary to the throne gave greater power to parliament and granted a greater degree of tolerance to dissenting churches. The next year, prominent pastor Increase Mather (1639-1723) of Boston appeared before the monarchs in England to negotiate a new charter for the colony. He succeeded in preserving many Puritan ideals even in the context of great social change. During this transitional period numerous pressures were threatening the old order in New England, not just from across the sea but from within. The older model of a social covenant within cohesive villages with a meeting house on the common was eroding.

New Englanders during this period were no different from other Europeans in their beliefs regarding portents, supernatural phenomena, and the efficacy of magical practices. It was in this context that accusations of witchcraft erupted in Salem Village in 1692. The debacle was initiated when two teenage girls began to demonstrate fits or seizures that were described as supernatural possessions. Several women were accused of being witches and causing these possessions. One of them was an enslaved Native American woman from Barbados named Tituba (dates unknown), who was owned by one of the ministers, Samuel Parris (1653-1720), the father of one of the young girls involved. Stories of visitations by the devil and numerous episodes of witchcraft soon spread throughout the region. Ministers and magistrates alike, struggling to understand and respond to what was happening, launched a disastrous series of trials that eventually resulted in nineteen executions.

Within a year the hysteria had passed. Several more persons were convicted in 1693, but the governor issued a pardon. A number of clerical leaders stepped forward even in the midst of the trials to oppose them. Cotton Mather (1585-1652) argued that the spectral evidence used in the witch trials, in which witnesses testified to seeing the forms of accused witches who were afflicting them, should be inadmissible in the courtroom and that the trials must stop. Judge Samuel Sewell (1652-1730), an earnest Congregationalist, confessed before the church the sinfulness of his participation in a judicial process that had run amok. In the decades following the trials, a number of key witnesses recanted their testimony and publicly acknowledged the harm that their testimony had caused. These were the last trials for witchcraft in British America, although prosecutions continued in Europe for another century. By the end of the 1690s it was clear that times were changing in Puritan New England.

Colonies of Virginia, New Amsterdam, Maryland, and Pennsylvania

While the Puritans were seeking to carry out their holy experiment in New England, other English settlers were establishing colonies along the eastern seaboard. Virginia, as was noted earlier, began as a private corporation but in 1624 was made a royal colony. During the period of the English Civil War the colonists in Virginia succeeded in gaining greater control over their own affairs, building upon a tradition of an elected assembly that dated from 1619. Anglicans loyal to the crown dominated Virginia's religious life through the sixteenth century, although a strong Puritan element could be found as well. Unlike in New England, where Christian spirituality was rooted in village life and every village had a meeting house and a well-educated pastor, the Church of England organized parishes in Virginia that were spread out to include plantations some distance from one another. Social life centered on the courthouse rather than the church. Clergy were few in number and sometimes of low moral character. Significant steps were taken to stabilize church life in the 1690s with the arrival of James Blair (1656-1743) as commissary of the bishop of London, the establishment of the College of William and Mary, and more serious efforts to recruit clergy. In London Thomas Bray (1658-1730) was instrumental in forming the Society for the Promotion of Christian Knowledge (SPCK) in 1698, and then as an agent of the new missionary organizations for the Church of England went to Maryland, a colony that, as we will see below, was initially founded in 1632 to provide a haven for Roman Catholics from England, to found new Anglican congregations.

The Netherlands entered the colonial enterprise in North America when the Dutch West Indies Company purchased land from Native Americans on the lower end of the island of Manhattan in 1626 and named the colony New Amsterdam. Over the next several decades, Dutch settlers spread throughout the island and up the Hudson River. In 1652 the Dutch government granted independence to the New Netherlands, but it proved to be short-lived. Twelve years later, England claimed all territories from Virginia to Massachusetts, and English warships sailed into New Amsterdam, which was renamed New York, in honor of the Duke of York. Although the colony was thereafter under English governance, no one Christian party was able to establish dominance, and the colony proved to be a home to a number of different groups, including a group of Jews, some of whom had recently been forced to leave the Portuguese colony of Brazil.

A member of the Irish nobility, a Roman Catholic named Cecil Calvert (1605-1675), who was Baron of Baltimore, received a royal charter from Charles I in 1632 to start a new colony on the Chesapeake Bay. Calvert named the colony Maryland in honor of Queen Henrietta Maria (1609-1669), wife of Charles I (1600-1649) and a Roman Catholic from France. The colony was to be open to all Christians, but its specific purpose was to provide Roman Catholics from England a place of refuge. From 1650 to 1658 Puritans from Virginia controlled the colony, but the Calvert family was able to regain control and continued to keep Maryland open to Roman Catholic settlers after that. While the majority of the colonists who settled in the colony were Protestants throughout the period, Roman Catholics were able to exercise their religious life without persecution, giving Maryland a distinct place in the history of the founding of these eastern colonies.

One of the most important colonial experiments in religious toleration in North America began in 1681 when the king of England granted a tract of land in North America to William Penn (1644-1718) to pay off a debt owed to Penn's father. William Penn was a member of the Society of Friends, or Quakers. The Quakers believed that the inner light of Christ could be found in every human being, and eschewed many elements of formal Christian religion such as ordained clergy and the sacraments. Persecution in England and New England alike landed many of them in jail, and in some cases even cost them their lives. Now they were given an opportunity to plant a colony built on their own principles. The result was the establishment of the city of Philadelphia in 1682 on land that Penn purchased from the indigenous Delaware peoples. He then proceeded to lay out a visionary city with parks arranged carefully amid the grids of streets. Although the city and colony were dominated by Quakers, members of other Christian communities were welcomed to Philadelphia and Pennsylvania. In 1683, only a year after the colony was established, a group of German immigrants seeking to escape persecution for their nonconformist religious beliefs were granted permission to settle just north of Philadelphia in what soon became known as Germantown.

Africans in North America

The system of chattel slavery that was instituted in America was unlike any other before it in history. It was a well-planned system carried out on a global scale. It was also a system built on physical bodily distinctions that required an extensive theoretical apparatus be developed, giving rise to the modern theories of "race" and racism. As such, it was designed to extend captivity forever, to keep the subjugated in permanent subjection. The effectiveness of the system can still be seen in the manner in which modern racism continues to operate long after the abolition of slavery in many societies.

The struggle for abolition of the African slave trade did not begin with Europeans. It began with African captives themselves, who resisted their enslavement and transportation across the Atlantic to work in America. There were numerous reports of rebellions on board slave ships, and of ship crews having to kill and subdue Africans who were resisting. Africans were chained on board the ships to keep them from jumping overboard in the middle passage and committing suicide, a form of resistance among those who chose death over the horrors to which they were being subjected.

The resistance continued in America as Africans retained their religious and cultural memories, but mixed them with the new religious and cultural worldviews of their European masters. Captives who were sold in markets in various regions of America and forced into perpetual servitude continued to retain hopes of going back to Africa. Many believed they would be reborn in Africa after death. Where possible, they found ways to escape into the wilderness country, where the Europeans could not reach them. The first abolitionist sentiments were lodged in the active resistance of enslaved persons, and in the hidden character of religious and cultural memories preserved in myriad ways. The first abolitionist societies were the communities of maroons that took shape in various colonies under European control. As Africans began to convert to Christianity, they retained these abolitionist sentiments. The form of Christianity that they created in America was from its inception an Africanized religion, abolitionist at the core, and capable of sustaining people's struggle and hope across many centuries.

The history of Africans in the English colonies in North America before 1650 is relatively undocumented. A Dutch warship brought Africans to Jamestown in 1619, and they were immediately forced into servitude. The legal status of these first African immigrants was not clear. Many Europeans crossed the Atlantic as indentured servants. Normally seven or ten years were assigned for an indentured servant to work off a debt or pay off a crime, after which the person was to be freed. Those who came from Europe to Virginia during the first decades of the seventeenth century had their full names and the date of their arrival listed, to mark the beginning of their period of service for legal purposes. Those who came from Africa did not have full names listed or dates recorded, indicating that the colonial authorities regarded European and African forms of servitude differently. The difference had much to do with Africans being considered "non-Christian," however, as English law regarding such matters typically only applied to Christians. Baptism had traditionally changed that condition, but in North America that would change.

The name "Antonio the negro" (dates unknown) appears in the Virginia census of 1625. He had arrived in the colony in 1621 as a servant. The name suggests he had been originally taken by the Portuguese. Anthony Johnson, as he was later known, eventually gained his freedom and married another African, named Mary (dates unknown). They are later listed as owning a farm and having servants.

By 1640 the climate was shifting in both Virginia and Massachusetts. African servants began to find that their indentured status was extended even if they had been baptized. In 1641 the Puritans in Massachusetts made slavery of Africans perpetual, and committed the children of African slaves to servitude as well. This latter was a condition that had never been applied to the children of indentured servants from Europe. In 1662 Virginia likewise made children of an African mother enslaved for life. Virginia law later made all enslaved persons who arrived in America who were not Christian when they arrived enslaved for life. The law was intended to cover Africans, Native Americans, and those of mixed ancestry. By 1750, some fifty thousand enslaved persons a year were being imported by British ships to American colonies. The slavocracy was fully in place in the English colonies in America.

As we have seen, seventeenth-century Christianity in North America was predominantly European in its various forms. If they practiced their Christian religion at all, migrants to America generally did so in ways that their ancestors in Europe had done. In the sixteenth century, most European nations followed the rule that the religion of the ruler would be the religion of the region. In America the principle of established Christianity generally followed in the colonies that Europeans founded, although in some cases the close proximity of differing national churches and constantly changing political winds brought a greater degree of pluralism. Notions of toleration were beginning to take hold by the end of the seventeenth century, and if a dis-established church was not yet a reality, there were still important signs on the horizon that separation of church and state was under way.

Christianity was undergoing a different kind of pluralization in America, being brought about through the increasing engagement of people of African descent now living in an African disapora, and Native American people becoming Christian. The numbers of those in the latter group remained relatively small, but, nevertheless, the presence of Native Americans and the effects of their cosmologies were beginning to appear in subtle, yet distinct ways. African influences in various regions throughout America were no less subtle at the beginning, although by the end of the seventeenth century they were becoming more religiously visible and distinct. The stage was set for a new set of global mission efforts, a new set of challenges, and a new set of awakenings and revivals for Christianity globally in the eighteenth century.

Suggestions for further reading

Bowden, Henry Warner, *American Indians and Christian Missions: Studies in Cultural Conflict.* Chicago: University of Chicago Press, 1981.

Gutierrez, Ramon A., *When Jesus Came, the Corn Mothers Went Away: Marriage, Sexuality, and Power in New Mexico, 1500-1846.* Palo Alto, CA: Stanford University Press, 1991.

Noll, Mark A., *A History of Christianity in the United States and Canada.* Grand Rapids, MI: Eerdmans, 1992.

Marty, Martin E., *Pilgrims in Their Own Land.* New York: Penguin, 1985.

Miller, Perry, *The New England Mind: The Seventeenth Century.* Reprint, Boston: Beacon Press, 2000.

Walsh, H. H., *The Church in the French Era: From Colonization to the British Conquest.* Toronto: Ryerson, 1966.

Weber, David J., *The Spanish Frontier in North America.* New Haven: Yale University Press, 1992.

12

Europe in the Seventeenth Century

Rationalism and science

"Philosophy is written in this grand book, the universe, which stands continually open to our gaze," wrote the Italian scientist Galileo Galilei (1564-1642) in *Il saggiatore* ("The Assayer"), a work on astronomy that he published in 1623. Reading such a grand book, he continued, requires one to learn the language in which it is written. The language of the universe is mathematics, and its characters the geometric figures of circles and triangles. Reading and understanding the universe depend first and foremost on the study of mathematics and science. Galileo's view of the universe was unfolding in the midst of an intellectual environment whose dominant language was Christian piety and praise, and whose characters were Christian dogmas. The two systems of thought were bound eventually to collide.

The rediscovery of ancient learning had been the cornerstone of the humanists' platform during the fifteenth and sixteenth centuries. This in turn led to a renewed emphasis on the religious and intellectual authority of the past. The intellectual movements of the Reformation and the Renaissance both took the return *ad fontes*, or "to the sources," that is, to ideas that their proponents thought had been long ignored or forgotten, to be the most effective basis for needed social, religious, and cultural renewal. In the seventeenth century a number of leading intellectuals went the other way, at least as far as social and cultural renewal were concerned. It was not the "rediscovery" of things forgotten, but the "discovery" of things never known before, or of things that were new, that became the goal of learning and knowledge. Eventually the notion took hold that the newer an idea was, the better or more accurate it was bound to be.

In sixteenth-century Christian Europe true knowledge of the world still ultimately derived from God. Reason might be an important tool, but reason worked upon information that ultimately was provided by means of divine revelation. The church had to oversee the exercise, production, and distribution of knowledge in all of its various guises. Women and men could manipulate and reorganize various kinds of knowledge, but knowledge was in an overall sense finite, and subject to the control of the church. This began to change in the seventeenth century. Reason, the human capacity to weigh, judge, evaluate, and interpret, began to grow in importance as a reliable source of knowledge and the best means of reaching truth. Furthermore, reason took as its subject matter not only authoritative texts from the past. Reason could work directly and immediately on the world that was at hand, as it was perceived through the senses, to arrive at conclusions that could be judged to be true. The horizons of thought thus began to expand, seemingly in infinite directions that were as vast as the universe itself was proving to be.

Throughout the seventeenth century in Europe knowledge could be organized broadly into two categories or camps. The first entailed knowledge derived from sacred sources; the second entailed knowledge derived immediately from the world. The first employed methods of interpretation sanctioned by church authority; the second employed methods of study that were increasingly being moved beyond church sanction. Over the course of the century, the church more and more came to be considered limited in overseeing the former, which entailed doctrine and morality. Concerning the latter, the methods used by human beings to discover what was true concerning the world around them were constantly being improved. Consequently, what counted as valid knowledge was increasingly becoming determined by methods that were no longer under church control. Furthermore, the world was coming to be understood as a realm that, even if it was not entirely known, was for all intents and purposes entirely knowable by science. Consequently, the need for God in such a world decreased in direct proportion to the increase in new knowledge about the world.

The revolution in knowledge that was taking place is symbolized by a revolutionary turn in consciousness that took place over the course of the sixteenth and seventeenth centuries. At the beginning of the sixteenth century most Europeans considered the earth to be at the center of the universe. A humanist from Poland, Nicolaus Copernicus (1473-1543), sometime after 1510 began to circulate in writing a theory that the sun and not the earth was at the center. The earth rotated around the sun, he argued, rather than the sun rotating around the earth. Copernicus published a full defense of his theory only in 1543, in *De revolutionibus orbium coelestium* ("On the Revolutions of the Heavenly Spheres"), which appeared shortly before his death. Although he had the support of at least one prominent Lutheran theologian at the time, the theory was considered by other church leaders to be heretical.

Little more came of the matter, however, until almost half a century later, in 1596, when a German mathematician and astronomer named Johannes Kepler (1571-1630) published a defense of Copernicus's theory in a book titled *Mysterium cosmographicum* ("The Cosmographic Mystery"). Kepler offered a more general cosmology that sought to build a bridge between astronomy and mathematics on one side, and theology on the other. In Italy, Galileo embraced the Copernican theory as well, supported in part by his observations through the new instrument he invented that he called a telescope. His work soon brought him into conflict with the church. In 1616, at the instigation of Pope Paul V (1552-1621) and under the guidance of Cardinal Robert Bellarmine (1542-1621), the Inquisition, which in 1542 had been renamed the Sacred Congregation for Doctrine, determined that Copernican theory regarding the universe was heretical.

When Galileo sought to defend the theory in 1632 in a book published in Italian titled *Dialogo sopra i due massimi sistemi del mondo* ("Dialogue Concerning the Two Chief World Systems"), he quickly found himself called before the Inquisition. Convicted of heresy the following year, Galileo was placed under house arrest and forbidden to publish anything for the rest of his life. His final work, *Discorsi e dimostrazioni matematiche, intorno a due nuove scienze* ("Discourses and Mathematical Demonstrations concerning the Two New Sciences"), was smuggled out of Italy to the Protestant nation of the Netherlands, where it was published in 1638. Almost another century would pass before the theory would find full acceptance by church officials.

Key to the advance of new knowledge, as the story of Galileo illustrates, was the use of new instruments. But even more important was the manner in which the gathering of data for use as evidence began to weigh more heavily in the work of scientists. The performance of experiments that produced conclusions that others could reproduce when the experiment was repeated became the cornerstone of the new system of knowledge that emerged in the seventeenth century. The name that is associated above all others with what came to be called the scientific method is Francis Bacon (1561-1626).

Bacon was from an English upper-class family. He entered Trinity College in Cambridge University at the age of twelve, and after graduating traveled for a time through Europe before returning to England to pursue a career as a lawyer. He eventually rose to serve as attorney general and then as lord chancellor under James I (1566-1625) before personal debt and charges of bribery forced him out of government.

Bacon is best remembered for developing a new inductive method for science. *Novum Organum* ("New Instrument"), published in 1620, sketched out the contours of his method. He conceived it to be offering an alternative to the logic of the ancient Greeks, most notably Aristotle's syllogism. His alternative came to be known as inductive reasoning. One had in the first instance to study a phenomenon itself to discover its form or cause, using comparative methods to find commonalities and differences, and arriving at explanations that derived from facts. His work laid the groundwork for the development of full-fledged experimental science. At the same time Bacon was a philosopher. He saw the world as a problem to be solved and harnessed in order to increase human good. He did not oppose Christian teaching. His *Essays* from 1601 and other writings were full of biblical references. His own personal Bible contained enough notes to suggest he read it thoroughly. But his inquiries took him beyond the established boundaries of inherited Christian knowledge and were an important building block for a new worldview.

Another important building block in the construction of what eventually became known as the modern worldview was provided by the French philosopher René Descartes (1596-1650). Descartes was by all accounts a faithful Roman Catholic thinker. Aware of Galileo's difficulties with the church, he exercised greater caution in presenting his own work. The more religiously tolerant political environment of the Netherlands also provided him a more hospitable environment for publishing his ideas.

Descartes spent eight years in the Jesuit school in Anjou, France, and a year studying law at the University of Poitiers before joining the army in the Netherlands for a short time. In 1618 he met Isaac Beeckman (1588-1637), a well-known mathematician, who introduced him to the field. Over the next decade Descartes traveled through various parts of Europe, much of which was in the grip of war between Protestant and Catholic forces, before settling in the Netherlands in 1628. His book *Le monde* ("The World"), a work on physics that defended the Copernican heliocentric solar system, was set to be published in 1633 when word came that Galileo had been condemned by the Sacred Congregation for Doctrine in Rome on account of his book *Dialogue*. Fearful of facing the same consequences even in Holland, Descartes decided to put off publication of the work and turned his attention to more general philosophical concerns. Four years later he published in French *Discours de la méthode pour bien conduire sa raison, et chercher la verité dans les sciences* ("Discourse on the Method of Rightly Conducting the Reason and Seeking Truth in the Sciences"), followed in 1641 by the publication in Latin of *Meditationes de prima philosophia, in qua Dei existentia et animæ immortalitas demonstratur* ("Meditations on First Philosophy in which the Existence of God and the Immortality of the Soul Are Demonstrated"). These two volumes alone were enough to secure his place in the history of the modern world.

Descartes was looking for a secure pathway to knowledge. Such a pathway, he argued, was best taken through a method of doubt. One can arrive at the greatest assurance of the truth by setting aside all foregone conclusions or prior knowledge, systematically removing them by doubt. Radical doubt in this way will clear the field of uncertainty and allow one to arrive at an unshakeable foundation for knowledge of what is real and true. Descartes worked through a series of thought experiments where he doubted even the existence of God before he arrived at the point where he could not doubt there was someone who did the doubting. One can in this way know with assurance that one exists. *Je pense, donc je suis,* he wrote in French. Later it was translated into Latin, *cogito ergo sum* ("I think, therefore I am").

From this starting point, he then went on to build a radically dualistic philosophical world that organized the world into a thinking human subject, the "I" who gazes, and the objects that the subject gazes upon. These distinctions correlated with mind, which was immaterial, and physical bodies, which are material. From Descartes' philosophy a radical ontological division arose that came to characterize the rationality of the modern era, a rationality that was also radically at odds with the originating worldviews of ancient biblical texts as well as with much of Christian theology prior to the seventeenth century. This ontological dualism came in time to characterize much of modern social and cultural thinking: reason and emotion; civilized and primitive; and even science and religion. In each case, the sure foundation for knowledge was provided by the former, which was taken to be normative.

The philosopher remained a faithful Roman Catholic to the end of his life. His philosophical work, however, provided the foundations for a revolutionary turn in European philosophy that was as far reaching as that of Copernicus.

Descartes' method put the thinking human subject, usually conceived to be a European male, at the center of the universe. Knowledge of the world, including knowledge of God, came to be regarded as a function of the thinking subject. Reason, and the reasoning subject who exercised it, came in a short time to be enthroned above scripture, tradition, and even the papacy as the source of authority and the trustworthy guarantor of knowledge.

Descartes' ideas quickly spread throughout Europe among members of the intellectual and academic communities. In Amsterdam they found a critical reader in a Jewish lens grinder named Baruch (Benedict de) Spinoza (1632-1677). Born into a family of merchants who were originally from Portugal, at the age of twenty-three Spinoza was expelled by the Jewish religious leaders from the community in Amsterdam on account of his philosophical ideas. In several philosophical treatises, including *Ethica ordine geometrico demonstrata* ("Order of Ethics Geometrically Demonstrated," usually referred to simply as "Ethics"), which was published after his death, Spinoza argued that God was an impersonal or abstract reality. God and the world were not different in substance. The universe was infinite, although complex, but there was ultimately no separation or difference between God and nature. Spinoza eventually came to argue against Descartes' mind-body dualism or the dualism of mental and material realities as well. All reality is determined by underlying laws, he asserted. God was not so much a first cause as an integrated dimension of this complex reality. Nothing is contingent, nothing happens by accident, and there is no such thing as "free will." One can see why the Jewish community in Amsterdam might have expelled him from their midst, given the manner in which such ideas challenged traditional religious beliefs of Jews and Christians alike.

Wars of religion and European realignment

Descartes had opened the second chapter of his book *Discourse on Method* relating an episode that provided him the free time necessary to engage in his extended philosophical reflections. "I was then in Germany, where I had gone because of the desire to see the wars which are still not ended; and while I was returning to the army from the coronation of the Emperor, I was caught by the onset of winter." The coronation to which he was referring was most likely that of Emperor Ferdinand II (1578-1637) in Frankfurt in 1619. The conflict was the Thirty Years War, which had broken out the year before between Protestants and Catholics.

The Peace of Augsburg in 1555 left central Europe politically unstable for it allowed rulers to determine the religion of their realms (the phrase in Latin was *cuius regio, eius religio*). By the early years of the seventeenth century, regional tensions between Protestant and Catholic princes in Germany rose to a breaking point. Protestants formed an Evangelical Union in 1608 under the leadership of Frederick IV, the elector of Palatinate (1574-1610). A year later Catholics responded by forming the Catholic League under the leadership of Duke Maximilian of Bavaria (1573-1651). In Bohemia, Protestants resisted the efforts of

Ferdinand II to appoint two Catholic administrators to rule in his stead, throwing them out a window that was at least twenty meters above ground. The revolt quickly fanned into full war, between German Protestants to the west and the Catholic powers of central Europe. Before the war ended, three decades later, Spain, Sweden, Denmark, Poland, France, and even the Ottomans would all be involved.

Central Europe was devastated by waves of warfare as Protestant and Catholic armies fought back and forth. By the time a settlement was achieved in the Treaty of Westphalia in 1648, Europe had become politically and culturally transformed. The Treaty of Westphalia marks a significant development in the emergence of the modern nation-state. Spain's power was considerably diminished, and Portugal even regained its independence in 1640. Sweden became a larger regional power, and France reigned supreme in western Europe. More important, however, were the historical processes that one can see at work. For the first time in Europe, territorial boundaries of nations were demarcated, and the notion of the sovereign state introduced. The modern nation-state was in the process of emerging. Europe was set on a path that would eventually transform the political face of the entire world.

The Treaty of Westphalia had significant religious repercussions throughout Europe as well. By all accounts, this was the last religious war in Europe. The notion that governing political entities should not be bound to a particular Christian confession or creed began to take hold. Political life began to be constructed on the basis of national, rather than religious, categories of identity. Europeans still went to war with one another and religion was still a matter of national identity, but after 1648 nations in Europe no longer went to war with one another for religious reasons. The idea of a fully religiously neutral state did not take hold right away, but the roots of what come to be called "secularization" or the "secular state" in Europe in later centuries can be traced to the Treaty of Westphalia in 1648.

Europe as a whole in the seventeenth century was steadily expanding its global presence. Advances in science and technology gave European nations an increasing advantage over those in other regions of the world. Over the course of the sixteenth century, Spanish and Portuguese fleets came to dominate the world's oceans, and the trade that flowed across them. The defeat of the Spanish Armada off the coast of England in 1588 marked the apex of Spanish global power. Spain's colonial empire was overextended, and despite the extraction of large amounts of gold from the Americas, its national coffers had become relatively depleted. The British and Dutch were becoming better sailors, with better navigational instruments, better knowledge of the world, and more accurate mapmaking skills. Furthermore, the northern European colonial powers had discovered that far more wealth could be generated by extracting products from their overseas colonies for sale at home than by extracting precious metals. After 1600 Dutch and English ships began shaving off portions of the Portuguese and Spanish colonial empires and building colonies of their own.

The Dutch, a majority of whom were what can be described as moderately tolerant Calvinists, and the English, who vacillated among Anglican, Puritan, and Roman Catholic sentiments, engaged periodically in warfare at sea during the 1650s and 1660s. From 1652 to 1654 ships from the two nations battled in the Baltic and North Sea, and in the English Channel. A decade later, warfare between the two nations moved out to their growing colonial empires.

In 1664 the Dutch colony of New Netherlands (present-day coastal New York and New Jersey) was taken over by the English. According to the treaty that brought an end to the conflict, Suriname, in South America, remained in Dutch hands while Dutch lands in North America, including Delaware, were turned over to the English. English settlers had already been developing colonies south of these Dutch holdings since 1607 and north of them since 1620. With the transfer of the Dutch colonies along the Middle Atlantic region in 1664, much of the east coast of what is now the United States was united under English colonial rule. England had also been attacking Dutch colonies in Africa during this period. For the first time, European nations at war with one another were carrying out their battles on three continents.

Roman Catholic reforms amid internal tensions

Pope Clement VIII (1536-1605) declared 1600 to be a year of jubilee for the church, the twelfth such to be declared by a pope. The city of Rome was told to be prepared for an expected three million pilgrims who would come to celebrate the event. Churches were repaired. Paintings, frescoes, statues, and new works of music were commissioned for the grand year. Large amounts of the Vatican's funds were spent on the preparations. Looming in the background was the century of schism the church had just been through and the divisions caused by Protestants. The artwork that was commissioned for the jubilee seemed to underscore the violence that had resulted from these divisions. Martyrdom was again a predominant theme, as seen in works such as Stefano Maderno's (c. 1576-1636) sculpture of St. Cecilia, dedicated in 1600 and located today in the church of Santa Cecilia in the Trastevere neighborhood in Rome. This is not to say that the mood was grim in Rome for the year of jubilee, for it was not. The burst of new works of music in particular points to the vibrant nature of the spirit of the era. A new musical form known as opera, which had only been introduced three years earlier, in 1597, in Florence, was introduced in the city. By the end of the century Pope Clement IX (1600-1669) would be writing librettos. Music in general began to be written with richer harmonies, more daring melodies, and more intricate counterpoints. More than a century would pass before these new developments would come to be known as Baroque, but the movement was already under way in early-seventeenth-century Rome.

The papacy continued to be directly involved in political affairs of various European states through the seventeenth century. Popes sometimes negotiated treaties between warring nations. They provided funds to support military campaigns against the Ottomans or against Protestants in the Thirty Years War. Urban VIII (1568-1644) was pope for twenty-one of those thirty years. During this time he worked to extend papal territories and to shore up the defenses of papal lands. He spent large amounts of papal money on armaments. He was also a strong patron of Roman Catholic missions. It was Urban who allowed other religious orders to begin work in China, which had been reserved by Pope Gregory XIII (1502-1585) for the Jesuits alone. He also prohibited enslavement of indigenous peoples in America, a prohibition that had the unintended effect of increasing the African slave trade. Concerned to reconvert Protestants and Protestant rulers, he commissioned renewed Roman Catholic efforts in this endeavor.

Urban had one of the longest reigns of the century, but Gregory XV (1554-1623), who only reigned for three years, may have had a greater influence on the global church. Gregory was the first pope to have studied at a Jesuit school, and the education seemed to have turned his mind and heart to the world. At the request of a Capuchin and a Discalced Carmelite, in 1622 Gregory established a special Congregation of Cardinals for overseeing all foreign missions, *Congregatio de propaganda fidei* ("Congregation for the Propagation of the Faith"). Roman Catholic missions took on a new dimension under papal oversight with the formation of this congregation in Rome. Other reforms that Gregory undertook included lessening recommended punishments for witchcraft and raising the requirements by which a person could be found guilty of a crime deserving death.

Given the new philosophical currents, warfare, and changing political conditions in seventeenth-century Europe, one might be led to assume that Catholic Christianity was in decline on the continent. Such was not the case, not yet at least. There were in fact strong movements of renewal and revitalization. After the religious upheavals of the sixteenth century, the reforms passed at the Council of Trent began to take effect in various local contexts. One could nevertheless find ample evidence of moral conditions that needed to be improved. Prostitution was common, and dueling was still popular. Many of the soldiers who had fought in the Thirty Years War were mercenaries whose pay was whatever booty they could seize. The war caused large movements of people, and many of them sought refuge in cities, overwhelming their resources. Cities already were growing, with increased need for education and for institutions dedicated to caring for children who were without homes. The bubonic plague returned to Europe, first in Italy in 1630-1631, and then later in France and finally in London where it hit in 1664-1665. Over 100,000 died in London before the plague was extinguished, ironically by the Great London Fire of 1666, which killed people, rats, and fleas indiscriminately.

Social moral reform was clearly needed throughout Europe. It was not the philosophers or scientists who took up this call, nor for the most part the clerical leadership of the churches. In the seventeenth century those who became the vanguard of social reform in Roman Catholic contexts were most often members of new religious communities. Often they had been educated and inspired in schools run by the Jesuits. Rome was clearly the center of the Roman Catholic Christian world in the seventeenth century, but the most important currents for Catholic spiritual renewal flowed from France.

At the end of the sixteenth century, France flirted with the notion of a religiously plural state. The Edict of Nantes, issued in 1598, extended to the Huguenots or French Calvinists legal permission to practice their religion in their homeland. Such tolerance began to erode, however, under the powerful and lengthy rule of Louis XIV (1638-1715). Only five years old when he assumed the throne (actual rule was exercised by Cardinal Mazarin [1602-1661] until Louis came of age), the so-called Sun King was one of the first monarchs in Europe to assert the divine right of the king, the claim that kings derived their right to rule directly from God and not through the other members of the nobility who either elected them or supported them with their oaths of loyalty. Not surprisingly, Louis's reign was marked by absolutism, increased nationalism, and the development of Gallicanism, the belief that French kings should exercise control over the church and its property under their realm. Toleration of Huguenots came to an end in 1685 when Louis revoked the Edict of Nantes, forcing as many as 200,000 French Protestants to leave the country. With the emigration of such a large number of citizens, many of them members of the growing urban middle class and many of them wealthy merchants, and with his military and budget overextended, Louis XIV and France with him begin to decline, a decline that would continue well into the eighteenth century.

Francis de Sales (1567-1622) is one of the most important figures in seventeenth-century European Christianity in this regard. Born in a castle in Savoy, Francis was initially headed for a career in law. While studying at a Jesuit college, however, he went through a period of personal struggle in which he came to doubt his own salvation before taking a vow of chastity and dedicating his life to religious service. After completing his studies, and to the dismay of his father, he became a priest with a commitment to working for the spiritual formation and renewal of lay people.

De Sales was ordained in 1593 by the bishop of Geneva. The city of Geneva remained firmly under Calvinist control at the end of the sixteenth century, but in the towns and countryside along the southern shore of Lake Geneva, Calvinist and Catholic worlds intersected. The Roman Catholic bishop of Geneva resided in Annecy, a small city some 35 km to the south of Geneva in French-controlled territory. It was here that de Sales first served in ministry, eventually rising to become bishop of Geneva. Shortly after his ordination he began traveling through the region along the southern shore of Lake Geneva both to minister to Roman Catholics in the region and also to convert Protestants to the Catholic faith. Refusing to engage Calvinists in controversy when they approached him, he concentrated on preaching a clear and simple message. In order to reach more people, he wrote small leaflets, which he reportedly slipped under doors of houses in the region, making him a pioneer in the use of Christian tracts. On one occasion he visited Theodore Beza (1519-1605), the leader of Protestant Geneva; and although neither succeeded in converting the other, by all accounts their discussion appears to have been cordial. By the end of his life de Sales was reported to have been responsible for as many as seventy thousand Protestants converting to the Roman Catholic faith.

De Sales is best known as the author of *Introduction à la vie dévote* ("Introduction to the Devout Life"). This devotional guide offered practical instructions for lay people seeking to experience the presence of God in their everyday lives without denouncing the world. Individual chapters covered such matters as how to gain the most spiritual benefit from confession, how to practice meditation, what kinds of amusements a spiritual person can pursue (he frowned upon dancing), and how to conduct a spiritual inventory of one's own personal life. *Introduction to the Devout Life* brought spirituality, for centuries the province of religious orders, to the cook, the businessman, and the farmer.

One of the persons who benefited from de Sales's spiritual direction was a widow, Jane Frances de Chantal (1572-1641), who lived in Dijon. De Chantal was married for eight years and had four children when her husband was killed in a gun accident. In her grief and loneliness she sought spiritual direction, which came at first in the form of a spiritual vision. Then in 1604 the vision was confirmed in a sermon she heard de Sales preach in Dijon during Lent. She began corresponding with de Sales and in 1610 founded the Congregation of the Visitation, which was the fulfillment of her vision. Although the Congregation was originally founded to care for the poor and the sick, it quickly turned more toward contemplation and private devotion.

Another friend of St. Francis de Sales was the irenic Cardinal Pierre de Bérulle (1575-1629). Born in Champagne, France, Bérulle was educated by the Jesuits. In his early years he demonstrated considerable zeal for converting Huguenots to the Roman Catholic faith, but after entering the priesthood he turned his interest more toward reforming the Catholic priesthood and developing spiritual resources for lay women and men. Friend of Francis de Sales and advisor to René Descartes, Bérulle helped to found several new communities for women. Bérulle's spirituality focused on the incarnate Jesus. It combined mystical experience with reading of scripture and commitment to missions. He is credited with having founded what became known as the "French School of Spirituality," a movement for renewal that had wide-ranging effect through the seventeenth century not only in France but in America.

Cardinal Bérulle was also the spiritual advisor to another important figure in the period, Vincent de Paul (1581-1660). De Paul was the founder in 1625 of the Congregation of the Mission of St. Vincent de Paul, better known as the Vincentians. Ordained in 1600, he was captured five years later by Muslim seafarers in the Mediterranean and sold as a slave in North Africa. Two years later, in 1607, he was freed after he succeeded in converting his Muslim owner to the Christian faith. Following further study in Rome, he returned to France, where he served as chaplain and spiritual advisor to a number of prominent members of the French aristocracy while developing ministries among the poor. By the time of Vincent's death in 1660 there were Vincentian houses in France, Italy, Tunis, Algiers, Poland, Ireland, and Madagascar.

In 1625, the year he founded the Vincentians, de Paul met Louise de Marillac (1591-1660). The illegitimate daughter of a prominent member of the nobility, she was widowed at thirty-four. About that time she met de Paul and the two began corresponding. Eight years later, the two cofounded the Daughters of Charity, an order that took a special interest in helping abandoned children and feeding and caring for prisoners. De Marillac sought to establish clinics and schools in villages throughout France. Women in the order were encouraged to go out into the streets to work with the poor.

The Ursulines were a religious order that proved to be especially important in the development of both devotional practices and ministry for women in the seventeenth century. Founded in 1535 by Angela de Merici (1474-1540) in Brescia, in northern Italy, in 1604 they opened their first convent in France to train young women. The Ursulines were the first Roman Catholic order founded specifically for the education of women, a development that marked a critical milestone in Roman Catholic spirituality. They were also among the first women's orders to send women as missionaries into other parts of the world. A small group of Ursulines, led by Marie Guyart (also known as Marie de l'Incarnation, 1599-1672), journeyed to Quebec, Canada, in 1639 where they founded an Ursuline house that provided medical services and engaged in the education of Native American children.

One of the most important figures in Roman Catholic Europe in the seventeenth century was Cornelius Jansen (1585-1638). Born in Holland, he graduated from the University of Louvain in Belgium. During his studies at the university, he discovered an affinity for the writings of St. Augustine and an aversion to Aristotelian thought. His disregard for the latter put him at odds with a number of other leading theological voices of his day, for although Aristotle was being rejected by a new generation of philosophers and scientists in Europe, most Catholic theologians continued to follow Thomas in matters of doctrine, and Thomas was clearly a student of Aristotle. After spending several years in France, Jansen returned to Louvain in 1616, where he became the head of one of its colleges. Over the next two decades he engaged in sustained theological controversy with the Jesuits, who were growing in influence at the university, and continued his studies on Augustine, intending to write a definitive work on the theology of the early Christian saint.

Jansen believed that the Jesuits harbored heretical tendencies. He specifically charged them with being semi-Pelagians, the doctrine that holds that human beings have a certain if limited capacity or ability to cooperate with God in achieving their own salvation, which they exercise by seeking God. The Jesuits did indeed teach what could be called a more generous anthropology that placed less emphasis on personal inability and more emphasis on personal free will in the work of salvation, thereby maximizing the spiritual value of an individual's own efforts. The Jesuits defended the thoughtful application of human reasoning as being thoroughly consistent with Catholic teaching.

Jansen's massive treatise, *Augustinus,* which worked out his arguments against the so-called semi-Pelagians, was not published until two years after his death. The work was immediately condemned by the Vatican as heretical, mainly for what Rome thought to be its Calvinist leanings. Jansen was dead by then, but his cause was taken up by his supporters. One of them, Jean Duvergier de Hauranne (1581-1643), had been a friend since their student days together at Louvain. Duvergier had become the abbot of the monastery at Saint-Cyran and the spiritual director to a community of nuns at Port Royal, near Paris. The convent had once been part of the Cistercians, but under the direction of their abbess, Mother Marie Angélique Arnauld (1591-1661), had become an independent community. Mother Angélique, as she was known, led Port Royal to become a center for what soon came to be called Jansenism.

Following the death of Duvergier, who ended up spending several years in prison for his activities, a new leader for the Jansenist cause stepped forward, the brother of Mother Angélique, Antoine Arnauld (1612-1694). In 1653 Pope Innocent X (1574-1665) issued a condemnation of five statements that had been extracted from Jansen's writings. Arnauld responded by denying the statements were actually what Jansen had written. Nevertheless the condemnation stood. Some who were involved found themselves being denied the sacraments because of their Jansenist views.

In 1646 a government official broke his hip. The two doctors who treated him during his recovery were Jansenists. They took the opportunity to introduce two of his children, Jacqueline Pascal (1625-1661) and her better-known older brother, Blaise Pascal (1623-1662), who had already gained a reputation as a brilliant young mathematician, to the Jansenist teachings. Six years later, in 1652, Jacqueline joined the community at Port Royal, doing so over the initial objections of her brother. Two years later, however, in November of 1654, Blaise Pascal had a dramatic personal religious experience. He recorded the event on a page that he carried with him the rest of his life. "Fire," he wrote. "God of Abraham, God of Isaac, God of Jacob, not of philosophers and scholars. Certainty, certainty, heartfelt joy, peace. God of Jesus Christ." Pascal's view of religion was at once deeply experiential and intellectual. He sought to hold together feeling and reason, arguing that sound judgment required both. In this vein he defended passion as a trustworthy pathway to truth. "The heart has its reasons, which reason does not know" was entry 277 in his book *Pensées* ("Thoughts"), which was published after his death.

Before long Blaise Pascal was regularly visiting Port Royal and actively defending not only the Jansenist cause, but his friend, Arnauld, against the attacks of their opponents, especially the Jesuits. In 1656, Arnauld and a number of the faculty were expelled from the Sorbonne. Louis XIV wanted the conflict resolved to keep the French nation united; the Jesuits wanted the pesky Jansenists silenced; and the popes wanted to reduce Gallicanism and increase papal authority in France. Finally, in 1660, Louis XIV at an assembly of French clergy ordered the five statements of Jansenism condemned. Those who would not comply were to be imprisoned.

During this period Pascal weighed in against the Jesuits through a series of anonymous letters written supposedly by an observer in Paris to a friend in the provinces. *Lettres provinciales* ("The Provincial Letters"), eighteen in all, attacked the Jesuit positions. Chief among the objects of criticism was the Jesuit use of casuistry, a pragmatic form of moral reasoning that allowed for case-by-case reasoning, and probabilism, a form of moral reasoning that allowed one to follow the most lenient opinion, even if it was a minority position among the authorities of the theological tradition. The Jesuits' arguments, Pascal ridiculed, were being framed carefully so as not to place too great a burden on their upper-class penitents. The Jesuits could argue any point and even both sides of a point, making right wrong and wrong right, Pascal claimed. Their lax view of sin, along with the high view of human ability, was in direct opposition to the Augustinian view held by the Jansenists.

The Jesuits in seventeenth-century France were formidable opponents. In the years following the Council of Trent, monastic orders in general had grown considerably in influence within the church. The number of regular priests, or those who were members of a religious order that followed a rule, was estimated to have grown to be about the same as the number of secular priests, or those who worked in local parish churches under the authority of diocesan bishops, in Europe. Moreover, regular priests were often better educated than secular priests. Regular priests belonged to orders that could often mobilize connections and resources on a far greater scale than secular priests could imagine. The orders were busy founding new schools, organizing mission work on a global scale, and in many cases providing the impetus for reform.

Among the orders, the Jesuits majored in higher-level education. In Roman Catholic Europe they also succeeded in becoming confessors and advisors to many in the upper levels of society. By the end of the seventeenth century, they had more than 16,000 members throughout the world. Over the course of their first two centuries they had founded more than 1,000 schools, 740 of which survived past the year 1750. Numerous political and religious leaders, not just in Europe but in other continents as well, were being educated by the Jesuits. The Italian musician Biacomo Carissimi (1605-1674) served as the maestro at the Jesuit German College for forty-four years. In 1651, Jesuit John Baptist Riccioli (1598-1671) created the first map of the moon, naming thirty-five lunar craters for Jesuit scholars. These are just a few examples of their educational accomplishments.

The Jesuits were also the Vatican's chief tool for pursuing Protestants, witches, and others who were judged to be heretics, including now the Jansenists. The fourth vow that every Jesuit took in the seventeenth century was a vow of obedience to the pope, which entailed in part a vow to go wherever he was sent. The Jansenists could hardly be expected to have toppled such a powerful order. On the other hand, after 1667 the controversy died down somewhat, especially after a more conciliatory pope came to occupy St. Peter's See in Rome. Jansenism continued to stand for a more rigorous approach to moral concerns, a greater emphasis on human sinfulness, and consequently a greater emphasis on the work of grace in redemption.

Jansenists were often accused by their opponents as being Calvinists. They were not, but enough parallels between Jansenism and Calvinism existed for the charges to stick. Another movement within the Catholic Church during the seventeenth century that also had parallels with certain streams of Protestant spirituality was Quietism. Quietism can describe any religious approach that teaches surrender, passive reception, and "quietness" to be the best means of access to the divine. The quietist in any tradition seeks to empty the self in order to passively receive spiritual essence. For this reason quietists are often closely associated with mystics. Earlier centuries in Europe had produced notable examples of quietistic spirituality, including Meister Eckhart, Tauler, Henry Suso, and Thomas á Kempis, whose book, *De imitatione Christi* ("The Imitation of Christ") written in the 1420s, is often considered a classic in the tradition. Even Francis de Sales talked about the need for one to practice willful indifference in order to give oneself completely to God. This basic approach to the spiritual was often called being "quiet of mind" (*quies mentis*). Unlike the much more academic movement of the Jansenists, the Quietist writers had a very large following. Their doctrine was much less complicated and seemed to speak to the deep longings of peasants and princes alike. It is a major reason why many of their writings are still in print in the twenty-first century.

Miguel de Molinos (1640-1697) was a Spaniard who also studied with Jesuits, at Valencia, and then was ordained at age twenty-two. He gained an early reputation for his brilliant speech and the ability to present arguments forcefully. Many, including the future Pope Innocent XI, sought his advice and counsel. In 1675 he published a work titled *Guida spirituale: che disinvolge l'anima e la conduce per l'interior cammino all'acquisto della perfetta contemplazione e del ricco tesoro della pace interior* ("A Spiritual Guide Which Disentangles the Soul and Brings It by the Inward Way to the Getting of Perfect Contemplation and the Rich Treasure of Eternal Peace"). Originally published in Italian and Spanish, the book quickly appeared in Latin, French, and German as well. Mystical knowledge proceeds not from reason but from experience, the opening pages of the work asserted. It is not invented, but proven. It does not even come through reading books, but through an infusion of the Spirit who communicates grace even to the lowly. To this end, *Spiritual Guide*, as it was best known in English, instructed its readers, which soon included over twenty thousand in Naples alone and even Queen Christina of Sweden, on practices of meditation and contemplation that would quiet the soul and allow God to speak to it.

De Molinos had his opponents in the church, but any immediate persecution was forestalled by his friendship with the pope. The inactivity he prescribed looked better to some than the strict moralism of the Jansenists. In time, however, opposition to him increased. Some took quietism to be an argument for offering quiet prayers in the liturgy, or replacing confession. De Molinos was also accused of having not such passive relations with female penitents. Although de Molinos was never found guilty of any immoral behavior, in 1688 the pope condemned sixty-eight propositions of his book and sentenced him to life in prison. With characteristic consistency, passively and quietly de Molinos accepted the sentence and spent the last nine years of his life in prison. His influence, however, was not so easily imprisoned.

Jeanne Marie Bouvier de la Motte (1648-1717), better known as Madame Guyon, was the most influential proponent of quietism. A native of northern France, at the age of sixteen she had been unwillingly married to a man twenty-two years her elder. The marriage was an unhappy one, and the daily pressure of the situation led her to withdraw on a regular basis into silent prayer and contemplation during the twelve years that her husband lived. Four years after his death, in 1681, she left her two surviving sons with family members, and with her daughter departed for the Duchy of Savoy near Geneva. There she gathered around her a community of *nouvelles Catholiques*, or converted Huguenots. The following year she completed her first book, *Les torrents spirituels* ("Spiritual Torrents"), which she initially circulated privately. Three years later, in 1685, one of her friends had her second book, *Moyen court et tres facile pour l'oraison* ("A Short and Very Easy Method of Prayer") published, making it available to a much larger, although not always sympathetic, audience. Other works eventually followed, including commentaries and a spiritual autobiography. Meanwhile Madame Guyon, along with several supporters, in 1686 moved to Paris.

Central to the Christian life, taught Madame Guyon, was the soul's contemplation of God. Such contemplation led to pure or disinterested love of God, and thereby to perfect union with God. The new life that resulted was one of perfection in which the soul no longer lived and worked on its own. Rather, it was God who lived and worked within it. The soul's perfection became God's perfection, and its love became God's love. Lost in the divine sea of love, one lived beyond the distinctions of action and meditation, or even virtue and meanness.

The climate in France was not the most favorable for these ideas. The year 1685 was the year that the Edict of Nantes was revoked, and Louis XIV was moving against any form of religious pluralism or toleration. The French ambassador to Rome played a major role in having Miguel de Molinos charged with heresy that same year. Three years later de Molinos was found guilty for teaching ideas that were similar to those of Madame Guyon. Such ideas could, and at times did, lead people to claim to have achieved spiritual perfection or spiritual maturity, so that they no longer needed the church's intervention through confession and the other sacraments. In addition, Madame Guyon quickly gained a considerable following, including some who were people of influence, many of them women. A movement that included influential women but also had the ear of the common folk was bound to be troubling to the king.

In 1688 she was arrested and held for several months until she published a retraction of her ideas. Even after her release, however, her writings continued to circulate and be read, and her circle of friends and followers continued to grow. Faced with increased opposition, she requested of the king in 1694 that a panel of judges review her writings for heresy. The panel was formed, and in 1695 returned with a verdict of guilty. Although she issued a second retraction, Madame Guyon was again imprisoned, this time for seven years in the Bastille. In 1703 she was finally released into the custody of her eldest son, with whom she lived quietly the final years of her life. Her works continued to be read by many, however, who found her spiritual teachings inspiring.

Three important movements within Protestantism

Protestantism in the seventeenth century was a diverse, dynamic, and at times balance-upsetting force. The impulses that gave rise to protesting Christians in Europe in the sixteenth century varied, as had the languages and national contexts in which these efforts of reform emerged. Although the various churches or groups recognized in one another, and were seen by Rome, which was usually their common enemy, to have a certain kinship, rarely were they able to unite. The paradox of the Protestant principle was that it championed the freedom to appropriate Christian faith in a personal and genuine way, but this brought with it the freedom to divide, often with acrimonious consequences. Added into the mix were the process of new European state formation that was taking place and the growing political aspirations of an increasingly wealthy merchant class. Both of these became important factors in the development of Protestant churches in the seventeenth century.

Cutting across the various national and confessional formations of the seventeenth century, one can discern several distinct streams or currents of spirituality that flowed through Protestant Christianity in the period. Arguably the dominant current, or at least the one that had the greatest political impact on both church and state in the era, was a stream that has come to be known as scholastic orthodoxy. This form of Protestantism focused on theological precision in confession. Its defenders were concerned to get their ideas right, then to pass along these correct ideas to church leaders and through them to the laity who made up the congregations of the church. True doctrine was considered to be the key to a healthy, or orthodox, Christianity.

Protestantism rejected the central, organizing office of a papacy that could ensure adherence to an orthodox standard, leading its advocates to go looking for an alternative source of authority. In the seventeenth century they found it in confessions, relatively brief summaries of what were considered to be essential theological beliefs that groups of congregations and church leaders agreed on and took to be authoritative and binding. Scholastic orthodoxy embraced such confessions as a means of protecting the church from grievous errors. It was the task of theologians of the church to expand on these confessions, providing clearly written summaries and elaborating on them by developing further their arguments. The model was the scholastic theologians of previous centuries, such as Thomas Aquinas. Indeed, the works of Protestant scholastic theologians read very much like Aquinas, with questions, possible answers, and the solution. By getting the doctrines correct, these Protestants believed, Christians would be able to live rightly. Right belief leads to right practice.

A second stream within Protestantism can be called the rise of "the religion of the heart." This stream shared much with the Catholic quietists and spiritual reformers examined above, and indeed there was considerable reading of one another's work and even dialogue among some of the major figures. Proponents of religion of the heart were never mere sentimentalists, but were concerned to recover the experience, purity, and completeness of faith that was expressed in piety and works of charity. Whereas Protestant scholastics turned to Aristotelian logic to argue their case, proponents of religion of the heart sought to reason more affectively and in more personal terms.

The English Puritans declared that they wanted to purify the English church of external practices that they deemed to be "papish," that is Roman, and idolatrous, or what the Puritans deemed to be the improper use of images. What these English Puritans were ultimately concerned about, however, was a genuine inner experience of Christian life that did not rest on what they considered to be external formalities. In a similar manner, German Pietists, who will be examined below, sought to recover what they considered to be the more mystical and experiential dimensions of Luther's teachings, rooted in earlier German mystical writers. Pietists acknowledged the need for a church to adhere to correct doctrine, but they were more concerned with how Christians lived their lives. Like the emerging scientists of their age, they emphasized the experiential or experimental process, and looked for results that could be observed. Truth was found in experience, they believed, and could be observed in actions. True religion was a matter of the heart, they said, not the head, as they supposed their scholastic counterparts to believe.

English Puritans and German Pietists placed considerable emphasis on personal devotional practices and the need for an individual appropriation of faith. They taught and expected members of the church to have an inward experience such as that described by the mystics. But both the Puritans and the Pietists remained firmly committed to the church and to its external sacramental practices. Some went further along the lines of inward religion, however, weakening considerably their emphasis on external sacraments, scripture, or church authorities. They often made their appeal to immediate forms of divine inspiration, sometimes received in the form of dreams or from an inner voice. The Quakers, for instance, taught that everyone had within them an inner light.

Closely associated with what might be called the "inner light" stream of spirituality was one that took on more apocalyptic forms of expression and belief. Millennialism had long been a factor in Western Christianity. Millennial expectations flourished among some of the early Protestant groups. In the seventeenth century millennialism began to grow in a number of new directions, especially among Calvinists who in the previous century had not been particularly open to such beliefs. Millennialists looked for the return of Christ or the inauguration of his reign on earth, many taking these to be imminent. Some took the work of the church to be participation in the building of this kingdom, while others were more pessimistic about the possibility of such endeavors. At times, as seen in the English revolution, their political theology could lend support to revolutionary efforts against what they considered to be "worldly" or unspiritual government. Over the course of the seventeenth century currents of mission and millennialism began to merge, creating a new sense of urgency in mission.

The third current of Protestant spirituality grew out of a desire to see religion reformed along the lines of the new view of the world that was emerging from the work of scientists and mathematicians. The roots of this stream reached back into the humanist tradition of previous centuries. In the seventeenth century its adherents began to challenge traditional Christian doctrines such as the Trinity more forcefully. Its chief articulations often came in the form of philosophy rather than theology, an indication of the manner in which its advocates sought to move from special to more general forms of revelation as a basis for understanding and the truth. Deists, early Unitarians, and even the work of the philosopher John Locke (1632-1704) were specific instances of this particular stream.

Developments in German Lutheranism

Lutheran churches in the first half of the seventeenth century struggled to survive. Germany, its historic homeland, was a political patchwork of independent states and free cities. Several German states had banded together to form the

Evangelical Union in 1608. Austria, Bohemia, and other parts of eastern Europe were under Habsburg rulers who claimed the title of Holy Roman Emperor because of their descent from Emperor Ferdinand I (1503-1564), younger brother of Charles V (1500-1558). The Habsburgs were Roman Catholic, but they had earlier accepted Protestant churches in areas where the rulers were Lutheran. By 1610 that was changing. As noted earlier, a revolt by Protestants in Bohemia against the effort to install Catholic administrators in the government in 1618 ignited a war that would last for three decades. In 1630, as Protestant forces were about to collapse, King Gustaf II Adolf of Sweden (or Gustavus Adolphus Magnus, 1594-1632), with help from the French, invaded. Swedish forces took and then occupied much of central Germany for more than a decade until the Peace of Westphalia brought the war to an end.

Lutheran churches in Germany had been united since 1580 by the *Book of Concord.* In some places where Lutherans and Calvinists lived side by side, in the sixteenth century ministers had moved easily back and forth between the two traditions. Theologians met for common discussions, and congregations even shared resources. By 1600, however, the lines of identity had significantly hardened. Lutherans and Calvinists proved to be bitter opponents of each other. To protect any tendencies toward Calvinism on the one side and Roman Catholicism on the other, especially in light of the aggressive missionary work of the Jesuits, Lutheran church leaders sought to ensure that pastors and lay people alike were properly informed regarding the emerging dogmatic differences among them. Older patterns of scholastic argumentation re-emerged in what was self-consciously for many a theology of retrenchment.

Among the notable Lutheran theologians of the period was Johann Gerhardt (1582-1637). Gerhardt studied at the universities of Wittenberg, Jena, and Marburg, and later taught at Heidelberg and then Jena. Involved both in practical church matters and theology, his writings included works of a polemical, dogmatic, and practical nature. His most important work was a nine-volume *Loci communes theologicae* ("Topics of Theology"), published between 1610 and 1622. In these volumes he provided an exhaustive explanation and defense of Lutheran doctrine and practice, using Aristotelian logic and scriptural proofs. He was one of the first to formally locate the doctrine of scripture at the beginning of a theological system, for scripture anchored the rest of theology. Gerhardt argued a theory of inspiration that extended all the way to the Hebrew vowel points, a position that his Roman Catholic opponents easily exploited since those vowel points were provided by Jewish rabbis who edited the Hebrew Masoretic text many centuries after the close of the Christian canon. Like most Lutherans of his day, Gerhardt combined academic scholarship with personal piety and pastoral sensitivities. He was known for maintaining daily devotions with his family, but also for visiting his students in their homes when they were ill. His most widely read work was *Meditationes sacrae* ("Sacred Meditations"), written when he was only twenty-two.

At the age of fourteen, Gerhardt came under the influence of the writings of another German Lutheran, Johann Arndt (1555-1621). Arndt had studied at the universities of Helmstadt, Wittenberg, Strasbourg, and Basel (the last an institution whose faculty were Reformed) before becoming a pastor. Exposed by his travels through Germany and Switzerland to both Lutheran and Calvinist doctrines, he looked for an irenic means of bridging their differences. Arndt was also concerned to combat the more general condition of what he described as the impenitent life, whereby people could confess Christian belief yet lead what he considered to be an un-Christian life. In this regard he had little use for scholasticism, for orthodox doctrine alone could not renew Christian life in the churches. Arndt was accused by some of his contemporaries for harboring unorthodox opinions, but this was not true. He clearly was within the confessional boundaries of Lutheranism. His main concern was to reinvigorate Lutheran churches with a less sterile and contentious theology, recovering something of the spirit of Martin Luther's own original mystical theology.

Arndt's best-known work was *Vier Bücher vom wahren Christentum* ("True Christianity in Four Books"), published in the years 1605 to 1610. The work came to exercise an enormous influence after his own life, reaching far beyond the borders of Lutheranism to Roman Catholic readers on one side of the European Christian spectrum and Mennonites on the other. Arndt organized the work loosely along the lines of what he perceived to be the Christian order of salvation. The book was intended to be an aid to growth in Christian faith, or to the unfolding of salvation in the Christian life. True Christianity brought about renewal of individual lives, the churches, and even the nation, he believed. While he did not shy away from criticizing other theological ideas, he generally tried to avoid as much as possible polemical or controversial statements. His main concern was for the development of the inner Christian life in daily practice.

The popularity of *True Christianity* continued to grow long after Arndt's death, with translations soon appearing in several European languages. When the publishers in Germany wanted to issue a new edition in 1674, they turned to a younger scholar named Philipp Jakob Spener (1635-1705) to write a new introduction. Spener was educated in Strasbourg and was serving as a Lutheran pastor in Frankfurt. The year after the new edition of Arndt's *True Christianity* appeared, Spener's own work, *Pia desideria* ("Pious Desires"), was published.

As a pastor, Spener shared many of Arndt's concerns about what appeared to him to be deficiencies in the spiritual life of the common people, clergy, and even civil authorities of his time. He saw the possibility of change, however, and offered his own constructive proposals as a conclusion. Several of these measures, including the organization of *collegia pietatis,* or small meetings of church members who gathered in homes for study and discussion, and *Kinderlehre,* or children's classes on Sunday afternoons, he had already begun to implement. Such gatherings, argued Spener, should occupy Christians instead of gambling, drinking, and other impious activities. Sermons ought to address practical concerns rather than more dogmatic issues. The Bible ought to be at the center of Christian life and devotion. Lay members of the congregation needed to be more involved in decision making and leadership. Love rather than disputation should be at the top of the theological agenda.

Spener's work was not without its detractors. Critics targeted in particular the *collegia pietatis,* or small group meeting. His opponents argued that the sermon was the best means of advancing Christian faith, and that allowing members of the church, including women, to gather and to discuss theology or the Bible could easily lead to doctrinal deviations. Civil authorities in some places forbade church members to gather in such ways because they perceived in them a potential threat to civil order, especially if women were involved. Nevertheless, Spener's work persisted, and throughout Germany the reforming ways of what were being derisively called "Pietists" started to take hold.

Developments in Reformed Churches in continental Europe

Churches that identified themselves as part of the Reformed movement and that followed the teachings of John Calvin took root in the sixteenth century in Switzerland, southern Germany, parts of Bohemia, various parts of France, throughout the Netherlands, and across England and Scotland. They organized themselves for the most part along regional or national lines according to the various national language bodies that had emerged over several hundred years of cultural history in Europe. There was considerable communication among the leadership of these churches. One of the most important developments they undertook to institutionalize from the sixteenth century was the formation of collective bodies of ruling elders and pastors that took the place of a bishop or bishops in their midst as the head of the church.

Reformed theology in the Netherlands in the last decades of the sixteenth century became identified with the nationalist struggle against Spanish rule. The formation of the Union of Utrecht in 1568 had been a major step toward open rebellion against Spain. Spanish forces had retaken the southern region of the Netherlands, but the northern provinces, with their growing merchant class, maintained relative independence. These merchants, as noted in an earlier chapter, formed the Dutch East India Company in 1602.

By 1600 a second and even third generation of Calvinist theologians were at work in universities across the Netherlands. A more moderating spirit was on the loose throughout the region. Jacobus Arminius (1559-1609) was one of the most able minds among them. Originally from Oudewater, his birth name was Jacob Harmenszoon. Oudewater was one of the cities that had declared independence from Spain, and most of his family was killed in 1575 when Spanish forces retook the town and killed most of its inhabitants. Arminius used the Latin form of his name thereafter, in part to obscure his Dutch national identity. After completing studies at Leiden, Geneva (with Theodore Beza), and Basel, Arminius returned to the Netherlands in 1588 and became a pastor in Amsterdam. In 1603 he became a professor in theology at the University of Leiden. His lectures on the nature of salvation soon landed him at the center of controversy.

Arminius challenged the position held by his teacher, Beza, and most other followers of Calvin that God unconditionally elects a limited number of human beings for salvation. A year following his death in 1609, a group of his followers issued a *Remonstrantiae,* summarizing their position. They were soon being called "Remonstrants" (Protesters), a term that echoed the first generation of sixteenth-century evangelical reformers who also stood over against an estab-lished view of theology. The Remonstrants argued that the human will is free and may act to decide for God in the process of salvation. Salvation comes through the preaching of God's word, but its realization, and thus the Christian's election, is conditional insofar as it is based on the human being's response to God. God foreknows what each person's response will be without predetermining it. Salva-tion is open to all human beings, since Jesus' sacrifice was for all people. Human beings can resist God's grace in the offer of salvation, however, and even those who come to believe may turn away and thereby lose their salvation.

A synod was called by four of the seven of the United Provinces in 1618 to meet in Dordrecht (Dort) to respond to the 1610 statement. An international del-egation of Reformed scholars representing eight countries met over the course of six months. A number of members of the Remonstrants party appeared before the gathering to argue their case. At the conclusion of its work the synod issued a statement in Latin titled *Iudicium synodi nationalis, reformatarum ecclesiarum Belgicarum, habitae Dordrechti anno 1618 & 1619* ("Decision of the National Synod of Reformed Churches of the Netherlands in Dort in 1618 and 1619"), or simply *Canones Synodi Dordrechtanae* ("Canons of the Synod of Dort"), which was soon translated into several European languages. The statement responded to each of the five points of the Remonstrants' platform. Human beings are totally depraved as a result of original sin. God's election is unconditional and does not in any sense depend on human choice. The effects of the atonement of Jesus Christ are limited to those who belong to the elect. God's grace is irresistible, and God will assure that those who are members of the elect will persevere in their salvation to eternal salvation. These five points quickly became a touchstone of Calvinistic orthodoxy throughout northern Europe, due in part to the interna-tional representation at the synod. Several supporters of the Remonstrants were imprisoned, and one of their leaders, Johan van Oldenbarnevelt (1547-1619), was beheaded for treason.

One of the supporters of the Remonstrants was the person who would become known as the "father of international law," Hugo Grotius (or de Groot, 1583-1645). Grotius was legal advisor to the Land's Advocate of Holland, the head of the most powerful of the various states that made up the Netherlands. In the years immediately following the Synod of Dort, the Remonstrants continued to be supported by some of the more powerful political figures in the Netherlands. Grotius joined the effort, arguing for greater religious toleration. He succeeded only in solidifying the opposition, which by now included Maurice of Nassau, the Prince of Orange (1567-1625), the son of William the Silent. Grotius, along with van Oldenbarnevelt and several others who supported the Remonstrants, was arrested in 1618. Grotius was sentenced to life in prison in a castle. Three years later with the help of his wife he escaped and fled to Paris. He remained in exile from the Netherlands for the rest of his life.

In 1609 while he was still in the Netherlands Grotius published *Mare liberum* ("Free Sea"). In its pages he argued that the seas are open territory and therefore free for all nations to use. The principle eventually became the cornerstone of international law regarding the open seas. Grotius also made a major contribution to natural law and just war theory in his book *De jure belli ac pacis* ("Of Laws of War and Peace"), a volume published in 1625 that he wrote while in Paris, in the midst of the Eighty Years War between Spain and the Netherlands and the Thirty Years War in central Europe. *De jure belli ac pacis* was noteworthy in that its arguments rested not on biblical or Christian principles but on natural laws that Grotius believed could be shown to be common to all humanity. A later work in Christian theology, *De veritate religionis Christianae* ("On the Truth of Christianity"), that was published in 1627 sought to solve some of the major conflicts among the various branches of Christianity by similarly finding common ground. Regarding the doctrine of the atonement, Grotius offered in that volume what came to be called the "governmental" or "moral example" theory regarding Christ's suffering and death. Christ's death, he argued, was God's way of demonstrating to the world divine displeasure with sin and was primarily ethical in its implications.

Another important Dutch theologian from the years following the Synod of Dort was Johannes Cocceius (1603-1669). Cocceius was originally from Bremen. After completing his studies at the universities of Franeker and Hamburg, he launched on a career as a scholar, teaching Bible and theology at Franeker and then later at the University of Leiden. Cocceius was one of the first to systematize Calvin's covenantal themes biblically, developing a full-fledged covenantal, or federal, theology. The notion that God's grace is dispensed in human history through distinct covenants went back at least to St. Augustine. Cocceius took these ideas and worked them out as a full-fledged biblical theology.

One of Cocceius's conclusions was that Sabbath observance was a Jewish practice and not strictly binding on Christians. The position brought him considerable opposition, most notably from Gijsbert Voetius (1589-1676). A delegate at the Synod of Dort, Voetius is usually remembered for his vigorous defense of scholastic methods in theology and for his opposition to the new ideas of René Descartes. His four-volume *Politica ecclesiastica* ("Church Polity"), which was published from 1663 to 1676, offered a defense of Reformed polity and explored a variety of issues in the training of ministers and in the work of the church. Voetius was also one of the first Reformed theologians to work out a full-fledged theology of missions, arguing that Christians needed to seek to plant new churches in regions where there were currently no existing Christian communities. He encouraged Dutch trading companies to sponsor missions as part of their work, laying the foundations for Protestant overseas missions from the Netherlands in the seventeenth century.

Voetius taught for a number of years at the University of Utrecht. One of his students was Anna Maria van Schurman (1607-1678), who in 1636 became the first woman ever to be admitted to a university in Holland. Born in Cologne, she moved as a child to Utrecht before entering the university, where she studied law and became proficient in Greek, Latin, Hebrew, Arabic, and Syriac. With Jean de Labadie (1610-1674), a French Jesuit who had converted to Calvinism, van Schurman eventually formed a community in Amsterdam devoted to contemplation and prayer. Her book *Dissertatio de ingenii muliebris* ("Whether a Christian

Woman Should Be Educated"), which first appeared in 1640, challenged traditional social roles ascribed to women.

In Switzerland, which provided the initial home for Reformed theology, one of the most influential scholastic theologians of the seventeenth century was Francis Turretin (1623-1687). Turretin was born and raised in Geneva, where his grandparents, who were originally from Italy, had moved several decades earlier after becoming Protestants. Francis had studied with a number of influential Reformed theologians in Geneva, Paris, Utrecht, and elsewhere before returning to Geneva to become the pastor of the Italian-speaking congregation there in 1648. Several years later he was appointed a professor at the university.

During his time in Paris, Turretin earned a name for himself as a theologian in his controversy with Moise Amyrault (1596-1664), a Huguenot who challenged the notion of a limited atonement to argue that the death of Christ was sufficient to cover the sins of all humanity. Turretin rigorously defended the Synod of Dort on this point, as he did on all other matters of doctrine. His own mature system, *Institutio theologiae elencticae* ("Institutes of Elenctic Theology," that is, "theology serving to refute") was published in three volumes from 1679 to 1685 and is nearly 1,800 pages in length. It stands as the most complete systematic exposition of Calvinist scholastic theology in the seventeenth century.

Reformed theology was clearly entering a new stage of development by the last decades of the century as theologians of the movement in England, the Netherlands, Scotland, and Switzerland sought to build on Calvin's work. The *Formula consensus ecclesiarum Helveticarum* ("Formula of Consensus of the Church of Helvetica"), which was published in 1675, marked a significant milestone in the development of Reformed scholasticism. John Henry Heidegger of Zurich (1633-1698) was its primary author, although he had help from Turretin and Lucas Gernler (1625-1675) from Basel. Most in Reformed Churches in Switzerland received it as being a continuation of the *Confessio Helvetica prior* ("First Helvetic Confession") of 1536 and *Confessio Helvetica posterior* ("Second Helvetic Confession") of 1562. The 1675 *Consensus* asserted that the inspiration of scripture extended to the letters in the original words of the biblical text, parsed the doctrine of original sin carefully regarding the manner by which its effects are communicated to all humankind, and limited salvation to the nation of Israel in the first dispensation and the church in the second.

One of the more ecumenically minded figures from the beginning of the seventeenth century was David Pareus of Heidelberg (1548-1622). A student of Zacharias Ursinus (1534-1583), Pareus served as a pastor before joining the faculty at Heidelberg in 1598. His book of 1614, *Irenicum, sive de unione et synodo evangelicorum concilianda liber votivus, paci ecclesiae et desideriis pacificorum dicatus,* argued that there was sufficient agreement on matters of essential doctrine between Lutherans and Calvinists for the two traditions to unite. To this end he called for a general evangelical synod. Pareus's plea was ignored by most of his contemporaries, but it represents an important early ecumenical Protestant effort.

A different kind of ecumenical voice in the period belonged to Jan Amos Comenius (1592-1670). Originally from Czechoslovakia, Comenius was a pastor among the Brethren, a community that traced its roots back to Jan Hus in the fifteenth century. Forced by the Thirty Years War to become a refugee, he spent several decades traveling through Sweden, Poland, Hungary, Germany, and England before spending his final days in the Netherlands. Comenius was one of the first persons to advocate universal education for all children, a position he first set forth in his book *Didactica magna* ("The Great Didactic") in 1633. His book *Orbis Pictus* ("The World in Pictures"), a textbook for children that he published in 1658, is considered by many to be the first children's book to include pictures.

Anabaptists

Anabaptists had been among the most severely persecuted religious groups in continental Europe in the sixteenth century. By the end of the century one of the Anabaptist groups, the Mennonites, had emerged as relatively stable. Their churches were throughout the Netherlands, in several cantons in Switzerland, and in a small area of Germany. One of the Mennonite leaders in Switzerland, Jakob Ammann (1644?-1730), in 1693 began an effort to reform the community in Bern. Discipline among the faithful was being relaxed, he complained. Specifically, he argued, the practice of "shunning" (*Meidung*), in which members of the community refused even to speak to someone who has been judged to have grievously sinned until the person has sufficiently repented, needed to be restored. Ammann believed that the practice needed to be applied even to married members, meaning the couple would need to separate if one were "under the ban." Ammann also held strict views on personal appearance, calling for untrimmed beards for men and uniformity in dress for both genders. He disallowed any attendance in a state-sponsored church, and argued that only Amish would be saved. Many other Mennonites felt that his position was too strict, leading to a division within the ranks of the church. Followers of Ammann, who became known as Amish, moved first in Germany, and then migrated for greater freedom to a new colony called Pennsylvania in North America beginning in the 1730s.

Reformed ferment and civil war in England

The death of Elizabeth I in 1603 in England marked the end of the reign of the House of Tudor. Elizabeth had no heirs, so members of her government turned to James VI of Scotland (1566-1625), who became James I of England as well. During his rule the English language witnessed some of the greatest literary accomplishments in its history, including the works of William Shakespeare (c. 1564-1616), and in 1611 the publication of a new translation of the Bible that James had commissioned. The translation, which came to be known as the King James Bible, soon became the standard English version. James's rule was also marked by increasing tensions with parliament, which he eventually refused to convene. Before assuming the throne of England he had already published several works arguing for a stronger theory of a sovereign monarch. The rule of kings, he argued, was grounded in authority that derived directly from God. His views clashed with a growing body of political thought that held the authority of kings to be derived from the authority of the lesser members of the nobility who elected them and supported them in their rule.

James continued Elizabeth's policy of restricting the Roman Catholic religion, especially for those who refused to take an oath of allegiance to the English crown. Several attempts on his life by supporters of the restoration of the Roman Catholic Church in England only served to harden his resolve. On the other hand, James was cautious in his dealing with Puritans. Puritan leaders had at first hoped the new king would bring changes that they supported, but soon their hopes were dashed. The number of dissenting church bodies was growing, and James took a harder stand against them, although later in his reign he relaxed many of the restrictions.

James's greatest problems were financial. Without parliament, he had no effective way to raise taxes. Poor management of the royal finances and growing inflation throughout Europe, caused in part by the increase in circulation of gold that came from America, took their toll. By the time his son, Charles I (1600-1649), came to power in 1625, the royal finances were on the verge of bankruptcy. Charles asserted even more forcefully than his father the doctrine of the absolute power of monarchs, a move that alienated many among the nobility. Shortly after ascending to the throne he married Henriette-Marie de France (1609-1669), the daughter of King Henry IV (1553-1610) of France and a devout Roman Catholic. The marriage only served to further alienate many of his subjects. Unable to raise funds, and with a noncompliant parliament, Charles sought to impose a new set of shipping taxes on coastal towns.

Events reached a crisis point in 1639 when Charles's efforts to impose episcopal rule on the churches in Scotland led to war between the two nations. Faced with the need to fund his campaign against the Scots, Charles was forced to call parliament back into session. Once seated, parliament in 1641 passed an act that declared it could not be dissolved without its own consent, providing it with a legal basis to continue to meet apart from the king's declaration. At the end of the year it presented the king with a list of grievances and ordered the archbishop of Canterbury, William Laud (1573-1645), imprisoned for his strenuous opposition to the Puritan cause. The following year, open civil war broke out between supporters of parliament and supporters of the crown.

Over the next four years the two sides fought throughout England. Parliament continued to meet at Westminster Palace while Charles was forced to leave London. In 1645 parliament ordered the execution of Archbishop Laud. The following year the royal army was decisively defeated, and Charles I was imprisoned. From his prison cell, however, the king continued to communicate with his supporters. Two years later war broke out again between forces loyal to the king and forces supporting parliament. Lured into battle on the royal side by the promise of a presbyterian form of government for their churches, an army from Scotland joined the side of Charles I. Following the defeat of the combined Scottish and royal forces in 1648, parliament this time tried the king for treason. In 1649 Charles I was executed.

Following the execution, parliament declared England to be a commonwealth under republican government and without a king. One of its members, a Puritan named Oliver Cromwell (1599-1658), who had risen through military rank in battle, was commissioned to invade Ireland with the purpose of bringing it back under English rule. The conquest of Roman Catholic Ireland was brutal. With Ireland under English military control, Cromwell then invaded Scotland in 1651, defeating its armies and imposing direct English rule there as well. Two years later Cromwell dissolved parliament and declared himself Lord Protector of the Commonwealth. This lasted until his death in 1658, when parliament reconvened, abolished the protectorate, restored a limited monarchy, and invited Charles II (1630-1685), the son of the executed king, to return from exile in the Netherlands and assume his father's throne. The Act of Uniformity passed in 1662 restored episcopal rule throughout the Church of England, and restored the *Book of Common Prayer* in worship.

The English Civil War marked the apex of Puritan ascendency in English political life. Early in the first years of war, the Puritans, who dominated in parliament, called for an assembly to make changes in English church life. Charles I refused to sign the act, but parliament proceeded on its own to appoint members and convene the assembly, which met in the church known as Westminster Abbey, thereby giving the gathering the name the "Westminster Assembly." Over the next nine years some 150 clergy persons and 30 lay persons met in more than 1,000 sessions. Some Scottish theologians participated, but for the most part the body was made up of English church leaders. Puritans dominated the assembly, with most favoring a presbyterian form of government, although there were some congregationalists represented among them as well. No supporters of the episcopal form of church government attended, and no representatives of groups that advocated separation of church and state were participants.

Parliament originally charged the assembly with revising the *Thirty-Nine Articles* of the Church of England, but within a year the body's mandate was expanded to examine more broadly matters of church discipline and governance, and to introduce a more thoroughly Reformed theological perspective into the life of the churches in England. Among the documents that the assembly produced along these lines were a new *Directory for the Public Worship of God, The Westminster Confession of Faith*, and both a *Larger* and a *Shorter Catechism* designed for religious instruction and formation.

The documents of the Westminster Assembly, produced in the midst of a revolutionary context, represent the high-water mark of English-speaking Reformed scholasticism. In rational, rhythmic questions and answers, the *Shorter Catechism* moves from the most general doctrine of the chief end for humanity (which is "To love God and enjoy him forever") to consideration of the advent of sin, election, redemption, Christology, the meaning of each of the Ten Commandments, and the meaning of the Lord's Prayer. The *Westminster Confession* covered matters of belief, church life, and the relationship of the church to civil authorities. Its carefully crafted arguments defined Christian life in rational and scholastic terms that were intended to govern a national church. After the Restoration in 1661, however, congregations that were part of the Church of England abandoned the *Westminster Confession* and returned to the *Thirty-Nine Articles* as their standard for doctrine. Those nonconforming congregations that adhered to a presbyterian form of governance but were not part of the established state church continued to look to the *Westminster Confession* as their standard.

The period of the English Civil War was a time of great religious ferment. As the social order was dissolving, a number of "prophets" arose to give voice to new millennial expectations. In 1640 the office of censorship collapsed and publishing simply exploded throughout England. In 1640 there were virtually no newspapers in the land, but by 1645 there were over seven hundred publications that offered news of current events. In the two-year period between 1640 and 1642, the number of books published in England grew almost one hundredfold. Most of these works were religious treatises. It was also a period of great democratization in literacy and publishing. Most of the twenty thousand books printed in England between 1640 and 1660 were written by those whom the university-educated considered "illiterates."

Many of these new voices claimed to have received visions from God, or to have received special revelations about how to live. Some, like the London tailor named Lodowicke Muggleton (1609-1698), who taught a form of quietism and claimed to receive direct revelations, attained a moderate following, in his case called Muggletonians. Others were joined together loosely, as in the case of the Ranters, who were often accused of radical antinomianism, or the Seekers, who were anticlerical. Between 1649 and 1651 the Diggers sought to create agrarian communes and abolish private property, while the Fifth Monarchists believed that the English Civil War was ushering in the final apocalyptic battle and would lead through violent revolution to the establishment of the millennial reign of Christ on earth.

The Quakers

Among the most important of the new spiritual movements that emerged from this period was a body of believers who were led by George Fox (1624-1691). Fox was raised in the Church of England. At the age of eleven he had an experience of conversion, but by the age of nineteen was recording his painful longings for a more vital experience of the Spirit, and for a purer and more dedicated church. Plagued by the inconsistencies he perceived all around him between religious profession and practice, Fox was encouraged by family and friends to seek the counsel of a priest. The experience only convinced him further of the corruption of the church, and instead this apprenticed shoemaker looked inward.

Fox began to spend long periods of time in meditation through which he came to what he considered to be a greater understanding of God. He called these sessions "openings." In them, he later reported, he would hear a voice that he identified as belonging to God, or to Jesus Christ, instructing him about an issue or a particular decision he should make. He believed that these experiences were instances of direct revelation, and that they were available to all human beings.

Although he was without any formal education, Fox began to speak publicly about these experiences in 1648. His preaching took him out into the open fields, in town markets, and even in "steeple-houses," as he called church buildings. He proclaimed a message of primitive Christian simplicity and began to develop a following of "children of the light," or "friends" as he called them. His message included a call to women to preach, an idea that was quite at odds with the dominant religious order of the day.

Fox believed that the true light of God was available to all human beings inwardly. People of all religions, not just Christians, could experience it if they sought it. At their meetings his followers would gather in silence and wait for the Spirit to speak through anyone in attendance. They were soon being called Quakers, at first a derogatory term that was attached to them either because members were said to quake when the Spirit came upon them, or, as another tradition has it, because an English judge once said he quaked when Fox was brought before him on charges and warned the judge that he should tremble at the word of the Lord. Those in the movement preferred the title the Religious Society of Friends, and simply to be known as Friends.

Fox taught that the inner light of Christ could be found in all people. At Quaker meetings women, as well as men, were allowed to speak when the Spirit moved them. This allowed women to have a much greater ministry in the Society of Friends than they could practice in any other religious community in Europe in the seventeenth century. One of the major women figures among the first generation of Friends was Margaret Fell (1614-1702). A member of the upper class, she met Fox in 1652 and soon afterward had opened her home, Swarthmoor Hall, located in northwestern England, to hold Quaker meetings. In 1664 she was imprisoned for refusing to take an oath. During her incarceration she wrote a brief pamphlet titled *Women's Speaking Justified* in which she defended the practice of women preaching the gospel. Toward the end of their lives Fox and Fell married, although they were not able to spend much time together mostly because of Fox's constant travels on behalf of the Society.

Like many spiritual teachers who were from among the less-educated and economically lower social classes, Fox had a strong social message. He criticized the moral injustice of judges and spoke against the oppression of the poor. He also spoke against taking up arms in warfare, recognizing social rank, and swearing oaths, including those of loyalty to a king. His activities landed him in prison on a number of occasions, which he took to be an opportunity to come into closer contact with the common people. By the early 1660s, as many as one thousand of his followers had joined him in being imprisoned for their beliefs. Still the movement grew, and not just among the poor. A number of merchants and other influential members of society joined the ranks of the movement. Some of Fox's followers traveled to America, where they sought to spread their message. Fox himself in 1671 traveled to Barbados and Jamaica in the Caribbean, and then to Maryland in North America where he met with Native Americans, whom he said also had the light of the Spirit of God in them. By the time he died, the Society of Friends, or Quakers, could be found in England, the Netherlands, the Caribbean, and North America.

Three years after his death, Fox's *Journal*, which detailed many of his visions and the words received from God and served as an important foundation for Quaker teaching, was brought into print by a member of the Society named William Penn (1644-1718). Penn's father had been an admiral in the English navy and had extensive land holdings in Ireland. At the age of twenty-two William underwent a conversion and joined the Society of Friends, which led his family to throw him out of their house. Penn and Fox became close colleagues, and Penn began to write tracts for the movement. He ended up in prison several times in the 1660s, and was released only when his father paid a fine.

In 1682 Penn proposed a plan to Charles II intended to assist the Quaker cause. The king owed a large debt to the estate of William Penn's now-deceased father. In return for the debt, Penn proposed Charles award him a sizable land grant in North America, to which members of the Quakers as well as other dissenting groups could immigrate. Thus was founded the colony of Pennsylvania ("Penn's Woods"). Penn intended it to be a place open to people of other religions, and without slavery.

Baptists and the emergence of the Free Church ideal

Among the most important movements that emerged from seventeenth-century England to become a major new force in world Christianity were the Baptists. In 1609 in Amsterdam the leader of an English-speaking congregation named John Smyth (1570-1612) came to the conviction that baptism is valid only if it follows upon the individual's profession of faith. The members of the congregation were separatists who had emigrated from England to avoid imprisonment because of their opposition to government control of the church. Smyth had been ordained in the Church of England, but in the Netherlands had encountered Mennonites and had become convinced of the propriety of their position on baptism. Without a recognized clergy person to perform the rite, Smyth first baptized himself, then his entire congregation.

Several years later a member of Smyth's congregation who was a merchant, Thomas Helwys (c. 1575-1616), took the lead in writing a confessional statement for the congregation. *A Declaration of Faith of English People Remaining at Amsterdam in Holland*, which is often regarded as the first English Baptist confessional statement, was first published in 1611. The following year Helwys returned with a small group of the congregation to England to found the first Baptist congregation in London. Helwys was quickly imprisoned, where he died four years later. Nevertheless, the notion of a separated church, that is, free from government control, made up of members who had been baptized after a public profession of faith took root.

Most of the first generation of Baptist leaders in England embraced the doctrine of the general atonement identified with the Remonstrant party in the Netherlands. Salvation was open to anyone who chose to believe in Christ, they believed. These Baptists followed John Smyth in adhering to a strict congregational form of polity that did not recognize any authoritative body or bishop beyond the local congregation. Without any central authority to enforce doctrinal teaching, a number of Baptists began to embrace the dominant Calvinist position, which held the atonement was particular, which is to say, it extends to cover the sins only of those who were predestined or elected by God. In 1644, in the midst of the English Civil War and excluded by parliament from the Westminster Assembly, leaders from seven of these particular Baptist churches in London drew up what became known as the *London Baptist Confession.*

Over the next decade several revised editions of this original *Confession* were issued by gatherings of Baptist leaders. The Restoration in 1662 brought a new time of persecution. In 1677 a group of Baptist leaders again gathered in London to forge a new *Confession,* but were prevented from making it public for another twelve years. In 1689 some one hundred Baptist church leaders endorsed and published the 1677 document, which is now generally known as the *Baptist Confession of Faith of 1689.* What are often called the "Baptist distinctives" are set out clearly in this document. "God alone is Lord of the Conscience, and hath left it free from the Doctrines and Commandments of men," states Article 21. The true church is a gathered congregation whose members are baptized after a profession of faith. The two ordinances of the church (so-called because Christ clearly ordered or "ordained" them) are baptism and the Lord's Supper. The two offices of leadership in the local church are bishops or elders and deacons. On matters regarding controversy in matters of either doctrine or administration, churches that are in communion with one another are to elect messengers who meet to advise on such matters, but such bodies do not exercise administrative rule.

One of the most influential Baptist writers of the Restoration was John Bunyan (1628-1688). The son of a poor family of tinkers who made their living mending household pots, Bunyan spent time in Cromwell's army before turning to a religious vocation and being ordained as a deacon in 1655. Although lacking a formal education, he began preaching in Baptist churches and gained a considerable following. After the Restoration, Charles II began imposing new restrictions on nonconforming religious worship services. Late in 1660 Bunyan was arrested for preaching without a license and sent to prison. Twice he was released, only to be reimprisoned for his nonconformist preaching, until 1675 when Charles II began to relax the strict prohibitions. During the last decade of his life Bunyan returned to lead his congregation, which grew considerably in size. His sermons often criticized the ways of the wealthy and lifted up the place of the poor in God's kingdom.

While in prison Bunyan began writing the work that would enter his name in the registry of great spiritual literature, *The Pilgrim's Progress from this World to That Which Is to Come; Delivered under the Similitude of a Dream Wherein Is Discovered the Manner of His Setting Out, His Dangerous Journey, and Safe Arrival at the Desired Country.* The allegory tells the story of a traveler named Christian, who, directed by one named Evangelist, journeys from the City of Destruction through numerous difficulties and challenges to eventually arrive at the Celestial City, which is the goal of the soul.

Bunyan's Christian pilgrim was journeying through the period of the Restoration. Toward the end of it Charles II had again succeeded in dismissing parliament and re-establishing strong monarchical rule. Charles II died in 1685 and was succeeded on the throne by his brother, James II (1633-1701), who held even stronger views on the absolute power of the monarch. A decade before James publicly acknowledged his earlier embrace of Roman Catholicism, which meant that a Roman Catholic now was head of the Church of England. In 1687 James issued the "Declaration of Indulgence," which called for relaxation of all restrictions on Roman Catholic and nonconforming churches alike. Alarmed by the act, the archbishop of Canterbury and six other bishops protested. James had them arrested for sedition.

Several members of the nobility then appealed to the royal couple William of Orange from the Netherlands (1650-1702) and Mary (1662-1694), who was the daughter of James II, to intervene. William and Mary agreed to invade, and in 1688 landed on English soil. Seeing most of his army deserting him, James abdicated and left for France. In 1689 William and Mary were declared by parliament to be the joint rulers of England. Scotland and Ireland were soon added to their reign. The so-called Glorious Revolution was complete.

Religious toleration in England

Before the year was out parliament passed the Act of Toleration. For the first time, a number of nonconformist groups were recognized. Their members were still required to take an oath of allegiance to the throne, thereby continuing the legal exclusion of Quakers. Roman Catholics were not granted full recognition, but restrictions on Catholics even came to be relaxed. Clearly in England the notion was emerging that even though one church was established, the social order could tolerate a number of what were beginning to be called "denominations." Belonging to a particular church was a matter of choice that an individual was considered free to make. Religious toleration and a plurality of Christian denominations were seen as going hand in hand.

Two significant English philosophers from the second half of the seventeenth century contributed significantly to shaping the broader transformation in religious thinking that was taking place during this period. The first emerged from the period of the English Civil War. Reason had championed science and invention but had also given rise to skepticism and doubt. None saw this with greater clarity than Thomas Hobbes (1588-1679). A strict materialist, he understood "spirit" to be another term for "mind" or "intellect" or "will," and religion to be entirely a matter of morality.

Hobbes was decidedly pessimistic when it came to matters of political theory, where his impact was most felt. In his influential treatise of 1651, *Leviathan, The Matter, Forme and Power of a Common Wealth Ecclesiasticall and Civil,* he argued that without government, human beings would live in a state where all could lay claim to everything, leading to a state of utter chaos and civil warfare. In order to avert such a situation, human beings form social contracts among themselves for some to rule and others to be ruled. Those who are ruled must cede their rights to a ruler in order for the contract to function. Hobbes argued that the most efficient form of government in this case was a sovereign, or absolute ruler. The despotic element that inheres in such rule is but the price society pays for peace. An absolute sovereign, on the other hand, is not bound by any single party or likely to be persuaded by any particular special interest, and can therefore better play the role of a disinterested judge. Although he argued for an absolute monarch, Hobbes did not argue on the basis of hereditary right but on the basis of an implicit covenant or contract that was formed between ruler and ruled. The notion drew on theological concepts regarding covenants that were being forged in Reformed theology while at the same time advancing a basis for later monarchical constitutional rule.

A second major English philosophical figure from the last half of the seventeenth century, who was already noted, was John Locke. Locke was from a Puritan family. His father had served in parliament's forces during the civil war. After studying medicine, he began his career as a medical doctor, but quickly showed an interest as well in matters of state. Forced to flee to the Netherlands on suspicion of involvement in a plot against Charles II, he returned with Mary in 1688 in the Glorious Revolution.

Like Hobbes, Locke was mindful of the dangers of social chaos that can ensue under weak political rulers. But he was more optimistic concerning the manner of social contract that could be worked out between rulers and ruled. Locke believed in the innate goodness of humanity and argued that toleration, including in matters of religion, was a means to bring out this innate goodness. His twin concerns were then to reduce authoritarianism of rulers and of institutions, and to encourage toleration or liberal acceptance of others. In doing so, Locke grounded his political and social theory in the notion of the fundamental rights of the individual that must be protected, including the right to life, liberty, and property, over against the rights of a sovereign ruler or state. Of these, the right to property was the most important for ensuring individual freedom. Human beings, he argued, enter into social contracts with those who govern them in order to protect their property and their selves.

Throughout his life Locke claimed to be a Christian. He was an enthusiastic supporter of Deism, however, a school of thought that held that God had created the universe but had then stepped back to let the universe proceed under the innate laws that were created within it. He applied the notion of rational laws to human society, leading him to formulate the law of supply and demand in the marketplace for instance. His 1695 volume, *The Reasonableness of Christianity,* sought to establish the truthfulness of Christianity on a rational basis that could in turn be verified by the mind through observations of the empirical world. Religion for Locke tended to be most effective when it concerned itself with matters of morality and ethics.

A clearer Deist statement came from the earlier philosopher Lord (Edward) Herbert of Cherbury (1583-1648). Lord Herbert was among the first in England to attempt to write on comparative religions. In his 1645 book *De religiones Gentilium errorumque apud eos causus* ("On the Religions of the Nations, Their Errors and the Causes"), he argued that all religions have a common core of belief. Where they differ shows only matters of error creeping in. Herbert identified what he considered to be the five core beliefs of all religions: the existence of a deity, the obligation to reverence such a power, the identification of worship with practical morality, the obligation to repent of sin and to abandon it, and divine recompense in this world and the next. Like Galileo, whose words opened this chapter, Herbert believed in the power of the human mind, of all human minds, to observe and arrive at the truth of things, not only regarding matters of astronomy and physics but on matters of religion and morality. Amid such an intellectual climate questions concerning the exclusive truth about God being confined to one branch of Christianity, or even to Christianity in general, were bound to arise. Toleration, pluralism, and rationalism were being joined together in a new European intellectual synthesis that was emerging.

Suggestions for further reading

Bireley, Robert, *The Refashioning of Catholicism, 1450-1700.* Washington, DC: Catholic University of America Press, 1999.

Campbell, Ted A., *The Religion of the Heart: A Study of European Religious Life in the Seventeenth and Eighteenth Centuries.* Columbia: University of South Carolina Press, 1991.

Cragg, Gerald R., *The Church and the Age of Reason, 1648-1789.* New York: Penguin Books, 1960/1970.

Daniel-Rops, H., *The Church in the Seventeenth Century.* Translated by J. J. Buckingham. London: Dent, 1963.

Jacob, Margaret C., *The Radical Enlightenment: Pantheists, Freemasons and Republicans.* Boston: Allen & Unwin, 1981.

Neill, Stephen, *Anglicanism.* London: Mowbrays, 1958/1977.

Old, Hughes Oliphant, *The Reading and Preaching of the Scriptures in the Worship of the Christian Church, V: Moderatism, Pietism and Awakening.* Grand Rapids, MI: Eerdmans, 2004.

Stein, K. James, *Philipp Jakob Spener: Pietist Patriarch.* Chicago: Covenant Press, 1986.

Ward, W. R., *Christianity under the Ancien Régime, 1648-1789.* Cambridge: Cambridge University Press, 1999.

13

Orthodox Churches and Christian Identity in the Seventeenth Century

Churches among empires

Orthodox churches in the seventeenth century were for the most part located in eastern Europe, western Asia, and northeast Africa. Four major political powers governed this portion of the world in the seventeenth century, two of them Muslim empires. In Persia, the Safavid dynasty, whose founders had come from a Sufi order known as Safaviyya, had converted to Shi'a Islam, which they established as the official religion of their realm. The Safavid rulers faced the Mughul empire to the east and a more aggressive Ottoman empire to the west. Mesopotamia, today the nation of Iraq, was the frontier between the Safavid and Ottoman states. Those Orthodox churches that managed to survive in Mesopotamia and Persia in the seventeenth century found themselves facing not only continuous Muslim religious expansion, but now the pressures of Catholic and Protestant missions from the West.

For their part, the Ottoman Turks, who were Sunni Muslim, considered the Safavid to be as much their opponents as were the Christian European nations to the west. Turned back from the gates of Vienna in 1683, the Ottomans turned their attention to consolidating their past gains and keeping their Christian antagonists to the west at bay. At the same time the Ottomans looked north and east. They began expanding their control over the regions of Armenia and Georgia, while Mesopotamia saw continuous warfare. The city of Baghdad changed hands several times between Safavid and Ottoman rulers in the sixteenth and seventeenth centuries. Orthodox churches in Egypt, Palestine, Anatolia, Serbia, Albania, Armenia, and even Georgia all had to live under conditions set by Ottoman Muslim rule in the seventeenth century. These churches were also increasingly forced to contend with what amounted to fellow Christian missionary pressures from the West.

The third political entity was Russia, a state that in the course of the seventeenth century was expanding greatly from its original form as the Muscovy kingdom. Russia's Orthodox Church sought to define both its ecumenical relations with other patriarchs in Muslim-ruled territories to its south and its own theological identity as a Russian Church more clearly. In 1589 the Russian Church elevated the metropolitan of Moscow to the rank of a patriarch, an act that was recognized by the ecumenical patriarch in Constantinople. Within the Russian Church, the notion that Moscow was the third Rome and successor to Constantinople was strong. But this Russian Christian identity was not being forged in a vacuum. Questions concerning the church's relationship to political rulers took a new turn in 1613 with the founding of a new dynasty under Mikhail Romanov (1596-1645).

During this period a fourth political force, a newly formed federation of Poland and Lithuania under Roman Catholic rulers, was expanding to the east. The Union of Lublin, which was signed in 1569, joined the kingdom of Poland and the grand duchy of Lithuania in a single commonwealth ruled by a parliament and a monarch who was elected by the princes. Polish-Lithuanian forces began expanding to the east, reaching as far as Moscow in 1610 and extending political control over the city of Kiev and across the Dnieper River. Orthodox churches that were located in these regions continued to find themselves also to be the object of missions from the Catholic West. The rebellion of Cossacks, semi-independent communities of Slavic descent with strong military training, in 1648 in the Ukraine helped shift control of Kiev from Polish-Lithuanian to Russian rulers. An invasion by Sweden in 1655 further curtailed the Polish-Lithuanian Commonwealth, for the most part ending its political control over areas where Orthodox churches resided.

Of these four political powers, it was the Ottoman Turks who were the most important players in the world political scene in the seventeenth century. When the Ottomans subdued Egypt in the sixteenth century they not only extended their power into a third continent, Africa, but further enriched their coffers. By controlling the trade of the whole eastern Mediterranean region, the Ottomans became the wealthiest, most powerful player in the region. Constantinople had been a city of only forty thousand at the time of its conquest in 1453. Within one hundred years its population had multiplied tenfold. The Ottomans had undertaken an aggressive urban development plan that included mosques, schools, and public buildings, making Istanbul one of the greatest cities in the world.

In matters of trade, the Ottomans were content for the most part to be on the receiving end of mercantile activities. The Ottoman territories continued to sit at the crossroads of east and west. Enormous amounts of silk, mostly coming now from Persian producers, continued to pass through Ottoman markets where it was sold to merchants from Italy or France, many of whom became semipermanent residents. Traditional Islamic law regarding *dhimmi* (*zimmi* in Turkish), or "protected minorities," did not extend to these resident foreigners from the Christian West. Islamic law allowed for the extension of safe-conduct pledges to travelers passing through Muslim-ruled territories, but not for foreigners who resided as merchants for extended periods of time. To accommodate these Western merchant communities in their territories, the Ottomans had centuries earlier begun to grant *ahidnames*, or what in Europe were called "capitulations." These grants extended by the sultan to various European nations allowed citizens from these countries to reside in Ottoman territories to conduct trade without being subject to Islamic law. In the seventeenth century the use of these capitulations grew considerably, and was extended to the Dutch and English, whose ships began for the first time showing up in the eastern Mediterranean. The capitulations were a significant source of benefit to the Ottomans through the trade that they fostered, but they also served to increase the foreign influence of Western Christians in various regions of the Ottoman empire.

The sixteenth century saw the Ottoman empire achieve its apex under Suleiman the Magnificent (1494-1566). In the last decades of the sixteenth century and continuing into the seventeenth century, direct rule within a highly structured social order based on promotion through military service had begun to give way within the Ottoman world to a more decentralized form of government. Sultans in the seventeenth century exercised less direct rule over their empire, and many of the provinces became semi-independent entities. This was due in part to the fact that sultans and many of their viziers, or advisors, in the seventeenth century lacked the direct military experience that had been common for those who ruled earlier in the empire, but also because those who were on the margins of the empire were increasingly finding ways to challenge the centralized power of the sultanate.

This pattern was replicated in the lives of churches in regions of the world under Ottoman rule. By establishing their political control over Syria, Palestine, and to a limited degree Egypt, the Ottomans originally restored to a significant degree the administrative authority of the ecumenical patriarch over the Orthodox churches that embraced the Chalcedonian formulation concerning Jesus Christ of "two natures in one person." But now in the seventeenth century, power shifted in subtle ways from the patriarch, whose office was located in the Phanar neighborhood in Istanbul, to leadership in the provinces.

Orthodox communities in the Balkans

As noted above, the Ottoman empire in the seventeenth century was beginning to show signs of weakening central authority. Regional rulers were gaining more control over the administration of affairs of state. Orthodox churches in the Balkans in particular reflected this tendency, which was manifested not only in an increase in their exercise of local administrative rule but in the growing consciousness of distinct ethnic and religious identity. Various national saints were becoming more important in the lives of churches in the region, as were national Christian political heroes and the new martyrs that the Ottomans had helped to produce. The growing trade with western European nations was bringing increased contact with and influences from the West into the Balkans.

The expulsion of Jews from Spain at the end of the fifteenth century resulted in Spanish Muslims settling in Ottoman territory. The number of Roman Catholic missionaries increased as well under the capitulations. Islamic law prohibited Muslims from converting to another religion, so these Catholic missionaries in Ottoman-controlled territories directed their efforts toward the Orthodox communities. The result was an increasingly diverse religious world as these churches learned to live side by side in new ways. The Muslim writer Evliya Çelebi (1611-1682) was a native of Istanbul and traveled widely through the Ottoman empire, documenting aspects of cultural and social life in great detail. He noted in Sarajevo that a number of churches, synagogues, and mosques had recently been built.

Roman Catholic presence was even more pronounced in Croatia, which was in effect the frontier between the Hapsburg and the Ottoman empires. The Ottomans had been turned back at the battle of Sisak in 1593, and Austrian control over the region strengthened considerably. Croatia had been long been home to both Catholic and Orthodox communities, but in the seventeenth century the Roman Catholic strength in the Balkans increased considerably. The Jesuits first arrived in city of Zagreb in 1606 and took up residence in what had earlier been a Dominican convent. They were reportedly invited by officials who were interested in expanding education in the city. The following year the Jesuits opened a high school, and in 1632 finished the construction of Saint Catherine's Church, an edifice that continues to stand as a monument to Baroque architecture.

One of the more important events in Catholic-Orthodox relations in Croatia was the Union of Marča in 1611. Orthodox monks several centuries earlier had established a monastery at Marča, near the city of Ivanićgrad, which had become the center of Orthodox Christian life in the region. In 1611 leaders from the monastery reached an agreement with representatives of Rome to become a uniate church. By papal decree in 1611 the eparchy (or diocese) of Križevci was established and a new bishop appointed. Churches that joined the eparchy were allowed to continue to worship in Croatian, following the eastern Orthodox liturgy, but were required to insert into their services of worship an acknowledgement of the pope in Rome. Needless to say the move stirred considerable opposition from other Orthodox Church leaders.

Advance on the northwestern edge of the Ottoman empire reached a turning point in 1683, when an Ottoman army led by Grand Vizier Merzifonlu Kara Mustafa Paşa (1634-1683) moved one last time against the Austrian empire. The siege and eventual conquest of Vienna seemed a sure thing when an estimated 150,000 Ottoman troops were met by an army of only 11,000 Hapsburg soldiers. The pope intervened, however, convincing the future Polish king, Jan Sobieski (1629-1696), to send an army to aid his former Austrian enemies. Sobieski arrived with more than 50,000 troops and the belief that his cause was blessed by God to help restore Christendom in the East. In the ensuing Battle of Vienna the Turks were indeed turned back. Over the next sixteen years Austrian forces under Hapsburg rulers continued to press against Ottoman rulers in Hungary and Transylvania, reaching all the way to the city of Sarajevo, which Austrian forces burned in 1697. Two years later the two sides signed the Treaty of Karlowitz, which ceded Hungary and Transylvania to the Austrian rulers. The Ottoman empire was no longer taken to be a serious threat to any of the emerging western European nations.

One of the unintended side effects of the Hapsburg-Ottoman conflict at the end of this period was a regional migration that reshaped the religious landscape of the Balkans. During the period of warfare, Austria had encouraged the Serbians, who since the famous Serbian Battle of Kosovo in 1389 had been living under Muslim political and cultural domination, to rebel. The Serbians did so, but when the war was over, the Treaty of Karlowitz left Serbia under Ottoman rule, and Western forces withdrew from Serbian territory. The Hapsburg invited Serbs to migrate, an invitation that proved to be irresistible to many war-weary occupants. Thousands did so, including Arsenije III Čarnojević (1633-1706), the Archbishop of Peć and Patriarch of the Serbs, leaving large areas of the Serbian territories vacant. Human nature tending to abhor such a territorial vacuum, Muslims of various ethnic identities soon moved into what had been Christian Serbian villages and towns. Life for the Serbs in Austrian territories, including that of their archbishop, was not easy. Life for the Serbian Christians who remained under Ottoman rule became even more difficult as the Muslim population of the Balkans increased significantly. The Balkans, the only remaining Ottoman hold on western European soil, became one of the most ethnically and religiously mixed landscapes in the world at the time.

The Maronite Church in Lebanon

The Maronite Church traced its history in Lebanon, which was historically part of Syria, to the fourth-century monk known as St. Maron. After the Arab conquest in the seventh century, their communities found refuge in the mountains of Lebanon, where they survived under independent leadership. During the period of the Crusades, the Maronites aligned themselves with Rome and became the first of the Eastern churches to enter into an agreement forming a uniate church. Maronites had struggled under Egyptian Mameluke rule, but after Ottomans took control of the region in the sixteenth century, the Maronites entered into a limited alliance with the Druze, a distinct Islamic group in Lebanon that had sided with the Ottomans and had been awarded with local political offices as a result. Toward the end of the sixteenth century a powerful Druze leader began to consolidate power, leading to open rebellion against the Ottoman rulers, who eventually crushed his efforts in 1635. Three years later France declared itself to be the protector of Christians in the Ottoman empire, including the Maronites. The declaration was relatively unenforceable, but indicates the degree to which the situation of Christians under Ottoman rule was becoming a matter of Western political concern.

More important for the Maronites were the resources of education and scholarship that were developing through relations with the Catholic West. In 1584 the pope established the first Maronite College in Rome for the training of Maronite priests. Maronite monks at the Saint Quzhayya monastery in Lebanon received delivery of a printing press from the West in 1610 and were the first to publish works in Arabic. It remained the only working press publishing in Arabic for more than a century. As a result of this press, the monastery would play an important role in later centuries in an Arab-language renaissance. The printing press was also a major influence in bringing the Bible into Arabic at a later date.

Abraham Ecchellensis (his Arabic name was Ibrahim al-Haqilani, 1605-1664) was one of the most important Maronite scholars of the century. Born at al-Haqil, Lebanon, Ecchellensis studied at the Maronite College in Rome, concentrating on languages and theology. After being ordained a deacon in Lebanon, he returned to Italy where he taught Arabic and Syriac in Pisa and then in Rome. His work in both languages and theology eventually earned him a position as an interpreter for the body providing oversight for Roman Catholic missions, *Propaganda fidei*. In this capacity he helped to revise the Arabic version of the Bible for missionary use among Muslims. Ecchellensis later traveled to Paris, where he taught Syriac and Arabic. He published a Syriac grammar earlier in 1628, and helped to produce the Syriac and Arabic portions of the Paris Polyglot Bible that was published from 1629 to 1654. His translation of Arabic sources regarding the Council of Nicaea was a significant contribution to theological scholarship. For the last four years of his life he was the scriptor for Syriac and Arabic at the Vatican Library.

Theological conflicts in the ecumenical patriarchate

The Maronites were not the only Orthodox Christians in the Ottoman empire to be influenced by contacts with the West. The influence of Western theological ideas reached as high as the office of the ecumenical patriarch at one point, in the person of Kyrillos Loukaris (known in the West as Cyril Lucaris, 1572-1638). Loukaris was born in Crete at a time when the island was under Venetian control. His family gave him the name Constantine, but he took the name Kyrillos (or Cyril) at the time of his ordination in Constantinople. After studying in Venice and Padua, he spent time in Wittenberg and then in Geneva, where he was exposed to Calvin's teachings. After the Union of Brest in 1596 he was appointed as a special envoy to the region on behalf of the Orthodox cause, and he taught theology for several years in one of the Orthodox training schools for priests. In Kiev he saw the growing influence of Polish Catholics and what he considered to be Catholic oppression of the Orthodox Church, fueling what was already a strong antipathy toward the Roman Catholic Church.

In 1602 Loukaris was elected patriarch of Alexandria, and then in 1621 the Ottoman sultan chose his name from among the nominees by the church to become the ecumenical patriarch. Concerned to keep out the Roman Catholic influence, Loukaris authored in Latin a *Confessio* ("Confession"), which he had published in Geneva in 1629. The *Confession* was strongly Calvinistic in character, creating a furor among other Orthodox Church leaders. Opposition especially from the Jesuits in Istanbul added to his problems with the sultan. Other Western ambassadors to the Ottoman court in Istanbul who were from Protestant regions not surprisingly supported the patriarch. Caught in the midst of various intrigues between Jesuits and Protestant emissaries in the city, and facing the hostility of others from his own church, Loukaris was deposed and then reinstated six different times. In 1638, as the sultan was preparing to go to war against Persia in

Armenia, he received a report that the patriarch was trying to stir up Cossacks in the Ukraine against the Ottomans. Loukaris was killed on board ship, his body thrown into the Bosporus.

Controversy over his *Confession* did not die with the patriarch. Over the next several decades, at least six different synods passed judgment on the document. Loukaris made no effort to hide the fact that his aim in the work was to reform the Orthodox Church along Calvinist lines. To this end he sent to study at universities in Switzerland, the northern Netherlands, and England a number of promising scholars, including Metrophanes Kritopoulos (1589-1639), who would later serve as the patriarch of Alexandria from 1636 to 1639. Loukaris was particularly well disposed toward the Anglican Church, and had a lively exchange of correspondence with several archbishops of Canterbury. The patriarch was concerned to increase the education levels of Orthodox priests, and was responsible for setting up the first Greek-language printing press in Istanbul in 1627. A number of books and manuscripts that Loukaris acquired from the West can still be found in the library of the ecumenical patriarchate in Istanbul today.

Among those Orthodox leaders who responded to Loukaris were several who turned to Roman Catholic sources for help. Petr (Peter) Moghila (1596-1646) became metropolitan of Kiev in 1633. In 1639 he published a Greek text titled *Orthodoxos Homologia tēs Katholikēs kai Apostolikēs Ekklesias tēs Anatolikēs* ("Orthodox Confession of the Catholic and Apostolic Eastern Church"). Moghila's *Confession*, which was written as a catechism, was clearly intended to refute many of Loukaris's Calvinist doctrines, but showed strong Roman Catholic influences in a number of places, such as in its explanation of the Eucharist. After being edited by several other Orthodox theologians, the *Confession* was approved by a synod of Russian and Greek theologians who met in Jassy, Romania, in 1642.

Dositheos Notaras (1641-1707) became the patriarch of Jerusalem in 1669. In 1672 he convened the Synod of Jerusalem, which considered Loukaris's earlier *Confession*. The Synod issued a direct, point-by-point refutation of the *Confession,* focusing on the doctrines of free will, the church, the sacraments, and the veneration of icons as points of special concern. Against both Roman Catholic and Protestant teachings, it rejected the ancient addition of the *filioque* in the Western version of the Nicene Creed. Orthodox, Roman Catholic, and Protestant theologies were clearly offering distinctive ways of understanding Christian faith.

The Coptic Church and the Ottomans

Egypt is located on the continent of Africa, but in the sixteenth and seventeenth centuries continued to be part of the Ottoman world. The Coptic Church continued to be bound historically as well to the wider Orthodox community of communions, and to Constantinople. The Ottoman conquest of Egypt in 1517 had little immediate effect on the lives of Coptic Christians in Egypt, since the Ottomans for the most part kept in place the political structure that they took over from the Mamelukes, including most of the local administrative rulers. In the seventeenth century conditions for the Copts became even more strenuous, however, as the power of the Ottoman viceroys, or *pashas,* increased. During the papacy of John XV (r. 1619-1634) the Copts began to pay not only the general tax and the *jizyah,* or special tax levied by Muslim rulers on *dhimmis*, but a third new tax called the *gawali,* which was assessed on each person. In 1664, all taxes were consolidated into one "obligation of the great sultan." Before 1664, taxes were paid to various local rulers or to the local mosques. After 1664 in Egypt, all taxes were collected from Coptic Christians by the *pasha,* who in turn would distribute them to the various administrative units and mosques in the land. This new system enabled the *pashas* to retain more money and to enforce collections more directly. Its harshness reached such a point, however, that Christians would leave their villages and live in the mountains before tax collection periods.

Other new restrictions were imposed on the Coptic community in Egypt in this period. In addition to the traditional Muslim restrictions such as the one prohibiting Christians from riding horses, Copts were now forbidden to walk on the right side of the street, or to wear clothes of any color other than blue. During the tenure of Pope Mark VI (r. 1650-1660) in particular, these laws were rigorously enforced. Copts had to wear bells on their necks, and the men wear black turbans in public baths. Coptic Christian women faced restrictions on venturing outside their quarters. Marriages moved out of churches and into private homes to keep them from drawing the attention of neighbors and being disrupted. Copts in some places were even forbidden to enter their churches for prayer and worship.

Such prohibitions could often be relaxed with payments of money that essentially amounted to bribes. Much of Coptic life in relation to political rulers in Egypt came to be regulated through such payments. Matthew III (r. 1634-1649) was elected pope after the death of John XV. Upon his consecration, the *pasha* informed the Coptic leaders that a newly consecrated pope was obligated to pay the treasury an additional sum of money. The viceroy determined the amount to be 4,000 dinars, forcing the Coptic leaders in Cairo to borrow funds to make the payment. Matthew III decided to travel to Upper Egypt to pay a pastoral visit to his churches and to take up a collection to help pay back the borrowed sum. The trip was reportedly successful on both counts. Four decades later, upon the death of Pope Matthew IV (r. 1660-1675), authorities in Cairo would not grant permission for the pope's burial before the Coptic community came up with additional sums of money.

The end of the seventeenth century saw a number of natural disasters add to the difficulties that the Coptic community faced. In 1686, drought followed by pestilence brought about a considerable number of deaths among them. Nine years later drought struck again. This time the accompanying pestilence took the life of the pope. In spite of these natural disasters and the continuing harsh conditions imposed by Egypt's Muslim rulers, the Copts managed to survive, and in some places even flourish. Churches were renovated from time to time, although such efforts could produce serious backlashes. On one occasion the *pasha* was visiting the town of al-Mahala al-Kubra in the delta region when he noticed the city's large church building in good repair. The *pasha* ordered the immediate demolition of the church and a school erected in its place to make sure that the church was not rebuilt.

Monasteries continued to play an important role in the life of the Coptic Church through this period. Reports from two European visitors to the monastery of St. Antony, located in the mountains in a desert region approximately 150 km southeast of Cairo, provide a glimpse into their condition. A French soldier named Jean Coppin (c. 1615-1690) described having to enter the compound in 1638 by being lifted by a pulley over walls that were more than 8 meters high. Several decades later, in 1672, a German Dominican named Johann Michael Wansleben (d. 1679) visited the same monastery. He had a similar experience of entering by means of a pulley over the wall, as there was no gate, he noted. A strong stone tower stood in the middle of the monastery where the monks kept their provisions, and to which they could take refuge when they were attacked. According to Wansleben, the bell in a belltower at St. Antony's was the only bell remaining in all of Christian Egypt. Wansleben, who was a student of Ethiopian and Coptic languages, reportedly purchased several manuscripts from the monks to take back to Europe. Both visitors noted the paintings on the walls of the monastery representing biblical figures and saints.

Life for Coptic Christians under Ottoman rule was clearly growing harsher. At the same time, the capitulations that the Ottoman sultans granted to Western nations had the effect of making life for the foreign Roman Catholic community, and the priests who served them in Egypt, relatively easier. The 1536 capitulation granted to the king of France gave French subjects in particular exceptional privileges in Egypt. The sultans' aim in granting these treaties was to stimulate Western investments in trade, business, and schools. French subjects living in Ottoman territories were not bound by Ottoman law and were not taxed as *dhimmis*. French Catholics in Egypt were allowed to purchase property, build schools, and support missionary projects, while the Copts faced increasing taxes and growing restriction on their lives.

Throughout the seventeenth century Rome continued its efforts to bring the Coptic Church under its jurisdiction. Catholic efforts were also directed toward converting Copts directly to the Roman Catholic rite. The Capuchins began working in Cairo in 1630, and by 1675 the Jesuits had established a mission in the city. A school was established by the Capuchins and opened to Coptic children in an effort to persuade Copts to become Catholic. In 1694, an Arabic translation of the accounts of the Council of Chalcedon was translated and printed by Catholic missionaries in Upper Egypt, in another attempt to convert the Copts to Catholicism. A 1696 report from the French consul in Egypt, however, notes that the Catholic missionaries had not been very successful in these efforts directed toward the Copts. The French missions were more successful in winning converts in Egypt from among merchants belonging to other Christian communities living in the Ottoman world. For their part, Coptic popes were drawn into some of the wider theological debates that were taking place in world Christianity in the seventeenth century. Pope Matthew IV in one of his letters addressed the issue of the real presence in the Eucharist, most likely in response to Protestant teachings.

The city of Jerusalem continued to hold a significant place in the spiritual landscape of both Catholic and Orthodox communions in the seventeenth century. Roman Catholics in Istanbul sought to secure from the Ottoman sultan at one point a *firman,* or edict, granting Rome administrative authority over Christian holy places in Jerusalem. The effort brought together the various Orthodox leaders and local Muslim rulers in Palestine, who all opposed it. Pilgrimages to Jerusalem were a vibrant part of the spiritual life of Christians from many traditions. For Coptic Christians making the journey from Egypt, such pilgrimages entailed the payment of two additional taxes, one to leave Egypt and another to enter the Holy Land. Nevertheless, many Copts, including their popes, made the journey often. For a period of twelve years, pilgrimages from Egypt were interrupted by local warfare among Muslim groups in the Sinai. The economic loss due to the interruption eventually led the sultan to appoint a special *pasha* to the region to restore peace.

Through the seventeenth century the Coptic Church continued to hold a special relationship with the Ethiopian Orthodox Church. The Ethiopian *abuna,* or patriarch, was appointed by the Coptic pope in Cairo. These *abunas* continued in the seventeenth century to be Coptic, not Ethiopian. They could often find themselves facing difficulties with monks and local clergy in Ethiopia, as well as with the Ethiopian kings, and with the growing presence of missionaries and merchants from Europe. In the 1630s the Ethiopian king closed the border to any foreign travelers coming from Egypt into Ethiopia in an attempt to stem the tide of European missionaries entering Ethiopia from the north. Ethiopia, as we have seen in a previous chapter, in the seventeenth century was more fully integrated into the political economy of the Indian Ocean.

One of the figures who helped inform the Christian world outside Egypt of the life of the Coptic churches in the seventeenth century was Yusuf ibn Abu Dhaqan, better known in the West as Joseph Barbatus or Abudacnus (c. 1575?-1643). Abu Dhaqan was born in Egypt and raised as a Coptic Christian. He arrived in Rome in 1595 with a letter from the Coptic pope, Gabriel VII, to the Catholic pope, Clement VIII. Shortly after that he converted to Roman Catholicism, although he continued to defend Coptic theology and practices in his later writings. From Rome he moved to Paris, and then in 1610 took up residence in Oxford University, where he taught for a time. He later taught at Louvain before moving on to eastern Europe and then to Istanbul where he worked for European governments in the court of the sultan. Abu Dhaqan's book, *Historia Jacobitarum seu Coptorum in Ægypto, Lybia, Nubia, Æthiopia tota, & parte Cypri insulae habitantium,* was published in 1692 and translated several decades later into English as *The True History of the Jacobites of Egypt, Lybia, Nubia, &c, their origine, religion, ceremonies, laws, and customs, whereby you may see how they differ from the Jacobites of Great Britain.*

Armenian Christians between Russia and the Ottomans

On the eastern frontier of the Ottoman empire lay the ancient Armenian homeland and the city of Etchmiadzin, where the catholicos of the Armenian

Orthodox Church historically resided. In the seventeenth century there were still in fact two claimants to the office of catholicos of the church. Back in the eleventh century, as the Armenian homeland had come under Muslim rulers, the catholicos moved from Etchmiadzin to the region of Cilicia, in what is now the southeast of Turkey but at the time was still a part of the East Roman or Byzantine empire. Late in the fourteenth century Cilicia was taken by the Ottomans, who recognized the catholicos there as the head of the Armenian churches under their rule. Other Armenian Church leaders in Etchmiadzin several decades later, however, elected a new catholicos in the ancient cathedral of that city. The act was intended to return the spiritual authority of the church to its ancient homeland, but its effect was to leave the church with two catholicoi, although in time the spiritual primacy of the catholicos in Etchmiadzin came to be acknowledged by the wider Armenian community throughout the world.

The Ottomans meanwhile, shortly after conquering Constantinople in 1453, encouraged the establishment of an Armenian patriarch in Istanbul, in the Kumkapi neighborhood of the city where a large Armenian community lived. The patriarch was technically under the spiritual authority of the catholicos, but due to the fact of his proximity to the sultans, he came to exercise a significant degree of administrative authority within the empire. The Ottoman sultans from time to time handed to the Armenian patriarch in Istanbul administration not just of Armenian affairs in the empire but those of the various non-Chalcedonian millets, or religious "nations," including the Copts, West Assyrians, East Assyrians, and Maronites, allowing him to handle the collection of taxes, settle disputes, and generally manage judicial affairs within the community. A second Armenian patriarch had been recognized in Jerusalem centuries earlier. In 1644, shortly after the Armenian homeland was divided by the Turkish-Persian war, the patriarch of Jerusalem declared himself to be the catholicos, without gaining the support of either the Ottoman rulers or the other churches.

The Jerusalem patriarch's effort to claim the title of catholicos was precipitated in part by the growing chaos in the ancient Armenian homeland. The Safavid emperor Shah Abbas the Great (1587-1629) launched an invasion into Ottoman-controlled Armenia in 1603. As the Ottoman forces counterattacked, the shah forced a large part of the Armenian population, including the entire population of the city of Julfa, a city known for its silk merchants, into exile across the Araxes River into Persian territory. Estimates of the number of displaced Armenians range into the hundreds of thousands, and many died in the migration. Some were eventually forced to march all the way east to the Safavid capital of Isfahan, in modern Iran, where they were settled in a district along the Zayandeh River, which became known as New Julfa (Nor Jugha).

At New Julfa, Armenians in the Persian world found a new home. No Muslims were allowed to reside in the district. Armenians, on the other hand, were allowed to build churches, ring bells for worship, drink wine, and engage in other activities that were otherwise supposed to be forbidden under Islamic law. These forced immigrants were soon flourishing both culturally and economically as their mercantile activity prospered. From exile they also helped build Armenian culture globally. It was an Armenian bishop from Persia, Oskan Erewanc'i (1614-

1674), who traveled to Amsterdam where he oversaw the first publication of an Armenian Bible in 1666 by one of the several Armenian publishing houses that had been established in the city by then.

In 1639 the Armenian homeland was effectively divided by the Ottomans and Safavids into western and eastern regions. Faced with the prospect of continuing Muslim opposition, a number of Armenians began to look to the north and place their hope in the Third Rome, Moscow. An envoy was sent in 1659 from New Julfa to Tsar Alexei Mikhailovich Romanov (1629-1676) with a special gift, a golden, jewel-bedecked throne that was intended to be an inducement for him to come to the Armenians' aid. Alexei, however, was preoccupied at the time with securing his borders against Polish-Lithuanian armies and with a challenging patriarch at the head of the Russian Church. Other Armenians chose a more direct approach to liberation. Bands claiming the ancient title of "Princes of Artsakh," the name of the first anti-Persian Armenian princes, or *meliks,* in the fifth century, engaged in open rebellion in Armenia. The region of Artsakh had never been fully subdued by any foreign ruler, providing Armenians with a powerful symbol of national dignity and zeal for freedom.

Kurds between Christians and Muslims

The land of the Kurds, or Kurdistan, is a mountainous region to the south of Armenia, spanning territory that is part of the contemporary nations of Turkey, Iraq, and Iran. The Kurdish people had long been fiercely independent, and even though they lived under various empires as far back as the time of Alexander the Great, they had never been fully conquered or incorporated into the dominant social and political systems of those empires. The Kurdish language, an Indo-European tongue unrelated to either Turkic or Arabic, reveals some of this independence. By the seventeenth century a significant percentage of Kurds were Sunni Muslims, but they resisted for centuries the domination by various other Muslims who ruled in the region. Many belonged to the Alevi, which had emerged from one of the Shi'a branches of Islam with strong Turkish Sufi influences. Still others were Yazidis, a more localized faith that has roots in ancient Mesopotamian tradition but incorporates elements of Zoroastrian, Sufi Islamic, Manichaean, and Christian traditions. Like neighboring Armenia to the north, Kurdistan was divided between the Ottoman and Safavid empires in the seventeenth century. Unlike their Armenian neighbors, the Kurds had not been subjected to forced deportations and remained closely tied to the rugged region of their traditional homeland.

The Kurds had long lived in proximity to Armenian and East Syrian Christians in the region. In 1667 they were joined by Roman Catholic missionaries in the region from Europe. These first Western missionaries were Capuchins, and they came to the region with the stated intentions of "evangelizing" other Christians, namely the East Syrians, whom they considered to be "heretical." The Capuchins set up mission stations in the cities of Aleppo and Mosul, operating under the capitulation the French government had received from the Ottoman sultan in Istanbul. Since the Capuchins were formally directing their mission toward other Christian communities, whom the Ottomans considered millets, they were allowed to engage in mission activities.

Within a year the Capuchins began studying the Kurdish language and directing some of their missionary efforts toward the Kurdish people they encountered. At first they had the support of some Armenian priests who translated for the Capuchins. The first two Kurdish Yazidi sheiks were converted and baptized, taking the names Peter and Paul (dates unknown). The Capuchins expected that other Yazidis would quickly become Christian en masse, following their leaders. Back in Paris word of the efforts led to a new fund being established by supporters of the Capuchins to assist the effort among the Kurds. Local Armenian resistance to the Capuchin efforts formed as well, however, as the Armenians were more concerned about developing resources for their own communities in the region. The Armenians were especially interested in the educational resources that the Jesuits had to offer. The growing rivalry in the region between the two Catholic orders coupled with the Armenians' withdrawal of support brought an end to the Catholic effort among the Kurds in the seventeenth century.

The East Syrian Church continues to decline

The story of the East Syrian Church, which was often called "Nestorian" in the West, was one of continuing decline in the seventeenth century. The East Syrian Church, as was seen in an earlier chapter, divided into two lines of patriarchal succession in the sixteenth century. The split started over issues of patriarchal succession, but were compounded when one of the patriarchs entered into communion with Rome in the 1550s. In 1607 the patriarch of the "old" East Syrian branch, Mar Eliyya VIII (r. 1591-1617), sent word to the pope that he was ready to enter into communion with Rome. The effort was later repudiated by his successor, but it shows the degree to which the patriarch was willing to go to seek help. Little in the way of actual benefit was ever gained from these efforts, although through the seventeenth century both patriarchs from time to time initiated them.

Finally, in 1662, Mar Shimon XIII (r. 1662-1692), patriarch in the "new" branch that had first entered into communion with Rome in the 1550s, under pressure from others in the church, broke formally with Rome and moved the patriarchal residence to the city of Kotchanes (or Qochanis). The two lines of tradition were not rejoined, however, leaving two patriarchs in the land. Then in 1672 in Diyarbakir (or Amid as it was also known) where the Capuchin missionaries had been active, an East Syrian bishop named Yūsuf (Joseph, d. 1707), from the church whose patriarchal see was located in Alqosh, formally announced his conversion to the Roman Catholic faith and left for Rome. He returned a decade or so later with the title "Patriarch of the Chaldeans," which had been bestowed on him by the pope in 1681. A number of other local East Syrian churches joined themselves to his patriarchate, creating in effect a third line of East Syrian tradition. Yūsuf returned to Rome and abandoned the title in 1696, but Rome appointed a successor, Mar Joseph II Sliba Maruf (r. 1696-1713), as Patriarch of the Chaldeans.

Living under Safavid Iranian and Ottoman Turkish rulers, the situation of all three lines of this ancient communion continued to wane as the seventeenth century closed. Churches saw their numbers reduced as families quietly drifted away or died out. They had no presence in any major city in the region. Educational efforts directed toward preparation of priests were nonexistent. Fewer men and women entered the monasteries. Some support came from Roman Catholic missionaries, but it was provided with the intention of generating greater loyalty toward Rome rather than helping the churches to develop their own local resources. Continued, if erratic, persecutions drove many of these minority religious communities farther into the mountains to live, having the effect of further isolating these Christians.

Orthodoxy in Russia and the Ukraine

Orthodoxy in seventeenth-century Russia and the Ukraine is inseparable from the politics of Tsarist Russia. Moscow proudly embraced both its title and responsibilities as the Third Rome. In light of the political threats posed by the Polish-Lithuanian Commonwealth to its west and from the Ottoman empire to its south, the title proved to be politically expedient as much as it was spiritually or culturally important. Russia in the seventeenth century was becoming the bulwark of world Orthodoxy. Within this emerging new Orthodox Russian empire, relations with churches from the West as well as with the more ecumenical patriarchate and the Second Rome, Constantinople, were to play a significant role.

Seventeenth-century Russian Orthodox history can be roughly divided in half. In the first half of the century, the church was caught in the midst of wars. Its theology and identity both reflect much of this bellicose environment. A great deal of the conflict related to the Ukraine, which under the Treaty of Pereyaslav was finally reunited with Russia in 1654. The second half of the century was a more peaceful period, politically as well as theologically, although it was marked by a significant schism in the church. Challenges to the Russian Orthodox worship, theology, and practice came from the Tsars, Roman Catholics, and Protestants. By the end of the century, the Russian Orthodox Church found itself not only divided, but becoming cut off from other Orthodox churches of the world in its relationships.

The various Protestant and Roman Catholic churches in western Europe in the seventeenth century were becoming more transnational or intercultural. Lutherans were found in regions of Germany, Sweden, Norway, Denmark, Poland, Latvia, and Lithuania. The first book known to be printed in Lithuanian, *Catechismusa prasty szadei* ("Simple Words of Catechism"), which first appeared in 1547, was by a Lutheran named Martynas Mazvydas (1510-1563). Roman Catholics were found in most regions of Europe as well as in Latin America, Africa, and various coastal regions of Asia. Reformed or Calvinist Christians were found in Switzerland, regions of France, the Netherlands, England, Scotland, Ireland, and Hungary. The Orthodox churches, however, were increasingly defined by language and land in the seventeenth century. The Russian Orthodox Church was Russian speaking and, for the most part, located on Russian lands. While the church was formally still in communion with the ecumenical patriarch in Istanbul, there was little formal communication or communion between them. Centuries of fighting with Lithuanians and Poles in the western regions had reduced the Russian Orthodox Church there. Russian Orthodox believers who lived in Roman Catholic lands, as we have seen, were expected to honor the authority of the pope, even if they were allowed to retain their Orthodox worship as uniate churches.

The seventeenth century in Russia began with what has been called the Time of Troubles (*Smutnoe Vremia*). In 1598 the weak but pious Tsar Fyodor I Ivanovich died, ending the 800-year-old Rurik (or Muscovite) Dynasty. Boris Godunov (r. 1598-1605), who had been ruling as regent for Tsar Fyodor, emerged to take power. Godunov was of Mongol descent but was married to the daughter of one of the most feared operatives of Ivan the Terrible (1530-1584). However, Godunov had been selected by Ivan himself on his deathbed to serve at the head of a council to govern as regent since Fyodor was judged as unable to rule. Gudonov's rise to power was calculated and precise. Years before, the younger brother of Tsar Fyodor, Dimitrii, had some claim to the throne but was exiled and mysteriously killed. Upon Fyodor's death many of the boyars did not want a non-Russian to rule, but the Patriarch of Moscow, seeing the need for a strong leader, proposed Gudonov as Tsar, and the *zemsky sobor* (national assembly) unanimously affirmed the choice.

It was not a good time in Russia. In addition to the continuing wars with the Polish-Lithuanian Commonwealth and with Sweden, a major famine struck between 1601 and 1603, taking an estimated 100,000 lives through starvation and disease in the regions around Moscow alone. Lawlessness plagued the countryside as groups of people banned together to rob or pillage for food or money. In 1605 Godunov died, and his sixteen-year-old son became tsar, assuming the title Fyodor II (1589-1605). Into this volatile situation stepped a pretender who claimed to be the recently expired son of Ivan the Terrible, Dimitrii, who had supposedly miraculously survived an assassination attempt on his life. False Dimitrii, as he came to be known in Russian history, had come from Poland, where he had gained the support of several powerful members of the Polish nobility. His conversion to the Roman Catholic faith in 1604 brought him the support of the Jesuits in Poland as well. The Jesuits secured a promise from the pretender that he would claim Russia for the Catholic Church if he were to gain power. False Dimitrii then made his way back to Moscow with an "army" of disgruntled Cossacks, eager Poles, and an assortment of troops from various members of the Polish nobility who supported him. His chances of success would have been negligible had not a number of boyars turned to him in 1605 to be their next tsar. Fyodor II was assassinated

False Dimitrii's reign was short-lived, in part because of his penchant for all things and all friends Polish. He maintained a Polish-Lithuanian guard, straining his relations with the very boyars who had supported him. His marriage later that year to Marina Mniszech (c. 1588-1614), a Polish Roman Catholic, violated Russian tradition that a wife of a ruler convert to the Orthodox faith before marriage and appeared to seal his fate. Two weeks after his wedding False Demitrii was killed in the Kremlin. His remains were burned, and his ashes reportedly shot from a cannon toward Poland. One of the boyars who had helped bring False Demitrii to power as well as helped end his reign was named tsar without gaining wide support. Meanwhile a second, then a third False Demitrii appeared to lay claim to the Russian throne.

The end of the Time of Troubles came in 1613. The Poles seized control of a number of Russian cities, monasteries, churches, and other landmarks, including the Kremlin in Moscow. Numerous monasteries were destroyed, and a number of priests and monks were killed. Patriarch Hermogen (1530-1612), who had been known earlier in his ministry as a priest and then bishop for his successful missionary efforts among various non-Russian ethnic groups, including Muslims, in the region that he served, and who had been elevated to the patriarchate in 1606, had been imprisoned in Moscow by Polish troops occupying Moscow. From prison he continued to encourage the Russians to resist, which reportedly led to his death when his Polish captors refused to give him food. At the end of 1612 Russian forces finally were able to enter Moscow and liberate it from Polish occupation.

In 1613, with much of Moscow in ruins, the boyars in the *zemsky sobor* elected sixteen-year-old Mikhail I Fyodorovich Romanov (1596-1645) to be the next tsar. Mikhail was the son of Fyodor Nikitich Romanov (1553-1633), who at the time of his son's election was being held as a hostage in Poland. Fyodor had once been a powerful *boyar*, but fearing him to be a rival, Boris Godunov forced both Fyodor and his wife, Xenia (d. 1631), into monastic life. Fyodor, now known as Filaret, subsequently became a priest, and then under False Demitrii became metropolitan of Rostov. He had been sent as an ambassador to the Polish king during the war, but when the Russians retook Moscow, the Poles made him a prisoner. Mikhail began referring to his father, who was being held in exile in Poland, as metropolitan of Moscow. But for the next eight years the Russian Church was without a patriarch.

Filaret was finally released by the Poles in 1619. Less than a month later a synod of the Russian Church elected him patriarch of Moscow. The Orthodox patriarch of Jerusalem, who was visiting Moscow at the time on a fund-raising mission for the church in Jerusalem, participated in both the synod and the subsequent service of consecration. Filaret concluded the service in the traditional Russian way by riding through the streets of Moscow on a donkey.

Over the next fourteen years, son and father ruled Russia as a diarchy. The patriarch was responsible for introducing a number of reforms, such as encouraging bishops to establish more effective schools for the training of priests. He encouraged the expansion of the printing industry and was involved in issuing new and corrected editions of liturgical texts. Concerned especially about the influx of Protestant and uniate Catholic religious ideas in books being imported from the West, he corresponded with Greek Orthodox Church leaders in search of support for his own educational efforts. The patriarch was also involved closely in matters of state, such as tax reforms and military concerns.

The tsar, on the other hand, not only was interested in matters of governance of the state, but he took part in reforming religion as well. One of the issues that became a major point of controversy toward the end of his reign concerned the liturgy. Russian Orthodox worship had been greatly influenced by the tradition of monastic offices. Worship in the regular church on Sunday could last six to eight hours in length, with a liturgy that was highly repetitious. To save time, priests had begun to conduct various parts of the liturgy at the same time, a practice known as *mnogoglasie* (polyvocality). While the practice allowed for shorter worship services, it meant that very little of what was said could be understood by the laity. Those who opposed the innovation were called *bogoliubtsy* (or "zealots," literally, "lovers of God"). They wanted to maintain the full liturgy, but also supported other reforms such as increasing preaching and improving education. The tsar called for reforms that would in effect reduce the repetitions and thereby shorten the liturgy while facilitating the laity's understanding of what was being said, which put him somewhere in the middle between those who practiced *mnogoglasie* and the zealots.

Tsar Mikhail died before any reforms could be instituted, but his son and successor, Alexei Mikhailovich Romanov (1629-1676), continued the effort. Several councils, or *sobors*, were called to deal in part with this issue. A council in 1649 sided with those who supported *mnogoglasie*, but a second council in 1651 took the opposite stand. The zealots, led by the tsar's confessor, Stephen Vonifatiev (d. 1656), pushed for efforts to curb the drunkenness of priests, encourage better sermons, and introduce harmony in signing. Improving the education of priests remained a primary concern of the reforming zealots as well. In seventeenth-century Russia theological education was confined almost entirely to the monasteries, and available only to monks. Vonifatiev and the other zealots sought to develop resources for educating all priests.

The reforming zealots found their cause advanced significantly by the election of a new patriarch in 1652. Vonifatiev was offered the position, but he was getting old and decided not to take on the office. His choice was a bright, decisive, impatient, if at times stubborn, abbot named Nikon (1605-1681). Born Nikita Minin into a family of peasants, he ran away from home as a child and lived in a monastery. As a young man he married and then was ordained as a priest, but after losing all three of his sons in one year, he convinced his wife to join him in taking monastic vows. Affairs of the monastery soon took Nikon, as he was now known, to Moscow, where he met Tsar Alexei. The two struck up a close relationship immediately. Alexei appointed Nikon to be the head of a powerful monastery a few years later, then in 1648 metropolitan of Novgorod. By the time of his election in 1652 to the office of patriarch, Nikon was already identified with the zealots. Chief among his concerns was to bring about educational reform in the church, and to this end in particular he began looking south, to the Greeks, for direction.

Nikon was not alone in looking toward Constantinople during this period. Alexei received a number of delegations of Greek merchants, monks, and priests, some of whom were seeking Russian support for churches and some who had raised the possibility of Russia eventually "liberating" Constantinople from the Ottomans. An invasion of the Balkans was considered, and the notion of the Russians celebrating Mass alongside the Greeks in Constantinople offered up as a realization of Russia's spiritual calling. Nikon in turn began to argue that the

Greeks were better educated, and that their liturgical books in particular were more reliable. With the help of advisors from Kiev, which after 1654 was firmly under the tsar's rule, as well as Istanbul and other Orthodox centers, he began to introduce a far greater number of liturgical reforms than the members of the zealots before him had contemplated.

Icons continued to play a central role in Russian Orthodox spiritual life, as they did in other Orthodox communities. In Russia, however, Baroque influences from the West had begun to appear in more recent paintings. Nikon criticized this development as a departure from Orthodoxy. He ordered that the homes of members of the nobility be searched to find such offending works, and that the eyes in these "heterodox" icons be gouged out before the icons were burned. Other changes concerned practices in the worship service. Nikon was particularly concerned to bring the Russian Church into conformity with Greek liturgical practices. He ordered that the sign of the cross be made with three fingers, as the Greeks did, rather than with two, as Russians traditionally did, for instance, and ordered the procession in the liturgy move counterclockwise, which was the Greek practice, rather than clockwise, as Russians had done.

Such changes may seem small, but critics of the moves saw them as amounting to a major shift in the Russian spiritual ethos. Moreover, Nikon based these reforms largely on the premise that the Greek liturgical texts were superior since they were the source of the Russian translations, a premise that others would question. Those who resisted the efforts, who came to be known as Old Believers, were exiled to monasteries far from Moscow. Several died from the harsh conditions of their treatment.

Resistance from these Old Believers nevertheless grew. At the same time Nikon's relationship with Tsar Alexei began to grow distant. After an argument with the tsar, the patriarch suddenly and unexpectedly resigned, retreating to a monastery. The tsar delayed the election of a new patriarch for several years, as the status of Nikon was debated by his ecclesiastical advisors. Finally, in 1666, the tsar convened a council to consider the patriarch's formal status. The Orthodox patriarchs of Antioch and Alexandria were both invited to attend, to help legitimate the decisions of the council since they were to touch in part on the status of the patriarch. Both journeyed to Moscow and participated in the event, thereby lending the authority of the ancient Greek church to the council.

At the end of its deliberations, the council found Nikon guilty on a number of counts and formally deposed him as patriarch. Nikon was returned to being a simple monk and sent into exile in a monastery outside Moscow. The council affirmed the changes that Nikon had supported, however, continuing the effort to bring the Russian churches into greater conformity with Greek Orthodox practices. A number of Old Believers who opposed these changes were excommunicated and sent into exile.

The Old Believers found their main spokesperson in the archpriest Avvakum Petrovich (1621-1682). Avvakum had once served in the Kazan Cathedral, which was located on Red Square, but in 1653 had been forced into exile by Nikon. A decade later he had been allowed by the tsar to return to Moscow. In early 1667, at the conclusion of the council that had deposed the patriarch, Avvakum, along with other leaders of the Old Believers, was again sent into exile by the tsar, this time to Siberia. In exile the archpriest wrote his autobiography, *Zhitie Protopopa Avvakuma, Im Samim Napisannoe* ("Life of Archpriest Avvakum as Written by Himself"), a work that was published only after his death but eventually came to be regarded as a classic work of Russian literature.

Prominent among the Old Believers were a number of women from among the ranks of the upper class. Among the early martyrs of the movement for instance was Boiarynia Feodosiia Morozova (1632-1675). Widowed at the age of thirty, she joined the Old Believers and became a nun, taking the name Feodora. In 1674 she was imprisoned for her beliefs and was starved to death the following year. An account of her life and ordeals, titled *Povest' o Boiaryne Morozovoi* ("Tale of Boiarynia Morozova"), was published and circulated by her family after her death, helping to spread both her fame and the cause for which she died even farther.

The death of Tsar Alexei in 1676 did not stop the persecution of the Old Believers, which continued under his son and successor, Feodor III (1661-1682). In 1682, in an effort to suppress the movement, a number of its leaders who were living in exile, including Avvakum, were sentenced to death. Avvakum was burned at the stake. Others had their hands cut off before being burned for signing themselves improperly with the cross. The numbers of those executed according to Old Believers' accounts reached into the tens of thousands. Other measures were taken as well to try to suppress them. Old Believers were ordered to wear special clothes to set them apart from others, a practice that had previously been exercised by Muslim governments toward religious minority communities. Many of the Old Believers moved to more remote areas, often establishing new colonies, especially to the north. The region of Latvia, which in the seventeenth century was divided between Poland (officially Roman Catholic) and Sweden (officially Lutheran) became a haven for Old Believers. Within the territorial boundaries of Tsarist Russia, official opposition could not kill the movement. Old Believers continued to hold on to the traditional Russian liturgical practices for centuries to come.

Old Believers actually separated from the main institutional structures of the state-supported Russian Orthodox Church in the middle of the seventeenth century. Another spiritual movement, whose members did not separate formally from the Orthodox Church but which nevertheless offered a distinctive spirituality, was known as *Khristovshchina* ("Christ-Faith"). The movement was founded around 1640 by a former soldier named Danila Filippovich (dates unknown) who claimed direct inspiration from God. Followers gathered secretly apart from the regular services of the Orthodox Church. They practiced a rigorous asceticism combined with what they considered to be primitive Christian spirituality. Great emphasis was placed on long fasts and self-denial, with members renouncing all sexual relations. Like the Quakers in the West, they believed in the immediate inspiration of the Holy Spirit in their lives as well. For the *Khristovshchina*, this took place especially during their gatherings when they practiced *radenie,* a form of ecstatic dance in which special illumination would come, often in the form of vivid visions. Members at these gatherings would often sing choruses celebrating the Holy Spirit, and, reminiscent of biblical accounts, many would speak in what they considered to be other languages while others would interpret. *Khristovshchina* retained the Jesus Prayer from Orthodox tradition, reciting regularly "Lord Jesus Christ, Son of God, have mercy on me." In many other regards they departed from traditional Orthodox spirituality, however, beginning with the belief that their founder was the messianic embodiment of Christ.

Such spiritual movements were an indication that the seventeenth century in Russia was a time of internal spiritual change. Much of this, however, was both caused and shaped by forces from beyond the immediate Russian context. Faced with growing pressures from the Catholic West, the main body of Russian Orthodox churches in the seventeenth century looked to the Greek tradition to its south for direction and renewal. At the same time the Russian Orthodox Church was spreading to the east, traveling with the migration of Russian peoples that had the support of the tsars. A group of fur traders reached the Pacific Ocean in 1639. Five decades later the boundary with China was finally established at the settlement of Nerchinsk. These traders and settlers moving to the east encountered sparsely inhabited regions whose indigenous peoples followed ancient shamanistic traditions. In the seventeenth century these indigenous peoples of Siberia began to convert to Orthodox Christianity, doing so through their contact with the priests and monks who had been sent by the tsars to provide for the religious needs of the expanding Russian communities. The Russian Orthodox Church was thus expanding as Russia politically was on its way to becoming an empire.

Suggestions for further reading

Aziz, S. Atiya, *A History of Eastern Christianity.* Notre Dame, IN: University of Notre Dame, 1968.

Baumer, Christoph, *The Church of the East: An Illustrated History of Assyrian Christianity.* London: I. B. Tauris, 2006.

Hupchick, Dennis P., *The Balkans: From Constantine to Communism.* New York: Palgrave Macmillan, 2004.

Moosa, Matti, *The Maronites in History.* Syracuse, NY: Syracuse University Press, 1986.

Pospielovsky, Dimitry, *The Orthodox Church in the History of Russia.* Crestwood, NY: St. Vladimir's Press, 1998.

Runciman, Stephen, *The Great Church in Captivity: A Study of the Patriarchate of Constantinople from the Eve of the Turkish Conquest to the Greek War of Independence.* Cambridge: Cambridge University Press, 1968.

Ware, Timothy, *The Orthodox Church.* 2nd ed. London: Penguin, 1993.

Part III

THE EIGHTEENTH CENTURY
Independence, Liberation, Awakenings

The world was rapidly shrinking in the eighteenth century as social, political, cultural, and religious interactions were becoming more global. European ships were the primary vehicles making the intercontinental connections, while Europe's growing material economy was the driving engine. The global divide between European nations and the nations and peoples of Asia, Africa, and America was becoming more pronounced as a result. Europe was at the center of the new global economic map, and its colonial efforts were rendering the rest of the world its economic periphery. Christian missions continued to ride the waves of colonial expansion through this period. Despite the fact that the relationship between colonists and missionaries was not always smooth, Christianity in Africa, Asia, and America in the eighteenth century was dominated by the effects of European colonial efforts.

The European slave trade, conducted mostly by people who claimed to be Christian, continued to play a significant role in shaping African Christianity through the eighteenth century. In the north of Africa, an Islamic revival under indigenous leadership reshaped the religious and political landscape, while in the south Dutch colonial rule was transforming the region. In east Asia, the memory of older Asian Christian forms continued to recede, leaving Christianity to be increasingly associated with Western colonial rulers and identified as a European religion. Large sections of India began in 1757 to come under the rule of the British East India Company, a private stock-holding company operating under British royal charter. In China, a decision made in Rome to end the practice of allowing Chinese Christians to practice ancestor veneration put the growth of Christianity in that empire on hold for the time being.

In Europe and its settler colonies in America, the eighteenth century witnessed the rise of the new liberal nation-state, dominated by the growing middle class, and culminating in revolutions in the colonies of British North America and in the European nation of France. Spain's control over its South American empire declined significantly over the course of the century, opening doors for political independence movements in those lands by the end of the century as well. The European intellectual landscape was dominated by the philosophical movement that came to be called the Enlightenment. Notions of political and intellectual freedom by the end of the century had begun to coincide, with religion, and state-dominated forms of Christianity in particular, often relegated to the side of authoritarianism and tyranny. A number of new movements seeking to address what seemed to some to be declining Christian affections among European peoples in general emerged in Protestant churches under the banner of Awakenings. They quickly spread beyond Europe, laying the foundations for a new global evangelical movement.

Orthodox churches in the eighteenth century under the Ottoman rulers began to experience new shoots of self-rule and independence. The long period of Muslim rule over Christians in eastern Europe was drawing to a close. The Ottomans continued to be a political force to be reckoned with by churches and their leadership throughout the region, but new national expressions and national churches began to appear. In places where territories under Ottoman rule came under European Christian rulers, strong and vital Muslim communities often remained, leaving Muslims living as political minorities in Christian states or under Christian rulers.

14

Africa in the Eighteenth Century

An overview

An observer of world history in 1700 could hardly be faulted for not expecting Christianity to have much of a future on the continent of Africa. In the north, Ottoman rule stretched from Egypt almost to the Atlantic Ocean. Christianity had all but disappeared from Libya, Tunisia, Algeria, and Morocco a thousand years earlier, and scattered efforts from time to time to replant it proved mostly futile. In Egypt, the Coptic Church and a much smaller community of Greek-speaking Christians who were in communion with the ecumenical patriarch persistently struggled to survive. A small but significant number of individuals from these churches had begun to join the Roman Catholic Church by the eighteenth century, doing so under the impact of Roman Catholic missions in the region. Christians had all but disappeared from Nubia. Franciscans who entered the country from Aswan, Egypt, and traveled through the northern region reported in 1734 that they found a few local Christian communities, but that the Muslim rulers of Nubia persistently sought to force them to abandon their faith. Only in the ancient Christian kingdom of Ethiopia in all of eighteenth-century Africa were Christians still in the majority. The continuous pressures of European colonial efforts were producing a more nationalistic church.

In West Africa, European colonial powers succeeded in establishing a series of forts along the coast of Ghana. These served as the points of contact for the growing trade in enslaved Africans, who were being shipped mostly to America. Christianity in West Africa was almost entirely confined to these forts populated mostly by European settlers and the children of mixed unions who were being raised within the forts. Contacts with Africans living in the vicinity of these forts resulted in a small number of Africans entering into the European social and cultural world, and undergoing Christian baptism. There was nothing that could be described as an indigenous Christian church in West Africa in the eighteenth century, however.

The central African kingdom of Kongo was still nominally Christian, but it had all but collapsed as a coherent political entity by the eighteenth century. Portuguese control over the area to the south, in the colony of Angola, was expanding. The Dutch colony at Cape Town on the tip of southern Africa continued to grow as well through the course of the century. Cape Town had become a multicultural and multireligious community as settlers from several European nations and some parts of Asia gathered in its confines. Conflicts with the indigenous Khoikhoi peoples increased in the region as Dutch expansion continued, and as people of European descent began to move inland to settle. A number of these Christian colonists of European descent from Cape Town who began in the eighteenth century to move inland to the more rugged territories to the north and east did so to escape what they considered to be the increasingly autocratic control of the Dutch East India Company over the colony. These seminomadic farmers and herders, known as *trekboeren*, or just *boeren* ("boers" in English), sought out isolated locations where they could settle and live. They often took with them their Bibles and guns, and little else in the way of material cultural goods.

The European slave trade in African bodies continued throughout the eighteenth century to dominate the material economy of Europe and Africa alike. Trade flourished despite the enormous economic disparity between the continents. Europeans gained financially far more than the Africans who were involved in the sale of human flesh. It is difficult to judge the full extent that the slave trade had on the continent of Africa, but few peoples from the continent were left untouched by it. In the eighteenth century both Catholic and Protestant European Christians were deeply involved. A number of individual Africans and Europeans raised their voices in protest through the course of the century against the slave trade, but the profits that were still to be made in the sale of human flesh proved to be a powerful counterincentive to justice.

Strengthening within Islam

Christianity in Africa through the eighteenth century lived in an uneasy relationship with Islam for the most part. Among the most important developments in Islam in the seventeenth century was the emergence of a number of revivalist movements in northern Africa. One of the most influential of these was a new Sufi order, the Tijānī or Tijaniyya, founded toward the end of the century in the 1780s. The order was organized by Sīdī 'Ahmad al-Tijānī (1737-1815), an Algerian who had moved to Fez, Morocco, to study. Around 1782 he began to experience a series of visions that he took to be a direct source of inspiration. Many of those who followed him soon were regarding these visions to be second only to the Qur'an and the Hadith in religious authority, thereby allowing them to bypass the lengthy succession of traditional Sufi teachers that were typically regarded as authoritative by the various branches. Al-Tijānī rejected a number of Islamic practices that he viewed as being Western-influenced corruptions of the original teachings of the Prophet Mohammed, such as conducting pilgrimages to tombs. Followers were taught to recite several times a day particular phrases or chants that he had selected in addition to maintaining the central practices or "Pillars" of Islam. While Al-Tijānī taught an ascetic and academic form of Sufi Islam, his opposition to those who dominated the various other Sufi schools of his day lent him the reputation for being anti-elite, and thus a proponent of the poor. He was more concerned with restoring traditional Islam, however.

The Tijānī movement spread rapidly across northwest Africa as far as Senegal and among the Fulani where it found widespread acceptance. By the eighteenth century a number of other branches of the Sufi movement were spreading through the region as well. Centuries of trade across the Sahara Desert had made Islam an indigenous religion in the sub-Saharan landscape. Islam in West Africa had generally coexisted for centuries alongside other indigenous traditions without significant conflict. Muslims lived mostly in the larger cities and towns, as these were the areas where merchant contact was strongest. Traditional African religious practices continued to dominate in the villages throughout the countryside.

In Mali, the city of Timbuktu, which was founded in the eleventh century, had by the sixteenth century become one of the most important Islamic centers for learning in the world. The Sankoré Madrasah, or Sankoré University, was housed in three mosques in the city, known as Djingareyber, Sankore, and Sidi Yahya. The Maliki branch, or school, of Sharia Islamic law dominated at the university. Muslim students who came to the institution would live, work, and study with one of the imams or sheiks who made up the faculty. The curriculum included the study of the Qur'an, grammar, literature, mathematics, science, and philosophy. The library of the university was made up of several hundred thousand volumes written in both Greek and Arabic and was held in over one hundred collections located throughout the city.

The combined influences of renewed scholarship spurred on by the university at Timbuktu and the new streams of Sufi spiritual piety found a fertile home among the Fulani people in West Africa in the eighteenth century. The Fulani were mostly nomads, and many of them had migrated to Hausa territory, where they lived and worked among the more settled Hausa towns. A new class of scholars emerged in the eighteenth century among the Fulani, called *torodbe*, or "revivalists." One of the most important of these Fulani revivalist scholars was Usuman Dan Fodio (Sheik Uthman ibn Fodio in Arabic, 1754-1817). Born in Degael, in the Hausa city-state of Gobir, at a young age he took to the study of Islam. A practitioner of Sufi spirituality as well, he soon drew around him a community of followers, or a school. Dan Fodio was an itinerant teacher and a prolific writer. He was also a popular political figure, criticizing the Hausa rulers for their heavy taxation, encouraging the education of women (his own daughters became scholars), and opposing the practice of female circumcision.

Opposition to his political activities forced Dan Fodio into exile in 1802. Backed by a growing number of followers who recognized him as a religious teacher as well as a political ruler, from exile he declared *jihad*, or "holy war," against the Hausa. Word soon spread among other members of the Fulani tribe as well as among a number of Hausa who were dissatisfied with the spiritual and social situation of their land. War broke out two years later, and by the time it was over in 1810 Dan Fodio was the head of one of the largest and most powerful political empires in Africa, the Sokoto Caliphate in northern Nigeria.

Dan Fodio identified himself as a *mujaddid*, or a "renewer of the faith," who appears only once a century or so. His visions and his own sense of calling were directed against what he considered to be a compromised form of Islam, as well as against the previous Hausa rulers in the region. The *jihad* that he successfully initiated was the first in a wave of new Islamic revivals that can safely be characterized as both politically and religiously intolerant. They were also directed against any Islamic absorption or accommodation with local religions, and would later feed into conflicts with Christians. The societies that these *jihadists* eventually established were politically stable and, for a time, financially prosperous. One of the major sources of their wealth came from slaving. Fulani traders in cities of the Sokoto Caliphate controlled much of the trans-Saharan slave trade that took Africans north to Muslim societies. To even a casual observer, by 1800 Islam appeared to be on the verge of dominating all of West Africa.

West Africa

More than two centuries of contact between West Africans and Portuguese along the coastal region produced little in the way of religious effects. The Portuguese were mostly interested in trading for slaves, which were provided by local African chieftains along the coast from raids conducted against neighboring peoples farther inland. In Central Africa the royal families of Kongo continued to be professed Christians; but there were few priests, and the level of Christian teaching was low. Both Capuchin and Jesuit missionaries conducted work in the region, but their efforts were not enough.

Little in the way of new Roman Catholic missionary work was undertaken in West Africa in the eighteenth century. In part this was due to a decline in Roman Catholic mission work globally. Europe, from where Roman Catholic missionaries were overwhelmingly recruited, was beginning to see a decline in the number of young men entering Catholic clerical life. The Catholic Church in northern European regions had lost many of its monasteries. France and Italy still sent large numbers of missionaries to work in other parts of the world, but friction between French and Portuguese kings and the Jesuits in their lands, related in a large part to the commercial interests of kings in both nations, led to the suppression of the Jesuits, including their missionary work in the French and Portuguese colonies after 1750.

One interesting episode in the history of Catholic Christianity in West Africa involved two young African boys who were sent to Europe at the end of the seventeenth century to receive a Christian education. The French tried to establish a trading settlement along the coast of West Africa in 1687. The following year the king of Assinie, which is now part of Côte d'Ivoire, sent two household servants with French Dominicans to return to France to be educated. The two servants, named Banga (dates unknown) and Aniaba (1673-c. 1720), were quite resourceful, convincing their Dominican captors that they were actually Assinie royalty. In France they were presented to King Louis XIV (1638-1715), who entrusted their instruction to the archbishop of Paris. Aniaba was baptized in 1691 and eventually both young men became officers in the French army. Both men eventually returned to the Côte d'Ivoire in West Africa, Banga first in 1695 and then Aniaba in 1701 after hearing of the death of the Assinie king. Shortly after returning, Aniaba renounced Christianity and had little further contact with the French. Nevertheless, he was one of the first Africans whose life became an intercontinental bridge with Christianity in Europe in the eighteenth century.

Protestants began appearing in West Africa in the middle of the seventeenth century as the Dutch, British, and later Danish began building forts to support their growing involvement in the slave trade. These newer European powers showed even less interest than the Portuguese in trying to spread their Christian faith among West Africans. A report by the director general of the Dutch West India Company in 1745 dismissed the possibility that Africans were ever going to convert to Christianity. So it is somewhat ironic that efforts to spread Protestant Christianity in West Africa were first initiated by West Africans themselves.

In 1725 a Dutch ship captain gave as a gift a young Fante-speaking African boy who had been sold to him along the coast of Ghana to one of the merchants from the Dutch West India Company in The Hague. The young boy, whose name may have been Asar, was renamed Jacobus Elisa Johannes Capitein (1717-1747), the family name bestowed in honor of the captain who brought him to Holland. Capitein grew up in the home of the Dutch merchant. He was educated in Latin, Greek, and Hebrew, and showed abilities in both painting and mathematics. At the age of eighteen he was baptized and two years later entered the University of Leiden to study theology.

Five years later in 1742 he completed a dissertation in Latin that ironically argued that slavery was compatible with Christian liberty, and was ordained to the ministry. Soon after that he made known his desire to return to West Africa to serve and was appointed to be the Dutch chaplain at the fort in Elmina along the coast of Ghana. More Dutch than Fante in his cultural identity by now, he married a Dutch woman in Elmina and set up a school for children in the fort. At the same time he did not entirely abandon his African heritage. Capitein served as tutor to the children of a local African chieftain. He prepared a catechism in Fante and translated the Apostles' Creed and the Ten Commandments, all of which were published in the Netherlands. The work in Elmina was difficult, and Capitein was fairly alone in the eighteenth century in his bicultural identity. His early death at the young age of thirty cut short his life's work before it could come to fruition. Nevertheless, his legacy as one of the first West Africans to become Protestant and one of the first Protestant missionaries to Africa from Europe is an important one.

A close contemporary of Capitein was Anton Wilhelm Amo (1703-c. 1756). A member of the Akan people, Amo was taken captive at the age of four and sold to Dutch merchants. They took him to Holland and presented him to the Duke of Brunswick-Wolfenbüttel in Germany. Amo was baptized and raised as a member of the duke's family. In 1721 he entered the University of Helmstedt and later completed a degree in law at the University of Halle with a dissertation on *De iure Maurorum in Europa* ("On the Legal Standing of Moors in Europe"). He then went on to the University of Wittenberg, where in 1734 he completed a second doctorate. His dissertation, titled *De humanae mentis apatheia* ("On the Apathy of the Human Mind"), presented a critique of Cartesian dualism, arguing that it is the body and not the mind that experiences sensation. Two years later he accepted an appointment as professor of philosophy at Halle, and in 1740 moved on to the University of Jena to teach.

Despite (or perhaps because of) these accomplishments, Amo faced a series of public attacks based on his African identity, leading him to decide in 1747 to return to West Africa. He arrived and located members of his family, but is reported to have faced opposition from the Dutch in the region who feared he might help stir opposition against them. Eventually he came to live at the Dutch Fort San Sebastian along the coast of Ghana, where he died, probably in 1756.

From the Danish Fort Christiansborg two other young African boys went to Europe in the eighteenth century and made themselves a name there. Frederik Pedersen Svane (d. 1789) and Christian Jakob Protten (1715-1769) were both sons of African mothers and Danish fathers serving as soldiers in Fort Christiansborg. Both were sent to Denmark to the household of King Frederick IV in 1727. Frederik had been greatly influenced by Pietism from Germany and showed considerable interest in helping to spread Christianity in other regions of the world. Both boys were baptized, the king serving as godfather, and were raised as members of the royal household. Both eventually attended the University of Copenhagen.

Frederik Svane tested the tolerance of Danish society by marrying a Danish woman named Catharina Maria Badsch (dates unknown). Shortly thereafter he was expelled from the school of theology. The young couple moved to Ghana in 1735 to begin work in ministry, making them possibly the first married couple to serve as Christian missionaries in Africa. Both suffered from even greater ridicule in Africa as a European-African couple. Pregnant with their son, Catharina returned to Denmark shortly after arriving, but Svane remained in Africa for another ten years, relearning his native Ga language in order to teach and preach in it, all the while longing to be rejoined with his wife and child. When he finally did manage to return to Denmark in 1745 he wrote about his experience in an autobiography that told of his ten years in West Africa. His final days were spent in study at Copenhagen.

Christian Jakob Protten (1715-1769) accompanied Svane to the court of Frederick in 1727. He too entered the University of Copenhagen in 1732, but three years later moved to Herrnhut, Germany, to live in a colony that was established by a group called Moravians who lived on an estate owned by German Count Nikolaus Ludwig von Zinzendorf (1700-1760) in Saxony. The Moravians were members of the Brethren from Czechoslovakia who had been forced to immigrate to Germany in the eighteenth century. Zinzendorf, who was a Lutheran, provided them political asylum and then became their spiritual leader. Their theology combined German Pietism, spiritual quietism, and an active missionary practice in a distinct combination. Protten lived at Herrnhut for a year before departing for the coast of West Africa in 1737 with another member of the community to serve as missionaries.

After several years of unsuccessful work along the coast of West Africa, due mostly to the opposition of the Dutch who controlled Fort Elmina, Protten returned to Germany in 1742. He then went on to work as a Moravian missionary on the island of St. Thomas in the Caribbean, which at the time was a Danish colony. Three years later he returned to Herrnhut and in 1746 married a woman named Rebecca Freundlich (1718-1780), who was also of African descent, had been also a Moravian worker in St. Thomas, and was the widow of a German Moravian named Martin Freundlich.

In 1757, despite the opposition of the leaders of Herrnhut, Protten returned to West Africa under the Danish West India and Guinea Company to serve in ministry at Christiansborg Castle, where he had originally lived as a child. He traveled to Herrnhut one last time in 1762 to retrieve his wife, Rebecca, and with her returned to Christiansborg in 1765 where he resided the rest of his life. Before he died he succeeded in writing several introductory grammar books for West African languages and translating a catechism. Rebecca lived another decade after him.

Although the British had begun to trade along the coast of West Africa as early as the 1560s, it was not until the eighteenth century that they succeeded in establishing a full presence in trading cloth, metals, guns, alcohol, and tobacco for slaves. During the eighteenth century, the British linked their trade in Asia, America, and Africa, connecting the continents into a British economic network that circled the globe. In the 1730s the British surpassed the Portuguese in slave trade, transporting an estimated 170,000 Africans to America during that decade alone. British goods were highly desired by West African rulers, who controlled their side of the trade equation with the European nations operating along the coast.

European traders in West Africa operated out of forts that the European companies built along the coast. Initially the European companies had simply seized the land on which the forts were built, but in time they had to pay for additional land. Europeans never came under the jurisdiction of local African chieftains, but they had to cooperate for supplies and for access to the markets. Africans learned the European languages and customs quicker than Europeans learned the African languages and customs, giving the African chieftains an upper hand in these local markets of West Africa. For European traders, success required accommodating to African customs and desires. The result was profitable for both sides. Europeans received a steady supply of slaves, but in return Africans received goods that they did not manufacture. During the last half of the eighteenth century, for instance, an estimated 20 million guns were sold to Africans. These guns, mostly British made, were used for hunting, defense, and capturing more prisoners among neighboring communities to enslave. Although the amount of trade was steadily increasing through this period, due to the increased competition in the region, European profits remained static or fell. The relative value of a firearm dropped from two guns being exchanged for one enslaved prisoner in 1682, to thirty-two guns for one enslaved prisoner in 1718.

The colonial empires of the Netherlands, Denmark, and England were run by merchant companies with royal charters rather than as direct operations under their respective national crowns. The purpose of these companies was strictly to make money. Unlike the earlier colonial efforts of Spain and Portugal, which were under royal control, there was no support for Protestant missionaries by these companies. Chaplains sailed on the companies' ships to provide religious services for those on board, and ministers were sent to be in residence at the forts to provide for the religious needs of the small number of settlers in them. But for the seventeenth century and the first decades of the eighteenth century, efforts to missionize outside the boundaries of the forts or settlements were for the most part not welcomed in places where the Netherlands, England, Denmark, or Sweden had colonial operations.

A report to the bishop of London on the dismal condition of religion in England's colonies in America led to the formation of the Society for the Propagation of the Gospel in Foreign Parts (SPG) in England in 1701. A year later it sent out its first missionaries to America. Although most of the work that the society conducted was geared toward European settlers in the English colonies, its charter stated that it was a society intended to effect the evangelization of enslaved Africans and Native Americans.

Thomas Thompson (1708-1773) was an SPG missionary working among enslaved Africans in the colony of New Jersey, in North America, in the 1740s when he asked to be commissioned by the society to go to West Africa. He sailed from New York to Cape Coast Castle in 1751, arriving the following year. The castle was primarily a holding prison for enslaved Africans who were waiting to be shipped to America. An ardent defender of the morality of slavery, Thomas nevertheless hoped to see Christianity spread among Africans. He also believed that the best candidates for achieving this end would be Africans themselves. With that goal in view, the following year he convinced a local African chieftain to allow three young Fanti boys to be sent to England to be educated. One of the boys died of tuberculosis in 1758, and another suffered a mental breakdown and died a decade later. The third, Philip Quaque (originally Kweku in Fanti, 1741-1816), was placed by the SPG in the home of a priest, who served as his tutor. Quaque was baptized in 1759, and then in 1765 was ordained by the bishop of London to return to Ghana the following year to serve as chaplain to the Europeans at Cape Coast and as a missionary to Africans, making him the first African to be ordained as a priest in the Church of England and the first English-speaking African to serve as a missionary.

Life in Cape Coast was not easy for Quaque. A year after arriving, his English wife, Catherine Blunt (d. 1767), died. He eventually married twice more. The English colonists at Cape Coast were generally indifferent, and in some cases even hostile, toward religion. For the most part they disliked having an African serve as their chaplain. Quaque had lost his ability to speak Fante fluently, hindering his ability to work among the Africans in the region. The SPG had trouble paying his full salary, forcing him to eventually try to supplement his income by working as a trader. He eventually sent his two sons back to England where they were educated, and one of them later helped him run the school for children at Cape Coast. Although his ministry is sometimes depicted as being a failure, the fact that he sustained for five decades the difficult conditions of serving on the boundary between European and African worlds in the eighteenth and early nineteenth centuries is remarkable.

Abolitionism begins

The Africans who journeyed to Europe in the eighteenth century faced considerable hostility directed against them for their Africanness. Building on centuries of cultural perceptions of Africans as "moors," Europe in the eighteenth century witnessed a growing racialized discourse that rendered African "blackness" as "inferior" and "other." In part this discourse served to undergird the European involvement in the African slave trade, and in part it served to buttress a growing sense of European cultural superiority.

Africans themselves posed the most effective challenge to such racialized discourse in Europe. The same was true for the nascent streams of abolitionism that by the middle decades of the eighteenth century were beginning to form in Europe. A key factor in the emergence of the abolitionist movement was the publication of several narratives written by Africans themselves, which helped stir public opposition to the global trade in African bodies.

Many northern Europeans, especially the Danish, English, and Dutch, were becoming aware of Africans as individuals in the eighteenth century. While this was an important factor in Europe's turn away from slave trade and slave holding over the course of the century, it was the writings of Africans themselves in Western languages, telling the plight of enslaved Africans, that played the major role in changing European public opinion. These African voices and the movement of liberation they helped inaugurate were integrally related to the development of Christianity in both Africa and in the West during this period. In the end the argument for the full humanity of Africans and for the inhumanity of the "peculiar institution" of slavery coincided.

The publication in 1789 of *The Interesting Narrative of the Life of Olaudah Equiano, or Gustavus Vassa, the African in His Own Words* proved to be a major factor in the development of public support in Europe for the abolitionist cause. In its pages Olaudah Equiano (c. 1745-c. 1800), who was also known as Gustavus Vassa, told the story of how he had been captured as a young child from an Igbo village near the Niger River by other Africans and sold into slavery, being taken first to Barbados and then to Virginia. From Virginia a British naval captain purchased him and took him to England, where Equiano was baptized and began to be educated. His seafaring skills kept him on ships, and eventually he ended up with a Quaker owner who allowed him to purchase his own freedom. Equiano continued to work on ships as a freeman, traveling to Turkey and on an expedition to the Arctic Ocean before settling finally in England. In 1792 he married Susannah Cullen, an English woman, and together they had two daughters.

Questions regarding the historical accuracy of Equiano's depictions of his early life have been raised in recent years due to the fact that his baptismal certificate from St. Margaret's Chapel in Westminster, England, lists his birthplace as South Carolina. This could be nothing more than the erroneous entry of a witness who misunderstood where the twelve-year-old boy was from. On the other hand, the historical effect of Equiano's vivid descriptions of the torture meted out to enslaved Africans, such as the muzzles placed over their faces to keep them from speaking, the manner in which they were chained to four stakes on the ground and then flogged, or the personal episode in which he was placed in cuffs by the British naval captain who was his master for preferring to be called Jacob rather than Gustavus Vassa, had a considerable historical impact in the last decade of the eighteenth century.

Equiano's formal association with the abolitionist movement in England began in 1774 with a visit to Granville Sharp (1735-1813), an ardent opponent of slavery in England. Sharp had been arguing in court in England for a decade prior to the visit that enslaved persons, upon setting foot on British soil, were automatically to be set free by law. Equiano visited Sharp to gain the latter's support in the case of a person of African descent who had been kidnapped and was being held on a ship. A decade later in 1783 Equiano again enlisted Sharp's help to raise a public outcry against an English sea captain who had thrown 132 enslaved Africans overboard at sea to drown in order to collect insurance money on them. The association of Equiano and Sharp in the abolitionist cause led to Equiano's being appointed as commissary steward for an expedition designed to relocate to West Africa a number of people of African descent in England in 1787. He was dismissed from the project, however, amid controversy when he exposed financial irregularities taking place. Toward the end of his life he became a prominent leader of a group of abolitionists of African descent in England who called themselves "Sons of Africa."

Equiano's religious story spans several continents and traditions as well. During the first eleven years of his life, he was exposed only to the indigenous African religion of his Igbo family. He was later baptized as a Christian in England after being brought there by the naval captain who was his master. By his own account, Equiano at one point considered resettling in Turkey and converting to Islam, before having a spiritual experience of grace and salvation while on a ship in Cadiz harbor in Spain that identified him with evangelical Christianity. Throughout his life he consistently demonstrated a deep love for the Bible, which he says was his only companion in all of his travels, beginning as a young boy when he first held the book to his ear in order to see if he could hear it talk. In 1777 he unsuccessfully petitioned the bishop of London to be ordained and sent to Africa as a missionary.

One of Equiano's close friends and collaborators in the abolitionist cause in London was Ottobah Cugoano (1757?-1801). Originally a member of the Fanti people in Ghana, Cugoano had been enslaved in 1770 and sent to Granada in the Caribbean. In 1772 his master brought him to England and then freed him. Like Equaino, Cugoano was moved by personal experience and empowered by education to speak out against the slave trade. Also like Equiano, he sought out Granville Sharp and joined the abolitionist efforts being organized in England in the last decades of the eighteenth century. In 1787 he wrote, possibly with the help of Equiano, *Thoughts and Sentiments on the Evil and Wicked Traffic of Slavery and Commerce of the Human Species.* The book notably placed blame for slavery on every person in Great Britain, who, he argued, to some extent shared responsibility for the horrors that were being perpetrated. He also followed Equiano's lead in speaking to the economic interests that were involved. The slave trade did not make good economic sense, he argued, for it detracted from the development of other commercial activities.

Cugoano's work received considerable recognition not only in England but in other parts of Europe. A French translation appeared within a year of its original publication. The manner in which it detailed the barbarity of practices carried out against slaves on plantations, such as having teeth extracted for eating a piece of sugar cane, helped to stir public opposition to the institution. While noting that if there were no buyers there would be no sellers, Cugoano nevertheless also acknowledged the role that Africans were playing in kidnapping and selling other Africans in the global slave trade. He cautioned that while Africans also kept slaves, their treatment was far better, and that those Africans involved in the trade in Africa could not know the misery they were causing in the Caribbean where their captives were being sold. The form of slavery that was being perpetrated by the overseers on plantations who were nominally at least Christian was far crueler. The irony that these Christian owners and overseers had no regard for the law of God or for human welfare was not missed on his readers. Cugoano's book provided a powerful weapon against both the slave trade and slave holding. Without question, it was these African Christian voices in the heart of the empire that proved to be most significant in turning the tide of public opinion in England at the end of the eighteenth century.

The expedition that Equiano had initially been appointed to serve on as commissary steward in 1786 represented a distinct moment of convergence of abolitionism, colonization, and Christian missions. It was also a story taking place on three continents, and resulted in the founding of the colony of Sierra Leone in 1787 in West Africa. The British colonies located along the Atlantic seacoast in North America had openly rebelled in 1776, leading to full-fledged war. During the course of the war, which came to be called the American Revolution, the British colonial governors offered any enslaved person freedom if they fought on the side of the British. As defeated British forces began to retreat from these colonies, a number of people of African descent went with them, taking up the British promise of freedom. Most of these former slaves were poor, and the majority of British people still did not fully welcome persons of African descent living in their midst. Efforts were made to resettle a number of these former slaves in the British colonies of Nova Scotia, the Bahamas, and Jamaica, but more than fifteen thousand persons of African descent ended up living in England.

Responding to the social blight caused by the influx of impoverished freed slaves, as well as to the racialized opposition to Africans, a group of benevolent politicians and other philanthropists in London formed the "Committee for Relieving the Black Poor." The plan the committee advanced was to send the impoverished descendants of Africans to a new colony that was to be formed in West Africa. The plan promised to give the repatriated Africans land and help them to develop commercially, whereby the new colonists would be able to repay the British government for the cost of repatriation. Granville Sharp was one of the leaders of the effort, and he enlisted a number of other abolitionists in the cause, including, as we have seen, Olaudah Equiano.

Sharp and several others among the plan promoters expressed strong Christian motives for the effort. Still others supported the cause for less-than-noble reasons, as a way to remove persons of African descent from England. The major problem that the plan faced was that the thousands of Africans living in England had originally come from hundreds of different locations. They had originally spoken many different African languages, and most spoke only English or another European language. Nevertheless, the plan went forward, and in 1787, after two initial attempts, more than four hundred passengers representing a mixture of African Americans, African Caribbeans, and African English, and including former soldiers, adventurers, craftspeople, appointed government officials, and several London prostitutes, left for "Granville Town" in West Africa.

The results were tragic. Within three months, a third of the group died from disease. Within a year, only 133, less than one-third of the original colonists, had survived. Rather than abandoning the plan, however, Sharp and others formed the Sierra Leone ("Lion Mountains" in Portuguese) Company in 1791. Empowered by an act of the British Parliament, the company began recruiting freed blacks from Nova Scotia who had fought with the British in the American Revolutionary War for the next round of settlement in West Africa.

Early in 1792, 1,190 former slaves and others of African descent sailed from Nova Scotia to the newly named "Freetown" in Sierra Leone. Unlike the first group from England, which included many miscreants, this group was mostly made up of dedicated Christians who had declared their purpose to be missionaries to Africa. Each of the five sailing vessels that left Nova Scotia was regarded as an individual Christian community, and each carried its own pastor. Together they were guided by a common biblical vision to bring Christianity and freedom to Africa. Most of those on the voyage also considered themselves to be African in heritage and identity. The trip back across the Atlantic was conceived to be repatriation. Insofar as this was true, it is with this expedition from Nova Scotia and the founding of Freetown and the colony of Sierra Leone that one can speak for the first time of an African church in West Africa.

The settlement was to be a Christian mission outpost in Africa. It was not envisioned to be an African Christian kingdom, however, nor a continuation of Christendom. The Sierra Leone settlers were filled with evangelical sentiments that fused abolitionist ideals and a political commitment to liberty with religious dissent and revivalism. The colony they founded was chartered by the English Parliament as a private company, but its leaders were committed to missions as much as commerce. The tens of thousands who eventually populated Sierra Leone in the early nineteenth century offered a prophetic African Christian witness that would become a harbinger for future liberation movements in Africa.

Southern Africa

The first Christians known to have visited southern Africa had been Portuguese who had first passed by at the end of the fifteenth century. The Portuguese continued through the sixteenth and seventeenth centuries mostly to stop along the southeastern coast of Africa on their way to and from India. Portuguese settlers eventually established trading factories in what is now Mozambique, and missionary work under the direction of Dominicans and then Jesuits followed. Goa was the center for all Portuguese mission work in eastern Africa as well as for Asia during this period. In the eighteenth century along the southeastern coast of Africa Islam had an established presence, but most of the inhabitants in the region were practitioners of indigenous African religious traditions.

The Dominicans had been the first to try to establish a Christian presence in Mozambique. Despite more than a century of work, however, they had mostly been unsuccessful in evangelizing Africans, or catechizing those whom they had baptized. An effort to train boys from Mozambique in Goa to serve as priests had limited success. Few, if any, returned to the region to serve. Lack of financial support from Europe in the eighteenth century led the Dominicans along the Zambezi River to turn to mining and trading. The Dominican priest Pedro de Trindade (d. 1751) was well known throughout the region for what the inhabitants considered to be his powers as a medicine man and healer. The reputation had been gained mostly by his success in developing an antitoxin for poisoned arrows. More significant for the history of the region, however, was his involvement in gold mining and slaving. The Dominican priest reportedly had as many as 1,600 slaves working in his gold mines and on his plantations at the peak of his operations. Faced with the threat of war from local people, Trindade was able to raise an army and defeat them, thereby frightening others in the region into submission. Not surprisingly in light of his extended political power, his parish grew quite a bit from the 1730s when he began working in the area until his death in 1751.

Both the Dominicans and the Jesuits who worked in Mozambique felt the impact of the decline in young men going into the Catholic priesthood in Europe in the eighteenth century. The effect on Catholic missions in Mozambique was greater than it was in Kongo, where Christianity had developed as a national religion and had established churches throughout the land. In the middle of the eighteenth century there were only ten priests to serve the whole Zambezi mission of the Dominicans, and only a few established parishes in or near towns where the Portuguese had trading settlements. The suppression of the Jesuits by the Portuguese crown in the last half of the century removed them entirely from Mozambique, where they had a presence in the south. Portuguese traders were interested in a number of items produced in the region, such as ivory, which was highly valued in Europe as a commodity. As in other parts of Africa, however, in the eighteenth century, slaves were the single most valuable commodity sought in the southeast.

Farther to the south, the growing Dutch colonial presence was reshaping the region. The Dutch first established the colony at Cape Town in the 1650s. The revocation of the Edict of Nantes in France by Louis XIV in 1685 brought an influx of French Huguenots seeking to escape the new climate of political intolerance in their homeland. Toward the end of the century various other groups from

Germany and England arrived to take up residence in the colony. For the most part these various European settlers showed little interest in local peoples except as cheap labor.

During the last half of the seventeenth century there had been several skirmishes between the Dutch settlers and the indigenous Khoikhoi people in the region, whom the Dutch called "Hottentots." By the eighteenth century the two sides had settled into an uneasy peace for the most part, which allowed trading to go on between them. There was little in the way of religious interaction between the European settlers and the indigenous Khoikhoi people, who were semi-nomadic farmers for the most part, living in small villages scattered throughout the region.

The Dutch brought slaves from other parts of Africa to the settlement shortly after it was established in the seventeenth century, but half a century later most Africans who lived in Cape Town were still adherents of indigenous religious traditions. A school was established to provide some literacy and to teach Christianity to the slaves, but for the most part Dutch masters were reluctant to allow their slaves to be baptized. Christianization in the colony was considered to be a useful tool only to pacify those forced to work as slaves. At the end of the seventeenth century the Dutch began to import ethnic Malay from the East Indies who were forced to engage in manual labor. The Malay were Muslims who retained their Islamic faith, thereby adding to the religious pluralism of eighteenth-century Cape Town.

German Pietists on their way to South India to serve as missionaries under appointment by the Danish king stopped off in Cape Town in 1706. Their published account of the visit several years later noted the dire state of Christianity in the colony, and particularly pointed out the lack of efforts to reach the enslaved population. Word of the conditions reached Count von Zinzendorf and the Moravians in Herrnhut, who responded in 1737 by sending one of their number, Georg Schmidt (1709-1785), as a missionary to Cape Town.

Schmidt was no stranger to difficulties, having already spent six years in prison in Bohemia for his religious convictions. In Cape Town he received little in the way of support from the other colonists, who did not recognize him as a pastor or priest since he had not been ordained by either the Dutch Reformed or German Lutheran churches. The Moravians combined an inward devotion to Christ with a commitment to reaching out to Christianize those who were on the margins of the European colonial endeavor. The Cape Town colonists feared Schmidt's efforts would encourage the Africans to resist Dutch authority.

Shortly after arriving, with the help of two Khoikhoi from the area who had learned Dutch, named Africo (d. 1756) and Kupido (or Kybodo, dates unknown), Schmidt decided to move some fifty miles east of Cape Town to a village along the Zonderend River to live among the Khoikhoi. Moravian missionaries typically supported their efforts by working as farmers, craftspeople, or traders wherever they went. Schmidt followed this pattern and began farming. He found the Khoikhoi language difficult to learn, so he depended on Africo and Kupido to serve as translators, but he soon began preaching and set up a small school for teaching Dutch and the basics of Christianity. Pressure from other European settlers in the region forced him the following year to move farther east, to a valley known as Bavianskloof, or the Vale of Baboons. There he continued his work, joined by a small group of Khoikhoi that included Africo and Kupido. Schmidt organized the group into an agricultural community, planting pear trees that came from Europe. The community grew to around fifty. Schmidt continued to run a school and in 1742 performed his first baptisms.

Word soon reached the Dutch authorities that Schmidt was performing baptism without what they recognized to be a valid ordination. A piece of paper that had arrived by post from Count von Zinzendorf earlier that year did not persuade them. Two years later Schmidt was forced to return to Europe where he hoped to be able to secure proper ordination in order to return to South Africa to continue his work. He never did make it back. Moravians were not permitted to return to Cape Town until 1792.

When three Moravian missionaries arrived that year to resume the mission work at Bavianskloof, they were met by an elderly woman who showed them a well-used New Testament in Dutch that she read from. Her name, she told them, was Magdalena Fredericks (d. 1800). Her birth name was Vehettge, but she had taken the name Magdalena (or Lena for short) after undergoing baptism by Schmidt some fifty years earlier. She had first met Schmidt at the village by the Zonderend River where he initially settled, and with her husband and several others, including Africo and Kupido, had moved to Bavianskloof with him. Lena, Africo, Kupido, and a fourth African named Willhem (d. 1756) were the original four whose baptisms forced Schmidt's departure from South Africa five decades earlier. Africo and Willhem died of smallpox in 1756. After that Lena returned to the village along the Zonderend River where Schmidt had originally settled, where she continued to hold prayer meetings and Bible readings under a fruit tree that Schmidt himself had planted. Although there had been no baptisms, the number of Christian believers grew under Lena's efforts through the decades.

The new Moravian missionaries re-established the community at Bavianskloof, which they renamed Genadendal (Valley of Grace). Lena began corresponding with leaders of the Moravian community in Germany, although poor eyesight forced her to depend on others to actually write her letters. She survived several bouts of severe illness and continued to serve as one of the leaders in the community, entertaining European visitors among other tasks until her death in 1800.

Genadendal continued to grow in the shadow of Dutch colonial suspicions. By the end of the century its numbers were over one thousand. The church bell rang every morning at 5:30 in the community, rousing its inhabitants to worship and work. Cycles of prayer were woven into the fabric of life as they had been at Zinzendorf's estate of Herrnhut in Germany. The town was neatly laid out with streets at right angles. Residents learned various crafts and trades. Everyone was expected to read and study the Bible. Europeans and Africans lived together with a significant degree of dignity and prosperity.

Ethiopia and East Africa

Ethiopia continued to be the place of strongest Christian presence in Africa in the eighteenth century. The century was marked by continuous tension among the three traditional institutions of religious authority, the emperor (or *negus*), the *abuna*, and the monasteries. External pressures from neighboring Muslim peoples, internal theological debates, and increasing conflict between the regional princes from among the various national or ethnic peoples in the Ethiopian empire and the emperor combined to increase the difficulties Ethiopians faced.

The waves of renewal that swept across Muslim North Africa and in part fed into the rise of the *jihadists* in West Africa reached Ethiopia in the eighteenth century as well. The pressure was especially acute in the south, where Islam was growing among the Oromo people. Derisively called "Galla" in Amharic, the Oromo were part of the Ethiopian empire, but they spoke their own language and not Amharic, the language that most Ethiopian Christians spoke in their day-to-day lives. Traditional religious practices among the Oromo included recognition of the high God and interaction with a host of lesser divinized ancestors through the mediation of male and female priests. Some among the Oromo had begun to convert to Christianity in the eighteenth century, but a larger number were converting to Islam. As the Oromo came to control much of the commercial trade in the south that reached to the shores of the Red Sea, the growth of Islam among them began to have economic consequences for Christian Ethiopia.

The seventeenth century had seen the rise of a new christological controversy among the monastic communities that divided the Ethiopian churches. Over the course of the eighteenth century that controversy continued, leading the churches into greater ecclesiastical chaos. On the one side were those who were members of what was called the House of Ewostatewos. On the other were those who belonged to the House of Takla Haymanot. The Ewostathians were rigorous nationalists, while those who were members of the House of Takla Haymanot, with its center at the ancient monastery of Dabra Libanos, were more willing to cooperate with Roman Catholic missionaries and were more accepting of Roman Catholic theology. The theological differences between the two sides were subtle and harkened back to the christological controversies of the fourth and fifth centuries in the ancient church. For the followers of Ewostatewos, the anointing of Christ was a sign of the divinization of humanity, the raising up of human flesh. For the monks of Dabra Libanos, the anointing of Jesus had nothing at all to do with union or divinization, but rather marked Jesus as the long-awaited Messiah or the second Adam.

For a brief time near the end of the eighteenth century, the two sides came close to resolving their differences under the leadership of Emperor Takla Giyorgis (r. 1779-1784). Giyorgis was particularly interested in religious matters. He had a reputation in the capital city of Gondar for strict observation of all fasts and celebrations of the church. He even presided over the baptism of several Oromo converts. By both example and personal persuasion he succeeded in bringing the two monastic houses together. In the end he was unable, however, to bring about theological reconciliation, in part due to the severe weakening of the emperor's power that was taking place during this period.

The condition of both the churches and the empire was further weakened by the increasing isolation of Ethiopia in the eighteenth century. Moving the capital inland toward the center of the country at Gondar was supposed to have made the imperial household more secure, but Gondar was far from the main avenues of commercial traffic that passed along the trans-Saharan trade routes to the Red Sea. The church in Ethiopia still depended on the Coptic pope in Alexandria for the appointment of its *abuna*, who continued to be an Egyptian. The continuing difficulties that the Coptic Church faced in Egypt, the expense of sending ambassadors to Alexandria when the Ethiopian national treasury was continuously falling short, and the impediments to travel and communication that Egypt's Islamic rulers set in place all contributed to the continuous disruptions in the office of the *abuna* at the head of the Ethiopian church.

Contact with European Christianity was mostly nonexistent through the eighteenth century. Catholic missionaries on several occasions tried to enter the country, which resulted in an execution in 1720. Two Franciscans were given permission in 1750 to stay in Gondar for several months, but little is known of their work there. In 1788 Rome ordained as bishop an Ethiopian named Tobia Ghebragzier (or Tobias Gebre Egziabeher, dates unknown). Bishop Tobia apparently had met Roman Catholic missionaries in Egypt and had gone to study in Rome before being ordained to return to Ethiopia to serve as a bishop. Allowed by Rome to celebrate the Mass according to the Ethiopian rite, he nevertheless appears to have been unsuccessful in making any converts in Ethiopia from 1790 when he arrived until 1797 when he returned to Egypt.

Churches and monasteries in Ethiopia fell into greater disrepair over the course of the eighteenth century everywhere except in Gondar, where the growth of the new capital resulted in a number of new churches being built. Ethiopian art and music began to reflect influences that came from earlier contact with Europeans during the century. Paintings became more naturalistic and music more complex. The century opened with Emperor Iyasu I (r. 1682-1706), one of the last effective leaders until the middle of the nineteenth century, on the throne. Although he sought to institute several reforms, he was assassinated by order of one of his sons, setting in motion two decades of political turmoil. In 1720 Dawit III (r. 1716-1721) took the side of the Ewostathians and ordered an assault on the monastery of Debre Libanos, which resulted in the massacre of the leading supporters of the House of Takla Haymanot.

The reign of Iyoas I (1755-1769) marks the beginning of what historians of Ethiopia often call *Zamana Masafent*, or the "Age of Judges." Iyoas I was deposed and then executed by a powerful regional prince from Tigray. Several other emperors suffered similar fates. During the last two decades of the century the princes came to exercise almost total control over the emperor and the land. From 1779 until 1800, Tekle Giyorgis I (1751-1817) was deposed and returned to the throne five times by the princes who by the beginning of the nineteenth century controlled the empire.

By the end of the eighteenth century the Ethiopian empire was fracturing into political pieces. A century of theological conflict, which at times had broken out into full-fledged violence and massacres, had left it spiritually depleted. The Ethiopian liturgy was still said in Ge'ez, an ancient version of the Ethiopian language that was no longer well understood. Ethiopian Christians spoke mostly Amharic by 1800, but even that language was not universally used throughout the country. Against this backdrop of political turmoil and spiritual decline the figure of Abuna Yosab III (r. 1770-1803) offers a brief glimpse of hope. Spiritual confidant and supporter of Giyorgis I, Yosab was a reformer. At one point he confronted an Oromo prince whose army was raiding Gondar. At another point he unsuccessfully sought to forbid the celebration of the Eucharist throughout the Ethiopian nation until much-needed social reforms were instituted. Yosab was a voice of conscience to a nation in decline. His death brought a considerable amount of national mourning.

Suggestions for further reading

Agbeti, J. Kofi, *West African Church History: Christian Missions and Church Foundations, 1482-1919.* Leiden: E. J. Brill, 1986.

Baur, John, *2000 Years of Christianity in Africa: An African Church History.* 2nd ed. Nairobi: Paulines, 2009.

Denis, Philippe, *The Dominican Friars in Southern Africa: A Social History (1577-1990).* Leiden: Brill, 1998.

Groves, C. P., *The Planting of Christianity in Africa, I: Up to 1840.* London: Lutterworth Press, 1948.

Hastings, Adrian, *The Church in Africa, 1450-1950.* Oxford: Clarendon Press, 1994.

Kalu, Ogbu, ed., *African Christianity: An African Story.* Pretoria, South Africa: Department of Church History, 2005.

Sundkler, Bengt, and Christopher Steed, *A History of the Church in Africa.* Cambridge: Cambridge University Press, 2000.

Werner, Roland, William Anderson, and Andrew Wheeler, *Day of Devastation, Day of Contentment: The History of the Sudanese Church across 2,000 Years.* Nairobi: Paulines, 2000.

15

The Eighteenth Century in Europe

On November 1, 1755, around 9:30 in the morning a powerful earthquake struck the city of Lisbon, Portugal. The consequences were devastating. What was not immediately destroyed by the earthquake, whose epicenter was located off the coast in the Atlantic Ocean, was destroyed by the tsunami that followed, or by the fires that were soon burning throughout the city. By the end of the day an estimated one-third of the 275,000 inhabitants of Lisbon had been killed. Every church in the city had been destroyed. The ships in the harbor, the vehicles that tied together the Portuguese "shoestring" empire that circled the globe, were tossed onto land like little toys. Much of Portugal's naval prowess in a single day was wiped out. The center of the vast Portuguese trading empire was defeated without anyone so much as lifting a sword.

For decades following the Great Lisbon Earthquake theologians and philosophers throughout Europe debated whether the event had been an act of judgment by God or simply a random event in a universe governed by the laws of science. Particularly ironic for some was the fact that the event occurred on All Saints Day, a holy day in the life of the Catholic Church set aside to remember the dead. The manner in which the earthquake had inflicted such damage on what many in Europe considered to be a Christian nation and a Christian colonial empire seemed to call into question the notion of a divine hand guiding human history. The quake proved to be particularly provocative to a young German philosopher named Immanuel Kant (1724-1804), from the Prussian port city of Königsberg, located on the Baltic Sea. Kant reasoned that it was not God but trapped gases beneath the earth that caused the earthquake. He was wrong, but his speculations can be credited with beginning the scientific field of study that today is known as seismology.

The effort by Kant and others to offer an alternative explanation for the earthquake rather than simply regarding it as an act of God was indicative of the increasing attraction that the new rational, scientific worldview had in European society. Science and rationality were advancing in tandem in this regard. The growing tendency to look for rational explanations for phenomena, and to see the universe as an ordered system operating under strict laws of cause and effect, went hand in hand with scientific discoveries and developments in technology.

René Descartes (1596-1650) argued in the seventeenth century that philosophical certainty is grounded in the experience of a thinking subject. The effect had been to increase philosophical reliance on the rationality that a thinking human subject exercised. The political notion that derived from this argument was that an individual thinking subject was politically to be regarded as a sovereign being. This idea directly challenged the political notion that the king or the state was sovereign, as well as the religious notion that the church, which claimed to represent God, was sovereign. The notion of the sovereignty of the individual gained symbolic ground across the course of the eighteenth century to provide the foundations for profound political transformations not only in Europe but elsewhere throughout the world.

Adding to the challenge that these ideas posed to the churches was the history of several centuries of religious wars that had proved to be so devastating to Europe. Significant numbers of thinkers in Europe began to question the notion of a religiously intolerant state, even if they did not reject the notion of an established church or of established religion in general. Some in Europe began to apply these notions of liberty and tolerance to other human beings who were not European, arguing for their application especially to persons of African descent who had been enslaved by Europeans. Ever so slowly arguments against slavery began taking hold, fueled in part by the growing personal contact between Africans and Europeans in Europe as much as by the growth of ideas of liberty and tolerance.

Here again churches in Europe found little in the way of their scriptures and histories that could serve as direct precedents to guide them. Churches came to be seen by many, including many among their own leadership, as being defenders of the status quo, a status quo that was seen by at least some as being violent and oppressive. Others within these churches, including some who were in leadership, were more willing to embrace in various degrees the concepts of liberty and toleration, theoretically as well as in practice. Christians could be found on both sides of these debates concerning the revolutionary changes taking place in eighteenth-century Europe. As a result the landscape of European Christianity became a more rugged and varied terrain.

The European Enlightenment

During the last decade of the seventeenth century an argument broke out among members of the French Academy, the body that was officially charged by the king with overseeing the rules of grammar for the French language. On one side were those who argued for the authority of ancient writers in matters of literature, culture, and art. On the other were members of a group who were styled the "moderns" because they argued for the superiority of the new ways of learning, in other words, for the superiority of the modern, over the past. The word took hold to describe the age that was under way.

Modernity might have in the first instance been called an aesthetic movement, with literary and artistic contours, but it was ushered in on the carriage of scientific thinking. Based on the experimental method that had been developed by Francis Bacon (1561-1626) in the seventeenth century, empirical science had made enormous gains in factual knowledge such as those of Isaac Newton (1642-1727). The eighteenth century saw those efforts continue, advanced by individuals who continued to identify themselves for the most part as Christian, and for that matter mostly Protestant. Outright atheism was still a rare phenomenon, at least as far as public pronouncements were concerned. This did not mean there was no divide between science and religion. By the eighteenth century the signs of such a gulf between the two were beginning to emerge in the intellectual life of Europeans. Most still saw science and religion as being compatible pursuits, but ever so subtly the manner in which the two proceeded began to diverge. As they did, the modern became associated with science while religion tended to be relegated to the ranks of the ancients, or antiquity.

Rapid developments in the areas of transportation, energy, agriculture, manufacturing, and construction were changing European life in the eighteenth century, giving credence to notions of progress and the superiority of the modern. Such advances were in no small part a result of the scientific method at work. Science and technology increased confidence in human ability to control and dominate the environment, leading in turn to questions about the manner or even the necessity of divine intervention in history. Scientific discoveries and the development of more complex and efficient technologies seemed to reduce the mystery and complexity of the universe for many. God seemed to be far away and, for some, unnecessary to the workings of the world. The traditional static, hierarchical, and ordered view of the universe gave way to a more dynamic and democratic world. The world of miracles and divine participation began to give way to a world that was mechanistically ordered and scientifically verifiable. This new way of understanding God in relation to the world was given its strongest expression in the school of thought called Deism, which first appeared in the seventeenth century and continued to spread throughout the eighteenth, but its effects were felt throughout the religious world.

There were a number of responses to these new ideas, from strong defense of traditional worldviews to outright rejection of the concept of a transcendent God. Most intellectuals searched for some middle ground that gave room for scientific discovery and advances while leaving room for God's creative activity in the world, even if the ongoing participation of the divine was greatly denuded. Some writers made greater room for human discovery and human reason over divine revelation and divine participation. The philosopher John Locke (1632-1704) had paved the way for a number of these ideas in his writings at the end of the seventeenth century. Locke's spirited view of a reasonable Christianity, coupled with the case he made for religious toleration, had a lasting impact on religious life not only in England, where the notion that one belonged to a church as a matter of one's own choice began to take hold, but in other parts of Europe as well.

The influence of John Toland (1670-1722) at the end of the seventeenth century has already been noted. In the eighteenth century he was joined by Matthew Tindal (1657-1733), whose book *Christianity, As Old as Creation* appeared in 1730 and quickly became known as the "Deists' Bible." Following the empirical principles of Locke, Tindal set reason over against revelation, or the natural over against the supernatural, in both cases regarding the former as a more reliable pathway to knowledge or understanding. By the middle of the eighteenth century in European intellectual circles, it was difficult to discuss Christian theology without assuming these dichotomies.

Tindal argued that true religion must be in accord with the nature of God, which is eternal, simple, and universal. True religion therefore must consist of eternal, simple, and universal principles that result in perfect or reasonable duties performed toward others and toward God. Both kinds of obligations or duties are fulfilled in moral actions or conduct toward others. True religion, according to Tindal, was defined as reasonable service toward others. No special revelation was needed to come to these conclusions. Furthermore, special revelation was unreasonable because it excluded some people. On this point the English philosopher and lawyer Anthony Collins (1676-1729) wrote even more forcefully. His *Essay concerning the Use of Reason in Propositions*, published in 1707, and *Discourse on the Grounds and Reasons of the Christian Religion,* published in 1724, advanced the claim that any revelation must conform to natural human ideas about God. Collins argued against the notion that the Bible was a special canon of truth, and disputed the authorship of parts of it such as the book of Daniel.

Locke, Toland, Tindal, and Collins all held fairly positive views as to what can be known about religion. For the most part they were also in agreement about what religion requires. These themes and ideas took on a slightly different cast in the work of several scholars from Scotland in the eighteenth century. Francis Hutcheson (1694-1746), often called the father of the Scottish Enlightenment, was born in Ireland to a Scottish Presbyterian family. He graduated from the University of Glasgow in 1712, having studied philosophy and theology, and was ordained as a Presbyterian minister. He returned to Ireland for some time and taught in a private academy before being called back to the University of Glasgow in 1729 where he assumed the chair in moral philosophy. In his philosophical writings Hutcheson argued that human beings had an innate sense of benevolence that informed morality and an innate sense of beauty that informed aesthetics. The ethical value of an action could be judged by the good that resulted from it, he argued.

One of Hutcheson's younger colleagues in the Scottish Enlightenment was David Hume (1711-1776). Hume followed Locke's theory of empiricism. Beginning with the notion that all knowledge is derived from experience, he concluded that absolute certainty in philosophy was unattainable. His skepticism was especially pronounced in relation to the trust that could be lodged in rationality. Hume famously noted that even the most basic element of reasoning as a cause-effect relationship can never be directly observed in the world but is always imposed upon events by an interpreter. He thought that passions more than reason dictated human thinking. His skepticism was especially on display regarding the existence of God, which he argued could neither be proven nor disproven. While such skepticism was not well received in many church quarters, Hume was viewed by his contemporaries as more of a critic of organized religion than as a promoter of unbelief; and no formal efforts were ever launched against him in his lifetime to prevent him from expressing such views.

Another younger colleague of Hutcheson who was not only one of his students at the University of Glasgow but a successor in the chair of moral philosophy was Adam Smith (1723-1790). In *The Theory of Moral Sentiments*, published in 1759, Smith took up Hutcheson's notion of an innate moral sense, which Smith took to be the capacity for sympathy, and offered it as the basis for moral life in society. Another similar innate tendency, that of self-interest, was at the heart of Smith's most important work, *An Inquiry into the Nature and Causes of the Wealth of Nations*, first published in 1776. *The Wealth of Nations*, as the book is generally known today, is often cited as one of the inaugurating texts in the field of modern economics.

The book opens by asserting that human progress in history arises from the division of labor. Labor results in the production of things of value, which human beings exchange in markets. Increased division of labor results in increased markets. The value of items exchanged in markets is not absolute, Smith noted, but is a function of supply and demand. Profits are the result of this function at work in markets, thereby creating wealth. Wealth in turn is the measure of well-being that results from human labor. The greatest wealth is generated by a free market, Smith argued. The best thing a government can therefore do to produce and accumulate wealth is allow free markets to work without interference. Smith argued that competing self-interests and the law of supply and demand would have a self-regulating effect upon a market. He called this an "invisible hand" promoting ends that were not necessarily those intended by the individuals involved in transactions, but in the end producing the greatest wealth and thus the greatest good overall. By this invisible hand self-interest becomes transformed into the common good. Although he did not necessarily intend the notion of the invisible hand of the marketplace to replace the invisible hand of God in history, the effect of *The Wealth of Nations* over time in the modern world was to create far greater reliance on markets, capital accumulation, and economic exchange for achieving the social good than on traditional religious practices.

Following Adam Smith in the chair of moral philosophy at Glasgow was Thomas Reid (1710-1796). Reid argued that there was a fundamental correspondence among objects in the world, the mind that grasped them, and the thoughts expressed in language that the mind has about objects. This correspondence was the basis for what he called *sensus communis*, or "common sense." Reid's position has also been characterized as direct realism. He argued that God created the world with innate moral principles that are akin to mathematical principles. Propositions regarding morality, like those regarding physics, are drawn from the world and are not merely ideas, sentiments, or beliefs that the mind has constructed. Reid's realism offered a Scottish counterpart to Locke's empiricism and Hume's skepticism.

Similar intellectual currents were flowing on the continent of Europe in the eighteenth century. Gottfried Wilhelm Leibniz (1646-1716) was a mathematician and philosopher remembered, among other things, for having devised the binary numeral system that is the basis for computing today. His metaphysical writings sought to offer a unified theory of reality that overcame the mind-body dualism of Descartes. His book *Essais de théodicée sur la bonté de Dieu, la liberté de l'homme et l'origine du mal* ("Essays of Theodicy on the Goodness of God, the Freedom of Humanity and the Origin of Evil"), written in French and published in 1710, coined the term "theodicy," which came to mean a defense of the goodness of God in light of the problem of evil in the created universe. Leibniz argued that because it was created by a perfect God, ours must be the best of all possible worlds, a position that the French philosopher François-Marie Arouet, who is better known by his pen name, Voltaire (1694-1778), lampooned in 1759 in his novel *Candide, ou l'Optimisme* ("Candide, or Optimism").

One of Leibniz's enduring legacies is his effort to try to mend the divide that separated Christian communions in Europe. During the last decade of the seventeenth century Leibniz engaged in correspondence with Jacques-Bénigne Bossuet (1627-1704), the Roman Catholic bishop of Meaux, in France, in an effort to find common ground for agreement between the Lutheran and Roman Catholic churches. He also sought to mend the breach between the Lutherans and Reformed Churches. His efforts sought to avoid the central issues that divided the churches, such as ecclesiology, the Eucharist, and the episcopacy, and instead focus on matters where there already seemed to be some agreement. While unsuccessful in these pursuits, he remains an important harbinger of later ecumenical efforts to heal divisions among the churches.

One of Leibniz's younger colleagues and an associate was Christian Wolff (1679-1754). Wolff taught for almost two decades at the University of Halle, a stronghold of Lutheran Pietism, until being expelled from the school and threatened by the king with death in 1723 on account of his theological defense of the use of philosophical reason. For the next seventeen years Wolff taught at the University of Marburg until a new king, Frederick II, also known as Frederick the Great (1712-1786), invited him to return to Halle. Wolff did so to great acclaim. Three years later, in 1743, Wolff became chancellor of the university, and two years after that was made a baron. His journey can be seen as marking the triumph of rationality over traditional orthodoxy in its pietistic forms at the very heart of the Pietist movement in Germany.

Traditional Christianity was but a stage in human development, now to be supplemented by reason, argued the German poet, literary critic, and philosopher Gotthold Ephraim Lessing (1729-1781). One of Lessing's major concerns throughout his life was the defense of human freedom in the exercise of religion, literature, and social life. His play *Nathan the Wise*, published in 1779, presented in a winsome manner the equality of Judaism, Islam, and Christianity, if lived out to the best of one's ability. All religions were equally reasonable and equally true, he seemed to be saying. Regarding the relationship between history and reason, Lessing argued that historical events, which are by definition accidental or contingent, could never provide an adequate basis for ascertaining metaphysical truths, which are by definition necessary or eternal. There was a "great ugly ditch" between the two that one cannot easily leap over, he argued. Historical reports of miracles as found in the Bible offer no basis for proof of the existence of God, he concluded.

Between 1774 and 1778, Lessing, who by then had taken the position of head librarian in Wolfenbüttel, published a series of extracts from a book he attributed to an anonymous writer. The essays, which quickly became known as the "Wolfenbüttel Fragments," were actually taken from an unpublished manuscript titled *Apologie oder Schutzschrift für die vernünftigen Verehrer Gottes* ("Apology or Defense for the Rational Reverers of God") by the philosopher and biblical scholar Hermann Samuel Reimarus (1694-1768). Reimarus had died several years earlier, but Lessing, wishing to protect family members from vindication, did not reveal the authorship of the works, so radical was their content deemed to be. Reimarus argued that everything that was true concerning both God and creation could be found apart from biblical revelation through reason. Concerning the Bible, he denied the reality of miracles. Jesus was a local preacher who landed himself in trouble with the Romans. After his execution, however, his disciples stole his body and invented the claim that he was the Messiah. Others before him had argued that the Bible was historically unreliable, but the work of Reimarus went further in this direction than anyone in Europe had previously dared to go.

The most important German philosopher in eighteenth-century Europe was arguably Immanuel Kant (1724-1804). The "German Socrates," as he has been called, turned the rational teachings of Leibniz and Wolff on themselves to question the new source of authority, or reason. His two groundbreaking works, *Kritik der reinen Vernunft* ("Critique of Pure Reason"), which was published in 1781, and *Kritik der praktischen Vernunft* ("Critique of Practical Reason"), which followed in 1788, sought to answer the basic question, "What is reason?" Kant concluded that all human knowledge was made up of perceptions of reality (*phenomena*), the way things appear to the senses, and *noumena*, things in themselves as they really are, as known—if they are known at all. As such, knowledge could never attain to things as they are in themselves but only to things as they are known by the human mind, which is dependent on the appearances of reality as perceived by the senses. Human reason is thus limited in its project, an idea that was not necessarily Kant's intention, however, for although he perceived the limits of human reason, he did not abandon his confidence in the human ability to make progress in knowledge by reason, especially when this was carried forward carefully (as in the sciences, which were then developing). In 1784 at the age of sixty, Kant wrote in a famous essay titled *Beantwortung der Frage: Was ist Aufklärung?* ("Answering the Question: What Is Enlightenment?") that Enlightenment is humanity's liberation from its own self-imposed tutelage to tradition, a tutelage that results from not having the courage to think critically on one's own. It holds in its grip most men (whom Kant compared to cattle) and all women (whom he called "the fairer sex"). *Sapere aude* ("dare to know"), he said, was the motto of Enlightenment. Those who dare to think on their own have "come of age" and thus are capable of both experiencing and exercising freedom.

One of the outcomes of Kant's critique of reason was to undercut arguments for the existence of God based on reason. Kant did not reject the existence of God, however; rather, he argued for God, but on the basis of an innate human consciousness of unconditional moral obligation. Such a consciousness of moral obligation, Kant argued, necessitates that humans posit the existence of God, freedom, and immortality. We could not have what Kant calls the unconditional categorical imperative ("Thou shalt not . . .") without a God and the freedom to follow the imperative. For Kant this moral imperative was the foundation for all religion.

In eighteenth-century France, the ideas of the Enlightenment took hold among a group of intellectuals who came to be knows as *philosophes*. They were motivated by many of the same concerns of tolerance and progress as their British and German counterparts. Ideas of political liberty and freedom were more pronounced in their works on the other hand. Official or state-sponsored persecution of Protestants was still a reality in eighteenth-century France, accounting in part for this stronger emphasis on political tolerance and freedom in the work of the French *philosophes*.

Jean Calas (1698-1762) was a Protestant merchant living in the city of Toulouse. In 1761 one of his sons was found dead. Because another of his sons had previously converted to Catholicism, Calas was charged with killing this son in order to prevent him from following his brother. Maintaining his innocence to the end, Calas was nevertheless found guilty and executed by an instrument of torture known as the breaking wheel, a device that crushed the body slowly. After his execution the family's property was confiscated, and his wife and daughters forced to live in convents.

The incident provoked a strong reaction from the skillful quill of Voltaire. *Traité sur la tolérance à l'occasion de la mort de Jean Calas* ("Treatise on Toleration"), which was published the following year, succeeded in having the sentence overturned posthumously. The incident was an important indicator of the influence Voltaire and other *philosophes* were gaining as public intellectuals.

Born in Paris and educated in a Jesuit school, Voltaire spent three years in England in his late twenties where he was exposed to the works of Newton, Locke, and others. His sharp and sometimes crude wit earned him expulsion from England, but not before he developed an appreciation for a constitutional monarchy and Shakespeare. He returned to France, where he lived for fifteen years with Gabrielle Émilie Le Tonnelier de Breteuil (1706-1749), the wife of the Marquis Florent-Claude du Chastellet and a mathematician, physicist, and translator of Newton's *Principia Mathematica* into French. He then spent a year at the court of Frederick the Great (1712-1786) in Germany before settling again in France in Ferney, near Geneva.

Much of Voltaire's work was in the form of poetry, plays, novels, and satirical essays. In these various works he attacked what he considered to be the superstition and intolerance of his day, especially those of the ecclesiastical institutions of the Catholic Church in France. *Écrasez l'infame* ("Crush the infamy!"), he cried. He was equally opposed to what he considered to be the oppression and violence of other religions, as seen in a letter sent in 1740 to Frederick that criticized Islam. "Superstition sets the whole world in flames; philosophy quenches them," he wrote in *Dictionnaire philosophique* ("Philosophical Dictionary") in 1764.

Another of the *philosophes* whose ideas fed the dramatic transformation of French society in the eighteenth century was Jean-Jacques Rousseau (1712-1778). Born in Geneva into a Protestant family, he converted to Catholicism at an early age and moved to northern Italy, giving up his Genevan citizenship. From there he moved to Paris until returning to Geneva in 1754 and reconverting to Calvinism. Forced to leave Switzerland a dozen years later because of some of the religious ideas found in his writings, he traveled to England for a time before returning to Paris in 1767 where he spent his remaining years.

Rousseau's political ideas can be encapsulated in a single word: *liberté* ("liberty"). In his *Discours sur l'origine et les fondements de l'inégalité parmi les hommes* ("Discourse on the Origin and Foundations of Inequality among Humanity"), published in 1755, he argued that human beings in their original, natural state were free and equal individuals unencumbered by the constraints of civil society. Human beings began to settle in communities where some claimed ownership of property, and as a consequence forced others into submission, thereby giving rise to inequality and oppression. In an effort to regulate such activities, governments of various kinds arose. All political systems exist as a form of pact, covenant, or contract among members of society, even if the manner or degree of inequality that they foster is different. Given the natural human propensity toward freedom, the best form of government is one that opposes inequality and supports life and liberty even of the famished masses, he concluded.

Du contrat social, ou Principes du droit politique ("The Social Contract, or Principles of Political Right"), which was published in 1762, followed up by expanding the ideas more fully. "Humanity is born free, but everywhere is in chains," he wrote in the opening pages. *The Social Contract* explored the strengths and weaknesses of democracy, aristocracy, and monarchy. It argued for mixed institutions and noted that in the end the preservation and prosperity of its citizens was the measure of a good government. In this regard, government ought to secure the rights and equality of everyone. Furthermore, if any form of government does not properly see to the rights, liberty, and equality of everyone, that government has broken the social contract that lies at the heart of political authority.

Rousseau's attitude and ideas regarding religion were best seen in his work *Émile, ou l'education* ("Émile, or On Education"), which was also published in 1762. For the most part *Émile* is concerned with child-rearing and education. One section, however, that sympathetically relates in some detail the views of a particular clergy person from Savoy whom Rousseau had met years earlier stirred considerable controversy, resulting in Rousseau's forced departure from Switzerland. The priest, and Rousseau by extension, argued against the notion of special revelation in favor of natural religion. All religions are good and pleasing to God. All religious truth can be found by observing the universe and exercising reason. To argue otherwise is to make God the cruelest and most unjust of tyrants. Human beings are not inherently incapable of finding the truth about God through reason and nature. On the other hand, the notion that God can be known only by special revelation that is known by a minority of humanity through the ages belies the notion of the justice of God. True religion in the end cannot be reduced to human institutions such as the church, the priest concluded. The righteous heart is the true temple of God, and the universal rule to love one's neighbor as one's self is the whole law. Faith and virtue are universal indications of this truth.

Both Voltaire and Rousseau were contributors to a grand project headed up by Denis Diderot (1713-1784) that sought to gather together and systematize all human knowledge in an *Encyclopédie, ou dictionnaire raisonné des sciences, des arts et des métiers* ("Encyclopedia, or a Systematic Dictionary of the Sciences, Arts, and Crafts"). The massive project, published between 1751 and 1772, eventually entailed thirty-five volumes with essays contributed by numerous authors. The most prolific, with almost eighteen thousand articles to his credit, was Chevalier Louis de Jaucourt (1704-1779). When the first volume was published in 1751, it was immediately condemned by French Catholic authorities for being antiroyal and opposed to the church. After much persecution, some public book burnings, and considerable delays, the final volumes to see print in 1772 were decidedly so. The *Encyclopédie* started on a religiously skeptical note, but by the time the last volumes were produced the work had become pronouncedly materialistic and in some cases even atheistic in orientation. What had started as a concern for freedom and open inquiry in the seventeenth century had turned antireligious by the end of the eighteenth century.

Not all of France was enthralled by the work of the *philosophes* in the eighteenth century. First of all, the movement was decidedly limited to a group of intellectuals, mostly men, drawn from the ranks of the growing middle class whose main income came through mercantile trade. A number of upper-class women supported them by providing funds and in some cases by extending the political protection of their husbands. Most of the *philosophes* shared Kant's belief that the common people had no real contribution to make to progress and reason. The vast majority of society, especially women, could only be expected to remain stranded in superstition and had to be controlled by religion. Only Rousseau sought to create political space for the full exercise of justice in society on behalf of those who were oppressed, but even he did not truly consider the possibility that women could exercise their freedom fully and equally in civil society. While the *philosophes* spoke of universal truths of God, they had little to offer in the way of concrete affirmations regarding other cultures and beliefs.

Opposition to the movement came mostly from supporters of the monarchy and clerics. These two strands of opposition generally converged in the eighteenth century. Defending the established church meant defending the political state that protected the church, and likewise defending the state meant defending the church that provided the state with a significant degree of what can be called symbolic or spiritual legitimation. The various opponents of the *philosophes* criticized them mostly for undercutting what were considered to be the foundations of social order, and for spreading irreligion, which it was feared would lead to social chaos. At times the opposition was extreme and unfounded. Yet others, such as the Dominican priest Charles-Louis Richard (1711-1794), provided a thoughtful and even prophetic critique of the *philosophes*. His *Exposition de la doctrine des philosophes modernes* ("Exposition on the Doctrine of Modern Philosophers"), published in 1785, argued that the ideas of these thinkers promoted materialism, rejected humanity's duties to God, and taught a morality based solely on self-interest and pleasure. The motivating factor behind all of these modern philosophers was self-love, which translated into concern for selfish interests and pleasures, he said. Richard's conclusion reflected the belief of many church leaders that the goal of the *philosophes* in the end was nothing less than the corruption of the faith and morality, and the eradication not only of religious observation but of law, conscience, justice, and virtue before God.

Italy in the eighteenth century was still a collection of independent political entities, including the Papal States, which were under the political rule of the bishop of Rome. The Catholic Church dominated virtually all aspects of life in Italy. The Waldensians, a community of Christians named for their founder, the twelfth-century reformer Peter Waldo, who shared much in common with Reformed and Lutheran churches, occupied a number of valleys in the Piedmont district in the northwest. Toward the end of the century Swiss Protestants founded a church in the northeastern city of Trieste, which was under the rule of the Hapsburgs of Austria, but otherwise Protestantism was unknown on the peninsula.

What was called the *Illuminismo* ("Enlightenment") in Italy was for the most part confined to a handful of scholars, mostly historians, such as Pietro Giannone (1676-1748), whose work on the relationship between church and state landed him in prison for twelve years. Another historian of the period, Ludovico Antonio Muratori (1672-1750), is best known for having discovered a fragment from a seventeenth-century Latin manuscript in the library of Milan that turned out to be a translation of a second-century Greek text listing those writings that were regarded as having apostolic authority. Named for its discoverer, the Muratorian Fragment, which was published is 1740, is widely regarded as being the earliest listing of a full New Testament canon. A third historian, whose work would greatly influence the development of historiography elsewhere in Europe in the nineteenth and twentieth centuries, was Giambattista Vico (1668-1744). Vico argued that Descartes' method of rational observation was suited to the natural world, which human beings did not create. The study of civil society or history, on the other hand, which was a realm that human beings had created, called for a different method of study. Vico argued that the methods of rhetoric or *phronesis,* "practical wisdom," or *prudentia,* were more suited to the study of history, which was the product of human choice. His book *Principi di scienza nuova d'intorno alla comune natura delle nazioni* ("Principles of New Science on the Common Nature of Nations"), which first appeared in 1725 and was republished in a longer edition in 1744, put this method to work, offering a universal interpretation of human history through distinct rhetorical or literary strategies.

The ascent of Philip V (1683-1746), grandson of Louis XIV of France (1638-1715), to the throne of Spain in 1702 led to a decade of civil war. Philip V was a member of the House of Bourbon. While his grandmother had been a sister of the king of Spain, his upbringing had been entirely French. Born in Versailles, he began studying Spanish only when he was named king in 1702. A number of the members of the Spanish nobility resisted this new ruler, which resulted in civil war. In response Philip turned to leading intellectuals who were identified with the *Ilustración* in Spain for support. The result was a far closer relationship between court and representatives of the Enlightenment in Spain than was true for any other nation in Europe in the eighteenth century.

A second distinctive characteristic of the Enlightenment in Spain was the far greater number of women who were associated with the movement's intellectual development. One of the most important supports for women in the Spanish Enlightenment was provided by a book written by a man, a Benedictine monk and scholar named Benito Jerónimo Feijoo y Montenegro (1674-1764). Feijoo's *Defensa de las mujeres* ("Defense of Women"), published in 1726, challenged the notion that women were defective or inferior to men in nature. Feijoo went so far as to criticize St. Augustine for teaching that in the resurrection women would be changed into men. Women demonstrated different characteristics than men in qualities such as beauty, gentleness, or candor, he argued, but in matters of intellectual and the critical ability to reason, they were fully equal to men. He argued for the ability of women to rule in government, but allowed on the purely functional basis that someone had to rule in order to avoid chaos that God had ordained men to rule in marriage.

During the latter half of the century, a significant number of women made major intellectual contributions to the Enlightenment in Spain. Josefa Amar y Borbón (1749-1833) translated numerous works from other languages into Spanish, and wrote a number of original essays on topics of education and social progress. The daughter of Irish immigrants, María Gertrudis Hore (1742-1801), became widely regarded for her poetry after being forced to retire to a convent in Cadiz on account of an adulterous affair that became public. In 1787 on the order of the king of Spain women were admitted into the Economic Society of Madrid, an organization that sought to advance education, agriculture, and economic development both in Spain and its colonial empire. Women in the organization belonged to a separate *Junta de Damas* ("Women's Committee"), which was originally headed by María Josefa Pimentel, Duchess of Osuna (1752-1834). Under her direction, the *Junta* helped to create schools and worked to alleviate poverty in Spain and throughout its colonies. Male intellectuals in other regions of Europe may have doubted the ability of women to participate in the Enlightenment, but in Spain a powerful group of women proved otherwise.

Renewal of Catholic life and worship

The intellectual work of the Enlightenment challenged the churches of Europe on social, cultural, religious, and philosophical grounds. The criticisms it mounted against traditional Christian teachings and against the cultural dominance of Christian institutions in European society had a lasting effect. At the same time the Enlightenment did not deal a mortal blow against Christianity, or against the institutions of religion in European society. Christianity in Europe in the eighteenth century proved to be far more resilient than either its critics or its defenders had imagined.

A number of renewal movements made their mark on European Christianity in the eighteenth century, in both Catholic and Protestant churches. In some cases such renewal movements were at least in part shaped in response to the efforts of the Enlightenment. While the church was being attacked in some of the salons and academic halls in Europe, there were other places, especially among the rural populations, where Catholic spiritual life was being significantly deepened. One such movement was the Company of Mary, or the Mulotins, founded by Louis Marie Grignion de Montfort (1673-1716) in Poitiers, France. Montfort already knew at the time of his ordination in 1700 that his vocation was to serve the poor. The following year he wrote in a letter that what the church needed was a small group of faithful priests dedicated to teaching the poor in rural areas and arousing sinners to devotion to the Blessed Lady. Faced with opposition from local priests, he traveled to Rome, where Pope Clement XI endorsed his efforts, granting him the title "Apostolic Missionary."

Shortly after starting the Company of Mary, Montfort started a women's order, called the Daughters of Wisdom. Marie Louise Trichet (1684-1759), who took the name Marie-Louise de Jésus, was its first and best-known member. The Daughters of Wisdom visited those confined to hospitals, opened schools for poor children, and operated orphanages. They shared Montfort's threefold spiritual emphasis on wisdom, the cross, and the Virgin. Members of both the Company of Mary and the Daughters of Wisdom became known after Montfort's death as Mulotins. Montefort's hymns, poems, and devotional books were popular throughout France. The movement's religious processions through town and its lively, celebrative liturgies attracted numerous followers, even if they also continued to raise the jealousies of local priests and bishops.

A similar missionary order devoted to reaching the rural poor, the Congregation of the Most Holy Redeemer, or the Redemptorists, was founded in 1732 in Scala, Italy, by Alphonsus Liguori (1696-1787). Liguori, who had come from a well-to-do family in Naples, had studied broadly in the humanities before practicing law and then turning to theological studies. After being ordained in 1726 he began working among the homeless in the areas around Naples and organizing "Evening Chapels" for young people. Sensing a call to foreign mission work, Liguori moved to the Chinese College in Naples where he served for a time as chaplain for missionaries in training. While there he met Marie Celeste Crostarosa (1696-1755), a nun who claimed to have mystical experiences. She told Liguori of a vision she had of a new religious order for women. He believed her vision, and in 1730 he helped her to found a new contemplative women's order known as the Redemptoristines. She then convinced Liguori that he was to found an order for men who would work with the poor. The result was the Redemptorists. At first its work was confined to Italy, but by the end of the eighteenth century the order had spread to other parts of Europe. Members dedicated their lives to preaching to the poor and to working with youth. Liguori, who was well educated and authored over one hundred works on spirituality and theology, defined the Redemptorist style of plain but thoughtful sermons.

Another Italian who founded a new religious order in the eighteenth century was Paul Francis Danei (1694-1774), better known as St. Paul of the Cross. Captivated early in life by the image of the cross, he responded in 1715 to the call of Pope Clement XI (1649-1721) for a crusade against the Ottomans who had gone to war against the Republic of Venice the previous year, not incidentally the last call to a crusade ever issued by a pope. Danei enlisted in the army in Venice as a volunteer, but while on his way to battle he stopped in a church for prayer where he had a change of heart and determined that bloodshed was not a spiritual answer. True devotion, he came to see, required an inner conversion, accompanied by prayer, penance, and service through the church. By 1720 he had become convinced that God was calling him to form a new community based on these principles. He shared his vision with his local bishop, who endorsed the proposal, outfitted Danei with a black tunic, and sent him out on preaching missions. Still a lay person, Danei wrote a rule for this new order that was to be organized around a life of poverty and devoted to the sufferings, or passion, of Christ. Joined at first by only his brother, he carried on for several years his itinerant preaching missions among the rural poor and began directing retreats for spiritual development.

The rule that he wrote was formally approved by the pope in 1725. By the end of the decade the two brothers, who were finally ordained in 1727, had been joined by several other priests and laymen. The new order, which had originally been known as the Poor of Jesus but was now called the Congregation of Discalced Clerks of the Most Holy Cross and Passion of Our Lord Jesus Christ, or simply the Passionists Congregation, was finally recognized by Rome in 1741. The community was dedicated to preaching and leading spiritual exercises especially among the poor, who were often Christian in name but for whom religion had little meaning. Passionists emphasized the sufferings of Jesus in their preaching, seeking to arouse the world from what their founders regarded as its spiritual slumber.

The Passionists emphasized contemplative forms of spiritual direction. Somewhat in contrast were the efforts of a traveling missionary preacher named Leonardo da Porto Maurizio (Leonard of Port Maurice, 1676-1751). A Franciscan who had been educated in Rome, Leonardo was initially assigned to serve as a missionary to China, but when he was prevented from going by a bleeding ulcer, he began instead an itinerant ministry of preaching across Italy. He often spoke in open squares in cities, or in fields in the country when the crowds became too big, his missions lasting up to eighteen days in a single town. His style of preaching was dynamic and expressive, using rhetorical tools to seek to bring his listeners to repentance.

Leonardo's message focused on the themes of the Immaculate Conception of the Virgin Mary, the adoration of the Blessed Sacrament, the veneration of the Sacred Heart of Jesus, and devotion to the Stations of the Cross. His sermons had a significant impact on Roman Catholic piety, especially in the growth of the importance of the Immaculate Conception, the doctrine that holds that the conception of Mary took place without the stain of original sin being passed on to her. He is personally credited with having set up 572 Stations of the Cross throughout Italy, including one in the Coliseum in Rome.

The efforts of Leonardo and other eighteenth-century preachers and spiritual directors in Italy were directed toward renewing Christian faith among populations where the church had decreased in importance in the life of the people.

They were especially targeted in Italy to the rural areas where economic conditions were especially harsh and the numbers of poor people were growing. Although these efforts were mostly directed toward people who had been baptized as children into the Christian religion, they were patterned after efforts being conducted in other parts of the world by Catholic missionaries who were working to convert new believers to the Christian faith. The notion of a "homeland mission" in regions that had previously been considered "Christian lands" was to have a profound effect in time on Christian ministry throughout Europe and its settled colonial regions.

The Jansenist controversy

In Italy, a number of these new orders and efforts consciously opposed the teachings of the Jansenists in France. With the revocation of the Edict of Nantes in 1685, not only did Huguenots begin to be persecuted, but others who were regarded as resisting the institutional authority of the Catholic Church began to feel political pressure. The days of limited tolerance were over. Chief among the persecuted Catholic groups were the Jansenists. By the time the papal bull *Unigenitus* was issued in 1713, formally condemning the teachings of its most important leader, Pasquier Quesnel (1634-1719), most of the Jansenists had already gone into hiding or had left France. Quesnel himself was already in Amsterdam, where he spent the remaining years of his life. In France, Louis XIV had ordered the convent of Port-Royal-des-Champs closed in 1709, and all of the nuns were forcibly removed. The bones of the dead in its graveyard were exhumed and plowed under.

Nevertheless, Jansenists survived, and through their illegal weekly publication *Nouvelles ecclésiastiques*, exerted considerable influence in Paris and throughout northern France. The increasingly autocratic rule of Louis XIV succeeded in increasing France's power and prestige internationally, but it also bred resistance at home. Jansenism proved to be an important intellectual vehicle for dissent, even if its home base at Port Royal had been destroyed. Up to a thousand priests were reported to have turned out to support Bishop Jean Soanen of Senez (1647-1740) when he was deposed and exiled in 1727 for his Jansenist theological leanings.

That same year a Jansenist deacon named Francois de Paris (1690-1727) died and was buried in the graveyard of Saint-Médard. Francois had a reputation for having lived a life of severe holiness. Shortly after his death, pilgrims visiting his gravesite claimed to experience healings and other miraculous events there. People visiting the site began to experience convulsions as well, with reports of women and men dancing ecstatically while claiming to be possessed by the Spirit, speaking in unknown tongues, and prophesying. The "Convulsionaries," as they were called, both women and men, were even by some reports performing the sacraments. In an effort to stop the movement, government authorities closed the graveyard at Saint-Médard in 1732, but the movement thereafter moved into private homes where it continued throughout northern France and the Netherlands.

Jansenism received new-found, if brief, support in the late 1740s from the Parliament of Paris, which took several steps to protect bishops and priests who refused to recognize the authority of the bull *Unigenitus*. Pope Benedict XIV (1675-1758) responded by ordering that those who opposed the bull were to be excluded from the sacraments. The king of France sought to enforce the papal order, leading to increased tensions between the king and parliament over control of the church in Paris. Jansenist influence in parliament also was put to use to oppose the Jesuits in Paris. In the seventeenth century the Jesuits, who had led the opposition against the Jansenists, exercised considerable influence within the government of France. But in 1682 a French council of bishops that had been convened by Louis XIV issued a Declaration of the Clergy of France, which asserted royal control over all aspects of the Catholic Church in France. Supporters of this position, which was known as Gallicanism, increasingly came to oppose the Jesuits as well, who strongly supported the institutional authority of the papacy in Rome. In the 1750s the Jesuit superior in Martinique borrowed a considerable amount of money to finance the expansion of a commercial development project there. When a shipload of merchandise was seized by a British warship at the outbreak of war between Britain and France in 1755, the Jesuits, facing financial bankruptcy, turned to the Parliament of Paris for relief. To make matters worse, the order succeeded in arousing the opposition of the mistress of Louis XV, the powerful Jeanne-Antoinette Poisson, Marquise de Pompadour, otherwise known as Madame de Pompadour (1721-1764).

In 1762 the Parliament of Paris succeeded in passing a law banning the Society of Jesus from France. The following year the order's colleges in France were closed, and all members of the society were required to sign a sworn statement repudiating their vows or be sent into exile. Under growing pressure from the Gallicans, the king gave his consent to the expulsion in 1764. The reasons for the suppression of the order in France were complex and varied, but at least one contemporary witness, Voltaire, believed that it was their opposition to the Jansenists that for the most part led to their demise.

By the time the Jesuits were expelled from France the order had already been suppressed in Portugal and its colonial territories for several years. The Jesuit conflict with the government in Portugal began in 1750 when Portugal signed a treaty with Spain that brought a number of Jesuit Reductions, or villages, among the indigenous Guarani people in South America under Portuguese colonial control. Ordered to leave their homeland, the Guarani rebelled, according to Portuguese colonial rulers, with Jesuit support. Members of the Society were ordered to leave all Portuguese colonial territories as a result. Then in 1758 members of the order were accused of playing a role in the attempted assassination of the king of Portugal, leading to the execution of an Italian member of the order who had been a missionary in Brazil and was now living in Lisbon. The following year all members of the Society were expelled from Portugal.

Nearly a decade later, in 1767, following the lead of both Portugal and France, the king of Spain issued an order expelling all Jesuits in Spain and its colonial holdings. News of the expulsion took the better part of the following year to reach all areas of the Spanish colonial world, but by the end of 1768 the Jesuits were gone from South America and the Philippines. The Jesuits were also forced out of Sicily and a number of other smaller kingdoms in Europe. Finally in 1773 Rome conceded to the pressure of the Catholic powers in Europe and suppressed the Order of Jesus within the Papal States as well. The Jesuits had simply become too powerful as an independent religious order. By the time they were restored as an order in the nineteenth century and returned to many places of the world to resume their work, they found that a host of new religious workers, Protestant and Catholic, had moved in to take their place.

Developments in Protestant intellectual and spiritual life

Scotland and England for much of the seventeenth century had been under a common monarch. In 1707 their parliaments agreed to finalize the relationship and form the United Kingdom of Great Britain. Five years later, the newly joined parliament passed the Church Patronage Act, which took the power to appoint clergy away from the elders of churches, a central component of Scottish Presbyterian practice, and vested it in the hands of patrons, which in most cases meant wealthy merchants or landowning members of the nobility. The effect was to call more pastors to pulpits who were favorable to the concerns of the most powerful laypeople in their churches, and especially to the concerns of the new middle class.

Scotland had already attained one of the highest literacy rates in Europe in the first decades of the eighteenth century. Clergy for the most part were expected to be well educated, and congregations came to expect sermons that were well-constructed literary works. Protestant worship in general throughout the eighteenth century in Europe was characterized by its emphasis on preaching. In Scotland, due in part to the effects of the Enlightenment philosophers on public life and in part to the effects of the Patronage Act, preaching began to be decidedly more moralistic, and even utilitarian in nature. Many called it a more "moderate" form of religion. Preachers in this school abandoned the older Calvinist tradition of strict delineation of doctrine. The Bible was still referred to throughout the sermon, but exposition of the text declined decidedly. Proponents of this new school of theology began to promote in their sermons practices they identified with social progress, improvements in agriculture, and even increased international trade. Thomas Chalmers (1780-1847), on the other hand, writing early in the nineteenth century, compared the sermons of the moderates to a winter's day: short, clear, and cold. The brevity and clarity are good, he warned, but the coldness can be fatal. Such sermons were like moonlight, incapable of ripening the harvest.

Similar currents of moderation were blowing through Protestant churches in continental Europe during the eighteenth century. Protestants in many places were still subject to persecution at the hands of national governments that were officially Roman Catholic, but even in these places one could find worshipping Protestant communities in major cities. In Germany, Switzerland, the Netherlands, and Scandinavia, Protestants enjoyed established church status. Here one could find similar forms of moderate Protestant theology emerging.

One of the exemplars of this moderate tradition was Jean-Frédéric Ostervald (1663-1747). Born in an upper-class family in Neuchâtel, Switzerland, he began his education in Zurich before moving on to schools in France, ending at the University of Paris as a Protestant scholar prior to the revocation of the Edict of Nantes. He then returned to Neuchâtel, where he served as pastor until his death. Ostervald sought to temper Reformed dogmatic theology with Enlightenment ideas and the devotional spirit of Pietism. The way to Christian unity, he argued, was through ethical cooperation and a renewed emphasis on the Bible rather than through creeds. He published his own revised translation of the Geneva Bible, which was soon translated from French into English and later became quite popular both in England and in the United States. While he was decidedly moderate in his theological ideas, Ostervald's homiletic style still harkened back to a previous century. Rather than preaching sermons on contemporary themes, Ostevald, in true Reformed fashion, would preach on a single verse or passage of scripture, employing other portions of scripture to interpret his chosen text. Sermons were long, focused, and exegetically carefully developed.

Unlike the stationary Ostervald, Jacques Saurin (1677-1730) moved around ecclesiastically as well as geographically. Born into a Huguenot family in Nimes, France, Saurin converted to the Roman Catholic faith after the revocation of the Edict of Nantes. However, contact with Reformed Christians in Holland, England, and Geneva helped to bring about his reconversion from Roman Catholic priest to Reformed pastor. Returning to the Reformed tradition, he brought with him into the pulpit some of the best of his Roman Catholic training and rhetoric, as well as a healthy dose of his French culture. Rather than using a *lectio continua* form of preaching (preaching through a book of the Bible), he chose to preach topical sermons. From his eventual pulpit in The Hague, where he lived and served for the last years of his life as an exile, he was involved with a community of thinkers who were hammering out the concepts of tolerance and the notion of the separation of church and state.

Saurin spoke directly to the issues of the day from the pulpit, including the rising interest in foreign missions among Protestants in Europe. One of his many sermons that was translated and published a number of times, *Sermon sur la penitence de la pecheresse* ("Sermon on the Repentance of the Unchaste Woman"), argued for equal respect for women in society and is considered an early feminist sermon. Another, *Sur l'éternité de Dieu* ("On the Eternity of God"), addressed issues concerning the universe and modern science. His defense of the faith employed concepts that were "reasonable" and "rational," using ideas considered to be part of the local context to move listeners beyond their local mindset. For over twenty years Saurin led the Huguenot congregation in The Hague, providing a model of what modern preaching could be, imbibing in the ideals of toleration, democracy, and independence.

The Swiss pastor and poet Johann Kaspar Lavater (1741-1801) was even more complex than Saurin in his adaptation of Enlightenment thinking and in his defense of what he understood to be the orthodox faith. In the tradition of Zwingli and Calvin, he preached in the *lectio continua* style each morning, usually preaching through the Gospels with breaks only for special sermons on

Christmas Day, Easter, and Pentecost. A preacher who had a bent for the rational, he also showed a love for the mystical and intuitive. Alongside his sermons he published poems and songs. His study on physiognomy, or the study of faces, in an effort to determine character or personality was popular for a time, until the field became generally discredited. Lavater associated with people of means and influence in the Swiss city of Zurich (he even tried to convert the great Jewish philosopher Moses Mendelssohn [1729-1786]), and was friends for most of his life with the German poet Johann Wolfgang von Goethe (1749-1832).

Pietism and the religion of the heart

On the opposite side of the Protestant religious spectrum in the eighteenth century were a cluster of movements that came to form an evangelical consensus around the need or desire for more experiential forms of Christianity. Pietism was one of these. Originating in Germany the previous century, Pietism championed what its proponents regarded as a more heartfelt form of religion. Its advocates opposed what they considered the cold orthodoxy of their opponents, who were often chastised for defending rational dogmas at the expense of conversion experiences. Pietists valued the experiential dimensions of religion, and expected one to appropriate these on a personal, narrative level. Its most influential leader, as we have seen in Chapter 12 above, was Philipp Jakob Spener (1635-1705). When Frederick III, elector of Brandenburg (later Frederick I of Prussia, 1657-1713), sought to found a new university in 1691, he turned to Spener for assistance. The new university at Halle quickly became the center for Pietist learning in Germany and throughout the world.

August Hermann Francke (1663-1727) was already a Pietist when he met Spener in 1689 in Dresden. Specializing in biblical languages, Francke had been teaching at Leipzig at the time, but that same year was removed from his position because of his Pietistic beliefs. Two years later, when he was expelled from the city of Erfurt for again promoting Pietism, Spener invited him to join the faculty of the new University of Halle, which was in the process of being established. Francke moved to Halle in 1694 and spent the rest of his life on the faculty.

The year Francke moved to Halle he also accepted a call to serve as pastor of a parish in Glaucha, a poor district on the outskirts of Halle. The entire region around Halle still showed the economic effects of the religious wars of the first decades of the seventeenth century, but Glaucha was particularly destitute. Its main commercial enterprise was the brewing industry, and its numerous taverns attracting unemployed workers, prostitutes, and other poor people. In addition to his work in teaching biblical languages and hermeneutics at the university, Francke soon found himself involved as a pastor addressing numerous social problems.

In 1695 he established a school for the children of destitute families in Glaucha, supported by charitable donations from wealthier members of the community in Halle and by tax grants from the elector. To prepare teachers for the school, he opened a special teachers' college, the *Seminarium selectum praeceptorum*, the following year. The curriculum of the school for children included religious instruction, reading, writing, mathematics, and physical education. The quality of the program soon attracted the attention of wealthier members of the Halle community, who began to send their own children to be educated. At first the children from the various classes were mixed, but within a few years a separate program for the children of wealthier families, called the *pädagogium,* was established. The fees that Francke charged wealthier families helped support the entire educational program. A separate orphanage was built and opened in 1701, and a publishing house, bookstore, and drugstore the following year. Similar schools were soon opened in other cities, including one in Königsberg, which later graduated Immanuel Kant. In 1710, with the financial support of Baron Carl Hildebrand von Canstein (1667-1719) of Berlin, Francke started the Cansteinsche Bible Institute, which began printing inexpensive Bibles and other religious literature from Halle, first in German but eventually in other languages as well. By the time of Francke's death in 1727, more than two thousand students were enrolled in the various school programs, and ten thousand copies of the Bible were being printed and sold annually. The entire complex of operations eventually came to be known as *Franckesche Stiftungen*, or the Francke Foundation.

Heinrich Wilhelm Ludolf (1655-1712), a German diplomat with broad international connections, was a friend of the Francke family. In 1699 he introduced Francke to a new effort being undertaken by the Church of England, the Society for Promoting Christian Knowledge, which was being organized to support missionary work in the British colonies. Francke began corresponding with the society. Through Ludolf and others in England, Francke's attention was drawn toward the needs of the Orthodox churches in the East. In 1702 he opened at Halle the *Collegium Orientale Theologicum* ("Oriental Theological College"), intended to train students in the languages of the Eastern Orthodox churches (Russian, Greek, Slavic, and even Arabic) as well as to prepare leadership from these churches for ministry. Several students from Greece attended the school in the first decade of the eighteenth century with little success. Far more important were the students from western Europe that the school prepared who went as missionaries to other parts of the world. Francke's interest in ecumenical efforts was widespread, but he was especially interested in developing relationships among Protestant churches. He corresponded with church leaders of various Protestant confessions throughout both western and eastern Europe, and in numerous colonial locations, including the British colonies in North America. Largely due to Francke's efforts, Halle continued to be the center not only of Pietism in Germany and Scandinavia throughout the eighteenth century, but one of the most important centers for missionary and ecumenical efforts taking place throughout the world as well.

One of the graduates of Francke's *pädagogium* in 1716 was Nikolaus Ludwig, Graf von Zinzendorf (1700-1760). A godson of Jakob Spener, Zinzendorf had been raised in a Pietist home. After finishing at Halle, he went on to complete a degree at the University of Wittenberg before settling in 1722 on the estate of his grandmother, which he renamed Berthelsdorf, in the southeastern part of Saxony, near the border of Bohemia. His plan was to build a Christian community on these grounds along the lines of a Pietist conventicle, maintaining a common life of devotion and service. A short time later he opened up part of his land to resettle a group of religious refugees from Moravia. These Moravians, as they were soon called, were members of the *Unitas Fratrum,* who were the followers of Jan Hus but who were now being forced by Catholic rulers to immigrate. Zinzendorf permitted them to build a village, which they named Herrnhut.

The numbers of refugees quickly grew, and with it dissent. Things were at a crisis in 1727 when Zinzendorf, who was not yet ordained, moved in among them and began to organize the community. With others in the community he wrote out a document that they called the "Brotherly Agreement," which was intended to bring about peace. Several months later, after an all-night prayer meeting, the community experienced a powerful religious revival that later came to be known as the "Moravian Pentecost." Members of the community wept, called for public repentance, and began continuous hourly prayer.

Under Zinzendorf's leadership a distinctive community soon emerged. Members were divided into what Zinzendorf called "choirs," organized by age and gender, for worship and work. Women held leadership positions alongside men. Schools were set up for children. The hourly prayers that began with the revival continued, along with daily scripture readings. Zinzendorf began writing hymns and theological study books for the community. Several new liturgical services were introduced, the most notable being foot washing and what Zinzendorf called the "love feast." Marriage was considered a sacrament, and the entire community was involved in celebrating the consummation of marriages among their members.

Zinzendorf's theology was a rich, if eclectic, mixture of themes and traditions. Following the experience of the Moravian Pentecost, he retained a prominent place for the Holy Spirit in all aspects of work. He often referred to the Spirit as "Mother," since, he reasoned, this most accurately describes our relationship to her. His doctrine of the Trinity was often expressed as Father, Mother, and Son. Moravians paid considerable attention to the passion of Christ in their theology. The emphasis reached a troubling point of excess in the 1740s, a period that became known among the inhabitants of Herrnhut as the "Sifting Time." Excessive sensual devotion in Zinzendorf's theology led to what were considered by some to be erotically charged practices that focused on descriptions of Christ's wounds. But even after the controversy subsided, the Moravians' emphasis on the blood and passion of Jesus remained strong.

Zinzendorf was often suspect within his own Lutheran church. The first years at Herrnhut he served as the community's religious leader without any official clerical recognition. In 1735 Zinzendorf was finally ordained to ministry, then two years later consecrated a bishop by two bishops in Berlin, one of whom was a member of the Moravian community. His ecumenical commitments were strong. Zinzendorf reached out to a number of Protestant leaders in other communions and even proposed a program of cooperation among the various Protestant confessional traditions in matters of mission and service. He developed a relationship with Roman Catholics, including a friendship with the Jansenist cardinal archbishop of Paris, Louis Antoine de Noailles (1651-1729). Moravian communities paralleled Catholic monastic orders with their daily disciplines of worship, song, and prayers, as well as in their work for the poor and their missionary vocation. As they spread around the world, many Moravian communities looked like monastic orders, with the only difference being that the Moravian communities were composed of married couples and families.

And spread throughout the world they did. By the time Zinzendorf was ordained, he had already begun to send out members of the Herrnhut community as missionaries. In 1731 in Copenhagen he met a former slave from the West Indies named Anthony Ulrich (dates unknown) who had been baptized. Zinzendorf invited Ulrich to return with him to Herrnhut to share with the rest of the Moravian community his story of the condition of slaves in the Caribbean. As a result two members of Herrnhut, David Nitschmann (1690-1772) and Johann Leonhard Dober (1706-1766), went the following year to the Danish colony on the island of St. Thomas in the Caribbean where they began working among the slaves. Nitschmann soon returned to Herrnhut and was ordained by the Lutheran Church as a bishop in 1735 before going to the British colony of Pennsylvania in 1741, where he spent the rest of his life. Zinzendorf himself visited the Caribbean as well as New York and Pennsylvania where he worked with Native Americans and helped to start a Moravian mission among them. By the time of his death, Moravians had established communities from Greenland to South Africa, and in several places in North America and the Caribbean.

August Gottlieb Spangenberg (1704-1792) had been on the faculty at Halle before his relaxed attitude toward doctrinal differences forced him to leave in 1733. Previous contacts with Zinzendorf led him to Herrnhut, where he went on to become its leader after Zinzendorf's death in 1760. In 1735, however, he and twenty-five other Moravians from Herrnhut were on a ship named the *Simmonds* on their way to a new British colony called Georgia, in North America, to start a mission among Native Americans. On board the same ship were two brothers, John Wesley (1703-1791) and Charles Wesley (1707-1788). The Wesleys were ordained priests in the Church of England and were heading to Georgia to serve as missionaries as well. En route to Georgia, John studied German in order to communicate better with the members of the Moravian community. At the end of the trip he confessed that their confidence during the stormy passage had impressed him deeply.

Three years after first meeting the Wesley brothers, the Moravians in Georgia were introduced to another young Anglican priest named George Whitefield (1714-1770), who was in Georgia for a short time. Whitefield was an associate of the Wesleys from the days when they had been at Oxford together. All three had belonged to an organization they called the "Holy Club," whose members met early each morning for worship, kept regular hourly prayers during the day, and sought to engage in outreach ministries to the poor and the imprisoned. Others at Oxford jeered them, calling them "Methodists" because of their methodical ways of holiness. The name stuck.

Wesleyan movement and evangelical revivalism

Two years after his first meeting with the Moravians in Georgia, Whitefield sold the missionaries from Herrnhut property in Pennsylvania where the Moravians then moved their work. Whitefield by that time was already gaining fame as an itinerant preaching, leading what came to be called "awakenings," or "revivals." The son of a widowed innkeeper, Whitefield had been literally born and raised in a tavern in Gloucester. He worked his way through Oxford, serving as an attendant to other students. A dramatic conversion experience in 1735 turned his life toward a religious vocation; and after being ordained by the bishop of Gloucester, he began itinerant preaching.

From his days growing up in a tavern, where he had witnessed local plays, Whitefield had been drawn to drama. He put this experience to good use, developing a style of preaching that was strongly theatrical in presentation. Quickly the sermons of the young Anglican priest began to draw crowds, larger than any local church could hold. In part due to the crowds, and in part due to opposition of other priests who closed their pulpits to him, Whitefield began preaching in open fields, a practice that violated Church of England canons. Some of his open-air meetings were held near mines, others out in fields, where people from nearby towns or cities could gather to hear him. Some listeners greeted these meetings with ridicule or disdain, throwing rotten food and shouting curses at him as he preached. But others responded positively, undergoing what came to be popularly called "conversions."

Whitefield crossed the Atlantic in 1738 to take a position as a priest in Georgia, but returned the following year to England to try to raise money for a new orphanage that was modeled after the one in Halle. In 1740 he returned to North America, this time to preach a series of public sermons in cities along the eastern seaboard from New England to the Carolinas. Before the end of his life he had traveled to North America seven times; in addition to preaching throughout England and Scotland, he traveled twice in Ireland and once to the Netherlands to lead revivals. At one of the open-air revivals in Cambuslang, Scotland, in the summer of 1742, an estimated thirty thousand people heard him preach.

By the end of his life, Whitefield had preached thousands of sermons. Some of these were published during his lifetime, but others appeared only after his death. During his lifetime he also published his journals, various letters, and narrative accounts of revivals. Although he was staunchly Calvinist in his theological leanings, an issue over which he differed sharply with the Wesleys, he engaged in numerous ecumenical relationships, not only with the Wesleys but with Lutherans and Moravians. And although he was both an owner (in Georgia) and a staunch advocate of slavery, he was also one of the first Europeans to preach to the enslaved of African descent in America. Upon his death he was eulogized in a poem by Phillis Wheatley (1753-1784), the first African-American woman to be published in a European language.

Among Whitefield's closest associates in England were John and Charles Wesley. The story of their ministry properly begins with their mother, Suzanna

Annesley Wesley (1669-1742), who by all accounts exerted the most important early spiritual influence on their lives. Raised in a Puritan home, Suzanna Annesley had been taught theology, the Bible, ancient languages, and the arts and sciences by her father. At the age of twelve she came to the surprising conclusion that the Anglican Church was the true church, leaving her Nonconformist family tradition behind. Upon marrying Samuel Wesley (1662-1735) they moved to the rural parish of Epworth, where Suzanna raised and educated her nine surviving children (out of nineteen children born).

As a parent, Suzanna was methodical and strict. Both boys and girls were to be trained in every way, and even after they became adults, school was still in session, for she believed that the spiritual responsibility for her children lasted her entire lifetime. Her many letters to John contain numerous theological discussions. She was strongly supportive of the Armenian theological point of view that John and Charles Wesley both came to embrace, and abhorred the Calvinist doctrine of predestination, which she believed charged God with being the author of sin. Although years later John Wesley would give credit to the English theologian William Law (1686-1761) for having been the immediate source of one of his most distinctive, if controversial doctrines, it was most likely from his mother that he first heard about the concept of Christian perfection.

Both Charles and John went on to Oxford, where they were exposed to the works not only of the Western theological tradition but to many of the ancient Christian writers from the Greek, Coptic, and Syriac traditions of the East. John graduated with a bachelor's degree from Christ Church College and was ordained in 1725. The following year he received a fellowship at Lincoln College in the university, and after completing a master's degree in 1727 went to work in the parish with his father. Two years later he returned to serve as a fellow, or tutor, at Lincoln College. The appointment allowed John to preach without having been appointed by a bishop to a specific parish. Charles completed his bachelor's degree that same year at Christ College and stayed to complete a master's degree in 1733. Charles had already organized the Holy Club in 1729 when John returned, but John soon became its leader. In its discipline one can see the early outlines that would later come to characterize the entire Methodist movement.

In 1735 the Wesleys headed off to Georgia in North America. John wrote in his journal aboard the *Simmonds* that they would arise at 4:00 for an hour of private prayer, study the Bible together for two hours, and then teach the children on the ship, provide counsel, study the church fathers to compare their understanding of the biblical text, and preach extempore on the ship. John also remarked that Charles wrote some hymns. As noted above, they also met Moravians on the voyage. Once in Georgia, the mission was a fiasco. John got into a romantic relationship with a young woman who was the niece of a judge in the colony, whom he then spurned. She promptly married another man. Wesley refused to serve her Communion on account of this, and she sued for defamation of character. Within a few months John left Georgia a defeated man.

Back in England in 1738, the brothers turned to the Moravians for spiritual guidance. Peter Böhler (1712-1775), the first Moravian to be ordained by the hand of Zinzendorf and soon to be on his way to America, had just established a Mora-

vian community called the Fetter Lane Society. In their conversations with the
Wesleys, the Moravians focused on the question of whether or not the brothers
had really experienced the assurance of pardon. In May of 1738 at a Moravian
meeting at Aldersgate, after listening to a portion of Martin Luther's *Preface
to the Letter of St. Paul to the Romans* being read, John wrote, "I felt my heart
strangely warmed. I felt I did trust in Christ, Christ alone for my salvation. . . ."
Within two weeks John was off to visit Germany. His reception at Herrnhut was
cold, but he had a fruitful time at Halle.

Upon his return to England, John Wesley began to distance himself theologically from the Moravians, whom he considered to be too passive in their
approach to holiness. John's own preaching showed increased confidence and
vigor. Whitefield invited him to join him in preaching in open fields, which Wesley did. Although the two had differences and eventually separated over issues of
doctrine, their work as revivalists continued to link them in ministry. Whitefield
had organized several new societies in Bristol as a result of his revival preaching, and upon departing for Georgia, he turned over their spiritual direction to
Wesley. Soon Wesley was organizing his own societies. Members were drawn
at first from among those who heard his sermons, but these members were soon
recruiting others. From their inception, the Methodist societies were highly organized. Each society was divided into several bands. Bands in turn were divided
into classes. Classes were gender specific, and met regularly for spiritual counsel
and direction under a class leader. Band meetings prepared members to receive
Communion and took up special offerings.

Wesley appointed the local leadership for these groups, many of them lay
people. In 1743 he published a set of rules that they were to follow. The following year he gathered a small group of leaders from these Methodist societies
for what became an annual conference for teaching and handling administrative matters. Wesley himself began training and appointing lay preachers whom
he then appointed to circulate among the societies to supplement his preaching.
His published sermons and notes on scripture provided the doctrinal standards
for the movement. He also published his journals, which narrated his day-to-
day experiences and reflections. Wesley abridged and edited over the course of
several decades a fifty-volume collection of what he considered to be Christian
classics for devotional use and theological instruction among societies. He also
published several worship services that he adapted for his movement, including
a covenant renewal service intended to be used on New Year's Eve. Traveling by
horseback, he logged more than 200,000 miles over the course of his lifetime of
service as he visited his members and provided spiritual oversight for the growing movement.

Through these efforts Wesley offered a vision of realizable holiness for daily
life. Salvation was a progressively ordered affair according to this vision. One
moved from a state of prevening grace to being justified and then sanctified
in Christian life. John Wesley believed that one could even attain to a state of
practical Christian perfection this side of eternity, a position that some in the
movement, including his brother Charles, did not fully embrace. This perfection,
argued John, was neither in knowledge nor in moral life such that one no longer

had the capacity to sin. It was instead perfection of love whereby one could attain a state in which one truly and entirely desired to love that which was of God.

Following the lead of his mother's teaching, Wesley rejected a strict understanding of the Calvinist doctrines of predestination and limited atonement. He taught that God foreknew all things, including who would accept the message of salvation, but that God allowed human beings to resist grace, and even allowed those who were Christians to turn away. Those who did fall away from salvation, Wesley believed, could later return to grace and be restored both in the societies and before God in eternity.

Although often identified as a conservative supporter of the monarchy in his political views, on other social issues Wesley was a forceful voice of reform. The efforts he undertook as a student at Oxford for outreach ministries to prisoners and to the poor established a pattern for the Methodist societies for years to come in England. Wesley taught his members to save money and created what amounted to incipient credit unions among his societies to help those in need. In 1774 he published a pamphlet titled *Thoughts upon Slavery,* in which he forcefully condemned the institution as barbaric. The Africans who were being enslaved were not only fully human but they came from well-organized societies, thereby refuting the notion that slavery was improving their condition. He described the inhuman conditions associated with the slave trade and appealed to his readers to join the effort to abolish it.

Wesley never intended his Methodist societies to leave the Church of England. He intended them to be a means of spiritual renewal for those whom the ministry of the Church of England seemed to him to be failing to reach, especially among the poorer social classes. Methodists were expected to participate in the sacramental life of their local parish while participating in the society for spiritual growth in holiness. For this reason the meeting times of the societies were set not to conflict with regular worship services in local Anglican parishes.

Toward the end of his life Wesley, though lacking episcopal standing, took the controversial step of ordaining several of his followers as priests, or elders. He did so to serve the growing Methodist movement in Scotland, Ireland, and in America. Criticized severely for taking such a step, he defended it on the basis of the need for ordained leadership to provide sacramental services to Methodists in these regions. There was precedence, he said, for such ordinations in early Christian history. In 1784 Methodists in North America, following the colonies' break with England, organized themselves under several of these clergy into a separate church body, apart from the Church of England. Methodists in England followed suit after John Wesley's death in 1791 to become a separate communion.

The Methodists in England boasted a significant number of capable leaders besides John Wesley, women as well as men. Wesley began appointing women as class leaders in 1742. At first Wesley sought to identify what these women did in the societies as "exhorting," but by 1760 he was forced to recognize that what women such as Mary Bosanquet (1739-1815) and Sarah Crosby (1729-1804) were doing was preaching. Others such as Hester Ann Rogers (1756-1794), who was John Wesley's housekeeper, were recognized as leaders in the movement on account of what others perceived to be their advanced spiritual state.

Among the most influential Methodists after John Wesley himself in the eighteenth century in England was his brother Charles. If John provided the organizational genius of the movement, Charles gave the Methodists their theology. He did not do so, however, by writing treatises on doctrine or books in systematic theology. Instead, it was the hymnody of Charles Wesley that gave the Methodists their theological voice. By the end of his life Charles had penned more than five thousand such hymns. Some of these, such as "O for a Thousand Tongues to Sing," which was written on the first anniversary of his own experience of receiving an assurance of pardon, became almost universally known and loved by Christians of all traditions throughout the world.

Not all who were part of the evangelical revival in England in the eighteenth century came under Wesley's theological umbrella. Whitefield for one, although being identified with the Methodists, remained a staunch Calvinist. Another who had been part of the Fetter Lane Society in 1739 but then sided with Whitefield rather than the Wesleys was Selina Hastings, the countess of Huntington (1707-1791). In 1748 she appointed Whitefield to be her personal chaplain, and funded more than sixty chapels where Whitefield's followers could gather. Until 1779 these chapels were considered part of the Church of England, but later most of them became part of the Congregational Church. The countess was also responsible for funding a number of schools, including Trevecca, a school for training preachers to help carry on the evangelical revival in Wales, and others that were dedicated to teaching the children of the poor.

Others who were identified with the wider evangelical revival of the eighteenth century in England stayed more clearly within the Anglican Church. One such person, John Newton (1725-1807), was a sailor and later a sea captain serving on slave ships carrying human cargo from Africa to England. During these years he professed several times to have had various conversion experiences, although none was strong enough to lead him to forgo his vocation. Finally after a stroke, he abandoned his work as a sea captain, and in 1764 he was ordained to the priesthood in the Church of England. As curate of Olney Parish, Newton had the opportunity to convince a young politician named William Wilberforce (1759-1833), who had recently experienced an evangelical conversion, to stay in parliament rather than go into parish ministry. Newton eventually joined the abolitionist cause along with Wilberforce and renounced his years as a slave-ship captain. His most enduring contribution to the history of Christianity was, however, writing and publishing the hymn "Amazing Grace" in 1773.

Wilberforce was from a wealthy merchant family, and he began his political career by being elected to parliament at the age of twenty-one, while still a student at Cambridge. His evangelical conversion experience several years later turned him even more forcefully in a philanthropic direction. By the late 1780s he was publicly supporting the abolitionist movement and introduced his first legislative bills to try to abolish the slave trade. In 1792 he was influential in starting the colony in Sierra Leone, and finally in 1807 was able to see the passage of An Act for the Abolition of the Slave Trade. Slavery itself would not be abolished by England until 1833, the year of Wilberforce's death.

Expansion of "Free" Churches

Methodists in England, like the Moravians and Pietists in Germany, for most of the eighteenth century existed on the margins of the established church (Anglican for the Methodists, Lutheran for Moravians and Pietists). Only after John Wesley's death did the Methodists in England in 1795 establish themselves as a separate communion. Other church bodies in England and in continental Europe, including Mennonites and other Anabaptists, Baptists, and various other dissenting churches in Great Britain, over the course of the eighteenth century found political conditions gradually relaxing. The reign of Queen Anne (1665-1714) from 1702 to 1714 was particularly difficult for the dissenting congregations, but in the decades that followed many found themselves not just surviving, but thriving. Members of Free Churches in eighteenth-century England could not attend the major universities, but several dissenting academies were founded to provide education for their children. For many dissenting and Free Church leaders, theological education was for the most part informal. New ministers were simply trained in the homes of pastors through hands-on experience.

Among the various Anabaptist communions, the Mennonites in the eighteenth century were the most prominent. During the second half of the seventeenth century, a number of Mennonites immigrated to the Palatinate region in Germany. Some of these Mennonites began to immigrate to North America beginning around 1707, settling in Pennsylvania where they established agricultural communities. Others who stayed in the Palatinate became known for their effectiveness in turning some of the poorest soil in the region into productive farms. One of the Mennonites of this period, David Möllenger (d. 1787), became known as the "archfarmer" of Palatinate. In Russia, the empress Catherine II (1729-1796) passed a religious freedom act in 1788 that attracted Mennonites to immigrate to Ukraine where, as in the Palatinate, they helped increase agricultural production significantly.

The relaxing political climate allowed Mennonites to become more settled. A number of their members even began to prosper financially. Looking to increase the level of education of pastors, the first formal Mennonite school for theological education was opened in 1735 in Amsterdam at the Lamb Church. By the 1760s Mennonites in the Netherlands were erecting substantial buildings, and by 1765 the first organ was installed in a Mennonite church in Utrecht. Prayers, which in Mennonite worship were previously said in silence, now began to be spoken aloud as in other churches. Mennonites still remained largely marginalized for their beliefs in pacifism and nonresistance, but in many other respects they were becoming more like their Reformed and Lutheran neighbors.

This is not to say that the Mennonite congregations entirely lost sight of their distinctive history. A significant aspect of that history resided in the Mennonite memory of martyrdom and suffering. In 1660 a Flemish Mennonite named

Tieleman Jansz van Braght (1625-1664) published a collection of martyrdom stories from across the centuries, highlighting the more recent stories of Anabapist martyrs over the past centuries. The original title of the volume was more than seventy-five words in length, but it became known after its second edition in 1685 simply as *Martelaersspiegel* ("Martyrs' Mirror"). The work was translated into German and published by the Mennonite community in Ephrata, Pennsylvania, in 1749 and then republished again in Germany in 1780. An English edition appeared in 1837. Along with the stories of martyrs through the centuries the massive volume contained poetry, a collection of Mennonite confessional statements, and a treatise on the true church. *Martyr's Mirror* helped Mennonites who were immigrating to a number of new regions in the eighteenth century both in Europe and in America maintain their distinct community values and spirituality.

Developments in church music

One of the most remarkable developments in Christianity in the eighteenth century in Europe concerned music. The most prolific hymn writer in the English language was unquestionably Charles Wesley, whose contributions have already been noted. The contribution of John Newton was noted above as well. Joining them in the eighteenth century in writing in English were such persons as William Cowper (1731-1800), whose compositions include "There Is a Fountain, Filled with Blood"; the Anglican clergyman Augustus Montague Toplady (1740-1778), who is best remembered perhaps for his hymn "Rock of Ages"; and Philip Doddridge (1702-1751), whose hymns were also influential and whose devotional book *The Rise and Progress of Religion in the Soul* was a major impetus for Wilberforce's conversion.

One of the most important of these English writers was Isaac Watts (1674-1748). The son of Nonconformist parents (his father first laid eyes on young Isaac while in prison), Watts grew up singing only the Psalms in worship, as was still the practice in the Reformed tradition. After attending one of the dissenting academies, he went on to serve as a pastor of an independent church in London. Toward the end of his life he was reported to have attended a Unitarian church, and published but then retracted a pamphlet titled *A Solemn Address to the Great and Blessed God*, in which he questioned the doctrine of the Trinity. His most enduring contribution to the life of Christians throughout the world without question came in the more than six hundred hymns that he published during his lifetime, including works such as "When I Survey the Wondrous Cross" and "Joy to the World."

Churches throughout Europe in the eighteenth century were developing more elaborate forms of music, making use of new or improved instruments. Over the course of the century the musical form generally known as Baroque, with its more colorful, polyphonic tonality, gave way to Classical music with its more structured order and lesser complexity. The development of secular opera in Italy found its counterpart in sacred music in cantatas and oratorios. Accompanying these developments in musical form were changes in instrumentation. The pipe organ went from being a smaller and often portable instrument over the course of the eighteenth century to become the massive cathedral instrument known today. In Italy the harpsichord, a plucked keyboard instrument with only one volume, was transformed in 1711 by Bartolommeo Cristofori (1655-1731) into a *gravicembalo col piano e forte*, or a "harpsichord with soft and loud," otherwise known as the piano. Other instruments coming into popular use in this period were the English horn, oboe, clarinet, and bassoon. With the newer instruments and the larger and more dramatic musical forms came the need for orchestration. The Italian Roman Catholic composer Alessandro Scarlatti (1660-1725) was a major influence in this development.

Austria boasted Wolfgang Amadeus Mozart (1756-1791) and Joseph Haydn (1732-1809), among others. The German composer Ludwig van Beethoven (1770-1827) is often regarded as the greatest, if the last, of the eighteenth-century Classical musicians. The impact of these developments on religious music can be seen best in two figures from the century, Johann Sebastian Bach (1685-1750) and George Frideric Handel (1685-1759).

Johann Sebastian Bach was born into a musical family. His father was a trumpeter and violinist. At a young age, Bach's uncle introduced him to the organ. He went on to study music at Lüneburg and after graduating supported himself during his early years as a court musician. In 1723 he accepted the position as director of music for a large Lutheran church in Leipzig, where he remained the rest of his life. His Lutheran sensitivities were evident throughout his work. Bach often began compositions with the words *Jehu juva* ("Help me Jesus"), and many of his manuscripts were completed with the phrase *Soli Deo gloria* ("Glory to God alone"). Moreover he was prolific, with more than two hundred sacred cantatas and other pieces of writing to his credit. One of his best-known works is *Matthäuspassion* ("St. Matthew Passion") from 1727, a work that puts the twenty-sixth and twenty-seventh chapters of Matthew to music, sung by a double choir and accompanied by a double orchestra. In his position as director both of the school and of the church in Leipzig, Bach was able to write cantatas on a weekly basis. Most of these were based on biblical passages or themes, which he carefully researched in scripture, which is evident from the abundance of notes found on the pages of his personal Bible. Bach was one of the most important names in orchestration and choral arrangement in his day. He introduced these into worship in new and lasting ways.

A second great name among musical composers of the eighteenth century whose works had a profound effect on religion and worship was another Lutheran named George Frideric Handel. Born in Halle, Germany, and educated in Halle and then Italy, Handel spent most of his working years in England. Although he largely wrote secular music for a living, his most famous work was an oratorio titled *Messiah*, which was written in 1741 in London and debuted the following year in Dublin, Ireland. The work narrates with full orchestration the prophecy, arrival, suffering, and exaltation of the Messiah, doing so entirely with words derived from the King James Bible. It has often been called the most famous oratorio ever written.

Handel's *Messiah* successfully brought the sacred text of the Bible to a wider world, but it also brought what was for many a nonsacred style of music into the church. Not all were pleased with either development. Many church leaders were opposed to having passages from the Bible sung in opera houses, where the oratorio was often performed. Handel defended the endeavor as being consistent with his Lutheran beliefs, but others disagreed. Such concerns were in fact more widely reflected throughout the various branches of Christianity in Europe in the eighteenth century. Many from among the more conservative sectors of the Reformed tradition still supported the exclusive use of Psalms in worship in these churches. In 1749, Pope Benedict XIV issued a papal bull, *Annus qui nunc vertentem*, which decreed that only the organ, stringed instruments, and the bassoon were permitted for use in worship. All other instruments, including kettle drums, oboes, flutes, and trombones, were prohibited. Only slowly did many churches open up to the breadth of instrumentation that was becoming common in the courts of the nobility, or in theaters and opera houses throughout Europe in the eighteenth century.

Impact of the Industrial Revolution on European religious life

The revolution taking place in music in the eighteenth century in Europe eventually had the effect of changing worship in Christian churches of all traditions. Another revolution taking place at the end of the century would have an even greater impact. Developments in technology had been increasingly transforming the social order for several centuries. Toward the end of the eighteenth century the speed of such changes rapidly accelerated, in effect revolutionizing the material economy, the social order, and eventually the global environment. The name that is usually given to this development is the "Industrial Revolution." The development was primarily driven by steam.

Steam had long been recognized as a potentially important source of mechanical power, but it was not until the first steam engine was invented in the late seventeenth century that its energy was actually harnessed. A Scottish mechanical engineer named James Watt (1736-1819) by 1765 had figured out how to use steam energy to drive a piston efficiently enough to make it effective. A decade later he was able to transform the linear motion of a piston into rotations, thereby turning a wheel. Soon steam engines made of iron were not only pumping water out of mines, the original purpose for which they were invented, but were also turning the wheels of mills and looms, enabling the expansion of production on a scale never before imagined. By the end of the century, engines built on the basis of Watt's patented invention were driving vehicles on land (the train) and sea (the steamship).

Steam engines enabled the production of goods such as textiles to expand at enormous rates toward the end of the century. With the development of these manufacturing centers, called factories in England, the Industrial Revolution was fully under way. Production quickly moved from homes and small shops to factories in the 1770s and 1780s, where work could be performed on a much larger scale.

The new factories were owned by wealthy individuals who invested large sums of money to build and operate them in hopes of eventual returns. They also required large numbers of workers, who were paid wages based on hourly labor. At first, factories were built outside cities; but by the end of the eighteenth century they were being built inside urban areas because of the greater concentrations of laborers that the cities offered. The opportunities that factories offered for wage employment in turn served to draw more people to these cities, rapidly increasing the density of the urban industrial population and straining resources that cities had to sustain their inhabitants materially, socially, and culturally. Churches in urban areas for the most part were not prepared to respond to these new urban realities.

Steam engines mostly burned coal. Coal had been mined for centuries for use as a fuel in heating and in the production of iron; but with the development of the steam engine, coal mining grew rapidly, requiring more workers who labored under difficult conditions. Burning of coal also began to impact the wider environment in ways that would not be recognized for centuries. All of these new social conditions and realities posed unprecedented challenges to churches and church leaders.

The French Revolution creates a new world for Christianity

If steam revolutionized the material economy of Europe toward the end of the eighteenth century, events in France revolutionized the political economy. Early on the morning of July 14, 1789, a crowd of several thousand gathered outside a fortress known as the Bastille in Paris. The fortress also served as a prison, but the crowd was not seeking to liberate the handful of inmates who were being held there. They were after the gunpowder that they had heard was being stored in the facility. Paris had been gripped by social unrest for weeks. Famine had driven up the cost of basic foods, including bread. The French government had borrowed heavily to finance several wars and was facing bankruptcy. Recognizing the mounting crisis, a group of leading members of the French nobility forced King Louis XVI (1754-1793) to call a meeting of the Estates General, a body made up of representatives from the three estates, or sectors, of French society, the church (the first estate), the nobility (the second estate), and the commoners (the third estate), to try to solve the national crisis. French monarchs had long ruled with near absolute power. The Estates General was purely an advisory body and had no legislative power. No king had even called a meeting of the body since 1614. Deteriorating social conditions forced Louis XVI to call it to convene in an effort to gain wider support from the population.

Historically the first and second estates, which represented less than 5 percent of the French population, controlled the deliberations of the Estates General. But when the body finally convened in May of 1789 in Versailles, where the royal family resided outside Paris, things were clearly different. The third estate, which represented the commoners, had by the end of the eighteenth century grown socially far more powerful because of the enormous growth of wealth among the urban merchants in their ranks, the so-called bourgeoisie. Unable to reach agreement as to how power would be distributed among the three sectors of the assembly, members of the third estate withdrew and in June formed a new general representative body known as the National Assembly. Enough members from the other two estates joined them to force the king to recognize the new assembly. Insurgents in Paris, fearing that the king would call in the military to suppress the new body, took to the streets looking for arms and munitions, which is why they were storming the Bastille on July 14. The date is typically cited as the start of the French Revolution.

In August the National Assembly, now officially known as the National Con- stituent Assembly, published *La déclaration des droits de l'homme et du citoyen* ("The Declaration of the Rights of Humanity and of the Citizen"), a document that was influenced by the Declaration of Independence that had been passed by the Continental Congress representing the thirteen British colonies in North America several years earlier, in 1776. The French statement declared among other things that all human beings are born free and equal, that sovereignty resided in the nation as a whole (and thus not in the king), and that all human beings had the right to participate equally through representatives in determining laws that would govern them. During deliberations of the National Assembly, members who took more traditional or conservative positions would sit on the right during discussions, while those identified with more revolutionary positions would sit on the left of the deliberation hall, thereby giving rise to one of the basic identifying metaphors of modern political discourse. In October some seven thousand women marched the fifteen km from Paris to the palace in Versailles where the royal family resided, forcing not only Louis XVI and his wife, Marie Antoinette (1755-1793), but the entire National Assembly to move inside the city of Paris.

In 1790 the Assembly passed a law making all members of the clergy employ- ees of the state and banning all monastic orders. Administration of all church lands, estimated to be approximately 15 percent of the territory of France, was transferred to the state. All clergy were to swear an oath of loyalty to the French state (few did), and bishops were to be elected locally by priests. From Rome Pope Pius VI (1717-1799) condemned these actions, but there was little he could do to oppose them.

In June the following year, the royal household tried to escape from Paris to get to the city of Montmédy on the eastern border, but were captured and returned to Paris under guard. In September the Assembly completed a new constitution that retained the monarchy, and all of its members resigned, agreeing not to stand for election to a new body, now called the Legislative Assembly, which was to be formed with greater direct representation through the popular vote. By this time the city government of Paris, known as the Paris Commune, was becom- ing more radicalized, and popular insurrection soon forced the formation in the following year of yet another new legislative body, this one called the National Convention. Following a national election in which all males were permitted to vote, the National Convention convened on September 20, 1792. Two days later it officially declared the monarchy to be abolished.

By the beginning of 1793 France was in chaos. War had broken out with sev- eral neighboring nations that were concerned about the chaos spreading to other parts of Europe. In Paris the newly constituted National Convention found Louis XVI guilty of conspiring against them and had him executed by the guillotine in January. A new nine-member Committee of Public Safety was created in April to take over executive powers of national government in the absence of a king. The revolutionary leader, Maximilien François Marie Isidore de Robespierre (1758-1794), was elected to join the body and soon dominated it. By summer Paris was under a reign of terror, guided by Robespierre's conviction that terror was equated with justice and thus a virtue. Anyone deemed by him to be an enemy of the revolution was executed. No record was kept of how many were killed, but estimates range from fifteen thousand to forty thousand. Among those sent to the guillotine were Marie Antoinette and other members of the nobility.

The National Convention declared a new Cult of Reason to be the national religion of France. A statue of the Goddess of Reason was installed in the cathedral of Notre Dame in place of the Virgin Mary. A new calendar was instituted, with September 22, 1792, the day that the monarchy had been abolished, declared to be day 1. The decimal system became the basis for most calculations. Each day was divided into ten hours of one hundred minutes each. Weeks were redefined as ten days in length, with three weeks to a month. The twelve months were given newly invented names based on terms associated with each season. The names of traditional Christian saints associated with various days of the year were replaced with names of animals, plants, minerals, or tools.

By 1794 the reign of terror had run its course. Robespierre himself was arrested on 9 Thermidor (July 27) and executed the next day. Yet another constitution was drafted and approved by popular vote, and in 1795 a new bicameral legislative body, called the Directory, came into being, with an executive directory of five exercising executive functions. The same year the national Academy of Science completed work on a unified decimal system of weights and measurement, the metric system. The Directory lasted four more years until 18 Brumaire (November 9) of Year VII (1799) when a general from the army named Napoléon Bonaparte (1769-1821) staged a coup d'état and overthrew the government, establishing himself at the head of a new national legislative body called the Consulate.

Napoléon's arrival marks the beginning of a new era in European history. The continent at the end of the eighteenth century was a far different place than what it had been for centuries. During the French Revolution for the first time in many centuries a European nation had officially disestablished any form of Christianity as its official religion. Over the course of the century, what became known as "the modern world" had, as Kant noted, come of age.

In this modern world the relationship between state and church in European society would be dramatically changed. Such change had been in the works for several centuries as various communions or churches found themselves outside the bounds of official state recognition in one way or another. Over the course of the eighteenth century throughout Europe there was in general a gradual relaxing of state persecution of dissenting or nonconforming groups, be they Catholic or one of the increasing number of groups that identified themselves with the Protestant or evangelical cause.

Among many of these Protestant or evangelical churches, internal fracturing accelerated throughout the course of the eighteenth century. This was due in some instances to an increased desire for spiritual renewal or heightened spiritual experience, as seen in the case of the rise of the Methodists. In others it had to do with resistance to the state. At the 1732 General Assembly of the Church in Scotland, an act was passed to strengthen the control of appointments of clergy by patrons, who were wealthy members of the nobility but also increasingly merchants from the middle class. A handful of ministers protested, and were all deposed. They soon formed what they called the Associate Presbytery. Others joined them, setting in motion a century of fragmentation that would leave Presbyterians in Scotland divided into numerous church bodies over the next century.

Meanwhile the main body of Presbyterians who formed the Church of Scotland slowly but persistently moved in what perhaps could be described as a more moderate direction theologically. Sermons became shorter and preaching was more thematic rather than following either the traditional lectionary, as Anglicans did, or a book of scripture. Titles of sermons from the century reveal a greater emphasis on morality and ethics, and less on the classic Lutheran or Reformed doctrines of sin, repentance, and grace.

Church life and worship patterns were changing. A large number of clergy, especially those serving rural parishes, received comparatively less in the way of financial compensation than they had in previous centuries, and a number bordered on being impoverished. In many places clergy began to lose social status, or were no longer regarded as highly as priests and pastors had been in previous centuries in European life. Centuries of religious conflict, coupled with centuries of at times unsavory church involvement in political affairs, had lessened the overall regard for church leaders throughout Europe.

Efforts to reform church life and renew spiritual life in western Europe in the sixteenth century began to be looked at by many, Roman Catholic, Anglican, and Protestant alike, as a high period for Christianity in European history. In contrast, the flowering of the Enlightenment was beginning to be seen by some at the end of the eighteenth century as responsible for the decline of Roman Catholic, Anglican, and various Protestant Christian communities throughout Europe.

The eighteenth century was a time of exciting new ideas regarding experimental science, toleration, freedom, and human ability. The various theologies of churches, those consciously worked out in the universities but also those bubbling up from grassroots locations throughout European societies, benefitted from these new ideas. The new confidence in science reduced traditional dependence on divine intervention as an explanation for events in history. Some pastors and theologians moderated the manner in which they explained the world to themselves and others. The supernatural realm, dominated by signs and wonders, began to give way to more rational explanations and a greater emphasis on the natural course of events. The vast majority of Christians in all churches or communions continued to hold on to what they considered to be classical orthodox doctrines, without question. This was not a century of large-scale desertion of historic Christian beliefs. There was an increased amount of emphasis placed on experiential dimensions of Christian faith on the other hand. One sees this especially in the various movements that claimed to be, or can be identified as being, part of the wider movement of "awakening" (Catholic and evangelical) that was taking place. Among Roman Catholics, devotion to the suffering of Christ stirred in many a profound re-awakening of the sense of faith. Among the evangelicals and Pietists, a new experience of grace and conversion gave authenticity to Christian belief that many believed had been lacking before. Such experiences of awakening developed alongside and in some instances offered a counterpart to the intellectual efforts of the Enlightenment that were taking place in Europe throughout the eighteenth century. Drawing deeply on mystical traditions reaching back centuries in Christian life, they seemed to arouse mere church attenders from their slumber.

Europe was becoming modern, but it was also becoming more of a global force in the eighteenth century. The colonial enterprise was bringing more and more people into contact and under European political control. European businesses were gaining enormous profits from the various colonial ventures that were under way. Both Portugal and Spain decreased during the eighteenth century as global colonial powers, but the northern European nations of the Netherlands, England, and Sweden increased. Where Roman Catholic missionaries, sponsored by cooperating kings, had dominated global missionary enterprises in the sixteenth and seventeenth centuries, in the eighteenth century Protestant missionaries began to make their appearance, not just as chaplains to European colonial settlers but as agents seeking to spread Christianity to people holding other religious commitments or beliefs. The form of Christianity that succeeded in taking hold in new places was usually at first strongly identifiable as European in its cultural expressions. Over the course of another century or two, that would change.

Suggestions for further reading

Atkin, Nicholas, and Frank Tallett, *Priests, Prelates and People: A History of European Catholicism since 1750.* New York: Oxford University Press, 2003.

Campbell, Ted A., *The Religion of the Heart: A Study of European Religious Life in the Seventeenth and Eighteenth Centuries.* Columbia: University of South Carolina Press, 1991.

Hempton, David, *Methodism: Empire of the Spirit.* New Haven: Yale University Press, 2005.

McLeod, Hugh, *Religion and the People of Western Europe, 1789–1989.* 2nd ed. New York and Oxford: Oxford University Press, 1997.

McMahon, Darrin M., *Enemies of the Enlightenment: The French Counter-Enlightenment and the Making of Modernity.* New York: Oxford University Press, 2001.

Old, Hughes Oliphant, *The Reading and Preaching of the Scriptures in the Worship of the Christian Church, V: Moderatism, Pietism and Awakening.* Grand Rapids, MI: Eerdmans, 2004.

Ward, W. R., *Christianity under the Ancien Régime, 1648-1789.* Cambridge: Cambridge University Press, 1999.

16

The Orthodox World
in the Eighteenth Century

The world of Orthodox Christianity was already complex at the dawn of the eighteenth century. By the end of the century, it had become considerably more so. Orthodox churches had long been spread across three continents. For centuries their congregations had been worshipping in a variety of languages. Since the fifth century, following the Council of Chalcedon, they had been divided into three major theological families that differed over their understanding of how the humanity and the divinity of Jesus Christ were to be understood in relation to each other. The various churches shared in common the historical legacy of Constantinople, Antioch, and Alexandria, the three ancient cities that both institutionally and symbolically shaped the great traditions of Orthodox Christianity. How they understood this legacy, and whom they considered the legitimate patriarchs occupying these sees differed considerably, however, among the various communions that made up the Orthodox world in the eighteenth century.

In the eighteenth century Russia was the imperial center of the Orthodox world, having in effect replaced Constantinople whose patriarchal see continued to be dominated politically, if not culturally, by the rulers of the Ottoman empire. Most Greek-speaking churches now lived within the Ottoman empire, which extended from modern Turkey to Mesopotamia, incorporated much of Armenia and Georgia, and since 1517 had dominated Egypt. In Syria the patriarch of Antioch, who was in communion with Constantinople and continued to be recognized as the spiritual leader of the church of Antioch by a significant number of Christians in that part of the world, now lived in Damascus. His counterpart in Alexandria had long resided in Cairo. They joined the patriarch of Moscow in being the most important spiritual leaders of the Orthodox churches that embraced Chalcedon.

There were other Orthodox communions in Asia and Africa that did not accept Chalcedon, but that equally claimed the ancient heritage of Orthodox tradition. The Armenian, West Syrian, Coptic, and Ethiopian churches affirmed in stronger terms the unity of the two natures (divine and human) in Jesus Christ after the incarnation, while the East Syrian Church (by the eighteenth century often called the Chaldean Church) placed more emphasis on the distinction of the two natures. While all five of these communions shared historically in the common Orthodox tradition, the four that are covered in this chapter shared in common the experience of being marginal communions within states that were under Islamic religious rule.

In the twelfth century during the Crusades, the Maronite churches in Lebanon had entered into communion with Rome under what came to be called a uniate agreement. The arrangement allowed the Maronites to maintain their distinct Orthodox faith and practice while affirming the primacy of the bishop of Rome with whom they were now regarded as being in full communion. Rome had forged similar uniate agreements with other Orthodox churches in Lithuania and Ukraine at the end of the sixteenth century and in Ottoman territories twice in the seventeenth century. In both locations a significant number of Christians had not accepted the agreements, thereby introducing new schisms that had further divided churches that were already severely weakened. Several new efforts for union were launched in the eighteenth century, leading to still further fragmentation and division among the churches in the Orthodox world.

The Russian Orthodox Church and the tsars

No other name dominates Russian political and cultural history in the eighteenth century as does that of Peter the Great (1672-1725). Historical judgment regarding this powerful Russian tsar is divided. On the one hand, he sought to introduce a number of reforms to enable Russia to develop economically and culturally. On the other hand, he often employed brutal methods in doing so. He was not a benevolent ruler, and was not above using the apparatus of state-sanctioned violence to accomplish ends that he thought were for the greater good. The son of Tsar Alexei by a second marriage, Peter was only ten years old when the boyars determined that he and his half-brother, Ivan, would be joint tsars, while his half-sister would in effect run the government from behind the throne. By 1696 he was reigning alone, however, and ready to transform Russia as it entered the eighteenth century.

The Ottoman empire posed the major strategic challenge to Russia on its southern border. Hoping to secure the assistance of other European powers in an alliance against the Turks, Peter undertook an extended trip though western Europe in 1697 and 1698. For much of the time he traveled under the guise of being simply a Russian diplomat, a ruse that allowed him to move about freely in the nations he visited. While the delegation failed to secure very much in the way of military support for Russia against the Ottomans, Peter gained extensive knowledge of western Europe. He visited shipyards in the Netherlands, had his portrait painted in England, and engaged in face-to-face diplomatic negotiations with leaders in Germany. He even attended services in Lutheran churches and a Quaker meeting.

Upon his return to Russia the impact of the voyage was soon made clear. The young tsar introduced Western styles of clothing at court, and ordered that all noble males, except for members of the clergy, were to shave their beards or pay an annual tax. Late in December of 1699, just in time for the year 1700 to dawn, he ordered the adoption of the western European calendar that dated year 1 from the birth of Jesus, replacing the older traditional Russian calendar that dated everything from what was assumed to be the beginning of creation. This moved the New Year to January 1, eight days after the birth of Christ, from September when the Russian calendar had traditionally celebrated the day. Schools throughout Russia were ordered to increase the level of mathematics and geometry taught, and young men were forbidden to marry until they could pass exams in the subjects.

In matters of government Peter embraced the notion of an absolute monarch, an idea that had gained support in several western European nations. Toward the end of his reign he even took the title "Emperor of Russia." At the same time he moved against the traditional Russian boyars, making administrative appointments to civic offices on the basis of merit rather than inheritance, and attempting to appoint a new senate to replace the older council of boyars who exercised considerable power in matters of state. In military affairs he instituted a number of initiatives, among them the establishment for the first time of an official Russian navy, and the building of the first Russian naval base in the port city of Taganrog, on the Sea of Azov to the north of the Crimean peninsula.

One of his most important contributions to Russian cultural life was the creation of a new city that bore his name and became his capital, St. Petersburg. In 1700 Peter joined other northern European powers to go to war against Sweden, which controlled the entire Baltic Sea region at the time. Russian armies succeeded in capturing a Swedish fort on the Gulf of Finland that opened up into the Baltic Sea. Three years later Peter began to build a new city at the site, bringing in forced laborers from across Russia. French and Italian architects were engaged to design buildings, creating what became known as the "Petrine Baroque" style, characteristic of such buildings as the Peter and Paul Cathedral that was begun in 1712. That same year Peter moved his capital from Moscow to St. Petersburg, which served as the capital of Russia for the next two centuries.

Peter's impact on public life reached into every sector of Russian society, including religion. In 1700 upon the death of the patriarch, Peter decided not to name a successor but appointed instead an interim. For the next two decades Stephen Yavorsky (1658-1722), who was originally from Poland, had studied in Kiev, and was the metropolitan of Ryazan, handled the affairs of the patriarchal office. In 1718 Peter appointed an even more trusted advisor, Feofan (Theophanus) Prokopovich (1681-1736), the bishop of St. Petersburg, who was originally from Kiev and had been educated in the West, to undertake revision of the synodical structure of the church in advance of a new patriarchal appointment. The result of Prokopovich's effort was a document known as the *Dukhovny Reglament* ("Spiritual Regulation"), which was put into effect in 1721.

Peter's Spiritual Regulation established in place of a patriarch a new governing body called the Most Holy Synod. The synod was initially made up of ten members and included major bishops as well as several lay persons. Under the new rules, the tsar appointed the procurator, who presided over the body. The first two procurators were bishops, but eventually lay members, who often came from the ranks of the military, were named to preside, thereby assuring the dominance of state over church. The body quickly grew to become a political bureaucracy, headed at times by procurators who lacked considerably in anything that could remotely be called spiritual leadership. The fact that the plan had been endorsed by the ecumenical patriarch in Istanbul as well as several other patriarchs in the Mediterranean world, however, helped to legitimate the synod as an alternative to a patriarch in the Russian Orthodox Church.

The Spiritual Regulation defined the church as an association of people organized as citizens for the betterment of the state. The tsar was defined as the head of the church, much like the king or queen was head of the Church of England. Bishops and priests were instructed to break confession and turn in to secular authorities anyone who spoke against the tsar or his government. Those who refused could be punished by torture or death. Under the new code, new restrictions were imposed on monastic life, in part to try to prevent monasteries from becoming centers of religious resistance. Monks were forbidden to have paper or ink in their cells. New restrictions on men entering monastic life were imposed, including prohibitions of anyone with a criminal background, and no woman under the age of fifty was permitted to take monastic vows, a regulation ostensibly intended to encourage women to fulfill their secular duty to be wives and mothers. The overall effect was to greatly diminish the ranks of the orders within a short period of time.

Increasingly the Orthodox Church in Russia found itself dealing with the influence of Western theological and spiritual thought, including Roman Catholic, Anglican, and Lutheran. Prokopovich, the principal author of the Spiritual Regulation, leaned strongly in the direction of Lutheran theological thinking. By contrast Yavorsky, who was appointed as the first procurator of the synod in 1721, leaned toward Roman Catholic views. His book *Kamen Very: Pravoslavnym cerkve synom na utverždenie i duxovnoe sozidanie. Pretykajuščimsja že o kamen' pretykanija I soblazna, na vozstanie I ispravlenie* ("The Rock of Faith: For the Affirmation and Spiritual Creation of the Sons of the Holy Orthodox Church. For Those Who Stumble against the Block of Stumbling and Temptation unto Restoration and Correction"), which was completed in 1718, supported the traditional notion of the patriarchate in opposition to what were considered Lutheran views. Peter opposed him on this and prevented the publication of the book. The same year the tsar ordered all Jesuits to be expelled from Russia.

One of Peter's less successful innovations was the effort to Westernize the schools of Russia. A number of new schools were founded apart from church control, but most did not last long. Within the various institutions of education under ecclesiastical control, teachers began to be appointed from the Ukraine, many of whom had been trained in Poland and by Roman Catholic missionaries. The education of priests in particular began to incorporate Latin, which exposed Russian churches to more Western ideas but at the same time did not help them when it came to providing pastoral care or leading worship in either Russian or Church Slavonic. The effect was to subtly distance priestly formation from the people whom the priests were to serve, creating a divide that lasted until the 1790s when the Moscow Academy began again to teach in Russian. Not just the language of theological instruction, but the content of the ideas began to show Western influences that tended to alienate clerics from the people. The Moscow Academy began to include in its curriculum not only ancient Roman and Greek classics but the works of Thomas Aquinas, the Roman Catholic theologian from the West.

Westernization continued after Peter's death. His second wife, a Polish Catholic, was born with the name Marta Helena Skawrońska, adopted the name Catherine I (1684-1727), and became Orthodox. She reigned for two years, and was succeeded by Peter's grandson, Peter II (1715-1730), who died of smallpox. Peter's niece, Anna Ivanovna (1693-1740), took the reigns of government next in 1730, pursuing a harsh course of policy similar to that of her uncle. She sent some twenty thousand dissidents off to Siberia, for example. She also continued to support Prokopovich. As chancellor she appointed a German named Heinrich Johann Friedrich Ostermann (or Andrei Ivanovich Ostermann, 1687-1747), whose love for Luther was matched only by his hate for Orthodoxy. Monasteries were closed, church lands were confiscated, and some of the priests who resisted, especially those who were suspected of Roman Catholic leanings, were tortured and killed.

Another daughter of Peter the Great, Elizabeth Petrovna (1709-1762), seized the throne from Anna's designated successor, who was only an infant, and continued the policies of Westernization. Six months after Anna's death, Catherine II (1729-1796), the German-born wife of Anna's designated heir, took over the throne after her husband was deposed. Originally named Sophie Friederike Auguste von Anhalt-Zerbst-Dornburg, she assumed the name Catherine upon her conversion to the Orthodox faith from Lutheranism in 1744 prior to her marriage. She only began learning Russian around the same time. Through the second half of the century under this series of powerful women leaders, Russia continued to move closer to the West politically, culturally, and spiritually.

The effects of church policies begun under Peter the Great and continued by the women who ruled in the last half of the century were felt acutely in monastic life. By the 1760s the number of monasteries in Russia had been reduced by half as a direct result of the Spiritual Regulation. Numerous women and men who had once found refuge in monasteries were rendered homeless as a result. During the last half of the eighteenth century there was considerable growth in new women's communities, or *zhenskie obshchiny*. Many of these were founded as semi-monastic lay communities, providing shelter for widows, the aged, and orphans. A number of them were eventually granted full monastic recognition by the church in the nineteenth century, which saw a revival of monasticism overall within the Russian Orthodox tradition.

Three eighteenth-century *starets,* as the great Russian monastic spiritual elders were known, helped lay the foundation for that revival in the Russian Orthodox tradition. The first was Paisii (or Paisios) Velichkovskii (1721-1794). Originally from the city of Poltava, in Ukraine, as a teenager he had gone to Kiev to study theology, but left after three years as he found the emphasis on Latin texts and Western ideas to be unsettling. After visiting a number of monasteries in Ukraine and Romania, he eventually settled on Mount Athos in Greece. Over the next decade or so he not only became adept at ancient hesychastic spiritual practices but was part of a larger effort to edit and correct a collection of spiritual teachings from the ancient Orthodox tradition that had been undertaken by Greek monks on Mount Athos. The *Philokalia* ("Love of the Beautiful"), as the collection was known, was eventually published in the West, in Venice, in 1782. Velichkovskii's translation of the work into Slavonic was published in Moscow in 1793 under the title *Dobrotolyubie*. The edited volumes in the collection quickly proved to be a major influence in rejuvenating Orthodox spirituality in monasteries throughout Russia. Velichkovskii meanwhile returned to Romania where he continued the work of editing and translating ancient texts, set up a printing press to publish them, and began to train lay people in hesychastic spiritual practices during his last years.

Tikhon of Zadonsk (1724-1783) was born into a poor family on the outskirts of Novgorod. Originally named Timofey Sokolov, at sixteen he entered one of the new seminaries for training priests that was established in Novgorod. He soon proved to have gifts as a scholar, continuing on to teach Greek and philosophy in the seminary after graduation. At age thirty-four he entered monastic life and took the name Tikhon, and eventually being ordained as a bishop before retiring in 1768 to the monastery at Zadonsk. Throughout his years of service Tikhon was concerned about promoting both the educational and spiritual training of clergy. As bishop of Voronezh in 1765 he opened a seminary for training priests and brought in teachers from nearby Kiev. His own numerous publications touched on matters of pastoral care, spirituality, the Bible, liturgy, and theology. Many of these were directed toward the pastoral and spiritual needs of lay persons in the church.

Theologically, Tikhon integrated an enormous range of influences in his work. First and foremost was the Bible, demonstrated in his own writings but also in the manner in which as a bishop he expected every priest in his diocese not only to be educated in biblical studies but to read devotionally from the New Testament each day. Next was the body of Orthodox theological tradition, including the ancient theologians of the church East and West. But Tikhon also engaged Western theological sources, most notably Johann Arndt's *True Christianity*, which had been translated into Russian in 1735. In 1776 after retiring to the monastery Tikhon published a book of his own in Russian under that same title.

Seraphim of Sarov (1759-1833), the third of these monastic reformers, was born Prokhor Moshnin but took the name Seraphim when he entered the monastery at Sarov in 1777. Shortly after being ordained as a priest he left the monastery in 1794 in order to live alone as a hermit in the forest outside Sarov. Ten years later he was forced to return to the monastic community after being severely beaten by a gang of thieves who sought to rob his cottage in the forest and left him unable to walk upright the rest of his life. As a young boy Seraphim had been healed after having a vision of the Virgin Mary. In 1815 after another vision of the Virgin, he began a ministry in which others came to him for prayer, especially for healing. Seraphim placed a great deal of emphasis on the work of the Holy Spirit in Christian life. Like Velichkovskii and Tikhon, he sought to reach out to lay people in his spiritual teaching and not confine spirituality to the life of the monastery. He also left behind a body of spiritual wisdom in the form of conversations recorded with followers and a number of hymns that he composed.

The seventeenth century had witnessed a major schism in the life of the Russian Orthodox Church centered around the reforms introduced by Patriarch Nikon in 1652. Those who opposed the reforms, known as Old Believers, became the target of intense state persecution. Nevertheless, many congregations, scattered throughout Russia, often in isolated rural regions, survived. Without bishops to ordain new priests, by the 1680s the Old Believers were becoming less dependent on sacramental life and more focused on texts, both the Bible and other writings, for spiritual sustenance. As the eighteenth century opened, their numbers were growing, mostly from peasants who were joining their congregations in the countryside. Peter the Great relaxed official persecution of the movement and instituted a double tax on its members instead. Many saw this as an indication of government acceptance. Their congregations were often led by elders who were lay people, and by 1700 they were developing their own schools, based in the congregations, for teaching their older traditions of liturgy and theology. Traditional styles of dress were enforced, and prohibitions against certain foods as well as alcohol were introduced.

Despite their common commitment to maintaining the old traditions, the Old Believers were far from unified as a movement. Without bishops (none with Old Believer ties had survived the initial purges of the seventeenth century), the main question confronting them was how to provide the sacraments. Some who were called *beglopopovtsy* ("fugitive priests") sought to convince regularly ordained priests from the dominant Russian Orthodox Church to join them, thereby enabling them to continue to practice sacramental life. Others argued instead for doing away with sacraments entirely and thus with the need for priests, thereby earning them the name *bezpopovtsy* ("without priests"). In apocalyptic tones, some among this latter group reasoned that the times were so corrupt that even the sacraments had to be dropped in order for the church to be kept pure and ready for the end of time. Many of the *bezpopovtsy* argued that in place of sacraments with valid priests, anyone who had a sincere desire to commune was actually participating in a spiritualized form of the mysteries. A more disembodied or spiritualized conception of the sacraments took the place of traditional Orthodox understanding. Early in the eighteenth century the ranks of the *bezpopovtsy* were split again, this time over the issue of marriage. Marriage was a sacrament, according to Orthodox teaching. Without priests to celebrate it, some reasoned, all true Christians were called to live in celibacy.

One such celibate community without priests formed along the Vyg River in 1694. Men and women lived together at first in semimonastic fashion, but after 1706 women lived separately some 20 km away. Both communities survived by farming and trading, the women managing many of their own affairs even though they were still considered to be under the authority of the men. Among the leaders of the Vyg community were Andrei Denisov (1664-1730), his brother Semen Denisov (1682-1741), and their sister Solomoniia Denisova (exact dates unknown). Andrei and Semen owned a sizable library and wrote several volumes defending their beliefs. Both brothers, however, criticized their sister for writing letters in secret without their approval.

In the middle of the eighteenth century a group known as *Doukhobors* appeared in Russian history. The name means "Spirit Wrestlers" and was first used derisively, but later was adopted by members of the movement who continue to go by it still today. The origins of the group may have been in the late seventeenth century, but they were clearly organized as a community in the Ukraine by the 1740s. Some suggest that the movement had its roots in mystical teachings from the West; others that they were influenced by followers of John Hus, and still others that they were influenced by Quakers. From 1755 to 1775 their leader was a peasant named Siluan Kolesnikov (d. 1775), about whom little else is known.

Doukhobors believed that all human beings had within what they called "the living word," and therefore did not need the authority of scripture, church, sacraments, or priests. They took bread, salt, and water as basic symbols of life to be represented on their tables during worship, which consisted mostly of prayers and hymns. The group clearly had Christian roots, maintaining Christian holy days and taking many of their teachings from Christian scriptures. They put a greater degree of emphasis on the humanity of Jesus in their teaching and were strict pacifists. Members lived communally in rural areas and supported themselves mostly through agriculture. Because the *Doukhobors* were mostly peasants they at first attracted little attention from either the government or the Orthodox Church, but by the end of the century their pacifist teachings began to generate opposition from the government, leading to the first wave of exile, some to Finland and others to join Mennonites at the beginning of the nineteenth century in sparsely populated southern Ukraine.

Russia under Peter the Great began to look to the West politically and culturally. At the same time Peter the Great turned the Russian gaze farther east, seeking to expand into lands adjacent to territories that had historically been considered part of the nation. The church played a major role in Peter's thinking in this regard. He ordered the Bible to be translated into several other languages and that priests be sent to establish churches in regions where he was expanding his empire. Russian explorers and missionaries eventually crossed the Bering Sea to reach Alaska in the eighteenth century, a story that will be explored in chapter 19.

Orthodoxy under the Ottomans in the Balkans and west Asia

Orthodox churches within the Ottoman empire continued to face major challenges as minority communities in a Muslim empire throughout the eighteenth century. The most important official for Orthodox churches in the Ottoman empire continued to be the ecumenical patriarch, whose appointment had to be approved by the sultan and who essentially served at the will of the sultan. Under these conditions, bribes and corruption were a regular part of the process of gaining access to the office. For Orthodox Christians, the office of the patriarch was the main vehicle of access in turn to the Ottoman political machine. A small group of wealthy Greek Orthodox merchants joined a handful of ecclesiastical leaders and scholars in the small section of Constantinople known as the Phanar quarter where the ecumenical patriarchal office was lodged to handle the business of running the church.

Everything had a price. Within the empire, the various national regions had to pay tribute to the Ottomans, for which local rulers had to exact money. In the middle of the century, Moldavia had to pay seven thousand gold pounds to the sultan and Walachia fourteen thousand gold pounds. For the right or privilege to rule these regions, which were predominantly Christian in population, a successful candidate would have to pay thirty thousand to fifty thousand gold pounds in bribes. Whoever eventually got to be appointed to local leadership would simply tax the people heavily in order to pay back the debts, usually expecting church leadership to support the endeavor. One can see how corruption could become endemic.

The decline can also be measured in more quantifiable terms as the number of Muslims living in areas of Albania, Serbia, Bulgaria, and Greece continued to grow. The Balkans had been almost entirely Christian before the arrival of the Ottoman rulers, but by the eighteenth century large portions had become predominantly Muslim. The number of Christians converting to Islam had slowed considerably by the eighteenth century. In some places factors of geography, such as proximity to Christian influences from Austria or how mountainous a region was, were a factor. In other places the resistance of local Christian leaders proved to be important. Christians in Albania rebelled several times against their Ottoman Turkish rulers, but systematic efforts to Islamicize the population through immigration and mandatory military service so wore down the people that by the year 1800 over two-thirds of the population was Muslim.

Ottoman domination had also fragmented Serbia during the seventeenth century, the effects of which continued into the eighteenth. Serbs in the south were often forced to fight with the Turks against their own relatives in the north. Those in the north were fighting to defend the Christian faith, but often along with Roman Catholics, leaving many Orthodox Serbs defending Latin Christianity. Several new Serbian martyrs helped solidify resistance and provide a glimpse into the nature of Christian life in the region. Damascene of Gabrovo (d. 1771) was a monk in the Serbian Hilander monastery. After being appointed abbot, he appealed to the Ottoman rulers to repay a large debt that they owed the monastery. Through intrigue and deception, Damascene was falsely accused of having taken a Muslim woman into his house, and was given the opportunity to either convert to Islam or be hanged. He refused to convert, stating not only his innocence but that he was born an Orthodox Christian and would die as such. Rejecting Jesus Christ would be the same as rejecting eternal life, he said. Accordingly he was hanged, his name entering the ranks of the Serbian saints who resisted.

Theodore Sladich (d. 1788) was another figure from the period who opposed Ottoman policies of heavy taxation. He also opposed the spread of influences that were coming from western Europe, especially the introduction of new forms of education that appeared to him to be reducing the importance of traditional religious teachings. During Lent of 1788, Theodore and 150 of his followers publicly preached against paying the heavy taxes to the Turks, linking such resistance to demonstrating one's love for God and the saints. For their testimony, all were burned alive. The episode demonstrates the degree to which religious and political forms of resistance were joined.

The ethnic identity of Serbs, Bulgarians, and many others continued to be shaped by what they considered to be oppression, and their resistance to it. While most of those involved in the history could not see it at the time, in the eighteenth century the Ottoman empire was in a period of slow political and economic decline. In the context of this decline, and to a degree on account of it, volatile religious divisions gave rise to nationalistic impulses in the Balkans. The decline of the Ottomans registered as well among Christians to the north of the Balkans. Defeated by Russia in the war of 1768 to 1774, the Ottomans were forced to give up control of Crimea and the region of Ukraine on the northern shore of the Black Sea, and to allow Russian influences over the Orthodox communities in Moldavia and Wallachia (today Romania) to grow.

The revitalization of Orthodoxy in the Balkans and elsewhere under Ottoman rule was primarily the result of the work of monastics whose teachings and writings inspired devotion mixed with nationalism. The growth of printing presses in eastern Europe and western Asia through this period aided the renewal. Among the monks whose influence spread widely throughout the Orthodox Church in the last half of the eighteenth century, Nicodemus of the Holy Mount (or Nicodemus the Hagiorite, 1749-1809) and Macarius of Corinth (1731-1805) were especially important. These two monks became the principal leaders of the *kollyvades*, a reform movement that began on Mount Athos in 1754 and spread throughout the Orthodox world. The *kollyvades* derived their name from the plate of boiled wheat that Greek Orthodox traditionally ate after memorial services commemorating the dead. Some of the monks on Mount Athos wanted to be able to work at building a church on Saturday, and proposed moving the weekly Saturday service commemorating the dead to Sunday. This conflicted with Orthodox practice, however, for Sunday, which commemorated the Resurrection, was never to be a day of fasting, which eating the boiled wheat would symbolize. The effort to keep the memorial service from being moved to Sunday quickly grew into a much broader revival of traditional Orthodox spiritual life and practice.

Nicodemus was born on the island of Naxos and was originally given the name Nicholas. He studied for a time at the Evangeliki, a new school in Smyrna that had been founded in 1733 by Greek merchants with connections in the West, and then at the age of twenty-six moved to Mount Athos to become a monk. Macarius was already archbishop of Corinth when he visited Mount Athos shortly after Nicodemus had arrived there. The two quickly became friends and began collaborating on a critical edition of the *Philokalia*, mentioned above. The *Philokalia* provided a virtual library of ancient Orthodox spirituality. Although its texts spanned more than a millennium, it was presented in such a manner as to make it seem a contemporary work. Its greatest importance to the wider *kollyvades* movement that it helped to spread was to provide a fuller basis for *hesychasm*, the disciplined inward spiritual practice that focused on reciting the Orthodox "Jesus Prayer" and brought about mystical spiritual union between a believer and God.

Among the collaborators on the *Philokalia*, which included the Russian monk

Paisii, who was noted above, Nicodemus was the most prolific. From the days at the Evangeliki he encountered Western theological texts and was especially drawn to Roman Catholic spirituality. The *Spiritual Exercises* of St. Ignatius of Loyola provided Nicodemus with the format for a book of spiritual meditations of his own. He translated and published in Greek another classic of Roman Catholic spirituality from the West, *Il combattimento spirituale* ("The Spiritual Combat"), by Lorenzo Scupoli (1530-1610). His biblical scholarship was displayed in the introduction to the Pastoral Epistles of the New Testament that he published, while the *Pedalion* ("Rudder"), a critical collection of canons of the church from the days of the apostles through the various regional and ecumenical synods that he published, demonstrated his grasp of Orthodox canon law. Nicodemus also published several works on the lives of saints, and a number of hymns that he either composed or edited.

The fact that an Orthodox teacher as important as Nicodemus, whose *Pedalion* had such influence on Orthodox life, was also drawing upon Roman Catholic sources was indicative of the growing influence the West was having in the Orthodox world. In Lebanon the Maronite Church, which had for centuries been formally in communion with Rome, was a major influence in this direction. Maronites supported several important academic institutions, including the Maronite College in Rome, founded in 1584. In 1610 Maronite monks at Qozhaya set up a printing press for publishing works in Syriac.

Among the most important Maronite Church figures of the eighteenth century were four priests who were members of an extended Assemani family (*Sam'an* in Arabic is Simeon). Joseph Simeon (1687-1768) was the oldest. After completing studies at the Maronite College in Rome and being ordained, he went to work in the Vatican Library, building its collection of manuscripts from the East. From 1715 to 1717 and again from 1735 to 1738 he traveled to monasteries and churches throughout Egypt, Lebanon, Damascus, and Syria, collecting ancient manuscripts, which he then deposited in the Vatican's holdings. The collection included numerous manuscripts in Greek, Syriac, Coptic, Hebrew, Arabic, and Armenian, and a catalogue of additional materials in the various collections he had visited. Simeon's younger brother, Joseph Aloysius (1710-1782), assisted the elder Assemani in his efforts and taught Syriac in Rome. A nephew, Stephanus Evodius (1707-1782), served as archbishop of Apamaea, Syria, until taking over as head of the collection in the Vatican Library after the death of his uncle. Stephanus eventually became a member of the Royal Society of London. Grandnephew Simeon (1751-1821) taught Eastern languages in the seminary at Padua. Together these four family members were a major influence in bringing together in the Vatican Library one of the most extensive collections of Christian manuscripts ever assembled from across the centuries and throughout the Christian world.

The removal of manuscripts from Orthodox monasteries across Egypt, Palestine, and other parts of the Christian East would eventually become a major issue of contention between Roman Catholic and Orthodox communions. Another issue was the continuing tendency of Roman Catholic missionaries in these regions that were traditionally under Orthodox jurisdiction to win converts to the

Catholic faith. Far more contentious for relations between Catholic and Orthodox communities were developments in the aftermath of the election of a new Greek patriarch of Antioch in 1724.

Seraphim Tanas, better known as Cyril VI (1680-1760), was born in Damascus. His uncle, who was a bishop, had supported union with Rome in the late seventeenth century. Seraphim spent eight years in his twenties studying in Rome before returning to Syria where he was ordained by his uncle to the priesthood. In 1724 Seraphim was elected patriarch of Antioch and took the name Cyril VI. In Istanbul the ecumenical patriarch viewed the election as providing a dangerous opening to Roman Catholic involvement. He declared the election to be invalid, excommunicated Cyril, and appointed Sylvester of Antioch (1696-1766) to the patriarchate in his stead. Cyril was forced to flee, taking refuge in a Maronite monastery. Other bishops and priests who supported him were removed from office or forced into exile.

In 1729 Pope Benedict XIII (1649-1730) in Rome officially recognized Cyril's appointment and invited him along with those bishops and priests who supported him to enter into communion with Rome. In 1730 a constituting synod was held in Lebanon. Before a delegation from Rome representing Benedict, Cyril made his profession of faith, and the Greek Melkite Catholic Church was formed. Although technically it was under the jurisdiction of the Congregation for the Propagation of the Faith, the body that oversaw all Roman Catholic missionary efforts, churches were allowed to retain their Orthodox liturgy and ordain priests according to Orthodox practice. Churches were not allowed to be in communion with other Orthodox who were not in communion with Rome, however, which led to a schism among the churches under Antiochene jurisdiction. From that point forward there were two claimants to the ancient patriarchal see of Antioch in the Chalcedonian tradition, one in communion with the ecumenical patriarch in Constantinople and the other in communion with the pope in Rome.

One of the deacons who supported Cyril and became a part of the Melkite Catholic Church was Abdalla Zakhir (1684-1774). Zakhir was a goldsmith who had studied Arabic in Aleppo before returning to Lebanon where he pursued further studies with French Roman Catholic missionaries. In 1733 shortly after the Greek Melkite Catholic Church had been formed, he designed and built a new printing press in al-Shuwayr, Lebanon, engraving the Arabic letters by hand himself. It was one of the first presses outside Europe to print Christian theological works in Arabic, which Zakhir published along with works in Greek and Latin. Under his influence, as well as others in Lebanon and Syria, the Greek Melkite Catholic Church began to develop many more resources for theology and worship in Arabic instead of Greek or Syriac.

The formation of the Greek Melkite Catholic Church further exacerbated the attitude of many in the ecumenical patriarchate toward Rome and the West in general. Making matters worse were the continued efforts by Roman Catholic missionaries to engage in proselytism in areas under Hapsburg rule as well as in the various districts of the Ottoman empire where the capitulations were in effect. The question was raised by members of the Orthodox clergy as to how they should regard the baptisms performed by Catholics or Protestants when those so baptized later sought to join an Orthodox church. Ancient Orthodox ecumenical councils had rejected the validity of baptism performed by those who were considered "heretics." In light of this practice, should Orthodox priests accept baptisms performed by Catholic and Protestant clergy, and only require those who had received them to undergo chrismation to join an Orthodox church, or must the individual be baptized again? In 1755 the ecumenical patriarch Cyril V (r. 1748-1757) issued a decree rejecting the validity of baptisms performed outside the Orthodox Church, even if they were done in the threefold name of the Trinity. Roman Catholics, Protestants, Armenians, and all others who had undergone the rite of initiation in a church that was not part of the Orthodox communion were to be rebaptized if they were to become part of an Orthodox church. The decree was signed by the Greek patriarchs of Alexandria and Jerusalem as well. Some among the Russian Church, most notably Nicodemus the Hagiorite, supported the decree, but the Russian Church as a whole never accepted the decision and continued to allow bishops and priests to recognize the validity of baptisms performed by Catholics and Protestants, requiring only that the individual undergo chrismation (or confirmation) upon entering a Russian Orthodox Church. For their part, Roman Catholic, Lutheran, and Calvinist churches in the West, as well as many other Orthodox bodies in the East, continued to recognize the validity of Orthodox baptisms.

Coptic Church in the eighteenth century

The eighteenth century was one of the most difficult in the long history of the Copts both as a church and as a people. Excessive taxation continued to burden the community. Harassment, discrimination, and pervasive injustice were the norm for day-to-day Coptic life. Monasteries continued to provide education for those entering into church service, as well as for lay people who sought to work in the world. Some Copts were able to find work in government service because of their education, while others were able to make their living as merchants. The Copts as a people were always faced with economic challenges, however, and in the eighteenth century they were increasingly moved to the margins of Egypt's commercial and industrial life.

The political situation in the eighteenth century did not help their position much. Since the early sixteenth century, the Ottomans had ruled Egypt as a vassal state in their empire. From Istanbul the sultan appointed a pasha, or governor, over Egypt, but most administrative affairs were left to the local Mameluke rulers, called *beys*, who came to office through hereditary family connections. Several times during the first decades of the century open conflict broke out among the main Egyptian ruling families. In 1747 open civil war broke out, forcing the pasha to flee to Istanbul and leaving the country to the rule of competing Mameluke beys. Over the next two decades the Ottomans continued to appoint pashas from Istanbul who at times were even able to reside in Cairo, but could do very little to bring Egypt back under their control. Cairo meanwhile became the scene of regular murders, robberies, and looting. Traditional laws against Christians, such as the prohibition for them to ride a horse, were vigorously enforced again. Copts were permitted to ride only donkeys, and only when there were no members of the ruling Mamelukes on the street passing by.

In the midst of this difficult century a brief window of relative peace opened up for the Coptic community. A former Christian of Georgian origin who had been kidnapped and sold in Istanbul as a slave to one of the ruling Egyptian families and had converted to Islam began a meteoric rise to power in the 1760s. Ali Bey (d. 1773), as he was known, soon attracted the attention of the sultan in Istanbul, who issued a decree in 1769 ordering Ali to be dispatched. One of Ali's political allies intercepted the messenger carrying the decree to Cairo, and Ali used it as the occasion to declare himself the ruler of an independent Egypt. Enough other members of the various ruling factions in Egypt followed him to make the claim credible. Ali quickly turned his attention to the south and across the Red Sea to Arabia, and in six months armies loyal to him successfully captured most of the western region of the Arabian Peninsula, including Mecca. The following year an army under his son-in-law conquered Damascus. Ali Bey was able to negotiate a diplomatic agreement with Russia to secure its support against the Turks, and a commercial agreement with Venice that opened Egyptian ports to international trade. His son-in-law, however, secretly began to negotiate with the Ottomans. In 1772 the son-in-law turned against Ali Bey, defeating him the following year outside Cairo. Ali himself died from wounds received in battle. His reign had been short, but for Copts it was a time of relative opening. For several years some of the more restrictive laws had been relaxed, and Copts had even been able to serve in government. Two of Ali's most trusted secretaries had even been Coptic scribes.

After the death of Ali Bey, the situation for the Copts quickly deteriorated to its brutal past. A new pasha was appointed who again enforced the laws against the Copts. Members of the community were allowed to use only what were considered Christian names. They were forbidden to wear brightly colored clothes or to move into houses considered to be too large. Women were not allowed to go out of their houses on certain festival days to celebrate in public. Soldiers of the pasha regularly looted Coptic homes without consequence.

The final days of the eighteenth century brought about a dramatic change in Egypt's history. A French army under the command of a general named Napoleon invaded Egypt, landing in Alexandria on July 1, 1798, and took Cairo a few weeks later. Napoleon's ostensible reason for invading Egypt had been to curtail the growing British presence in India. Historians differ as to whether this was in fact the main reason, or if the French general was not already patterning himself after such ancient military leaders as Alexander the Great. In any case, the Egyptians were not prepared for the well-equipped French army, allowing Napoleon to enter Cairo without resistance on July 25. The British navy, however, attacked and destroyed the French fleet near Alexandria, thereby cutting Napoleon off from his supply lines. A year later after several indecisive battles with Ottoman forces in Egypt and Palestine, Napoleon himself slipped away, leaving the remaining French army to surrender to the British and Ottomans in 1802.

The French campaign had been short, but it nevertheless had a significant impact on Egyptian society. The French introduced a number of new laws and set up new courts for hearing cases during their time in Cairo, introducing legal practices that had been forged in an earlier period in the West. They brought with them new crops from France, such as apples and peaches, many of which remained after they left. Egyptians saw firsthand some of the newly developed material resources Europeans had at their disposal, including new forms of weaponry. French engineers even proposed the idea of a Suez Canal that would link the Mediterranean Sea and the Red Sea, thereby facilitating travel and trade between the continents. Napoleon brought with him more than 150 scientists, who sought to document everything Egyptian. One of their discoveries was the Rosetta Stone, the inscription that allowed Egyptian hieroglyphics to be translated for the first time. In their retreat, the French took not just knowledge of Egypt with them back to Europe but a sizable number of works of art and culture, giving considerable impetus to the development of the study of Egypt back in Europe.

Coptic attitudes toward the French invasion were ambiguous at best. On the one hand, the French tended to favor the Copts, hiring them as scribes and relaxing regulations against them. On the other hand, the French were invaders, and Copts like other Egyptians resisted the foreign occupation of their land. After the French departed, conditions for the Copts quickly returned for the most part to what they had been before the invasion. The lasting impact of Napoleon's adventure upon Coptic life was to be found in the development of interest in Coptic history and culture in France and other parts of Europe in the nineteenth century, bringing wider international attention to the condition of this minority community in Egypt and opening the door for the development of new international connections.

Even more ambiguous for the Coptic community in the eighteenth century were the continued presence and work of Roman Catholic missionaries. Catholic missionaries continued to operate generally under the legal authority of the capitulations, which allowed European nations to establish districts for trade in cities throughout the Ottoman empire, although by the eighteenth century they were not entirely confined to them. Roman Catholic missionaries were not allowed under Ottoman law to target Muslims for conversion, but proselytism of other Christians for the most part was. Alarmed by the growing influence of Roman Catholics in his empire, the Ottoman sultan at one point in the 1730s issued a decree forbidding members of Orthodox churches from attending Roman Catholic services, but this was not regularly enforced.

In Egypt, such Catholic activities were generally directed toward the Copts. By the 1730s Catholic missionaries had made their way to several cities in Upper Egypt where they established mission programs and were sending younger Coptic boys to Rome to be educated as priests. In a number of places the schools that Roman Catholic missionaries established locally made an important contribution to educating members of the Coptic community. On the other hand, by seeking to have members of the Coptic community become Roman Catholic, they were generating divisions in the church and creating problems for the Coptic community regarding such matters as marriage and the inheritance of property. At one point a group of Coptic Church leaders petitioned the Egyptian government in Cairo to prevent Coptic proselytes who had become Roman Catholic from being released from paying the traditional *jizyah*, or tax levied under Islamic law upon all non-Muslim males, an indication of at least one reason conversion was attractive as well as suggesting the numbers were enough to generate concern.

In 1741 Catholic missionaries in Jerusalem were successful in convincing a Coptic bishop named Amba Athanasius (dates unknown) with his congregation to enter into communion with Rome. Pope Benedict XIV (1675-1758) subsequently consecrated the Coptic bishop as metropolitan of Alexandria. Athanasius in turn appointed a Coptic priest as vicar apostolic in Egypt. Within a few years Athanasius had returned to the Coptic communion, but Rome continued to appoint new vicar apostolics for what soon was known as the Coptic Catholic Church. Emboldened in part by the growing number of Copts who were becoming Roman Catholic, a delegation from Rome visited Egypt at one point to formally invite the Coptic pope in Cairo to recognize Roman supremacy, with little success. More problematic were the issues of conflict within the Coptic community that the formal presence of a Coptic Catholic Church posed. By the end of the century an agreement had been reached with delegates from Rome that Copts and Catholics were not to intermarry, that priests from either communion could not attend to the pastoral needs of the other communion, and that disagreements between the two communions ought no longer end up in Islamic courts, but that disagreements would be settled between the two heads of the churches in Egypt. The agreement was signed by a delegate from Rome as well as by the Coptic pope and several lay delegates.

Partly as a result of the growing encounter with Roman Catholics, the Coptic Church in the second half of the eighteenth century witnessed a sizable number of fresh theological works among the Copts. Bishop Michael of al-Bahnasa (dates unknown) wrote a detailed defense of the faith, criticizing Chalcedonian theology and the *filioque*, or the doctrine that the Holy Spirit precedes from the Son as well as the Father. Pope Mark VII (r. 1745-1769) authored several works on the sacraments and on the liturgy and spirituality. Yusab (Joseph), bishop of Jirja and Akhmim (1735-1826), wrote more than thirty treatises on matters of theology, exegesis, liturgy, spirituality, and morality. There was also a noticeable increase in the copying of manuscripts, especially in the second half of the century. In spite of the challenges of the period, Coptic Christianity was able to experience intellectual and spiritual renewal from within as it became more engaged with other Christian communities, especially those in the West, from without.

Armenian Christianity in the eighteenth century

Armenians by the eighteenth century had become a global diaspora community. Their traditional homeland located between the Black and the Caspian seas was divided between the Ottomans and the various Persian dynasties, while Russia over the course of the eighteenth century was increasingly becoming a political force in the region. Outside the territorial homeland, Armenian communities continued to thrive through mercantile activities from the Netherlands to India. A number were employed by the Dutch East India Company in various regions of Asia where they served as administrators of the Dutch colonial enterprise. Others were employed in various courts throughout Europe, in Germany and Austria, or in Russia. Since the sixteenth century when they had been openly courted by the Mughul rulers to locate there, Armenians had been growing in both numbers and in economic power in Mughul India.

A number of Armenians lived within the Ottoman empire but outside their traditional territorial home. In the area of what is now central Turkey, the traditional catholicos of Sis exercised leadership over churches in the region, but for the rest of the Ottoman world the Armenian patriarch of Constantinople, who resided in Istanbul, was the most important figure. The Ottomans expected him to collect taxes from Armenians living throughout their empire as merchants, even those in Egypt, as well as to handle matters of internal community affairs, including the administration of justice in civil matters. In the eighteenth century the Ottomans did not distinguish between Armenians who were members of churches that identified themselves with the traditional Armenian Orthodox tradition and those who were becoming Roman Catholic, creating difficulties within the community when it came to matters of marriage, inheritance, and property.

Within the historic Armenian homeland, which in the eighteenth century was divided politically between Ottoman and Persian rulers, the *meliks*, or princes, were able to exercise a degree of effective local rule. Several times in the eighteenth century one or more of these local princes tried to stage a national uprising, often with the hope for assistance from Russia or one of the European nations, but with little success. The Safavid empire in Persia was in disarray at the beginning of the eighteenth century. The Ottomans took advantage of an invasion of Afghanis in the 1720s to take control of most of Armenia; but under a powerful Persian general named Nader Afshar (1698-1747), Persian forces regained control of the region. In an effort to turn back Ottoman control, Nader reached out both to Armenians who lived in the eastern region of their ancient homeland and to the catholicos in Etchmiadzin, securing their support. After taking back the region he granted the princes greater local autonomy and even invited the catholicos to his coronation several years later.

Toward the end of the century Russian influence was on the rise. Peter the Great had taken an increased interest in Armenian affairs earlier in the century, and an Armenian archbishop had been recognized as having jurisdiction over Armenian churches in Russian territory. Following his reign, however, Russia showed little interest in the Armenian territory for half a century. By the 1770s migration of Armenians into Russian territories was on the rise, dramatically so after Russians defeated Ottomans in war. From New Julfa in Persia Armenians had been negotiating between Russia and Persians for some time. Those connections grew as well.

During the course of the century Armenian cultural life flourished in a variety of ways both in the territorial homeland as well as in its diasporan locations.

In various places throughout the world where Armenians were located in the diaspora they generally settled in urban areas. They continued to use the Armenian language in their day-to-day interactions within their own neighborhoods in these cities, including in worship and in publications. They also began to interact with the dominant cultures around them, making for what would today be called a cosmopolitan understanding. Several new printing presses began to operate in Istanbul under the direction of the Armenian patriarch in the city, resulting in more than a hundred new volumes and translations published in Armenian there. Toward the end of the century a group of Armenian intellectuals in India formed what they called the Madras Group. One of the members of the group, Movses Baghramian (dates unknown) in 1772 published a small book titled *Nor tetrak vor kochi hortorak* ("New Booklet of Exhortations"), calling for armed struggle and national liberation. The book was influenced in part by ideas that were emanating from the West, but also by the long history of Armenian resistance in the territorial homeland.

One of the more notable figures in Armenian cultural history from the century was Harutyun Sayatyan (1712-1795). Known as *Sayat-Nova*, or "King of Songs," he is often considered one of the greatest musical composers in Armenian history. His compositions continue to be sung in Turkish, Persian, and Armenian today. Killed in Haghpat by Persian invaders in 1795, he also became a figure of national martyrdom and resistance.

Like the other smaller Orthodox communities in the East, Armenian Orthodoxy in the eighteenth century felt the effects of Roman Catholic mission efforts. Mechitar of Sebaste (or Sivas, 1676-1749) was born in Turkey of an Armenian family. As a young man he entered the monastic order and was ordained an Armenian Orthodox priest in 1696. Contacts with Roman Catholic missionaries led him to try to go to Rome to study. He was unable to do so, but in 1700 he went to Istanbul and the following year joined the Roman Catholic Church that was located there. With a small group of others, he formed a new community in Istanbul that called themselves Mechitarists.

When word of the effort reached Rome, the pope almost immediately granted official recognition to the group and sent several others from Armenian backgrounds to assist. Opposition from the Armenian Orthodox patriarch in Istanbul forced Mechitar to move the community to Venetian-controlled territory several years later, in 1706. The community moved again in 1717 to San Lazzaro, an island inside the Venetian Lagoon to the south of the city. Originally organized under the rule of St. Anthony as were other Armenian monasteries, the Mechitarists soon adopted the Benedictine rule. Mechitar himself was concerned with preserving Armenian texts—not only biblical translations but early Christian translations in Armenian—and Armenian cultural life in diaspora; however, he was equally concerned with developing a Roman Catholic order.

The Mechitarists carried out their work in territory under Western Christian rule. Other Armenian Church leaders sought to develop an Armenian Catholic tradition inside Ottoman lands. Sometime around 1680, Melkon Tazbazian (1654-1716), who was the son of an Armenian merchant from Mardin, converted to Roman Catholicism through contact with Catholic missionaries in Mosel and went into the priesthood. After studying in Rome and being ordained, he was consecrated as a Roman Catholic bishop and returned to live in the region of Mosel. Forced to leave by the local authorities a short time later, he made his way to Istanbul where he was eventually imprisoned for his efforts to build a new Roman Catholic congregation there.

While in prison in Istanbul he met Abraham Ardzivian (1679-1749), an Armenian priest who had been ordained in 1706 by the catholicos of Sis, and since 1710 had been serving as bishop of Aleppo. Whether Ardzivian already harbored Catholic sympathies before his encounter with Tazbazian is not clear, but by 1719, after meeting Tazbazian, Ardzivian clearly had come to support communion with Rome. That same year he made his way to Lebanon to a Maronite monastery at Kreim where he was able to resume administration of the affairs of his church in Aleppo from a distance.

Ardzivian was finally able to return to Aleppo in 1738. Two years later a small group of local Armenian bishops who shared his commitments to Rome, including one whom Ardzivian himself had ordained, elected the bishop to the office of patriarch. Two years later the new patriarch traveled to Rome, where the pope recognized his election and bestowed on him the title of patriarch of the Armenian Catholic Church. Ardizivian returned to Kreim where he spent the last years of his life building the new Armenian Catholic Church, one more uniate body with Rome.

Syrian Orthodoxy in Persia

In 1722 the shah of Persia was overthrown by an invading army of Afghans who had been previously subjugated under Safavid rule. Russia and the Ottomans, both neighboring states, took advantage of the situation by seizing bordering Safavid territories. Fourteen years later Persian forces under a general named Nader Afshar (1698-1747) finally defeated the last of the Afghans. Nader did not have sufficient support from the other Persian nobility to be able to claim the title of Shah of Shahs at first, but finally, in 1736, he was able to do so, thereby establishing a new, if brief, dynasty.

One of Nader's concerns was to turn back the Ottoman advance into areas in the west that had been previously under Persian control. In the mid-1730s he launched a campaign to regain Baghdad and the region around Mosel, on the Plains of Nineveh. A number of Syrian Orthodox churches in the region were destroyed in this campaign, in part due to the perception that they supported Ottoman rule. At the same time Nader reached out to Armenians who lived in the eastern region of their ancient homeland and who had previously been under Ottoman rule. He granted the princes greater local autonomy and even invited the catholicos from Etchmiadzin to his coronation in an effort to win their support against the Ottomans. Following Nader's assassination in 1747, Persia was divided among several competing dynastic factions.

The Syrian Orthodox were already severely weakened by centuries of oppression and struggle. A handful of families dominated what had become little more than a regional collection of churches living in mountainous regions, supporting a handful of remaining monasteries, but nevertheless possessing an ancient memory of faith. The patriarchal see had been moved far from the centers of Persian political life and for more than a century had been passed down from uncle to nephew in an effort to sustain the church apart from governmental involvement. During most of the last century two claimants contended for the title of patriarch, leaving questions of authority among the churches quite open for dispute.

In 1766 Mar Ignace Michael III Jarweh (1731-1800) became bishop of Aleppo. He already had previous contact with Jesuits in the region, and through their influence apparently already came to the decision that union with Rome was the best route for the Syrian Orthodox to follow. A little more than a decade after his election, in 1775, Rome formally recognized him as being in full communion as a bishop, not requiring of him any further service of consecration. Six years later Ignace was elected patriarch of the Syrian Orthodox Church; but when he announced his earlier embrace of the Catholic faith and sought to bring the entire church with him into communion, several other Syrian Orthodox bishops withdrew and elected another to be patriarch. Ignace was forced into exile in Lebanon, where he became the patriarch of a new branch that was recognized by Rome, called the Syrian Catholic Church.

During this period the Zand dynasty, which came to power in 1750 in the wake of Nader's assassination, ruled Persia. The Zand rulers began to open the ports of Persia to trade with the British East India Company, effectively spreading Britain's economic reach into the region. In 1779 the last Zand ruler was assassinated and after several years of internal struggle, in 1794, a member of the Qajar tribe named Muḥammad Khān Qājār (1742-1797) succeeded in having himself named Shah of Shah, thereby establishing a new dynasty that would last until 1925.

Islam and Christianity

Orthodoxy was going through major transitions in the eighteenth century. Many of the same factors precipitating change in the Orthodox world were affecting the wider Islamic world in which a large number of Orthodox communities lived as minority peoples. More than a set of religious beliefs, Islam provided the inspiration for several major cultural formations from the Mediterranean to India. Islamic societies had for centuries excelled in science, industry, and the arts. Now in the eighteenth century these great Islamic cultures and political empires appeared to be stagnant, if not in decline. Especially in matters of science, those nations or empires where Islam was the official religion were materially unable to match the growing European body of knowledge and resources.

The Mughal empire in South Asia had flourished since the middle of the sixteenth century and was still able to control much of northern India; but in the eighteenth century encroaching European powers, most notably the British, effectively supplanted its ability to govern. After the death of Aurangzeb in 1707, the Mughal empire began to fragment and disintegrate. The Persian empire was in political turmoil through much of the eighteenth century, passing through several dynasties and ruled for a time by foreign Afghanis until witnessing the establishment of the Qajar at the end of the century. The Ottoman empire, which spanned three continents, found itself increasingly incapable of exercising effective rule over all of the regions under its control. Even more important, the Ottoman rulers were unable or unwilling to gain a share of the growing global economy that had become unleashed in the eighteenth century. Merchants in Europe were making enormous profits, giving them considerable political and social power, enough to effect a fundamental revolution not only in how their societies were governed but how the world was organized. In the Ottoman world, trade was controlled in large part by important Orthodox families, the *phanariots*, and by members of the Christian ethnic minorities such as the Armenians. Generally speaking, a strong Muslim merchant class did not emerge in the eighteenth century within the Ottoman empire.

Orthodox communities felt the impact of the West in religious and cultural terms. A number of Roman Catholic and Protestant intellectual leaders in the West also found themselves challenged by many of these new intellectual and cultural forces that were unleashed in Europe in the eighteenth century. For better or worse, in most cases Catholic and Protestants in the West struggled to accommodate them. Orthodox churches in the East experienced those same challenges at a greater distance. Except in Russia, where the policies of Peter the Great sought to Westernize the nation culturally, most Orthodox communities experienced the impact of Western science and culture in the form of European nations extending political influence by means of their navies or their trading companies. Where they encountered the West religiously it was usually in the form of missions seeking to proselytize Orthodox believers. These efforts were successful enough to create a problem for the Orthodox churches. Large enough numbers of the various Orthodox communities living in the Ottoman empire either joined the Roman Catholic Church or became part of uniate churches to cause Orthodox concern.

The challenge that the West began to pose to Muslim communities and the Islamic world of the eighteenth century, however, was far more political in nature, but it would be *experienced* as a clash of civilizations and religions. Within the Ottoman world, it was illegal for one to convert from Islam to Christianity. Muslims from Morocco to India neither embraced the new ideas coming from Europe that took their origin in the Enlightenment nor did they quickly adopt Western innovations in warfare and science. The effect was to create a geopolitical and social imbalance for the next century between what in the eighteenth century still looked like the union of faith and culture of Christendom in the West and the *dar-al Islam* ("house of Islam") in the East.

One place where these challenges played out acutely in the eighteenth century was the Arabian Peninsula. Arabia was nominally part of the Ottoman empire, but as in other parts of their political domains, by the eighteenth century the Ottomans exercised little political influence over the region, other than to collect taxes. Throughout much of Arabia, popular religious cultural practices had grown over the centuries, often under the cover of Sufi or Shi'a innovations and often associated with practices around shrines at gravesites dedicated to holy men and women. Imam Mohammad Hayyat ibn Ibraaheem al-Sindi (d. c. 1750) came from Sind, in current Pakistan, to Medina where he began to teach what he considered a restored version of Islam grounded in the Qur'an and Hadith. One of his students was Muhammad ibn Abd-al Wahhab (1703-1792), who saw himself as a reformer of Islam called to put into action his teacher's call for purging the religion of corrupt, innovative, and idolatrous practices. Mosques were to be simple, graves were to be without elaborate markings, and the veneration of saints was to end. Prohibitions against both drinking of alcoholic beverages and smoking tobacco ought to be enforced. His ideas were preserved in a number of works that he authored, among the best known being *Kitab at-Tawhid* ("The Book of Unity").

Abd-al Wahhab was able to gain a small following and implement some of these ideas in his hometown of 'Uyayna, in central Arabia, until these followers destroyed the local gravesite of a well-known Muslim saint, thereby incurring the opposition of local political authorities. Forced to go into exile in 1740, Abd-al Wahhab was offered refuge by a prince named Muhammad ibn Saud (d. 1765) in the town of Ad-Dar'iyah in central Arabia, near the city of Riyadh. The Saudi sheik took up the cause of reform as espoused by Abd-al Wahhab and linked it with the political mission of creating a new independent state. Over the next four decades, his son, Abdul Aziz ibn Muhammad ibn Saud (d. 1803), successfully extended the control of the house of Saud over most of the Arabian Peninsula, including the holy cities of Mecca and Medina in 1802. This first Saudi state would not last long. Ottoman forces invaded Arabia and brought the independent state to an end in 1818. Nevertheless its successors would rise again several times to refound an independent Saudi state, founded on the reforming ideals of Abd-al Wahhab, which taken as a school is often called Wahhabi, or as adherents preferred, Salafi (Arabic for "ancestors"). Islam had found a new center of intellectual and spiritual renewal that would have a major impact for centuries to come.

Suggestions for further reading

Atiya, Aziz S., *A History of Eastern Christianity*. Notre Dame, IN: University of Notre Dame Press, 1968.

Geraci, Robert P., and Michael Khodarkovsky, *Of Religion and Empire: Missions, Conversion and Tolerance in Tsarist Russia*. Ithaca, NY: Cornell University Press, 2001.

Hovannisian, Richard G., ed., *The Armenian People from Ancient to Modern Times, XI: Foreign Domination to Statehood: The Fifteenth to Twentieth Century*. New York: St. Martin's Press, 1997.

Hupchick, Dennis P., *The Balkans: From Constantinople to Communism*. New York: Palgrave Macmillan, 2002.

Jenkins, Philip, *The Lost History of Christianity: The Thousand-Year Golden Age of the Church in the Middle East, Africa, and Asia—and How It Died*. New York: HarperCollins, 2008.

Panikkar, K. M., *Asia and Western Dominance: A Survey of the Vasco Da Gama Epoch of Asian History, 1498-1945*. London: George Allen & Unwin, 1953.

Pospielovsky, Dimitry, *The Orthodox Church in the History of Russia*. Yonkers, NY: St. Vladimir's Seminary Press, 1998.

Rahman, Fazlur, *Islam and Modernity: Transformation of an Intellectual Tradition*. Chicago: University of Chicago Press, 1982.

Rogich, Daniel M., *Serbian Patericon: Saints of the Serbian Orthodox Church, I*. Platina, CA: St. Herman Press, 1994.

Runciman, Stephen, *The Great Church in Captivity: A Study of the Patriarchate of Constantinople from the Eve of the Turkish Conquest to the Greek War of Independence*. Cambridge: Cambridge University Press, 1968.

Vernadsky, George, *A Source Book for Russian History from Early Times to 1917, II. Peter the Great to Nicholas I*. New Haven: Yale University Press, 1972.

Ware, Timothy, *The Orthodox Church*. 2nd ed. New York: Pelican, 1993.

17

Christianity in East and Southeast Asia amid Colonial Conflicts

China and self-inflicted Christian wounds

Late in 1703, a newly appointed papal legate, Charles Thomas Maillard de Tournon (1668-1710), arrived in southeastern India. De Tournon was of French descent and had grown up in the city of Turin, in northern Italy. Two years earlier he had been appointed as papal legate for India and China and ordained patriarch of Antioch. He stopped in southern India on his way to China, where he was planning not only to take a general account of the state of the Catholic mission there but to report Rome's decision that Chinese Christians were no longer allowed to continue to practice certain rites associated with Chinese ancestral veneration as the Jesuits had done. In India several Capuchins quickly brought to de Tournon's attention the fact that the Jesuits there were engaged in similar missionary practices, allowing Indian converts to wear items of dress that were associated with particular Hindu castes or deities, for instance, and omitting on account of Hindu sensitivities the use of saliva in the prebaptismal ceremony of *effeta*, or "opening of the ears." The following June, just before departing for China, de Tournon issued a decree forbidding what were called the Malabar Rites. He also evaluated the work of Joseph Vaz in Sri Lanka, and was impressed enough by his mission to seek to nominate Vaz to be vicar apostolic for Sri Lanka, an appointment Vaz declined.

Rome's concern was that the purity of Catholic faith was being compromised and thus salvation was being jeopardized by allowing converts to Christianity to continue certain practices or rites that were associated with other religions. Pope Clement XI (1649-1721) was also concerned about reports of conflict between Dominicans and Franciscans who were involved in mission work in southern China, mostly in Fujian, and the Jesuits in Beijing. The Dominicans and the Franciscans were without episcopal oversight. De Tournon's appointment was in part an effort to address that need.

The papal legate arrived in Macao in the spring of 1705 and before the end of the year was in Beijing. At first he was welcomed by the Kangxi Emperor (1654-1722), the third Manchu ruler of the Qing dynasty, but the welcome was soon withdrawn when the emperor learned that the papal legate had come to put an end to the practice of Chinese Christians observing certain traditional rites. Chief among these was the practice of ancestor rites of veneration, which the Chinese considered essential to maintaining the social order but Rome interpreted as being sacrifice and worship, and thus idolatry. A year earlier in Rome, some 8,000 km from Beijing, Clement XI had confirmed the papal legate's decision regarding the rites in India and reasserted his opposition to allowing the Chinese to continue to practice rites that were associated with Confucian life and culture. When de Tournon sought to enforce the papal decision in 1707, the emperor had him imprisoned in Macao, where the papal legate soon died, but not before being made a cardinal by Rome.

Five years after de Tournon's death, Pope Clement XI issued a papal bull titled *Ex illa die*, which decreed in strongest terms that the Jesuit practice of adapting Christianity to aspects of Chinese life that were considered religious was to be halted. Chinese Christians were to be permitted to practice customs and traditions that did not appear to be religious in nature. The pope stated that the church had no interest in matters such as managing households or governing the state. But customs or practices that appeared to contradict Christian religious beliefs were to be forbidden. To this end God must be called *Deus* (the generic Latin term for deity) not *Shangdi* (Chinese for "Lord on High") or *Tien-zhu* ("Lord of Heaven"), as the Jesuits had done. Christians were not allowed to participate in, or even to watch, the Chinese spring and autumn Confucian rites being performed. Most important, Chinese Christians were not to participate in any aspect of the traditional rites venerating Chinese ancestors, for such rites were considered by the pope to be incompatible with Christianity under any circumstances. Clergy who persisted in allowing such practices were declared excommunicated.

De Tournon's successor remained intractable regarding Rome's decision on the matter, leading the same emperor, who had once studied under the Jesuits and who in the 1690s had issued an edict of toleration for Christianity, now formally to proscribe it. Europeans were too parochial to be able to understand Chinese ways, he concluded, and their presence would only destabilize Chinese life.

Over the next two decades, Roman Catholic missionaries in China struggled to maintain their churches and members. Judging from reports on baptisms coming from the various missionary orders, by 1700 there were an estimated 200,000 Chinese Catholics with as many as 150 Western Catholic missionaries. In 1724, Kangxi's son and successor, the Yongzheng Emperor (1678-1735), issued an edict expelling most of the Western missionaries. Only a few Jesuits were allowed to remain in Beijing, and any further practice of Christianity, such as performing baptisms, was strictly forbidden. The Jesuits who remained were allowed to practice their religion. The new emperor even employed one of them as an official court artist and commissioned him to do particular paintings. On their part, the Chinese Christians were left mostly without clerical leadership, yet many continued to practice aspects of their Christian faith, baptizing their own children as well as other orphaned children that they took in, for instance.

By the 1730s church buildings in China were actively being torn down. By 1742, when Benedict XIV (1675-1758) issued the final blow to the Jesuit policy in his bull *Ex quo singulari*, forbidding any further discussion of the issue, the number of Chinese Christians is estimated to have dropped to around 125,000. In the 1740s the fifth ruler in the Qing dynasty, the Qianlong Emperor (1711-1799), reaffirmed the proscription against Christianity and had seven Catholic missionaries executed, one of them publicly beheaded, for their activities. This same emperor oversaw the aggressive international expansion of Chinese interests and influence into present-day Myanmar, Vietnam, and Turkestan. China was coming into increased contact, and in some cases conflict, with the British, French, and Russians, all of whom were considered to be Christian nations. The Qianlong Emperor continued to employ Jesuits in his court as advisors on foreign affairs, as well as astronomers, artists, teachers, and architects. European Christians ran the important Chinese Bureau of Astronomy until 1827. The emperor even allowed the Jesuits to maintain their religious faith, celebrate the Eucharist, and maintain hours of prayer, for instance. Priests were not to be engaged in any activities that the emperor deemed intended to encourage Chinese to convert to Christianity, however. For the most part, the Jesuits who remained in Beijing cooperated with this policy.

Outside of Beijing and the imperial court, communities of Christian faith continued to survive even without priests. Of the approximately 120 churches in China identified in the 1720s, three-fourths of them were located in the south, far from the political center of the country. During a period of persecution in 1784-1785, the regions hardest hit were those that still could boast foreign priests in the north and northwest. In some areas of China there was actually some growth of Christianity in the last decades of the eighteenth century. In Sichuan, a province that was receiving many migrants from the east and where there was greater tolerance of popular religions, the number of Christians is estimated to have grown from under five thousand to more than forty thousand by the end of the century. Similar growth was seen in Inner Mongolia, Guzhou, and Yunan. In all of these cases, leadership was indigenous, without Western presence. Small communities of Christians met for prayer and worship on a regular basis. Some of them practiced baptism, but without priests they did not celebrate the Eucharist.

Farther to the west were two regions that remained all but untouched by Christian influences during the eighteenth century, Nepal and Tibet. Tibet was a fairly organized kingdom at the time, although China was encroaching on its political and religious sovereignty. Nepal was a valley region made up of three small city-state kingdoms, the largest and wealthiest being Kathmandu. Christians had visited Tibet before the year 1000, but there is no evidence of any surviving Christian community. In 1624 Jesuits first visited Tibet, but a papal decree in 1702 assigned the region to the Capuchins to evangelize. In 1707 two Capuchin missionaries on their way to Lhasa, in Tibet, arrived in the city of Kathmandu in Nepal, where they were able to work for four years before hunger and disease forced them to close the mission.

The Jesuits returned to the region in 1715 when an Italian named Ippolito Desideri (1684-1733) and a Portuguese named Manoel Freyre (1679-c. 1725) arrived in western Tibet. A year later they arrived in Lhasa and began writing works in the Tibetan language. An invasion by the Zunghar Khanate, which had risen to power in the seventeenth century in what is now Kazakhstan, forced the Jesuits to leave Lhasa for a time. Meanwhile the Capuchins had arrived in 1716 in Lhasa and were exerting their claim to exclusive rights from Rome to work in Tibet. In 1721 the Jesuits received word that Rome was recognizing the Capuchin claim, and they were ordered to leave. By this time Desideri had composed five works in Tibetan, including a two-part dialogical apologetic work arguing against transmigration of souls and the belief that everyone could be saved by one's own religious practices or beliefs and a detailed account of observations on Tibet and its Buddhist practices. By 1728 Desideri was back in Rome where he unsuccessfully defended the Jesuit case for a mission in Tibet. In 1733 *Propaganda fidei* finally ruled on the case against the Jesuits. Desideri was forbidden to publish any of the works he had completed on Tibet, including both the travel accounts and the detailed scholarly arguments with Buddhism. They remained unpublished until the end of the nineteenth century.

The Capuchins continued to work in Lhasa until 1745 when resistance from the Tibetan Buddhist teachers, or *lamas*, led to their expulsion. Only a handful of Tibetans had become Christian, but their refusal to receive the blessing of the Dalai Lama, who was not only the head of the Gelugpa school of Buddhism in Tibet but who exercised political control over the central part of the country, along with their rejection of a number of Buddhist practices, was perceived to be a threat to the state. Among the notable literary achievements of Capuchins from this period were works by Francesco Orazio Olivieri della Penna (1681-1745), who produced the first published Tibetan dictionary with over thirty-five thousand Tibetan words, a translation of Cardinal Bellarmine's *Christian Doctrine* in Tibetan, and the translation of several Tibetan works into Italian.

A little more than two decades later, in 1769, the fragile Capuchin mission in Kathmandu in Nepal similarly came to an end. Only two churches had been built in the fifty years that the Capuchins sought to build a Christian community in the region. When the king finally ordered them to leave in 1769 the fifty or so Nepalese who joined the church went with them into exile in northern India where a Nepalese Christian community in exile began to grow. Nepal itself would not see another Christian mission effort for almost two more centuries.

Korea

Throughout Asia in the eighteenth century the relationship between Christianity and ruling regimes was often delicate. Christianity grew in Japan and China through the first part of the seventeenth century, only to suffer major setbacks when the imperial will shifted or when new rulers came to power. The same was true in Korea, with one major difference. Korea was a closed kingdom, often called "the Hermit Kingdom," and did not allow foreigners in. Consequently it was not initially the recipient of any Western mission in the eighteenth century. Christianity first came to Korea in the century through the efforts of Koreans who had encountered the new religion through writings that came from China, and then through contacts with the Jesuits in the imperial court in Beijing.

The work of Ricci and the other Jesuits in China had given voice to a form of Christianity that sought not only to be Chinese but self-consciously Confucian. Although that voice had been muted by papal decrees and Chinese imperial action, the expressions were still circulating in the form of books and in the person of the Jesuits, who were still in residence in Beijing toward the end of the century. Twice a year an embassy came from the Yi dynasty king of Korea in Seoul to show respect and pay tribute to the more powerful Chinese emperor in Beijing. One of the leaders of the Korean embassy in the winter of 1783-1784 brought his son, Lee (or Yi) Sung Hun (1756-1779), with him. Lee was a member of the Korean ruling class of Confucian scholars, known as *yangban*. He had already been reading Chinese Christian literature, including works by Ricci that had been taken back to Korea by an early delegation from Seoul. In the 1770s these works were circulating among a group of younger intellectuals in Korea. Collectively the doctrines were known as *sohak*, or "Western leaning." Lee and several of these younger Confucian scholars were impressed by the new school of thought and sought to follow its teachings. While in Beijing, Lee sought out one of the Jesuits, Jean Joseph Grammont (1736-1812), and after receiving further instruction was baptized at the Xishiku (or Beitang) Cathedral, which had been founded by Jesuits in 1703 near the Forbidden City. Now bearing the Christian name Peter, Lee returned to Korea with a number of additional books on Christian teachings as well as crucifixes and other items to support his new faith. He was soon spreading the word to others.

Chief among the points the Jesuits in Beijing emphasized to Lee was the instruction that Koreans who became Christians were not to engage in rites venerating their ancestors. Rites of ancestor veneration were as important in the Korean national ideology as they were in China, if not more so. Confucianism was central to the ruling ideology of the Yi (Lee) dynasty (also known as the Joseon or Chosen dynasty), which had been in power in Korea since the end of the fourteenth century. The devotion of son to father ("filial piety"), which could be considered the paradigm for all other relationships in Confucianism, was mirrored by the relationship of people to king. Ancestral veneration was the basic expression of filial piety across generations. As such it was considered by Korea's rulers to be essential to the entire ruling social order.

Word about the new teaching that had gained a small foothold through Lee quickly reached Korea's rulers, who labeled it a deviant teaching. In 1785, only two years after Lee's baptism, the Korean king issued an edict outlawing Catholic teaching and requiring the practice of ancestral rites. The new Christians refused to do so and were quickly labeled enemies of the state. Later that same year another imperial edict was issued, this one banning all books that were being imported from China. The following year Kim Pomu (d. 1786) became the first Korean Catholic to be tortured and martyred for his faith. Clearly these new ideas were not welcomed in the Hermit Kingdom.

Lee and the several other early followers of Christian teaching in Korea were scholars from the upper class of *yangban*, but the movement quickly spread to the middle class of artisans and merchants in Seoul, the *jungin* (or *chungin*), and among members of the lower class (or *sangmin*), in the city. The attraction was due in part to the opposition Christian teaching received from the government, and in part due to the intrinsic egalitarianism the new teachings seemed to imply with their resistance to ancestor veneration. The Yi dynasty had become increasingly oppressive of the Korean population. A large percentage of Koreans had been forced into labor, and poverty throughout the nation was considerable. The spread of Christian teachings among members of the middle and lower classes posed a problem for the community, as members of the *yangban* could not easily associate in public with those of other classes considered beneath them without attracting the attention of the ruling authorities. The young Christian community in Seoul found a solution to this by meeting clandestinely in the house of one of its members who dispensed medicinal herbs. Members of all classes had medical needs, and thus their activities at this particular location drew less attention.

In 1787 the young community decided to organize itself more formally. They elected one from among them as a bishop and several others as priests, and began to administer the sacraments as they had observed the Jesuits in Beijing practice them. Two years later Lee sent a letter to the bishop of Beijing by way of one of the Korean delegates that year. The letter outlined the steps that the Korean community had taken and asked for the bishop's advice. The response they received was a strict rebuke, forbidding them to practice the Eucharist any longer without a properly ordained priest. The Korean community was also strictly instructed that they were not to participate in any *chesa*, or ancestral rites, in Korea, an issue that had begun to cause some to leave the Christian community. In 1795 a Chinese priest, Chou Wen-mu (?-1801), finally arrived from Beijing under cover to begin to provide the sacraments to the Korean Christians. Despite the fact that several more members of the community were executed for their faith, Chou could report to the bishop in Beijing that there were some ten thousand Christians in Korea by 1800, spread across a wide section of central and northern Korea. According to one source from 1800, more than two-thirds of the Christians were women, with one-third of these from the lower classes or slaves.

One of the most remarkable leaders of the earlier community was a woman named Kollumba (or Columba) Kang Wansuk (1761-1801). An upper-class woman originally from the south, she had moved to Seoul after her husband divorced her because of her embrace of Christian teachings. Her house in Seoul soon proved to be a center for Christian activities. The Chinese priest Chou lived there in hiding from 1795 until shortly before his execution in 1801, making her home the center for his ministry. Chou appointed Kang *yo-hoejang*, or women's catechist, a role that she excelled in. Among the women she instructed were several members of the royal family. Kang was an enthusiastic advocate of women's celibacy. She also most likely played an important role in administering the sacraments of confession, baptism, and Eucharist in her home on behalf of Chou, who spoke very little Korean and often remained out of site even during worship services as she spoke the words of the Mass in Korean, translating for him.

An important source of information about Kang's life and work, and indeed about much that was taking place in the first years of Christianity in Korea, comes from a letter written by a Korean named Alexander Hwang Sayong (1774-1801) on a piece of silk approximately 63 by 38 centimeters in size and addressed

to the bishop in Beijing. Hwang was from a *yangban* family. He had completed
his studies and passed with high marks the Confucian scholar exams that were
required for entry into government service. Sometime around 1796, however, he
came into contact with Christian teaching and converted under the ministry of
Chou. He was in hiding at the time that he composed the silk letter (*baekseo*),
which was made up of 13,311 tightly written Chinese characters and intended to
be sewn into the fabric of a garment so that it could be smuggled out to China. Its
bearer, a Christian who was part of the annual embassy to China that year, was
to hand deliver it to the Catholic bishop in Beijing. Unfortunately both he and the
letter were intercepted before reaching the border and turned over to the Korean
government.

According to the letter, a severe persecution of Christians was under way in
Korea. In an effort to keep from exposing others, Chou had turned himself in
and been executed, as had Kang, who was decapitated. Hwang speculated that
the reason for the resistance to Catholic teaching was in part the Korean government's narrow adherence to Confucian ideas, which made it fear what it considered strange. He described the persecution that was under way, and asked the
bishop in Beijing to send a request to the pope asking him to solicit the Chinese
emperor's intervention in affairs in Korea. The Chinese should intervene militarily, he said, to force the Korean emperor to recognize Christianity. Furthermore,
the letter went on, Christian nations from the West should be invited to send an
army and a fleet of warships to force Korea to open its doors to Western priests.
The letter only confirmed the Korean rulers' concerns about Christianity being
a seditious force. Hwang was captured and executed, joining nearly two hundred
others who soon became known as the first generation of Christian martyrs in
Korea. Another four hundred Korean Christians from the Seoul area were exiled,
while still others went into hiding throughout the countryside.

Vietnam, Cambodia, and Thailand

Like Korea, the kingdom of Vietnam in the eighteenth century lived very
much in the shadow of China, its imperial neighbor to the north. Vietnam had
a long, bittersweet relationship with China, borrowing much in the way of religion, culture, and politics, while struggling to maintain its independence as a
kingdom. Catholic Christianity found a foothold in Vietnam in the sixteenth
century. Jesuit missionaries in Vietnam sought to adapt the Christian message
to Confucian and Buddhist worldviews. Accordingly, Catholic Christianity in
Vietnam became much more indigenous in the seventeenth century. Now in the
eighteenth these efforts to indigenize Christianity in Vietnam became entwined
with the Rites Controversy in China, whose repercussions spilled across the border. In the 1720s the bishop assigned to Vietnam excommunicated the superior
of the French missionaries serving in the south for allowing Christians to continue to practice rites associated with Buddhism and Confucianism. Franciscans
and Augustinians had a growing presence in the country, and although they had
historically opposed the Jesuit efforts to adapt Catholic faith to local religious

contexts, they were proving to be effective agents of church growth. By 1750 the Franciscans had established forty-four churches in Vietnam and Cambodia.

The Le dynasty officially ruled Vietnam since the fifteenth century, but by the end of the seventeenth century real power was in the hands of two power-ful ruling families, the Trinh Lords in the north and the Nguyen Lords in the south. Although the two often battled, by the late seventeenth century they had reached an uneasy truce. In the south conditions under the Nguyen Lords over the course of the eighteenth century had become increasingly oppressive due to heavy tax burdens and various wars with neighboring states. In 1771 three broth-ers from the village of Tay Son launched a rebellion. They had soon gathered an army from among the peasants in the region. In each of the towns where they seized control, the Tay Son redistributed wealth and property, opening up food stores, abolishing taxes, dividing the land among the peasants, and destroying legal records and registrations. As the rebellion spread, it gained support from dissident scholars, merchants, and members of the military. Within a decade the rebels had seized control of much of southern Vietnam from the Nguyen Lords.

The Tay Son brothers initially negotiated a peace agreement with the Trinh Lords, who controlled the north. But then in 1786 the youngest of the three broth-ers, Nguyen Hue (1753-1792), marched with an army against the north, attacking and destroying the Trinh forces. Hue marched on to Hanoi, where the nominal Le emperor still resided. The emperor, Le Hien Tong (1740–1786), gave his daughter to Hue in marriage, shortly before dying. The new Le emperor, Le Chieu Thong (r. 1786-1788), fled to China, where he asked the Qing rulers to intervene. A large Chinese army marched into Vietnam against Hue and the Tay Son forces three years later. But while the Chinese were celebrating the New Year (*Tet* in Vietnamese), Hue launched a surprise attack that completely routed the Chinese army. The victory solidified Tay Son control over most of Vietnam, even if only briefly. Nguyen Hue was proclaimed Emperor Quang Trung, thereby bringing an official end to the Le dynasty. Nguyen Hue's rule as emperor of a united Vietnam lasted only six more years, but in that time he succeeded in achieving some land reforms that benefited peasants and introduced a modified Vietnamese script.

Meanwhile, earlier in 1777, as the Tay Son rebels were completing their campaign in the south, one of the members of the ruling Nguyen Lords, a fifteen-year-old boy named Nguyen Anh (1762-1820), managed to escape the Tay Son rebels and made his way to a Catholic seminary in the Mekong Delta area. There he met Pierre Joseph Georges Pigneau (1741-1799), better known simply as Pigneau de Behaine. Originally from France, Pigneau de Behaine had been sent as a missionary by the Société des missions étrangères de Paris (the "Paris Foreign Mission Society," MEP) to southern Vietnam ten years before. He had published a Vietnamese-Latin dictionary and several catechetical works before being consecrated as bishop and appointed apostolic vicar for the region.

After meeting the young Nguyen Anh, Pigneau de Behaine traveled to India, where he pleaded the case for French intervention against the Tay Son. Receiv-ing no encouragement there, he traveled to Paris in 1786 and presented the case before Louis XVI, receiving the French king's commitment to assisting the res-toration of Nguyen rule. When the promised assistance was not forthcoming, the bishop took it upon himself to raise the money from French traders back in India, and with their help secured four warships to join the fight against the Tay Son rebels. The French introduced European military techniques and supplies to the Vietnamese forces supporting Prince Nguyen Anh, who recaptured Saigon in the south in 1788. With the death of Emperor Quang Trung (Nguyen Hue), the Tay Son rulers in the north were left without an effective leader. The new emperor was only a ten-year-old boy, without a supporting administration to help. Anh seized the opportunity and began moving militarily against the north. By 1794 Pigneau de Behaine himself was directly involved in the fighting. The French bishop died of dysentery while commanding forces on the battlefield in 1799. Nguyen Anh went on to complete his victory over the remnants of the Tay Son rebels in 1802, founding that year the Nguyen dynasty, which lasted in Vietnam until 1945.

To the west of Vietnam, the eighteenth century proved to be rather challenging for the kingdom of Cambodia. Over the course of the century Vietnamese rulers annexed a number of provinces that had historically been part of Cambodia. Their policy of encouraging Vietnamese to settle in them created new ethnic conflicts in the region. In 1769 Thailand (or Siam) invaded Cambodia from the west and attempted to install a puppet king. The effort failed, but further lands that had historically been under control of Cambodian kings, including Battambang and Angkor, were annexed by the Thai. Forced labor was extracted from Cambodians living in the area to help build canals in Thailand and to help the Thai in turn fight against Burma (now Myanmar) farther west. In addition to the repeated foreign invasions, Cambodians suffered from cholera and smallpox, which reached epidemic proportions. Food production was a continuous problem, resulting in widespread starvation throughout the land.

Christianity faced challenges of its own in Cambodia in the eighteenth century. Catholic Christianity was a foreign religion twice over. The Catholic priests were almost all European missionaries. In addition, the apostolic vicars who served the Christian communities in Cambodia were stationed either in Ayutthaya, the capital of Thailand, or in southern Vietnam. When bishops visited the missions they oversaw in Cambodia, they were traveling from what were considered for the most part enemy territories. Bishops needed to make compromises to be allowed to stay in Vietnam or Thailand. Throughout the century, suspicion on the part of many Cambodians toward Christianity was high.

Christian communities in Cambodia were also divided along lines of authority. One Roman Catholic faction was made up of Portuguese loyalists who maintained their allegiance to the older Portuguese *padroado* authority. The other faction looked to the newer apostolic vicars, who were French, for authority. Although the future was with the apostolic vicars, Portuguese influences were still strong in the church in eighteenth-century Cambodia. Adding to the Portuguese loyalists were a few Japanese priests whose families had migrated from Japan to Vietnam to avoid persecution, and who had eventually settled in Cambodia. These priests also supported the old *padroado* system and worked against consolidating the Cambodian church under the leadership of the apostolic vicars. The conflict intensified in the early decades of the century, resulting even in several priests being killed. By the end of the century, this civil war within the Cambodian Catholic Church had mostly subsided, but not before sullying the church's public face.

Christian communities in Cambodia were few and scattered. The center of Catholic life in Cambodia was north of Phnom Penh, along the Tonle Sap River and Lake. These communities were largely composed of people of Portuguese, Japanese, Chinese, or Vietnamese descent, with various mixtures thereof. There were very few indigenous Cambodians among them in the eighteenth century. One of the most important figures in the development of an indigenous church was Gervais Levavasseur (1730-1777) of the MEP. The "Apostle of the Khmers," as Levavasseur is often called, arrived in 1768 and began to learn the Cambodian language with the help of Buddhist monks. Within a few years he had translated prayers, written a catechism, and compiled a Khmer-Latin dictionary. Levavasseur saw the need to train local clergy, and was instrumental in establishing a seminary for training Khmer candidates for the priesthood. He also helped establish a religious order for women on the pattern of the *Dong Men Thanh Gia* ("Lovers of the Cross"), which had been started in the seventeenth century in Vietnam. The first sisters were young girls of mixed ethnicities and Portuguese names, but eventually a number of Khmer women joined the community.

Among the most important of Levavasseur's contributions was the personal journal that he kept during his years of service. It has provided historians with a valuable source of information not just about the development of Khmer Christianity but about the political and cultural context of Cambodia in the eighteenth century. Regarding other religions, Levavasseur thought it was important to study the position of other religions in order to engage their teachers effectively in interreligious arguments and discussions. Although he remained committed to evangelizing those who espoused other faiths, he saw the importance of engaging in dialogue with them around religious ideas and teachings.

The Philippines

In June of 1700 the governor of the Philippines sent a letter to Madrid stating that he did not see the need for starting a seminary in his colony. He thought the church would best be served by having a pure Spanish clergy, with priests trained in Spain. His new archbishop, Diego Camacho y Avila (served 1695-1712), was of a different mind. Camacho believed the church would best be served by having local clergy, or "Indios" as he called them, being ordained. For the most part the attitude of the governor won out. Fifty years later only 142 of the 569 parishes in the Philippines had local priests. Christianity continued to be defined as a European-dominated religion in the Philippines as it was in many other parts of Asia throughout the eighteenth century.

The Philippines were the most distant outpost of Spain's far-flung colonial empire. Although the Spanish claimed the entire archipelago to be their colonial holdings, for the most part their political control was confined to the coastal regions of the major islands. The farther one traveled inland through the rugged interior regions, the less Spanish political and cultural influences could be found. In the mountainous regions of the Philippines numerous indigenous peoples in the eighteenth century continued to govern their villages and practice customs that they had followed for centuries. The overall number of Spaniards who came to the Philippines, even in the Manila area, was always relatively small. Manila itself meanwhile was a crossroad for merchants and other travelers from across Asia. A rich array of Spanish, Asian diasporan, and indigenous cultures characterized life in the islands in the eighteenth century. At the same time a distinctive Filipino culture was emerging. In the eighteenth century Filipinos developed a particular kind of horse cart called the *kalesa*, which was brightly colored, extravagantly decorated, and not quite like anything else in the world.

The mixing did not mean Spanish rule was widely welcomed among the indigenous peoples. A number of local insurrections were mounted against the Spanish governors and friars, providing a testimony to the independent spirit of the Filipino people that survived through the colonial period. In many cases the only Spanish presence in villages or in the countryside was in the form of the friars who were seeking to Christianize the local populations. While the friars did not come armed, they were able to summon Spanish military force when necessary, making them targets as well of many of these local indigenous insurrections. The lack of a national organizing structure on the part of the insurrections kept them, on the other hand, from being able to mount a successful effort in the eighteenth century.

Two important rebellions stand out in symbolic significance in the eighteenth century. The first was a brief revolt that ran from 1762 to 1764 in a northwest region of the island of Luzon known as Ilocano. Diego Silang y Andaya (1730-1763) was an Ilocano who worked as a messenger between the priests in his region and Manila. In 1762 British forces took Manila. Frustrated with the oppressive Spanish rule, the complicity of the priests, and the economic hardships of foreign domination, Silang, who had already begun to organize a rebellion, sought and received assurance from the British that they would come to the aid of any uprising against the Spanish back home in Ilocos Norte (northern Ilocano). Silang began to assemble his forces to attack the city of Vigan, but no British support ever arrived, however, and before Silang could launch the rebellion he was assassinated by a Spanish-Ilocano mestizo who was paid by church officials for his deed in honor of the Virgin Mary.

At that point Diego Silang's widow, María Josefa Gabriela Cariño Silang (1731-1763), assumed leadership of the rebellion. She was a mestizo who had married Diego only a few years earlier, in part because she learned of his intentions to lead an insurrection. She had been a close advisor and confidante of her husband and upon his assassination rallied and regrouped the troops. On September 10, 1763, still without the promised British support, the rebels attacked Vigan. The Spanish, however, were prepared. Gabriela Silang survived and retreated to the wilderness, but several days later was captured and hanged in the city square with the other insurrectionists.

A rebellion in Bohol Island in the Visayas led by an indigenous worker named Francisco Dagohoy (d. before 1829) lasted much longer, running from 1744 until it was finally suppressed in 1829. Forced labor and heavy taxation were already taking their toll from the indigenous people in Bohol, but the flash point for Dagohoy's rebellion was the refusal of a Jesuit priest to provide Dagohoy's brother with a Christian burial due to the fact that he had died in a duel. The young man's body lay outside the church for three days. Seeking to avenge his brother's honor, Dagohoy began organizing others to take up the fight against the Spanish. Within a short period of time over three thousand did so, taking off for the mountains to live in caves where the Spanish could not find them. From their mountain hideouts the Boholian rebellions began raiding coastal towns, killing local Spanish officials and priests and burning down churches. The Jesuit priest who had refused Dagohoy's brother a Christian burial was one of those killed. The Spanish government sent in troops to put down the rebellion and religious embassies to try to negotiate a peace, with no success. One of the offers the emissaries made was to replace the Jesuits with secular priests, an indication that there was more widespread authoritarianism being practiced by the Jesuit priests in the region. Still the rebels refused, holding out until 1829, when Spanish forces finally brought it to an end.

Catholic Christianity was still the official religion of the Spanish colonies, but in the Philippines even in places where Spanish influences dominated, the people mixed indigenous elements with Spanish Catholic beliefs and practices more freely than they did in other parts of the Spanish empire. The Virgin Mary became the object of especially strong devotion, but in the process she also came to resemble a number of traditional goddess figures known throughout the islands. A church council in Manila in 1771 tried to restrict the devotion to Mary out of fear that it had become too great, with little apparent success. For many Filipinos, devotion to Mary was the central element of their religious life, displacing even regular attendance at Mass in religious importance.

Fiestas had also become popular throughout the Philippines by the eighteenth century. These public festivals and celebrations were held not only to commemorate the great holy days of the Christian calendar but also the feast days of numerous saints whose names came to be associated locally. Catholic friars had long practiced various forms of self-flagellation as part of their spiritual exercises, emulating Christ's suffering on the night of his execution. In the Philippines the practice took root among the lay people and became associated with public festivals and parades. The same church council of 1771 that tried to tone down devotion to Mary also forbade the practice of public self-flagellation, also with little apparent success.

Spanish attitudes toward indigenous peoples in the Philippines were generally hostile, as seen in works by authors such as the Jesuit Pedro Murillo Velarde (1696-1753), whose *Geografia historica de las islas Philippinas* ("Historical Geography of the Philippine Islands") depicted Filipinos in ways that were overwhelmingly negative. Spain's interests in the islands were primarily economic. In the last decades of the century a number of new cash crops were introduced, including indigo, tea, mulberry trees (for silkworm production), opium, sugar, peppers, poppies, and hemp. The Philippines even became for a time the largest producer of tobacco in the Spanish empire. Such cash crops for the most part did not bring benefits to the indigenous Filipinos who were under the *frialocracia*, or "friarocracy." Friars acted as local civil and law enforcement authorities. They provided health care and education, collected taxes, and reported on any seditious activities. Some were concerned about the welfare of the indigenous people, and through their work Christianity continued to spread through the islands.

Life for women in most places in the Christian world was harder than for men in the eighteenth century. The Philippines were no exception. Under the Spanish, both men and women were required to pay tribute and to provide conscripted labor. But women bore additional burdens in families and communities under the authoritative rule of men. Very few Spanish women traveled to the Philippines, which meant that most Spanish men took wives or partners from among the indigenous peoples. Traditional male power was often amplified by the cultural power imbalance within such relationships.

The Philippines, like other parts of the Spanish empire, became home to a number of women's religious orders and *beaterios*. Due to the much smaller number of Spanish women in the islands, however, in the Philippines the founders of these orders were much more likely to be Filipino or mestizo. One such woman, the founder of the first local indigenous order for women in 1684, was Ignacia del Espíritu Santo (d. 1748). Ignacia was from a culturally mixed background, her father being Chinese and her mother Filipino. Raised among Chinese Christian converts, in 1684 she refused marriage and instead requested spiritual direction from a Jesuit priest who advised her to remain a virgin and serve Jesus Christ. She did so and soon had a sizable following of other women, due in part to her exemplary life of prayer, devotion, and works of charity. She became known for encouraging the other sisters who followed her with the saying, *Nasa diyos ang awa, nasa tao ang gawa*, which loosely translated means, "Do your best and God will do the rest." She and her companions followed a religious rule patterned on the *Spiritual Exercises* of Ignatius Loyola, and took the name *Beaterio de la Compañia de Jesus*. The rule was approved in 1726.

From its inception the *Beaterio de la Compañia de Jesus* was entirely composed of indigenous women who dedicated their lives to serving the poor and the needy. By the time Ignacia died at age eighty-five, she had already passed on leadership. The order, later called the Religious of the Virgin Mary, was fully recognized in 1755 by the king of Spain, with support from the archbishop of Manila, who noted in his support the importance of their work in education and charity.

The Dutch East Indies

South of the Philippines was another archipelago of islands where the Dutch East India Company (VOC) had established its presence. The "Seventeen Directors" of the VOC, known as the "Heeren XVII" were businessmen. Chief among their concerns was the goal of making money. But they also held strong Reformed Christian convictions, which included opposing the Roman Catholic Church and spreading the Reformed faith. Over the first two centuries of the VOC's existence, the company sent out approximately a thousand members of the clergy, built numerous churches and some schools, and published Bibles, prayer books, and devotional books for what they called the "Indies." Most of these efforts were intended to provide for the religious needs of the Dutch workers and colonists under the VOC, but by the middle of the eighteenth century, portions of scripture and devotional books had been published in Malay, Taiwanese, Tamil, and Sinhalese, including an entire translation of the Bible into Malay. Two editions were produced, one in 1733 using Latin script, and one in 1758 using Jawi, the localized Arabic script. Melchior Leydekker (1645-1701) began the project and completed the translation up to Ephesians 6:6 when he died. Following his death the VOC made finishing the project a low priority, so that it took another thirty-two years before the translation was completed and printed. The VOC as a whole did not place a strong emphasis on Christian missionary activity.

Priests in the Philippines worked for the king of Spain. In a similar manner the *predikanten*, or "pastors," in regions under the VOC worked for the Seventeen Directors and often were outright employees of the company. A missionary college was opened by the VOC in 1622 in Leiden, but it was very expensive to run and closed only a decade later. Roman Catholicism was banned on Dutch lands until the beginning of the nineteenth century. Lutherans were similarly excluded by the Dutch from the colonial holdings. The first Lutheran church was finally built in Batavia in 1743, more than a century later than the first Lutheran church in the Netherlands.

The typical Dutch *predikant* working for the VOC was in a very difficult position. He may have been required to collect taxes from the very people he was seeking to serve. Often he was asked to pray for God's blessing on the Dutch soldiers as they went out to battle against local Malay or East Indian people. Such an alliance with the invading troops did little to advance Christianity among indigenous people.

Under these conditions pastoral leadership was hard to find. *Predikants* who were not well qualified to pastor in the Netherlands were often sent overseas. Both quality and quantity were problematic. In 1660, there were only twenty-one Dutch ministers in all of the Indies, down from twenty-eight in earlier years. In 1730, there were thirty-four, but in 1776, their numbers were back to twenty-two, and only five of these could preach in a language other than Dutch. The ministers were paid by the VOC, which was in decline during the last years of the eighteenth century. The VOC assets were finally transferred to the Dutch government in 1798, causing turmoil in the ranks of the clergy. Throughout this period there were always more Roman Catholic priests who were more skilled, working in the East Indies with much larger groups of people, even though they were officially outlawed by the VOC.

For the sake of maintaining a lucrative and growing trade, the VOC developed good relations with the Muslim leaders. The VOC directors made several treaties and alliances with Muslim sultans that protected the local Muslims from Christian missionaries in the islands where the VOC traded. VOC ships even took Muslims to Mecca to enable them to fulfill the requirements of the *hajj*, or pilgrimage to Mecca. Ironically conditions were better for a local Muslim imam serving under the Dutch than it was for a Roman Catholic priest. By such actions Dutch colonialism in the eighteenth century can be seen as having actually aided the continuing spread of Islam through Southeast Asia, especially among the inhabitants of Indonesia.

Christianity was also spreading through the islands, even if slowly and unevenly. Large numbers of Christians were reported in the Molucca region of Amboina, Ceram, in the Banda Islands, and to the south in Timor in Talaur and the Sungi Islands. By 1800, about six thousand to ten thousand Christians lived on the island of Roti, west of Timor. At Roti, Dutch Protestants, supported by the VOC, began to teach the local rulers Malay. Some of these rulers were converted by 1729, and they in turn established Malay schools that taught the newly translated Malay Bible. By 1754 there were six of these Malay schools on the small island, and by 1765 they were all self-supporting and staffed by Roti teachers. Thus, Christianity came to the island and converted most of the people using the new *lingua franca*, Malay. Roti remained more of an oral language, and some basic Christian doctrine can still be heard chanted today by local Rotinese, even though Malay is the commonly used language.

South Asia

Just to the north of the Dutch VOC lands lay the Malay Peninsula, another region the Dutch took from the Portuguese. In the eighteenth century the local people were mostly Muslims and spoke Malay. Seeking to reduce the influence of the Portuguese in the region, the Dutch established themselves in Malacca (Melaka), the northernmost port city in their East Indies possessions. As in Ceylon, the Roman Catholic Church was already established in and around Malacca when the Dutch arrived. The strongly anti-Catholic Dutch persecuted Catholics with some vigor, while doing little to promote Protestantism. By the end of the century the British began to dislodge the Dutch when Captain Francis Light established a British foothold on the island of Penang in 1786. Light was a captain in the British East India Company (EIC), so once again a company, with no interest in Christian mission work, set down roots in colonial Asia. Only with the introduction of the "Pious Clause" in the charter of the EIC in 1813 were Anglican clergy permitted to work in British colonies in South Asia.

On the Indian subcontinent, Portuguese, British, French, Danish, and Dutch all had established colonies by the end of the eighteenth century. The various settlers, traders, soldiers, and administrators who were part of these European efforts were Christian, at least in name if not particularly observant of their faith. The Portuguese and French governments provided a significant degree of support for Catholic priests in the areas they controlled. By contrast, Protestant Christians associated with the British, Dutch, and Danish East India companies were without much support and endured numerous problems in eighteenth-century India.

One of the more remarkable stories of the era took place in the small Danish colony on the Coromandel Coast in the southeastern part of India. Two young

German Lutherans, Bartholomäus Ziegenbalg (1682-1719) and Heinrich Plüt-schau (1677-1752), arrived on July 9, 1706, in Tranquebar. They had been sent by King Friedrich IV of Denmark to begin a mission in the region to the local popu-lation. Fearing that such efforts might endanger Danish trade, however, the local colonial administrators in Tranquebar did little to welcome or support them. At first they concentrated their efforts among the mixed families of Portuguese and Tamil living in the region, but eventually gained converts from among Tamil-speaking people who lived outside the colony.

Ziegenbalg and Plütschau were both Pietists from Halle. Friedrich's court preacher at the time was also a Pietist, and it was through him that the two Ger-mans were brought into the Danish king's effort to launch a mission in Tranque-bar. Further financial support for the effort came from Anglicans in London, making the effort international and interconfessional. Neither Ziegenbalg nor Plütschau had what could be called formal missionary training. Nevertheless, their method and experience came to have a significant impact on future gen-erations of Protestant missionaries. The two Pietists began with the assumption that all people had been created by God in the divine image. As a result, Indians already knew, though imperfectly, about God. Ziegenbalg in particular believed that he had been chosen and sent by God to communicate a more perfect under-standing of who God was, as revealed through Jesus Christ. To do so, however, he had to learn the local languages, in this case Tamil and Portuguese, and trans-late the message of the gospel especially into Tamil.

Ziegenbalg also sought to find places of contact between Christian teach-ings and the ideas that he found in the religious texts of India that the Brah-mins studied. He also entered into what could be considered sociological and anthropological research regarding the religious world he was encountering. One of Ziegenbalg's outstanding works, written in 1713, was titled *Genealogie der malabarischen Götter* ("Genealogy of the Malabar Gods"). Ziegenbalg requested his mentor, A. H. Francke, in Halle, Germany, to publish the work, but Francke replied that European theologians and Christians lived in a different sphere than the missionaries in Tranquebar, and that the interaction with Indian religious principles that the book demonstrated was not relevant to Europe. Regarding Ziegenbalg's work in general Francke is reported to have opined that the mis-sionaries were sent to exterminate heathen ideas in India, not to spread heathen nonsense in Europe.

One of Ziegenbalg's priorities in Tanquebar was education. He had learned much that was valuable from Francke's orphanage at Halle and sought to adapt those insights to the Indian colonial context. At the request of and with the help of local Tamils who had become Lutherans, Ziegenbalg founded in 1707 two public schools, one for boys and the other for girls. He introduced Euro-pean scientific methods of study in medicine and astronomy, and is credited with being the first to bring a printing press to the region and the first to set the Tamil language to type. He was most concerned with issues of language when it came to Christian mission work, and was adamant that the Bible be read and understood in the mother tongue of the people, in this case Tamil. He only began his study of Tamil around 1706 when he first arrived in the region, but by 1711 Ziegenbalg had translated the entire New Testament into the language. He believed that the Indian Christians who had a strong understanding of the Bible would be the best agents for building an Indian Church. The young Tamil converts he trained became school teachers, catechists, and pastors. In 1717 Ziegenbalg translated a systematic theology from German into Tamil to provide more advanced theological resources for these church leaders. He also helped the Indians build several churches for worship. By the time of Ziegenbalg's death, there were approximately 250 Indian Lutherans in Tranquebar. They came from different groups, making the church a meeting place for people from different castes.

Growth in the mission only stirred up further opposition from the colonial government. The primary goal of the colony was to gain wealth through trade, with little attention paid to the welfare of the common people in the region. The goal of the mission was equally singular: to enable these same common men and women to have access to knowledge of Christ, which entailed literacy and education. The two goals remained incompatible for some time, making conflict between colonial authorities and the missionaries inevitable.

Despite local resistance, the mission grew, proving to have an influence on Hindus in South India as well as on Europeans who read the intriguing correspondence that Zigenbalg sent home. Letters from Tranquebar were printed in Halle as periodic reports. These *Hallische Berichte* ("Halle Reports") had far-reaching influence on Germans, Danes, and English readers across Europe. Anglican leaders of the Society for Promoting Christian Knowledge (SPCK) helped the missionaries in Tranquebar by sending them a printing press, literature, and educational tools such as globes. The printing press in particular quickly revolutionized the dissemination of Tamil literature.

In 1718, Ziegenbalg baptized Arumugam Pillai (1698?-1745), a Vellalan convert from Shaivism, and gave him the symbolic name Aaron. After serving the mission as a school teacher and catechist, Pillai was ordained on December 28, 1733, thus becoming the first Indian Lutheran pastor. Another influential Indian Lutheran leader was Rajanayakan (1700-1771). He grew up as a Roman Catholic and was a member of the "Pariah Caste." After having read Ziegenbalg's Tamil translations of the Gospels, he became a Lutheran and served the mission as an evangelist. He was prevented from being ordained, however, because upper-caste Indian Lutheran converts would not receive Communion from his hands, an indication that the effects of caste differences still made an impact on church life in Tanquebar.

There were other Lutheran missionaries who contributed to the work in Tranquebar as well. John Philip Fabricius (1711-1791) translated the whole Bible into Tamil, correcting Ziegenbalg's diction as he did so. Christian Friedrich Schwartz (1726-1798), who knew Tamil, Marathi, and Persian, worked among Hindus and Muslims, negotiating treaties with rulers, raising orphan children, visiting the poor and sick, and serving as a chaplain to the troops of the English East India Company. One of the Tamil Christian leaders Schwartz baptized was a Brahmin widow named Rasa (1750-1802), who took the name Clorinda upon her initiation into the Christian faith in 1778. Two years later she founded a church in Tirunelveli, the first Protestant congregation in that city and a church that continues to exist today.

The colonial desire for wealth and power were without question intertwined with the work of European-based missions in the eighteenth century. To a significant degree, however, these factors were less operative among German Lutheran Pietists. The Pietists were more idealistic, and more immediately concerned with evangelism. Lutheran missionaries in the region of Tranquebar did not have the support of the British or French, who by the end of the century were the dominant colonial powers. If anything, the mission work of these German Pietists was hampered by the antagonism that they faced from the British East India Company as well as by the changing political situation in Denmark. By the end of the century, the Lutheran efforts were marginalized for the most part, but it was not without lasting importance in the life of Christianity in India.

The Mughal empire, which was officially Islamic and ruled most of India, was weakening significantly over the course of the eighteenth century. This in turn allowed local rulers, both Hindu and Muslim, to gain in power. One of these was a Muslim named Fateh Ali Tipu (r. 1782-1799), who came from the region of Bangalore and eventually exerted his rule as sultan across much of southern India. The greatest impediment to his effort was the British, whose interests in the south were growing. Tipu sought alliances with the Persians, Afghans, and even the French in his efforts to extend his rule. When the British openly opposed him, Tipu lashed back against the Christians in his territories, including those of indigenous Indian identity. Priests were arrested and church buildings destroyed. Some twenty-five thousand Christians in South Kanara were put in chains and marched off into exile in Srirangapatnam, with as many as ten thousand dying of disease and hunger on the way. Christian men were forced to undergo circumcision and take Muslim names. Women were given to Muslim men in marriage. Over the next decade, Tipu's religious policy softened considerably, but by then the Christian population had been dramatically reduced. The British conquered the region and killed Tipu in 1799, putting an end to his nascent Muslim kingdom in South India.

Throughout India, Europeans were settling mostly in coastal regions and establishing centers for trade. Strong local governments served the interests of European colonists who often entered into alliances with local rulers in an effort to legitimate their presence and stabilize the region. Over the course of the eighteenth century the British proved to be most successful in this policy, effectively establishing their supremacy in the Indian subcontinent as colonial rulers by the end of the century. But Britain's colonial expansion in India coincided with a massive trade imbalance with China. The British had little in the way of goods that were of interest to the Chinese to purchase. China, on the other hand, had a number of goods that the British desired, chief among them was tea. British tea consumption grew 200 percent in the first half of the eighteenth century. By 1820 the British were importing 30 million pounds of tea per year. It was an expensive habit. More importantly, the British had little in the way of goods that the Chinese wanted. Chinese merchants expected gold or silver in exchange for the tea, cotton, and other items that the British sought, which had the effect of driving up Britain's trade imbalance with China in the eighteenth century.

The British needed a disposable product to trade with China to offset this trade imbalance. They found it in opium from India. In 1757 the British East India Company succeeded in conquering the region of Bengal, and by 1773 the company had taken control of the entire opium production in the region, which the British then exported to China. Although the Chinese had outlawed the importation of opium, both on account of the unhealthy effects it had on individuals and society and in an effort to protect its own poppy crops, the British ignored the ban and continued to export opium from India to China. The effect was eventually to reverse the balance of trade between the British and China. By the third decade of the nineteenth century nearly four times the silver was flowing out of China to Britain as was coming in to China. The trade in opium had a tremendous impact on China's relationship to the West in the nineteenth century. The fact that these European states were still identified in much of Asia as being Christian nations tainted the integrity of Christianity throughout Asia for another century.

As the foreign presence increased and expanded in India, indigenous religions responded with renewed vitality. Guru Gobund Singh (d. 1708) regularized the sacred texts of the Sikhs and their Khalsa Order of purity, established schools, and codified their external marks of identity such as *Kesa* ("unshorn hair"), *Kangha* ("comb for the hair"), *Kachha* ("pair of underpants"), *Kara* ("iron bracelet"), and *Kirpan* ("sword"). Several European missionaries derided Hinduism, thereby indirectly helping its resurgence through the backlash such efforts precipitated. Western missionaries often failed to understand Indian beliefs on Indian terms. This failure, coupled with the renewed vitality the indigenous religious traditions of India began to show in the eighteenth century, produced an Indian religious renaissance in the nineteenth century that would continue to shape the subcontinent in the twentieth.

A final note about global politics and the ongoing struggles of race, cultural expansion, and religion in Asia, Africa, and Latin America is in order. In Goa, the Portuguese resisted the leadership of local Goans, who were often mixed race, in the church, but they were more than willing to use the same Goans for military expeditions in Africa. Racism and political domination made for a volatile mix that destabilized the social order and put Christians in the middle of unhealthy battles. As a result of this tension and the new ideas of liberty and freedom coming from France, a Christian-led revolt, the "Conspiracy of Goa" (or "Conspiracy of the Pintos") was launched in 1787. Local people looked for help from the Catholic Church and especially the pope in Rome, from France, and from local Muslim rulers. The revolt was put down, but many more would follow until India's independence finally came 150 years later.

Christianity in India in the eighteenth century was especially caught in the contradictions and tensions of global political forces. A number of streams of global Christianity met in India, including the St. Thomas (or Syrian Orthodox), Syro-Malankara, Roman Catholic, Dutch Reformed, Lutheran, and Anglican. The older Indian churches for the most part accepted the caste system as an established social institution. Syrian Orthodox Christians, for example, were considered to be equal to the Nayars of Kerala who in the caste hierarchy were next to the Brahmins. Traditions that were transplanted from Europe, while not entirely rejecting the Indian caste system, as was seen above, were on the whole less committed to upholding it and more likely to allow it to be challenged in the congregations that they founded.

In 1751, the Orthodox tradition that continued to use Syriac in all liturgical matters was given a boost by the arrival of Syrian prelates from West Asia bearing sixty-four Syriac manuscripts. Oddly enough, the Dutch provided some support for the Orthodox, both because of their access to the spice trade and because they opposed the Roman Catholics. Struggles and open conflicts pertaining to leadership marred the Syrian Orthodox community during the eighteenth century. In 1700 there were about fifty thousand Syrian Christians in the south.

Mar Thoma IV (r. 1688-1728) and Mar Thoma V (r. 1728-1765) both looked to Rome for some validation of their leadership positions. Mar Thoma V was almost ignored as a leader because he could not gain any outside support for his community. Finally, in 1770, Mar Thoma VI (r. 1765-1808) received from the patriarch of the Syriac Orthodox Church a hand cross, a crosier, or shepherd's crook, and a letter that gave him the new episcopal name of Mar Dionysios I, thereby strengthening the Orthodox identity of the Syrian Christians in the region. Mar Dionysios I proved to be a strong leader, but he was also a vacillating leader. At one point he conducted a Roman Catholic Mass but later declared himself again to have returned to the Orthodox faith. These ecclesiastical flip-flops troubled the Syrian Orthodox community. Some of his followers became and remained Roman Catholics who followed a heavily Latinized Orthodox rite. They celebrated their holy days in a very austere manner and trained their clergy in a seminary run by Carmelites and Jesuits. The reading list of the seminarians was limited, but it included Malayalam books published in the first decade of the eighteenth century, the accounts of several Malabar synods, instructional materials for catechism and the sacraments, doctrinal treatises, and a collection of homilies. Over the course of the century the Syrian Roman Catholic priests gradually lost their understanding of Syriac, so that the Syriac Mass became meaningless, even to the priests.

In spite of these and other limitations, Roman Catholic communities continued to grow in eighteenth-century India, especially in the area now covered by the modern southern states of Karnataka, Kerala, Tamil Nadu, and Andra Pradesh. Other Roman Catholic communities arose in regions mostly, but not exclusively, where Portuguese, British, Dutch, Danish, or French traders established colonies. Bombay, which was controlled by the British, had about eleven thousand Catholics in 1713, but even with the influx of Christian refugees, the Catholic population was under ten thousand at the end of the century. In the area of west Bengal, Roman Catholic communities had a similar fate. At the beginning of the century there were about forty thousand Roman Catholics in Bengal. The region began as a Portuguese settlement, was later Dutch, and was finally English. As a result, support for Roman Catholic work waned during the century.

The dissolution of the Jesuits in 1773 and the increasing power of the British curtailed Roman Catholic activity. Indeed, the British resistance to missionary work hindered the development of Christianity throughout the subcontinent.

Suggestions for future reading

Bays, Daniel, ed., *Christianity in China: From the Eighteenth Century to the Present.* Malden, MA: Wiley-Blackwell, 2011.

Charbonnier, Jean Pierre, *Christians in China: A.D. 600 to 2000.* Translated by M. N. L. Couve de Murville. San Francisco: Ignatius, 2007.

Iversen, Hans Raun, et al., eds., *It Began in Copenhagen: Junctions in 300 Years of Indian-Danish Relations in Christian Mission.* Chennai, India: ISPCK, 2008.

Jeyaraj, Daniel, *Bartholomäus Ziegenbalg: The Father of Modern Protestant Movement.* Chennai, India: ISPCK, 2006.

Moffett, Samuel Hugh, *History of Christianity in Asia, II: 1500-1900.* Maryknoll, NY: Orbis Books, 2005.

Neill, Stephen, *The Story of the Christian Church in India and Pakistan.* Grand Rapids, MI: Eerdmans, 1970.

Pomplum, Trent, *Jesuit on the Roof of the World: Ippolito Desideri's Mission to Tibet.* New York: Oxford University Press, 2010.

Ponchaud, François, *Cathedral in the Rice Paddy: 450 Years of History of the Church in Cambodia.* Paris: Le Sarmeny, 1990. Standaert, Nicholas, ed., *Handbook of Christianity in China, I: 635-1800.* Leiden: Brill, 2000.

Uhalley, Stephen, Jr., and Xiaoxin Wu, eds., *China and Christianity: Burdened Past, Hopeful Future.* Armonk, NY: M. E. Sharpe, 2001.

18

South America and the Caribbean in an Age of Revolution

The Caribbean

The Caribbean Sea is nearly three million square kilometers of tropical waters bounded by a string of islands stretching from Cuba to the Antilles on the north and east, and by the coastal regions of South and Central America on the south and west. In the eighteenth century it was a crossroads of global trade and politics, a place of pirates and plantations where Europeans, Africans, and Native Americans interacted under continuously changing political fortunes. One could hear a number of European languages being spoken throughout the region: Spanish in Yucatán, Cuba, and Puerto Rico; Danish in St. Thomas; English in Jamaica; French in Saint-Domingue (after 1804 known as Haiti); and Dutch in parts of the Antilles, as well as in settlements along the coast of South America. A scattering of Jewish communities, mostly made up of merchants and their families, dotted port cities throughout the Caribbean region. The number of Africans, the vast majority of them enslaved and forced to labor on plantations, continued to grow through the century, increasing the African religious and cultural influences throughout the region and adding strong African tones to the European colonial languages that dominated. The number of people of indigenous descent was small but stable. Many of them were descended from mixed parentage, of Native American mothers and European fathers. Their presence was mostly marginal to the dominant society.

The Caribbean was often a dangerous place to travel in the eighteenth century. British, French, Danish, Dutch, and Spanish warships all rode its winds and plied its waves, seeking to protect the merchant ships of their native lands while attacking the ships and harbors of others. A significant number of these warships and their crews, called buccaneers or pirates, operated outside the boundaries of any national legal jurisdiction. They mostly attacked Spanish galleons because that was where the gold usually was. Other ships carried human cargo, as enslaved Africans continued to be imported to work in the growing plantation industry in the region. These same ships took sugar and rum on to ports in North America or western Europe before returning to Africa loaded with goods to begin again the cycle of trade.

In the eighteenth century sugar was still the dominant agricultural product grown in the Caribbean. Most of it went to feed the growing European and North American demand for sweetness. Plantations became much larger as this demand grew, and production increased with larger fields, advances in technology, and more slaves. In 1775, an estimated 19,000 Europeans (mostly British) with an estimated 193,000 slaves lived and worked on the plantations of Jamaica. Throughout the region the ratio of Europeans to Africans was similar. The Portuguese, Spanish, and then Dutch had been the most active traders shipping enslaved Africans across the Atlantic in the seventeenth century. In the eighteenth century dominance passed on to the British who ended up transporting approximately 2.5 million Africans to the Caribbean and South America between 1690 and 1807. The enslaved Africans continued to work under horrid conditions with little, if any, legal or human rights afforded to them. Births among the enslaved were low in the Caribbean, and disease and death rates were quite high, making the continuous importation of new captives necessary to sustain the system. Despite the stringent conditions of oversight under which they labored thousands managed to escape, often forming communities of what were called "maroons" living in rugged interior regions.

Most Europeans who had originally settled in the Caribbean came in search of wealth. There was little in the way of Christian conviction or commitment to spiritual life that inspired people to relocate from Europe to the region. Later generations of European descent, called *criollos* in Spanish ("creoles" in English), continued for the most part to show little interest in practicing Christianity. With few bishops or ordained clergy, whatever passed for Christian life in Caribbean societies was mostly administered by secular colonial rulers. In the British colonies, the governor functioned as a sort of lay bishop, administering the affairs of the churches as an "ordinary." Governors were primarily concerned with upholding social order and protecting property rights, especially the claims of slaveholders to the right to hold their enslaved captives as private property. Governors were loyal to the laws of their home nations and usually sought to promote whatever interests their national churches might have in the region. Although the eighteenth century saw the rapid advance of notions of inherent human rights in Europe, in the colonies such ideas were applied only to the ruling families of European descent.

In theory, conversion of persons of both African and Native American descent was enjoined on colonial political leaders by the ruling church bodies in Europe, but in practice little was done to bring Christian teachings to enslaved Africans in ways they could understand. European rulers from time to time instructed colonial governments to provide opportunities for teaching Christianity to enslaved Africans on their plantations as well as others in colonial societies, taking care to be sure such practices did not encourage notions of emancipation or question the right of plantation owners to hold slaves. Despite such cautions, plantation owners and colonial rulers were highly resistant toward anyone who might take up missionary work among slaves. The danger of fanning emancipatory hopes was judged to be too high.

Into this mix of political and economic concerns in the Caribbean in 1732 came a group of Moravian missionaries from Herrnhut in Germany. Moravian interest in the Caribbean, it will be recalled, dated from a year earlier when Count Zinzendorf (1700-1760) had been in Denmark attending the coronation of the king of Denmark and had met Antony Ulrich (dates unknown), a Christian of African descent from the Caribbean island of St. Thomas. Ulrich pleaded with Zinzendorf for missionaries to be sent to his island to help Christianize the people and thereby alleviate the suffering of the enslaved. Ulrich even went to Herrnhut to make his case before the entire Moravian community. After one of his sermons, members of the community drew lots to decide who would be sent to begin to work among the slaves in the West Indies. The task, as was noted earlier, fell to Johann Leonhard Dober (1706-1766), a potter, and David Nitschmann (1695-1772), a ship's carpenter. The two left for St. Thomas on August 21, 1732.

Dober and Nitschmann began visiting plantations in St. Thomas to preach to the enslaved members of the community living on them. Although the Moravians accepted slavery as a legitimate institution, their efforts were nevertheless opposed by the plantation owners who feared the Moravians would stir up insurrection. These fears were intensified the following year by a rebellion on the nearby Danish-held island of St. John. After only four months in St. Thomas, Nitschmann returned to Germany to report on the mission work. Dober continued on for another two years before being summoned to return to Germany in 1734 to be ordained. Other Moravians arrived in nearby St. Croix that same year to work among the enslaved there, but within twelve months most had died.

In 1736 Frederick Martin (1704-1750) arrived in St. Thomas from Herrnhut to continue the mission that Dober had begun. Shortly after arriving he visited the home of an eighteen-year-old woman named Rebecca (1718-1780). Born in Antigua of mixed European and African descent, she had been sold as a slave to a Dutch plantation owner on St. Thomas. There she had been exposed to Christian teachings and had undergone baptism by a Roman Catholic priest visiting from Puerto Rico, an act that led her owner to set her free. Rebecca was attracted to the teachings of the Moravians, which included an openness to the Spirit and to the leadership of women in the church. Martin quickly involved her in the mission work, as she spoke the Dutch dialect that the enslaved on the island used, and as a free woman she could travel freely throughout the island. Within a short time she was proving to be a particularly effective witness, especially among the enslaved women on the island. She held Bible classes for them and began teaching them to read. A congregation was formed among the enslaved on one of the plantations, the first Moravian community in America.

A year after Martin arrived, another German Moravian, Matthäus Freundlich (d. 1741), arrived, and a year after that Martin presided over the wedding of Matthäus and Rebecca. Problems soon arose, however. The Danish authorities on the island did not recognize the Moravian's ordination and thus the validity of the wedding. They put Rebecca and her husband in prison for living together unlawfully. Rebecca and Matthäus refused to undergo a second wedding service, claiming that they were legally married. Furthermore, Martin refused to swear a public oath because of his convictions, a crime that was punishable by jail as well. The issue was not resolved until Zinzendorf himself visited the island and intervened to have them released. Matthäus and Rebecca decided to take their infant daughter and go to Herrnhut in Germany. Unfortunately, Matthäus and the daughter both died on the way, but Rebecca made it to the Moravian headquarters where in 1746 she was ordained, making her quite likely the first woman of African descent to undergo the rite in a Protestant or evangelical church tradition. Four days after her ordination Rebecca was married to Christian Jakob Protten (1715-1769), a Ghanaian by birth who, as was noted in an earlier chapter, was also at Herrnhut during these years. A decade later Christian Protten returned to Ghana, where he served as a missionary, translating scriptures and other materials and building a congregation. Rebecca Protten did not join him until the last years of his life. She continued in Ghana after his death, living another decade in a house along the coast.

George Liele (1750-1820) was the first Baptist of African descent to plant a church in the Caribbean. Born on a plantation in the English colony of Virginia, he was converted at the age of twenty-three and while still enslaved was licensed to preach as a Baptist. After traveling for some time from plantation to plantation to preach, in 1774 he formed with several other persons of African descent a congregation in Silver Bluff, South Carolina, in 1774. In 1775 Liele was ordained by the congregation as a Baptist minister, an ordination that was recognized by the other Baptists of European descent in the region. The following year war between the British government in England and the British colonies in North America broke out. The British forces held the city of Savannah, Georgia, during much of the war. Many enslaved persons, including Liele, made their way to British-held territories where they were given their freedom. In 1783 as the British withdrew, many of these newly freed men and women went with them. Liele migrated to Kingston, Jamaica, where he began preaching and had soon established a Baptist church. By the end of his life several other churches had spread from his efforts in both Jamaica and the Bahamas.

Methodists first showed up in the Caribbean in 1759 when a plantation owner in Antigua named Nathaniel Gilbert (dates unknown) along with two enslaved persons returned from a trip to England during which they met John Wesley and been converted to the Methodist way. Gilbert began a Wesleyan society on his plantation. Following his death, leadership passed on to two women of African descent, Mary Alley (dates unknown) and Sophia Campbell (dates unknown). The first Wesleyan chapel was built in Antigua in 1783. Three years later Bishop Thomas Coke (1747-1817) arrived from England to organize the first Wesleyan conference. An indefatigable bishop, Coke visited a number of other islands in the Caribbean over the next two decades spreading the Wesleyan message. Methodism in the Caribbean from its first days drew together people of European and African descent, both free and enslaved, but its major growth was among those of African heritage. By 1804 there were over 14,000 members in Methodist societies throughout the region. Only 112 were of European descent.

Jan Willem Kals (1700-1781) was born in Düren Berman, in the Netherlands. Although he had studied with Jesuits in Utrecht, he was thoroughly Reformed in his theological commitments. The Jesuit's concern for those of other nations may have had an effect on his manner of ministry, however. Appointed in 1731 to serve the Dutch settlers in the colony of Surinam, he soon began working among the indigenous people in the region as well. Kals urged his parishioners to join him in efforts to reach those outside the Dutch community. He strongly opposed the colonial leaders' involvement in the lucrative African slave trade. His argument for the better treatment of both indigenous peoples and Africans was simple: we all are entitled to the full knowledge and teaching about God. Schools should allow all peoples to attend together, no matter what the color of their skin or their place of origin. Such views might have sounded reasonable and consistent with the tenets of Christian faith, but among the soldiers, sailors, businesspeople, and church leaders of Surinam, they gained very little hearing. Within two years Kals was put on a boat and sent back to the Netherlands by the authorities. He continued his advocacy for evangelizing Africans and Native Americans upon his return, challenging his fellow citizens with books such as *Neerlands hooft- en wortel-sonde: het verzuym van de bekeringe der heydenen* ("The Netherlands' Main and Root Sin, the Neglect of the Conversion of the Heathen"), and later, *Nuttige en noodige bekeeringe der heiden in Suriname en Berbices* ("Useful and Needful Conversion of the Heathen in Surinam and Berbice").

In the 1700s, the Roman Catholic Church in the Caribbean did not expand as much as Protestant churches did. Globally, as we have seen, Roman Catholic missionary work was in decline, in part because of the dissolution of the Jesuit order, and in part because of the diminishing colonial power of Spain and Portugal. Roman Catholic congregations throughout the Caribbean still depended heavily on European priests and friars for pastoral services and leadership. Although there were a number of lay groups active in Roman Catholic regions, these did not provide for the sacramental life of Catholics. The lack of priests was augmented by the coming of Jesuits in the previous century, but their work was terminated in the 1750s and 1760s, leaving a huge void in the Catholic religious world there. With fewer priests to provide not only pastoral and sacramental services but catechism or instruction as well, the effectiveness of Catholic education in the faith declined. At the same time, indigenous religious beliefs as well as rituals, practices, and beliefs brought from Africa continued to fuse with traditional Catholic devotion to the saints. Both traditional indigenous as well as African practices flourished in an increasingly hybrid form of Catholicism among people who had been baptized.

Native American and European Catholic forms of spirituality merged in places throughout the islands of the Caribbean, but the African-European Catholic religious mixing that created *Vodou* (or *Voudun*) in Saint-Domingue (Haiti) and *Santeria* in Cuba was especially strong. Vodou and Santeria both focused upon a range of lesser deities, or *orishas,* who were mostly associated with West Africa and whose devotion was roughly parallel to the place of saints in traditional Roman Catholic devotional life. Practitioners sought out the help of one or more spirits, or orishas, to address day-to-day concerns. The encounter was often through ecstatic practices of worship and dance over which a priest (*houngan* in Voudou, *santero* in Santeria) or a priestess (*mambo* in Voudou, *santera* in Santeria) presided. Such worship sometimes involved blood sacrifices of chickens or other animals. During worship, which often involved frenzied dancing and the use of drums, the mambo or houngan typically became possessed by one or more orishas. Other participants in the ceremony often followed suit in a collective religious experience. Vodou and Santeria also involved the use of various charms, representative figures, and potions that could cause good or ill.

In the Caribbean, European secular and religious authorities alike generally opposed these religious practices, but they were unable to eradicate them. In Saint-Domingue the *Code Noir* strictly forbade African practices, and Catholic priests sought diligently to enforce the penalties prescribed for Vodou practices. Such efforts tended, however, not to drive Vodou out of the island so much as to drive it more deeply into the community. Traditional Catholic practices such as prayers to the saints and participation in the Mass became more pronounced in the worship experience without diminishing the African religious components.

One of the major fears voiced by plantation owners and civil authorities alike was concern that such nightly African and African-Caribbean rituals would lead to insurrection. And sometimes they did. There were incidents in which enslaved Africans and people of mixed descent rose up against plantation owners and their families after such worship. Far more often, however, the religious practices of African traditional origin served to address day-to-day difficulties and concerns. A general pattern of two-tiered religiosity eventually emerged. Christianity could be sincerely embraced to provide for eternal salvation and link the new believers to a more modern world, while African Traditional Religion provided resources for the exigencies of daily life such as maintaining health, bringing about healing, blessing crops and animals, and warding off evil spirits. A similar pattern developed in some Spanish- and Portuguese-speaking regions in South America in this period as well. To a degree it also carried over into the religious life of North America.

South America

Catholic Christianity was well-established as the dominant religion throughout South America by the beginning of the eighteenth century. More than two centuries of Spanish and Portuguese colonial rule had reshaped religious and cultural life across the continent. In remote places, especially in the mountains, where Catholic missionaries had not been able to reach, indigenous peoples continued to practice their ancestral religions. Diverse African religious practices, mixed to various degrees with expressions of Christianity, thrived on plantations where Africans labored. There was a scattering of small Jewish communities across the continent, and a number of Jewish sailors working on ships passed through harbor cities. Several colonies had been founded along the eastern coast by European nations where Protestant Christianity was the established religion, marking a Protestant presence. For the most part, however, South America could be safely described as a Catholic continent.

Catholic Christianity was part of the fabric of day-to-day life for most people, be they on plantations, in villages and towns, or in the major cities of the continent. Basic patterns and rhythms of life were not just Catholic but Iberio-American Catholic. They were deeply rooted in Spanish and Portuguese spirituality with its sense of tradition and duty, but were increasingly being expressed in uniquely "American" ways. The *confradias*, or confraternities or associations, of lay people that were found across South America were far more important in the life of the faithful there than were their counterparts in Spain or Portugal at the time. Confraternities had traditionally in European Catholic practice been organized for special purposes such as devotion to a particular saint or supporting a particular charitable cause. In South America they tended to be organized more on a community basis. For the most part confraternities in South America were segregated by ethnic origin or skin color, thereby functioning to reinforce the social stratification of the society. In 1772 a bishop in the diocese of Guatemala recorded 1,963 *confradias* with 145 different purposes and with extensive holdings in funds, real estate, cattle, horses, and mules.

As in the Caribbean, European, African, and indigenous Native American rituals and beliefs often merged to create a complex, hybrid Catholic spiritual identity. In South America this was especially the case among the indigenous peoples and peoples of mixed racial descent. In Mexico, for instance, *mestizaje*, or "cultural mixing," became a more general reality, shaping the cultural life of *peninsulares* (those who came from Iberia) and *criollos* (those of pure Iberian descent but born in America) as much as that of *mestizos* (people of mixed Native American and European descent), *mulatos* (people of mixed European and African descent), *indos* (people of Native American descent), *zambos* (people of Native American and African descent), and *negros* (people of African descent). Cultural mixing did not translate into social egalitarianism, however. South American societies were clearly hierarchical in their racial ordering. The social hierarchy placed people of European descent on the top and people of Native American and African descent on the bottom. The degree to which lineages of descent were mixed played an important role in establishing the location of those of mixed descent between the top and bottom. Generally the more European one looked or could claim to be, the higher in social and religious life one could expect to go. This created a complex social reality, for, by the eighteenth century, hardly anyone in South America who was not part of an isolated indigenous community or who was not a recent immigrant from Europe or Africa had not been affected to some degree by the mixing of peoples on the continent.

The complex social situation created by the reality of *mestizaje* accounted in a large part for the manner in which Catholic Christianity found expression in day-to-day life. On one end of the spectrum was what was often called "popular religiosity." These forms of expressions of Catholic faith tended to bypass or even resist the official expressions sanctioned by the priests and located within the church. Often either African influences were pronounced in these expressions, as seen along the central coast of Brazil, or Native American expressions, as in the high Mayan regions of Mexico and in the southern Andes. In both cases practices and traditions that had not been part of the European Christian heritage were incorporated within or underneath Roman Catholic practices and expressions. Saints were honored, but the specific characteristics were drawn from divine figures of Native American or African descent.

At the other end of the Catholic religious spectrum were expressions that maintained the dominant European heritage. This was most often true among communities where the population was almost entirely *criollos* or of *peninsulares*, where Roman Catholic practices, especially in the cathedrals, were maintained more or less as they had been for their ancestors in Europe. Over time even the manner in which *criollos* worshipped began to differ slightly from the way Catholics worshipped in Spain and Portugal. For the most part, however, a visitor from Iberia to a parish among *criollos* in South America would have found the worship experience quite familiar, and a priest arriving from Iberia would have had little difficultly serving his new members.

Between these two ends of the spectrum were a range of religious options. In some cases the form of Catholicism that was practiced incorporated aspects of popular religiosity that brought together the two in harmony. People would in effect follow both forms, keeping shrines to familiar saints in their homes while attending services regularly in the local parish church. Popular festivals in towns and cities, especially those associated with the days leading up to the season of Lent, were especially rich in the manner in which they gave expression to popular religiosity while maintaining their Catholic identity.

Three elements or practices were generally found throughout South America as common aspects of the Catholic faith. The first of these was strong devotion to the saints. The role of the saints in Christian life and the propriety of devotion being directed toward them had been reaffirmed at the Council of Trent in response to the Protestant rejection of the practice. In South America such devotion had taken root early in the colonial period as a dominant aspect of Catholic faith, more so than was the case for Catholics in Europe. Among indigenous peoples who had become Catholic, saints often served as intermediaries, spiritual power brokers, or change agents for whole families or villages. Mary and the other saints became important mediators between the people and the more distant powers of church and state that affected their lives.

Festivals of all kinds likewise were more important in South America than they were in Catholic life in Europe. In the early years of the Spanish and Portuguese conquests, festivals celebrating particular saints had been used as means for evangelizing local populations. These festivals quickly took root among these local communities, which appropriated them as their own. Members of various communities or regions would decorate special carts to be used in processions or parades, and would create colorful costumes with local themes that would be worn only in the festivals. In some places older religious and cultural traditions were incorporated into these events. In Cuzco (or Cuszco), Peru, for instance, the Incas had traditionally practiced a festival in honor of their king and ancestors that was similar to what European Catholics had practiced in Iberia. After the conquest, Catholic priests leading festivals dedicated to saints who had lived in

Europe would often find the local Incas wearing skins of mountain lions as they had previously done to honor their indigenous king and ancestors. These local people would offer thanks and praise to rivers, lakes, and mountains alongside the saints and members of the Holy Trinity, blending the two forms of celebration. Festivals were often organized by confraternities, which made them occasions for strengthening community solidarity. In Brazil, for instance, members of African confraternities would often prepare for local festivals sponsored by the church and held during the day, but then would hold additional celebrations on their own in the evening, introducing their own dances and practicing their own form of worship.

Pilgrimages were the third important form of religious devotion that had been introduced from Spain and Portugal and had come to characterize Catholic faith throughout South America. The idea that certain places bore special significance in the sacred realm and that traveling to such places to honor sacred persons or events brought increased spiritual benefits was common not only among European settlers, but among persons of African descent and from the First Nations in America. Numerous sacred sites dotted the landscape of South America long before the first Europeans arrived. In places such as Pachacamac, near Lima, Peru, people had journeyed to find blessings or healing long before the European conquest. In many cases the sacredness of such sites was transferred from one religion to the other. This was the case of the sacred Aztec mountain where the vision of the Virgin of Guadalupe had taken place in Mexico, as well as in the sacred Inca town of Copacabana on the shore of Lake Titicaca in Bolivia where a basilica, also dedicated to the Virgin Mary, was built. Pilgrimages continued, but under Catholic auspices.

In other cases a more recent miracle or occurrence marked the significance of a site that became the destination for pilgrims. One of these is the basilica dedicated to *Nossa Senhora de Conceição Aparecida* ("Our Lady of the Conception of Aparecida") in Brazil. According to tradition, in 1717 the Portuguese governor was passing through the village of Guaratingueta, and the people decided to hold a celebration in his honor. Three men, Domingos Garcia, João Alves, and Filipe Pedroso (dates unknown) went fishing in the Paraiba River to provide fish for the meal. At first their efforts were unsuccessful, but then their net pulled in a small statue of the Virgin Mary. The head was missing so they threw their net back again, and miraculously it brought up the head. They reattached the head to the body of what turned out to be a 150-year-old statue, praying for a blessing as they did so. Soon their net was full of fish. Recognizing the miracle, they took the one-meter-tall statue to the home of Pedroso. Word got out about the miracle, drawing visitors from near and far in search of blessings and answered prayers. Over the next fifteen years people continued to come to the site in increasing numbers, leading eventually to the building of a larger chapel for her in the 1740s and a full basilica a century later. The basilica with the statue still stands today, drawing pilgrims in devotion to the patron saint of Brazil.

In the eighteenth century these various religious practices were largely regulated by provincial councils and synods that for the most part were extensions of the patronage exercised by the kings of Spain and Portugal. The overwhelming majority of priests, monks, and friars who provided leadership were European or *criollo*. The church provided most social services, such as care for orphans, care for the sick, and education. Whether in the city, on a plantation, or on a *reduccione,* virtually everyone was baptized shortly after birth. Although weekly worship was not always possible, most people participated in annual confession and Eucharist during Holy Week. One of the reasons for the near-perfect attendance was that the tax list was usually used to call people for confession. Failure to show could be a tax liability and could lead to excommunication. The church, working hand-in-glove with the viceroys and governors, helped maintain a unified sense of order throughout the society.

Catholic Christianity did not reach every part of South America in the eighteenth century. There were still communities, mostly in remote regions, where indigenous religions were practiced. Catholic missionaries continued to try to convert these peoples, many of whom lived in *reducciones*, or settlement towns. The attitude of these missionaries was often quite patronizing. Europeans in general tended to treat indigenous peoples as legal minors or children who needed to be taught and disciplined. This was not always the case, however, as there were some who demonstrated considerable respect for indigenous peoples. Jesuits working among the Abipones of the Chaco noted the honesty of the people, who were able to live without locks on their doors. Augustinians working in the Amazon noted that the so-called savages had a stronger faith in the creator than many of their European co-religionists. At the same time the Jesuits and Augustinians did not romanticize indigenous peoples the way a number of intellectuals in Europe did from a distance, with their theories of the "noble savages" in places like Brazil. Missionaries who were working directly with indigenous communities tended to be more realistic in their appreciation, even in their most patronizing moments.

Mission efforts succeeded in extending the borders of Christian society geographically as well as spiritually through the eighteenth century in South America. Mission work often became institutional development. One of the best examples of this is the case of Baltasar Jaime Martínez Compañón y Bujanda (1737-1797). A secular priest who was appointed bishop of Trujillo, Peru, and then of Bogotá by the king of Spain, Martínez Compañón was deeply concerned about extending the ministry of the Catholic Church among indigenous peoples. He published the first detailed map of the Peruvian region, founded six seminaries, organized twenty new towns for indigenous peoples, and moved seventeen other such towns to safer regions. He founded fifty-four primary schools and four boarding schools for indigenous peoples, established forty-one new parishes, and laid out six new roads. Another example of such efforts is the Spanish Franciscan Antonio Margil (1657-1726). Margil traveled widely through Central America on foot in order to serve the local indigenous people. In addition to evangelizing, he also helped to develop the missionary colleges of Cristo Crucificado in Guatemala City and Nuestra Señora de Guadalupe in Zacatecas. Both of these schools, carrying on Margil's efforts, were dedicated to training friars for work among the indigenous people.

Europeans from countries other than Spain and Portugal, while not common in the eighteenth century in most parts of South America, were nevertheless appearing often enough to make a contribution. Protestants could not legally work in Roman Catholic lands, but Protestant influences were beginning to be felt. Thomas Falkner (1707-1784) was an English Calvinist who traveled to the Guinea coast hoping that the better climate would prove to be a remedy for his bad health. Nearly dead when he arrived, the Englishman was left in the care of a Jesuit priest. Falkner soon not only recovered but converted, undergoing baptism as a Catholic in 1731 and shortly thereafter joining the Jesuit order. Falkner went on to become a missionary in the viceroyalty of La Plata, in Argentina, but his greatest contribution was made in his study of Patagonian plants and his speculations regarding herbal remedies, making him arguably the first Catholic missionary in South America to give medical care for the sick a central place in his ministry.

Martin Dobrizhoffer (1718-1791) was a Bohemian Jesuit missionary who labored for eighteen years in what is now Paraguay among the Abipón at a time when this seminomadic people were being forced off their hunting lands by the Spanish colonial government. Dobrizhoffer's writings provide an important historical record of the Abipón people, whose women were tattooed with ashes and blood and whose men were expert archers. The Apibón were incorporated into the great Guaraní Indian system, but after the suppression of the Jesuits in 1767 Dobrizhoffer quietly returned to Europe and found his way to the court of Empress Maria Theresa of Austria (1717-1780) as preacher. She was fascinated by his stories and urged him to write them, resulting in a three-volume work Dobrizhoffer published in 1784 in Latin as *Historia de Abiponibus, equestri bellicosaque Paraquariae natione* ("History of the Abipones, an Equestrian People of Paraguay"). The longer subtitle of the book explained that it contained a wealth of information concerning not just the people and their villages, but the rivers, cities, wild animals, amphibians, insects, reptiles, fish, birds, trees, and plants in the region. The book was soon translated into German, with an English translation appearing several decades later.

Social upheavals

Across the span of the eighteenth century, ideas from France and England made their way to South America. The works of John Locke (1632-1704), François-Marie Arouet de Voltaire (1694-1778), and Jean-Jacques Rousseau (1712-1778) were all read and discussed with great interest in the last decades of the century by members of the *criollos* class. Ideas about *liberté* and *égalité* were attractive to some, but for the most part were viewed by members of the ruling population as being a threat. Only 15 percent or so of the population in South America were *penisulares* or *criollos* of unmixed European descent in the eighteenth century, however. Change was in the air, but the sources of rebellion and the ideas that guided them most often did not come from Europe. Instead they arose from the experiences of the indigenous, the enslaved, and the oppressed who were politically, socially, and often religiously on the underside of Spanish power.

Life for the Mayan people in Mexico and Central America was becoming more difficult in the first years of the eighteenth century. Spanish authorities were increasing the amounts they extracted from the people, both in taxes and labor. Mayans were finding themselves increasingly forced out of their villages or off of their traditional lands. In the midst of this deteriorating social situation, a young Mayan woman named María de la Candelaria (dates unknown) from the village of Cancuc in southern Mexico in 1712 received what she claimed to be a vision of the Virgin Mary. Other members of the village believed her. They built a small shrine to honor the apparition, and soon pilgrims from the surrounding Mayan countryside came to worship there. The Spanish authorities disputed the authenticity of the apparition, however, labeling it idolatrous. De la Candelaria's supporters responded by denouncing the king and taking up arms. A group of them took control of the village of Cancuc, killing the local priests and several of the *criollos*, while setting up their own priests at the shrine of the Virgin Mary. Spanish troops from Guatemala responded quickly, crushing the rebellion before the year was out. The Spanish executed more than one hundred of the movement's leaders, but they failed to capture de la Candelaria. For several years after that, the Spanish continued to search for her among the Mayan people, who refused to turn her in despite bribes and torture.

Another indigenous uprising coming at the end of the century was that of Túpac Amaru II (1742-1781, born José Gabriel Condorcanqui), which began in 1780 in Cuzco, Peru. Condorcanqui was a direct descendant of the last Inca emperor, Túpac Amaru (1545-1572). Born of mixed indigenous and Spanish ancestry, Condorcanqui had been raised as a Christian and studied at the Jesuit school San Francisco de Borja. A political appointment by the governor in the region provided him an opportunity to witness firsthand the Spanish mistreatment of his fellow indigenous people in the mines and villages. After several years of unsuccessful protests, Condorcanqui took to open rebellion. Assuming his ancestral Inca name, Túpac Amaru II, he organized several thousand followers who took up arms to follow him. The rebels succeeded in capturing and executing the Spanish governor in 1780. They failed to gain the support of the *criollos*, however, due mostly to the economic impact that the rebellion had on the region. Within a year Amaru was captured, and in May of 1781 on the same plaza in Cuzco where his ancestor had been executed, Amaru was forced to watch as the other members of his family were killed, then had his tongue cut out before being beheaded. His body was subsequently quartered and his remains spread throughout the countryside.

Amaru's followers continued for some time to mount rebellions in other parts of Peru. Inspired by Amaru's efforts, Túpac Katari (born Julián Apasa Nina, c. 1750-1781) mounted a similar rebellion in Bolivia. Katari raised an indigenous force of about forty thousand to besiege La Paz. His efforts soon failed as well, and in November of 1781 he was executed. But still the movement did not die as scattered outbreaks and rebellions continued throughout the last decades of the century.

One of the most important successful revolutions against European colonial rule in South America or the Caribbean was led by François-Dominique Toussaint Bréda, better known as Toussaint L'Ouverture (1743-1803) in Saint-Domingue (or Haiti). A self-educated slave who had gained his freedom around the age of thirty, Toussaint L'Ouverture had been instructed in the Catholic faith and undergone baptism by the hands of a priest of African descent named Pierre Baptiste Simon (dates unknown). By 1791 word of the French Revolution, with its ideals of equality and liberty, had reached the colony of Saint-Domingue. A slave rebellion broke out, and while Toussaint L'Ouverture was not involved in the preliminary battles, he soon entered the fray and became a major leader of the effort. Over the course of the next decade as France continued to go through turmoil and British and Spanish forces sought to take advantage of the situation by seizing the colony, Toussaint L'Ouverture skillfully guided the people of the colony toward full independence. By the end of the decade he succeeded in wresting control of all areas of government from French colonial rulers, establishing a state in which persons of African descent played the dominant role in governing. The Roman Catholic Church continued to be officially established in the new independent nation, which in 1804 was renamed Haiti, reflecting Toussaint L'Ouverture's strong Catholic commitments. The French government sent an expedition against the former colony in 1802 to try to bring it back under their rule. The effort ultimately failed, but not before Toussaint L'Ouverture was taken captive and transported back to France, where he died the following year in prison. Haiti, however, was after 1804 a free nation, and under Toussaint L'Ouverture the first to abolish slavery in the Americas.

The quest for freedom in South America and the Caribbean radiated beyond the geographical region to reach as far as Europe at the end of the eighteenth century. Juan Pablo Viscardó y Guzmán (1748-1798) was a Jesuit of European descent who had served in Peru before his order had been suppressed and he had been forced to move to Italy. A year after the defeat of Amaru's uprising, word of the effort reached Viscardó, who moved to London for a short time to try to help the cause by supporting it before the British government. After returning to Italy, and then later moving to France, Viscardó in 1791 finished an essay in French titled *Lettre aux Espagnols-Américains* ("Letter to the Spanish Americans"). The essay circulated for several years among his friends before being published in London and Philadelphia at the end of the decade. Drawing on ideas from a number of sources and continents, Viscardó called for the independence of nations in South America and the Caribbean from their colonial rulers. His work in turn helped inspire other independence efforts as they began to gain renewed strength in the first decades of the nineteenth century.

Through the course of the eighteenth century, kings in Spain who belonged to the House of Bourbon sought to introduce a number of changes intended to increase manufacturing and improve the economy of the nation. In the colonial regions under Spanish control in America these reforms translated mainly into administrative restructuring that was intended to make government more efficient. The military was strengthened, and more *criollos* were incorporated into its lower rank as officers. The political role of the church was reduced, with more military officials than bishops receiving appointments to power. These latter efforts reached their peak in 1767 with the expulsion of the Jesuits.

Despite their diminishing influence in matters of colonial government, for the most part church leaders in Spanish colonies in South America steadfastly supported the colonial order. This translated into their consistent opposition to the various rebellions, or struggles for independence as their proponents considered them, that broke out across the century in Spanish territories. The leadership of the church in these areas was still made up almost entirely of *penisulares* or *criollos*, whose European ancestry secured for them a place of colonial privilege. Most of these church leaders comfortably sided with the colonial authorities. Some in the church, mostly Jesuits, sided with the indigenous people and the enslaved in these uprisings, but with the suppression of the order, their impact was minimized. Members of other religious orders often held large tracts of land with slaves and indentured servants laboring on them. The income these lands generated helped fund church projects, including colleges that in the long run served to provide educational opportunities for descendants of African and indigenous peoples. Nevertheless, members of the various orders generally sided with the existing colonial arrangements of power and wealth throughout the continent, sustaining repressive conditions for the lower classes. Economic disparities abounded, and the church for the most part was not willing to challenge them, nor were the European colonial powers that continued to benefit from these arrangements.

Throughout Central and South America, and across the Caribbean, these struggles were part of a larger global current at the end of the eighteenth century. Large numbers of Europeans had crossed the Atlantic, and large numbers of Africans had been forced to cross during the preceding two centuries. Now, by the end of the eighteenth century throughout Central and South America, and across the Caribbean, the descendants of these peoples, along with the remnants of the indigenous peoples who survived the onslaught of European colonial rule and diseases, were busy working together to construct not only new identities but new nations. Notions of freedom and liberty were mixed in with this new nationalism throughout the hemisphere. Churches throughout the hemisphere south and north would find themselves forced to address these shifting political winds in a variety of ways by the beginning of the nineteenth century.

Suggestions for further reading

Barnadas, Joseph M., *Journals of Jean François de La Perouse*. London: Hakluyt Society, 1984.

Bethell, Leslie, ed., *The Cambridge History of Latin America, I: Colonial Latin America*. Cambridge: Cambridge University Press, 1984.

Dayfoot, Arthur Charles, *The Shaping of the West Indian Church, 1492-1962.* Gainesville: University Press of Florida, 1999.

De Laperouse, Jean François de Galaup, *Journals of Jean François de La Perouse.* Translated by John Dunmore. London: Hakluyt Society, 1984.

Desmangles, Leslie G., *The Faces of the Gods: Vodou and Roman Catholicism in Haiti.* Chapel Hill: University of North Carolina Press, 1992.

Dussel, Enrique, ed., *The Church in Latin America, 1492-1992.* Maryknoll, NY: Orbis Books, 1992.

Goodpasture, H. McKennie, *The Cross and the Sword: An Eyewitness History of Christianity in Latin America.* Maryknoll, NY: Orbis Books, 1989.

Humboldt, Alexander von, *Personal Narrative of Travels to the Equinoctial Regions of America during the Years 1799-1804.* Translated and edited by Thomasina Ross, 1852.

Jaenike, William F., *Black Robes in Paraguay: The Success of the Guaraní Missions Hastened the Abolition of the Jesuits.* Minneapolis: Kirk House, 2008.

Penyak, Lee M., and Walter J. Petry, eds., *Religion in Latin America: A Documentary History.* Maryknoll, NY: Orbis Books, 2006.

Ribeiro, Darcy, *Las Americas y la Civilizacion.* Caracas, Venezuela: Biblioteca Ayacucho, 1992.

Rogonzinski, Jan, *A Brief History of the Caribbean, From the Arawak and the Carib to the Present.* Revised ed. New York: Plume, 1999.

Shepherd, Verene A., ed., *Women in Caribbean History: The British Colonised Territories.* Princeton, NJ: Markus Wiener Publishing, 1999.

Weber, David J., *Bárbaros: Spaniards and Their Savages in the Age of Enlightenment.* New Haven: Yale University Press, 2005.

19

North America Undergoes Awakening and Revolution

Michel-Guillaume Saint-Jean de Crèvecoeur (1735-1813) was born in Normandy, France, and educated by the Jesuits before immigrating first to England and then on to North America in 1755. After traveling through the Great Lakes region, he settled as a farmer in Orange County, north of New York City, around 1760 and became an English citizen. He also began writing his observations of his new land, drawing on his travels as well as on reports he gathered from others. He finally published the work in 1782 under the name J. Hector St. John de Crèvecoeur. *Letters from an American Farmer: Describing Certain Provincial Situations, Manners, and Customs, Not Generally Known; and Conveying Some Idea of the Late and Present Interior Circumstances of the British Colonies of North America* delineated what for de Crèvecoeur appeared to be a new national identity that was emerging in the colonies. He simply called it "American." Of particular interest to him was the manner in which not only people of diverse European national cultural identities were becoming blended as one in this new identity, but the manner in which members of various Christian confessional traditions were able to live and worship alongside one another peacefully, especially in the mid-Atlantic colonies. The religious persecution that had so often characterized the history of Europe had ceased here in America, he reported. The American had left behind the ancient prejudices of Europe to become a new person.

De Crèvecoeur set his new American identity against the background of its European antecedents. He owned enslaved persons of African descent who worked on his New York farm, and although toward the end of his life he expressed moderately abolitionist views, *Letters from an American Farmer* assumes the normative nature of what came to be called the "peculiar institution" of slavery in American life. Nowhere in the pages of his work does one read a glimmering of expectation that the African would eventually become part of this new "American" mixing. Equally absent from the construction of this new identity were the original inhabitants of the land, the Native Americans, whom de Crèvecoeur thought to be incapable of assimilation into the new American identity. In stark contrast to the experience of societies in the Caribbean, Central

432

America, and South America where "mixing" had been common, the normative American in *Letters from an American Farmer* is decidedly "white."

De Crèvecoeur's work was an important landmark in the emergence of a new American identity, but it was an identity that had been in the making for some time. Important to that process was the particular history of the colonization of North America and the reasons why individuals had gone there from Europe. The Caribbean, Central America, and South America were originally colonized by Spanish and Portuguese conquistadors in search of gold and other forms of wealth. The colonies that emerged from their endeavors were either Spanish or Portuguese in identity. Other European powers began to colonize in the Caribbean and along the eastern coast of South America and in the Caribbean in the seventeenth century. People of diverse European background eventually also began to mix in these areas, especially in the Caribbean. Nevertheless, Spain and Portugal dominated the political and cultural landscape, and the Roman Catholic Church was firmly established.

Along the eastern seaboard of North America the pattern of colonization was quite different. Most of the first settlers who established colonies there were Protestants of various national confessional identities, and most were traders or merchants. Even those who came for religious purposes, such as the Puritans in New England or the Quakers in Pennsylvania, were predominantly merchants. The colonies that they established were primarily agricultural in their economic base. Merchants and not soldiers dominated the initial North American colonial enterprise in the east. The French, English, Dutch, Swedish, German, and Spanish were all represented in colonies from Quebec to Florida by the eighteenth century. Even though the colonies from New England to Georgia were all under English rule by the beginning of the eighteenth century, they continued to be inhabited by people of diverse national European descent, allowing various national European identities to overlap and interact.

Several colonies provided a home to various dissenting religious groups, such as Huguenots from France or Baptists from England. Some of these immigrants from Europe brought their religion purposefully, seeking to preserve and even enhance or purify their beliefs, while others were seeking to escape the religious persecution they had experienced in Europe. Those who came for religious purposes often came as families, a practice that was far less common in the seventeenth and eighteenth centuries in South and Central America. Entire communities sometimes transplanted themselves from England or Germany to colonies along the eastern seaboard of North America. The family was deeply embedded in the self-understanding of these communities and played a major role in shaping de Crèvecoeur's "new" American.

Mixing of African and European cultural practices already began in the seventeenth century in the English colonies, especially in the south where the proportion of persons of African descent within the population was higher. The notion of a mixed class of people located between European and African did not take hold in North America as it did in South American and the Caribbean. By the beginning of the eighteenth century the English colonies had in place a number of laws that defined people clearly as being either of African or European descent. A binary racial caste system arose within these colonies that took deep root legally and socially. Most persons of African descent in the English colonies along the Atlantic seaboard by 1700 were bound in a legally sanctioned form of perpetual slavery. The dominant form of labor they were engaged in was agriculture, although many were artisans or domestic workers in both rural and urban areas. Most farms in the English colonies were small, and the ratio of persons of African descent to those of European descent considerably lower than in the Caribbean and parts of South America such as Brazil. Africans interacted much more with Europeans as a result in North America, which is perhaps why the legal separation was so strong.

Communities of free Africans emerged in several major urban areas in the eighteenth century, most notably in Philadelphia, but even here the boundary between African and European, black and white, was firmly fixed. Mixed offspring between the two peoples were not uncommon, due mostly to the predatory sexual practices of male owners of female slaves in what was in effect legally sanctioned rape. The mulatto children of these unions were not considered a third class, however, as they generally were in South America. In the English colonies in North America the children of an enslaved mother were legally considered enslaved, even if the father was of European descent and free. The binary framework of black-white existence was fixed by law and generally considered absolute.

The interaction between Native Americans and European colonizers was also quite different in the English colonies of North America than it was in Central and South America. Indigenous people did not become as mixed with European peoples through intermarriage in the English colonies in North America the way they had in South America. In the eighteenth century, Native Americans were literally being relegated to the edge of colonial experience, continuously pushed off their ancestral lands and forced to migrate westward before the advancing wave of the frontier in order to survive. Communities of Native Americans continued to reside within the colonial frontiers throughout most of the century, but their numbers were steadily diminishing in proportion to the advancing numbers of European descendants, and the land on which Native Americans lived was steadily being confiscated from them. By the end of the century forcible deportation to the western frontier had become standard policy.

The frontier was only a few hundred miles from the coastal region at the beginning of the eighteenth century. By the end of the century it extended significantly westward beyond the Ohio and Mississippi rivers and around the Great Lakes. European expansion into these areas came in waves. The first to come were traders and trappers, followed closely by troops. A string of small settlements and forts emerged, connected by the mostly male adventurers who crisscrossed the region, mapping its terrain and increasingly populating the expanding frontier of colonial life. Migrating families came next, mostly to establish farms. By the end of the century new urban areas were emerging around the Great Lakes and along the rivers that served as the major transportation passageways through the region.

The religious character of the English colonies in North America was changing as the eighteenth century began. In New England the Puritan political experiment had fairly well run its course, and a greater degree of toleration accompanied
by a new sense of rationalism was taking hold. Although the Church of England
was officially established in New York and the Quakers exercised considerable
cultural power in Pennsylvania, the reality was that in both these colonies, as
well as in New Jersey and Delaware, the diversity of Protestant confessions prevented any one body from gaining complete political control. Dutch Reformed
congregations continued to gather in New York and New Jersey even though the
colonies were now under English control. Those who had favored a Presbyterian
form of church government over strict Congregationalism had been forced out
of New England in the seventeenth century to take refuge in Long Island and
New Jersey. The first Presbyterian congregation in New York City was founded
in 1717, despite the fact that the Church of England was officially established in
the colony. The Church of England was also officially established in the southern
colonies, but even in those places there was considerable theological diversity,
due in part to the diversity that the Church of England harbored within itself.
Participation in public worship was generally strong. By some estimates as many
as 80 percent of the population attended services regularly in cities along the
eastern seaboard in the first decades of the century in the south.

Congregationalists and Baptists had no problems providing for their own
leadership needs in the colonies, since these churches could ordain individuals
they deemed called and qualified from among their own ranks. For Anglican
congregations, it was another matter. The colonies were considered mission territories under the oversight of the bishop of London. There was no bishop in
America, which meant that a candidate for the priesthood had to travel to England to be ordained. Increased support came from England after 1702 in the form
of ordained priests supported by the Society for the Propagation of the Gospel in
Foreign Parts (SPG), but even this was not sufficient to meet the pastoral needs of
churches. Anglican congregations in the American colonies turned to lay leadership, or "readers," who were chosen from among their own ranks and who led
services, often even preaching, but who did not administer the sacraments. The
authority of the vestry in these churches likewise grew as these elected leaders
often filled the gap of a missing clergyperson.

Revivals and awakening in the North American context

One of the lingering theological questions left from the Puritan experiment
in New England concerned the question of whether one could know with assurance the state of one's eternal salvation. Puritanism as a whole had held firmly
to the doctrines of predestination and divine election. God alone deemed who
was regenerate from among the total body of humanity, and one could never be
sure in this life if one was indeed numbered among the elect. At the same time
the Puritans had placed considerable emphasis on the experiential dimension
of "true" religion and expected a person to demonstrate signs of regeneration

or conversion in behavior and lifestyle. Preaching was generally the preferred means by which conversion was brought about among the Puritans, although by the end of the seventeenth century some Puritan leaders such as Solomon Stoddard (1643-1728) were teaching that the Eucharist, or as he preferred to call it, "Communion," was also a "converting ordinance." Stoddard argued that all persons should be admitted to the Communion table whether or not they were deemed to be already converted in the expectation and hope that participation in the rite would bring conversion about.

The emphasis on conversion echoed themes that were prominent in European Pietism at the end of the seventeenth century. Theodorus Jacobus Frelinghuysen (1692-1747) had come into contact with those teachings before coming to America. Originally from Germany, Frelinghuysen had been ordained in the Reformed tradition before going to the Netherlands where he was re-ordained by the Classis of Amsterdam to be sent to New Jersey in 1720 as the pastor of several Dutch Reformed Churches in the Raritan River Valley. In New Jersey he quickly began preaching the need for conviction of sin leading to a conversion experience that resulted in a holy or disciplined life. Unlike Stoddard, Frelinghuysen practiced a closed Communion, admitting to the table only those whom he and the elders of the church deemed to be worthy. Under his preaching, a number of conversions were recorded, and weekly attendance at worship services in his churches began noticeably to grow. Some of these new attendees were lapsed members of the congregation, but others were people who had been baptized in a church of a different confessional tradition, or who were without significant previous experience with religion. Personal conviction rather than an inherited national religious identity became the basis on which new members entered into the life of his congregation.

William Tennent (1637-1745) had been born in Ireland and educated in Scotland at the University of Edinburgh before being ordained in 1706 by the Anglican Church of Ireland. In 1718 he immigrated to America. Eight years later he was called to be the pastor of two small Presbyterian congregations in Neshaminy, Pennsylvania. Tennent also preached the need for conversion, although he placed more emphasis on growth in the Christian life to maturity. His most important contribution was in the small school that he founded for training future ministers. Tennent had already been preparing his four sons for ministry when in 1727 he opened the school in a log cabin in Warminster, Pennsylvania. The Log College, as it was derisively known by those who opposed his theological perspective, is often credited as the first training school for Presbyterian pastors in North America. Two of its most important graduates were Tennent's own sons, Gilbert Tennent (1703-1764) and William Tennent Jr. (1705-1777). Both followed their father in preaching the need for a conversion experience. Both Tennent sons served churches in central New Jersey, where they joined Frelinghuysen in his efforts. One of Gilbert Tennent's best-known sermons, "The Danger of an Unconverted Ministry," which he preached in 1740, extended the commitment to conversion to striking out against what he deemed to be members of the clergy who were without divine calling or authority.

Late in 1733, a young pastor in Northampton, Massachusetts, named Jonathan Edwards (1703-1758) began to notice a new openness among the members of his congregation to what he considered the experiential dimensions of religion. He described it as a "softening," and noted that it was accompanied by what he considered to be an increase in piety among his congregation. Edwards was the grandson of Solomon Stoddard, who, as was noted above, had argued for the converting effects of Communion. Edwards had come to Northampton several years earlier to serve as the assistant to his grandfather, and had assumed the pulpit after Stoddard died in 1729. A native of Connecticut, at thirteen years of age Edwards had entered the newly founded Collegiate School, which by the time he was ready to graduate in 1720 had been renamed Yale College. After further study at Yale toward a master's degree, he served for a few months as a supply pastor for the new Presbyterian church in New York City and then as a pastor in Bolton, Connecticut, before returning to Yale in 1724 to serve as a tutor. In 1727 he accepted a call to the Congregational Church in Northampton and was ordained.

By the time he was preaching at Northampton Edwards had already published his first essay, a sermon titled *God Glorified in the Work of Redemption by the Greatness of Man's Dependence upon Him, in the Whole of It* (1731). In it he argued that the glory of God was made manifest through the experience of absolute dependence of human beings on the divine in their redemption. Redemption was experiential for Edwards. It entailed a sensible acknowledgment and resulted in manifestations of holiness in moral life, the means by which Edwards understood human beings to be capable of participating in the divine nature. He placed a great deal of emphasis on the condition of the heart, by which he meant religious feelings or affections. One of Edwards's most important contributions in this regard over the course of his lifetime was to shift the emphasis in theology from one's beliefs in doctrines alone to the realm of affections in determining the case for an individual's salvation. Tasting the sweetness of God was the end of the study of divine truths for Edwards.

By 1734 the fires of revival were dimming in the Northampton congregation. According to Edwards's *A Faithful Narrative of the Surprising Work of God in the Conversion of Many Hundred Souls in Northampton* (1737), a major reason for the decline of the revival spirit was the dampening effect of a suicide committed by one of the members of the community who suffered from melancholy. It took the arrival of the English revivalist, George Whitefield (1714-1770), in 1739, to help stir the flames anew not only in Northampton but throughout the colonies.

Whitefield had visited Georgia for several months in 1738 at the suggestion of John Wesley (1703-1791). After returning to England and being ordained, Whitefield began to preach in open-air gatherings, a practice that quickly drew the criticism of the bishop of London. Whitefield returned to America later that year, arriving in Philadelphia toward the end of 1739 where he began preaching in public. The result was astonishing, as tens of thousands gathered to hear him. Reportedly thirty-five thousand came to hear his farewell sermon before he left for New York, where again tens of thousands came out to hear the English revivalist. Early in 1740 Whitefield made his way to Georgia, where he founded an orphanage. Toward the end of the year he went back north where he preached for Jonathan Edwards in the Northampton church for several days in October.

Whitefield eventually made five more trips to America to preach in what were called "revivals," the last ending in 1770 in Newburyport, Massachusetts, where he died and was buried. A revival was a specific form of public worship that featured preaching and was intended to stir up an experience of conversion among its listeners, who might or might not be already baptized as Christians. Whitefield's preaching in particular is often credited with having unleashed in cities up and down the eastern seacoast of the English colonies in North America a collective experience of revival that went far beyond the immediacy of religious conversion to become a major social and cultural phenomenon. The Great Awakening, as it came to be called, was under way, and Whitefield was its major attraction. Whitefield spoke to tens of thousands, many of whom traveled considerable distances to hear him. Reports of his sermons were published in newspapers, making his evangelical appeals a public theology. Furthermore, his message cut across the lines of confessional identity, creating a common theology among adherents. Although his own theological commitments were strongly Calvinist, Whitefield liked to tell his listeners that there were no Presbyterians, Quakers, Baptists, Methodists, or even Catholics in heaven. They were all simply known as Christian there, he would say. A number of persons of African descent attended Whitefield's meetings and others that followed in his wake, marking the beginnings of a distinctive African American church tradition that emerged from the fires of revival as well.

If Whitefield was the most important preacher of the Great Awakening in America, Edwards was without question its most important theologian. Indeed Edwards has often been called the first, if not the most important, North America theologian. He was also a compelling preacher in his own right. One of his best-known sermons, "Sinners in the Hands of an Angry God," which was delivered in Enfield, Connecticut, in 1741, compared sinful humanity being held by God over the pit of hell to a spider being held by its thread over a fire. The sermon was not necessarily typical of his oratory style, however, for Edwards could be quite eloquent in his appreciation for the world around him. As a pastor, on the other hand, his legacy was uneven. Throughout his years in Northampton, Edwards was involved in a number of controversies with the members of his church. He was often at odds with the tendency of some to frequent taverns and to engage in other practices that he considered lewd. At one point he stirred the ire of many by publicly exposing several young men in the congregation who had been circulating a midwife's manual and sexually taunting young women with the information they found in it. The breaking point came in 1748 when Edwards attempted to restrict church membership and admission to Communion to those whom he considered to be truly converted. After two decades of pastoral service, with the consent of the other clergy in the region, Edwards was voted out by the congregation.

From Northampton he moved to Stockbridge, Massachusetts, where he took a position serving as a missionary pastor to a Native American people known as the Housatonic. Not knowing their language, Edwards was forced to preach through an interpreter, with little in the way of positive results. Though his practice of ministry might have been unremarkable through these years, he continued to write and publish in areas of theology, philosophy, and ethics. He was well aware of the ideas coming from Europe that were part of the new scientific worldview. Edwards strenuously opposed the shift from a theocentric to a more anthropocentric understanding of the world, but at the same time he embraced aspects of the experimental thinking and showed keen powers of observation as well as considerable appreciation for the natural environment. A strong understanding of divine providence and a firm commitment to the coming millennial reign of Christ on earth shaped his theology of history, but Edwards had a more universal sense of providence and the reign of Christ than many of his predecessors or associates. Christ's reign would encompass all the earth one day, he believed, even if it started in New England and through the efforts of the churches to redeem society.

In 1757 Edwards accepted a call to become the president of a new college in Princeton, New Jersey, that the Presbyterians had recently formed, succeeding his son-in-law in the position. Before he could assume his presidential duties he died from smallpox. Several members of his family had been exposed, and Edwards, seeking to avoid the disease, underwent a procedure that had recently been introduced from England that tried to inoculate persons using pus or scabs from someone who was already infected. Edwards contracted the disease and died in 1758.

The legacy of Jonathan Edwards did not end with his death, but continued on in the work of a number of his family members and followers who came to be known as the New Light Calvinists. Samuel Hopkins (1721-1803) was one of the ablest of Edwards's successors in this regard. Hopkins argued against the notion of original sin in favor of actual sin being the cause of human damnation. Joseph Bellamy (1719-1790) was another of the New Light leaders. Bellamy took Edwards's emphasis on the experiential dimensions of religion even further in a pragmatic direction.

Edwards and the other leaders of the Great Awakening were not without their theological critics. On the one side were the defenders of more traditional Puritan and Calvinist theologies who came to be called the Old Lights. Old Light proponents such as Moses Mather (1709-1806) argued that the New Light theologians placed too much emphasis on human experience and not enough on divine truth. Revivalism encouraged enthusiasm, disrespect for the church, and disobedience to authority overall, they contended. These latter points were shared by critics of the Great Awakening on the other side of the aisle that tended to identify itself as being more liberal. These critics included Charles Chauncy (1705-1787) and Jonathan Mayhew (1720-1766). Chauncy was often identified among the Old Lights, but his affirmation of an innate universal moral sense in humanity that could be located apart from grace led him to a more self-consciously liberal theological direction later in life. Mayhew likewise sought to emphasize the goodness of God over the threat of the wrath of God as an invitation to experience grace. Both distrusted what they perceived to be the religious excesses of revivalism.

One of the best ways to see the impact of the Great Awakening not only upon religion in North America but on the wider society is through the lens of a woman named Sarah Osborn (1714-1796). Osborn was originally from England and had migrated to Newport, Rhode Island, with her family at the age of twelve. As a teenager she had, against her parents' wishes, attended a church that was identified with older Puritan teachings. When she was nineteen her first husband died at sea. Osborn remained single for nearly a decade after that. During this time she went through a series of experiences of being filled with terror and doubt over being lost, followed by periods in which she experienced a sense of complete surrender, repentance, and fulfillment of grace and joy. Finally in 1740 she was "awakened" from the cycle as a result of hearing a sermon by George Whitefield.

Shortly after experiencing her awakening, Osborn organized in her home a "Religious Female Society," which she intended to provide support for the work of the church. The original concept had been to hold a gathering of women for prayer and Bible study, but soon men and children were attending as well, as were both enslaved and free persons of African descent. At one point she was reported to have hosted five hundred people each week in her home in Rhode Island.

Osborn wrote extensively about theology and her experience of grace. Her pastor, the New Light theologian Samuel Hopkins, who was mentioned above, reported at one point that she had already written over fifty books, including a commentary on Genesis. Several of her writings defended women's exercise of their own ministry. Revivalism triggered democratic impulses in this regard, rendering all equal before God in the experience of conversion, and calling all who would be followers of Christ to be engaged more deeply in a life of service and devotion. Osborn did not become an itinerant preacher, but she meditated on the messages she heard from other preachers and wrote out her reflections, generating a body of spiritual theology that emerged from her own context. She was opposed to any tendency to view salvation as a human effort, as if human beings could achieve salvation on their own, for this would mean that human beings would exercise control over God. At the same time, human beings were expected and required to take responsibility for their own spiritual growth and transformation, she believed. To this end, members of her society were encouraged to keep spiritual journals, meditate on God's grace, and pursue various special disciplines on birthdays and other special occasions throughout the year. Reading the Bible devotionally was a constant discipline that undergirded all the rest.

Osborn's story points to the importance of both experience and literature in the Great Awakening. Critics of the time pointed toward the tendency to place what they considered too great an emphasis on religious experience alone, but in fact a great deal of energy throughout the Awakening in North America was expended in writing and reflecting. In this regard the Great Awakening was a notably literate affair, undergirded by a significant body of scholarly literature. Osborn's fifty books might have been more than the norm, but she was no eccentric in this regard. Thomas Prince (1687-1758) was pastor of Old South Church in Boston and one of the first historians of the North American experience. He was also the editor of the first religious periodical in North America, the *Christian History*, which made many of the sermons of the Great Awakening, as well as devotional and theological writings of past generations, available to a wider public. Revival sermons, testimonies, and theological reflections on the experience kept not only Prince but a number of printers in business through the period. Edwards's output might have been among the greatest in eighteenth-century America, but it was a part of a burgeoning movement of publishing that made the Awakening part of a larger cultural phenomenon.

Africans develop a distinct form of Christianity

The Great Awakening marks a new beginning in North American church life not only for people of European descent but for those of African descent as well. Indeed, the emergence of a distinct African American church tradition in North America can be traced to the effects of the Great Awakening of the mid-eighteenth century. Africans and their descendants had been exposed to Christian beliefs and practices from their first days on the shores of America. In South America and across the Caribbean persons of African descent began early on to merge to a variety of degrees traditional African and European Catholic religious forms. The story was somewhat different in North America, where there was less mixing of traditions. A small number of persons of African descent were registered as members of churches through the seventeenth century, and by the beginning of the eighteenth efforts to evangelize among the enslaved population were being undertaken. But it was not until the middle decades of the century, beginning with the Great Awakening, that large numbers of African Americans embraced Christianity. As they did, they gave rise to a distinctively new Christian form, effectively converting Protestant Christianity from Europe into a distinct and often independent African form of Christianity. The literary impulses of the Awakening were felt among persons of African descent as well. By the last decades of the eighteenth century, a number of biographies had been put into print, along with works of poetry and other devotional writings. The beginnings of a sustained public campaign to end both the slave trade and slavery can also be traced to the Great Awakening, despite the fact that many of its leaders, including Whitefield and Edwards, owned slaves.

One of the most important developments from the middle decades of the seventeenth century was the emergence from the plantations of the South of a distinctive African American form of Christianity that has often been termed "slave religion." Most of the Africans who were being brought to work in the English colonies in North America passed through the Caribbean, where they had been initially exposed to the Christian beliefs of the European captors. In North America they continued to be at least vaguely exposed to Christian beliefs and practices, with little effect. Some of the enslaved Africans were Muslims, and although there is little evidence that Islamic practices were followed in America, Islamic cultural influences survived. Others were already Christian when they arrived in the English colonies. In 1739 some fifty enslaved persons of Angolan descent staged a rebellion along the Stono River in St. Paul's Parish,

South Carolina. They claimed to be Christian and by contemporary accounts were seeking to head south to Florida where they expected the Spanish in St. Augustine to free them. Those involved in the Stono River Rebellion were the exception, however, regarding their religious identity. Most of the Africans living in the English colonies along the east coast were adherents of traditional African religions, even if by the first decades of the eighteenth century those practices were weakening.

Anglican missionaries from the SPG began to evangelize among the enslaved population during the first decade of the eighteenth century using traditional means of catechism in preparation for baptism, with little success. Baptists began to form churches in the southern colonies in the period just before the Great Awakening, beginning with the work of the Armenian Baptist preacher Paul Palmer (d. 1747), who founded the first Baptist church in North Carolina in Camden County in 1727. A small number of Africans joined Baptist churches in areas such as in the Tidewater region of Virginia, where blacks and whites worshipped together for a time. After the initial wave of revival preaching by Whitefield and others in the 1740s, a new effort was made by white revivalists such as the New Light Presbyterian Samuel Davies (1723-1761) to reach African Americans. Davies had been born in Delaware, studied at the Log Cabin College, and took Presbyterianism to Virginia in the 1740s and 1750s before returning north to serve as the president of the College of New Jersey after the death of Jonathan Edwards.

Members of these various confessional traditions all were preaching to the enslaved during this period. In some cases, mainly among the Baptists, persons of African descent could be admitted to membership along with persons of European descent in the church. Most of the time white evangelists set up special meetings on plantations for the enslaved. Concerned not to stir hopes for emancipation, the sermons they preached often included support for the institution of slavery. Those who heard these sermons often memorized the biblical passages being quoted. Filtering out the message about bondage, they recreated both the worship experience and the essentials of Christian belief in a new context. The first reports of independent gatherings of enslaved persons on plantations date from the 1750s. More information emerged from oral narratives of enslaved persons that were gathered decades later. These were often clandestine affairs, as they sought to avoid attracting the attention of white masters. Gifted orators among the enslaved community were recognized by the communities as preachers, while liturgical forms of music and prayer were adapted to African cultural patterns. For the most part the independent church that emerged on plantations was invisible to the dominant white community, for whom such gatherings were often considered seditious.

The Great Awakening not only strengthened African American hopes for freedom. It helped stir impulses among Africans for writing. Lucy Terry (c. 1730-1821) was born in Africa and had been sold into slavery as a baby. In the 1740s she was living in Deerfield, Massachusetts, when the Great Awakening came through and she was converted. Her owners allowed her to undergo baptism. In 1746 a band of Native Americans attacked several families of European descent in Deerfield. Terry composed a poem about the event, which she titled "Bar

Fights" (a "bar" was an open field). Although the poem was not published until 1855, it is often regarded as the first formal literary work by an African American in North America.

Jupiter Hammon (1711- c. 1806) was a third-generation enslaved North American of African descent in Oyster Bay, Long Island. Raised as a Christian, he went through an awakening sometime in the 1740s and became a local preacher among his fellow African Americans in the community. Hammon had also been educated in the household of his owners, and served as a bookkeeper in the family business. In 1761 his first work appeared in print, a poem titled "An Evening Thought: Salvation by Christ with Penitential Cries," which he had written on Christmas Day in 1760. Several other poems and three sermons were subsequently published. In 1786 Hammon appeared before the African Society in New York to deliver a speech on the subject of freedom. Published by the Quakers the following year, his "Address to the Negroes of the State of New York" was a landmark in African American efforts to achieve emancipation. While Hammon had personally come to accept his condition of servitude, he encouraged younger persons of African descent to work for their gradual emancipation. He lifted up education in particular, as well as the development of Christian virtues in one's personal life, as important means in this regard. Hammon drew on the recent experience of the War of Independence (also known as the Revolutionary War, or the American Revolution) that the colonies had undertaken against England to lift up the value of liberty, applying the experience to black people as well as to whites. There is only one heaven and one hell for blacks and whites alike, he noted. All are going to end up together in these places in the end.

In 1778 Hammon published a poem titled "An Address to Miss Phillis Wheatly" [sic]. The work was addressed to his younger contemporary, Phillis Wheatley (1753-1784), whose *Poems on Various Subjects, Religious and Moral* had been published five years earlier in 1773 in London. Wheatley was originally from Gambia, West Africa. At the age of eight she had been kidnapped by slave traders and sold to a family in Boston. Recognizing her intellectual gifts, her owners allowed her to be educated. Wheatley learned Greek and Latin at a young age, but became especially interested in English poetry. Two of her first poems, "An Address to the Atheist" and "An Address to the Deist," written in 1767 when she was fourteen years of age, illustrate well her religious convictions. The poem that first established her reputation, however, was "An Elegiac Poem, on the Death of that Celebrated Divine, and Eminent Servant of Jesus Christ, the Late Reverend, and Pious George Whitefield," which was published in the year of the revivalist's death in 1770. Wheatley was only seventeen years old at the time. The composition gained the attention of Whitefield's supporters not only in America but in England, giving her an immediate international reputation.

In 1773 Wheatley traveled to England with a member of her owner's household. There she was able to arrange for the publication of her entire collection of poems, making her the first African American woman to be published in either England or America. Returning to Boston that same year, she was eventually emancipated by the family with whom she lived. A decade later she married another free black in the city, but she died shortly after that in abject poverty and without having published any further works of poetry. Despite the shortness of her life, her impact was significant. Not least of her achievements was demonstrating that a woman of African descent could not only be educated but could write and publish.

In 1772 Wheatley was called to defend the authenticity of her work before a group of clergy in Boston that included Charles Chauncy, who was noted above. Chauncy and the others in the group found it hard to believe that a black woman had written such poems. She defended herself before their tribunal, demonstrating her ability to read in several languages and reciting works of poetry by heart. The names of her inquisitors appeared in the frontispiece of her book when it was published, making them witnesses to the authenticity of her work. Wheatley, like Hammon, supported the cause of emancipation. Like many others, she struggled to understand the enslavement of Africans through a lens of divine providence. God was at work in the situation, she believed, seeking to bring new order through the chaos that had engulfed Africa and its peoples. In every human breast, however, God had implanted a desire for freedom that was impatient with oppression and panted for freedom, Wheatley wrote in one of her letters. Not incidentally, that letter was part of an exchange with the first Native American to publish in English and a Presbyterian clergyperson, Samson Occom (1723-1792), who is noted below.

Missions to Native Americans in the eastern colonies

Native Americans were steadily relegated to the frontiers of colonial life in North America over the course of the eighteenth century. The steady expansion of European immigrants had the effect of pushing this frontier continuously westward over the century. Concern for the rights and well-being of Native Americans was scarce, even among church leaders of the period. There were notable exceptions, but for the most part the history of Christian encounters with Indian communities in the English colonies was a tragic affair.

Amid that backdrop the notable exceptions were significant. As was noted earlier, Moravians in South Africa had become concerned for the fate of enslaved Africans in America. This led them to take their mission efforts to the Caribbean. In 1735 the first Moravians landed in Georgia, where they intended to work among the descendants of Africans and the Native American community. In 1741 the Moravians purchased a track of land in Pennsylvania owned by George Whitefield. Whitfield had been purchasing land during his revival tour, and had an agent managing the properties. The Moravians bought over five hundred acres on which they established two communities, which they named Bethlehem and Nazareth. Their main objective was to establish a mission to the Lenape peoples in eastern Pennsylvania.

August Spangenberg (1704-1792) was assigned leadership of the new effort. Two decades later Spangenberg purchased 100,000 acres of land in North Carolina from its English owner and led the expedition to survey and develop the tract, which he called Wachau and which later became known as Wachovia. Moravians began settling in what is now the Winston-Salem area of North Carolina, leading to a second center for their life and work in North America. From these two main centers, Moravians sent out additional missionaries to Georgia, Delaware, Ohio, Indiana, New York, and Connecticut.

One of the better-known Moravian leaders in these efforts was David Zeisberger (1721-1808), who worked among the Lenape and Iroquois and Delaware for six decades. One of his most significant accomplishments was a Christian village he established in Ohio that was known as Shoenbrunn ("Beautiful Spring"). At its peak over four hundred members of the Lenape people lived, worked, and worshipped there. The village had sixty dwellings, including a church building, and a civil code was drawn up for the community, the first such legal code in Ohio. The village was abandoned in 1777 during the War of Independence, and Zeisberger led some of the former residents later to Ontario, where they lived peacefully in a settlement named Gnadenhütten ("Shielded by Grace").

Although the Moravian missions were not large in number, their impact was significant. Moravians were responsible for the education of almost all the Cherokee leaders in Georgia. They participated regularly in negotiations regarding land rights and business deals with Native Americans in Georgia. The personal journals of Moravians from Bethlehem, Nazareth, and other communities they founded contain numerous accounts of these encounters and provide a rich body of documentation for Native American encounters with European immigrants during the period.

The Collegiate School was founded in 1701 in response to what its supporters perceived to be the growing theological laxness of Harvard. Yale College, as the school was soon known, also played an important role in training several missionaries who sought to take Christianity to the Native American community. John Sergeant (1710-1749) graduated from Yale in 1729 and began working with the Housatonics in western Massachusetts five years later. He became fluent in the Algonkian (Algonquian) dialect and translated a number of catechetical works to support the evangelizing effort. Sergeant regarded the culture of his Native American interlocutors with considerable disdain. He advocated the removal of Native American children from their families in order to board them in special schools that would teach them English culture, a necessary component in his mind to Christianization. Jonathan Edwards succeeded Sergeant in the position at Stockbridge after the latter's death.

David Brainerd (1718-1747) also attended Yale for a time, although he was expelled before he could graduate for voicing strong opinions regarding the spiritual condition of several of his teachers. Brainerd worked for a while with Sergeant in Stockbridge, Massachusetts, before accepting a call from the Presbytery of Newark, New Jersey, to open a mission to the Lenape in western New Jersey with support coming from Scotland. Eventually his congregation numbered around 150. Tashawaylennahan, better known as Chief Moses Tunda Tatamy (c. 1690-1760), was the first Lenape whom Brainerd baptized as he launched the work. Tashawaylennahan had purchased land from the descendants of William Penn in the Lehigh Valley of Pennsylvania near the Delaware River and gathered a small community of Lenape on it. Following his death the land, known as Tatamy Place (now the borough of Tatamy, Pennsylvania), was seized by its European neighbors. Early in the twenty-first century the land was the subject of legal action as descendants of the Lenape sought to reclaim it through court action. As for Brainerd, tuberculosis forced him to relinquish his pastoral charge in 1746. He spent the last year of his life as a guest in the home of Jonathan Edwards in Northampton, where he died. Edwards's biography of him, *An Account of the Life of the Late Reverend Mr. David Brainerd*, first published in 1749, came to exercise a great deal of international influence on Protestant missions in subsequent years.

Eleazer Wheelock (1711-1779) graduated from Yale in 1733. Two years later he accepted the call to become the pastor of the Second Congregational Church of Lebanon, Connecticut, a charge he held for the next thirty-five years. A strong supporter of the Awakening, Wheelock was also a firm proponent of education and had opened a school for learning Latin in his home. His life changed dramatically in 1743 when a young Algonquian-speaking Mohegan named Samson Occom (1723-1792) came to his school. Occom was from the area of New London, Connecticut, and had recently been converted in one of the revival services conducted in the region. He had heard of Wheelock's school and had come to study divinity. For four years Occom worked under Wheelock's tutelage before launching out on his own. He eventually was ordained by the Presbytery of Suffolk in Long Island, New York, in 1759. In 1766 Wheelock convinced Occom to make a trip to England to raise funds for a new school Wheelock was seeking to found to teach both Native Americans and European immigrants. The trip was successful, and in 1769 Dartmouth College opened its doors in Hanover, New Hampshire. Occom and Wheelock soon parted ways, however, over what Occom perceived to be the slacking commitment of the school to the education of Native Americans. In 1786 Occom moved with a group of Native Americans from Long Island on to territory of the Oneida in upstate New York where they founded Brothertown as a Christian village.

Occom is widely regarded as the first Native American to publish works in English, which include *A Short Narrative of My Life* (1768) and *A Choice Collection of Hymns and Spiritual Songs* (1774). Several unpublished manuscripts are still held in the New London Historical Society. In the 1770s he exchanged letters with Phillis Wheatley, the African American poet noted above. One of her letters to him, published in the *Connecticut Gazette* in 1774, indicates that they shared a strong opposition to slavery and a concern for the treatment of Native Americans and African Americans alike.

Missions to Native Americans in the West

While graduates of Yale and others were undertaking a new round of mission work among Native Americans in the eastern regions of North America, in the Far West it was Franciscans who were opening new efforts to bring Christianity to the indigenous peoples in the eighteenth century. The Catholic mission to California was part of the overall effort to extend Spanish colonial sovereignty along the western seacoast of what is now divided between Mexico and the United States. In the eighteenth century this region, along with what was known as New Mexico, was part of Spanish America. The fact that it is territorially part of North America, however, and today is a part of the United States, suggests it be considered as part of this larger story.

By the eighteenth century the Catholic Church was institutionally well established throughout most of Central and South America. In the region known as California, which includes what today is divided between the states of Baja California in Mexico, and California, Nevada, and Arizona in the United States, Christianity was still in a period of initial expansion. The Spanish first landed in Baja California in Mexico in the 1530s. A decade later their ships explored the coast farther north. Much of the area they found to be desert or inaccessible coastline, discouraging them from any significant settlement efforts for the time being. Franciscans established a mission presence throughout the region known as New Mexico in the sixteenth century, but had not gone farther west into California. It was not until Russia began expanding its presence to the north along the coast of what is now Alaska in the 1740s that Spain decided it needed to increase its colonial presence in California as a political countermove.

The first mission effort in California was led by the Jesuit Eusebio Francisco Kino (1644-1711). Born in the north of Italy, and educated in Austria and Germany, he entered the Jesuit order in 1677 and was sent to New Spain as a missionary in 1681. Shortly after arriving in Mexico he changed the spelling of his name from Chini, as it was originally in Italy, to Kino, by which he was known thereafter. From his first effort to establish a mission in San Bruno in Baja California in 1683 until his death in 1711 in what is now the state of Sonora in Mexico, Kino was an indefatigable missionary, explorer, educator, agricultural pioneer, and human rights advocate. Some fifteen missions were eventually established under his leadership, while his exploration of the geography of the region resulted in the publication of numerous maps. His defense of the rights of the indigenous people in the region, known as Pimas, and his opposition to slavery earned him the trust of the local population. His efforts to open roads and chart the rivers increased trade and led to overall economic development throughout the region. Kino introduced a number of agricultural techniques and a variety of new seeds that improved farming and the quality of life among the Pimas. He is often remembered as the "apostle" to the region by Christians there today.

In 1767 the Jesuits were expelled from Mexico by order of the king of Spain. A year later the *visitador general*, who was appointed by the king of Spain to oversee religious affairs in the colonial regions, handed the responsibility for the California missions over to the Franciscans. A few months later he appointed the Dominicans to take charge of these missions in Baja California and instructed the Franciscans to open up a new effort to the north in Alta California among the Chumash, Salinan, and Ohlone peoples. In 1769 the first of these new Franciscan missions was founded in San Diego. A small contingent of Spanish troops accompanied them, building a fort that almost immediately attracted the attention of local indigenous Native Americans. The variety of Spanish metal goods proved to be an initial attraction to the local peoples, but conflict soon erupted between the local population and Spanish troops. The Franciscans decided to move their mission several miles away from the Spanish fort to distance themselves from the troops. A few baptisms were recorded, and several Native Americans came to dwell in the Franciscan mission; but conversions were generally slow. The major obstacle the Franciscans faced came from the behavior of Spanish troops in the area, who committed a number of atrocities in the surrounding villages. At one point several years after it had been initially established, the Franciscan mission itself was burned to the ground, but the Franciscans rebuilt and continued their efforts.

The first leader of the Franciscan effort in California was Junípero Serra (1713-1784), who, shortly after starting a mission in San Diego, opened a second in Monterey. A year later in 1771 he moved the site of that work to the Carmel Valley in order to be closer to the local villages. The mission, known as San Carlos Borromeo de Carmelo, became the center of the Franciscan project, which eventually resulted in the establishment of twenty-one missions along the California coast reaching as far north as San Francisco. Funding came from a special offering that had been started in Spain for these purposes. Typically, several Franciscans under an appointed superior would identify a suitable site on which they would build a central church and several additional surrounding buildings in which they would dwell. The missionaries would often bring an initial cache of items that they would use to trade with local populations, thereby establishing contact. Members of these local communities would then be invited to come and live in and around the missions in order to learn to be Christian. The Franciscans would introduce new crops and construction skills. Eventually they would establish schools. The original plan that Serra devised called for a secular priest to be sent within ten years of the founding of a mission and a large portion of the work to be turned over to local leadership, but the Franciscans soon found that to be an unrealistic plan. Secularization did not come about until several decades into the nineteenth century.

There were some reports that suggest the Franciscans employed tactics that were harsher than an invitation, that they captured members of the local population and forced them into labor. An account by a French visitor to California in 1786 reports that the Franciscans treated the local people like little children, putting them in stocks for behavioral infractions and using corporal punishment. They expected the local people who had joined the mission to follow a rigorous spiritual discipline that called for seven hours of labor and two hours of prayer each day, with four to five hours of prayer on Sundays and feast days. Without question, harsh methods of coercion were at times employed by the Franciscans, but it was not the general practice. And while the spiritual discipline of the Franciscans was undeniably rigorous, it was not unlike that of other Franciscan communities around the world. Compared to the history of other mission efforts in America before the nineteenth century, the Franciscan effort in California was relatively peaceful.

Far more problematic for the mission effort was the growing military presence of the Spanish in the region. Accompanying Serra on his first visit in 1769 was Gaspar de Portolà i Rovira (1716-1786), who had been appointed governor of the entire California region (Baja and Alta). A short time after establishing his fort at San Diego, Portolà continued north along the coast, establishing a Spanish military presence before resigning his charge in 1770. The next governor, Pedro Fages Beleta (1734-1794), quickly began to clash with Serra. In 1773 Serra traveled back to Mexico City to file formal charges against Fages before the viceroy. Thirty of the thirty-two charges were upheld, and Fages was removed. Nevertheless, conflicts continued to be reported between the military and the missionaries.

Despite such problems, by the end of the century the Franciscan mission effort in California was firmly established. The Spanish military presence meanwhile continued to grow as well. In 1804 Spain separated Baja California from Alta California administratively, prefiguring what would eventually become the border between Mexico and the United States in the region. Winds of change were blowing. From the east, the former British colonies along the Atlantic seacoast from Georgia to New England had successfully fought a war of independence and were establishing themselves as a new nation. Russian, French, and English were all becoming more involved in the politics of the Pacific. In California, the missions served as a mediating presence between Native Americans and the wider global political forces that were affecting local lives. They would not be able to continue to do so as effectively in the nineteenth century, which brought rapid changes to the region. Nevertheless, the basis of Catholic Christianity in California was well enough established to survive these new cultural winds of the next century.

To the east of California, the eighteenth century was a time of conflict and declining Spanish colonial control in the territory known as New Mexico. Franciscans began to establish their work in New Mexico at the end of the sixteenth century, but open revolt broke out in 1680, forcing for a time both the Spanish military and the Franciscans to withdraw from most of the region. Spain quickly reconquered the area, but the Franciscans were forced to allow greater autonomy among their indigenous charges, including greater expressions of indigenous religious practices.

The Pueblos among whom the Franciscans worked were in fact a variety of tribes or peoples. Most were primarily agricultural workers. The Pueblos occupied themselves mostly with farming, supplementing their food supply with hunting. By the eighteenth century they were also trading, among themselves but also with the Spanish, who took goods to markets in Mexico and Spain. Seeking to increase their presence to the north of the territory, the Spanish also offered land grants to individuals who would farm or raise livestock. New towns such as Chimayó, located halfway between Santa Fe and Taos, were the result. The numbers of new settlers these efforts brought to the region were not large, but the economic effects were nevertheless significant. The combined pressures of increased Spanish military presence seeking to protect these new settlers, a growing economy, and the perceived weakness of the Pueblos that the Franciscans served helped to draw increased attention from other nations in the region, including the Comanche, Navajo, Apache, and Utes. By the middle of the century, the Comanche had become the dominant power among the various Native

American nations. Their regular raids on Spanish towns and Franciscan missions were a constant threat to the efforts of settlers and missionaries alike.

During the last decades of the century, the Spanish took a more aggressive stance, launching a major raid in 1779 against Comanche forces near Pueblo, Colorado. Skirmishes with the Comanche continued for another seven years until a peace treaty was finally signed in 1786. One effect the constant warfare had upon the churches was to prevent any further Catholic mission efforts among these various nations that were at war with the Spanish. The generally nomadic life of the Apache and the Comanche as well did not allow for the kind of settled mission that the Franciscans had established in New Mexico. Finally Spanish preoccupation with European political events prevented full-fledged military expansion of the colonial effort north of the New Mexico territory, leaving the region steadily plagued by warfare.

Christianity in New Mexico during the eighteenth century was undergoing a steady process of becoming the religion of the indigenous. The Franciscan missions had been successful in part in bringing various Pueblo peoples into the church. Some of the new settlers who moved to the region were *criollos* of European descent, but far more were *mestizos*, of mixed European and indigenous descent. Another group that came to make up a significant part of the population in New Mexico were called *genízaros*. These were Native Americans of various nations who had been taken captive, mostly as children and mostly by the Comanche, and sold into slavery to the Spanish who employed them mostly for herding. While virtually all Native American nations from the region, including Comanche themselves, were represented among them, a large percentage had been Navajos. Most of them eventually achieved emancipation after a number of years of work. Having been raised as Spanish, however, they did not return to their original communities. Instead they resettled throughout New Mexico, especially along the frontier areas where the Comanche and others continued to raid. Most *genízaros* in the eighteenth century were Catholic, having adopted both Spanish culture and religion, although there were constant reports among priests that accused them of continuing to follow traditional Native American practices, which the priests considered "witchcraft."

The War of Independence

Whatever side one might have been on regarding the methods of the Great Awakening and their theological underpinnings, the experience had been one of the first to cross the boundaries separating the English colonies along the eastern seaboard of North America. A new national identity was appearing. Fanning the flames of this new identity were ideas of liberty and equality that emanated from Europe, more from the Scottish Enlightenment than from continental Europe. Equality in particular was proving to be an ambiguous notion. Some defended these notions of liberty as extending to all human beings, but for the most part the conversation of the period assumed that full political liberty and the right to vote applied only to those who were land-holding members of the educated classes, who were the most powerful element in colonial society. The rise of a new, educated merchant class was allowing colonists to begin rethinking the notion that the landed aristocracy alone ought to enjoy such rights.

Against this background the mercantilist constraints imposed by English government on its colonies, which led the English ruling class to view the colonies as existing primarily to produce wealth for the crown, were causing conflict. A significant number of colonial leaders on the American side of the Atlantic by the 1760s were feeling economically, if not politically, oppressed by their English rulers. Pastors in the colonies began to pick up the theme. By the 1760s a number of them were including references to political events in their catechetical instructions or in their sermons on Sunday mornings. The new political rhetoric was being drawn mainly from Puritan covenant theology but was linked to what in English political theory had been an antiroyalist Whig ideology. Their opponents on both sides of the Atlantic, who supported the royalty and hereditary forms of government, came to be called Tories.

The Puritan concept of a divine covenant entailed not only the individual's relationship with God but the relationship of a people or nation. From the 1620s in Massachusetts the notion had taken root that the colonists, like ancient Israel, had entered into a special covenant relationship with God that entailed on the colonists' part the obligation to live responsibly before God to be a light to the nations. Such a divine covenant took precedence over obedience to kings at times, especially when the king was far enough removed in England to impede enforcement of royal decrees, or when royal decrees were determined to be contrary to what the Puritans deemed to be revealed of the divine will. The notion of being a chosen people trusted by God with a historical mission found expression in the Great Awakening among such proponents as Jonathan Edwards. By the middle of the eighteenth century these ideas were being mixed with the new political theories emerging from the Enlightenment that emphasized the contractual nature of the social covenant between governors and the governed. Preachers added to this the doctrine of original sin, which emphasized the need for checks on the powers of rulers. Uncontrolled political power, these preachers reminded their hearers, opened the door to uncontrolled evil. It was the duty of citizens to resist such unchecked powers and to separate themselves from such evil. The result was a unique American form of civil religious discourse that helped define an emerging nation as special, but not unrestrained.

Both Congregationalists and Anglicans had relied on the legal establishment of their churches for support during the colonial period. Roman Catholics for a time had seen their church legally established in Maryland, but by the eighteenth century they had been displaced by the Anglicans there as well. Quakers had been established in Pennsylvania, but allowed a significant degree of toleration. Baptists and Presbyterians were not established. Both had begun to develop congregations apart from official establishment or recognition by secular government. The voluntary principle of church membership took hold during the Great Awakening to a significant extent. The notion of religious freedom became part of the wider package of freedoms that were becoming discussed in various colonial legislative assemblies.

North America had seen a decade of war between English and French armies and their various allies on either side among Native American nations. At issue was control of the lucrative trade around the Great Lakes, through the Ohio River Valley, and down the Mississippi River. One of the military leaders of the Virginia militia who fought on the side of the English was Major George Washington (1732-1799). When he was not serving in the militia, Washington was a planter who raised tobacco as well as other crops. Washington owned a number of slaves, although he left provisions in his will for their emancipation and support.

Following the war between England and France, the issue of taxes began to heat up in the colonies. The English crown in particular was in need of funds, and the wealth of the merchants in its thirteen American colonies was simply too inviting not to become the object of legislation. From the colonists' side these taxes came to be seen by a significant number of leaders as increasingly unfair. Not only were they excessive, but they seemed to violate an established English legal principle of the participation of the governed in the decisions of government, including the imposition of taxes. The ideas of radical republicanism began to take hold, voiced by Patrick Henry (1736-1799) in Virginia, Samuel Adams (1722-1803) and John Hancock (1737-1793) in Boston, and Benjamin Franklin (1706-1790) and Thomas Paine (1737-1809) in Philadelphia. Hancock was reportedly the wealthiest person in the American colonies at the time, an indication of the support the new republican ideas held among the merchant class.

Open hostility between the colonies and England broke out outside Boston in 1775. A gathering of representative legislators from most of the colonies had gathered in Philadelphia the previous year and petitioned the English crown for relief, to no avail. Delegates from all thirteen colonies gathered again in a Second Continental Congress in 1775 and continued to meet through the following year when on July 4, 1776, they signed a "Declaration of Independence" that had been drafted by Thomas Jefferson (1743-1826). The document cited what it called "the Laws of Nature and of Nature's God" as justifying the dissolution of the political bonds between the colonies and England. All human beings are created equal, the document stated, and are endowed by their creator with a number of inalienable rights, including life, liberty, and the pursuit of happiness. When a government becomes destructive of these rights, it is the right of the governed to alter or abolish it. The die was cast. The colonies were in full rebellion. George Washington was appointed commander in chief of the Continental army.

War lasted until 1781, when the last British army in North America was trapped in Yorktown between troops of the Continental Congress and a French fleet that had come to the aid of the revolutionaries at the last moment. In a peace treaty signed in Paris in 1783, England ceded all claim to its colonies south of the Great Lakes and east of the Mississippi. The former colonies were left on their own to develop a new national structure for governance and the place of religion in society. What became the principle of extending freedom of religion to all churches came into being, however, not so much because of theological conviction that it was the right thing to do as much as the realization that freedom for one's own church would be uncertain if freedom was not also granted to others. And the theoretical grant of religious freedom to all, really meant freedom for Protestants and other non-Roman Christian groups. Practically speaking, both Jews and Catholics found themselves considered interlopers in a Protestant ascendancy.

Freedom of religion in the new nation

Three years after the signing of the Peace of Paris, representatives from several of these former colonies gathered in Philadelphia, this time to draw up Articles of Confederation that were intended to provide the framework for a new national government. The result of this first effort was soon perceived to be a failure due mostly to the weakness of its central government. In 1787 delegates from the various former colonies gathered again in Philadelphia, this time to hammer out a new framework. By the end of the year they had drafted a new Constitution. James Madison (1751-1836) of Virginia was its main author.

This new Constitution called for the former colonies to unite to form a new nation, to be known as the United States. The government would be divided into three branches, handling legislative, executive, and judicial functions. A series of checks and balances assured that no one branch could dominate the other two. The legislative branch was divided into a Senate and a House of Representatives, with representatives elected from the various states according to different formulas that balanced the power of larger states against that of smaller ones. The head of the executive branch, known as the president, was to be chosen by an electoral college made up of delegates who had been elected by the individual states for this purpose. Members of the judiciary were chosen by a process that involved both of the other two branches, and were guaranteed independence by serving for life.

The new Constitution made no provision for a king or other form of hereditary ruler. Instead, all offices were to be filled by either election or appointment, based on the will of the people. The preamble of the new Constitution showed a pronounced historical debt in this regard to the covenantal tradition of Puritan theology. "We the People of the United States, in Order to form a more perfect Union," read its opening line, echoing a tradition of church covenants that stretched back to Salem, Massachusetts, more than 150 years before. This did not mean, however, that that framers of the new Constitution envisioned universal suffrage. Only males were allowed to vote or hold office under the new Constitution, and among males, only those of European descent, not African Americans. The soaring rhetoric of inalienable rights of all that had infused the War for Independence was now a thing of the past. Not only did the new Constitution recognize the legality of chattel slavery in the new nation, but for the purposes of calculating the population, it called for African-Americans to be counted as only three-fifths of a person.

The Constitution was set to take effect after nine of the new states had ratified it. Three did so before the end of 1787, with nine more doing so the following year, enough to put the new government into motion. Delegates to the electoral college were selected late in 1788, and in the spring 1789 they in turn met to elect George Washington to serve as the first president of the nation. The Constitution called for a new federal district that was not a part of any state to be created as the capital for the new government. A site measuring ten miles by ten miles was selected by Washington on the border between Virginia and Maryland, and in 1791 the new city named Washington, in the federal District of Columbia, came into being as the capital of the new nation.

Prior to ratifying the Constitution, a number of states had set as a condition for doing so the inclusion of a set of provisions that were intended to strengthen the rights of individual citizens over against the new, more powerful federal government. To Madison again fell the task of drafting these amendments, ten of them in all, that were approved by the states in 1791 following the process set forth in the body of the original Constitution.

One of the most notable elements of the new political order, inscribed in the First Amendment of the new Constitution, was the prohibition against an established religion in the new nation. The United States was the first nation-state rooted in the European reality of Christendom to so disestablish Christianity. Some European nations had relaxed restrictions and increased the degree of toleration that was practiced regarding religious diversity, but in all of them some church was officially established as the religion of the state. Now in these new United States was enshrined the principle that the government could neither establish any form of religion nor prohibit the free exercise of any form of religion.

Thomas Jefferson was one of the major proponents of disestablishment in the new nation. Several years earlier he had promoted a Bill for Religious Freedom in Virginia that foreshadowed the First Amendment of the U.S. Constitution in this regard. For Jefferson, freedom of religion entailed freedom from both coercion and compulsion in matters of faith. It meant the freedom to express any religion an individual may choose to follow, or the freedom not to be religious, making it in effect legal to be an atheist. For Jefferson and others in the period, the range of religion that they had in view was the diverse forms of Christianity and Judaism. They were not without awareness that there were other religions in the world, but Jefferson and the other framers of the Constitution assumed that Christianity would continue to be the dominant religion in the United States. Nevertheless, they did not move to limit the definition of accepted religions to Christian and Jewish traditions. Instead, they left open the possibility of the freedom to practice Islam and Eastern religions, as well as the right of Native Americans to retain their indigenous religious traditions. Religion would continue to play an important role in the civic life of the new nation. A general recognition of God as creator and governor of history, more compatible with Deism at times than with traditional forms of orthodox Christianity or Judaism, found expression in numerous ways in the public discourse of the new nation. As a matter of law, however, religion was left to one's own individual choice and reason, causing the entire question of religion to migrate in no small degree from the public to the private realm of affairs in national life.

The varieties of religion in the early United States

Among those most affected by disestablishment in the new nation were Jews and Catholics. There were approximately two thousand Jews living in the United States at the time of its formation. Most were of Spanish or Portuguese descent, and most were living in New York, Philadelphia, Charleston, South Carolina, or Newport, Rhode Island. Jews had first come to Newport in the middle of the seventeenth century. By the middle of the eighteenth century they had organized themselves into a congregation that they called Yeshuat Israel ("Salvation of Israel") and in 1763 completed building a synagogue. At the time of the War of Independence there were thirty families in the community. Most made their living as merchants, clerks, or ship owners. Several had come from Portugal where they had lived as Christians, but after arriving in Newport they had reclaimed their Jewish identity, in some cases undergoing ritual circumcision.

In August of 1790, Moses Seixas (1744-1809), the warden of the synagogue in Newport, Rhode Island, presented a letter to President Washington that he wrote on behalf of the congregation on the occasion of the new president's visit to the city. The children of the "Stock of Abraham," the letter began, joined with the other citizens of the city to welcome the president to Newport. While they had been deprived of the rights of citizenship in the past, it went on, they applauded the fact that the new government now promised to extend the rights of citizenship to all people, refusing to sanction bigotry or persecution. God was at work in these affairs of state, the letter affirmed, for which the members of the congregation gave thanks. As the angel had guided their ancestors through the wilderness to the promised land, so may the president be guided through difficulties and dangers of these days, it concluded. Washington replied shortly after that with a letter of his own addressed to the congregation. He affirmed the full citizenship of the members of the community and echoed Seixas's sentiments that there be no sanction of bigotry or persecution in the new nation. He concluded by wishing the children of the "Stock of Abraham" good will, praying that the "father of all mercies" not only shed light upon all, but bring all to everlasting happiness. Both letters were later published in the New London *Connecticut Gazette*.

A month before the exchange of letters with the Jewish community in Newport, Washington penned a letter to several prominent Roman Catholics from Maryland who had written earlier to congratulate him on his election as president. Chief among the signatories of the letter of congratulations was John Carroll (1735-1815), who only four months earlier in 1789 had become the first bishop of the newly formed Roman Catholic diocese of Baltimore. Washington was well acquainted with Carroll and the other prominent Catholic leaders who had signed the letter. His reply noted his hope that as the human race became more liberal, they would increasingly recognize that all are equally entitled to the protections of government. He recalled the support the new nation had received from Roman Catholics during its recent War of Independence, and especially the role they had played in securing the support of the Roman Catholic nation of France.

Carroll had been born in Maryland. The son of a prominent business family, he went to Belgium for his education where he became a Jesuit. With the suppression of the Jesuit order in 1773, Carroll returned to Maryland and organized the parish of St. John the Evangelist, in what is now Silver Spring, which he served as priest. The British colonies in North America were considered mission territories by Rome and were under the ecclesiastical jurisdiction of the vicar apostolic of London, England, itself at the time having no dioceses but considered mission territory as well by Rome. At the time of Carroll's return there were only twenty-one other priests serving in Maryland and Pennsylvania, the two colonies that had shown the greatest degree of toleration toward Roman Catholics. Most of these priests were German in background, and like Carroll were Jesuits. While some were settled, most carried on itinerant ministries, traveling from town to town to serve the pastoral needs of Roman Catholics scattered through the colonies. There were no women's religious communities in the English colonies. Women who sought to pursue religious vocations had to go elsewhere to join a community.

During the War of Independence Carroll had supported the colonists' effort. At one point he had even been tapped to join a delegation along with his cousin, Charles Carroll (1737-1832), who was the only Catholic to sign the Declaration of Independence and a member of the Continental Congress representing Maryland, to go to Montreal to seek French support for the revolutionary effort. With the end of the war and independence from England secured, the question of apostolic oversight for the Catholics in the new nation was up in the air. The clergy of Maryland petitioned Rome for the appointment of a Superior of the Missions, which was granted in 1784. Carroll was appointed to the position. Four years later the priests again petitioned Rome, this time requesting permission to elect one from among their ranks to become a full bishop, thereby elevating their territory to the rank of diocese. Permission was granted, and in 1789 Carroll was elected first by the clergy and then confirmed by Rome as the bishop of Baltimore, the first Roman Catholic bishop in the United States. Two years later he convened the first synod with all his twenty-two priests participating.

One of Carroll's major concerns was for education. Shortly after being named Superior of the Missions, he began plans for a school for young people. A plot of land near the Potomac River just outside the village of Georgetown was secured in 1789, and two years later under the direction of several former Jesuits, Georgetown Academy, later known as Georgetown College, opened it doors. While the school was under Roman Catholic leadership, it was open to students of all religious professions from its inception. Two years later, now-Bishop Carroll took up the matter of training priests for the new diocese. This time he turned to the Society of Saint-Sulpice in France. In 1791 four Sulpicians opened the doors of St. Mary's Seminary in a former tavern that Carroll purchased on the edge of the city of Baltimore. Five students came from France to form the first class.

Carroll was committed to a church with an American identity. He supported the notion of a pluralistic state in which no religious body would be established. Often he had to defend the Catholic religion against attacks from Protestants who were opposed to Catholics sharing equally in the new nation. He was a tireless promoter of the reading of scriptures and was instrumental in getting an Irish immigrant named Mathew Carey (1760-1839), who owned a printing shop in Philadelphia, to publish the Rome-approved Douay-Rheims translation of the Bible for English readers in America. Carroll also promoted the use of English for portions of the liturgy in worship services in Catholic churches in America. In 1806 he oversaw the beginning of construction on the Cathedral of the Assumption, which was finally completed in 1820, five years after his death. In 1808 Baltimore was elevated to the ranks of an archdiocese with four other dioceses formed in Boston, New York, Philadelphia, and Bardstown, Kentucky. Archbishop Carroll ordained bishops for these new dioceses and convened the first provincial council in 1810. By the time of his death the Roman Catholic Church was firmly in place in the United States.

Among the many letters Washington received wishing him and the new nation well through the years of his presidency were a number that were from various Masonic lodges located throughout the colonies. Washington had been baptized as a child in the Church of England in Virginia. During his time in Philadelphia, during the first Continental Congress, he had attended a variety of religious services, including those of Quakers and Roman Catholics. Washington was also a Freemason, a quasi-religious organization which by the 1790s had secured a firm place in American civic life.

Freemasonry had obscure origins in European society prior to the eighteenth century. Adherents claim to have descended from ancient secret societies with rituals passed down from the days of Solomon and the building of the Temple, or from Egypt and the building of the Great Pyramids. The documented history of Freemasonry traces the movement to the labor guilds of European cities that emerged in the period between 1000 and 1500 C.E. Skilled workers were free to travel from city to city, unlike many others who were often tied by social custom as well as law to the lands on which they had been born. The lodges or housing that these workers occupied functioned as community centers. These lodges gradually assumed more and more social functions and became fraternities. With the development of cities, they also took on aspects of esoteric societies, and after 1600 became in many places associated with the emerging new middle class of merchants and their intellectual supporters in the Enlightenment. In 1717, four of these lodges in London came together to form a Grand Lodge with a constitution that established a uniform order and set of rituals. The Grand Lodge began issuing charters to those seeking to organize other lodges under its leadership. Freemasonry as a fraternal movement emerged from that gathering, with secret initiation ceremonies, degrees of membership, founding charters from a recognized mother lodge, and a body of rituals that employ highly religious symbols.

Freemasonry spread to England's colonies in the 1730s. Benjamin Franklin was elected grand master of the Philadelphia lodge in 1734. Washington joined in 1752. In 1775 a free African American named Prince Hall (c. 1735-1807), along with fourteen other African Americans living in Boston, were initiated into an English Freemason lodge by British soldiers. After the English soldiers left, they continued to meet as a separate lodge under the charter they received. From Boston the movement spread to other cities as free African Americans began organizing separate lodges under charter from the original lodge in Boston. In 1791 members of these various lodges organized the African Grand Lodge of North America and elected Prince Hall as its first grand master.

Freemasonry played a significant role in civic life in the early years of the American republic. Freemasonry borrowed heavily from religious life in developing its rituals. It shared with Deism and other religious movements of the European Enlightenment a basic belief in a supreme being who governs the universe, and did not hesitate to identify this being with the God of Christian and Jewish traditions. Candidates for membership in a lodge were expected to express their belief in God. According to tradition, at the last moment before his first inauguration, Washington borrowed a King James Version of the Bible from a local Masonic lodge in New York City to place his hand upon while swearing his oath of office.

In many ways Freemasonry served as a civil religion. Freemason symbols appeared on the currency of the new nation. The symbol of the eye within a pyramid that was incorporated into the currency of the new nation was borrowed from Masonic tradition. Washington incorporated Masonic rituals into the ceremony accompanying the laying of the cornerstone for a new federal capitol building in 1793, and after his death his funeral service included both Christian and Masonic rites. The common use of such Masonic symbols and terminology especially concerning the supreme deity helped establish a more general religious language without establishing any particular church.

Forming new churches

The War of Independence brought a series of far-reaching changes to American religious life. Not least of these was the establishment of an independent Episcopal Church apart from the Church of England. Most of the priests serving congregations in the English colonies had remained loyal to England during the war, despite the fact that a significant number of those leading the independence effort were baptized members of the Church of England. By the end of the war these congregations were in disarray. Many loyalists had chosen to depart with the British troops from cities like Boston and New York. One loyalist who remained was Samuel Seabury (1729-1796). Originally from Connecticut, he had been ordained to the priesthood in England and had served in New Jersey and New York. In 1783 a group of clergy in Connecticut decided that the time had come for there to be a bishop on American soil. Seabury was elected to the position.

Four months later he set sail for England to undergo consecration, only to find out that as an American he was unqualified to be consecrated because of the requirement that bishops in the Church of England take an oath of loyalty to the king. The Scottish church on the other hand had no such requirement, so late in 1784 Seabury was consecrated in Aberdeen. Seabury returned to Connecticut, where the following year he began ordaining clergy for the American churches. He brought with him the Scottish Rite, which he continued to use for the Eucharistic liturgy in place of the English Rite that had been mostly used before. In England, meanwhile, the government changed its requirements to allow future bishops for foreign churches to be ordained without taking an oath of loyalty to the English crown.

Two other bishops for the American church were ordained in England in 1787. Then two years later at a convention held in Philadelphia, representatives from across the new United States met to draw up a new constitution for an independent Episcopal Church. A new *Book of Common Prayer* was adopted for the American church shortly after that. In 1792 Seabury and others began consecrating bishops on American soil. The newly formed Episcopal Church continued to be in communion with the Church of England, but henceforth was an independent body with its own episcopal leadership, liturgy, and institutions of learning.

John Wesley had briefly served in Georgia in the 1730s before returning to England where he went on to become the driving force in the Methodist movement. Wesley had encountered the Moravians in Georgia and continued to carry on a relationship with them in England, even hosting Zinzendorf (1700-1760) upon the latter's visit to the island. Whitefield was part of the Methodist movement as well in England, although he and Wesley eventually parted ways over doctrinal differences. The evangelical revival that Whitefield, Edwards, and others had led in America waned through the middle decades of the eighteenth century in America, but it did not die out entirely. It became highly interconfessional, however, as a new generation of itinerant evangelists came of age. Zinzendorf, the leader of the Moravians, visited the English colonies and tried to unite the movement in 1742 by hosting the first meeting of what came to be called the "Pennsylvania Synod." More than one hundred persons from Lutheran, Reformed, Quaker, Mennonite, and Church of England confessional traditions participated. Eventually the effort came to naught, as leaders of these various communions differed with Zinzendorf over doctrine, or suspected him of merely seeking to build the Moravian ranks.

During the 1730s and 1740s, Moravians had been especially active among German settlers in eastern Pennsylvania. In response, a group of these settlers wrote to Halle asking for a regular Lutheran pastor to provide them with leadership. Heinrich Melchior Mühlenberg (1711-1787), a graduate of Halle and a committed Pietist, responded in 1742. Over the course of the next four decades Henry Muhlenberg, as he became known in English, organized new Lutheran churches, founded a ministerial synod, and worked to build stronger pastoral leadership for Lutherans up and down the eastern seaboard. Another graduate of Halle, John Christopher Hartwick (1714-1796), arrived in New York in 1746 to serve Lutheran settlers located along the Hudson River Valley near Rheinbeck, New York. He later moved to the region just south of Cooperstown, New York, to start a utopian community that bore his name. Upon his death Hartwick left funds to start a Lutheran school of theology, which opened in 1797 in New York City in the home of still another immigrant Lutheran pastor from Germany, John Christopher Kunze (1744-1807). Hartwick Seminary later moved to the town of Hartwick, where it continues as a college today.

The arrival of Methodists in America beginning in the 1760s provided the fan that helped rekindle the smoldering embers of evangelical revival and renewal. Robert Strawbridge (d. 1781) and his wife, Elizabeth Strawbridge (dates unknown), were from Ireland, where they had first joined the Methodist movement in the late 1750s. Robert became a lay preacher and gained a reputation for effectiveness. Sometime around 1760 the couple arrived in Maryland, settling as farmers just outside Baltimore. Within a few years they began holding Methodist meetings in their home. The first convert in North America to Methodism was recorded in 1763 under the ministry of Elizabeth, and the first Methodist baptisms were performed by Robert that same year. Robert also began traveling to other cities to preach in homes or on street corners. By 1766 Methodist groups were reported to have been organized by him in Baltimore and Georgetown. Strawbridge preached as far away as Philadelphia and Trenton, New Jersey. For the most part, those who gathered and continued to meet in these places had some previous exposure or involvement with the evangelical revivals dating back to the 1740s. Strawbridge's preaching became a catalyst for their renewal.

About the same time Strawbridge was arriving in Maryland, two cousins named Philip Embury (1729-1775) and Barbara Ruckle Heck (1734-1804), also from Ireland, were arriving in New York. Embury and Heck were German in national background. They were part of a larger community from the Palatine region that had gone to Ireland a generation or so earlier. A significant number of them had joined the Methodist connection after Wesley preached in Limerick in 1752. A carpenter by trade, Embury was also a lay preacher, but in New York the new immigrants did not immediately pursue their religious activities. Sometime in 1766, however, at the prompting of Heck, the group began to hold a Methodist class meeting in her home. One of these first members in New York was a slave whom the Hecks had purchased, a woman of African descent named Betty (dates unknown). The meetings grew, and the following year Heck and Embury had to move to a larger space. They eventually secured property on John Street in lower Manhattan on which to build a small chapel. The Wesley Chapel on John Street opened its doors in 1768 with more than four hundred people in attendance at the first services. Embury preached while Heck organized band meetings. Two years later, Heck and Embury resettled in upstate New York, where they gathered a fresh Methodist congregation. After the War of Independence, Heck moved on to Canada, where she ended her days in Ontario, leaving the work in New York to others to continue.

Thomas Webb (1724-1796) was a captain in the British Army who fought against the French in Canada in the 1750s. Converted at a Moravian worship service back in England, he joined a Wesleyan society in 1765, and although he had no formal training in theology, within a few months he was preaching at their services. A year later he decided to sell his commission in the army and cross the Atlantic again, this time to serve as a Methodist missionary. Webb joined Embury and Heck in New York City, but traveled as well to New Jersey and into Pennsylvania, where he quickly was able to organize a Methodist society in Philadelphia in 1767, drawing it from the wider Evangelical network in place in the city and building on the work of Strawbridge from the year before. In 1768

Webb was back in New York City for the completion of the new chapel on John Street, which he played a major role in helping to fund.

One of Webb's signature actions in his sermons was to place his sword upon his pulpit, telling his listeners that he was now a soldier for a different cause. The reminder of his former commission proved to be his undoing during the War of Independence, however. Webb was interned on suspicion of being a British spy. Only the direct intervention of George Washington allowed him to return to England in 1778, where he completed his days.

In England, John Wesley was kept abreast of these developments by reports from a variety of sources, including letters and firsthand accounts of other clergy-persons returning to Europe from America. In 1769 he sent three lay preachers, formally recognizing the work in America as a new circuit. That same year the Methodists in Philadelphia, who now numbered around three hundred, purchased an unfinished church from a German Reformed congregation on Fourth Street, renaming it St. George's. Two years later Wesley again sought volunteer preachers to help build the work in America. This time a young man name Francis Asbury (1745-1816) responded.

Asbury was from a working-class family background in England. At a young age he was already showing intellectual promise, this despite spending only a few short years in formal schooling. At fourteen, in response to the prompting of his mother, he began attending a Methodist society and was converted. By sixteen he was preaching, and at age twenty he entered the ranks of John Wesley's itinerant lay preachers. In 1771 he was only twenty-seven years of age when at the annual conference held at Bristol Wesley called for workers to go to America. He arrived in Philadelphia later that year, and by the end of 1772 had almost doubled the membership of the society there. Asbury began visiting the other Methodist societies in the colonies as well. Two years later he was joined by several other lay preachers whom Wesley sent, one of whom was designated as the head of the societies in America. It was Asbury, however, whom Wesley looked to as his general assistant for the work.

The War of Independence posed a significant challenge to the fledging work of the Methodist preachers in America, more so than it did for many other confessions. Methodists were still ecclesiastically regarded as part of the Church of England. Wesley was known to be a supporter of the crown and opposed the independence effort. Most of the Methodist leaders who had been sent from England left during the war. Only Asbury stayed, and he saw his movements curtailed in several states. Nevertheless, the Methodists survived. None of the preachers who had begun the work in America were formally ordained in the Church of England. Their ecclesiastical status derived from being appointed by Wesley as lay preachers and nothing more. This did not prevent them in some cases in America from performing baptisms and even administering the sacrament of Communion. Mostly, however, they ministered through preaching and holding regular revival meetings. Despite opposition, their societies continued to meet under local leadership through the war.

With the conclusion of the war, the Methodists faced the new challenge of being now part of an independent nation. Recognizing the need for more formal ecclesiastical structures, especially in regard to sacramental life, Wesley sought help from the hierarchy of the Church of England. Finding none coming, he took things upon himself to set in motion the development of an independent Methodist Episcopal Church. Thomas Coke (1747-1814) was a priest in the Church of England who had come into the Methodist connection in 1776. In 1782 Wesley appointed him head of the work in Ireland. Two years later Wesley appointed Coke superintendent of the work in America. Although Wesley was not a bishop, he proceeded to ordain two other members of his society as full elders or priests to work in America, claiming that the extraordinary need of his societies there warranted such a break with tradition. Coke was issued a further certificate for Asbury and dispatched to the new nation where Wesley intended Coke and Asbury to be cosuperintendents.

Upon his arrival, Coke met with Asbury, who refused to accept the appointment without the other Methodist preachers having a say. A conference was called for Baltimore for Christmas Eve, 1784. Some sixty Methodist preachers gathered at the event, whose first order of business was to address the question of leadership. They moved quickly. On Christmas Day, the conference ordained Asbury as a deacon. The following day, they held a service of ordination as elder Philip William Otterbein (1726-1813), a minister in the Reformed Church in Baltimore who had been ordained in Germany and had become well acquainted with the Methodists, joined with Coke in laying hands on Asbury. The third day the conference voted to make Asbury and Coke bishops, disregarding Wesley's directive to call them superintendents. A prayer book prepared by John Wesley was adopted, as was a modified set of Articles of Religion. The name "Methodist Episcopal Church" was adopted, and an additional twelve new preachers were ordained by the entire conference before it ended its work.

One of the preachers who attended the Christmas conference was an African American named Harry Hoosier (c. 1750-1808). A former slave who had been emancipated when his master had become Methodist, Hoosier had likewise become a Methodist and began traveling with Asbury as a servant. Sometime around 1780 Asbury began allowing Hoosier to preach to the African American slaves who attended the Methodist meetings with their European American masters. Hoosier usually followed Asbury with a sermon, although on several occasions he substituted for him. His fame as a preacher grew significantly, mostly for the emotional fervor that he brought to his sermons, but also for his tendency to weave the sermon and song together. Hoosier was unable to read, but he would memorize large passages of scripture that he could recite from heart when preaching. Even though he was said by some to be the greatest preacher in America at the time, he suffered repeatedly from discrimination, even from his own Methodist colleagues. Hoosier, for instance, was not allowed to join in the vote at the Baltimore Conference in 1784 because of his African identity.

Methodists were not the only group in America to ride the currents of the Great Awakening toward the end of the century. The Baptist movement in the English colonies had likewise been given a boost by the evangelical impulses of the mid-century revivals. Among Baptists, Methodists, and other evangelical groups, conversion took the place of catechism as the pathway to church membership. The same pattern was repeated in determining preparation and fitness for ministry. Churches that identified with the evangelical movement valued demonstrable evidence of conversion more than they did demonstrable evidence of education in their ordained leadership. This in turn opened the door to both members and ordained leaders who came from among the ranks of the lower social classes for whom the privilege of education was generally unavailable. It especially opened the door to African American membership and leadership.

The experiential emphasis of Methodists and Baptists in matters of religion subtly resisted the impact of rationalism that was increasingly coming to affect other Protestant traditions in the English colonies over the course of the eighteenth century. Methodists and Baptists, like Moravians and several other smaller communities, continued to embrace visions and signs as valid means of religious discovery through the century long after most of the descendants of New England Puritanism had abandoned them. Methodists and Baptists were more receptive of emotional demonstrations in worship. This in turn provided an important point of contact with traditional African cultural practices that continued to find expression among African descendants in America. African Americans in turn imparted to the evangelical experience of America greater vibrancy in expression than was known among their counterparts in Europe. Such experiences as shouting in worship, which in America came to be nearly synonymous with the Methodist experience by the early nineteenth century, were drawn as much from African as from European cultural roots.

The Methodists did not spread much farther south than Maryland prior to the 1780s. Asbury visited South Carolina for the first time after the Baltimore Conference. When they did begin to spread south, the Methodists did so mostly along the frontier regions where people of European descent were settling after 1780. Baptists on the other hand began to grow in the South during the Great Awakening, and continued to plant new churches. In 1707, representatives from five Baptist churches in and around Philadelphia formed the first Baptist Association in the English colonies. By the end of the century there were at least thirty-five such associations, with more than 750 Baptist congregations spread throughout the new nation.

Isaac Backus (1724-1806) was a leading Baptist figure in New England during the latter part of the century. His church was in Middleborough, Massachusetts, a state in which the Congregational Church remained officially established even after the U.S. Constitution was ratified. Backus argued that Baptists ought not have to pay taxes to the state to support these established churches. He was also a supporter of higher education and was one of the founding trustees of the College in the English Colony of Rhode Island and Providence Plantations, which later became known as Brown College.

John Leland (1754-1841) was originally from Massachusetts, but in 1775, after undergoing a conversion, he moved to Virginia, where he began an itinerant ministry, planting new Baptist churches and organizing the Virginia Association. Leland, like Backus, was a forceful advocate for the separation of church and state. In 1787 Leland threw his support, and with it the support of the state Baptist Association, behind James Madison and the ratification of the new Constitution in exchange for a promise for an additional guarantee for religious freedom in the document. Upon the eventual adoption of that guarantee in the First Amendment, Leland celebrated the fact that people of any religion, whether "pagan," Muslim, Jew, or Christian were eligible to run for office or hold a government position in the new nation.

Benjamin Randall (1749-1808) was one of the last persons to be converted under Whitefield's ministry in New England in 1770. Ten years later he was ordained to be the founding pastor of a new Baptist church in New Durham, New Hampshire. Although he had originally embraced Whitefield's Calvinism, Randall became a strong advocate for the Armenian position regarding free will. Within two years a dozen other Free Will Baptist churches had been founded across New England under Randall's influence. Contrary to many of his contemporaries, Randall demonstrated an openness to experience of direct mediations of the Spirit that help him both in understanding doctrine and in guiding his congregation. His own personal mystical experiences, including what at one point appears to have been a spiritual trance, were influential in this regard. This openness to spiritual experience allowed for those who might otherwise not be regarded as eligible for ministry to participate in leadership in the churches. Under Randall the Free Will Baptists in New England opened the doors for women to serve in the office of exhorter, allowing them to participate in conferences of the church alongside ordained ministers and ruling elders.

Over the course of the nineteenth century the United States would prove to be the birthplace of a number of new religious movements that came to be regarded by the larger majority of Christians as being outside the boundaries of orthodox Christian belief. One of the first of these new movements began in England in the eighteenth century and moved to the American colonies in the 1770s. Two years prior to the arrival of Heck and Embury in New York, twenty-two-year-old Ann Lee (1736-1784) began attending Quaker meetings in Manchester, England. From a young age she worked in the textile factories alongside others from families of workers. She also showed a reluctance to marry, to which her father responded by forcing her at age sixteen into a union with a man named Abraham Standley (dates unknown). Defying usual English practice at the time, Ann continued to use her birth surname the rest of her life. She eventually became pregnant eight times, but only four children were born live, and none of them survived past the age of six.

The group of Quakers that Lee joined had been earlier influenced by a band of religious refugees from France who called themselves prophets and were traveling through England in the 1740s. Known as *les trembleurs* ("the tremblers") from their practice of shaking in worship, they went from town to town, teaching that the second coming of Christ and the advent of his millennial rule on earth were imminent. The Manchester Quakers embraced these notions and were soon being called "Shaking Quakers," a name that was later shortened simply to the "Shakers." Members of the society, including Lee, began traveling from town to town, preaching the imminent second coming of Christ and practicing their ecstatic worship in public.

In 1772 Lee was imprisoned on charges of profaning the Sabbath on account of her dancing and shaking. While in prison, she had a vision that crystallized

her understanding of both human sexual relations and her own millennial vocation. The vision revealed to her that the root of all human depravity was sexual
activity that led to natural generation. No one could follow Christ in the work of
regeneration without first abandoning the works of natural generation and the
accompanying gratifications of the flesh. Entrance into this new teaching brought
one into the millennial age.

Upon hearing of Lee's vision, others in the group took it as a sign that pointed
toward her being the anointed one who was to come, the second coming of the
Christ, thereby completing the revelation of God as male and female. The group
began calling Lee "Mother Ann." Manchester as a whole did not prove to be
receptive of the revelation of a female Christ, however, and persecution by the
civil authorities increased. The fact that Lee and her group publicly advocated
complete renunciation of sexual activity between men and women did not help
their cause. Facing increased opposition, in 1774 Lee set sail to New York with a
small band of followers that included her husband.

The husband abandoned the group soon after their arrival in Manhattan. The
rest of the small band went to work to raise money to purchase property upstate.
A year or so later they were able to move to Watervliet, New York, outside
Albany. There they resided for several years without attracting much attention
other than that of the local authorities in Albany who suspected them of being
British sympathizers during the war. In 1780, in the midst of a local revival, a
Baptist minister named Joseph Meacham (1742-1796) heard about Mother Ann's
group and journeyed to their community in Watervliet to meet her. Upon hearing
Mother Ann's message he became the first convert in America. Others soon fol-
lowed, and the ranks of the Shakers grew.

Local opposition grew as well, including brief spells in prison for the members. Mother Ann and her followers, however, were not to be deterred. A small
group of them, under Mother Ann's leadership, launched a mission trip through
Massachusetts and Connecticut. In each town they visited, they would preach
the renunciation of all works of the flesh, and demonstrate their unique form of
ecstatic dancing in worship, which they said was the means for entering into the
millennial kingdom of Christ. In town after town they were hounded by mobs
and beaten. Yet their message received a hearing. Young women dissolved their
engagements, married women abandoned their husbands, and a number of couples ended their sexual relations to enter into the millennial church together.

Mother Ann died in 1784, and leadership of the community passed on to
others, both men and women. No one else was proclaimed after her to be the
second coming of the Christ. The Shakers believed that this was the unique
role that fell solely to Mother Ann—the second coming, this time in the person
of a woman. Shakers who joined the community literally became part of the
millennial kingdom of Christ come on earth. Death no longer separated them
from one another, which is why Shakers continued to receive regular visitations from Ann Lee and other saints in the community even after they had gone
through physical death.

By the first decades of the nineteenth century Shaker communities, or
gatherings, had spread from New York to Massachusetts, Connecticut, Maine,

Pennsylvania, Ohio, and Kentucky. Shakers lived in strictly celibate communities, and thus depended entirely on conversions for gaining their new members. In these communities, men and women lived in separate, but symmetrical, communal quarters. Women often worked in the shops and fields, while men sometimes worked in the kitchens. During the week there were organized times for women and men to meet together and learn to relate to each other as equals. Women were taught that they had to learn to love men without feeling lustful, while men were warned that their lusting after women was the sign of their sinful nature, and that it must be given up entirely in the millennial kingdom. They grew their own food and made most of what they used in their own workshops. They often sold seeds and other goods to help support their communities. Property was owned communally, and most decisions were made by the elders in ways that maintained the collective sense of identity in the community. They were strict pacifists and abstained from any association with the outside world that was deemed to be sinful.

Shakers never numbered more than ten thousand believers, but their impact was widely felt through the culture. Sinlessness entailed cleanliness, order, and simplicity in the Shakers' millennial kingdom of Christ on earth. With this vision in mind they designed their buildings and made their own furniture. Shaker rooms were built with pegs on the walls so that furnishings could be lifted and the floors swept clean each day. The design of their furnishings was distinctive for its simplicity, beauty, and functionality. Likewise, labor was regarded as a highly spiritual activity and guided by their vision of millennial holiness. Applying the principles of Mother Ann's teachings to their everyday economy, Shakers became highly industrious. The number of patents held by members of the movement in the nineteenth century ran into the thousands. A Shaker woman invented the circular saw by applying the principles of the spinning wheel to the milling of lumber in a Shaker wood shop.

Mother Ann often said that she was married to Jesus in her Christhood. Theirs was a spiritual relationship of equality, not one in which she was a submissive wife. Women's subordination was a result of original sin, she taught. Mother Ann believed that Adam and Eve had fallen in the Garden of Eden by engaging in sexual relations before God had pronounced them good, that is, before they were mature and ready. The result was the sorrow and curse of Eve, tied up with her childbearing and her subordination to her husband in marriage. Thus marriage, according to Shaker teaching, was by definition a part of sinful life and a practice only of this age. Renunciation of sexual relations in the millennial kingdom meant renunciation of the curse of childbearing and freedom from marriage. In this way men and women were seen as being restored to the original equality Adam and Eve were intended to have in the Garden of Eden.

The image of God that was restored by the revelation of Jesus and Mother Ann was a dual one. God, according to Shaker theology, was thus a duality of male and female, mother and father, and not a Trinity. The image of God the Heavenly Father was complemented and completed by the image of God the Heavenly Mother, sometimes associated with the Holy Spirit. The duality of God was in turn reflected in the duality of Jesus and Mother Ann, and the equality of men and women in their millennial kingdom on earth.

African American churches emerge

George Liele (c. 1751-1828) was born in slavery on a plantation in Virginia. At a young age he moved to Georgia with his master, who was a Baptist deacon. In Georgia, Liele began attending Buckhead Creek Baptist Church, and in 1772 he underwent baptism. Shortly after that, he began preaching with great effect, leading his master to emancipate him in order to allow him to itinerate. During the War of Independence, Liele moved to Savannah and under British protection organized a congregation of African Americans. Among the members of the group were Andrew Bryan (1737-1812) and David George (c. 1740-1810). In 1782 the British withdrew from Savannah. Liele decided to go with them, relocating to Kingston, Jamaica. Two years later, he started a new Baptist church there, which had grown within five years to a congregation of over 350. Liele was also instrumental in founding other Baptist churches throughout the island. Most of his members were enslaved, which led to suspicions of many plantation owners on the island. On one occasion Liele was even imprisoned on charges of sedition. Added to his burdens was the poverty of the members of the congregation, which forced Liele to work as a teamster, in addition to carrying on his pastoral duties, in order to support himself and his family.

One of Liele's most important steps for the development of the Baptists in America was his decision to baptize Andrew Bryan in 1782 before the British evacuated the city. Bryan was originally from South Carolina, and within a few years of his baptism, he was exhorting others of African descent on plantations in the area. In 1790 a white plantation owner allowed Bryan to build a small structure near the town of Yamacraw in which he was allowed to hold religious services for persons of African descent, both enslaved and free. In 1788 a white Baptist clergyman ordained Bryan, who by this time had a church of approximately fifty members; he named the congregation the Ethiopian Church of Jesus Christ. Two years later, with more than two hundred full members, the church changed its name to the First African Baptist Church and was accepted into membership in the Georgia Baptist Association. In 1794 the congregation purchased land and moved to Savannah. By the time of his death in 1812 the congregation had almost 1,500 members.

While in Savannah Liele was joined by David George and a group of about thirty from his church in Silver Bluffs, which was located on the South Carolina side of the Savannah River. George had been converted several years earlier under Liele's preaching. He was originally from Virginia, but had escaped from the plantation and had been living for some years in hiding among Native Americans before ending up again on a plantation in Silver Bluffs. Following his conversion he had been baptized by another Baptist minister in the region and in 1774 had organized a small congregation among the slaves on the plantation that he served as a lay preacher. In 1778 George made his way to Savannah with the others from his congregation after the plantation owner abandoned his property. In Savannah George underwent baptism again, this time at the hands of Liele. When the British evacuated the city four years later, some of the members of the group returned to the plantation in Silver Bluffs. The rest of the group went with George to Nova Scotia, in Canada, where under George's leadership they organized a new Baptist church.

Nova Scotia through these years was being overwhelmed by both black and white immigrants who were escaping the war to the south. Being one of the more prominent black leaders, George was especially vulnerable to attacks. At one point a riot broke out in the town of Shelburne as George was attempting to baptize two whites. At another point his house was attacked and destroyed by unemployed soldiers. Soldiers also disrupted worship meetings at the church at night, threatening the lives of members. Nevertheless, George persisted. He planted seven other black Baptist churches during the decade or so that he was in Nova Scotia.

In 1792 the opportunity to move on to West Africa presented itself to George and some of the members of the original Silver Bluffs church. The Sierra Leone Colony, noted in a previous chapter, was being formed. Persons of African descent in both England and Canada were being invited to go. George was among those who accepted the offer and in 1792 was on one of the fifteen ships taking settlers from Nova Scotia to West Africa. In Sierra Leone, George helped again to start a Baptist church, the first in the colony.

While Liele, Bryan, and George were forging the institutional beginnings of the Black Baptist church in Georgia, Lemuel Haynes (1753-1833) was busy becoming the first person considered black in English-speaking North America to serve as the pastor of a white congregation. Haynes was born in Connecticut to a white mother and a black father. He was abandoned by his parents shortly after birth, and was raised on a farm by a white couple as an indentured servant. As a child he demonstrated intellectual gifts but never received any formal education. After serving in the Continental Army during the War of Independence, he was licensed in 1780 in a Congregational church and five years later was ordained. In 1788 he accepted a call to the white congregation in Rutland, Vermont, where he served for the next thirty years. Haynes preached more than five thousand sermons over the course of his time in Rutland. He wrote extensively in opposition to slavery, arguing that liberty is equally precious to black and white alike while bondage is intolerable to both. He comfortably blended traditional Calvinist theological commitments with republican political ideals. Recognizing the importance of his life and work, Middlebury College awarded Haynes an honorary graduate degree in 1804. Nevertheless, for reasons that remain obscure, the congregation voted to end his pastorate in 1818. Haynes moved on to become the pastor of the South Granville Congregational Church in Granville, New York, where he finished his days.

Among the most important African American religious leaders of the eighteenth century was an African American Methodist named Richard Allen (1760-1831). Allen was born in bondage to a slave-holding Quaker family. At a young age he and several other members of his family were sold to a man in

Delaware, where Allen grew up. At the age of seventeen Allen was converted to Christianity under the preaching of Freeborn Garretson (1752-1827), an itinerant Methodist preacher who espoused strong abolitionist views. Allen's master was converted shortly after that under the same preacher. According to Garretson, slaveholders were not going to find mercy on Judgment Day. Convicted of his sin, Allen's owner decided to allow the enslaved persons he owned to go to work to pay off his investment and gain their freedom. For several years Allen sawed wood, made bricks, and drove a wagon until he had raised the necessary funds to purchase his own freedom.

By this time Allen had also been licensed by the Methodist as an exhorter. After purchasing his own freedom, he took to the road and began an itinerant ministry of preaching, traveling through Delaware, New Jersey, and eastern Pennsylvania for several years. Allen preached to whites as well as to blacks on these trips. In his autobiographical account of these years he described one occasion of a mostly white congregation being, in his words, "slain of the Lord" under the impact of his sermon.

In 1786 Allen settled in Philadelphia, where he attached himself to St. George Methodist church and began ministering to the growing African community in the city. He began each day by preaching at the 5:00 A.M. service at the church and often preached several more times a day for various services. Allen also began to organize. In 1787, he and several other African Americans from the church, including Absalom Jones (1746-1818), another formerly enslaved African who had purchased his own freedom, established the Free African Society, a religious benevolence organization that provided fellowship and mutual financial aid to free Africans and their descendants in the city.

Such activities brought a sizable number of new African American members into St. George Church. In response to the increasing number, the church decided to add a second-floor gallery, or balcony, around the inside. A number of the African members supported the effort with pledges. Soon after the balcony was completed, however, the white leadership of St. George, without consulting Allen and the other African members, decided that the Africans would thereafter have to sit in the gallery upstairs. During prayer one Sunday morning in 1792 while Allen, Absalom Jones, and several others were on their knees, white elders from the congregation tried to remove them bodily from the main floor. The Africans finished their prayers and, according to Allen, departed as a body so that the church would no longer, in his words, be "plagued" with their presence.

They went to a plot of land on Fifth St. in Philadelphia on which they dug a cellar and erected a simple preaching structure. Allen believed it to be the first African meeting house built in the United States. The group called their congregation the African Church and voted to affiliate with the Episcopal Church. Allen, however, continued to hold his Methodist connection because it was under them he had been converted, but also because he was convinced that the manner of preaching and the discipline of the Methodist church best suited the needs of African Americans. Methodist worship allowed for more enthusiastic expression than did the Episcopal Church. Allen recognized a greater cultural affinity between the African heritage and Methodist identity on these points.

In 1794 the Free African Church, now called St. Thomas' African Episcopal Church, formally asked Allen to become its pastor. He turned them down, and Absalom Jones accepted the call instead. Allen then turned his attention to a lot on Sixth and Lombard Streets that he had purchased several years earlier. An old blacksmith's shop was bought and hauled onto the property where it was transformed into a church house. A group of ten other African Methodists joined Allen there in founding Bethel African Methodist Episcopal Church where they could worship in Methodist style yet apart from the white Methodists of St. George. Bishop Asbury, whom Allen had known for several years, joined in the opening celebration at Bethel Church in July of that year.

The trustees of St. George continued to insist on trying to run the affairs of the Bethel congregation, demanding various payments and sending over white preachers who failed in Allen's view to meet the needs of the Africans. The struggle eventually led to a court battle. At stake for the African American congregation was its ability to control its own affairs, including making decisions regarding the property and appointments of preachers. Finally in 1799 Bishop Asbury ordained Allen a deacon in full standing in the Methodist connection. Allen was then appointed by Asbury to serve as the pastor of the Bethel church. By then the congregation had grown from its initial ten members to more than one hundred. By 1805 the church numbered 457, and by 1813 it had grown to 1,272. In 1810 Philadelphia's African population numbered just under 10,000, giving some indication of the level of Allen's and Bethel's influence within the black community in the city.

Allen's struggle with the white Methodists did not end with his ordination and appointment. He would eventually go on to lead Bethel and several other congregations to form an independent African Methodist Episcopal Church in 1817. Several other free African Methodist Church movements emerged alongside Allen's work in the nineteenth century, carrying on the tradition of freedom and discipline in a new context in America.

Developments in Canada

David George's sojourn to Nova Scotia illustrated at once both the connections and the distances between England's thirteen colonies along the middle Atlantic seaboard and its colonies to the north. The French originally claimed all the coastal regions of the eastern Atlantic seaboard north of Virginia, naming the region "Acadia." French settlers established a colony on Saint Croix Island, at the mouth of the Saint Croix River, which today separates the U.S. state of Maine from the Canadian province of New Brunswick. Scottish settlers began arriving in the 1630s as England laid claim to the region as well. Following their defeat in 1763 the French ceded control of the region to England, leading to the expulsion of a number of French settlers from what is now Nova Scotia, New Brunswick, and Prince Edward Island.

By the middle of the eighteenth century Nova Scotia's population was mostly descended from Scottish immigrants. An influx of Irish immigrants in the second half of the century changed the religious composition of the population, and brought Irish priests who sought to establish pastoral ministry among them. An uprising by descendants of the Irish immigration at the end of the century was one indication of the tensions that characterized life in the region. Henry Alline (1748-1784) was born in Newport, Rhode Island, but moved with his family to Nova Scotia in 1760. Converted in 1775, he soon began preaching throughout Nova Scotia and Prince Edward Island. He emphasized in his sermons the experiences of remorse for sin, overwhelming grace, and the transformation of life. Although the Congregationalists originally issued him a license to preach, they withdrew it after he was accused of fanaticism, forcing him to take his message to barns and open fields. Alline wrote some five hundred hymns during his short life, dying at the age of thirty-five of tuberculosis as he was preparing an evangelistic tour of New Hampshire.

The Methodist preacher William Black (1760-1834) followed in Alline's footsteps in Nova Scotia. Black immigrated to Nova Scotia from England in 1775 with his family, who were Methodists. These Methodist immigrants held worship services in their homes, and at one of these meetings in 1779 Black had a conversion experience. Two years later, without any direct connection with Wesley in England, he began an itinerant ministry of preaching on his own. Black wrote to Wesley in 1782, requesting help. Wesley replied by encouraging him to establish a relationship with the Methodists in the colonies to the south. Black responded by traveling to Philadelphia late in 1784 where he joined Coke and Asbury in time to attend the Christmas Conference in Baltimore at the end of the year. Coke eventually sent several ministers to Nova Scotia, including Freeborn Garretson, to help the Methodist efforts there. Black was eventually ordained a Methodist elder in 1789, but by then his organizing work and his itinerant preaching had helped establish the Methodists firmly in Canada.

In the treaty of 1763 that ended the war between France and England, France ceded all of its territories in America to England, including those of Quebec, which was by then a well-established French district. The transfer of political dominion greatly affected the Catholic majority who populated the region. The Catholic Church had been officially established throughout Quebec prior to 1763. Now suddenly the churches faced a changed political context. Jean-Olivier Briand (1715-1794) had been ordained in France in 1739 and had first come to Quebec in 1741. In 1766 he was consecrated as bishop in Montreal. The move was a positive one for the churches, as Briand proved to be both an irenic leader with strong pastoral sensitivities and an adamant opponent of the American Revolution. It was Briand that John Carroll visited with a delegation from the Continental Congress in 1776, seeking French support for the independence effort. Briand reportedly excommunicated Carroll for his pro-independence stance.

An ill-advised invasion of Quebec by the Continental Army in the War of Independence in 1775 and 1776 proved to be short-lived. The English colonist's forces quickly withdrew. Of far greater concern to Briand was the precipitous decline in the priests serving in the region. From 1759 to 1764, the number of priests dropped from 196 to 137 in Quebec. On the other hand, more than half of those who remained had been born in New France, marking a sharp contrast to the experience of Catholics in Spanish and Portuguese South America.

For their part, the British had a love–hate relationship with their French Catholic subjects. After 1763 the British paid the salary of the Catholic bishop, forcing them to treat him as if he were a bishop in the Church of England. At the same time the British expelled not only the Jesuits, whose order was being suppressed by Rome anyway, but the Capuchins and other orders in the colony. The effect was to bring about an end for the most part to ministry among Native Americans. In 1774 the English Parliament passed the Quebec Act, giving the French "island" colony greater autonomy in matters of law and religion. In some ways Catholics in Quebec were better off under British rule than they had been under French rule. They were certainly better off than Catholics were in England. The Quebec Act had the effect of placating the French Canadians and keeping them from coming to the aid of the Continental Congress in its war of secession from England. Briand supported the British effort, refusing the Eucharist to any who supported the rebellion and rejecting the efforts by his fellow Roman Catholic, John Carroll, to seek support for the independence cause. Canada became a safe haven for loyalists and Catholics alike.

During the War of Independence a trickle of Loyalists crossed the border into Canada to settle. Their numbers increased significantly after 1781, and continued for the rest of the decade. Some had served in the British army and no longer felt they had a place in the new American republic. Most settled in the area just north of Lake Ontario and Lake Erie. Most were English-speaking, and a sizable number were members of the Church of England, at least in name. The British government, seeking to accommodate the new immigrants, purchased some 1,000 square kilometers of land from the Mississauga Nation in 1787. Six years later they built a fort on the north shore of Lake Ontario on a harbor formed by the Toronto Islands. The fort was originally named York until its name was changed in the nineteenth century to Toronto. Loyalists who moved to the region were awarded two hundred acres of land on which to settle and farm. York quickly grew to become the focal point for travel and commerce through the region.

Recognizing the increasing potential for conflict between the newer English-speaking immigrants from the United States and the older French-speaking population of Quebec, the British Parliament in 1791 passed the Constitutional Act, dividing the Province of Quebec into Upper and Lower Canada. Lower Canada, so named because the lower end of the Saint Lawrence River passed through it, was the traditional French province while Upper Canada, to the south and west, comprised what is now mostly Ontario. English law applied to Upper Canada with land grants for the support of the Church of England clergy, while Lower Canada continued to be allowed to follow traditional French law, including government support for the Roman Catholic Church and land ownership. An English educational system was implemented in Upper Canada while the French educational system continued in Lower Canada. Two separate representative governing bodies were formed, each with an upper house and a lower house. In 1793 York became the capital of Upper Canada while Montreal continued to serve as the capital of Lower Canada. Canada was effectively divided into French and English regions.

Russian Orthodox missions in the Northwest

On the far western shores of North America, the Russian empire was beginning in the eighteenth century to make its presence known. Russia had been expanding politically and culturally to its east through the first decades of the century. The expansion was driven by commercial interests as much as it was politically motivated by the desire to extend the empire. On both counts it had a significant religious impact on the regions into which Russian traders and soldiers were moving. The Russian Orthodox Church was the first to establish a Christian presence in what is now Alaska in North America, a fact that would be significant for the development of Orthodox Christianity in North America.

From 1725 to 1741 Russian naval forces under the command of Vitus Bering (1681-1741), who was originally from Denmark, explored the northwest Pacific region, including the straits that now bear his name, and reached Alaska. Also involved in these expeditions was Aleksiei Chirikov (1703-1748), who has the distinction of being the first Russian to set foot in Alaska. The first permanent Russian colony was not begun until several decades later when a merchant named Grigorii Shelekhov (1747-1795) organized a settlement expedition in 1784, landing on Kodiak Island and naming the bay after one of his ships, Three Saints. Shelekhov is credited not only with founding the Russian-American Company in 1799, but with organizing what amounts to the first Orthodox church and mission in Alaska.

The first Russian settlers in Alaska were mainly interested in furs, for which they traded with the Unangans, whom the Russians called Aleuts. Initial conflicts with some of the indigenous people led to the death of some two hundred Unangans during the first months of the colony. The introduction of new diseases took far more lives among the indigenous peoples of Alaska, as it had in other parts of the continent when Europeans first arrived in the sixteenth century. The Russian settlers at Kodiak forced some from among the Unangans to work for them, and took some women as wives. It was mostly these wives and the children of the Russian settlers who were born from their unions who were the first among the Unangans to be baptized as Christians, in many cases by settlers who were lay people, as part of an effort to incorporate them into Russian culture.

The history of Christianity in Alaska took a decided turn in 1793 when eight monks and two novices traveled to Alaska from the monastery of Valaam on Lake Ladoga, in northern Russia. The monastery had been deeply affected by the recently translated *Philokalia* of Paisii (or Paisios) Velichkovskii (1721-1794). The monks brought a copy of the work with them in 1794. The mission was headed by Archimandrite Ioasaph (1761-1799). Originally named Ivan Ilyich Bolotov, he had studied in the seminary at Tver and was named an archimandrite in 1793, the year he left St. Petersburg under the direction of the Holy Synod to go to Alaska.

The missionaries quickly set to work learning local languages, translating the liturgy, and seeking to teach indigenous people about Christianity. The main obstacles they faced came mostly from the other Russian colonists, whose abuse of the indigenous peoples Ioasaph reported to the Holy Synod. Determining that Alaska needed its own bishop to deal with such problems, the Holy Synod in

1796 decided to consecrate Ioasaph as bishop of Alaska. The service eventually took place in Irkutsk, in Siberia, in 1799. Bishop Ioasaph was subsequently killed in a shipwreck while trying to return to Alaska.

Even the death of the first Orthodox bishop of Alaska could not hinder the work that was already going on among the indigenous peoples. By 1800 over ten thousand members of several indigenous ethnic groups along the coastal region had been baptized. The approach the Orthodox missionaries took was to affirm continuities they found between the cultures of the indigenous peoples and Orthodox faith in such matters as the sacredness of the natural world or respect for all of life. They then would add on specifically Christian teachings about God, Christ, the Spirit, and the church. Early on in the enterprise the missionaries had argued for setting up schools to train indigenous leaders as priests for the churches that they were starting, rather than sending candidates back to Russia. Officers of the Russian-American Company, which began operation in 1799, sought to block such efforts. Nevertheless, the foundations for an indigenous Orthodox Church had already been laid by the opening of the nineteenth century.

Suggestions for further reading

Bowden, Henry Warner, *American Indians and Christian Missions*. Chicago: University of Chicago Press, 1981.

Fay, Terence J., *A History of Canadian Catholics*. Montreal: McGill-Queen's University Press, 2002.

Finke, Roger, and Rodney Stark, *The Churching of America, 1776-1990: Winners and Losers in Our Religious Economy*. New Brunswick, NJ: Rutgers University Press, 1992.

Frey, Sylvia R., and Betty Wood, *Come Shouting to Zion: African American Protestantism in the American South and British Caribbean to 1830*. Chapel Hill: University of North Carolina Press, 1998.

Genovese, Eugene D., *Roll, Jordon Roll: The World the Slaves Made*. New York: Pantheon, 1974.

McAvoy, Thomas T., *A History of the Catholic Church in the United States*. Notre Dame, IN: University of Notre Dame Press, 1969.

Noll, Mark, *America's God: From Jonathan Edwards to Abraham Lincoln*. New York: Oxford University Press, 2002.

———, *A History of Christianity in the United States and Canada*. Grand Rapids: Eerdmans, 1992.

Old, Hughes Oliphant, *The Reading and Preaching of the Scriptures in the Worship of the Christian Church, V: Moderatism, Pietism, and Awakening*. Grand Rapids: Eerdmans, 2004.

Rabateau, Albert J., *Slave Religion: The "Invisible Institution" in the Antebellum South*. New York: Oxford University Press, 1978.

Sernett, Milton C., ed., *African American Religious History: A Documentary Witness*. Durham, NC: Duke University Press, 2000.

Index